CORELDRAW! 4
MADE EASY

CORELDRAW! 4
MADE EASY

Emil Ihrig and Sybil Ihrig
&
Martin S. Matthews and Carole Boggs Matthews

Osborne **McGraw-Hill**

Berkeley New York St. Louis San Francisco
Auckland Bogotá Hamburg London Madrid
Mexico City Milan Montreal New Delhi Panama City
Paris São Paulo Singapore Sydney
Tokyo Toronto

Osborne **McGraw-Hill**
2600 Tenth Street
Berkeley, California 94710
U.S.A.

For information on translations or book distributors outside of the U.S.A.,
please write to Osborne **McGraw-Hill** at the above address.

CorelDRAW! 4 Made Easy

34567890 DOC 99876543

ISBN 0-07-881961-X

Acquisitions Editor
Scott Rogers

Associate Editor
Kristin D. Beeman

Technical Editor
John Cronan

Project Editor
Edith Rex

Copy Editor
Judith Brown

Proofreaders
Kayla Sussell
Linda Medoff

Indexer
Valerie Robbins

Computer Designer
Stefany Otis

Illustrators
Marla Shelasky
Lance Ravella

Cover Designer
Compass Marketing

CONTENTS AT A GLANCE

1	Getting Acquainted with CorelDRAW!	1
2	Drawing and Working with Lines and Curves	21
3	Drawing and Working with Rectangles, Squares, Ellipses, and Circles	59
4	Adding Text	81
5	Using Magnification and View Selection	125
6	Selecting, Moving, and Arranging Objects	143
7	Transforming Objects	183
8	Shaping Lines, Curves, Rectangles, and Ellipses	217
9	Shaping and Editing Text	265
10	Cutting, Copying, Pasting, and Object Linking and Embedding (OLE)	289
11	Defining the Outline Pen	313
12	Defining Outline and Fill Color	349
13	Printing and Processing Your Images	401
14	Creating Special Effects	443
15	Combining CorelDRAW! Features	493
16	Using CorelCHART!	525
17	Introducing CorelSHOW!	559
18	Introducing CorelPHOTO-PAINT!	569
19	Introducing CorelMOVE!	585

A ▰▰▰ **Installing CorelDRAW! 4** **605**

B ▰▰▰ **Importing and Exporting Files** **613**

C ▰▰▰ **Tracing Bitmap Images** **629**

CONTENTS

Acknowledgments . . . . *xix*
Introduction . . . . *xxi*

1 ▇▇▇ Getting Acquainted with CorelDRAW! 1
  Starting CorelDRAW! 2
  The CorelDRAW! Screen 4
  CorelDRAW! Menus 7
  Dialog Boxes 11
    Roll-up Windows 13
  The CorelDRAW! Toolbox 14
    Drawing Tools 14
    Editing Tools 17
    Tools for Customizing the CorelDRAW!
      Screen 18
  Quitting CorelDRAW! 18

2 ▇▇▇ Drawing and Working with Lines and Curves 21
  Freehand Versus Bézier Mode 22
  Drawing Straight Lines 22
    Using the Status Line to Improve Precision 24
    Erasing Portions of a Line 25
    Constraining a Line to an Angle 26
    Clearing the Screen 27

Drawing Multisegment Lines 27
Drawing a Polygon 29
Straight Lines in Bézier Mode 30
Drawing Single Lines in Bézier Mode 30
Drawing a Polygon in Bézier Mode 31
Drawing Curves 32
Erasing Portions of a Curve 34
Drawing Multisegment Curves 35
Closing an Open Path 35
Full Color Versus Wireframe Modes 36
Drawing Curves in Bézier Mode 37
The Dimension Lines Feature 40
Using Dimension Lines 40
Increasing Precision 43
Setting the Grid and Displaying Rulers 43
Joining Lines and Curves Automatically 45
Adjusting the AutoJoin Threshold 46
Creating a Drawing Using Lines, Curves, and Polygons 48
Saving Your Work 54
Retrieving a File 55

3 ▬▬ **Drawing and Working with Rectangles,**
Squares, Ellipses, and Circles **59**
Drawing a Rectangle 60
Drawing a Rectangle from Any Corner 60
Drawing a Rectangle from the Center
Outward 62
Drawing a Square 62
Drawing a Square from Any Corner 62
Drawing a Square from the Center Outward 63
Practicing with the Grid 64
Creating a Drawing Using Rectangles and Squares 66
Drawing an Ellipse 70
Using the Rim as a Starting Point for
an Ellipse 70
Drawing an Ellipse from the Center Outward 71
Drawing a Circle 72
Using the Rim as a Starting Point for a Circle 73
Drawing a Circle from the Center Outward 73
Creating a Drawing Using Ellipses and Circles 74

4 ▰▰▰ **Adding Text** **81**

    Entering Text 82
        Selecting the Text Tool 82
        Text Strings and Paragraphs 83
        Selecting an Insertion Point 84
        Artistic Text Dialog Box 85
        Using the Keyboard and Mouse 86
    Entering Text 87
        Entering Text in the Text Dialog Box 87
        Using Keys to Move Around 87
        Using the Mouse 88
        Entering Text Directly on the Screen 89
    Aligning Text 90
        Left Alignment 90
        Center Alignment 91
        Right Alignment 92
        No Alignment 93
    Selecting a Type Size 94
    Selecting a Type Design 95
        Selecting a Font 95
        Selecting a Style 100
        Adjusting Text Spacing 102
        Adjusting and Comparing Spacing 106
    Working with Paragraphs 107
        Extracting Text from CorelDRAW! 110
        Merging, Importing, and Pasting Text into
          CorelDRAW! 113
        Putting Text in Columns 114
        Paragraph Attributes 115
        Hyphenation 116
        Using the Spelling Checker 116
        Thesaurus 118
        Find and Replace 118
    Using the Symbol Library 119
    Entering Special Characters 121

5 ▰▰▰ **Using Magnification and View Selection** **125**

    The Zoom Tool 126
    The Zoom-In Tool 128
        Defining the Viewing Area 128

The Zoom-Out Tool 134
Viewing at Actual Size 136
Fitting a Graphic in a Window 138
Viewing an Entire Page 139

6 ▬▬ **Selecting, Moving, and Arranging Objects** **143**
Selecting and Deselecting Objects 144
Single Objects 145
Multiple Objects 148
Selecting All Objects in a Graphic 153
Cycling Through Objects 153
Moving Objects 156
Moving a Single Object 156
Moving Multiple Objects 157
Moving at a 90-Degree Angle 159
Moving Objects with the Keyboard (Nudge) 162
Moving an Object Using Precise
Measurements 162
Copying an Object While Moving It 163
Arranging Objects 166
Reordering Superimposed Objects 166
Grouping and Ungrouping Objects 168
Combining and Breaking Objects Apart 170
Aligning Objects 173
Layers 177
Layer Features 178
Welding 180

7 ▬▬ **Transforming Objects** **183**
Stretching and Mirroring an Object 184
Stretching Horizontally 185
Stretching Vertically 188
Creating a Mirror Image 191
The Stretch & Mirror Command 192
Scaling an Object 196
Scaling with the Stretch & Mirror Command 199
Stretching and Scaling from the Center 200
Rotating an Object 201
Rotating with the Rotate & Skew Command 207
Skewing an Object 208

       Skewing with the Rotate & Skew Command 212
    Repeating a Transformation 213

8 ▬▬ Shaping Lines, Curves, Rectangles, and Ellipses ... 217

About the Shaping Tool 218
Selecting with the Shaping Tool 218
Shaping Lines and Curves 220
    Selecting a Line or Curve 220
    Selecting Nodes of a Line or Curve 222
    Moving Nodes and Control Points 226
    Editing Nodes 233
    Working with the Node Edit Roll-Up 233
Shaping Rectangles and Squares 253
    Rounding the Corners of a Rectangle 253
    Stretched, Rotated, or Skewed Rectangles and
      Squares 257
    Converting a Rectangle to a Curve Object 257
Shaping Ellipses and Circles 259
    Creating an Open Arc 259
    Creating a Pie Wedge 261
    Converting Ellipses and Circles to Curve
      Objects 262

9 ▬▬ Shaping and Editing Text 265

Editing Attributes for a Text String 266
Selecting and Editing Text with the Shaping Tool 267
The Character Attributes Dialog Box 269
    Reviewing the Dialog Box 270
    Editing Font and Style 271
    Editing Type Size 272
    Horizontal and Vertical Shift 273
    Creating Superscripts and Subscripts 274
    Editing Character Angle 274
Kerning Text Interactively 275
    Kerning Single Characters 276
    Kerning Multiple Characters 278
Adjusting Spacing Interactively 279
    Adjusting Inter-Character Spacing 280
    Adjusting Inter-Word Spacing 282
    Adjusting Inter-Line Spacing 283

Reshaping Characters 284

**10 ▬ Cutting, Copying, Pasting, and Object Linking
     and Embedding (OLE)** **289**
 About the Windows Clipboard 290
 Copy, Cut, Duplicate, Clone, or Delete 291
 Copying and Pasting Objects 291
  Copying and Pasting Objects Within
   a Picture 291
  Copying and Pasting Between Pictures 293
 Cutting and Pasting Objects 294
  Cutting and Pasting Within a Picture 295
  Cutting and Pasting Between Pictures 296
 Working with Different Applications 298
  Clipboard Memory Limits 298
  Transferring Objects to Other Applications 299
  Transferring Objects from Other Applications 300
  Object Linking and Embedding 300
 Duplicating and Cloning Objects 304
  Cloning an Object 307
 Copying an Object's Attributes 308

11 ▬ Defining the Outline Pen **313**
 Defining Outline Pen Attributes 314
 Using the Outline Pen 314
  Creating Objects with Default Attributes 316
  Customizing Outline Pen Defaults 322
  Selecting a Preset Outline Pen Width 323
  Editing Outline Pen Attributes of Existing
   Objects 325
 Outline Pen Hints 344
  Defining an Outline Pen for Text 344
  Varying Your Calligraphic Style 345
  Copying Outline Styles 346

12 ▬ Defining Outline and Fill Color **349**
 Defining an Object's Outline Color Attributes 351
 Outlining with Spot Color 352
  Setting New Outline Color Defaults 352
  Assigning Spot Color Outlines 355

Setting New Spot Color Outline Pen Defaults 356
Using the Pen Roll-Up for Outline Color 358
Outlining with PostScript Halftone Screen Patterns 359
Selecting Halftone Screen Patterns 360
Outlining with Process Color 361
Defining a New Color and Adding It to the
Custom Palette 364
Outlining with Black, White, or Gray 366
Copying Outline Color and Pen Styles 368
Defining Fill Color Attributes 369
Filling an Object with Uniform Spot Color 370
Filling an Object with PostScript Halftone Screen
Patterns 376
Filling an Object with Uniform Process Color 379
Assigning Process Color Uniform Fills 379
Filling with Black, White, or Gray 381
Custom Fountain Fills 381
Defining Linear Fountain Fills 382
Defining Radial Fountain Fills 386
Defining Conical Fountain Fills 389
Bitmap and Vector Fill Patterns 391
Using Bitmap Fill Patterns 391
PostScript Texture Fills 396
Fill Roll-Up Window 398
Fill Tool Hints 398
Copying Fill Styles 398
Using Fountain Steps to Enhance Previews and
Printing 399

13 ▬▬ **Printing and Processing Your Images** **401**
Output Devices 402
Preparing to Print 404
Printer Installation and Setup 404
Printer Timeouts 406
Disabling the Print Manager 407
The Print Setup Dialog Box 407
The Print Dialog Box 408
Using CorelMOSAIC! 408
Selecting the Print Command 411
Checking Printer Setup 412
Number of Copies 413

Pages 413
Printing Only Selected Objects 413
Tiling a Graphic 414
Scaling an Image 416
Fitting an Image to the Page 417
Printing to a File 418
Using Print Options 419
Printing File Information with a Graphic 420
Color Separations, Crop Marks, and
Registration Marks 422
Film Negative Format 428
Fountain Fill Steps 429
Flatness Setting for PostScript 430
Screen Frequency for PostScript 431
All Fonts Resident for PostScript 432
Using the Color Separator 433
Hardware-Specific Tips 435
PostScript Printers and Controllers 435
HP LaserJet Printers and Compatibles 437
HP DeskJet and PaintJet 438
Genuine HP and Other Plotters 438
Dot-Matrix Printers 438
Complex Artwork on PostScript Printers 438
Downloadable PostScript Error Handler 439
Printing PostScript Textures 440
Printing Complex Curve Objects 440
Printing Fountain Fills 441
300 DPI Printers Versus High-Resolution
Imagesetters 441

14 ▨ **Creating Special Effects** **443**
Using an Envelope 447
Creating and Duplicating Text 450
Straight Line Envelope 450
Single Arc Envelope 452
Two Curves Envelope 453
Using Ctrl and Shift with Envelopes 453
Unconstrained Envelope 455
Adding a New Envelope 457
Copy Envelope From 458
Clearing an Envelope 459

Creating Perspective Effects 460
    Using One- or Two-Point Perspective 461
    Using the Vanishing Point 463
    Adding a New Perspective 463
    Copy Perspective From 463
    Clearing a Perspective 464
Blending Objects 466
    Blending Two Objects 466
    Rotating the Blended Objects 467
Extruding Objects 472
    Extrude Roll-Up Window 472
    Depth and Direction 474
    Clearing an Extrusion 477
    Spatial Alignment 478
    Shading and Coloring 479
    Applying Extrusions to Open Paths 481
Using Contours 482
Using Powerlines 485
    Applying Powerlines to an Object 486
    Varying the Nib 487
    Using Pressure Lines 488

15 ▬▬ **Combining CorelDRAW! Features** **493**
Integrating Clip Art and Line Art 494
Fitting Text to a Path 500
    Fit Text To Path Roll-Up 501
    Using Fit Text To Path 504
Achieving Special Effects with Text and Graphics 514

16 ▬▬ **Using CorelCHART!** **525**
Charting Basics 526
Starting CorelCHART! 528
Creating a New Chart 530
Using the Data Manager 531
    Entering Data with the Data Manager 533
    Importing Data with the Data Manager 533
Customizing Charts 535
    Formatting Text 535
    Adding Labels 537
    Adding Graphics 538

Modifying Chart Elements 541
Creating Chart Templates 542
Chart Types 543
Bar Charts 543
Line Charts 548
Area Charts 549
Pie Charts 550
Scatter Charts 551
High/Low/Open/Close Charts 552
Spectral Maps 553
Histograms 553
Table Charts 554
3-D Riser Charts 554
3-D Scatter Charts 555
Pictographs 555

17 Introducing CorelSHOW! **559**
CorelSHOW! Overview 560
Getting Started with CorelSHOW! 560
CorelSHOW! Screen Elements 561
CorelSHOW! Tools and Modes 562
Previewing a Presentation 567
Other Tools 567

18 Introducing CorelPHOTO-PAINT! **569**
CorelPHOTO-PAINT! Overview 570
Getting Started with CorelPHOTO-PAINT! 570
CorelPHOTO-PAINT! Screen Elements 572
The Roll-Up Menus 573
CorelPHOTO-PAINT! Tools 575
Experiment with CorelPHOTO-PAINT! 582

19 Introducing CorelMOVE! **585**
Animation Basics 586
Getting Started with CorelMOVE! 587
CorelMOVE! Screen 588
CorelMOVE! Menus 588
Animation Information Dialog Box 588
Playback Options Dialog Box 589
CorelMOVE! Toolbox 589

Path Tool 589
Actor Tool 592
Prop Tool 596
Sound Tool 596
Cue Tool 596
CorelMOVE! Control Panel 599
Playback Controls 599
Opening a CorelMOVE! Animation 600
Timelines Roll-Up 601
Library Roll-Up 602
Cel Sequencer Roll-Up 603

A ▰▰▰ Installing CorelDRAW! 4 .... **605**
System Requirements 606
Installing the Software 608
Creating a Directory 609

B ▰▰▰ Importing and Exporting Files **613**
Bitmap Versus Object-Oriented Graphics 614
Using Help for Importing and Exporting 617
Importing: An Overview 618
Bringing in a File 619
Importing Bitmap Graphics 620
Importing Object-Oriented Graphics 620
Exporting: An Overview 621
Preparing for Exporting 621
The Export Dialog Box 621
Exporting to Bitmap Graphics Formats 623
Specifying a Bitmap Graphics Resolution 623
Exporting to Object-Oriented Graphics Formats 624
Exporting to an EPS Format 625

C ▰▰▰ Tracing Bitmap Images **629**
Creating a Bitmap Image 630
Importing a Bitmap Image 630
Autotracing an Imported Bitmap 632
Tracing Manually 637
Tracing with CorelTRACE! 640
Preparing to Use CorelTRACE! 641
Loading CorelTRACE! 642

Opening Files to Trace 642
Tracing a Bitmap with CorelTRACE! 644
Customizing Your Tracing Options 646

■■■■■ **Index** **651**

CORELDRAW! 4

ACKNOWLEDGMENTS

A number of people are responsible for this Fourth Edition of *CorelDRAW! Made Easy*. Bill Loyd and Erik Poulsen are responsible for updating a large number of the chapters, and John Cronan did an excellent job technically reviewing it all. The team assembled by Osborne/McGraw-Hill was superbly lead by Scott Rogers with invaluable editorial support from Edith Rex and Judith Brown. The original authors, Emil and Sybil Ihrig of VersaTech Associates are ever present with their tremendous initial work. All of these people put out a considerable amount of effort in a short period of time along with more than a little of themselves to produce an excellent product. Their effort and the results are greatly appreciated.

CorelDRAW! 4

INTRODUCTION

Since its initial release in January of 1989, CorelDRAW! has become the most talked-about graphics software package for IBM-compatible PCs. It is easy to understand why the program has received many major industry awards and received so much favorable attention. Quite simply, no other drawing package offers so many powerful drawing, text-handling, autotracing, color separation, and special effects capabilities in a single package. CorelDRAW! 4 continues this tradition by adding many new desktop publishing features including multipage documents, text controls, extensive bullets, and improved color separations with auto-trapping; many new artistic features including powerlines (lines with variable shapes), textures and fills, artistic styles to manage complex drawings, and weld capability to join the outlines of existing objects; and completely new technical illustration features including dimensioning, clones that mirror their master, attaching data to objects, and drag and drop symbol manipulation. If this isn't enough, CorelDRAW! 4 also has added a completely new application: CorelMOVE!, a multimedia animation package that provides the combination of sound, graphics, and 2-D animation for use in a presentation.

About This Book

CorelDRAW! 4 Made Easy is a step-by-step training guide to CorelDRAW! that leads you from elementary skills to more complex ones. Each chapter contains hands-on exercises that are richly and clearly illustrated so that you can match the results on your computer screen.

This book makes few assumptions about your graphics experience or computer background. If you have never used a mouse or worked with a drawing package, you can begin with the exercises in the early chapters and move forward as you master each skill. On the other hand, if you have experience in desktop publishing, graphic design, or technical illustration, you can concentrate on the chapters that cover more advanced features or features that are new to you. Even the basic chapters contain exercises that stimulate your creativity, so it is worth your while to browse through each chapter in order to gain new knowledge and ideas.

How This Book Is Organized

CorelDRAW! 4 Made Easy is designed to let you learn by doing, regardless of whether you are a new, intermediate, or advanced user of CorelDRAW!. You begin to draw right away and as the book proceeds, you continue to build on the skills you have learned in previous chapters.

The organization of this book is based on the philosophy that knowing how to perform a particular task is more important than simply knowing the location of a tool or menu command. The body of the book, therefore, contains step-by-step exercises that begin with basic drawing skills and then progresses to advanced skills that combine multiple techniques. The appendixes at the end of the book contain handy reference material that you can turn to when you need to review what you have learned.

The organization of each chapter will help you quickly locate any information that you need to learn. Each section within a chapter begins with an overview of a particular skill and its importance in the context of other CorelDRAW! functions. In most chapters, every section contains one or more hands-on exercises that allow you to practice the skill being taught.

Conventions Used in This Book

CorelDRAW! 4 Made Easy uses several conventions designed to help you locate information quickly. The most important of these are

✦ Terms essential to the operation of CorelDRAW! or the understanding of this book appear in *italics* the first time they are introduced.

✦ The first time an icon or tool in the CorelDRAW! toolbox or interface is discussed, it often appears as a small graphic beside the text; for example, the Pencil tool is displayed to the left.

✦ You can locate the steps of any exercise quickly by looking for the numbered paragraphs that are indented from the left margin.

◆ Names of keys appear as small graphics that look similar to the actual keys on your computer's keyboard (for example, Ctrl).

◆ Text or information that you must enter using the keyboard appears in **boldface**

C H A P T E R

CORELDRAW! 4

1

GETTING ACQUAINTED WITH CORELDRAW!

Welcome to CorelDRAW!. You have selected one of the most innovative and advanced graphics tools available for the PC. CorelDRAW! will sharpen your creative edge by allowing you to edit any line, shape, or character with ease and precision; fit text to a curve; autotrace existing artwork; create custom color separations and moving animation presentations; produce desktop publishing documents; and more. You can combine CorelDRAW!'s features to achieve many different special effects, such as placing a line of text or an object in perspective; folding, contouring, rotating, or extruding a line of text or an object; blending two lines of text or two objects; and creating mirror images, masks, and 3-D simulations. CorelDRAW! makes these and other capabilities work for you at speeds far surpassing those of other graphics programs.

To support your creative and technical endeavors, CorelDRAW! has a large number of fonts and clip-art libraries at your disposal. If the more than 50 fonts provided on the CorelDRAW! disk fail to meet your needs, you can use the over 750 fonts provided on the CD-ROM that comes with CorelDRAW!. Your software also supplies over 5000 symbols and over 3000 clip-art images, and you can obtain thousands more from industry vendors. You also have a library of over 125 animations and 400 cartoon figures to use in CorelMOVE!.

If you haven't installed CorelDRAW!, turn to Appendix A before continuing with this chapter.

Starting CorelDRAW!

To start CorelDRAW!, first turn on your computer. Next, you may or may not need to start Windows. If you do *not* automatically load Windows, use the first two instructions below for that purpose. If you already have Windows up on your screen, skip to the paragraph following the second step.

1. Change to the drive and directory of the hard disk in which you have installed Windows. If you are not in the correct drive, you need to change the drive by typing the drive letter followed by a colon. For example, type **c:** and press Enter. To then change the directory to the Windows directory, type **cd windows** or **cd***yourname*, if you have named the directory something else, and press Enter.

2. Type **win** and press Enter to start Windows. After an introductory screen and a few seconds, the Program Manager window appears on the screen, a sample of which is shown in Figure 1-1.

   Depending on how you or someone else last left Corel on your computer, the Corel window (representing the group of Corel Graphics) may be open, as shown in Figure 1-1, or you may see an icon at the bottom of the Program Manager window. If you don't see an open window with the title "Corel 4," look for an icon with that name, like the one on the left. If you don't see either the Corel 4 window or icon, open the Window menu and look there.

1

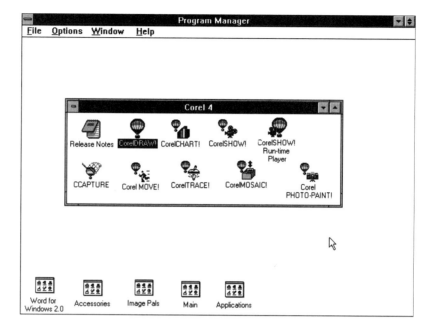

Program
Manager
window with
Corel
Graphics
group window
open
Figure 1-1.

3. *Click* on Window in the menu bar of the Program Manager window (with your mouse, place the mouse pointer on top of the word "Window" and press and release the left mouse button). The Window menu should open and look like this:

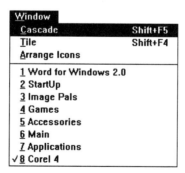

4. If you see "Corel 4" in the Window menu, click on it (place the mouse pointer on top of the phrase "Corel 4" and press and release the left mouse button). Your Corel group window should open.

CAUTION: If you don't see "Corel 4" in the Window menu, you need to turn to Appendix A and install CorelDRAW!. Do that now and then return here.

If Corel 4 is an icon, open it now.

5. *Double-click* on the Corel 4 group icon (place the mouse pointer on the icon and press and release the left mouse button twice in rapid succession). The Corel group window should open.

6. To start CorelDRAW!, double-click on the CorelDRAW! application icon (place the mouse pointer on the icon and press and release the left mouse button twice in rapid succession).

After a moment, an information screen is displayed, then the CorelDRAW! screen appears.

The CorelDRAW! Screen

You will see references to the various screen components of CorelDRAW! many times throughout the book. Take a moment now to familiarize yourself with these terms and their functions within the program. Figure 1-2 shows the location of each screen component.

Window Border   The Window border marks the boundaries of the CorelDRAW! window. By placing your mouse pointer on and dragging the border, you can scale this window. Refer to your Microsoft Windows user's guide for full details on how to scale a window.

Title Bar   The title bar shows the name of the program you are working in and the name of the currently loaded image. All files in CorelDRAW! format have the file extension .CDR directly after the filename. When you first load CorelDRAW!, the screen hasn't been saved yet, so the title bar reads "UNTITLED.CDR."

Minimize Button   You will find the minimize button at the upper-right corner of your screen. Click on this button to return to the Corel 4 group icon. When running as an icon within Windows, CorelDRAW! frees up memory that you can use to run another application. To restore CorelDRAW! to its previous size, position the mouse over the icon and double-click.

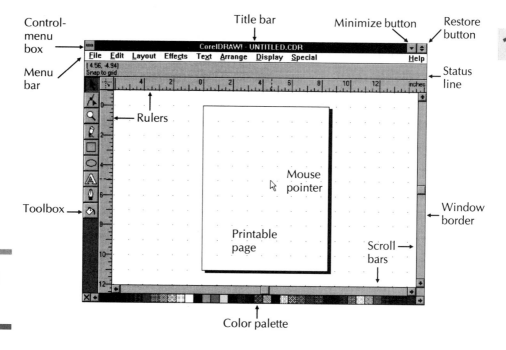

Control-
menu
box

Menu
bar

Toolbox

Title bar

Minimize button

Restore
button

Status
line

Rulers

Mouse
pointer

Printable
page

Window
border

Scroll
bars

Color palette

The
CorelDRAW!
screen
Figure 1-2.

Maximize Button   If you want to make the CorelDRAW! window fill the entire screen, click on the maximize button located next to the minimize button. This button then turns into the restore button, as shown in Figure 1-2. You can return the CorelDRAW! window to its previous size by clicking on the restore button once more.

Control-Menu Box   You can use the Control-menu box as another easy way to move, minimize, maximize, or otherwise change the size of the CorelDRAW! program window. To use the Control-menu box, simply click on the small bar inside the box, or press [Alt]-[Spacebar], and the Control menu will appear. Select the command you want by clicking on it. When you have finished, click anywhere outside the Control menu to close it. The Control menu is a Windows feature that is not needed by CorelDRAW!.

Menu Bar   The menu bar contains nine menus that you pull down by clicking on one of the menu names. See the section "CorelDRAW! Menus" later in this chapter for a brief summary of the command options in each menu.

Status Line   The status line contains a rich source of information about the image you have on your screen. When you first load CorelDRAW!, this line contains only a pair of numbers—the coordinates of the mouse pointer.

When you are drawing or editing images, however, it displays information such as number, type, and dimensions of objects you select and the distance you travel when moving these objects. The exact nature of the information displayed depends on what you are doing at the time. The status line offers invaluable aid to technical illustration or to any work that requires precision.

Printable Page Area   You create your images in the printable page area. The exact size of the page depends on the printer or other output device that you installed when you set up Microsoft Windows, as well as on the settings you choose through the Page Setup command in the Layout menu. When you first load CorelDRAW!, the screen displays the total printable page area. Once you learn about magnification in Chapter 5, you can adjust the area of the page that is visible at any one time.

Scroll Bars   The scroll bars are most useful when you are looking at a magnified view of the page. Use the horizontal scroll bar to move to the left or right of the currently visible area of the page; use the vertical scroll bar to move to an area of the page that is above or below the currently visible area. You will find more information on how to use the scroll bars in Chapter 6.

Rulers   The horizontal and vertical rulers that appear in Figure 1-2 may not appear on your screen. These are optional and must be specifically turned on by selecting Show Rulers from the Display menu. A dashed line in each ruler shows you where the mouse pointer is. You can see such lines at about 4.5 on the horizontal ruler and about 5.0 on the vertical ruler. These are the same as the coordinates in the status line. The rulers allow you to judge the relative sizes and placements of objects quickly and accurately.

Color Palette   The color palette at the bottom of the CorelDRAW! window in Figure 1-2 allows you to apply shades of gray on a monochrome screen or shades of gray and colors on a color monitor. Like the rulers, the color palette can be turned on or off in the Display menu. In CorelDRAW!, shading and color can be applied to either a character's or an object's outline, or its body.

Toolbox   The toolbox contains tools that carry out the most important and powerful drawing and editing functions in CorelDRAW!. Click on a tool icon to select a tool. The tool icon now appears on dark gray background. Other changes to the screen or to a selected object may also occur, depending on which tool you have selected. For a brief explanation of the function of each tool, see the section, "The CorelDRAW! Toolbox," later in this chapter.

With a basic understanding of the screen elements, you can get around the CorelDRAW! window easily. The next three sections of this chapter explore three types of interface elements—menus, dialog boxes, and tools—in greater depth.

1

CorelDRAW! Menus

When you pull down a menu, some commands appear in boldface, while others appear in gray. You can select any command that appears in boldface, but commands in gray are not available to you at the moment. Commands become available for selection depending on the objects you are working with and the actions you perform on them.

This book is a tutorial rather than a reference manual. As such, it organizes information about CorelDRAW! according to the task you want to perform and not by menu. You'll learn to use program menus by working with particular functions of CorelDRAW!. This section briefly describes the major purposes of each menu. These menus are shown in Figure 1-3.

The File Menu   The File menu in Figure 1-3a is similar in all Windows applications. Most of the commands in the File menu do not apply to the process of drawing. Instead, they cover program functions that deal with entire files at a time or with running the program as a whole. Examples of such functions are loading, saving, importing, exporting, and printing a file, as well as inserting an object and exiting CorelDRAW!. The most recent files you have worked with will be listed and can be easily opened by double-clicking on the filename.

The Edit Menu   The Edit menu in Figure 1-3b is also similar to other Windows applications. Use the commands in this menu to copy, *clone* (duplicate where the copy also receives any modifications made to the original), cut and paste objects or images, undo the last action you performed, copy or change styles or objects and text, and manage links with other applications.

The Layout Menu   The commands in the Layout menu, shown in Figure 1-3c, allow you to control the layout of pages. You can insert or delete pages, go from one page to another, set margins and page sizes, and work with layers that allow you to construct your drawing in multiple overlays. You can manage styles assigned to drawings, set attributes for grid and guidelines, and set the Snap To feature for grid, guidelines, and objects. The Layout and style menus use convenient submenus called "roll-up" windows. A roll-up window, or just "roll-up," is a dialog box that remains on the screen either at its normal size or "rolled up" in a minimized window. The roll-up will be fully discussed in the next section.

The Effects Menu   The Effects menu, shown in Figure 1-3d, allows you to create special effects with text and objects that transform the images. Among the tools available are Rotate, Skew, Stretch, and Mirror. These allow you to distort the image in specific ways. You can also place text or an object in an envelope and then shape that envelope to make the text or object appear to be in perspective or extruded. It also allows you to blend two lines of text or two objects. Two new features, Contouring and PowerLines, allow you to add contouring depth to an image, or to draw lines of varying width and depth. A more detailed discussion will be presented in Chapter 14.

The Text Menu   The Text menu shown in Figure 1-3e combines the text commands from other menus in one location. With CorelDRAW! 4 you have many features, such as Find and Replace, a spelling checker, and thesaurus. You have available a text roll-up to format text, and dialog boxes for setting character, frame, and paragraph attributes. An Edit Text dialog box displays font, style, and size attributes for quick changes.

The Arrange Menu   The commands in the Arrange menu, shown in Figure 1-3f, all have to do with the relative placement of objects within an image. Select the commands in this menu to move a selected object or group of objects, to combine, group, ungroup, or break apart selected objects, and to align objects and text. A new feature in CorelDRAW! 4 welds overlapping images together, making one object out of two. You will find more details about the Arrange menu commands in Chapter 6.

The Display Menu   The Display menu in Figure 1-3g has one very clear function: to help you customize the user interface and make the CorelDRAW! screen work the way you do. Use the commands in this menu to display or hide the rulers, status line, and color palette to set the screen for precision drawing, and to choose whether and how to display fully accurate, WYSIWYG (What-You-See-Is-What-You-Get) previews of your images.

The Special Menu   The Special menu in Figure 1-3h can be used for functions not found in other menus. You can use the Special menu to create patterns out of a selected object, line endings or arrows that can be attached to the end of a line, and symbols from a selected object. You also can extract text as an ASCII string for editing, and then merge it back into a drawing. Finally, the menu provides fine-tuning of many different program parameters using the Preferences option. Discussions about these options, which apply to a wide range of functions, appear in their respective contexts.

The Help Menu   The Help menu, shown in Figure 1-3i, allows access to an enormous wealth of online help features including a glossary and reference library. Through the Contents button you can choose help topics which cover the screen, commands, tools, and keyboard, and which also explain how to perform certain functions, as you can see in Figure 1-4.

By selecting Search For Help On from the Help menu, you can type in a word or choose one from a list and you will be shown all topics matching

CorelDRAW!
menus
Figure 1-3.

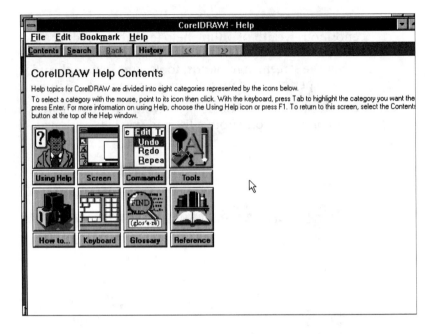

CorelDRAW!
Help Contents
Figure 1-4.

your search criteria. You can also get a quick look at how to use the comprehensive Help feature by selecting How To Use Help.

The final option on the Help menu, About CorelDRAW!, displays information on the current version of CorelDRAW! and other useful information on the number of objects and groups that are open, and on the available disk space on your C drive.

There are other ways in which you can get help. First, by pressing F1, the Help Contents option shown in Figure 1-4 is displayed, giving you the same eight categories of help that are available directly from the menu. Another method provides *context-sensitive* help. By pressing and holding down Shift followed by pressing F1, the mouse pointer changes to a question mark and arrow, as you are shown here:

You can then click on a menu command or screen item, and a help window will be displayed providing information on that particular subject.

Dialog Boxes

Some menu commands are automatic: Click on them, and CorelDRAW! performs the action immediately. Other commands are followed by three dots (an ellipsis), indicating that you must enter additional information before CorelDRAW! can execute the command. You enter this additional information through dialog boxes that pop up on the screen when you click on the command. This section introduces you to the look and feel of typical dialog boxes in CorelDRAW! and the new roll-up window.

Dialog boxes contain several kinds of controls and other ways for you to enter information. Compare the following descriptions with the screen elements in Figures 1-5 and 1-6 to familiarize yourself with operations in a dialog box. Look at Figure 1-5 first.

Diamond-shaped *option buttons* like those in Figure 1-5 present you with mutually exclusive choices. In a group of option buttons, you can select only one at a time. When you click on an option button to select it, the interior becomes dark.

Square *check boxes* in a dialog box offer you choices that are not mutually exclusive, so you can select more than one option simultaneously. Check boxes behave like light switches; you turn them on or off when you click to select or deselect them. When you turn on or enable an option in a check box, a check fills it. When you turn off or disable the option, the check disappears.

The larger rectangles in a dialog box are *command buttons*. When selected, a command button is highlighted temporarily, and usually CorelDRAW! performs the command instantly. When you click on a command button that has a label followed by an ellipsis, you open another dialog box that is nested within it.

A rectangle that contains numeric entries and that is associated with up and down scroll arrows is a *numeric entry box*. You can change the numeric values in three ways. To increase or decrease the value by a single increment, click on the up or down arrow, respectively. To increase or decrease the value by a large amount, press and hold the mouse button over one of the scroll arrows. You can also click on the value itself to select it, erase the current value, and then type in new numbers.

Rectangles containing units of measurement represent *drop-down list boxes* that are valid only for the associated option and dialog box. Click on the drop down list box as many times as necessary to change to the unit of measurement you prefer.

Figure 1-6 shows an example of a dialog box that contains different types of controls. Use the *text entry boxes* available in some dialog boxes to enter

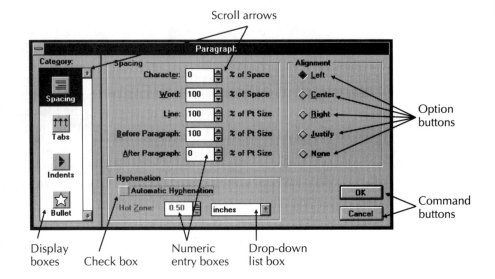

Representative
controls in a
dialog box
Figure 1-5.

strings of text. Depending on the dialog box involved, text strings might
represent filenames, path names, or text to appear in an image. To enter new
text where none exists, click on the text entry box and type the text. To edit
an existing text string, click on the string, then use the keyboard to erase or
add text. You will become familiar with the specific keys to use as you learn
about each type of text entry box.

The *list boxes* within a dialog box list the names of choices available to the
user, such as filenames, directory and drive names, or typestyle names. Click
on a name in the list box to select it.

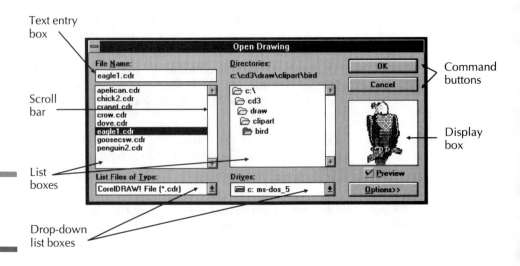

Additional
dialog box
controls
Figure 1-6.

Scroll bars accompany text entry boxes or list boxes when the contents of those boxes exceed the visible area in the dialog box. You can use the scroll bar to access the portions of the list that are outside of the currently visible area. To move up or down one name at a time, click on the up or down arrow of the scroll bar, respectively. To move up or down continuously, press and hold the mouse button over the up or down arrow of the scroll bar. Alternatively, you can click on the scroll bar itself, drag the scroll box, or press [Pg Up] or [Pg Dn] to move up or down the list box in large increments.

Some dialog boxes, such as the one shown in Figure 1-6, contain *display boxes* that show you just how your current selection will look after you exit the dialog box. You do not perform any action on the display box itself; instead, its contents change as you change your selections in the dialog box.

Some options in a dialog box may appear in gray, indicating that you cannot select them at the moment. On the other hand, a command button within a dialog box may appear in boldface, indicating that you can select it, and it also may have a bold outline around it. This command button represents the default selection. You can simply press [Enter] to activate that selection, exit the dialog box, and return to your graphic. The OK command button is normally the default. The OK button accepts and processes the entries you make in the dialog box. You can leave most dialog boxes without changing any settings by clicking on the Cancel button or pressing [Esc].

You will learn more about operating within dialog boxes in the context of each chapter in this book. The following section will acquaint you with the toolbox, the portion of the interface most vital to the operation of CorelDRAW!.

Roll-up Windows

Roll-up windows are a special form of dialog box that you can keep on the screen to allow faster access to the features provided in the window. Once you've chosen a roll-up from a menu, you can choose any of the offered features and watch them take effect. You can also move the roll-up by dragging its title bar. After you've completed a task, you then have the choice of either keeping the roll-up on the screen in its full size or rolling up the window to its minimized size by clicking on the arrow in the upper-right corner, as shown here:

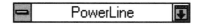

More than one roll-up can be kept on your screen at a time. A convenient way to display one or more minimized roll-ups is to choose the Arrange or

Arrange All option from the roll-up's Control menu, which is located in the upper-left corner of the roll-up window. When chosen, Arrange (one roll-up) or Arrange All (multiple roll-ups) moves the minimized windows into a single column starting in the upper-right or upper-left corner of the full CorelDRAW! window.

You can also remove any roll-up from the screen by double-clicking its Control-menu box, or by selecting Close from its Control menu.

The CorelDRAW! Toolbox

One of the features that makes CorelDRAW! so easy to work with is the economy of the screen. The number of tools in the CorelDRAW! toolbox (Figure 1-7) is deceptively small. Several of the tools have more than one function, and nested submenus *flyout* when you select them. This method of organization reduces screen clutter and keeps related functions together.

The tools in the CorelDRAW! toolbox perform three different kinds of functions. Some allow you to draw objects, others let you edit the objects you have drawn, and a third group permits you to alter the appearance of the screen so that you can work more efficiently. This section describes each tool briefly in the context of its respective function.

Drawing Tools

CorelDRAW! allows you to create or work with nine different types of objects, as shown in Figure 1-8. Because you use the same tools and

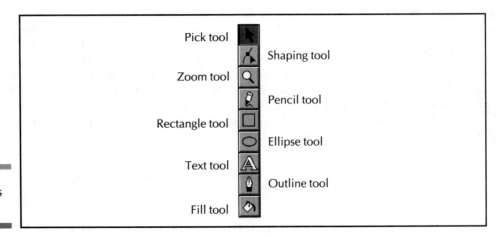

CorelDRAW!
toolbox icons
Figure 1-7.

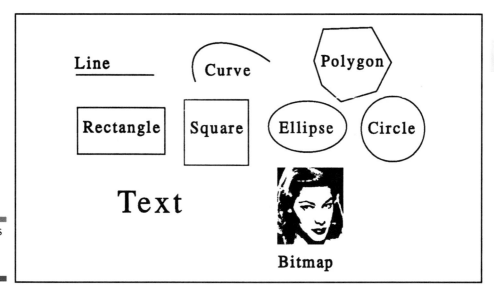

The nine types
of objects
Figure 1-8.

techniques for some of the objects, however, there are actually only five
different *classes* of objects. These classes, and the kinds of objects you can
design in each, are

✦ Lines, curves, and polygons

✦ Rectangles and squares

✦ Ellipses and circles

✦ Text

✦ Bitmap (pixel-based) images imported from a scanner or paint program

Does nine seem like a small number? Professional artists and graphic
designers know that basic geometrical shapes are the building blocks on
which more elaborate images are constructed. After you "build" an object
using one of the four drawing tools, you can use one or more of the editing
tools in the CorelDRAW! toolbox to reshape, rearrange, color, and outline it.

The four drawing tools—the Pencil tool, the Rectangle tool, the Ellipse tool,
and the Text tool—are all you need to create eight of the nine object types in
CorelDRAW!. You work with the last object type, a bitmap image, after
importing it. (See Chapters 13 and 17 for a fuller discussion of this subject.)

The Pencil Tool   The Pencil tool is the most basic drawing tool in the CorelDRAW! toolbox. This single tool allows you to create lines, curves, curved objects, and polygons. The Pencil tool can be changed from a single-mode freehand drawing instrument to a more sophisticated multimode instrument using Bézier lines and curves, or to one of three Dimension Lines modes. Freehand mode is the default and is used for less precise work. Bézier mode is selected from the flyout menu. Click on the Pencil tool, hold the mouse button down, and five icons, one for each drawing mode, are displayed, as

shown on the left. Bézier mode is used for smooth, precise curves, which remain so, even when magnified or distorted. The three Dimension Lines modes are used to place lines that show dimensions between two objects or locations, such as in technical drawings.

Chapter 2 guides you through a series of exercises that teach you all the basic CorelDRAW! skills for using this tool in all five modes.

To select the Pencil tool, press F5 or click on the Pencil icon once, and then move the mouse pointer into the white space on the page. When you select this tool, the mouse pointer takes the shape of a crosshair, the Pencil tool icon becomes highlighted, and the message "Drawing in Freehand Mode...", "Drawing in Bézier Mode...", or "Creating Linear Dimension..." appears on the status line.

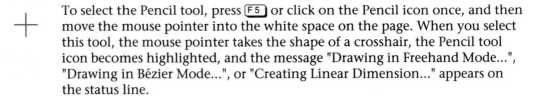

The Rectangle Tool   The Rectangle tool lets you draw rectangles and squares. You'll create your own rectangles and squares in Chapter 3. To round the corners of a rectangle, however, you need to use the Shaping tool, one of the editing tools in the CorelDRAW! toolbox.

To select the Rectangle tool, press F6 or click on the Rectangle icon once, and then move the mouse pointer into the white space on the page. The Rectangle icon becomes highlighted, the mouse pointer becomes a crosshair, and the message "Rectangle..." appears in the status line.

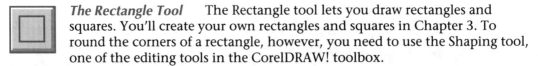

The Ellipse Tool   The Ellipse tool allows you to design ellipses and perfect circles. You can learn more about using the Ellipse tool in Chapter 3.

To select the Ellipse tool, press F7 or click on the Ellipse icon once, and then move the mouse pointer into the white space on the page. The Ellipse icon becomes highlighted, the mouse pointer becomes a crosshair, and the message "Ellipse..." appears in the status line.

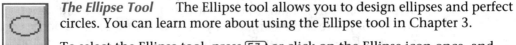

1

The Text Tool   The Text tool contains a flyout menu with three icons for choosing between text or symbols. You can enter text in one of two modes: as an artistically created string of letters, or as a paragraph such as you might use for a brochure. The text mode gives you access to more than 50 Corel Systems fonts (750 on CD-ROM) and to thousands of other commercial fonts as well. The symbol mode provides access to CorelDRAW!'s extensive symbol library. Chapter 4 teaches you how to enter text in CorelDRAW!.

To select the Text tool, press `F8` or click on the Text icon once, and then move the pointer into the white space on the page. The Text icon becomes highlighted, the mouse pointer becomes a crosshair, and the message "Text..." or "Curve..." appears in the status line.

If you "scribbled" on the page while trying out any of the drawing tools, clear the screen before proceeding. To do this, click on the File menu name and select the New command. The following dialog box appears:

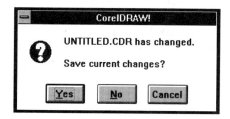

Select the No command button to exit the message box and clear the screen.

Editing Tools

Once you have created objects on a page with the drawing tools, you use a different group of tools to move, arrange, reshape, and manipulate the objects. The editing tools include the Pick tool, the Shaping tool, the Outline tool, and the Fill tool.

The Pick Tool   The Pick tool is really two tools in one. In the *select mode,* you can select objects in order to move, arrange, group, or combine them. In the *transformation mode,* you can use the Pick tool to rotate, skew, stretch, reflect, move, or scale a selected object. This tool does not let you change the basic shape of an object, however. Chapters 6 and 7 introduce you to all the functions of the Pick tool.

The Shaping Tool   The Shaping tool allows you to modify the shape of an object. Use this tool to smooth or distort any shape, add rounded corners to rectangles, convert a circle into a wedge or arc, modify a curve, or kern individual characters in a text string. Chapters 8 and 9 cover the basics of using this tool.

The Outline Tool   The Outline tool, like the Pick tool, functions in more than one way. Use the Outline tool and its associated flyout menu to choose a standard or custom outline color, or to create a custom outline "pen" for a selected object. Chapters 11 and 12 instruct you in the use of this tool.

 The Fill Tool   Use the Fill tool and its associated flyout menu to select a standard or custom fill color for selected objects or text. As you'll learn in Chapter 12, your options include custom colors, POSTSCRIPT screens, fountain fills, and POSTSCRIPT textures.

Tools for Customizing the CorelDRAW! Screen

 The third group of tools helps you customize the CorelDRAW! interface so that it works the way you do. Only one of these tools, the Zoom tool, is visible in the CorelDRAW! toolbox. The Zoom tool and its associated flyout menu let you control just how much of your picture you will view at one time. Use this tool when you need to work on a smaller area in fine detail, or when you need to zoom in or out of a picture. Chapter 5 will discuss the Zoom tool and its flyout menu in more detail.

Quitting CorelDRAW!

Now that you are familiar with the screen components, exit CorelDRAW! and return to the Program Manager. You can use the mouse, the keyboard and mouse, or the keyboard alone to quit CorelDRAW!.

Using the mouse, double-click on the Control-menu box in the upper-left corner, or display the File menu by moving the mouse pointer to the File menu name and then click once. Then, select the Exit command by clicking on it once.

Using both mouse and keyboard, display the File menu by clicking on the menu name. Then, with the File menu displayed, press X.

Using the keyboard alone, you can either press Alt-F to display the File menu and then press X, or press Ctrl-X.

TIP: If you have attempted to draw during this session, a screen message like the one shown here appears:

1

`UNTITLED.CDR has changed, Save current changes?`

Select the No command button to abandon your changes.

If you are like most CorelDRAW! users, you will want to begin drawing immediately. This book encourages you to draw. In Chapter 2 you will use the Pencil tool to begin drawing lines and curves.

C H A P T E R

CORELDRAW! 4

2

DRAWING AND WORKING WITH LINES AND CURVES

The Pencil tool icon is the most versatile tool in the CorelDRAW! toolbox. By using this tool in two different modes, you can create both straight and curved lines, and from these simple building blocks you can construct an almost infinite variety of polygons and irregular shapes. A third mode, Dimension Lines, allows you to place vertical, horizontal, and angular lines that display dimensions of objects or other lines on a page. Work through the exercises in this chapter to become thoroughly familiar with this most basic CorelDRAW! Pencil tool.

Freehand Versus Bézier Mode

The Pencil tool has two modes of drawing: Freehand mode, where curves mirror the movements of your hand on a mouse, and Bézier (pronounced "bay-z-air") mode, where curves are precisely placed between two or more points you identify. Drawing straight lines is very similar in the two modes, but drawing curves is very different. In the remaining sections of this chapter, Freehand mode, the default, will be discussed first, and then Bézier mode. Dimension Lines mode is discussed after the first two drawing modes.

Drawing Straight Lines

In the language of the CorelDRAW! interface, *line* refers to any straight line, while *curve* refers to curved lines, irregular lines, and closed objects you create with such lines. Drawing a straight line requires that you work with the mouse in a different way than when you draw a curved or irregular line. To draw a straight line in CorelDRAW! follow these steps:

1. Load CorelDRAW! if it isn't running already.

2. Position the mouse pointer over the Pencil tool icon and click once. The pointer changes to a crosshair as you move it off the icon, and the Pencil tool icon becomes darkened.

3. Position the crosshair pointer where you want a line to begin. This can be anywhere inside the printable page area.

4. Press *and immediately release (click)* the left mouse button, and then move the crosshair pointer toward the point where you want to end the line. A straight line appears and extends as far as you move the crosshair pointer, as in Figure 2-1. You can move the line in any direction, or make the segment longer or shorter.

5. When you have established the length and direction you want, complete the line by clicking and releasing the mouse button. As Figure 2-2 shows, a small square *node* appears at each end of the line to show that the line is complete and can be selected for further work.

6. Press [Del] to clear the line from the screen.

TIP: When you begin to draw a line, be sure to release the mouse button as soon as you press it. If you continue to hold down the mouse button while drawing, you create a curve instead of a straight line.

2

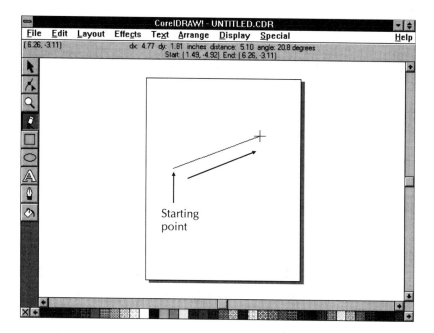

Extending a
straight line
Figure 2-1.

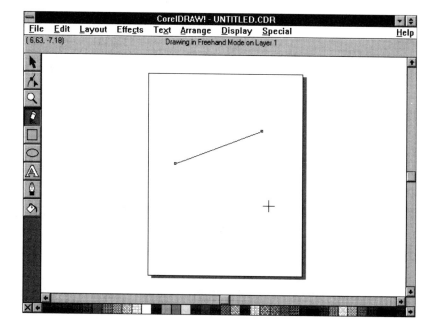

Nodes on a
completed line
Figure 2-2.

Using the Status Line to Improve Precision

Chapter 1 introduced you briefly to the status line and its potential for helping you draw with precision and accuracy. In the next exercise, pay attention to the useful information that appears on the status line.

1. With the Pencil tool still selected, begin another line by clicking the mouse button at a point about halfway down the left side of the page. The coordinates on the left side of the status line should be *about* 1.0, 5.5 (absolute precision is not important).

2. Move the mouse toward the right side of the page. Don't click a second time yet.

3. Notice that as soon as you clicked once and began to move the mouse, a message appeared on the status line, as shown here:

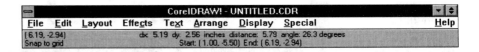

Look more closely at the status line. It includes information about the line you are drawing. The codes in the status line and their meanings are discussed next. (The measurements may be set as millimeters, inches, picas, or points. If your screen does not show the same measurement units as this book, you can change the setting in the Layout menu by choosing Grid Setup and then Grid Frequency. Set both the horizontal and vertical measurements to inches.)

dx The *dx* code refers to the *x*-coordinate or horizontal location of your line on the page relative to the starting point. The number following this code identifies how far your line has traveled (in other words, its distance) from that starting point along the X or horizontal axis. A positive number (one with no minus sign in front of it) indicates that you are extending the line to the right of the starting point, while a negative number indicates the reverse.

dy The *dy* code refers to the *y*-coordinate or vertical location of your line on the page relative to the starting point. The number following this code identifies how far your line has traveled (in other words, its distance) above or below that starting point along the Y or vertical axis. A positive number indicates that you are extending the line above the starting point, while a negative number indicates that you are extending it below the starting point.

inches The unit of measurement for the current *dx* and *dy* position indicators appears on the status line as well. The CorelDRAW! default is inches, but you can change it to millimeters or picas and points using the

Grid Setup command in the Layout menu. You'll gain experience with the grid later in this chapter.

2

distance   The number following this text indicates the length of your line relative to the starting point.

angle   The number following this text indicates the angle of the line relative to an imaginary compass, where 0 degrees is at the 3 o'clock position, 90 degrees is at the 12 o'clock position, 180 degrees is at the 9 o'clock position, and -90 degrees is at the 6 o'clock position.

Start and End   The pairs of numbers following each of these items represent the coordinates of the start and end points of the line.

Continue the preceding exercise with these steps:

4. Choose an end point for the line and click again to freeze the line in place. Note that the status line indicators disappear as soon as you complete the line, just as they did in Figure 2-2.
5. Press Del to delete the line before going further.

As you may have noticed, information appears on the status line only when you are performing some action on an object. This information makes CorelDRAW! especially powerful for applications requiring great precision, such as technical illustration.

Erasing Portions of a Line

In the following exercise, you'll practice erasing part of a line that you have extended but not completed. You can always backtrack and shorten a line in CorelDRAW!, as long as you have not clicked a second time to complete it.

1. With the Pencil tool still selected, choose a starting point for another line.
2. Move the pointer downward and to the right until the *dx* indicator reads about 5.00 inches and the *dy* indicator reads about -1.00 inches, as in the example in Figure 2-3.
3. Without clicking the mouse button a second time, shorten the line until the *dx* indicator reads 4.00 inches. Notice that the line you have drawn behaves flexibly and becomes shorter as you move the mouse backward.
4. Click a second time to freeze the line at *dx* 4.00 inches.
5. Before going any further, delete the line by pressing Del.

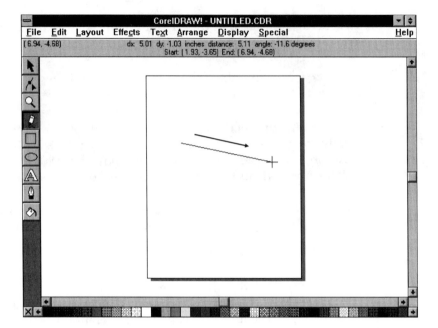

Extending a
line using the
status line
indicator
Figure 2-3.

Constraining a Line to an Angle

You need not rely on the status line alone to control the precision of your
drawing. You can also use the Ctrl key while drawing to *constrain* (force) a
line to an angle in increments of 15 degrees. In the following exercise, you'll
create a series of seven straight lines this way.

1. With the Pencil tool still selected, *press and hold* Ctrl and click the mouse
    button to choose a starting point for the line.

2. Release the mouse button, but continue holding Ctrl as you extend the
    line outward and downward from the starting point. Try moving the
    line to different angles in a clockwise direction. As the angle indicator in
    the status line shows, the line does not move smoothly but instead
    "jumps" in increments of 15 degrees.

3. Now, extend the line straight outward, so that the angle indicator on
    the status line reads 0 degrees. While still holding down Ctrl , click the
    mouse button a second time to freeze the line at this angle.

4. Release Ctrl . (Remember always to click the mouse *before* you release Ctrl .
    If you release Ctrl first, the line doesn't necessarily align to an angle.)

5. Draw six more lines in the same way, each sharing a common starting
    point. Extend the second line at an angle of 15 degrees, the third at an
    angle of 30 degrees, the fourth at an angle of 45 degrees, the fifth at an

angle of 60 degrees, the sixth at an angle of 75 degrees, and the seventh at an angle of 90 degrees. When you are finished, your lines should match the pattern shown in Figure 2-4.

Clearing the Screen

Before going any further, clear the screen of the lines you have created so far.

1. Click on the File menu to pull it down.
2. Select the New command.
3. A message box appears with this message:

`UNTITLED.CDR Has Changed, Save Current Changes?`

Click on the No command button to exit the message box and clear the screen. The Pick tool in the tool box is highlighted by default, just as when you first loaded CorelDRAW!.

Drawing Multisegment Lines

With CorelDRAW!, you can easily draw several straight lines in sequence so that each begins where the previous one left off. Use this technique both for

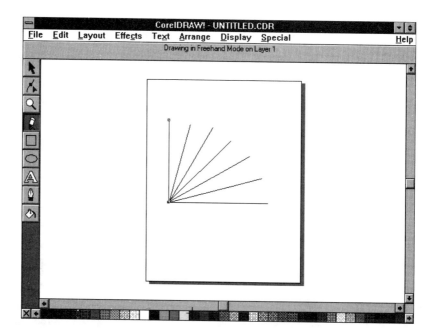

Constraining lines to angles in 15-degree increments

Figure 2-4.

drawing open-ended line figures and for constructing polygons. In the present exercise, you will construct a series of peaks and valleys.

1. Select the Pencil tool using a shortcut—press the ⟨F5⟩ function key. Then click to choose a line starting point. Extend a line upward and to the right.

2. When you reach the desired end point for the line, freeze it in place with a *double click* rather than a single click of the mouse button.

3. Move the mouse downward and to the right, without clicking again. The flexible line follows the crosshair pointer automatically.

4. Double-click again to freeze the second line in place.

5. Continue zigzagging in this way until you have created several peaks and valleys similar to those in Figure 2-5.

6. When you reach the last valley, click once instead of twice to end the multisegment line.

7. Press ⟨Del⟩ to clear the screen before proceeding.

TIP: If you make a mistake drawing, you can erase the last line segment you completed in one of two ways. You either press ⟨Alt⟩-⟨Backspace⟩ or select the Undo command in the Edit menu. Don't press ⟨Del⟩ when drawing a multisegment line, or you will erase all of the segments you have drawn so far.

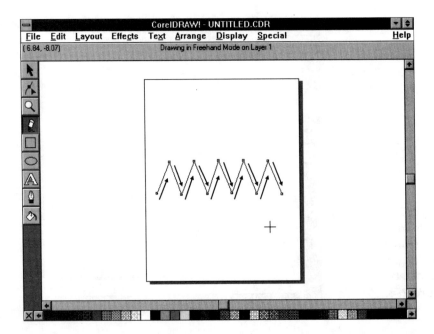

Drawing
multisegment
lines
Figure 2-5.

Drawing a Polygon

A *polygon* is a closed two-dimensional figure bounded by straight lines. You create polygons in CorelDRAW! by drawing multisegment lines and then connecting the end point to the starting point. In the following exercise, you'll create a polygon figure like the one in Figure 2-6.

2

1. Draw the first line, double-clicking at the line end point so that you can continue drawing without interruption.

2. Draw four additional lines in the same way, following the pattern in Figure 2-6. End the last line segment with a single click at the point where the first line segment began.

Did your last line segment "snap" to the beginning of the first? Or does a small gap remain between them? If you can still see a small gap, don't worry. In the section "Joining Lines and Curves Automatically," later in this chapter, you'll learn how to adjust the level of sensitivity at which one line will join automatically to another. If your lines did snap together to form an enclosed polygon, it will fill with a solid black color if the standard defaults are set. For now, clear the screen and begin the next exercise.

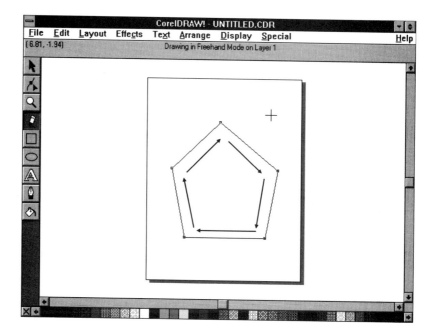

Drawing a
polygon
Figure 2-6.

Straight Lines in Bézier Mode

The Bézier mode of drawing is to identify end points or nodes and place lines or curves between them. Therefore, drawing straight lines in Bézier mode is very similar to drawing straight lines in Freehand mode. Try it next and see for yourself.

To use Bézier mode:

1. Select Bézier mode by pointing on the Pencil tool and pressing and holding the mouse button down until the pencil flyout menu appears, like this:

2. Click on the Bézier tool, the second from the left of the five icons on the flyout menu.

Your status line should now include the words "Drawing in Bézier Mode..."

Drawing Single Lines in Bézier Mode

Now draw a single line segment as you did earlier in Freehand mode.

1. Click on a starting point in the middle left of the page, immediately release the mouse button (if you hold down the mouse button, CorelDRAW! will think you are drawing a curve), and move the mouse pointer to the upper right of the page.

    Notice that the starting point is a solid black square. This starting point is a node, a point on a line that is used to define the line. When you start the line, the starting point is selected and is therefore black. Also, there is no line connecting the starting point and the mouse pointer, and no information in the status line except the coordinates of the mouse pointer. A line does not appear and there is no information in the status line because a Bézier line is not defined until you have placed at least two nodes.

2. Click on an end node. A straight line is drawn between the two nodes, as shown in Figure 2-7, and information now appears in the status line. The line segment, however, is called a "curve."

2

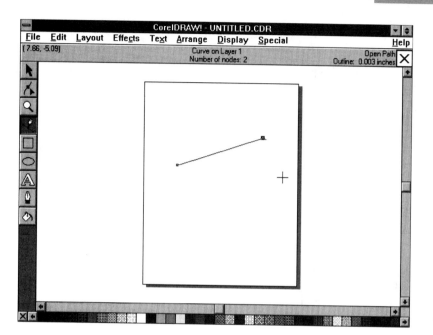

Drawing a Polygon in Bézier Mode

Unlike Freehand mode, you can continue to add line segments after clicking on an end node only once in Bézier mode. Do that next to build a polygon (your screen should still be as you left it after drawing the first Bézier line segment).

1. Click on two more nodes, one toward the lower right and the other toward the lower left. Lines will be added connecting the nodes.

2. Position the mouse pointer on top of the original starting node and click one final time. The result is a four-sided polygon like the one shown in Figure 2-8. If your sides join to form a polygon (that is, not an open shape), and you are using a fill pattern, your polygon will fill with the pattern defined as the default, such as a solid black color. Chapter 12 discusses this in more detail.

As you can see, there are many mechanical similarities between Freehand and Bézier drawing of straight lines. The results are virtually the same, but the screen looks very different during the creation of the lines. For straight lines there is little reason to use Bézier over Freehand.

Like Freehand mode, you can move the mouse pointer in any direction, including backward, over the path already traveled to "erase" the object

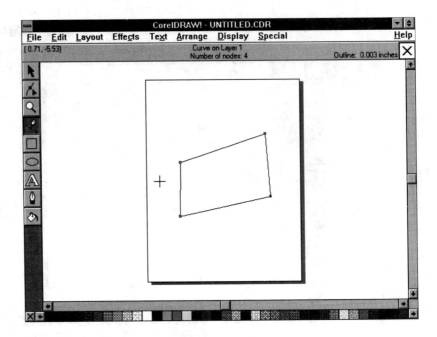

Bézier polygon
Figure 2-8.

before clicking on a node. After clicking on a node you can use Undo (either Alt -Backspace or choose Undo from the Edit menu) to erase the previous line (or curve) segment. If you want to delete the entire object (line or polygon) while it is still selected (you can see all of the nodes), press Del.

If you want to draw two or more Bézier line segments that are not connected, press the Spacebar twice, then draw your second line.

3. Press Del to clear your drawing. To return to Freehand mode, click on the Bézier Pencil tool and hold the mouse button until the flyout menu appears.

Now you can either release the mouse button and click on the Freehand tool, or you can continue holding the mouse button down and drag the mouse pointer to the Freehand tool, and then release the mouse button. You are returned to your drawing, in Freehand mode, ready to begin working with curves.

Drawing Curves

The Pencil tool has a twofold purpose in CorelDRAW!: you can use it to draw curved or irregular lines as well as straight lines. This section introduces you to the basics of drawing a simple curve, closing the path of a curve to form a closed curve object, and erasing unwanted portions of a curve as you draw.

To draw a simple curve:

1. Select the Pencil tool (in Freehand mode) if it is not still selected.

2. Position the crosshair pointer at the point on the page where you want a curve to begin and then *press and hold* the mouse button. The Start and End coordinates appear on the status line.

3. Continue to hold the mouse button and *drag* the mouse along the path where you want the curve to continue. Follow the example in Figure 2-9.

4. Upon completing the curve, release the mouse button. The curve disappears momentarily while CorelDRAW! calculates exactly where it should go. Then the curve reappears with many small square nodes, as in Figure 2-10. Note that when you have finished, the words "Curve on Layer 1" and the number of nodes appears in the middle of the status line, and the message "Open Path" appears at the right side of the status line. "Open Path" indicates that you have drawn a curved line, not a closed figure.

5. Press Del or select the Undo command in the Edit menu to clear the curve you have just drawn.

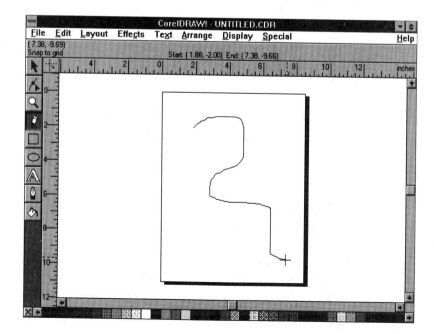

Drawing a
curve
Figure 2-9.

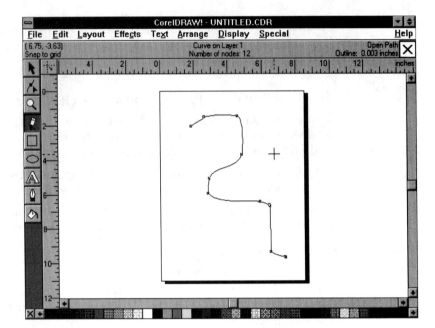

A complete
curve with
nodes
Figure 2-10.

TIP: To draw a straight line, click and release the mouse button. To draw a curve, press and hold the mouse button and drag the mouse along the desired path.

Erasing Portions of a Curve

Should you make a mistake while drawing a curve, you can backtrack and erase what you have drawn, as long as you have not yet released the mouse button. You use Shift to erase the portion of a curve that you no longer want.

1. Begin another curve by pressing and holding the mouse button over the point at which you want the curve to start.

2. Drag the mouse as desired. Do not release the mouse button yet.

3. While still holding down the mouse button, press and hold Shift and backtrack over as much of the curve as you wish to erase.

4. After you have erased a portion of the curve, release Shift and continue to draw by dragging the mouse in the desired direction.

5. Release the mouse button to finalize the curve. Delete the curve by pressing Del.

Drawing Multisegment Curves

Just as you drew multisegment lines, you can also draw multisegment curves. You can join two successive curves together automatically if the starting point of the second curve is within a few pixels of the end point of the first curve.

2

1. Select a starting point for the first curve and begin dragging the mouse.
2. Complete the curve by releasing the mouse button. Do not move the mouse pointer from the point at which your first curve ends.
3. Draw the second curve and complete it. The second curve should "snap" to the first.

If the two curved lines didn't snap together, you moved the pointer farther than five pixels away before starting the second curve. Don't worry about it at this point. CorelDRAW! has a default value of five pixels distance for automatic joining of lines and curves. In the "Joining Lines and Curves Automatically" section of this chapter, you will learn how to adjust the sensitivity of this AutoJoin feature.

Closing an Open Path

When you drew your first curve, the message "Open Path" appeared at the right side of the status line. This message indicates that your curved line is not a closed object, and therefore that you cannot fill it with a color or pattern (see Chapter 12). You can create a closed curve object with the Pencil tool, however. Refer to Figure 2-11 to create a closed outline of any shape for this exercise. You'll draw this shape as a single curve.

1. Before beginning the exercise, select New from the File menu to clear the screen. When a message box appears and asks whether you want to save your changes, select No.

   You may at this point want to set an option to fill a closed shape with a color or pattern. To do this you can select the Fill icon and click on the black color square. A Uniform Fill dialog box will be displayed. Ensure that a check mark is next to the Graphic option and click on OK. If you want more information, see Chapter 12.

2. Select the Pencil tool (Freehand mode).
3. Start the curve about midway across the page area.
4. Continue dragging the mouse to create the closed shape. Your drawing doesn't have to look exactly like the one in Figure 2-11. If you make a mistake, press (Shift) and backtrack to erase the portions of the curve that you do not want.

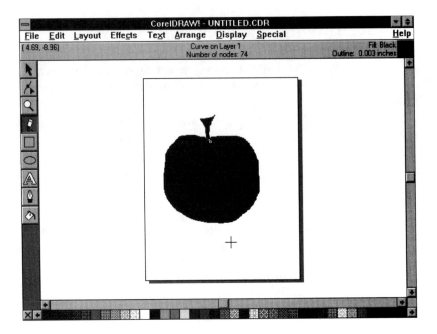

Drawing a
closed curve
object
Figure 2-11.

5. When you return to the point at which you began, make sure you are
    over your starting point and then release the mouse button. After a
    second the object reappears as a solid black shape.

Note that the message in the middle of the status line now reads "Curve" and
the number of nodes. At the right side of the status line, the message
"Fill:Black" appears, followed by a representation of a solid black color. This
indicates that you now have a closed curve object and that it is filled with
the default color, black.

Full Color Versus Wireframe Modes

In the last exercise and in the two previous polygon exercises, it was noted
that the polygon would fill with solid black color when and if the polygon
was closed and if the default settings were still in effect. As of CorelDRAW! 3,
the default drawing mode became *full color mode,* meaning that you can see
the full color of an object as you are working on it. In versions of
CorelDRAW! prior to 3, you could only see an object's color in what was
called *preview mode,* and you could not actually draw in this mode. In earlier
versions, all work was done in *wireframe mode,* where you could see only an
object's outline and therefore not its color. Although by default all work in
CorelDRAW! 3 and later is done in full color mode, you can switch to
wireframe mode when it is beneficial to work with an object's outline. You

do this by choosing Edit Wireframe from the Display menu. You can return to full color mode by again choosing Edit Wireframe to turn it off.

Drawing Curves in Bézier Mode

2

If you are like most people, drawing smooth curves in Freehand mode is very difficult, if not impossible. Of course, as you'll see in Chapter 8, CorelDRAW!'s Shaping tool allows you to clean up messy artwork very quickly. As an alternative, though, the Bézier mode of drawing allows you to draw smooth curves to start with—after a little practice.

The principle of Bézier drawing is that you place a node, set a pair of control points that determine the slope and height or depth of the curve, and then place the next node. The method is to place the crosshair where you want a node, press and hold the mouse button while you drag the control points until you are satisfied with their positioning, release the mouse button, and go on and do the same thing for the next node. When you have two or more nodes, curves appear between them reflecting your settings. This is very different from Freehand mode drawing and will take some getting used to. Dragging the mouse with the button depressed moves the control points in two dimensions and only indirectly identifies the path of the curve. Understanding how to handle control points, though, will help you use the Shaping tool in Chapter 8.

The only way to really understand Bézier drawing is to try it.

1. Clear your screen by selecting New from the File menu and choosing No in answer to the Save Changes message.
2. Momentarily hold the mouse button while clicking on the Pencil tool to open the flyout menu, and then select the Bézier mode icon.
3. Move the mouse pointer to where you want to start the curve and press and hold the left mouse button.
4. Move the mouse in any direction while continuing to hold the left mouse button, and you should see the *control points* appear—two small black boxes and dashed lines connecting them to the larger node, as shown here:

There are three principles involved in moving the mouse to set the control points:

✦ Begin by dragging a control point in the direction that you want the curve to leave the node.

♦ Drag the control point away from the node to increase the height or depth of the curve, and drag the control point toward the node to decrease the height or depth.

♦ Rotate the control points about the node to change the slope of the curve. The slope follows the rotational increment of the control point.

5. Drag the control point out away from the node toward 2 o'clock and swing it in an arc about the node. Notice how the two points move in opposite directions. Continue to hold the left mouse button.

6. Drag the control point in toward the node until it is about a half inch away from the node and swing it until the control point that you clicked on is pointing at 2 o'clock. Your node should look like this:

7. Release the mouse button and move the mouse pointer to where you want the second node to be—about two inches to the right and in line with the first node.

8. Again press and hold the left mouse button to set the node.

9. Drag the control point toward 5 o'clock so it is about a half inch away from the node.

10. Release the mouse button. A curve segment is drawn between the two nodes that should look like this:

11. Move the mouse pointer and press and hold the mouse button to set a third node about an inch below and in the middle of the first two nodes.

12. Drag the control point so it is about a quarter of an inch to the left of the node, at 9 o'clock.

13. Release the mouse button. A second curve segment will appear, as shown here:

14. Move the mouse pointer until it is on top of the first node you set and press and hold the mouse button.

15. Drag the control points until they are about a half inch away from the node and the top control point is aimed at 2 o'clock, like this:

2

16. Release the mouse button. A third curve segment appears, completing a curved triangle, which will be filled with solid black in full color mode.

Practice drawing other Bézier objects. Notice how moving the control points both in and out from the node and in an arc around the node can radically change the curve segment to its left (behind the node) and to a lesser extent, the curve segment to the right (ahead of the node). Also, notice how the number of nodes can affect the finished object. As a general rule, the fewer nodes the better, but there are some minimums.

A continuous curve like a circle should have a node every 120 degrees or three nodes on a circle like this:

A curve that changes direction, such as a sine wave, needs a node for every two changes in direction, as shown here:

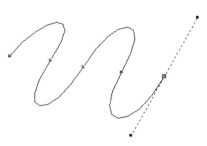

A curve that changes direction in a sharp point (called a cusp) needs a node for every change in direction, like this:

17. Clear the screen by selecting New from the File menu and responding No when asked to save the changes.

The Dimension Lines Feature

The Dimension Lines feature is new with version 4. Dimension lines can be used to display measurements, sizes, or distances, as you might need in technical drawings, for example.

CorelDRAW! offers three dimension line tools:

Vertical   Horizontal   Angular or Diagonal

Using Dimension Lines

Since the three dimension line tools operate similarly, you will experiment with just one of the tools. You will see how to draw and position a dimension line, using one of two methods to complete it. Follow these steps:

1. Hold the mouse while clicking on the Pencil tool to open the flyout menu. Select the vertical dimension line icon, which is the first dimension line with the vertical line.

2. Move the mouse pointer to the top left quadrant of the page and click the left mouse button to anchor the beginning point.

3. Experiment with moving the dimension line by moving the mouse pointer left and right, up and down. Move the pointer off the page as well. You'll see how the vertical dimension line can be positioned left or right, shortened, or lengthened by moving the pointer.

When you have seen what to expect in the vertical line movement, move the mouse pointer to the bottom right quadrant and click the mouse button.

4. Experiment again by moving the vertical line to the right and left. See how you can position it in exact locations.

2

Pull the line off the page to the right and place the pointer somewhere toward the top of the vertical line, then click the mouse button. The position of the pointer indicates where the dimension is to be placed on the line.

Figure 2-12 shows what your screen may look like. You can see the dimension label has been placed approximately where you clicked the final time.

TIP: You can change the format and placement of the dimension label by changing the settings in the Special menu, Preferences dialog box, and Dimension button. You can automatically center the label on the vertical line, and you can print it horizontally rather than vertically as it is in Figure 2-12. By pressing the Format button, you also can choose a default display pattern for how the dimension will be printed.

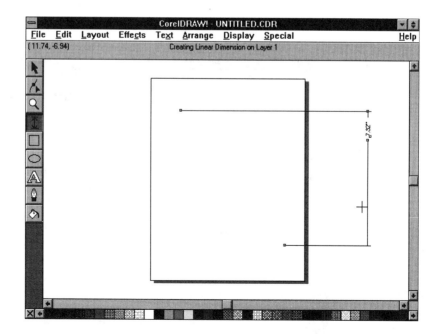

Using a
dimension line
Figure 2-12.

TIP: The units of measurement are the same as those set for the horizontal rulers. To change these, reset the Horizontal Grid Frequency setting in the Grid Setup dialog box found on the Layout menu.

Try this second method of placing a dimension line. This involves double-clicking on the final line placement rather than single-clicking on it.

1. With the vertical dimension line still selected, begin a new line. Place the mouse pointer somewhere in the top left quadrant of the page and click the mouse button as before.

2. Move the pointer to the bottom right of the page and double-click the mouse button.

Figure 2-13 shows an example and how the resulting lines differ. Depending on the requirements of the drawings, you can use either the first or second method to produce a dimension line shaped the way you need it.

TIP: The dimension label is printed according to the default font and point size. To change the default, select the Text Roll-up dialog box from the Text menu and reset the default values.

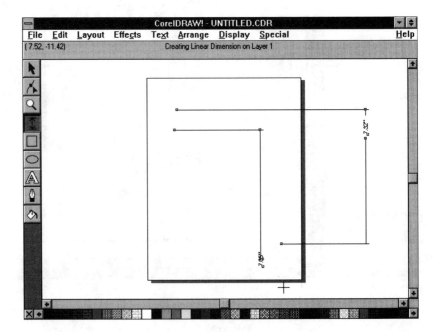

Using a different approach to draw a dimension line
Figure 2-13.

Increasing Precision

In addition to the mouse pointer coordinates and the other line and curve data displayed in the status line, CorelDRAW! has three features that aid in precision drawing. These are an adjustable grid that underlays the drawing surface and assists in aligning points and objects, a pair of rulers to give you a visual reference to where you are, and the ability to place nonprinting guidelines on the page for purposes of alignment.

2

The grid, the guidelines, and objects can optionally be given a magnet-like property that causes points or objects that are placed near them to be drawn to them. These are called Snap To Grid, Snap To Guidelines, and Snap To Objects. The Snap To property can be turned on and off, like the rulers, through the Layout menu. You can also turn Snap To Grid on and off by pressing Ctrl-Y. In addition, the Layout menu provides access to Setup dialog boxes for grids and guidelines. The Grid Setup dialog box allows you to display the grid on the screen (as a series of faint dots) and, when it is displayed, to determine the horizontal and vertical spacing of the grid. The Grid Setup dialog box also allows you to turn the Snap To Grid property on and off by clicking on its check box. With the Guidelines Setup dialog box, you can place guidelines with a very high degree of precision. You can also place guidelines by dragging them out of either ruler and placing them by visually aligning them in the opposite ruler.

This section shows you how to use the rulers and the grid to draw with greater precision. Guidelines will be used and discussed further in a later section.

Setting the Grid and Displaying Rulers

You will next make several changes to the settings for the grid and turn on the Snap To property. Then you will turn on the display of both the grid and the rulers.

1. Select the New command from the File menu to clear the screen of the shape you drew in the last exercise. Don't save any changes.

2. Select the Grid Setup command from the Layout menu. The dialog box in Figure 2-14 appears. The settings in your software may be different from the ones in the figure.

   You would use the Scale setting to establish a relationship between the CorelDRAW! drawing and another measurement standard, for example, as in architectural drawings where an inch equals so many feet. You will not set Scale now.

3. Adjust both horizontal and vertical grid frequencies to 16.00 per inch, if necessary. To change the value in the numeric entry box, press and hold the mouse button over the up or down scroll arrow until the number

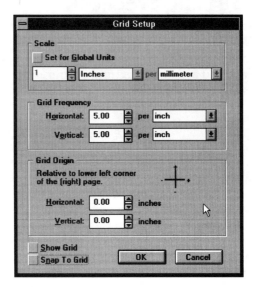

Grid Setup
dialog box
Figure 2-14.

changes to 16.00. Alternatively, you can click on the numeric value itself and type in the new number. To change the unit of measurement in the rectangular units box, just click on it until the word "inch" appears.

4. Click on Show Grid to turn on its display and then adjust the Grid Origin so the vertical position of the lower-left corner is at 11 inches. (Some versions of CorelDRAW! use the upper-left corner as the point of reference, in which case a vertical position of 0 is correct.) Check that the horizontal position is set at 0.0.

5. Look at the Snap To Grid check box. If no check mark appears in front of it, select it to make the grid active. If a check mark already appears in front of it, you don't need to do anything. Click on OK to save these settings and close the dialog box.

6. Reopen the Layout menu, click on the Snap To option, and notice that the Grid option now has a check mark next to it, showing the feature is turned on.

7. Choose the Show Rulers command from the Display menu. Since you have set the grid size to inches, the rulers will also display in inches, as in Figure 2-15. Notice that the zero point for both the horizontal and vertical rulers begins at the upper-left corner of the page area, as shown in the figure. This is a convenient way to set the rulers so that you can measure everything relative to that corner.

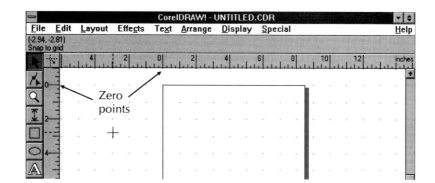

Displaying the rulers
Figure 2-15.

Joining Lines and Curves Automatically

CorelDRAW! has a feature called AutoJoin which causes lines and curves to "snap" together automatically when their end points are separated by a preset number of *pixels* (the smallest element on a screen—the "dots" with which everything is built). You can adjust the threshold number of pixels through the Preferences command in the Special menu.

Literal joining of two end points is important because CorelDRAW! classifies an object as being either open or closed. If an object is open, you cannot fill it with a color or shade. Try out the AutoJoin feature and then change the AutoJoin threshold and see the effect.

1. Select the Pencil tool (Freehand mode), then move the crosshair pointer to a point 1 inch to the right of the zero point on the horizontal ruler and 2 inches below the zero point on the vertical ruler. Notice that as you move the mouse, dotted "shadow" lines in each ruler show you the exact location of your pointer.

2. Click once at this point to begin drawing a line. The parameters in the status line appear.

3. Using the rulers and status line to help you, extend the line 4 inches to the right. The *dx* and distance parameters on the status line should read 4.0 inches, as in Figure 2-16. Click a second time to freeze the line in position. Notice how both the grid display and the grid's Snap To feature help you do this.

4. Move the crosshair pointer exactly 1/4 inch to the right of the end point of the line. Use the rulers to help you.

5. Press and hold the mouse button at this point and drag the mouse to form a squiggling curve.

6. Release the mouse button to complete the curve. If you began the curve 1/4 inch or more to the right of the line end point, the curve remains

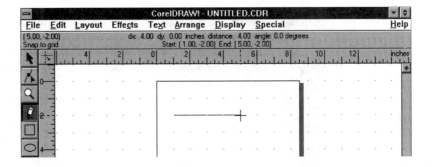

Extending a
line (*dx* = 4.00
inches,
distance =
4.00 inches)
Figure 2-16.

separate from the line and does not snap to it, as in Figure 2-17. In order
to make a curve snap to a line automatically at this distance, you'll need
to adjust the AutoJoin threshold value in the Preferences dialog box.
(You'll become familiar with this process in the next section.)

7. Select the New command from the File menu to clear the screen before
proceeding. Do not save any changes.

Adjusting the AutoJoin Threshold

The AutoJoin feature determines how far apart (in pixels) two Freehand or
Bézier lines or curves have to be for them to join together automatically. If
the setting in the Preferences-Curves dialog box is a small number, such as 3

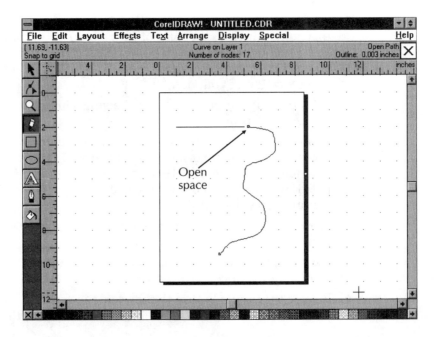

Curve failing
to snap to a
line (AutoJoin
value too low)
Figure 2-17.

or less, lines snap together only if you draw with a very exact hand. Use this lower setting when you want to *prevent* lines from joining accidentally. If your technique is less precise, you can set the AutoJoin threshold value to a number higher than 5 pixels so that lines will snap together even if you don't have a steady hand.

2

1. Select the Curves option from the Preferences command in the Special menu. The Preferences-Curves dialog box in Figure 2-18 appears. The default setting for the features in this dialog box is 5 pixels. You'll use some of the other settings later on, when you learn skills for which these settings are useful. For now, concern yourself only with the AutoJoin setting.

2. Set the AutoJoin value to 10 pixels by clicking several times on the up scroll arrow.

3. Select OK twice to save the new value and return to the drawing.

4. Now you can redraw the line and make the curve snap to it. With the Pencil tool selected in Freehand mode, redraw a straight line as you did in steps 1 through 3 of the previous section.

5. Move the crosshair to a point 1/4 inch to the right of the end point of the line and then press and hold the mouse button to begin drawing a curve.

6. Drag the mouse and draw the squiggling curve as you did in step 5 of the previous section.

7. Release the mouse button. This time, the curve joins automatically to the line, as shown in Figure 2-19.

8. Select New from the File menu to clear the screen before going further.

The AutoJoin feature has other uses besides allowing you to connect lines and curves. You can also use it to accomplish the following:

✦ Join lines to lines or curves to curves

AutoJoin in the Preferences-Curves dialog box

Figure 2-18.

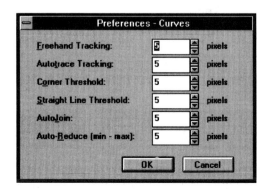

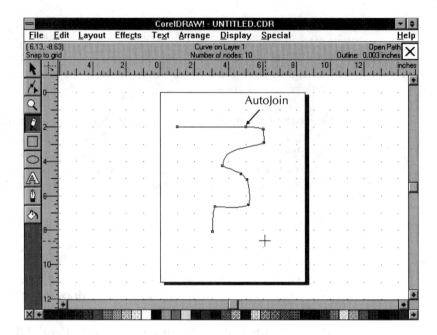

Curve
snapping to a
line (AutoJoin
value high)
Figure 2-19.

◆ Add a curve or line to the end of an existing curve, line, or object that
   you have selected

◆ Create closed curve objects and polygons by starting and ending a curve
   (or a series of line segments) at the same point

Creating a Drawing Using Lines, Curves, and Polygons

You have learned to create all of the simple objects—line, curve, closed
curve, and polygon—that you can make with the Pencil tool. In this exercise,
you'll bring together all of the skills you have learned by drawing a kite that
consists of lines, curves, and a polygon. Use Figures 2-20 through 2-28 as a
guide to help you position the start and end points of the lines and curves.

1. Turn on the rulers and show the grid (if they do not appear onscreen
    already) by selecting Show Rulers from the Display menu and Show
    Grid from the Grid Setup dialog box reached from the Layout menu.

2. Also from the Layout menu, select Snap to and then Guidelines. From
    the Display menu select Edit Wireframe. You have now turned on all of
    CorelDRAW!'s precision enhancement features.

2

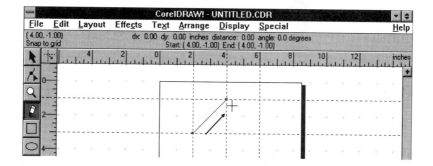

Guidelines in place
Figure 2-20.

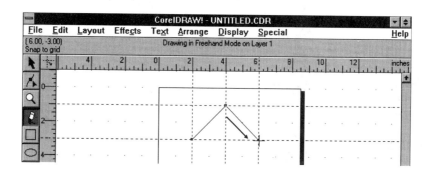

Drawing a kite: the first line segment
Figure 2-21.

Drawing a kite: the second line segment
Figure 2-22.

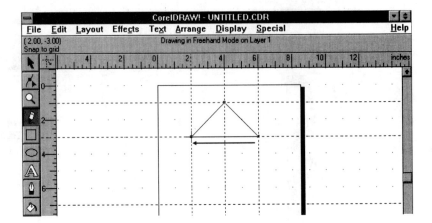

Drawing a
kite: the third
line segment
Figure 2-23.

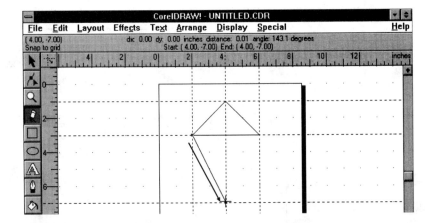

Drawing a
kite: the fourth
line segment
Figure 2-24.

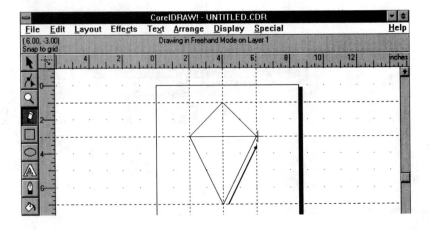

Completing
the basic kite
shape
Figure 2-25.

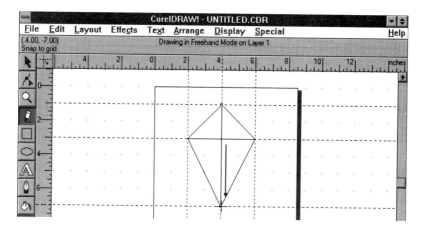

Drawing the
vertical
crosspiece
Figure 2-26.

Guidelines, nonprinting lines placed on a drawing by either dragging on a ruler or via a dialog box, are used like the grid to align objects in a drawing. Guidelines have two major benefits over the grid: They can be placed anywhere, not just on a ruler mark and, since they are continuous dotted lines, they provide a better visual reference than the grid dots. When a guideline is near a grid line, the guideline always takes priority. This allows you to place a guideline very near a grid line and have objects on a drawing retroactively—turning on Snap To Grid,

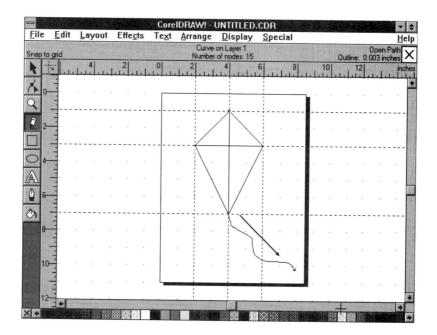

Drawing the
kite tail
(a curve)
Figure 2-27.

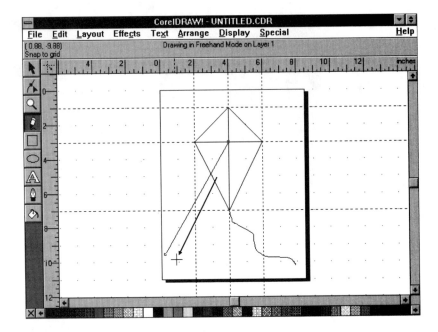

Adding a
string and
completing
the kite
Figure 2-28.

for example, will not move objects already on the drawing.

Since the drawing you are doing here uses only major ruler coordinates, you could very easily do it without guidelines. Use the guidelines anyway to see how they work and to use them as a visual reference.

3. With any tool, from any point on the horizontal ruler at the top of the drawing area, drag a horizontal guideline down to 7 inches below the zero point on the vertical ruler. (Move the mouse pointer to the horizontal ruler; press and hold the left mouse button while moving the mouse pointer and the dotted line that appears down to 7 inches; then release the mouse button.) You'll see that the Snap To Grid helps you align the guideline. Your screen should look like this as you are dragging the guideline:

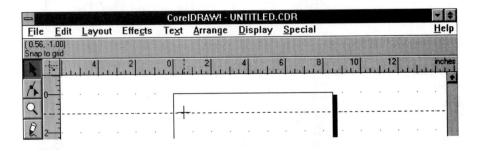

4. As you did in step 3, drag two more horizontal guidelines down to 3 inches and 1 inch, respectively, below the zero point on the vertical ruler.

   If you misplace a guideline, move the mouse pointer to it, press and hold the left mouse button until a four-headed arrow appears, then drag the line into proper position. You can drag a guideline off the page to get rid of it. Also, you can double-click on a guideline and get the Guideline Setup dialog box. From there you can move a guideline precisely or delete it.

5. Again as in step 3, drag three vertical guidelines to the right from the vertical ruler and place them at 6, 4, and 2 inches to the right of the zero point on the horizontal ruler.

   When you are done placing all of the guidelines, your screen should look like the one shown in Figure 2-20.

6. Select the Pencil (Freehand mode) tool.

7. Move to a point 2 inches to the right of the zero point on the horizontal ruler and 3 inches below the zero point on the vertical ruler and then click once to start a line.

8. Extend the line upward and to the right until you reach a point 4 inches to the right of the horizontal zero point and 1 inch below the vertical zero point. Use the status line information to help you and refer to Figure 2-21. Double-click and release the mouse button at this point. With the intersections of the guidelines at each of these points, the lines you are drawing jump to these points if you get anywhere near them.

9. Extend the next line segment downward and to the right as shown in Figure 2-22, until you reach a point 6 inches to the right of the horizontal zero point and 3 inches below the vertical zero point. Double-click at this point to add another line segment.

10. Extend another line segment horizontally to the left until you reach the starting point. Double-click at this point. The last line segment will connect to the first line segment and form a triangle, as shown in Figure 2-23.

11. From this point, extend another line segment downward and to the right until you reach a point 4 inches to the right of the horizontal zero point and 7 inches below the vertical zero point, as shown in Figure 2-24. Double-click at this point to complete this segment.

12. Now, extend a segment upward to the lower-right corner of the original triangle, as in Figure 2-25. Click just once to finish the line and complete the basic kite shape.

13. Next, add a vertical crosspiece to the kite. Since this line must be absolutely vertical, begin by pressing and holding [Ctrl] and then clicking once at the top of the kite.

14. While holding Ctrl, extend this new line to the base of the kite, as shown in Figure 2-26 and then click once. Release Ctrl. You are going to attach a curve to this line.

15. To attach a curve to the line, press and hold the mouse button and then draw a kite tail similar to the one in Figure 2-27. Release the mouse button to complete the curve.

16. Finally, add a string to the kite. While pressing and holding Ctrl, click on the point at which the crosspieces meet and extend a line diagonally downward and to the left until you reach the margin of the printable page area. Use Figure 2-28 as a guide. Click once to complete the line. Release Ctrl.

17. Your kite should now look similar to the one in Figure 2-28. Leave the kite on your screen for the concluding section of this chapter.

18. To remove the grid lines for Chapter 3, turn off the grid by selecting Grid Setup from the Layout menu. Click on Show Grid. The check mark will be removed.

Saving Your Work

As you work on your own drawings, save your work frequently during a session. If you don't save often enough, you could lose an image in the event of an unexpected power or hardware failure.

In order to save a new drawing, you must establish a filename for it. To save the kite you just drew, follow these steps:

1. Select the Save As command from the File menu to display the Save Drawing dialog box in Figure 2-29. The Directories indicator should show that you are in the C:\CORELDRW\DRAW directory of your hard drive. (Path names may vary, depending on how and where you installed the software. In the figure, directory \CDRAW is used instead of \CORELDRW.)

2. If the path is different from what you want or if you want to save the drawing in a different drive and/or directory, for example, C:\DRAWINGS as suggested in Appendix A, change to the correct drive and directory by double-clicking on the correct entries in the Drives and Directories list boxes. When you double-click, the selected path name will appear in the list box. If the drive or directory name you want is not visible in the Drives or Directories list boxes, position the mouse pointer over the up or down arrow in the scroll bar, then press and hold the mouse button until the path name becomes visible. You can then select the drive or directory name.

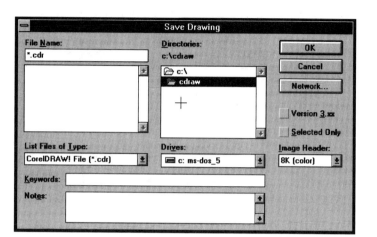

Save Drawing
dialog box
Figure 2-29.

3. Name the drawing by clicking in the File Name text entry box and then typing the desired name of your file. Delete the default characters if they are not what you want. Use no more than eight characters; CorelDRAW! adds the .CDR extension for you when you select the OK command button. In this case, type **kite**.

4. Save the file by clicking on the OK command button or pressing Enter. CorelDRAW! adds the extension .CDR to the file. You exit the Save File dialog box and return to your drawing. Notice that the title bar now contains the name of your drawing, KITE.CDR.

5. Select New from the File menu to clear the screen before continuing. Since you have just saved a picture, the Save Changes warning box doesn't appear.

The foregoing procedure applies only the first time you save a drawing. To save a drawing that has already been saved, either select the Save command from the File menu, or press Ctrl-S.

Retrieving a File

To open a drawing that you have saved, use the following procedure. In this exercise, you'll open the KITE.CDR file you just saved.

1. Select Open from the File menu. The Open Drawing dialog box appears, as in Figure 2-30. Its layout is very similar to the Save Drawing dialog box.

2. If you saved your file in a directory other than the default directory (the DRAW directory), select the drive and/or directory name from the Directories list box. Use the scroll bar if necessary.

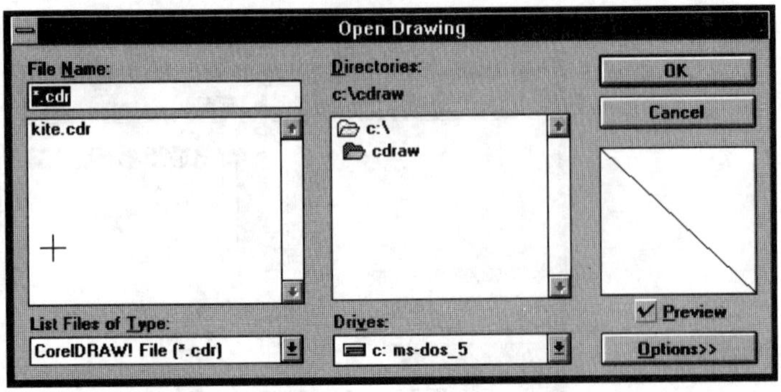

Open Drawing

File Name:	Directories:	OK
*.cdr	c:\cdraw	Cancel
kite.cdr	c:\	
	cdraw	

List Files of Type:	Drives:	☑ Preview
CorelDRAW! File (*.cdr)	c: ms-dos_5	Options>>

Open
Drawing
dialog box
Figure 2-30.

3. If you can't see the file KITE.CDR in the File Name list box, position the mouse pointer over the down arrow in the scroll bar and then press and hold it until the filename becomes visible.

4. Click once on the filename, KITE.CDR. The name appears in reverse video (white lettering on black or colored background—depending on the color options set) and displays in the File Name text box. Also, you will see a miniature of the drawing in the Preview box.

5. To open the file, select the OK command or press (Enter). After a moment, the file displays in the window and its name appears in the title bar.

6. Exit CorelDRAW! by pressing (Alt)-(F4), or by selecting Exit from the File menu.

TIP: There's a shortcut to opening a file once you are in the Open Drawing dialog box. Instead of clicking once on the filename and then clicking on OK, you can simply double-click on the filename.

That's all there is to it. You have created a complete drawing using the Pencil tool, saved it, and loaded it again. Along the way, you have learned how to do Freehand and Bézier drawing of both lines and curves, and to use the dimension lines, rulers, grid, guidelines, and status line to help you work.

COREL DRAW! 4

CHAPTER

CORELDRAW! 4

3

DRAWING AND WORKING WITH RECTANGLES, SQUARES, ELLIPSES, AND CIRCLES

The rectangle and ellipse are basic shapes that underlie many complex forms created by man and nature. In this chapter you will use the Rectangle tool to create rectangles and squares and the Ellipse tool to create ellipses and circles. As you work your way through the exercises in later chapters, you will apply a host of

CorelDRAW! special effects, fills, and shaping techniques to rectangles and ellipses to make them come alive.

Drawing a Rectangle

Using the Rectangle tool in the CorelDRAW! toolbox, you can initiate a rectangle from any of its four corners, as well as from the center outward. Having this degree of freedom and control over the placement of rectangles saves you time and effort when you lay out your illustrations.

Drawing a Rectangle from Any Corner

You can start a rectangle from any of its four corners. The corner that represents the starting point always remains fixed as you draw; the rest of the outline expands or contracts as you move the pointer diagonally. This flexibility in choosing a starting point allows you to place a rectangle more quickly and precisely within a drawing. Perform the following exercise to become familiar with how the CorelDRAW! interface reacts when you use different corners as starting points. To make your screen look like the figures in this chapter, click on the Display menu and make sure there is a check mark on Show Rulers, Show Status Line, and Edit Wireframe. If there is no check mark beside one or more of these items, click on the item to insert one.

1. Load CorelDRAW! if you are not running it already.

2. Select the Rectangle tool by placing the mouse pointer over the Rectangle icon and clicking once, and then moving the pointer out of the toolbox and to the right. The mouse pointer changes to a crosshair, the Rectangle icon is selected and the status line shows "Rectangle on Layer 1".

3. Position the pointer anywhere on the printable page area, press and hold the left mouse button, and drag the mouse downward and to the right along a diagonal path, as shown in Figure 3-1. The Width and Height indications in the status bar will change as you move the pointer.

4. Experiment with different widths and heights until you achieve the shape you want. You can easily modify the shape of the rectangle by redirecting the movement of the mouse. Notice that the upper-left corner, which was your starting point, remains fixed.

5. When the rectangle is the size and shape you want, release the mouse button. This action freezes the rectangle in place, and a node will appear at each of the four corners. The status line displays the messages "Rectangle on Layer 1", and "Fill:" followed by a black square, as in Figure 3-2. The "Fill:" message indicates that the rectangle has a default interior color of black. If you do not have Edit Wireframe selected in the

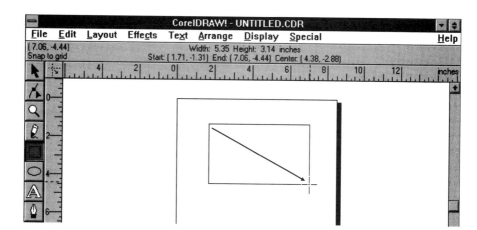

Drawing a
rectangle
Figure 3-1.

Display menu, the rectangle you made will be black. You will learn
more about fills in Chapter 12.

6. Press and hold the mouse button at a new starting point and then move
   the pointer along a diagonal path downward and to the left. Release the
   mouse button when the rectangle has the dimensions you want.
   Practice making several rectangles by starting at different corners.

7. While the last rectangle is still selected—has nodes at the
   corners—select Delete from the Edit menu or press Del to remove it.

8. Clear the whole page by choosing New from the File menu and clicking
   on No in answer to the "Save current changes?" question. Another way

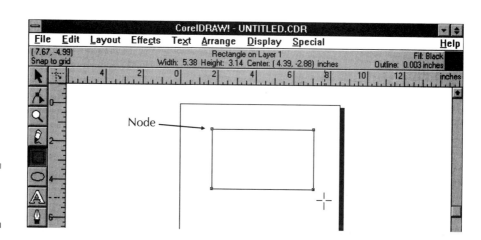

Completing a
rectangle
Figure 3-2.

to clear the page is to click on Select All in the Edit Menu and then press [Del].

The type of information appearing in the status line reflects the kind of object you are drawing. When you create a line, the status line displays the x- and y-coordinates, the distance (*dx,dy*) traveled, and the angle of the line. When you create a rectangle, the status line displays the width, height, start, end, and center. After the mouse button is released, the start and end are no longer shown.

Drawing a Rectangle from the Center Outward

CorelDRAW! allows you to draw a rectangle from the center outward. Using this technique, you can place rectangular shapes more precisely within a graphic, without having to pay close attention to rulers or grid spacing. The width and height indicators display the exact dimensions of the rectangle as you draw. Draw a rectangle now, using the center as its starting point.

1. With the Rectangle tool selected, press and hold both [Shift] and the mouse button at the desired starting point. Keep both [Shift] and the mouse button pressed as you move the mouse. As with any rectangle, you can draw in any direction, as you see in Figure 3-3.

2. Release both [Shift] and the mouse button to complete the rectangle.

3. Press [Del] to clear the rectangle from the screen.

Drawing a Square

In CorelDRAW!, you use the same tool to produce both rectangles and perfect squares. The technique is similar, except that you use the [Ctrl] key to constrain a rectangle to a square.

Drawing a Square from Any Corner

Follow these steps to draw a square. As with a rectangle, you can use any corner as your starting point.

1. With the Rectangle tool selected, position the pointer where you want to begin the square.

2. Press and hold both [Ctrl] and the mouse button and then draw diagonally in any direction. Note that the status line indicators show that the width and height of the shape are equal, as in Figure 3-4.

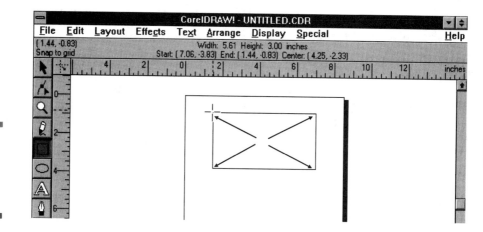

Drawing a
rectangle from
the center
outward
Figure 3-3.

3. To complete the square, release the mouse button first, and then release
   Ctrl. If you release Ctrl first, you might draw a rectangle with unequal
   sides rather than a square.

4. Press Del to clear the square from the screen.

Drawing a Square from the Center Outward

To draw a square in any direction, using the center as a starting point, you
must use both Ctrl and Shift, as well as the mouse button.

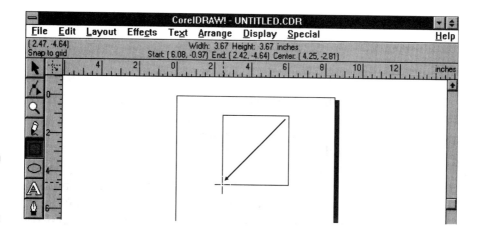

Drawing a
square
Figure 3-4.

1. With the Rectangle tool selected, position the pointer where you want to begin the square.

2. Press and hold [Ctrl], [Shift], and the mouse button simultaneously, and draw in any direction.

3. To complete the square, release the mouse button first and then release [Ctrl] and [Shift]. If you release [Ctrl] and [Shift] first, you might draw a rectangle with unequal sides, and the center might turn into a corner.

4. Press [Del] to clear the square from the screen.

Practicing with the Grid

If your work includes design-oriented applications such as technical illustration, architectural renderings, or graphic design, you might sometimes find it necessary to align geometrical shapes horizontally or vertically in fixed increments. In this section, you can practice aligning rectangles and squares while drawing; Chapter 6 will introduce you to techniques for aligning shapes after you have drawn them.

TIP: As you learned in the previous chapter, the grid in CorelDRAW! can either be invisible or a pattern of dots on the screen. Objects are aligned to the grid because of the Snap To feature that is similar to a magnetic attraction.

One way to align objects while drawing is to take advantage of the Grid Setup and Snap To Grid commands in the Layout menu. The process of aligning new objects to a grid consists of four steps:

◆ Adjusting the grid spacing

◆ Displaying the grid

◆ Displaying the rulers

◆ Enabling the Snap To Grid feature

Follow these steps to practice using the grid:

1. Pull down the Layout menu and select the Grid Setup command. The Grid Setup dialog box in Figure 3-5 will display.

2. Adjust both the Horizontal and Vertical Grid Frequency values to 2.00 per inch. To do this, press and hold the mouse button over the lower scroll arrow until the number 2.00 appears. Alternatively, you can drag across the current value and type **2.00**. Press [Tab] twice to go from

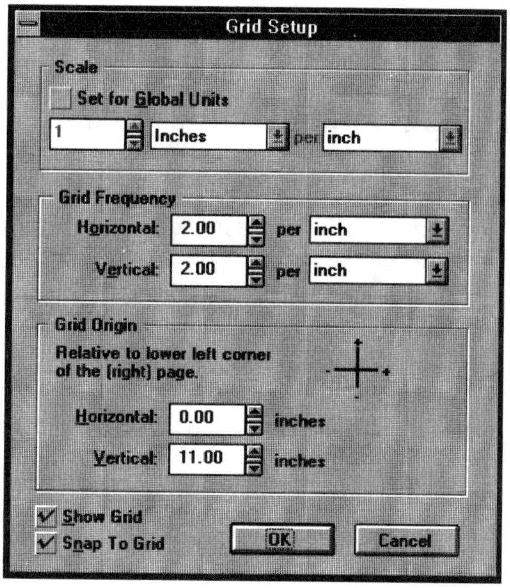

3

Adjusting Grid
Frequency to
2.00 per inch
Figure 3-5.

Horizontal to Vertical. If the selected unit of measurement is something
other than inches, click on the unit's drop-down list and choose "inch."

3. If they are not already checked, click on Show Grid and Snap To Grid,
   then click on OK to save these settings, and exit the dialog box.

4. Display the rulers (if they do not already appear on the screen) by
   selecting the Show Rulers command in the Display menu. A check
   mark will appear next to the command, indicating that the rulers are
   now active.

   With the Snap To Grid turned on, you can align and place objects
   automatically on the grid, and a message appears to that effect in the
   lower-left corner of the status line.

5. Open the Display menu and make sure there is a check mark next to
   Edit Wireframe indicating it is turned on. If there isn't, click on Edit
   Wireframe.

6. Next, select the Rectangle tool and position the pointer at the 1-inch
   mark relative to both the horizontal and vertical rulers. Even if you
   place the pointer inexactly, the corner of the rectangle will align
   perfectly to the 1-inch marks when you begin to draw.

7. Press and hold the mouse button and draw a rectangle 4 inches wide
   and 3 inches high.

8. Draw a second rectangle the same size as the first, beginning at a point 1/2 inch to the right and 1/2 inch below the starting point of the first. The extension of the mouse pointer in the rulers—a dotted line—should align exactly with the 1/2-inch marks on both rulers. The grid setting prevents you from "missing the mark."

9. Draw a third rectangle from a starting point 1/2 inch below and 1/2 inch to the right of the starting point of the second. Your three rectangles should align like the ones in Figure 3-6.

10. Select New from the File menu to clear all of the rectangles from the screen. When the "Save Current Changes?" message box appears, select No.

Now that you have practiced drawing all possible types of rectangles, you are ready to build a drawing with rectangular and freehand elements.

Creating a Drawing Using Rectangles and Squares

In the following exercise, you will integrate all the skills you have learned so far by creating a teacup that includes rectangles, squares, and freehand drawing elements. In the process, you will also learn how to adjust the relative smoothness of curved lines you draw with the Pencil tool. The adjustment involves a feature called Freehand Tracking, which controls how closely CorelDRAW! follows the movements of your mouse pointer when you draw curves.

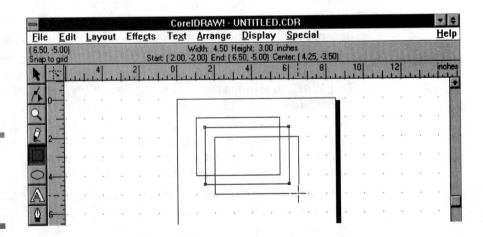

Drawing rectangles at 1/2-inch intervals
Figure 3-6.

To prepare for this exercise, select the Grid Setup command from the Layout menu and adjust both the Horizontal and Vertical Grid Frequency to 8.00 per inch. Both Show Grid and Snap To Grid should still be selected, and Show Rulers should be turned on. Refer to the steps in the preceding section if necessary.

When you are ready to create the drawing, proceed through the following steps, using the numbers in Figure 3-7 as a guide. If you wish, use the rulers as an aid in laying out your work.

3

1. Draw a rectangle (1) to represent the body of the teacup. It should be higher than it is wide.

2. Position your pointer at the right side of this rectangle and attach a rectangular handle (2) to the body of the teacup. The handle should touch the edge of the teacup but not overlap it; the grid settings you have chosen will prevent overlapping.

3. Draw a smaller rectangle (3) inside the one you just created (2) to make the opening in the handle.

4. Now select the Pencil tool and add a straight line (4) to the base of the teacup. (Freehand mode should be selected, not Bézier. If you need to change the drawing mode, click and hold on the Pencil tool until the flyout menu appears, then click on the leftmost icon.) This represents

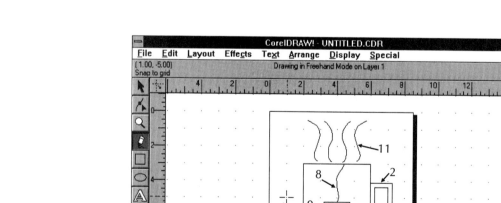

Drawing a teacup using rectangles, squares, and freehand elements

Figure 3-7.

the top of the saucer. Remember to press and hold Ctrl while drawing to ensure that the line remains perfectly horizontal; use the information in the status line if you need guidance.

5. Extend diagonal lines (5) and (6) down from each end of the top of the saucer. Check the status line indicators as you draw. The angle for the diagonal line to the left (6) should read –45 degrees, while the angle for the diagonal line to the right (5) should read –135 degrees. Again, press and hold Ctrl while drawing the line to ensure that the line remains on a 15-degree increment. Also, be sure to make both lines the same length. Each line snaps to the saucer base to form a multisegment line, as you learned in Chapter 2.

6. Now add another straight line (7) to form the bottom of the saucer. Remember to constrain the line using Ctrl . The saucer base snaps to the other line segments to form a single object, a polygon.

7. With the Pencil tool still selected, press and hold the mouse button and draw a curve (8) to represent the string of a tea bag. Does your string appear excessively jagged? If it does, you can adjust the Freehand Tracking setting in the next set of steps.

8. Before adjusting the Freehand Tracking value, erase the tea bag string you have just drawn by selecting Undo from the Edit menu.

9. Select the Curves option from the Preferences command in the Special menu to display the Preferences-Curves dialog box, as shown in Figure 3-8. You used this same dialog box in Chapter 2 to adjust the AutoJoin values. The default value in the numeric entry box next to Freehand Tracking is 5, but you are going to adjust it to a higher number to facilitate smoother curves.

10. Using the scroll arrow, adjust the sensitivity level in the Freehand Tracking option to 10 pixels. This is the highest number possible and causes CorelDRAW! to smooth your curved lines as you draw. Lower numbers, on the other hand, cause the Pencil tool to track every little dip and rise as you move the mouse.

11. Select OK twice to exit the dialog boxes and save your setting.

12. Now draw the tea bag string a second time. Your curve should be somewhat smoother now, more like the one in Figure 3-7.

13. Next, attach a tag to the string. Select the Rectangle tool again, position the pointer just below the bottom of the string, press and hold Ctrl and Shift simultaneously, and draw a square (9) from the center outward.

14. To add a center label to the tag, create a square (10) inside the first square. Select one of the corners as the starting point for this smaller square.

Preferences - Curves

Freehand Tracking:	10	pixels
Autotrace Tracking:	5	pixels
Corner Threshold:	5	pixels
Straight Line Threshold:	5	pixels
AutoJoin:	10	pixels
Auto-Reduce (min - max):	5	pixels

OK   Cancel

Adjusting the Freehand Tracking value for smoother curves
Figure 3-8.

3

15. To add a finishing touch to your drawing, create some steam (11) by selecting the Pencil tool and drawing some curves. Since you have set Freehand Tracking to a higher number of pixels, you can create more effective "steam."

16. Finally, save your drawing. Select the Save As command from the File menu and, after you select the directory you want to use, type **teacup**, as shown in Figure 3-9. When you click on the OK command button, CorelDRAW! adds the extension .CDR automatically.

17. Choose New from the File menu to clear the screen and prepare for a new drawing.

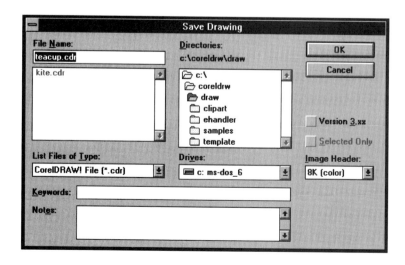

Saving the drawing as TEACUP.CDR
Figure 3-9.

Drawing an Ellipse

The Ellipse tool in CorelDRAW! allows you to create both ellipses and perfect circles. Follow the exercises in this section to create ellipses and circles of many different shapes and sizes. In later chapters, you will expand your skills and apply a rich variety of special effects and shaping techniques to these basic geometrical forms.

All versions of CorelDRAW! allow you to start an ellipse from any point on the rim. You can also draw an ellipse from the center point outward by using the (Shift) key. This second method allows you to place ellipses precisely within a graphic.

Using the Rim as a Starting Point for an Ellipse

You can initiate an ellipse from any point on its rim. This flexibility in choosing your starting point allows you to position an ellipse within a drawing, without sacrificing precision.

Since you cannot use a corner as a starting point for ellipses and circles, you can still use the width and height indicators as guides.

CorelDRAW! gives you an additional visual cue when you are drawing ellipses and circles. If your starting point is on the upper half of the rim, CorelDRAW! places the node at the uppermost point of the ellipse; if your starting point is on the lower half of the rim, CorelDRAW! places the node at the bottommost point of the ellipse. Perform the following exercises to become familiar with how the CorelDRAW! interface reacts when you choose different points on the rim as starting points for an ellipse.

1. Click on the Ellipse tool and position the pointer anywhere on the printable page area, press and hold the mouse button, and drag the mouse downward and to the right along a diagonal path, as shown in Figure 3-10. The indicators on the status line display the width and height of the ellipse.

2. When the ellipse is the shape you want, release the mouse button. This action completes the ellipse and freezes it in place. As in Figure 3-11, a single node appears at the uppermost point of the ellipse, and the status line changes to display the messages "Ellipse on Layer 1" and "Fill:" followed by a solid black rectangle. Press (Del) to clear the page.

3. Choose a new starting point and draw an ellipse from bottom to top. Press and hold the mouse button at a desired starting point anywhere on the bottom half of the rim and then move the pointer upward in a diagonal direction.

4. When the ellipse has the dimensions you want, release the mouse button. Note that the node is now at the bottom of the ellipse.

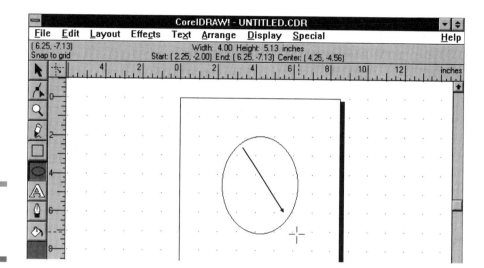

Drawing an
ellipse from
top to bottom
Figure 3-10.

5. Press ⌨Del to clear this ellipse from the screen.

Drawing an Ellipse from the Center Outward

CorelDRAW! allows you to draw an ellipse from the center outward, just as
you did with rectangles and squares. This feature offers you a more

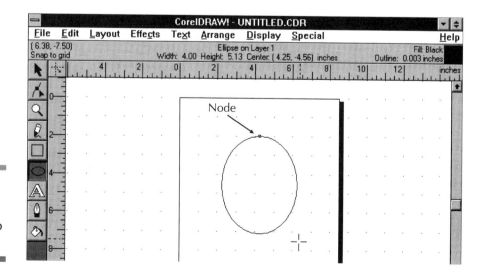

A completed
ellipse
showing the
node at the top
Figure 3-11.

interactive method of working, without sacrificing precision. The width and height indicators continue to display the exact dimensions of the ellipse as you draw. Practice drawing an ellipse using the center as a starting point with these steps:

1. With the Ellipse tool selected, press and hold both Shift and the mouse button at the desired starting point. Keep both Shift and the mouse button depressed as you move the mouse. As with any ellipse, you can draw in whichever direction you choose, as you see in Figure 3-12, in which an ellipse was drawn from its center outward.

2. Release the mouse button and then release Shift to complete the ellipse. Be sure to release the mouse button *before* you release Shift, or the ellipse may "snap" away from the center point you have chosen, and your center point will be treated as a rim point.

3. Clear the ellipse from the screen by pressing Del.

Drawing a Circle

In CorelDRAW! you use a single tool to produce both ellipses and perfect circles, just as you used the same tool to produce rectangles and squares. The technique is similar; you use Ctrl to constrain an ellipse to a circle. As with ellipses, you can choose either the rim or the center of the circle as a starting point.

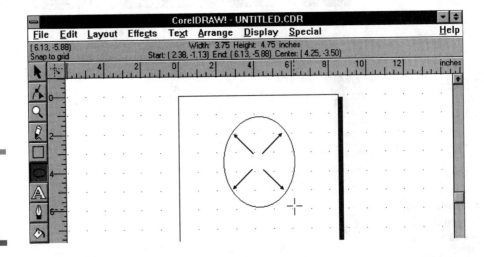

Drawing an ellipse from the center outward
Figure 3-12.

Using the Rim as a Starting Point for a Circle

Perform the following exercise to create a perfect circle, starting from the circle's rim:

1. With the Ellipse tool selected, position the pointer at a desired starting point.
2. Press and hold both Ctrl and the mouse button and draw diagonally in any direction. As you can see in Figure 3-13, the status line indicators show that both the width and the height of the shape are equal.
3. To complete the circle, release the mouse button and then Ctrl. Be sure to release the mouse button *before* you release Ctrl, or your circle may turn into an ordinary ellipse of unequal height and width.
4. Clear the circle from the screen by pressing Del.

Because of the way CorelDRAW! works, you arc actually creating an imaginary rectangle when you draw an ellipse or circle. That is why the status line indicator for a perfect circle displays width and height instead of diameter. The ellipse or circle fits inside the rectangle, as you will see more clearly when you begin to select objects in Chapter 6.

Drawing a Circle from the Center Outward

In the following brief exercise, you will draw a circle using the center as a starting point.

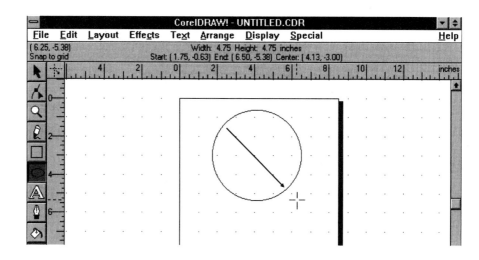

Drawing a
circle using
Ctrl
Figure 3-13.

1. With the Ellipse tool selected, position the pointer where you want to begin the circle.

2. Press and hold (Ctrl), (Shift), and the mouse button simultaneously and draw in any direction.

3. To complete the circle, release the mouse button and then (Ctrl) and (Shift). If you release the keys before you release the mouse button, you may jeopardize both your circle and its central starting point.

4. Clear the circle from the screen by pressing (Del).

Now that you have created some circles and ellipses using all of the available techniques, you can integrate these shapes into an original drawing. Continue with the next section to consolidate your skills.

Creating a Drawing Using Ellipses and Circles

The following exercise brings together all the skills you have learned so far. You will create a drawing (of a house and its environment) that will include ellipses, circles, rectangles, squares, and freehand drawing elements. The grid can assist you with some of the geometrical elements of the drawing; other elements you can draw freehand. Since this drawing will be wider than it is high, you will also learn how to adjust the page format from portrait (the default vertical format) to landscape (horizontal format). The first few steps get you into the habit of anticipating and preparing for your drawing needs before you actually begin to draw, so that you can draw quickly and without interruption. Use the numbers in Figure 3-14 as a guide in performing this exercise.

A high Freehand Tracking setting lets you draw smoother curves, and a high AutoJoin setting causes lines and curves to snap together even when their end points are a few pixels apart.

1. To prepare for the geometrical portion of the drawing, select the Grid Setup command from the Layout menu and adjust both the Horizontal and Vertical Grid Frequencies to 4.00 per inch. If you need help, refer to the "Practicing with the Grid" section of this chapter.

2. Change the page setup so that your page is wider than it is long. To do this, select the Page Setup command from the Layout menu. When the Page Setup dialog box in Figure 3-15 appears, select the Landscape option button to set the orientation to landscape. Exit by selecting the OK command button.

3. Select the Curves option from the Preferences command in the Special menu and set both the Freehand Tracking and the AutoJoin options to 10 pixels, if they are not already. Click on the OK command button twice to exit both dialog boxes.

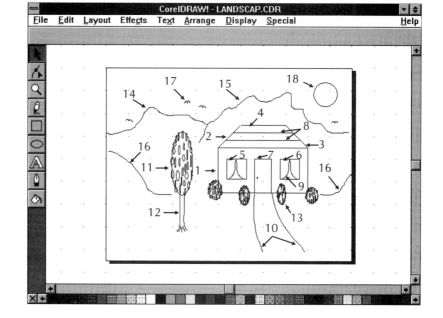

A drawing
using ellipses,
circles,
rectangles,
and freehand
elements
Figure 3-14.

3

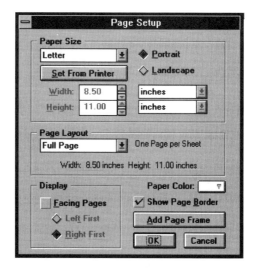

Page Setup
dialog box
Figure 3-15.

TIP: When you changed the page setup from portrait to landscape, the vertical ruler went back to its default of zero being in the lower-left corner. (You may remember that you moved the vertical zero to the upper-left corner in Chapter 2.) Change this again for this drawing, to provide a more normal reference.

4. Move the mouse pointer to the icon at the intersection of the vertical and horizontal rulers. Click and hold the mouse button and drag the ruler crosshair to the upper-left corner of the page as shown here:

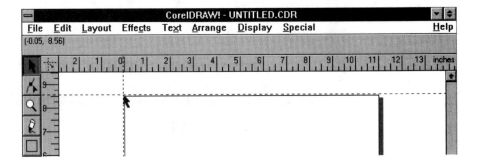

Notice that the lines snap to the corner grid point. Release the mouse button, and the zero point on the rulers will be opposite the upper-left corner of the page.

5. Select the Rectangle tool and position the pointer at the 5-inch mark on the horizontal ruler and the 3 1/2-inch mark on the vertical ruler. Draw a rectangle that extends from this point to the 9-inch mark on the horizontal ruler and to the 5 1/2-inch mark on the vertical ruler. This rectangle will compose the main element of the house (1).

6. Designing the roof of the house requires three steps involving constrained lines and automatic joining of lines to form a polygon. Select the Pencil tool and position your pointer at the upper-left corner of the "house." Extend a line (2) upward and to the right at a 45-degree angle. Remember to press Ctrl while drawing to constrain this line to the correct angle automatically. End the line at the 6-inch mark on the horizontal ruler and the 2 1/2-inch mark on the vertical ruler.

7. Extend a line (3) upward and to the left at a 135-degree angle. Remember to press Ctrl while drawing to constrain this line to the control angle automatically. When you reach the 8-inch mark on the horizontal ruler and the 2 1/2-inch mark on the vertical ruler, end the line with a double-click so you can continue with another line segment.

8. While continuing to hold Ctrl, extend a horizontal line (4) back to the first diagonal line (2) and single-click to end it. The two line segments should snap together and form a polygon that constitutes the "roof" of the house.

9. You will need smaller grid increments when drawing the next few objects. Select the Grid Setup command from the Layout menu again and set both the Horizontal and Vertical Grid Frequencies to 8.00 per inch. Select OK to save this setting and return to your drawing.

10. Create two square windows for the house. To create the first window, select the Rectangle tool and begin a square (5) near the left side of the house, a little below the "roof." Practice drawing a square from the center outward using the Ctrl-Shift key combination. Notice the dimensions of your square just before you complete it, so that you can draw a square of the same size in the next step. If you do not like the first square you draw, press Del immediately to erase it and try again.

3

11. Create a second square window (6) near the right side of the house. Make sure this square is the same size as the first and that it begins and ends on the same horizontal plane. The grid settings should help you place it correctly.

12. Make a rectangular door (7) for the house about halfway between the two windows. Use the rulers to help guide your movement. If you make a mistake, press Del or select Undo in the Edit menu to delete the rectangle and try again.

TIP: Change both the horizontal and vertical frequencies to 6.00 since you are trying to divide an inch into three equal parts in the next step.

13. To create planes of shingles for the roof, select the Pencil tool, press and hold Ctrl and draw two perfectly horizontal lines (8) across the roof.

14. Add asymmetrical curtains for the house by drawing some diagonal freehand curves (9) inside the windows. Remember to press and hold the mouse button as you draw to create curves instead of lines.

15. Draw a freehand sidewalk (10) that widens as it approaches the foreground of your picture.

16. Select the Ellipse tool and draw an elongated ellipse (11) to the left of the house. This represents the foliage of a poplar tree.

17. Select the Pencil tool and form the trunk of the poplar by adding some freehand vertical curves (12) beneath it. If you wish, you can add some small lines to the "foliage" of the poplar.

18. Select the Ellipse tool again and draw a series of "bushes" (13) immediately in front of the house. Use ellipses for the outlines of the bushes; create detail in the bushes by inserting a few ellipses and circles inside each one. Insert more ellipses to create a denser bush. (You can practice this technique on the poplar tree, too.)

19. Select the Pencil tool and create a mountain (14) behind and to the left of the house. Use curved instead of straight lines. Your mountain doesn't have to look exactly like the one in the figure.

20. Before creating the second mountain, select the Curves option from the Preferences command in the Special menu and set Freehand Tracking to 1 pixel. This will make the outlines of your subsequent freehand curves more jagged. Select OK twice to exit the dialog boxes and save the new setting.

21. Draw the second mountain (15) behind the house. Notice that the outline of this mountain looks rougher than the outline of the first mountain.

22. Continue by using freehand curves to add a little landscaping (16) beneath the mountain and, if desired, a few birds (17).

23. Select the Ellipse tool and create a sun (18) by drawing a circle from the center outward at the upper-right corner of the picture.

24. Save your drawing by selecting the Save As command from the File menu. When the Save As dialog box appears, select the correct directory, type **landscape**, and click on OK. CorelDRAW! adds the .CDR extension automatically.

25. Finally, if you want to leave CorelDRAW! for a while, choose Exit from the File menu to return to Windows. If you want to go on to Chapter 4 without leaving CorelDRAW!, choose New from the File menu to clear the screen.

Congratulations! You have mastered the Rectangle and Ellipse tools and created another masterpiece with CorelDRAW!.

CORELDRAW! 4

CHAPTER

COREL DRAW! 4

4 ADDING TEXT

CorelDRAW!'s advanced text-handling features let you turn text into a work of art. You can rotate, skew, reshape, and edit a character or a text string (a group of characters) just as you would any other object. You can perform these feats on Corel Systems fonts and on the extensive library of fonts available from other manufacturers. The more than 50 TrueType fonts provided on disk with your software and over 750 Adobe Type 1 and TrueType fonts provided on the CD-ROM look similar to standard industry fonts and will print on any printer with which CorelDRAW! is compatible. Since the Corel fonts are in the Windows standard TrueType format (and in Adobe Type 1 format on the CD-ROM) you can use your Corel fonts with all your Windows applications—a real bonus!

In this chapter, you will learn how to insert text into a drawing and select the font, style, point size, alignment, and spacing attributes of your text. You will also learn how to enter special foreign language or symbolic characters. After you have completed the exercises in this chapter, you will be ready to tackle more advanced techniques for reshaping your text (see Chapter 9), and converting other manufacturers' fonts to a format that you can use in CorelDRAW!.

Entering Text

The Text tool, the last of the four basic drawing tools in CorelDRAW!, is represented by a stylized capital letter "A." You use the Text tool to insert text into your pictures, just as you use the Ellipse or Rectangle tool to insert geometrical objects. The process of inserting text into a drawing can involve up to eight steps:

1. Select the Text tool.
2. Choose between a text string and a paragraph.
3. Select an insertion point.
4. Enter text.
5. Choose the point size of your text.
6. Set the alignment for the text.
7. Select a font and style.
8. Adjust the spacing between the letters, words, and lines of your text.

The sections that follow treat each of the preceding steps in greater detail. Since most of this chapter consists of exercises, however, the order in which you perform these steps may vary slightly from this list.

Selecting the Text Tool

You use the Text tool in CorelDRAW! to enter new text on a page. When you first load CorelDRAW!, the Pick tool is highlighted; in order to enter text, you must activate the Text tool. In the following brief exercise, you will adjust the page format and then activate the Text tool.

1. If the printable page area is in portrait format (vertical instead of horizontal), select Page Setup from the Layout menu and select

Landscape format. If you did the drawing exercise at the end of Chapter 3, the printable page area is already in landscape format. This is because CorelDRAW! always "remembers" the page setup you used the last time you created a new drawing.

2. For the same reason, open the Display menu and choose Edit Wireframe to turn off that feature.

3. Select the Text tool by positioning the mouse pointer over the tool. Then press and momentarily hold down the mouse button. A three-icon flyout menu appears, as shown here:

4

The icons represent the three uses of the Text tool: artistic text, paragraph text, and symbol entry.

The Artistic text entry icon on the left, which is the default, allows you to enter text in Artistic mode. The Paragraph text entry icon in the middle allows you to enter text in Paragraph mode. The distinction between the two modes is explained in the next section. The rightmost icon, in the shape of a star, allows you to access the extensive Symbols Library provided by CorelDRAW! 4. Symbols and their uses are discussed later in this chapter. Select Artistic text entry mode by clicking on the leftmost icon. The mouse pointer turns into a crosshair.

Text Strings and Paragraphs

Artistic text is designed to enter shorter text strings, such as titles, captions, and notes, that can be up to 250 characters long. Paragraph text is designed for larger blocks of text, such as copy for a brochure. A paragraph text file can have a number of paragraphs, but each paragraph can have no more than 4000 characters.

To enter text strings, you simply click the Artistic Text tool at the point on the page you want text to begin. For a paragraph, you drag a *frame*, a box to contain the text, from where you want text to start to where you want text to end. Frames can be linked so that a paragraph text file will flow from frame to frame.

Paragraph text provides many of the attributes of word processing. Text will automatically wrap at the end of a line; text can be justified (aligned on the left and right), as well as left-aligned, right-aligned, and centered; text can be cut and pasted to and from the Clipboard; you can adjust the space between paragraphs in addition to adjusting the space between characters, words, and lines; and you can create up to eight columns with a *gutter* (space between columns) that you define. Bulleted lists can be created using any of the symbols included with CorelDRAW! as bullets. Also, you can import text files created with a word processor, such as Microsoft Word or WordPerfect.

Selecting an Insertion Point

The *insertion point* is the point on the printable page where you want a text string to begin. Text aligns itself relative to that point. In CorelDRAW!, you can enter text directly on the page, or you can type it in a special dialog box, where you also select its attributes. To select an insertion point and prepare for the other exercises in this chapter, follow these steps:

1. From the Grid Setup dialog box in the Layout menu, make sure that Snap To Grid and Show Grid are on, and set both the Horizontal and Vertical Grid Frequencies to 2.00 per inch. If your screen does not already display rulers and/or the grid, select Show Rulers from the Display menu and Show Grid.

2. Position the mouse pointer at the top center of the page area at 5 1/2 inches horizontal and 1/2 inch vertical, click once, and type **CorelDRAW!** . Select the Edit Text option from the Text menu, or use the shortcut key combination Ctrl-T. The Artistic Text dialog box displays, as shown in Figure 4-1.

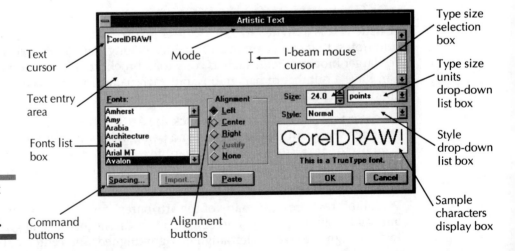

Artistic Text dialog box
Figure 4-1.

Artistic Text Dialog Box

Using the elements of the Artistic Text dialog box, you can enter text and then customize it in five different ways. Take a moment to become familiar with the layout of this dialog box and the way the keyboard functions within it.

The following paragraphs describe the components of the Artistic Text dialog box and their respective functions. Figure 4-1 points out the major components. The words "Artistic Text" in the title bar of the dialog box indicate you are in Artistic text, or text string, mode. If you use Paragraph mode you will instead see "Paragraph Text" in the Title bar.

4

Text Cursor   A flashing text pointer appears in the text entry area when you first call up this dialog box. You can type or edit your text string, or series of characters, in this window. A text string can include up to 250 characters. You can include an unlimited number of text strings in a single file.

Alignment Buttons   Use the alignment buttons to align your text relative to the insertion point. The default setting for this text attribute is Left. The dimmed Justify button is for justified (right and left alignment) paragraphs and is available only in Paragraph mode.

Fonts List Box   The Fonts list box contains the names of all the fonts from which you can choose, including those provided by CorelDRAW! 4 and any you may have from other sources.

Sample Characters Display Box   When you select a font, the sample characters display box will display in that font as much of your text as fits in the box. This gives you a true WYSIWYG example of the font. Additionally, CorelDRAW! adds a statement below the display box that indicates whether the font is a TrueType font supported by Windows 3.1 or a font created by another source, such as Adobe Type Manager.

Style Drop-Down List Box   Once you choose a font, use the Style list box to specify the style in which you want the font to appear. In CorelDRAW!, *font* refers to an entire character set that shares the same basic design (for example, Avalon), regardless of the size (for example, 10 points) or weight (for example, bold or italic). A *style* is narrower in scope. One style includes only a single weight (normal, bold, italic, or bold-italic) for a particular font. Although there are four possible styles for any font, some fonts are not available in all four styles, and the unavailable styles are therefore dimmed.

Type Size Selection Box   Use the type size selection box to choose the size for the text you enter. The default setting for this attribute is 24 points, but you can change this value by using the scroll arrows at the right side of the selection box. (See "Selecting a Type Size" later in this chapter.)

Type Size Units Drop-Down List Box   Click on the arrow in the type size units box to change the unit of measuring type sizes from points (the default) to inches, millimeters, or picas and points.

Spacing Button   The Spacing button gives you access to an additional dialog box where you can specify spacing between characters, words, or, if you are in Paragraph mode, paragraphs. See the "Adjusting Text Spacing" section in this chapter for detailed instructions on how to adjust spacing.

Paste Button   Clicking on the Paste button transfers the contents of the Windows Clipboard to the text entry area. If the Clipboard contains more than 250 characters, the excess will be cut off and not brought into CorelDRAW!.

Import Button   The dimmed Import button allows you to import a text file into CorelDRAW! if you are in Paragraph mode.

OK and Cancel Buttons   Click on the OK button or press Enter to save your attribute settings and display, onscreen, the effects of these settings on your previously (or newly) entered text. To exit the Artistic Text dialog box without saving any changes, click on the Cancel button or press Esc.

Using the Keyboard and Mouse

You can use both the mouse and the keyboard to move among attributes and among attribute settings in the Artistic Text dialog box. If you are using a mouse to move around in the Artistic Text dialog box, you can select a text attribute in four different ways: by clicking on an option or command button, by scrolling with a scroll bar or scroll arrow, by clicking on a selection box, or by choosing from a drop-down list box. You work with option or command buttons to choose justification and spacing; with scroll bars or scroll arrows to choose fonts or to display more text in the text entry box; with a selection box to choose from different text sizes; and with drop-down list boxes to choose styles and size units.

If you prefer to use the keyboard in the Artistic Text dialog box, you can select most text attributes using Tab, Shift-Tab, and the four arrow keys on your numeric pad. When you first enter the dialog box, the text cursor appears in the text entry area. To move from the text entry area to any of the attribute settings, click on the attribute setting, or press the Alt key along with the appropriate underlined letter. Then pressing Tab moves you from one attribute to the next, while the Shift-Tab key combination moves you between attributes in the reverse order. The order in which you move between attributes depends on which version of CorelDRAW! you have.

Now you are familiar with how to get around in the Artistic Text dialog box. The differences between the Artistic Text dialog box and the Paragraph Text dialog box are discussed in the sections later in this chapter dealing with paragraph text. In the following sections you will learn how to set text attributes for yourself.

Entering Text

Text can be entered either directly on the screen or through the text entry area in the Artistic and Paragraph Text dialog boxes. In the next section, you will become acquainted with the use of the text entry area, followed by some of the unique properties of direct onscreen text entry, including the use of the Text roll-up window. The exercises on text entry and manipulation will use both methods to let you see for yourself when to use one over the other.

4

Entering Text in the Text Dialog Box

When you first open the Artistic Text dialog box, the text entry area is automatically selected, as you can see by the text cursor in Figure 4-1. (On your monitor, the text cursor is flashing.) If you are not in the text entry area because of the previous exercises, click in the box now to return there. To enter a maximum of 250 text characters, simply begin typing. For this exercise, enter text in the following way:

1. Type **CorelDRAW!** at the flashing text cursor if it's not there already. Notice how "CorelDRAW!" appears in the sample characters display box in the current font.
2. Press (Enter) to begin a new line, type **Made**, and press (Enter) again.
3. On the third line, type **Easy**.

Your text entry area should now look like this:

Using Keys to Move Around

The way you use your computer keys to move around in the CorelDRAW! text entry area may differ from the way you use them in a word processor.

Whenever you have several lines of text in the text entry area, you can use the following keyboard commands:

✦ Press ⌷Enter⌷ to start a new line within the text entry area and begin entering text into it. The window will hold as many lines of text as you generate, as long as you do not exceed the 250-character limit.

✦ Press the ⌷↓⌷ key to move the text cursor down one line. (This does not apply if you are already on the last line of text.)

✦ Press ⌷Pg Dn⌷ to move the text cursor down to the last line of text. The text in the previous two lines may "jump" out of visual range, like this:

✦ Press the ⌷↑⌷ key to move the text cursor up one line. (This has no effect if you are already on the top line of text.)

✦ Press ⌷Pg Up⌷ to move the text cursor up to the first line of text.

✦ Press ⌷Home⌷ to move the cursor to the beginning of the current line.

✦ Press ⌷End⌷ to move the cursor to the end of the current line.

✦ Press the ⌷→⌷ key to move the cursor one letter at a time to the right.

✦ Press the ⌷←⌷ key to move the cursor one letter at a time to the left.

✦ Press ⌷Backspace⌷ to delete the character immediately preceding the text cursor.

✦ Press ⌷Del⌷ to delete the character immediately following the text cursor.

Using the Mouse

You can also perform some text entry operations using the mouse:

✦ Use the scroll bar at the right side of the text entry area to locate a line of text that is not currently visible.

✦ If you want to insert text at a given point, click at that point.

✦ To select one or more characters in a text string, position the text cursor at the first character you want to select and then drag the mouse across the desired characters. The characters appear highlighted, as shown here:

✦ You can delete a text string that you have selected in this way by pressing Del.

Continue to experiment with the keyboard controls and the mouse until you feel comfortable with them. Entering text directly on the screen, you will find, uses the same text editing techniques.

Entering Text Directly on the Screen

CorelDRAW! 4 allows you to type both artistic and paragraph text on the screen, with the attributes that you choose. The mechanics of entering the text are the same as entering it in the text entry area of the Artistic Text dialog box: you establish the insertion point by clicking the mouse on the screen, and you use the same navigating and editing keys as you did in the text entry area (Home, End, Backspace, Del, and the arrow keys).

4

To change the attributes of the text you enter, you can use either the Artistic Text dialog box or the Text roll-up window that lets you access the more common attributes. The following exercise repeats the previous text entry, but this time on the screen:

1. Return to the screen by clicking on the OK button.
2. Choose New from the File menu and click on No when asked if you want to save the changes to the current file, "Untitled.CDR." A blank page appears.
3. Choose Text from the menu bar and click on Text Roll-Up, or, using the keyboard, press Ctrl-F2. The Text roll-up window appears on your screen, as shown here:

The Text roll-up window lets you choose text alignment, font, type style, size, and units. The dimmed Frame button is not available with artistic text. The Character Placement button is used to adjust the attributes of selected characters in the text, such as superscript and subscript. The Paragraph button opens the Paragraph dialog box, which is covered in the section "Paragraph Attributes" later in this chapter. For any of your choices to take effect, you must choose Apply after changing the attributes.

TIP: You can use both the mouse and the Tab key to switch among the Text roll-up attributes, but the mouse works the best. Some of the attribute buttons do not allow you to easily see whether they are active.

4. Select the Artistic Text tool and place the insertion point at 5 1/2 inches horizontal and 1 inch vertical.

5. Type **CorelDRAW!**, press Enter, type **Made**, press Enter, and finally, type **Easy** and press Enter.

   You should be looking at the same text entry that you made earlier in the text entry area. Select Text Edit to verify this. When you are satisfied that it's the same, return to the screen by clicking the Cancel or OK button.

   As you probably noticed, the Text roll-up window is taking up some of the printable page.

6. Roll up the roll-up window by clicking on the up arrow in the upper-right corner.

Now that you have a feel for both the text entry area and direct-entry ways of adding text, the following exercises will guide you through text attribute usage.

Aligning Text

The next exercise involves deciding how you want to align the text. You have four choices available on the Text roll-up menu with artistic text: Left, Center, Right, and None. In Paragraph mode, you also have Justified (both left and right) alignment.

Left Alignment

Left is the default alignment setting. When you choose this setting, text will align on the page as though the insertion point were the left margin.

1. You will need to open the Text roll-up window by either clicking on the down arrow of the "rolled-up" title bar, or choosing Text Roll-Up from the Text menu. If the Left icon (leftmost icon on the top row, which turns on left alignment) is not selected, use the mouse to select it by positioning the mouse pointer over the icon and clicking once. The Left button darkens when you select it.

2. Select Apply from the Text roll-up window. The text that you entered displays on the page in the default font, left-aligned at the 5 1/2-inch mark, as in Figure 4-2. The text string has a default fill of black like other closed objects in CorelDRAW!.

NOTE: The type size in Figures 4-2 through 4-5 looks larger than what appears on your screen. The size has been increased from the default 24 points to 40 points so you can better see the text and the effects of alignment selections. You will do the same on your screen when you use the Size attribute.

3. Leave this text on the page and select another insertion point, at the 3-inch vertical mark and the 5 1/2-inch horizontal mark, just below the first text string.

4

Center Alignment

When you select Center alignment, the insertion point becomes the midpoint of any string you type. Perform these steps to compare center alignment with left alignment:

1. Type **CorelDRAW!** on one line, **Made** on the next, and **Easy** on the third line, as you did in the last section.

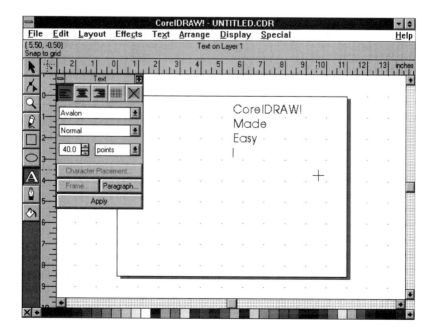

Left-justified
text
Figure 4-2.

2. Using the mouse, change to center alignment by positioning the mouse pointer over the Center icon (second from left icon on the top row) and clicking once.

3. Select Apply. The text you entered appears in the default font, center-aligned with respect to the 5 1/2-inch mark. Your page should now look like Figure 4-3.

4. Leave this text on the page. Select a third insertion point, this time at the 5-inch vertical mark and the 5 1/2-inch horizontal mark, just below the center-aligned text.

Right Alignment

When you select Right alignment, the text aligns on the page area as though the insertion point were the right margin. Perform these steps to compare right alignment with left and center alignment:

1. Type **CorelDRAW! Made Easy** on three lines as you did in the previous exercises.

2. Using the mouse, change to right alignment by positioning the mouse pointer over the Right icon (middle icon on the top row) and clicking once.

3. Select Apply. The text you entered appears in the default font, right-aligned with respect to the 5 1/2-inch mark. Your page should

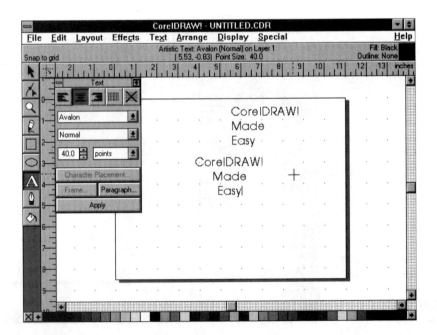

Center-justified
text added
Figure 4-3.

now look like Figure 4-4. Notice that the Text roll-up window remains on the screen.

4. Leave this text on the page. Select a fourth insertion point, this time at the 7-inch vertical and 5 1/2-inch horizontal mark.

No Alignment

When you select None for alignment, text displays on the page exactly as you enter it. This selection is useful when you want to add unusual spacing at the beginning of a line in a text string. Perform these steps to compare text with no alignment to text with left, center, and right alignment:

1. Type**CorelDRAW!** and press Enter.

2. On the second line, indent two spaces, type**Made** , and press Enter again.

3. On the third line, indent four spaces and type**Easy** .

4. Using the mouse, change the alignment to none by clicking on the None icon (rightmost on the top row).

5. Select Apply. The text that you entered appears in the default font, with the spacing exactly as you typed it. Your page should now look like Figure 4-5.

6. Clear the page of text by selecting New from the File menu. Do not save the changes. Notice the Text roll-up window remains on the screen.

4

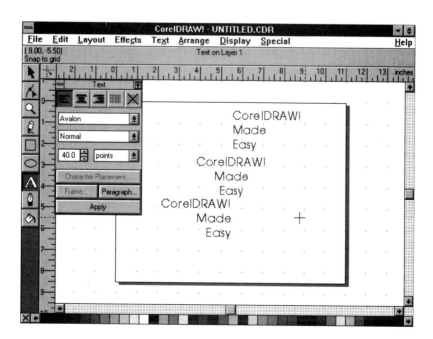

Right-aligned
text added
Figure 4-4.

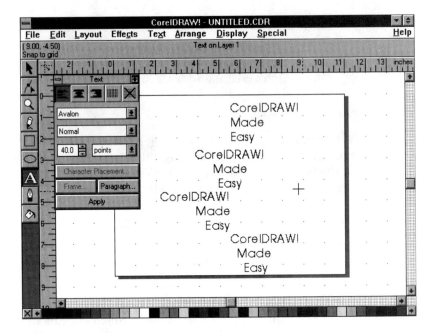

Unjustified
text added
Figure 4-5.

Selecting a Type Size

Normally, you will select alignment and font settings for a text string before you specify the type size, which is measured in points (72 points make up an inch). For this exercise, however, you will want to see results on the full page in a larger size than the default value of 24 points.

To change the default type size from 24 to 100 points using the mouse, follow these steps:

1. Position the pointer over the upper scroll arrow next to the Size box in the Text roll-up window and depress and hold the mouse button. As you scroll, the numerical value in the Size box increases.

2. Release the mouse button when the value in the Size box reaches 100.0.

3. Click on Apply. The Text Attributes dialog box will be displayed, as shown here:

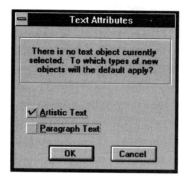

4

4. Click on the Paragraph Text check box to turn it off; only Artistic Text should be selected. Click on OK. The default for artistic text is now 100 points, and the default for paragraph text remains at 24 points.

5. Roll up the Text roll-up window. In the next section you'll return to the text entry area.

Selecting a Type Design

So far, you have used only the default font in CorelDRAW!. In this section, you will have the opportunity to experiment with some of the different fonts and styles supplied with your software.

Selecting a Font

Many books and trade magazines offer guidelines for selecting an appropriate font. A thorough discussion of the subject is beyond the scope of this book; however, when choosing the font to use in a CorelDRAW! graphic, you should consider the tone and purpose of your work, as well as your intended audience. Look at the two fonts in Figure 4-6, for example. You probably would not choose an elaborate, flowery font such as Paradise for a graphic that you would present to a meeting of civil engineers; a font such as Frankfurt Gothic might prove a better choice.

NOTE: The discussion of fonts in this and the following chapters assumes that you have loaded the fonts described onto your hard disk from the CD-ROM as described in Appendix A.

Practice selecting fonts in the following exercise.

Comparing
the "tone" of
fonts
Figure 4-6.

1. Select the Artistic Text tool and then select an insertion point that is at the 1 1/2-inch mark on both the horizontal and vertical rulers.

2. Type **Paradise**. Open the Artistic Text dialog box by choosing Edit Text from the Edit menu or by pressing   -Ⓣ. The dialog box appears, with the sample text box showing the word "Paradise" in the default font.

3. Select the Paradise font from the Fonts list box. You can select a font in one of four ways:

   a. *Click* With the mouse, click directly on the font name if it is visible in the list box. When you do this, the font name becomes highlighted, and a faint dotted outline surrounds it. If the font you want is not visible, use one of the following techniques.

   b. *Scroll continuously up or down the list* Position the mouse pointer on the up or down scroll arrow and then depress and hold the mouse button until the desired font comes into view. Click on the font name to select it.

   c. *Scroll up or down the list one line at a time* Position the mouse pointer on the up or down scroll arrow at the top or bottom of the scroll bar in the Fonts list box. Click repeatedly until the name of the font you want comes into view. Select that font name by clicking on it. This is the same as using Ⓣ or Ⓓ with the Fonts list box selected.

d. *Scroll up or down the list one list box at a time* Position the mouse pointer in the right scroll bar, not on a scroll arrow, and either above or below the scroll box, and click. The list will move up or down by the height of the list box. This is the same as using `Pg Up` or `Pg Dn` with the Fonts list box selected.

4. Set Alignment to Left if it isn't already.

5. Select OK to return to the page, where you will see the Paradise text string with the selected attributes, as shown in Figure 4-7. On your screen, nodes will appear between each letter.

6. Select another insertion point at the 1 1/2-inch mark on the horizontal ruler and the 3 1/2-inch mark on the vertical ruler.

7. Type **Avalon** and open the Artistic Text dialog box.

8. Select the Avalon font in the Fonts list box if it's not already selected.

9. Select OK to return to the page, where you will see the Avalon text string beneath the Paradise text string, as in Figure 4-8.

10. Select a third insertion point at the 1 1/2-inch mark on the horizontal ruler and the 5 1/2-inch mark on the vertical ruler.

11. Type **Aardvark** and open the Artistic Text dialog box.

12. Select the Aardvark font from the list box.

13. Click on OK to exit the Artistic Text dialog box. Your page now looks like Figure 4-9.

14. Select a fourth insertion point at the 1 1/2-inch mark on the horizontal ruler and the 7 1/2-inch mark on the vertical ruler.

15. Type **Dixieland** and open the Artistic Text dialog box.

16. Select the Dixieland font from the list box and notice that nonalphabetic symbols, rather than letters, appear in the sample characters window. This font, like the Geographic Symbols, Greek/Math Symbols, and Musical Symbols fonts, consists of symbols rather than letters.

17. Select OK to see the text on the page. Your page now resembles Figure 4-10. You will notice that even though you have entered all of the text strings at the same point size, some appear larger than others. Each font has its own characteristic width and height.

18. Clear the screen by selecting New from the File menu. Do not save any changes.

Practice trying out different fonts. When you are ready for the next section, clear the screen by selecting New from the File menu. You will learn how to select one of the four available styles for a given font.

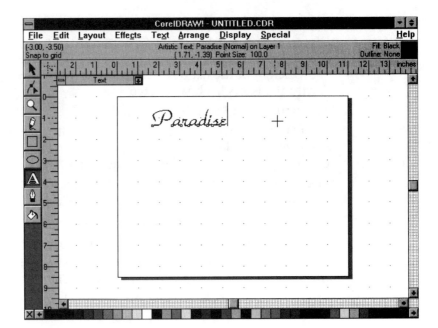

Text string
using the
Paradise font
Figure 4-7.

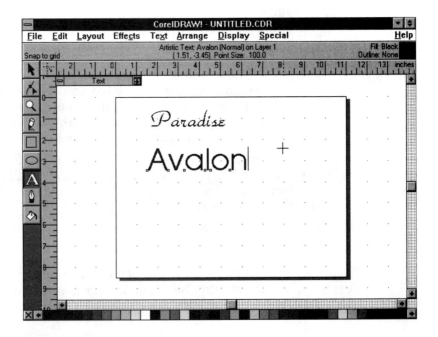

Text strings
using the
Paradise and
Avalon fonts
Figure 4-8.

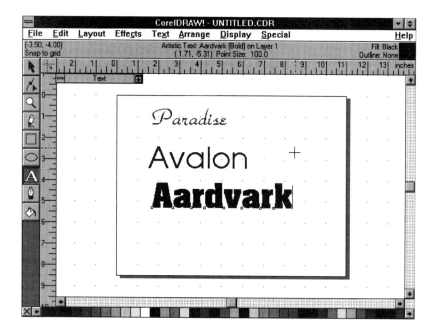

Comparing
Paradise,
Avalon, and
Aardvark fonts
Figure 4-9.

4

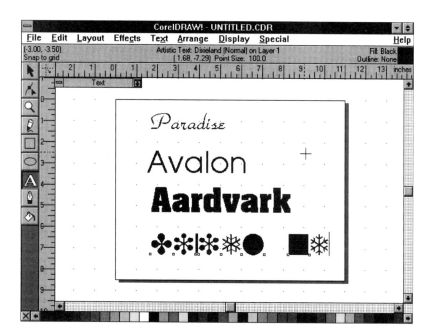

Adding a text
string from a
nonalphabetic
(symbol) font
Figure 4-10.

Selecting a Style

While you were experimenting with fonts in the foregoing exercise, you may have noticed that not all styles were offered for some fonts. This is because some fonts have only one or two styles available, while others have three or four.

Perform the following exercise to practice selecting available type styles for the CorelDRAW! fonts. This exercise uses the direct entry method and the Text roll-up window. The instructions are less descriptive since you should now have the tools to easily move through the menus.

1. In the Text roll-up, change the text size to 75 points and click on Apply. In the Text Attributes dialog box, confirm that only Artistic Text is checked and click on OK.

2. Select the Artistic Text tool and then choose an insertion point that is at the 1 1/2-inch mark on the horizontal ruler and the 2-inch mark on the vertical ruler.

3. Type **Frankfurt Gothic** and highlight the words by dragging across them from the "F" in Frankfurt to the "c" in Gothic, as shown here:

Frankfurt Gothic

4. Select Frankfurt Gothic from the font list box in the Text roll-up.

5. Select the Italic style in the style drop-down list box.

6. Select Apply to display the resulting text on the page, as in Figure 4-11. Leave this text on the page for now.

7. Select another insertion point at the 1 1/2-inch horizontal and 4-inch vertical ruler marks.

8. Type **Frankfurt Gothic** highlight the text, and select the Frankfurt Gothic font.

9. Select Bold in the style drop-down list box.

10. Select Apply to display the resulting text on the page, as in Figure 4-12. Click on a blank part of the screen to remove the highlighting.

11. Select a third insertion point at the 1 1/2-inch horizontal and the 6-inch vertical ruler marks.

12. Again, type **Frankfurt Gothic** but this time instead of highlighting the text by dragging, you will use the Pick tool.

The Pick tool is used to select, move, or arrange objects or text.

Chapter 6 provides an in-depth discussion on the use of the Pick tool, but it's necessary at this point to introduce the text-selecting properties of the tool.

4

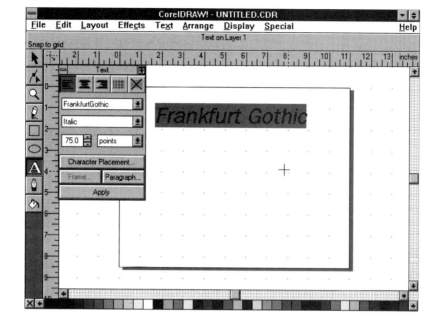

Text string in
Frankfurt
Gothic italic
Figure 4-11.

Comparing
italic and bold
type styles
Figure 4-12.

For CorelDRAW! to change the attributes of a text string, the string must be selected. In simple cases, where there is only one string, some attributes can be changed without you doing the selecting because CorelDRAW! "knows" which text to change. As you increase the number of text strings, you must highlight the text by dragging; or, if CorelDRAW! does not accept the attribute change, select it with the Pick tool.

13. Click on the Pick tool. If the text is not selected, place the mouse pointer on a letter in the text string and click once more. The words "Frankfurt Gothic" become surrounded by eight boundary markers. The full use of these boxes is discussed in Chapter 6, but for the purposes of text, they identify the text as being selected.

The Pick tool will be used again in later sections of this chapter.

CAUTION: Double-clicking on text with the Pick tool invokes the rotate and skew feature. If you accidentally do this, just click on the text again to get the selection boxes back.

14. In the Text roll-up window, change the font to Frankfurt Gothic and select Bold-Italic in the style drop-down list box.

15. Select Apply to display the resulting text on the page. Click on a blank portion of the screen to remove the highlighting. Your screen should resemble Figure 4-13.

16. Select New from the File menu to clear the screen before continuing with another exercise.

Take a few moments to practice selecting styles for other fonts. When you have finished, continue with the next section to learn how to adjust spacing when you enter a new text string.

Adjusting Text Spacing

The Spacing command button in the lower-left corner of either the Artistic or the Paragraph Text dialog box may be easy to overlook, but it can give you enormous control over text. When you select this button, the Spacing dialog box appears, which allows you to control the spacing between characters, words, and lines of text.

In this chapter, you are working with attributes only as you enter text. However, CorelDRAW! also allows you to adjust text spacing *interactively*. This means that even after text displays on the page, you can change the

Frankfurt Gothic

Frankfurt Gothic

Frankfurt Gothic

Comparing
italic, bold,
and bold-italic
type styles
Figure 4-13.

4

spacing of one character, several characters, or an entire text string without
going back to the dialog box. You will learn more about how to change
spacing attributes for existing text in Chapter 9.

Setting Up the Exercise

In the following exercise, you will have the opportunity to review what you
have learned thus far about setting all of the attributes in the Artistic Text
dialog box.

*If you have
forgotten how
to perform any
of these
functions, go
back to the
relevant section
and review it.*

1. Select the Artistic Text tool if it is not selected already.
2. Select an insertion point near the top of the page, aligned to the 5
   1/2-inch horizontal and 1 1/2-inch vertical marks on the rulers.
3. Enter four lines of text on the screen. Type your name on the first line,
   your address on the second, your city, state, and ZIP code on the third,
   and your telephone number on the fourth.
4. Click on the Pick tool to highlight the four lines of text. Open the Text
   roll-up if it isn't already displayed on your screen.
5. Change the type size to 50.0 points.
6. Select Center alignment.
7. Select Gatineau as the font and click on Apply.

8. Open the Artistic Text dialog box. It should look like Figure 4-14, except that the actual text on the screen will be your name and address, as you have entered them. Select the Spacing command button by clicking on it once. The Spacing dialog box in Figure 4-15 appears.

The Spacing Dialog Box

The Spacing dialog box features five options for adjusting spacing: Character, Word, Line, Before Paragraph, and After Paragraph. You will not change them at this point in the exercise, but take a moment to become familiar with your options.

Character The Character option controls spacing between each pair of characters within each word of the text. The default value is 0 percent of space width. In other words, CorelDRAW! inserts no space at all between characters unless you change that value. This measurement is relative, rather

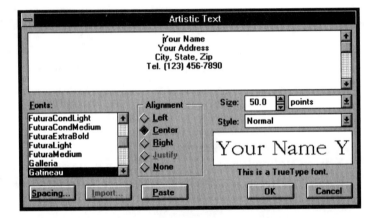

Settings:
Gatineau
normal, center
alignment,
50 points
Figure 4-14.

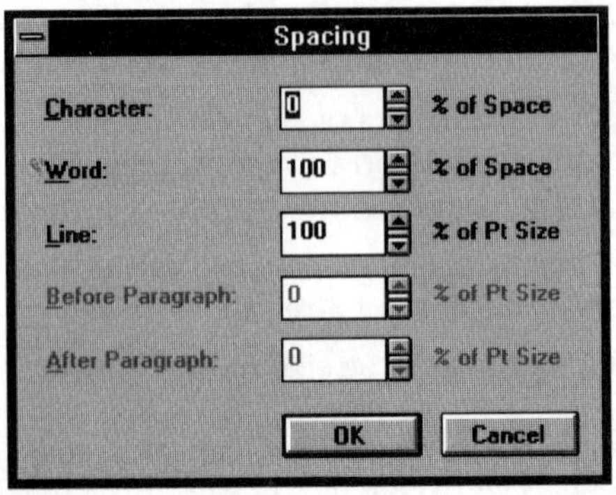

Spacing dialog
box
Figure 4-15.

than an absolute measurement, so that your spacing will stay constant as you scale your text or change the font. You can adjust the value of inter-character spacing in increments of whole percentage points using the scroll arrows, or you can type in the value.

Word   The Word option controls spacing between each word of the text that you enter. The default value is 100 percent of space width. You can adjust the value of inter-word spacing in increments of whole percentage points using the scroll arrow or by typing in a value.

Line   When your text contains more than one line, the Line option controls the amount of space between each line. In the printing industry, this type of spacing is also known as *leading*. The default value is 100 percent of the type size, which means that if your text size is 10 points, the total amount of space between two lines is exactly 10 points and no more. You can adjust inter-line spacing in increments of 1 percent.

4

Before and After Paragraph   If you are in Paragraph mode, and you have more than one paragraph, the Before and After Paragraph options control the amount of space between each pair of paragraphs. The default values are 100 percent of the type size Before Paragraph and 0 percent After Paragraph. If your text size is 10 points, the space between paragraphs will be 10 points. You can adjust the inter-paragraph spacing by increments of 1 percent.

You can adjust the values in the Spacing dialog box in two ways: by scrolling with the mouse or by using the keyboard.

To adjust values using the mouse only:

1. Position the mouse pointer on the up or down scroll arrow. If you want to increase the value, position it on the up arrow; if you want to decrease the value, position it on the down arrow.
2. Press and hold the mouse button until the value you want displays in the adjoining box and then release the mouse button.

To adjust values using the keyboard:

1. Use `Tab` or `Shift`-`Tab` to go from item to item in the dialog box. When you reach one of the spacing number boxes, the entire number will be highlighted. This means that if you type a new number, you will completely replace the original number.
2. Type in the value you want. To go to the next setting, press `Tab` or `Shift`-`Tab`.

Leave the spacing options at their default settings for the current text string and select OK twice. You exit the Spacing dialog box and the Artistic Text dialog box. Your text string has the default settings of 100 percent spacing between words, no extra spacing between characters, and no extra leading between lines, as shown in Figure 4-16. If your screen still has the select boxes around your text, click on a blank area of the screen and they will disappear.

Adjusting and Comparing Spacing

Now that you are acquainted with the way the Spacing dialog box works, you will create another text string, identical to the first except that its spacing values differ. You can then visually compare the results of your spacing adjustments.

1. With the Artistic Text tool, select an insertion point at the 5 1/2-inch mark on the horizontal ruler and the 4 1/2-inch mark on the vertical ruler, just beneath the last line of text on the page.

2. Type your name, street address, city, state, and ZIP, and telephone number on four separate lines.

3. Click on the Pick tool and then, if necessary, on the new text to highlight it. Use the Text roll-up to set the alignment, font, and size attributes to what they were (Center, Gatineau, and 50 points). Click on Apply.

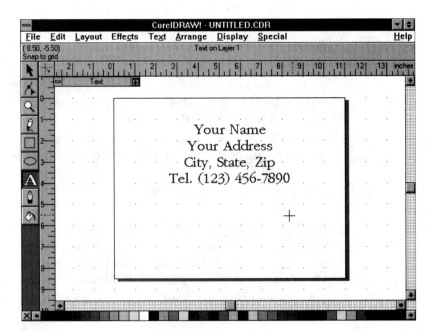

Address text string with default spacing attributes
Figure 4-16.

4. Open the Artistic Text dialog box and select the Spacing command button to display the Spacing dialog box.

5. This time, adjust the spacing in the Character number box to 50 percent, Word to 200 percent, and Line to 130 percent. This means that the space between characters will equal the width of half a space, the space between words will equal two spaces, and the space between lines will equal 1.3 times the height of the font itself.

6. Select OK twice to save these settings and exit to the page. The second text string now displays beneath the first. Your page resembles Figure 4-17.

7. Select New from the File menu to clear the screen. Do not save any changes.

4

Working with Paragraphs

So far in this chapter, all of your work has been in Artistic Text mode. This is fine for titles, captions, and other pieces of text that are only a few short lines. If you are creating a brochure, a flyer, or other documents where you need large blocks of text, you should use Paragraph mode. Paragraph mode offers several features that are valuable for large blocks of text and are not available in Artistic Text mode. Among these features are

✦ An increase in the character limit from 250 characters to 4000 characters

✦ Automatic word wrap at the end of each line

Comparing default and custom spacing attributes
Figure 4-17.

◆ Variable line length controlled by a frame, or bounding box, whose dimensions and attributes can be changed

◆ Justified (full left and right) alignment

◆ The ability to define up to eight columns with variable inter-column spacing

◆ The ability to paste text into the text entry area or onto the page from the Windows Clipboard

◆ The ability to import text created with a word processor

◆ Adjustable inter-paragraph spacing

◆ The ability to control text hyphenation

As with artistic text, paragraph text can be entered directly on the screen, or you can open the Paragraph Text dialog box and use the text entry area.

Try out Paragraph mode now with these steps:

1. Select the Paragraph Text tool (the middle icon on the Text tool flyout) and place the mouse pointer at 1 inch on the horizontal ruler and 1/2 inch on the vertical ruler.

2. Press and hold the mouse button while dragging the mouse pointer to 10 inches on the horizontal ruler and 8 inches on the vertical ruler, as shown in Figure 4-18, and then release the mouse button.

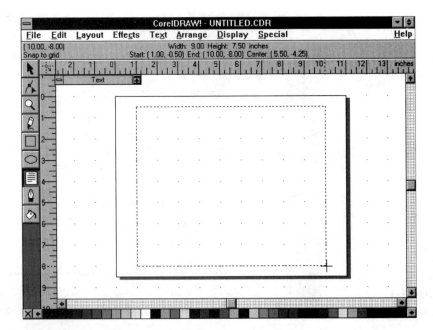

Forming the Paragraph mode bounding box or frame

Figure 4-18.

The frame dimensions of the paragraph will be set. After you release the mouse button, the insertion point appears at the beginning of the frame. Though the printable page area does not show that you are in Paragraph mode, the status line will display "Text on Layer 1."

3. Open the Paragraph Text dialog box by clicking on Edit Text in the Text menu.

As you can see in Figure 4-19, the Paragraph Text dialog box has a few differences from the Artistic Text dialog box. The title now reads "Paragraph Text;" the Justify alignment and Import buttons are turned on; and if you look at the Spacing dialog box you will see that Before and After Paragraph spacing can now be set. To the right of the text entry area is the paragraph selection box. Each paragraph in the paragraph text file is treated as a separate entity; you use the paragraph selection box to select the active paragraph.

4. Type several paragraphs, such as those shown following this step, and your Paragraph Text dialog box should look like Figure 4-20. It doesn't matter what you type as long as you have two or more paragraphs about as long as those shown. Press (Enter) only at the end of the paragraphs and let CorelDRAW! automatically wrap the text at the end of each line.

Here are two sample paragraphs you can type:

```
CorelDRAW!'s paragraph mode, first available in version 2.0,
provides many features that are valuable for entering large
blocks of text. Among these features are: an increase in the
character limit from 250 to 4,000 characters, automatic word
wrap at the end of each line, a line length that is controlled
by the size of the frame, full (both left and right)
justification, text hyphenation, and the ability to define up
to eight columns.
```

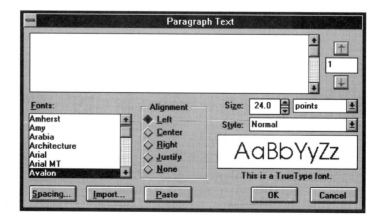

Text dialog box in Paragraph mode
Figure 4-19.

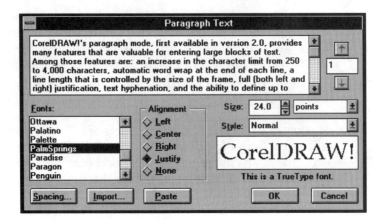

One of two
paragraphs
entered into
the Text
window
Figure 4-20.

Paragraph mode also allows you to paste text into the Paragraph
Text dialog box from the Windows Clipboard, import text files
created with a word processor, and adjust the inter-paragraph
spacing. Paragraph mode is used in building brochures, flyers,
and other documents where large blocks of text are needed.

5. When you are finished typing, click on Justify alignment, confirm 24
   points is the default size, select the Palm Springs font, and the Normal style.

6. Click on the Spacing command button, change Line spacing to 120
   percent and After Paragraph spacing to 90 percent. Click on OK twice to
   return all the way out to the page.

   When you return to the page, after a moment, the text will appear
   within the frame, as shown in Figure 4-21. It will not be terribly
   readable but now you can add or edit text directly on the screen. In
   Chapter 5, you will see how to magnify a portion of the page to be able
   to read it better.

   To preserve the typing you have done, save this file.

7. From the File menu select Save As, if necessary, change to the
   DRAWINGS directory, type **paratext** in the filename text box, and
   press (Enter) or click on OK.

Extracting Text from CorelDRAW!

CorelDRAW! includes a feature that allows you to extract text from
CorelDRAW! in a format that is usable in a word processing program. You
can modify the text in the word processor and then merge the text back into
CorelDRAW!, automatically reattaching all of the formatting, such as font,
size, and style, that was originally attached to the text. (In the word
processing program you will not see any of the formatting.)

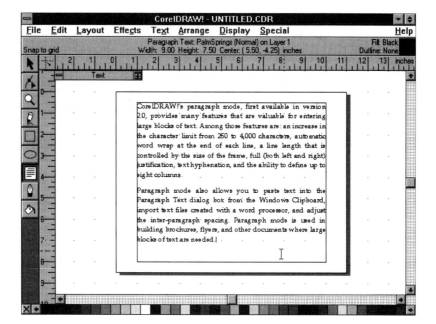

Paragraph text
as it is
displayed on
the page
Figure 4-21.

4

In this section you will extract the text you entered, bring that text into a word processor, modify it, save it, save it again as a plain text file, and place it on the Windows Clipboard. In the next section, you will bring each of these files back into CorelDRAW!.

Start by extracting the text from CorelDRAW!. The text you typed should still be on the screen, as shown in Figure 4-21. To extract it, though, you must select it with the Pick tool.

1. Select the Pick tool and click in the paragraph frame to select the text.
2. From the Special menu, select Extract. The Extract dialog box will open.
3. Make sure the DRAWINGS directory is selected, type **extrpara** in the File Name text box, and click on OK.

You have now written an ASCII text file containing the paragraphs you entered. In the following steps you will switch out of CorelDRAW! without closing it, open Windows Write, and edit that file. (Almost any word processor could be used in place of Windows Write.)

4. Open the Control menu in the upper-left corner of the CorelDRAW! window and select Switch To.
5. From the Task list, double-click on Program Manager. The Program Manager window will open.

6. Open the Accessories group (if necessary) and double-click on Write. The Write word processing program will open.

7. Select Open from the File menu, In the Directories list box, locate the DRAWINGS directory, to which you extracted the EXTRPARA.TXT file. If you installed CorelDRAW! according to the instructions in Appendix A, this is C:\DRAWINGS. In the List File of Type drop-down list box, choose Text Files (*.TXT) and then click on *extrpara.txt* in the File Name list box. The filename is displayed in the File Name entry box. Click on OK.

8. A dialog box will open asking, "Do you want to convert this file to Write format?" Click on No Conversion to preserve the ASCII text format. The text you entered in CorelDRAW! will appear on the Windows Write screen, as shown in Figure 4-22.

   The first two lines and the last two lines of text (the last line is blank) are reserved for CorelDRAW! to use in merging the text back in. It is, therefore, very important that you do not change these four lines, or CorelDRAW! will not be able to merge this file. You can change all other parts of the file except the first two and last two lines.

9. Modify any of the text you entered. In this exercise, it doesn't matter what you modify, as long as you can recognize the change when you get back to CorelDRAW!.

10. When you finish modifying the text, open the File menu and save the file under its original filename, EXTRPARA.TXT. This is the file that will be used to merge back into your CorelDRAW! PARATEXT.CDR file.

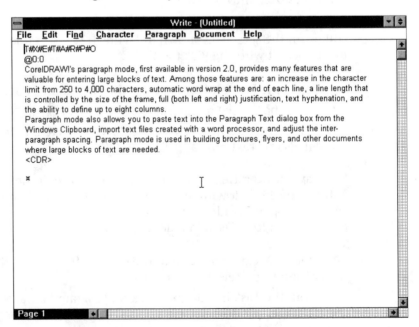

Paragraph text
in Windows
Write

Figure 4-22.

Now that you have saved the merge file, you can remove the first two and last two lines to make another text file that you can import into CorelDRAW!. Also, you will copy the remaining text to the Windows Clipboard and paste it into CorelDRAW!.

11. Delete the first two and last two lines of the file so you only have the text you entered (select the lines by dragging over them with the mouse and press (Del)).

12. From the File menu, select Save As, type **test.txt**, and click on OK. This is the file you will import.

13. Select all of the text you entered and have now modified by dragging over it with the mouse, and then from the Edit menu select Copy. This places a copy of the text on the Windows Clipboard.

14. Double-click on the Control menu to close Windows Write, and then open the Program Manager's Control menu and select Switch To.

15. Double-click on CorelDRAW! to switch to that program. CorelDRAW! will reappear on the screen.

Merging, Importing, and Pasting Text into CorelDRAW!

You now have four copies of the text you entered: the original file you saved in PARATEXT.CDR, the modified merge file EXTRPARA.TXT, the clean text file TEST.TXT, and finally, the copy on the Windows Clipboard. Use each of the last three of these copies to see how CorelDRAW! merges, imports, and pastes text from outside CorelDRAW!.

1. From the Special menu, select Merge-Back. The Merge-Back dialog box will open.

2. Double-click on EXTRPARA.TXT in the File Name list box. After a moment you will see the revised text displayed on the page. The copy of PARATEXT.CDR in memory has now been revised with the changes you made in Windows Write. All of the formatting in the original file has been maintained. If you had some graphic elements in the file, they would also remain unchanged. Only the words and their positions have changed.

3. Select New from the File menu to clear your screen. Save the revised file if you wish.

4. Select the Paragraph Text tool and draw a paragraph bounding box from 1 inch on the horizontal and 1/2 inch on the vertical ruler to 10 inches on the horizontal and 8 inches on the vertical ruler. Open the

Paragraph Text dialog box, note that your text settings, font, size, and style are still set.

5. Click on Import and then double-click on TEST.TXT. The revised text will be brought into the Paragraph Text dialog box, as shown in Figure 4-23.

6. Click on Cancel to throw away the imported text.

7. The frame that you established in step 4 returns to the screen. Press Ctrl-T to open the Paragraph Text dialog box.

8. Click on the Paste command button. Once again the revised text will come into the Paragraph Text dialog box, this time from the Windows Clipboard. The only difference is that now there is a carriage return at the end of each line.

You have now seen how you get text out of CorelDRAW! and how you can bring text back into CorelDRAW! in three different ways. Now look at how you can use columns in CorelDRAW!.

Putting Text in Columns

Many brochures, flyers, and other documents appropriate for CorelDRAW! put text into multiple columns instead of one wider column in an effort to make the text easier to read. Try it here. You should still be in the Paragraph Text dialog box with the revised paragraphs you pasted into the text entry area.

1. Click on Cancel to return to the screen. Your paragraph frame should still be selected.

2. Select the Text menu and choose the Frame option. The Frame Attributes dialog box will open, as shown in Figure 4-24.

Text imported into the Paragraph Text dialog box

Figure 4-23.

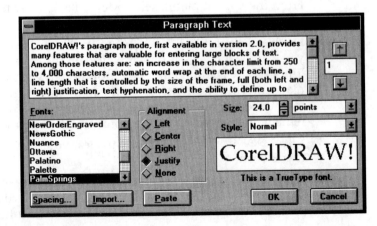

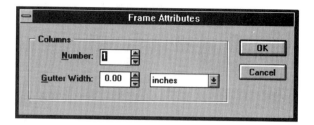

3. Type **2** for the number of columns, press Tab to move to the Gutter Width number box, and type **.5**.

4. Click on OK to close the Frame Attributes dialog box and return to the page layout. After a moment the text will appear in a two-column format, as shown in Figure 4-25.

5. Select New in the File menu to clear the page, and answer No to saving the current contents.

Paragraph Attributes

Paragraph attributes can also be set using the Paragraph dialog box shown in Figure 4-26. You open this dialog box using either the Paragraph button in the Text roll-up or the Paragraph option in the Text menu. With the

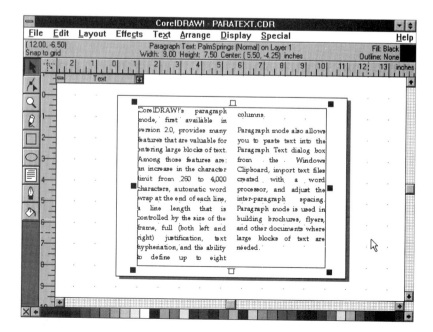

Text in
two-column
format
Figure 4-25.

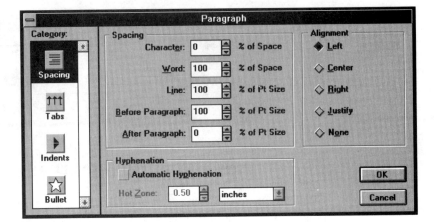

Paragraph
dialog box
Figure 4-26.

Paragraph dialog box you can adjust spacing, alignment, hyphenation (which is discussed in the next section), tabs (left, right, center, and decimal), indents, and the symbol attributes used for bulleted lists.

Hyphenation

When enabled by clicking on the Automatic Hyphenation check box in the Paragraph dialog box, CorelDRAW! will hyphenate words at the end of a line if three conditions occur: they begin before the left edge of the hot zone, they continue beyond the right edge of the frame, and a valid hyphenation break occurs within the zone. The *hot zone* extends from the right side of the paragraph text frame toward the left, according to the distance listed in the Hot Zone box. The unit of distance in the hot zone is the same as that currently entered in the units box. If a word begins in the hot zone and continues beyond the frame's right edge, it will wrap to the beginning of the next line.

Using the Spelling Checker

CorelDRAW! 4 allows you to spell check text in either Artistic or Paragraph Text mode. To use the Spelling Checker you can either highlight the text to check, which can be one word or an entire block of text, or you can type a word in the Word to Check entry box of the Spelling Checker dialog box. You open the Spelling Checker dialog box by choosing Spell Checker from the Text menu.

Note: Using the Pick tool will highlight your entire text selection.

Clicking on the Check Text button starts the spell checking. If a word is found that is not among the over 116,000 words in the dictionary, it will appear in the Word not found entry box, which replaces the Word to Check entry box. You can now have CorelDRAW! offer spelling alternatives by clicking on the Suggest button. If you click on the Always suggest check box, suggestions will always be provided. If you select one of the alternatives, the word appears in the Replace With list box, as shown in Figure 4-27. You can choose between replacing this particular occurrence or all occurrences of the word. If you don't want to replace the word with any of the suggested alternatives, you can ignore either one or all occurrences of the word. Finally, you can manually enter a word into the Replace With entry box.

4

The Spelling Checker dialog box also offers the ability to create one or more dictionaries of your favorite abbreviations, acronyms, and proper names. With such a word in the Word not found entry box, create a new dictionary with these steps:

1. Type a filename like MYDICTRY in the entry box under "Create a personal dictionary", next to the Create button.

2. Click on the Create button. The name you gave to the dictionary appears in the Personal Dictionary drop-down list box. Once you've

Spelling
Checker
dialog box
Figure 4-27.

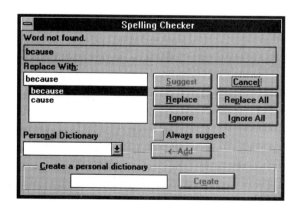

created one dictionary, subsequent dictionaries can be added by just typing the new name in the Create a personal dictionary entry box and clicking on Create.

3. Click on the Add button.

Clicking on the Cancel button closes the Spelling Checker, but does not undo any text changes you've made.

Thesaurus

CorelDRAW! 4's Thesaurus, shown in Figure 4-28, provides synonyms and definitions for selected (or manually entered) words. Simply highlight a word using the Text tool and open the Thesaurus from the Text menu. Or, open the Thesaurus and enter a word in the Synonym for text entry area, then click on Lookup. In either case, CorelDRAW! offers various definitions and synonyms. If you decide to replace the word in the Synonym for text entry area, highlight the word and click on the Replace button.

Find and Replace

New with CorelDRAW! 4 are two additional features to help you create accurate text. These are Find and Replace. The Find dialog box, shown in the following illustration, is opened by choosing Find from the Text menu. A text string up to 100 characters long is entered in the Find text box. Clicking on Find Next will move the insertion point from its current location in the paragraph text to the next occurrence of the selected text string. When the end of the document is reached, you will be prompted whether you want the search to continue from the beginning of the paragraph text. The Match

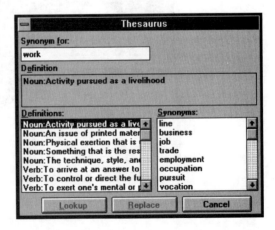

Thesaurus
dialog box
Figure 4-28.

Case option is used when you want an exact match, including upper- and lowercase, of a text string.

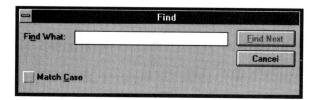

The Replace dialog box, shown in the next illustration, is similar to Find and is also found on the Text menu. With Replace you can replace the selected text with another text string. The Replace option can also match the case of the search string. You can replace single occurrences of the search string, with confirmation, or replace all the occurrences in the paragraph text.

4

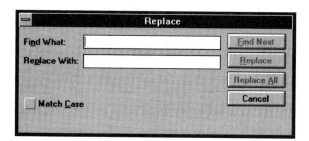

Using the Symbol Library

CorelDRAW! includes a library of over 5000 symbols that are stored and retrieved like characters in a font using the Text tool. The symbols are simple, but effective, drawings that are stored as vector images (unlike most clip art, which is stored as bitmap images). As a result, the symbols can be enlarged, stretched, rotated, and edited like any other CorelDRAW! objects without any loss in the quality of the image. Also, they take very little room to store. To use the symbols, you must install them on your hard disk. CorelDRAW!'s Install program will do this for you, as discussed in Appendix A.

The symbols are organized into over 50 categories; for example, Animals, Borders, Holidays, Space, and Weather. These categories are like fonts. You first select a category, and then from that category you select a particular symbol. The number of symbols in a category varies from 30 to 208, with the average around 80. Corel includes with CorelDRAW! a catalog of all of the symbols, giving each a number within a category. If you know this number, once you have selected a category you can enter the number and get the symbol. Also, as you will see in a moment, you can select a symbol from a display box once you have decided on a category.

Try this feature now by selecting several symbols.

1. Click on the Text tool, momentarily hold down the mouse button, and select the Symbols icon from the flyout menu. The Symbols roll-up opens, as shown in Figure 4-29.

2. Click on several categories in the drop-down list box at the top of the roll-up.

   For example, click on Computers. The first group of symbols of the category displays in the sample window.

3. Use the scroll arrows below the Sample window to see additional symbols in the Computers category.

Use steps 2 and 3 to look at a number of symbols. Notice below the scroll arrows, there is a Size number box where you can specify the initial size of a symbol when it is placed on the page.

In future chapters you will see how you can also size symbols that have already been placed on the page.

4. Change the size to 1 inch and then drag a symbol onto the page at 2 inches on both the horizontal and vertical rulers.

5. Drag another symbol to 4 inches on the horizontal ruler and 2 inches on the vertical ruler.

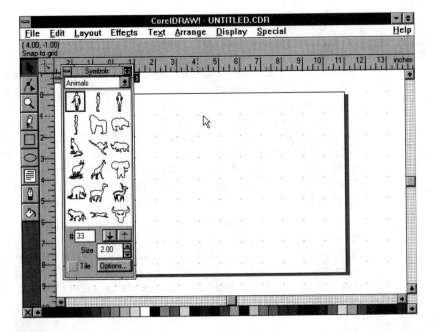

Symbols roll-up
Figure 4-29.

6. Drag other symbols to first 6 and then 8 inches on the horizontal ruler. When you are done, you should have a string of symbols, as in Figure 4-30.

The Symbol Library provides a good source of quick art that can be used for many purposes.

Entering Special Characters

CorelDRAW! includes five different proprietary character sets beyond the standard alphabet and characters that appear on your computer keyboard. You enter special characters either on the drawing page or in the text entry area of the Text dialog box, and can adjust alignment, type size, and spacing for these special characters, just as you can for alphabetic characters. The five character sets are Corel, Dixieland, Greek/Math, Musical, and Geographic.

4

✦ The Corel character set includes all keyboard characters, foreign language characters, currency symbols, and copyright and other popular commercial symbols. This character set applies to most of the fonts you have available in CorelDRAW! 4.

✦ The character set in the Dixieland font includes decorative and directional symbols and callouts.

✦ The character set in the Greek/Math font includes a variety of scientific and mathematical symbols.

✦ The character set in the Musical font contains common musical notes and notations.

✦ The character set in the Geographic font includes geographical, military, and industrial symbols.

A complete listing of the contents of each character set appears on the Character Reference Chart provided with your software. Also, the Dixieland, Musical, Geographic, and Common Bullets character sets are available as symbols in the Symbol Library. Each of the fonts is a category in the list box, and each of the characters is a symbol.

No matter which of the five character sets you are using, characters above ASCII 126 are not accessible by pressing a single key on your keyboard. To type one of these special characters, depress and hold Alt and then type the appropriate number on your numeric keypad. Be sure to include the 0 that precedes each number. For example, to type an ellipsis (. . .) in the Corel character set, type **0133**.

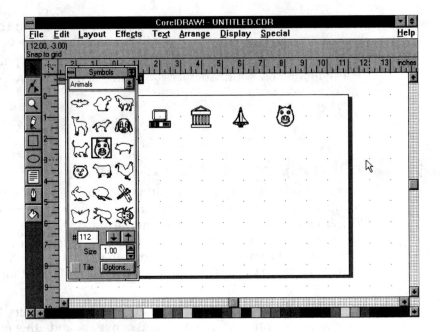

Sampling of
symbols on
the page
Figure 4-30.

CAUTION: The text you see in the text window of either the Artistic or
Paragraph dialog box uses the standard Windows character set. If you
are using a different character set, you must look at either the type display
box in the dialog box or on your drawing to see the true character set.

Always refer to your CorelDRAW! Character Reference Chart when you are
entering special characters.

CHAPTER

COREL DRAW! 4

5

USING MAGNIFICATION AND VIEW SELECTION

Until now, you have done your work in CorelDRAW! using full-page view, the default view when you load CorelDRAW! or open a file. But it has obvious limitations if you need to edit images or do fine detail work. The Zoom tool can customize the viewing area of your screen any way you wish. As you become familiar with this tool, you will experience greater drawing convenience and ease in editing.

The Zoom Tool

The Zoom tool, the third tool in the CorelDRAW! toolbox, resembles a small magnifying glass. Unlike the Pencil, Rectangle, Ellipse, and Text tools, the Zoom tool is not a drawing tool. It could be called a view adjustment tool, because it allows you to zoom in or out of the viewing area in a variety of different ways. Because the Zoom tool gives you complete control over the content of the viewing area, it helps enhance every object you draw and increases the usefulness of every tool in the CorelDRAW! toolbox.

The Zoom tool is really five separate tools. When you select this tool, the flyout menu shown in Figure 5-1 appears, giving you five tools for adjusting your viewing area.

Zoom-In   The Zoom-In tool allows you to zoom in on any area of a drawing that you select.

Zoom-Out   The Zoom-Out tool either zooms out of your current image by a factor of two or, if your screen currently shows a zoom-in view, returns you to the previous view.

Actual Size   The Actual Size tool lets you see your drawing in the actual size it will be printed.

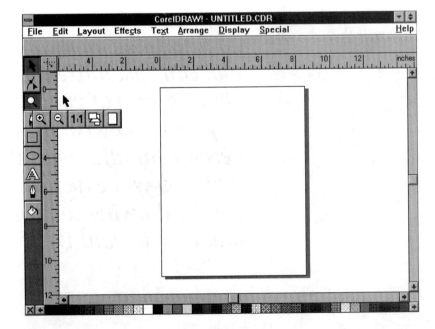

The five viewing options for the Zoom tool

Figure 5-1.

Fit-in-Window The Fit-in-Window tool lets you see all of the current drawing—everything you have placed on the page—in the current CorelDRAW! window.

Show Page The Show Page tool returns you to the default full-page view of your graphic.

In order to have something to magnify, switch to your map clip-art directory by using the Open option in the File menu. Then open the file USA_T.CDR that was provided with CorelDRAW!. If you installed CorelDRAW! using the default directories discussed in Appendix A, you can use the path you see here:

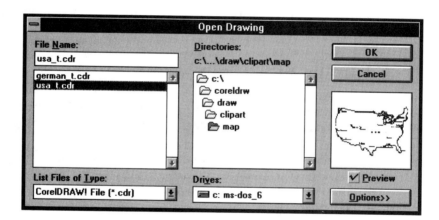

5

If this file is not available to you, open the landscape drawing you made in Chapter 3. When you have a picture on your screen, perform these steps:

1. Select the Zoom tool by positioning the mouse cursor over the Zoom tool in the toolbox and clicking once. The menu containing the five viewing options flies out below and to the right of the Zoom tool.

2. Select a tool from the flyout menu using either the mouse or your keyboard. To select a tool using the mouse, simply click on it, or drag the mouse cursor until you highlight the tool and then click. To select a tool using the keyboard, you must use individual function keys for each of the Zoom tools. (The Actual Size tool is not available through the keyboard.) The function keys and the Zoom tools they activate are

   ✦ `F2` Zoom-In

   ✦ `F3` Zoom-Out

✦ [F4] Fit-in-Window

✦ [Shift]-[F4] Show Page

All five of the Zoom tools except the Zoom-In tool perform their functions automatically when you select them. The following sections discuss each Zoom tool and present hands-on exercises for you to practice using these tools.

The Zoom-In Tool

The Zoom-In tool looks like the main Zoom tool, except that it is smaller and contains a plus sign. The Zoom-In tool is the most versatile of the five Zoom tools because it lets you define precisely how much of your picture you want to view at once. It is therefore invaluable for drawing fine details or editing small areas of a picture.

Defining the Viewing Area

Unlike the other Zoom tools in the flyout menu, the Zoom-In tool does not perform its function automatically. You have to define the zoom-in area in a series of four general steps. Try this yourself now on the map:

1. Select the Zoom-In tool by first activating the Zoom tool and then selecting the Zoom-In tool from the flyout menu or pressing [F2]. The mouse pointer changes to an image of a magnifying glass containing a plus sign.

2. Position the cursor at any corner of the area you want to magnify; usually it is most convenient to start at the upper-left corner.

3. Press and hold the mouse button at that corner and then drag the mouse diagonally toward the opposite corner of the area on which you want to zoom in. A dotted rectangle (a *marquee*) will follow your cursor and "lasso" the zoom-in area, as in the example in Figure 5-2.

4. When you have surrounded the area on which you want to zoom in, release the mouse button. The screen redraws, as in Figure 5-3, and the viewing window now contains a close-up view of only the objects you selected.

You can zoom in on successively finer areas of the screen using the Zoom-In tool. You must reselect the Zoom-In tool each time you wish to magnify further, however, for as soon as the screen is redrawn, CorelDRAW! automatically returns to the Pick tool. Simply select the Zoom-In tool again and select another area, as in Figure 5-4. The number of times you can zoom in depends on the type of monitor and display adapter you use. Try zooming

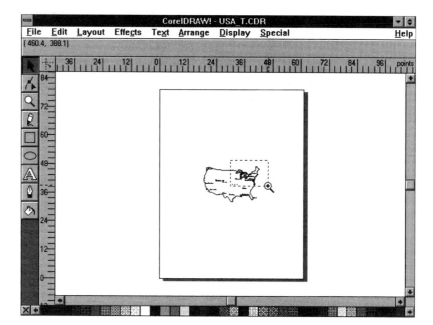

Selecting an
area with the
marquee
Figure 5-2.

5

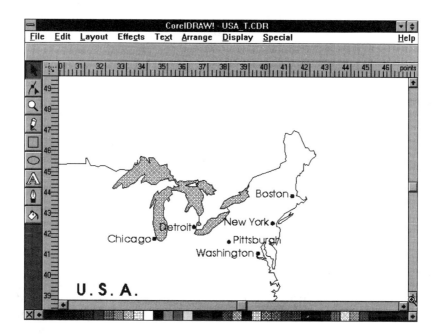

A close-up
view of the
selected area
Figure 5-3.

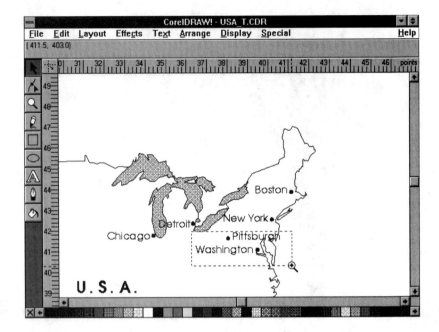

Zooming in a
second time
Figure 5-4.

in on progressively smaller areas; eventually, you reach a point where you are unable to zoom in any further. When this occurs, you have reached the maximum magnification possible for your monitor and display adapter. At that point, 1 pixel on the screen represents approximately 1/1000 of an inch. You must use another Zoom tool first before you can use the Zoom-In tool again.

TIP: You can set the right mouse button to zoom in, by a factor of two, on any point you select. Do this by choosing Preferences in the Special menu, then click on Mouse. A Mouse dialog box will appear, and you can select one of the five options. Click on 2X zoom and on OK, then on OK again in the Preferences dialog box. After setting the mouse button, a single click of the right button will zoom in, while a double-click will zoom out. The area where you click will be at the center of the new screen.

Zooming In and Editing TEACUP.CDR
The following exercise lets you practice using the Zoom-In tool on the teacup illustration you created in Chapter 3. You will edit this illustration by entering text inside a tiny area of the drawing, a function you couldn't

perform without using the Zoom tool. With this exercise you can also practice the text entry skills you learned in Chapter 4.

1. Select Show Rulers from the Display menu if the rulers do not already appear on the screen.

2. Make sure that a check mark appears in front of the Grid option on the Snap-To flyout from the Layout menu. If a check mark does not appear, select Grid on the flyout menu.

3. Select Grid Setup from the Layout menu and set both Horizontal and Vertical Grid Frequency to 16 per inch, and make sure both Show Grid and Snap To Grid are checked.

4. Select Open from the File menu, select the file TEACUP.CDR, and click on OK. If the teacup image is filled when it opens, select Edit Wireframe in the Display menu.

5. Select the Zoom tool and then select the Zoom-In tool from the flyout menu. The cursor changes into a replica of the Zoom-In tool as soon as you move into the drawing window.

6. Zoom in on the tag for the tea bag: Position the cursor at the top left corner of the tag, press the mouse button, and drag the mouse diagonally downward until you have surrounded the tag, as in Figure 5-5.

5

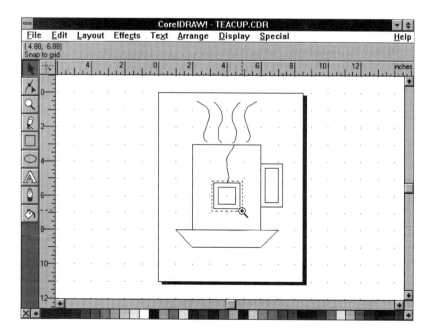

Lassoing the
tea bag
Figure 5-5.

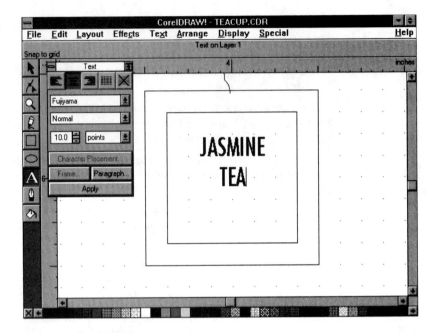

Placing text at
the insertion
point
Figure 5-6.

7. Release the mouse button. The screen redraws and displays only the tag and its immediate environment. Notice that in magnified view, the scale of the ruler changes from 1/4 inch to 1/16 inch.

8. Select the Text tool. The mouse cursor changes to a crosshair.

9. Select Text Roll-Up from the Text menu. In the Text roll-up, click on the center alignment button, select Fujiyama normal, and then 10 points.

10. Click on Apply. The Text Attributes dialog box appears. Select Artistic Text, if it does not already have a check mark next to it. Click on OK.

11. Position the cursor near the top center of the inner square of the tea tag and align it with a horizontal ruler marker.

12. Click once to select this location as the insertion point. Type the text, **JASMINE TEA** in all capital letters on two lines, as you see in Figure 5-6.

13. Click on the Pick tool and the text is selected. Choose Edit Text from the Text menu, and the Artistic Text dialog box appears, as shown in Figure 5-7.

14. Now click on the Spacing button, and the Spacing dialog box will appear. Make Character spacing 50 percent, Word 100 percent, and Line 150 percent, as shown here:

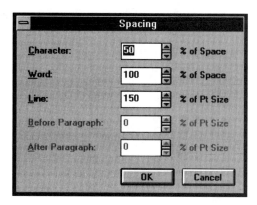

15. Select OK twice to return to the magnified display window. The text you typed now appears within the tea tag label, as in Figure 5-8.

16. Select the Save As command from the File menu. When the Save As dialog box appears, type **teacup2** in the File Name text entry box and then select OK.

17. Finally, double-click on the Control-menu box for the Text roll-up.

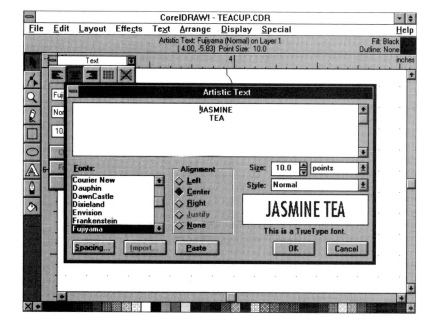

Text attributes
for JASMINE
TEA
Figure 5-7.

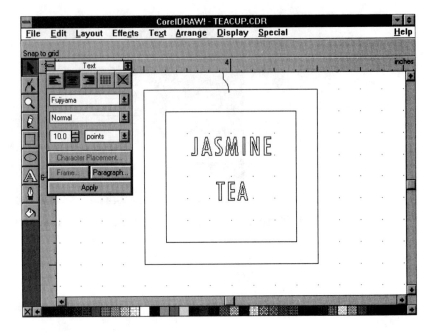

Entering text
in close-up
view
Figure 5-8.

The Zoom-Out Tool

The Zoom-Out tool looks like the main Zoom tool, except that it is a little smaller and contains a minus sign. As soon as you select this tool, it defines the zoom-out area for you automatically in one of two ways:

✦ If you are currently in an actual size, fit-in-window, or show page viewing magnification, selecting the Zoom-Out tool causes your current viewing area to zoom out (expand) by a factor of two.

✦ If you are currently in a zoom-in viewing magnification, selecting the Zoom-Out tool causes you to return to the previously selected view. You can therefore use the Zoom-Out tool to back out of successive zoom-ins one step at a time.

The maximum zoom-out you can achieve is a view that allows you to see one side of a 48-by-48-inch drawing.

To use the Zoom-Out tool, select the Zoom tool, and click on the Zoom-Out tool or press F3 . The cursor does not change shape when you select this tool, but the screen redraws according to the preceding rules.

In the following simple exercise, you will practice using both the Zoom-In and Zoom-Out tools while editing the LANDSCAP.CDR file that you created in Chapter 3. Remember the few extra circles and ellipses you drew inside the bushes of that picture? Now that you can see the bushes up close, you can add even more detail. Turn Snap To Grid off before you begin.

1. Select Open from the File menu and open the file called LANDSCAP.CDR that you created in Chapter 3. The image first appears in full-page view.

2. Select the Zoom tool and then click on the Zoom-Out tool to select it. You can still see the full page, but it now appears at half size, as in Figure 5-9.

3. Select the Zoom-Out tool again. This time, you zoom out only a little further. You cannot zoom out further than this.

4. Select the Zoom-In tool and then lasso the house and bushes. The screen redraws to include just these objects.

5. Select the Zoom-In tool again and magnify the bushes only.

6. Select the Zoom-In tool once more and lasso a single bush.

7. Select the Ellipse tool and add detail to the bush by inserting small ellipses and circles, as shown in Figure 5-10.

8. Now select the Zoom-Out tool. The screen displays the view you magnified in step 5, but the bush you worked on has more detail.

9. Select the Zoom-Out tool again. This time, the screen displays the view you selected in step 4.

5

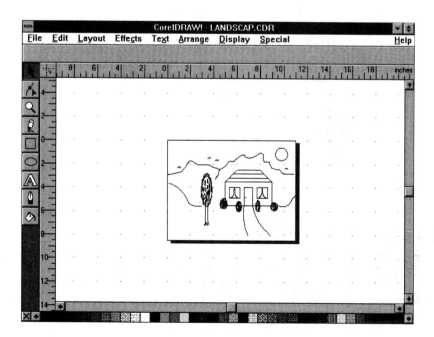

Zooming out to a 50 percent page view
Figure 5-9.

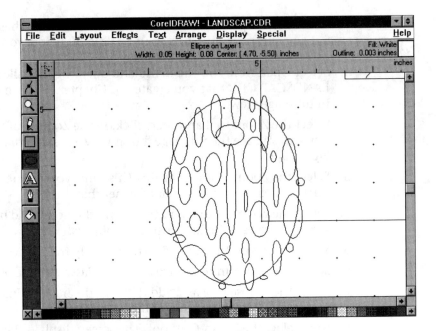

10. Select the Zoom-Out tool a third time. This time, the screen displays the full page at 50 percent of its size, as in step 2. The bush you edited probably looks denser than the others because of the detail you have added.

11. Select the Save As command from the File menu. When the Save Drawing dialog box appears, type **landsca2** in the File Name text entry box and then select OK or press Enter.

12. Select New from the File menu to clear the screen.

You have seen how the Zoom-In and Zoom-Out tools work well together when you are interested in editing a picture in minute detail. In the next section, you will learn how to achieve the kind of view that is useful when you want to print your image.

Viewing at Actual Size

When you want to see approximately how large your image will look when printed, use the Actual Size tool in the Zoom flyout menu. At a 1:1 viewing magnification, 1 inch on your screen corresponds to about 1 inch on the printed page. The amount of the page you see at this magnification may vary, depending on the way Microsoft Windows works with your monitor.

To achieve actual size viewing magnification, select the Zoom tool and click on the **1:1** tool. You can practice using this tool on the TEACUP2.CDR image that you edited earlier in this chapter.

1. Open the file TEACUP2.CDR using the Open command from the File menu. Unless you have a full-page, 19-inch, or 24-inch monitor, the full-page view of the image is too small to allow you to read the text you entered earlier in this chapter.

2. Select the Actual Size (1:1) tool. The screen redraws to display an area of your image similar to Figure 5-11. The actual area may vary because of the variety of monitors and display adapters available. At this viewing magnification, your text still appears small but it is legible.

3. Select the Zoom-In tool and lasso the tea tag with the marquee. The screen redraws to display only that portion of the image.

4. Select the Zoom-Out tool. Since you were in a 1:1 view previously, you zoom out by a factor of two.

5. Clear the screen by selecting New from the File menu.

The next section shows you how to fit an entire image within the viewing window. This is a different type of magnification than the 1:1 ratio.

5

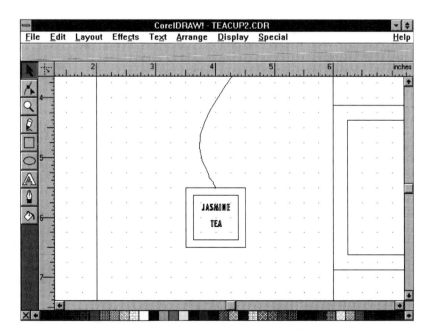

Viewing an
image at
actual size
Figure 5-11.

Fitting a Graphic in a Window

When the pictures you draw extend all the way to the edge of the page, they already fit within the viewing window. The Fit-in-Window tool is not of much use to you in such cases. When some blank space exists, however, you can use the Fit-in-Window tool to view everything you have drawn, but no more. This can be especially useful for small designs, such as logos.

To select the Fit-in-Window tool, first select the Zoom tool, then click on the Fit-in-Window tool or press F4. The screen redraws to fill the entire viewing area with the graphic image. Practice using this tool on one of the sample CorelDRAW! files in the following exercise.

1. Open the file APELICAN.CDR from the bird clip-art directory. If the image appears in wireframe mode, go to the Display menu and click on Edit Wireframe to remove the check mark. Note that there is some blank or "white" space at both the bottom and top of the page, as in Figure 5-12.

2. Select the fit-in-window view by selecting the Zoom tool and clicking on the Fit-in-Window tool. Now you see only the pelican, as shown in Figure 5-13.

Image with unused blank space at top and bottom
Figure 5-12.

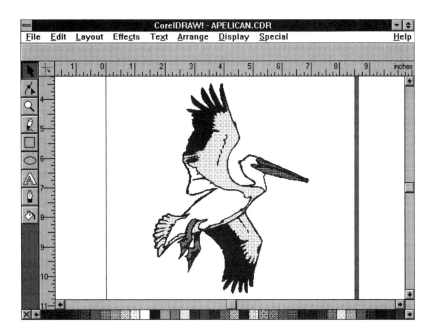

Fitting the
image within
the viewing
area
Figure 5-13.

Viewing an Entire Page

The full-page view is the default view when you load CorelDRAW! or open a
picture. It is easy to return to this view from any other view you have
selected. Simply select the Zoom tool and click on the Show Page tool or
press (Shift)-(F 4).

You have mastered all of the view selection tools, but there is still another
method, called *panning,* that you can use to control your viewing area.

Use the Zoom-In tool to select a small portion of the pelican. That portion
will fill the viewing area, and even though you see only the selected part, the
whole drawing has been expanded.

Regardless of which view you are in, you can always move beyond your
current viewing area to see what lies beyond it. This operation is called
panning and moves the image around on the screen so you can see different
parts of it. The horizontal and vertical scroll bars at the bottom and right
sides of your screen are the tools you use to pan a picture. The callouts in
Figure 5-14 point out the three different parts of the scroll bars you can use
for panning.

✦ To pan in small increments, click on a scroll bar arrow. The size of the
increment varies, depending on your monitor and display adapter

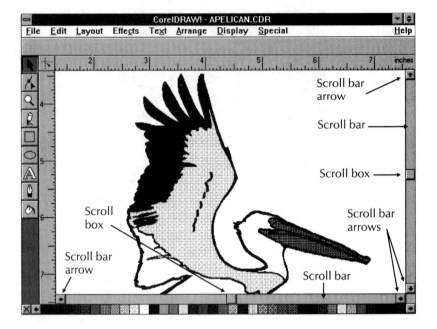

Using the
parts of the
scroll bar to
pan a picture
Figure 5-14.

combination. If you click on the right horizontal scroll arrow, the image
in the viewing window appears to move to the left. If you click on the
left horizontal arrow, the image appears to move to the right. This is an
excellent method to use when you need to edit an image in fine detail.

✦ To pan in large increments, click on either side of the scroll box, located
in the middle of the horizontal and vertical scroll bars. Once again, the
image appears to move in the opposite direction from where you clicked.
This method has only limited usefulness for editing, because the
movement of the screen is rather jumpy and unpredictable.

✦ To control the exact distance that you pan, position the cursor over the
scroll box and drag it across the scroll bar in the direction that you want
to pan. Release the mouse button when you reach the desired area.

Now that you are familiar with all of the Zoom tools and with the scroll bars,
you have complete control over the portion of your picture that you display
at any one time. In Chapter 7, you will put this new skill to work to help you
select, arrange, and move objects and text.

COREL DRAW! 4

CHAPTER

COREL DRAW! 4

6

SELECTING, MOVING, AND ARRANGING OBJECTS

In order to change the appearance or position of any object or text string, you must first select it. Once you have selected an object, you can move and rearrange it, stretch, scale, rotate, or skew it, give it a custom outline, or fill it with a color or pattern. Learning how to select an object is therefore an important prerequisite to mastering most of the skills in CorelDRAW!. Though you were introduced to the basics of text selection in Chapter 4, this chapter shows you the full capabilities of object and text selection.

You use the Pick tool, the first tool in the CorelDRAW! toolbox, to select objects and text. When you first load CorelDRAW!, the Pick tool is automatically active and remains active until you choose a different tool. If you are already working with one of the other tools, you can activate the Pick tool by clicking on the Pick tool icon in the toolbox.

TIP: Pressing the (Spacebar) once is a more efficient way to reactivate the Pick tool. This shortcut allows you to switch back and forth between tools quickly. To reactivate the tool you were working with before you selected the Pick tool, press the (Spacebar) again. Use this shortcut when you want to draw objects, immediately move, rearrange, or transform them, and then continue drawing.

The Pick tool performs more than one function; it has both a select mode and a transformation mode. The select mode includes all those functions—selecting, moving, and arranging—that do not require you to change the size or structure of the object. The transformation mode allows you to stretch, scale, rotate, skew, or reflect objects. This chapter covers the functions of the select mode; Chapter 7 will acquaint you with the use of the Pick tool in the transformation mode.

Selecting and Deselecting Objects

You can select objects only when the Pick tool is active. This tool is always active when you first open a picture, when you begin a new picture, and immediately after you save your work. To activate the Pick tool when you're using the Shaping tool or one of the drawing tools, you either press the (Spacebar) or click on the Pick tool icon once.

Once the Pick tool is active, you can select one or more objects by clicking on their outlines, by using (Shift) with the mouse, or by lassoing the objects. The technique you choose depends on the number of objects you are selecting, the placement of the objects within the graphic, and whether it's more convenient to select objects with the mouse or with the keyboard shortcuts.

The CorelDRAW! screen gives you three visual cues to let you know that an object is selected. First, a *highlighting box*, consisting of eight small rectangles called *handles*, surrounds the object. These markers allow you to stretch and scale the object, as you'll learn in Chapter 7. Second, one or more tiny hollow nodes appear on the outline of the object or group of objects. The number of nodes displayed depends on the type and number of objects selected. The nodes are the means by which you can change an object's shape, as you'll learn in Chapters 8 and 9. Finally, the status line tells you the type of object you have selected (rectangle, ellipse, curve, and so on) or the number of objects you have selected if you have selected more than one.

Single Objects

Any time you activate the Pick tool while working on a graphic, the Pick tool automatically selects the last object you created. If you want to select a different object, simply click once anywhere on the object's *outline.* Clicking on the inside of a rectangle or ellipse, or on an open space inside a letter, has no effect. Also, you must click on a point unique to that object; it cannot share that point with the outline of any other object. Only when an object is the same type and size as another object on top of it does it have no unique selection point available. For information on how to select superimposed objects without unique selection points, see the "Cycling Through Objects" section of this chapter.

To *deselect* an object or text string so that the tools or menu commands you use no longer affect it, click in any open area on the page. Alternatively, you can select a different object and thereby automatically deselect the previously selected object.

6

In the following exercise, you will practice selecting and deselecting single objects in the LANDSCA2.CDR file that you edited in Chapter 5. You will use the (Spacebar) to select objects that you have just drawn and the mouse to select other objects.

1. Make sure that the Show Status Line and Edit Wireframe commands in the Display menu are turned on, and that the Show Rulers command is turned off. Also, in the Layout menu, turn off Show Grid and Snap To Grid in the Grid Setup dialog box.

2. Open the LANDSCA2.CDR file. Note that when the picture displays on the screen, the Pick tool is already active.

3. Select the Zoom tool and then select the Zoom-In tool from the flyout menu and lasso the lower-right quarter of the picture. The screen redraws an area of the image similar to that in Figure 6-1.

4. Select the Pencil tool and use the mouse to draw a large pond in the lower-right corner of the picture. Be sure to connect the starting point to the end point, so that the curve representing the pond becomes a closed path that you can fill later. See Figure 6-2.

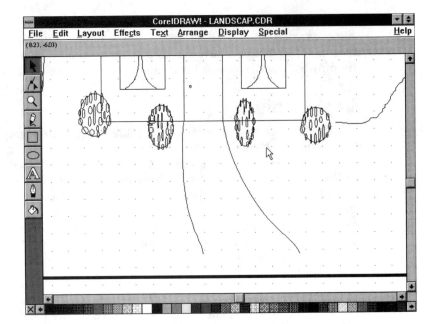

Magnifying
the lower-right
quarter of the
file LAND-
SCA2.CDR
Figure 6-1.

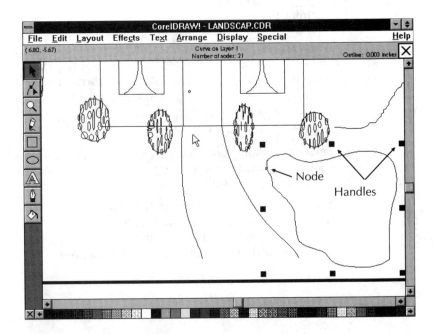

Using the
Spacebar to
select the last
object drawn
Figure 6-2.

5. As soon as the pond appears, press the (Spacebar) to activate the Pick tool. Since the pond is the last object you drew, CorelDRAW! automatically selects it. A highlighting box surrounds the pond, and the status line indicates "Curve on Layer 1," as in Figure 6-2.

6. Click on the outlines of the curve object again. As Figure 6-3 shows, black two-way arrows replace the handles of the highlighting box. Your second click has enabled the rotate and skew functions of the Pick tool. Click on the object's outlines again to toggle back to the select mode.

7. Now, zoom out of your magnified view using the Zoom-Out tool in the Zoom tool flyout menu. Practice selecting objects that you drew in previous sessions. For example, click on one of the curves that form the branches of the poplar tree. Each time you select a new object, the previously selected object becomes deselected; the highlighting box disappears from the previously selected object and surrounds the new one instead. The name of the currently selected object type always appears in the status line. If you select any objects within other objects (the detail inside one of the bushes, for example), you may notice that the highlighting box is sometimes much larger than the object itself. If several objects of the same type are crowded closely together, it may be difficult to tell which one you have selected. Use the Zoom-In tool to magnify a small portion of a crowded area before you attempt to select single objects.

6

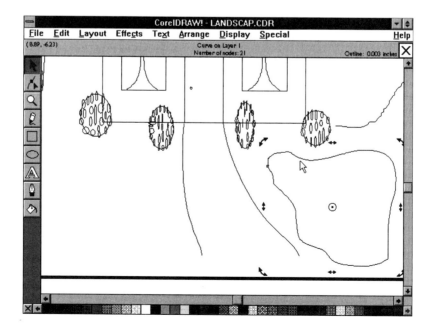

Enabling the transformation mode of the Pick tool
Figure 6-3.

8. When you have practiced enough to feel comfortable with selecting objects, select Save As from the File menu and type **landsca3.cdr** to save the file.

9. Select New from the File menu to clear the screen.

Multiple Objects

It's often more convenient to perform an operation on several objects simultaneously than to perform the same operation on a series of objects individually. Assume, for example, that you want to move the tree in the LANDSCA3.CDR file to another location within the picture. Since the tree consists of several separate objects, moving each component object individually would be tedious and might even lead to inaccurate placement.

CorelDRAW! gives you three alternative solutions to this type of problem. The first solution, simply *selecting* the objects, is appropriate when you want to keep multiple objects together only temporarily, without merging them into a single entity. For example, you might want to fill a certain number of objects in a picture with the same color or pattern or move them all by the same distance. You can select multiple objects by using the mouse and Shift key, by drawing a marquee around them, or by using the Select All command in the Edit menu. Your choice of technique depends on both the number of objects you want to select and their location within the graphic.

If the multiple objects are components of a larger whole and should remain together at all times, you might choose to *group* them, as you will learn to do later in this chapter. CorelDRAW! will still remember that grouped objects have separate identities. If the multiple objects belong together and contain many curves, you can choose to *combine* them into a single object. Combining objects, unlike grouping them, reduces the amount of memory they require and also allows you to reshape the entire resulting object.

You will learn more about the uses of grouping and combining multiple objects in the "Arranging Objects" portion of this chapter. The following group of sections lets you practice common methods of selecting multiple objects.

Selecting with the Shift Key

When you want to select a few objects at a time, you can conveniently select them one after another using the mouse and Shift together. The Shift key method is especially useful when the objects you want to select are not next to one another within the graphic. In the next exercise, you will practice selecting multiple objects using the following method:

✦ Select the first object by clicking on its outline.

✦ Depress and hold (Shift) and select the next object.

✦ Continue selecting objects in this way, holding down (Shift) continuously.

✦ When you have selected all desired objects, release (Shift).

To deselect one or more of the objects you have selected in this way, hold down (Shift) and click again on that object's outline. This action affects only that object; other objects in the group remain selected. To deselect all of the selected objects simultaneously, click on any free space.

Each time you select another object using (Shift), the highlighting box expands to surround all the objects you have selected so far. Objects that you did not select also may fall within the boundaries of the highlighting box, making it difficult for you to see just which objects you have selected. The following exercise shows how you can use the status line information and the preview window as aids in selecting multiple objects with (Shift).

1. Open the TEACUP2.CDR file that you edited in Chapter 5.

2. If the screen is not already maximized, use the maximize button to enlarge the size of the working area. Magnify the area that extends from the upper-left corner of the picture to the bottom of the tag on the tea bag.

3. Click on the leftmost wisp of "steam" above the tea cup to select it. A highlighting box surrounds the object, and the status line indicates that you have selected a curve.

4. Depress and hold (Shift) and click anywhere on the outlines of the text "JASMINE TEA." The message in the status line changes to "2 objects selected on Layer 1," but the highlighting box shown in Figure 6-4 seems to surround many more objects. It is difficult to tell whether you have selected the text string or one of the rectangles on the tea tag surrounding it. To find out, you need help from the preview window.

5. Press (Shift)-(F9) to display the preview window. Do not be concerned at this point that all of the objects in your drawing seem to blend into a solid black mass. You will learn how to edit the outlines and colors of individual objects in Chapters 11 and 12.

6. From the Display menu, choose Preview Selected Only to turn it on, and then click on Show Preview. These two commands cause only the currently selected objects to appear in a full-screen preview window. As Figure 6-5 shows, you can now be certain that you selected the correct objects.

6

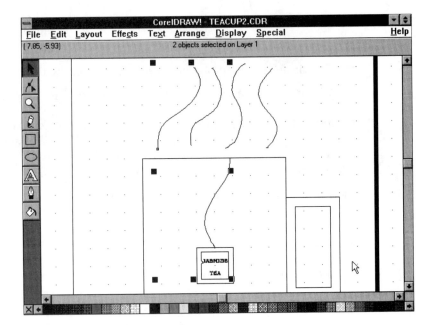

Selecting
nonadjacent
objects using
Shift
Figure 6-4.

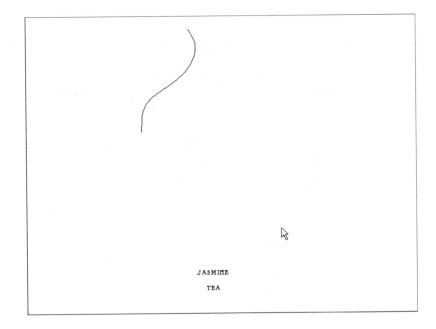

Using Preview
Selected Only
to confirm
object
selection
Figure 6-5.

TIP: If you cannot see the "steam" when it is selected, click on the Outline tool and again on the first or second line width in the first row of the flyout menu. This action ensures that selected lines and curves have a visible outline.

If you accidentally selected one of the tea tag rectangles instead of the text string, press F9 to return to the drawing, and deselect the incorrect object by holding Shift while clicking again on that object. When the highlighting box no longer surrounds that object, continue to hold down Shift and select the text string instead.

7. Still holding down Shift, select the rightmost wisp of "steam" and add it to the group of selected objects. The status line now displays the message "3 objects selected on Layer 1," and the preview window displays all three objects. Again, if you can't see the steam when it is selected, click on the Outline tool and click again on the first or second line width in the flyout menu.

8. Click on the Preview Selected Only command in the Display menu again to turn off this feature, and then select New from the File menu to clear the screen.

6

Selecting with the Marquee

If you need to select a large number of objects at once, using the mouse and Shift can be tedious. A shortcut is to draw a marquee around all of the desired objects with the Pick tool. The method for using a marquee is as follows:

✦ Position the mouse pointer just above and to the left of the first object you want to select. (You can begin from any corner of the group of objects, but the upper-left corner is usually most convenient.)

✦ Depress the mouse button and drag the mouse diagonally in the direction of the other objects you want to select. A dotted rectangle (the marquee) follows the cursor. Make sure that every object you want to select falls completely within this rectangle or CorelDRAW! will not select it.

✦ When you have enclosed the last object you want to select within the marquee, release the mouse button. The highlighting box appears, encompassing all of the objects within the selected area.

If you want to exclude some of the objects that fall within the selected area, you can deselect them using Shift. Lasso the entire group of objects first, depress and hold Shift, and click on a particular object's outline to deselect that object. You can also use the status line and preview window as "quality control" aids to guide you in selecting exactly the objects you want.

Perform the following exercise to gain skill at selecting objects quickly with the marquee. Use the Zoom tool for magnification, status line information, and the preview window to make the selection process more efficient. Use (Shift) to fine-tune your selection and add or subtract objects to or from the group you selected with the marquee.

1. Open the file LANDSCA3.CDR. Note that the poplar tree you drew in an earlier lesson contains several objects: the ellipse that forms the main body of the foliage, a few curves that form the foliage, and curves that make up the trunk. Since all of these objects are adjacent to one another, the tree is a perfect example of the types of multiple objects you can select easily with the marquee.

2. Select the Zoom tool and then select the Zoom-In tool from the flyout menu. Zoom in to display the left half of the picture. As soon as you have magnified this area, the Pick tool becomes highlighted again.

3. Position the mouse pointer above and to the left of the poplar tree. Drag the mouse downward and to the right until the marquee surrounds all of the component objects of the tree completely and release the mouse button. The highlighting box appears, and the status line indicates the number of objects you have selected, as in Figure 6-6.

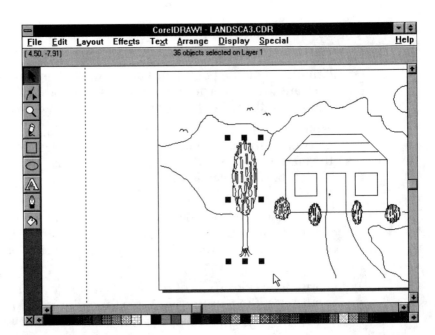

Selecting all component objects of the tree

Figure 6-6.

4. Depress and hold (Shift) and then click once anywhere on the outline of the ellipse that makes up the main body of the foliage. CorelDRAW! deselects it, and the status line shows there is one less selected object.

5. Click on any white space to deselect all of the objects and then select New from the File menu to clear the screen.

Selecting All Objects in a Graphic

If you want to perform an operation on all the objects in a graphic, you can select them by drawing a marquee. A quicker way to select all objects is simply to invoke the Select All command in the Edit menu. Using this command, you can be sure that you haven't left out any objects.

You now know several methods for selecting single and multiple objects. Most of the time, selecting objects is a straightforward process in CorelDRAW!. But what if your graphic contains many small objects or you want to select an object that may have several other layers of objects on top of it? The next section makes that process easy for you.

Cycling Through Objects

The object selection techniques you have learned so far in this chapter are adequate for most applications. However, when working with complex drawings containing many objects or superimposed objects, you may find it more convenient to cycle through the objects using (Tab). The following steps summarize this technique:

✦ Select an object near or on top of the object you want to select.

✦ Press (Tab). CorelDRAW! deselects the first object and selects the next object in the drawing. The "next" object is the one that was drawn just prior to the currently selected object. Each time you press (Tab), CorelDRAW! cycles backward to another object. If you press (Tab) often enough, you eventually select the first object again, and the cycle begins once more.

The following sections show you two different situations in which you might choose to cycle through objects in a drawing. The first section provides an example of objects that have other objects superimposed on them. The second section demonstrates how to locate and select small objects in a complex drawing.

Cycling Through Superimposed Objects

You may recall that in order to select an object in CorelDRAW!, you must click on a unique point on its outline, a point not shared by any other

6

object. This limitation does not apply to most superimposed objects, because you can usually see separate outlines. The only exception is when two or more objects are the same size and shape and overlay one another exactly.

Why might you choose to create two identical overlapping objects? You could achieve interesting design effects by varying the color and thickness of their respective outlines and fills, as shown in the example in Figure 6-7. The window shows that what appears to be a single rectangle in the editing window is actually two separate rectangles, each with its own outline color, outline thickness, and fill color. In Chapters 11 and 12, you will learn more about outlines and fill colors. For now, you need only know that to select the object in the background, you can select one object and then press Tab. The Fill box on the right end of the status line confirms which rectangle is selected, as illustrated in Figure 6-7.

Cycling Through Many Objects
There is another, more common use for Tab when selecting objects in CorelDRAW!. Clip art, technical illustrations, and other complex drawings often contain many small objects close together. Even in magnified view, trying to select one or more of these with the mouse can be difficult at best. To ease the process, you can select one object and then press Tab repeatedly until the minute detail you are looking for is selected. CorelDRAW! cycles backward through the objects, selecting them in the reverse order to which you drew them. To cycle forward through the objects in a drawing, press

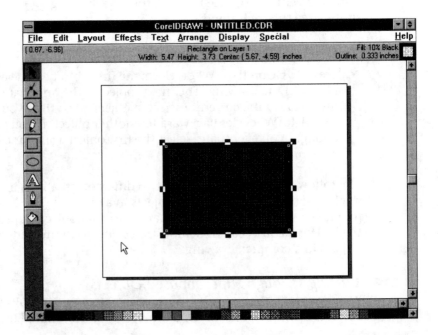

Example of
objects
exactly
superimposed
Figure 6-7.

[Shift]-[Tab]. Perform the following brief exercise to gain a clearer understanding of how the [Tab] key method of selection works.

1. Open the file EYE.CDR, which should be in your \DRAW\SAMPLES directory.

NOTE: You can view the EYE.CDR drawing in full color or wireframe mode by turning the Display menu option Edit Wireframe off or on, respectively. The full color mode will take much longer to appear on your screen due to the color memory requirements.

2. Choose the Select All command from the Edit menu. The status line shows you that there are 73 separate objects that have not been grouped or combined.

3. Click on any white space to deselect all the objects, then select the upper-left part of the EYE.CDR object by applying a marquee to it, as shown in Figure 6-8. Note that the marquee must begin off the page on the white screen, since otherwise an object on the art will be selected, and you will not be able to draw the marquee. Notice the status line says "11 objects selected on Layer 1" (your count might differ slightly depending on where you lassoed the eye), so you have actually selected a group of objects, not a single object. (You'll learn more about this later in this chapter under "Grouping and Ungrouping Objects.")

6

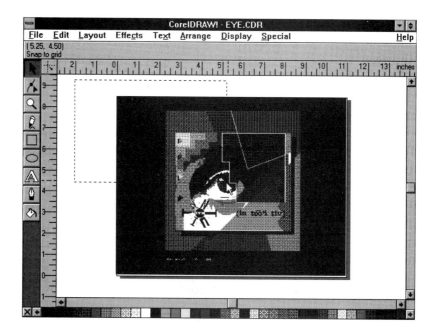

Cycling
through
multiple
objects in a
complex
drawing
Figure 6-8.

4. Press Tab several times. CorelDRAW! cycles through the other objects on the drawing each time you press Tab.

5. Press Shift-Tab several times. Now CorelDRAW! selects objects in the opposite order.

6. If you have the patience to cycle through all 71 objects, keep pressing Tab or Shift-Tab until CorelDRAW! selects the lassoed objects again.

7. Select New from the File menu to clear the screen before you proceed.

Now you are familiar with all of the available techniques for selecting any number of objects. In the next portion of this chapter, you will begin moving selected objects to other areas within the illustration.

Moving Objects

Once you have selected an object, you can move it by positioning the cursor over any point on its *outline* (not on the highlighting box) and then dragging the mouse along with the object to the desired location. The status line provides you with precise, real-time information about the distance you are traveling, the *x* and *y* components of that distance, and the angle of movement. You can achieve precision worthy of the most demanding technical illustrations if you choose to work with the status line and grid.

Factors such as the number of objects you want to move, whether you want to constrain movement to a 90-degree angle, and whether you want to make a copy of the object determine your choice of technique.

Moving a Single Object

The appearance of an object undergoes several changes during the process of moving it. Try the following simple exercise to become familiar with those changes.

1. If you have done the exercises earlier in this chapter, your drawing page is in landscape orientation. From the Page Setup option in the Layout menu, change this by selecting Statement as the paper size and then choosing Portrait.

2. Select the Ellipse tool and draw an ellipse in the upper area of the page.

3. Activate the Pick tool and the ellipse is automatically selected. (Recall that you can simply press the Spacebar to select the last object you have drawn.) The highlighting box surrounds the ellipse.

4. Move the mouse to any point on the outline of the ellipse, press and hold the mouse button, and begin dragging the mouse downward and to the right. The screen does not change immediately, because

CorelDRAW! has a built-in, three-pixel safety zone; you must drag the mouse at least three pixels away from the starting point before the object begins to "move." As soon as you pass the three-pixel safety zone, the mouse pointer changes to a four-way arrow, and a dotted replica of the highlighting box follows the cursor, as shown in Figure 6-9. This dotted box represents the object while you are moving it; as you can see in the figure, the object itself seems to remain in its original position.

5. When you have dragged the dotted box to the lower edge of the page, release the mouse button. The ellipse disappears from its original position and reappears in the new location.

6. Press Del to clear the screen before proceeding.

These are the basic steps involved in moving an object, but CorelDRAW! offers you additional refinements for moving multiple objects, constraining an object to move at a 90-degree angle, and retaining a copy of an object while moving it.

Moving Multiple Objects

6

The technique for moving multiple, selected objects differs very little from the way you move single objects. When more than one object is selected, you simply press and hold the mouse button on the outline of *any one* of the objects within the selected group. The entire group moves together as you

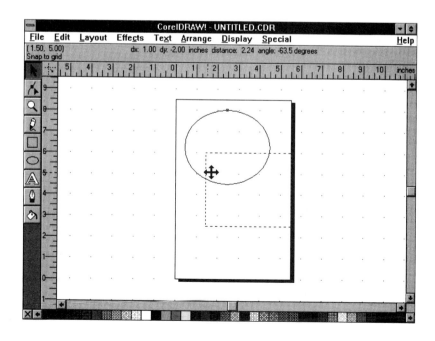

Dragging the dotted move box to move an object
Figure 6-9.

drag the mouse. Complete the following exercise to practice moving multiple objects in the LANDSCA3.CDR file.

1. Open the file LANDSCA3.CDR. The Pick tool is automatically activated when you open a new picture.

2. Draw a marquee and lasso the entire poplar tree in the foreground of the picture to select it. The status line displays the number of selected objects. If you are not sure whether you have selected all of the objects that make up the tree, get confirmation by turning on the preview window and selecting Preview Selected Only from the Display menu.

3. Position the mouse pointer over any of the outlines in the tree, and then drag the mouse until the dotted move box reaches the extreme right of the picture, as shown in Figure 6-10.

4. Release the mouse button. The tree disappears from its original location and reappears in the new location. The tree is now in part of the pond, so you will move the pond next.

5. Select the pond and move it to the left side of the picture where the poplar tree formerly stood.

6. Select the Zoom-In tool from the Zoom tool flyout menu and magnify the area around the leftmost bush in front of the house. Your viewing area should look similar to Figure 6-11.

Moving multiple objects to a new location

Figure 6-10.

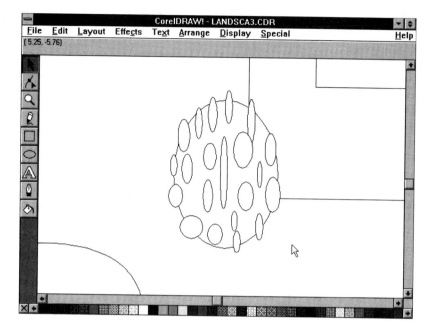

Magnifying
the area
around the
leftmost bush
Figure 6-11.

6

7. With the Pick tool, select (lasso) the entire bush, including the detail you drew inside it, and then move the bush a little to the left of the house.

8. Zoom out to full-page view. Your picture should now resemble Figure 6-12.

9. Save this altered picture as LANDSCA4.CDR and leave it on the screen.

Moving at a 90-Degree Angle

The techniques you have learned so far in this chapter apply to moving objects in any direction. But what if the nature of your drawing requires that you move objects straight up or down, or directly to the right or left? You could, of course, use the coordinates information in the status line to reposition the object precisely. But CorelDRAW! also offers you a more intuitive method of moving objects at an exact 90-degree angle using Ctrl. This is a convenient method for obtaining precision without slowing your drawing pace. Perform the following exercise to practice constraining the movement of objects vertically or horizontally.

1. With the LANDSCA4.CDR file still displayed, select one of the birds at the top of the picture.

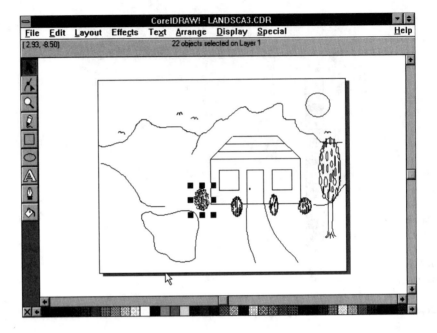

LAND-
SCA3.CDR
after moving
the multiple-
object bush
Figure 6-12.

2. Press and hold Ctrl and then drag the bird to the right. Even if you don't
   have a steady hand, the bird remains at exactly the same horizontal
   level of the picture. The information on the status line verifies the
   steadiness of your movement: both the *dy* indicator and the angle
   indicator remain at zero, as in the following illustration:

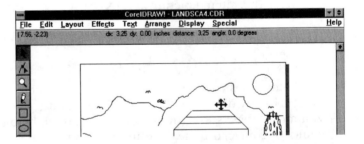

Release the mouse button first and then release Ctrl to reposition the
bird at the new location. If you release Ctrl first, the selected object is no
longer constrained and can move up or down relative to the starting
point.

3. Press and hold Ctrl and the mouse button a second time. This time drag
   the bird to the left of its current location. Again, the bird remains at the

same horizontal level, and the *dy* indicator remains at zero. This time the angle indicator displays 180 degrees:

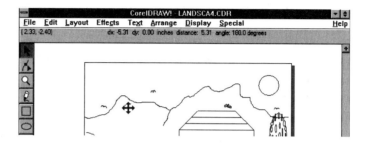

Release the mouse button and Ctrl when you reach a satisfactory location.

4. Press and hold Ctrl and the mouse button again and drag the bird directly downward. This time, the *dx* indicator remains at zero, and the angle indicator displays –90 degrees:

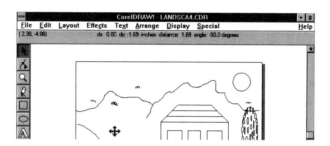

Release the mouse button and then Ctrl to reposition the bird at the new vertical location. If you accidentally release Ctrl first, the selected object is not constrained, and you can move it both horizontally and vertically relative to the original location.

5. Continue to depress both Ctrl and the mouse button and drag the bird directly upward. The *dx* indicator remains at zero, but the angle indicator reads 90 degrees:

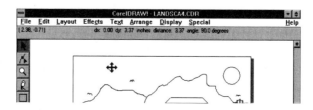

6. Continue practicing this technique with other objects in the picture.

Moving Objects with the Keyboard (Nudge)

As you moved objects in the preceding exercises, you probably found that it was difficult to move an object in very small increments with any precision—most people repeatedly overshoot the mark.

CorelDRAW!, version 2.0 and on, has a feature called Nudge, which allows you to use the arrow keys on your keyboard to move the selected object(s) by as little as 0.01 inch. The amount by which you move an object each time you press an arrow key, and the unit of measure, are determined in the Preferences dialog box reached from the Special menu. The default increment is 0.10 inch. Also, since you only have arrow keys pointing in 90-degree increments, nudging is always constrained to 90-degree increments. Follow these steps to practice nudging:

1. If you don't have a currently selected object, reselect one of the birds.
2. Open the Preferences dialog box from the Special menu and verify that the Nudge increment is set to 0.10 inch.
3. Press the ➡ three times and then press the ⬇ three times. The bird you selected should move to the right and down by 0.3 inch in each direction.

Practice this on your own for several minutes. Nudging can be very useful.

When you are finished, select New from the File menu but do not save any changes.

Moving an Object Using Precise Measurements

If you wish to move an object an exact measured distance, or to a specific location using coordinates, you use the Move command in the Arrange menu. A dialog box is displayed, which allows you to enter horizontal and vertical measurements, as shown here:

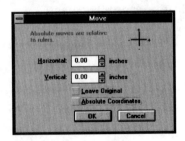

To move the object to the right horizontally or up vertically, enter a positive number; to move it to the left or down, enter a negative number. If you choose Absolute Coordinates, a box with nodes will appear in the dialog box, as shown here:

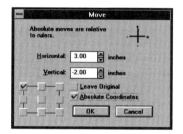

Follow these steps to move an object to precise coordinates:

1. Using the Ellipse tool, draw an ellipse anywhere on the page. Be sure it is selected.

2. Turn on the ruler guides if they are not on, and use the crosshair in the upper left of the ruler guides to reset the ruler origins, so that 0 appears on each ruler.

3. Select Move from the Arrange menu. Click on Absolute Coordinates.

4. On the node box, click on the center node, indicating that the center of the ellipse should be aligned to the coordinates.

NOTE: The "node box" represents the parts of the object that are used to align, i.e., if you clicked the upper-left box, the upper-left "corner" of the ellipse would align on the coordinates.

5. Enter **3** in the Horizontal coordinate box and **5** in the Vertical coordinate box. Click on OK. The ellipse will be relocated so that the center of the ellipse is aligned with the coordinates.

You can also leave the original object in place and move a copy to the specific location by clicking on the Leave Original check box.

Copying an Object While Moving It

You may recall that while you are moving an object, it seems to remain in place, and you appear to be moving only a dotted rectangular substitute. CorelDRAW! lets you take this feature a step further; you can make an identical copy of the object as you move it. The copy remains at the initial location while you move the original to a new location. This handy technique has interesting design possibilities, as you can discover for yourself by performing the next exercise.

1. Select the Grid Setup command in the Layout menu, set both Horizontal and Vertical Grid Frequency to 2.0 per inch, set Vertical Origin to 8.5 inches, and turn on Show Grid and Snap To Grid. Click OK. Then, from the Display menu, turn on the Show Rulers option and turn off Edit Wireframe. Since you just finished working on a picture in landscape (horizontal) mode, the blank page area is also in this mode. (If you worked on something else in the meantime, change to landscape mode now, using the Page Setup command in the Layout menu.)

2. Select the Text tool and then select an insertion point at the 1-inch mark on both the horizontal and vertical rulers. Type **Arrow** in upper- and lowercase. Select the word with the Pick tool, open the Text roll-up (in the Text menu), and set the text attributes to Bangkok normal and 100 points. Click on Apply and close the Text roll-up.

3. Press and hold the mouse button over the outline of any letter and begin to drag downward and to the right. Since you have set grid spacing in large units, the dotted move box travels and snaps in visibly discrete increments.

4. Continue holding down the mouse button. When the upper-left corner of the dotted move box snaps to a point 1/2 inch below and to the right of the starting point (about midway down and across the letter "A"), press and release the ⊕ key in the numeric keypad. At the left of the status line, the message "Leave Original" appears, as in Figure 6-13. The ⊕ key in CorelDRAW! is also called the Leave Original key.

5. Release the mouse button. An exact copy of the object appears at the starting point, and the original appears at the new location. (If nothing happens press and release the ⊕ key and the mouse more rapidly.)

6. Make four more copies of the text string in the same way, using the ⊕ key or right mouse button, and moving the text object in 1/2-inch increments downward and to the right. You should now have a total of six identical text strings.

7. Change the direction in which you move the text object. Make five additional copies as you move the text object downward and to the left in 1/2-inch increments. When you are finished, 11 identical text strings form an arrowhead shape. Your screen should look like Figure 6-14.

8. Select Save As from the File menu and save this picture under the name ARROW1.CDR.

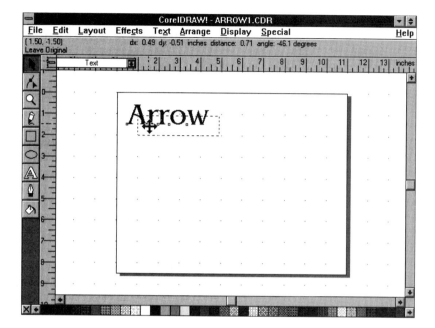

Copying an
object while
moving it
Figure 6-13.

6

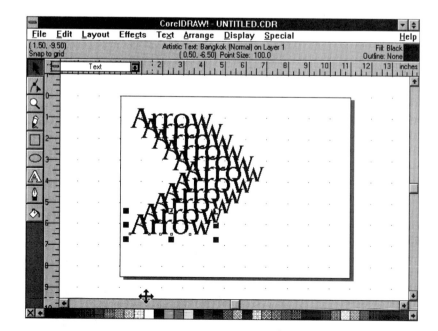

Preview of the
arrow design
Figure 6-14.

Using the preceding exercise as an example, you can probably think up additional design ideas for copying single or multiple objects as you move them. Go on to the later sections of this chapter to discover ways of changing the relative order of objects within a drawing.

Arranging Objects

In CorelDRAW!, you can change the order of superimposed objects, group and combine separate objects, and align objects relative to one another. All of these techniques are ways of arranging objects on the page. The Arrange menu contains all of the commands you will use in this chapter, plus a few others that are discussed in later chapters. The next four sections demonstrate the most common methods of arranging selected objects.

Reordering Superimposed Objects

When you draw a series of objects, CorelDRAW! always places the object you drew *last* on top of all of the other objects. If you could look at the ARROW1.CDR file in 3-D, for example, you would see that the first text string you created is beneath all of the others you subsequently copied.

You can change the order of objects at any time by applying one of five commands in the Order option of the Arrange menu to a selected object or group of objects. The five commands—To Front, To Back, Forward One, Back One, and Reverse Order—appear on a flyout menu, as shown here:

Arrange	
Move...	Alt+F7
Align...	Ctrl+A
Order	▸
Group	Ctrl+G
Ungroup	Ctrl+U
Combine	Ctrl+L
Break Apart	Ctrl+K
Weld	
Separate	
Convert To Curves	Ctrl+Q

To Front	Shift+PgUp
To Back	Shift+PgDn
Forward One	Ctrl+PgUp
Back One	Ctrl+PgDn
Reverse Order	

The To Front, To Back, Forward One, and Back One commands rearrange the selected objects *relative* to the other objects on the page, but they do not rearrange objects within a selected group. The Reverse Order command, on the other hand, rearranges the objects *within* a selected group, but it does not alter the relationship between the selected objects and the other objects in the picture. Practice working with these commands now, using the clip-art file SYMB483.CDR (of a jack-o'-lantern) that came with your software.

1. Select the Open command from the File menu and open the file SYMB483.CDR in your CELEBRAT clip-art directory.

2. Choose the Select All option from the Edit menu. When the drawing is selected, you'll see it's a group of 3 objects.

3. Choose the Ungroup command in the Arrange menu to allow rearrangement of the individual objects.

4. Select (lasso) the stem, eyes, and mouth of the pumpkin as shown here:

6

Be sure to include all of the eyes and mouth and other features but not the pumpkin shape. You have selected everything you want if you have selected 2 objects.

5. Press F2 to select the Zoom-In tool, click to magnify just the center portion of the image.

6. Pull down the Arrange menu and from the Order option flyout, select the To Back command. The entire group of selected objects disappears behind the background objects, as shown in Figure 6-15. When you apply this command to a group of objects, however, the relative order of the objects *within* the group does not change.

7. With the same group of objects still selected, select the To Front command from the Order option flyout on the Arrange menu. Now the objects reappear in their original order, in front of the background objects.

8. Leave these objects selected and select the Back One command from the Order flyout on the Arrange menu. This command moves the selected objects back behind the first layer beneath them. Since there is only one object behind the 2 that make up the face, this has the same effect as To Back.

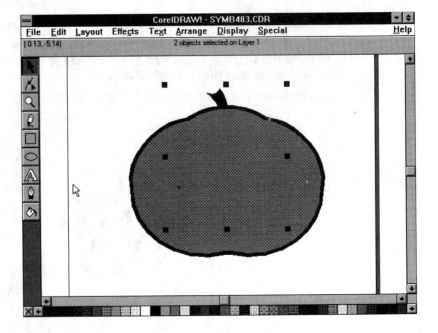

Using the To
Back
command on
selected
objects
Figure 6-15.

9. Select the Forward One command to return the objects to their original order on the screen. Leave this drawing on the screen for the next exercise.

Grouping and Ungrouping Objects

Selecting multiple objects with the marquee or (Shift) key is fine if you want to apply certain commands or operations to them on a one-time basis only. However, most drawings contain subsets of objects that belong together, such as the elements of a logo on a business card. If you want the same set of objects to form a single entity at all times, consider *grouping* them instead of merely selecting them.

To group multiple objects, you first select them and then apply the Group command in the Arrange menu. Thereafter, the group responds to any operation collectively. You can move, align, color, and outline them together, without individually selecting each component of the group. However, CorelDRAW! still "knows" that the component objects have separate identities. As a result, you cannot apply the Reverse Order command to a group or reshape the group using the Shaping tool. You can also create groups within groups, and then use the Ungroup command to break them down into their component objects again.

In the last exercise, all objects in the SYMB483.CDR file were selected and then ungrouped. Continue working with this file to become familiar with the basics of grouping and ungrouping objects.

1. The group made up of the word "face" should still be selected. The status line should display the message "2 objects selected on Layer 1," as shown in Figure 6-16.

2. Select the Group command in the Arrange menu. The status line message changes immediately from "2 objects selected on Layer 1" to "Group of 2 objects on Layer 1."

3. Open the Order flyout on the Arrange menu and notice that Reverse Order is dim—it isn't available, since the selected objects have been grouped. Select Ungroup and then select the Reverse Order command from the Order flyout of the Arrange menu. The 2 objects that used to form the group are now reversed in order—what was on top is now on the bottom relative to the other item in the group. The only change is *within* the group.

4. Select the Reverse Order command again from the Order flyout on the Arrange menu. The original order returns.

5. Select the Group command from the Arrange menu. The message in the status line changes back to "Group of 2 objects on Layer 1."

6. Press F3 to zoom out and return to a normal screen.

6

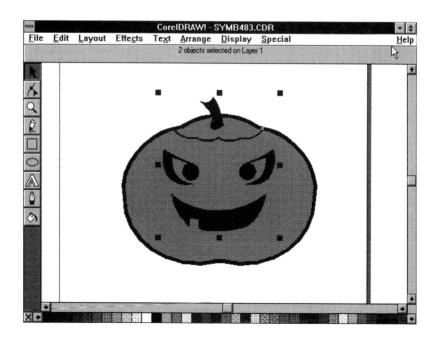

Grouping
multiple
objects
Figure 6-16.

7. Press and hold the mouse button at any point along the outline of any of the features of the face and drag the mouse with the selected objects to the bottom of the screen. The entire group moves together and relocates when you release the mouse button, as shown in Figure 6-17.

8. Practice moving the group around, ungrouping, forming new groups, rearranging the groups, and moving various objects in relation to one another.

Before and after grouping objects and text strings, look at the menus to see how grouping affects which commands you can and cannot select.

9. When you are done, select New from the File menu to clear the screen before proceeding. Do not save any changes to this picture.

Combining and Breaking Objects Apart

The Arrange menu contains two sets of commands that seem almost identical in content, but are actually two different operations: Group/Ungroup and Combine/Break Apart. Combining objects differs from grouping them in several complex respects that are beyond the scope of this chapter; you will gain more experience with the Combine command in

Moving the entire foreground group
Figure 6-17.

Chapter 15. In general, however, you use Combine in the following situations:

✦ When you want multiple objects to become a single object *that you can reshape* with the Shaping tool

✦ When the objects contain many nodes and curves and you want to reduce the total amount of memory they consume

✦ When you want to create special effects such as transparent masks, behind which you can place other objects

In these situations, simply grouping objects would not yield the desired results.

Later chapters contain several examples of creative uses for the Combine command. There is one interesting use of Combine, however, that you can practice in this chapter. Recall that when you first activated the preview window in this chapter, you couldn't distinguish the component objects of the TEACUP2.CDR file because they all contained a default fill of black. If you combine objects with other objects contained within them, however, the net result is a reverse video effect that makes alternating objects transparent and creates contrast. For a clearer understanding of how this works, try the following exercise.

6

1. Open the TEACUP2.CDR file. The window displays a solid black mass, as shown in Figure 6-18, because you haven't yet applied different fill colors or outlines to separate objects.

2. Press (Shift)-(F9) to go to wireframe mode and select both the larger rectangle that forms the outline of the handle and the inner rectangle. Use either the marquee or the (Shift) key method. When you are done, the status line should say "2 objects selected on Layer 1."

3. Select the Combine command from the Arrange menu. Press (Shift)-(F9) again to turn off wireframe, and the inside of the inner rectangle becomes transparent, as shown in Figure 6-19. This "special effect" occurs because the Combine command causes all overlapping areas in a graphic to appear transparent. Notice that the status line now refers to the combined object as a single curve object.

   Because of the hollow areas you created when you selected the Combine command, you can now distinguish the handle from the rest of the cup.

4. Save this file under the new name TEACUP3.CDR.

5. Select the newly combined handle, if it is not still selected, and then select the Break Apart command from the Arrange menu. All objects revert to their previous state and become black again.

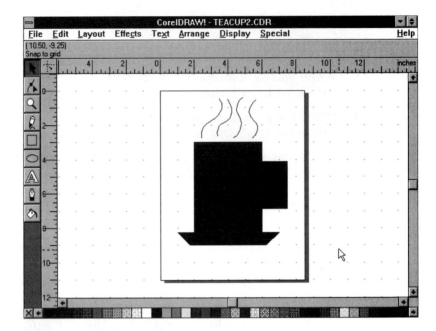

The tea cup
appears as
solid black in
the preview
window
Figure 6-18.

6. Clear the screen using the New command in the File menu. Do not save any changes.

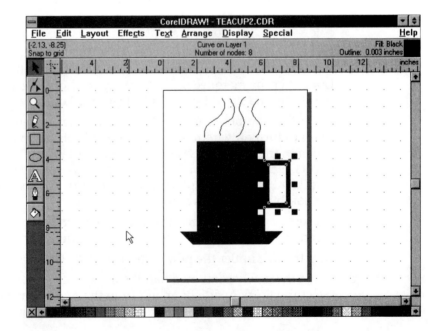

Using the
Combine
command to
create a
hollow inner
region
Figure 6-19.

Aligning Objects

Earlier in this chapter, you saw how you can move objects precisely using the Ctrl key as a substitute for the grid. The Align command in the Arrange menu offers you another quick and easy method for aligning selected objects without having to spend all of your drawing time measuring. To align objects, you simply select the objects, click on the Align command, and then adjust the horizontal and vertical alignment settings in the Align dialog box.

You could try to memorize the abstract effects of all 15 possible settings, but experiencing those settings for yourself might be more meaningful. In the following exercise, you will create the surface of a billiard table complete with six pockets, combine all the elements of the table into one object, and then add a billiard ball and apply various alignment settings to the ball and the table.

1. Start with the page in landscape orientation with the rulers and grid displayed, the Snap To Grid turned on, the horizontal and vertical grid frequencies set to 16 per inch, and wireframe mode turned on. Select the Rectangle tool and draw a rectangle 9 inches wide and 4 inches deep. This rectangle represents the surface of the billiard table.

2. Magnify the area of the page that contains the rectangle, select the Pencil tool, and draw six billiard "pockets," as shown in Figure 6-20. You

6

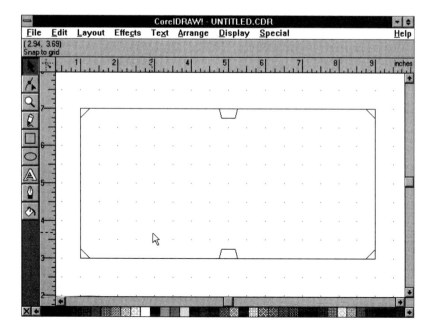

Billiard "table" with six "pockets"
Figure 6-20.

can draw the pockets either as curved or multisegment lines, as you wish.

TIP: If you want to draw the billiard pockets as curves, set Freehand tracking in the Preferences-Curves dialog box to 10 pixels and then magnify each area as you draw a pocket in it. The smaller the area in which you are drawing, the smoother your curves become. Zoom out when you have finished drawing the fine details.

3. Activate the Pick tool and draw a marquee around the billiard table to select both the table and the pockets, and then apply the Combine command in the Arrange menu. This combines the pockets and the table surface into a single object to prevent accidental realignment of the pockets later on in this exercise.

4. Select the Ellipse tool, press and hold Ctrl, and draw a perfectly circular "ball" in the center of the table.

5. Press the Spacebar to switch to the Pick tool and select the ball. Next press Shift and select the table, then select the Align command in the Arrange menu. The Align dialog box in Figure 6-21 appears.

The Align dialog box contains two areas of option buttons. The settings in the upper-right area of the dialog box pertain to the relative *horizontal* alignment of the selected objects, while the settings in the left part of the dialog box pertain to their relative *vertical* alignment. You can set horizontal and vertical alignment independently of each other or mix them, for a total of 15 possible settings. When multiple objects are selected and you choose the Horizontal Left, Horizontal Right, Vertical Top, or Vertical Bottom alignment option, CorelDRAW! repositions all but one of the objects. The object *last selected* remains in place. All other objects are moved to carry out the desired alignment. When you select Horizontal Center or Vertical Center

Align dialog box
Figure 6-21.

alignment, however, CorelDRAW! repositions all of the selected objects, unless one of them is already in the desired location.

6. Select Horizontal Left in the Align dialog box and then click on the OK command button. The billiard ball reappears in position 1 in Figure 6-22, aligned to the left edge of the table.

   If your screen does not look like Figure 6-22, you can see only half of your table, your table moved, and the ball stayed stationary, then you selected your table first and the ball last. The last object selected stays stationary, and previously selected items are moved the first time you do an alignment.

7. Select the Align command repeatedly and choose each of the numbered settings in the following list, one at a time. As you select each setting, check the location of the billiard ball against the corresponding call-out numbers in Figure 6-22. Six of the following settings will cause your ball to "go" into one of the billiard table pockets.

   (1) Horizontal Left
   (2) Horizontal Center
   (3) Horizontal Right
   (4) Vertical Top
   (5) Vertical Center
   (6) Vertical Bottom

6

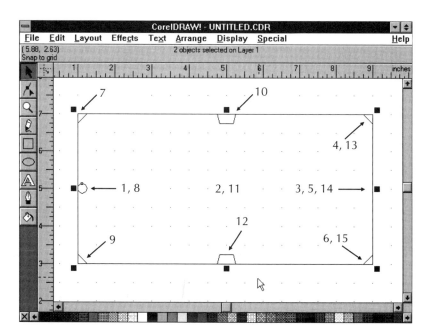

Results of
Align dialog
box settings
Figure 6-22.

(7) Horizontal Left-Vertical Top
(8) Horizontal Left-Vertical Center
(9) Horizontal Left-Vertical Bottom
(10) Horizontal Center-Vertical Top
(11) Horizontal Center-Vertical Center
(12) Horizontal Center-Vertical Bottom
(13) Horizontal Right-Vertical Top
(14) Horizontal Right-Vertical Center
(15) Horizontal Right-Vertical Bottom

If you do the above alignments without reselecting the ball and the table, you will notice that the first time you do the alignment to the horizontal left, the ball moves as you would expect. On the second alignment, the table moves, the third time, the ball moves again, and so on, switching back and forth between objects. If you want the table to remain stationary, you must reselect first the ball and then the table before each pair of alignments.

The Align dialog box has two additional options, Align to Grid and Align to Center of Page. When used, you want to set either of these options before setting the horizontal and/or vertical alignments. Try both of these options now.

1. Open the Align dialog box and click on Align to Center of Page. Notice that the Center Horizontal and Center Vertical alignment have also been selected as a default. Click on OK. The ball returns to the center of the table, and both objects are positioned in the center of the page as they were when you started this exercise.

2. Again select Align to Center of Page from the Align dialog box. Then click on Left Horizontal and Top Vertical and click on OK. The ball moves to the upper-left corner of the table, and the upper-left corner of the table moves to the center of the page, as shown in Figure 6-23.

In Align to Center of Page, the objects first position themselves in accordance with the horizontal and vertical alignment instructions, and then the common point of alignment is positioned in the center of the page.

1. Click on anything other than the ball or the table to deselect them both, then click on the table to select only it.

2. In the Grid Setup dialog box reached from the Layout menu, set both Horizontal and Vertical Grid Frequency to 2.

3. Using the arrow keys, nudge the table so that it is away from grid lines in both directions.

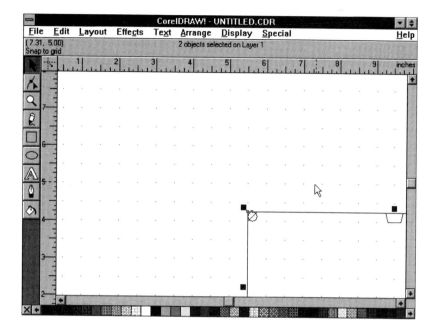

Upper-left
corner aligned
to center of
page
Figure 6-23.

6

4. Click on Left Horizontal and Top Vertical in the Align dialog box and select Align to Grid. Click on OK. The table will move to the nearest grid point that is up and to the left of the table's original position.

The Align to Grid command does not position objects in relation to each other, but rather it individually aligns objects (all that are selected) in relation to the nearest grid point in the direction specified by the horizontal and vertical alignment commands.

Experiment on your own, perhaps with other objects in drawings you have already created. Other objects may align in a slightly different way, depending on the order in which you select alignment settings.

When you are through practicing using the Align feature, clear the screen using the New command in the File menu. Do not save any changes.

Layers

CorelDRAW! has the ability to design your drawing in different layers. Just as you can stack transparencies on an overhead projector, you can design your drawing in distinct layers so that you can hide certain objects, prevent certain objects from being changed, and control the printing of the drawing by layer. This last feature is important in more complex drawings where printing time is a factor.

You probably noticed in the examples throughout this book that the status line displays the current object followed by the words "on Layer 1." This is the layer assigned to all new drawings. You can have as many layers as you want, but new objects are placed only on the active layer.

Layering is controlled by the Layers roll-up window, an option on the Layout menu. When opened through the Layout menu (or by pressing Ctrl-F3) the Layers roll-up appears.

The four layers that appear in the Layers roll-up are CorelDRAW!'s defaults: Layer 1, Guides, Grid, and Desktop. (The third layer, Grid, is active only if Show Grid is selected first.) The Desktop is active when you have multilayers. The highlighted Layer 1 is the active layer, and all new objects and text will be on it. A layer becomes active when you select and highlight its name in the Layers roll-up window.

The Guides layer contains any guidelines that you may choose. These are the same guidelines available from the Layout menu, and drawings made on other layers will snap to them. You can also draw on the Guides layer, by making it the active layer. The Grid layer is similar to the Guides layer, except you cannot make it the active layer. Consequently, it is a locked layer on which nothing can be drawn. The Grid layer is simply a series of points that can help you draw accurately in other layers.

Layer Features

Clicking on the right-pointing arrow below the title bar of the Layers roll-up opens a flyout menu, which allows you to create a new layer, or to edit, delete, copy, or move existing layers. Additionally, you can change the stacking order of your layers or use multilayering to select objects across any layer, except for locked or hidden objects.

Creating or Editing a Layer

When either New or Edit is selected, the Layer Options dialog box opens, as shown here:

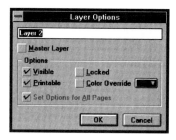

A text box identifies the name of the layer. You can rename the layer anything you want, using up to 32 characters. This dialog box can also be displayed by double-clicking on any layer's name in the scroll box of the Layers roll-up window.

The dialog box contains six check boxes. The first allows you to identify a layer as a master layer. If the Set Options for All Pages check box is also checked, all objects on the master layer will be displayed on all pages of the document. Other check boxes allow you to choose whether to make a layer visible or invisible on the screen, in order to see objects on a complex graphic more clearly. A layer may be printable or unprintable. It may be locked, whereby a layer cannot be accidentally edited. You can also set Color Override, which determines whether you see your object as a color outline or a black solid on the screen. (The default is a black solid.) You can change the color of the outline by clicking on the button next to Color Override. Checking the Set Options for All Pages check box for a layer will cause its objects to be displayed for all pages whether it is a master layer or not.

NOTE: If you double-click on a Guides or Grid layer's name in the Layers roll-up window, the Layers Options dialog box will open with an added Setup button. Depending on which layer is selected, the Guidelines Setup or Grid Setup dialog box will open when Setup is selected.

Deleting a Layer
To delete a layer, simply click on the layer name in the Layers roll-up window and then click on the right-pointing arrow. Choose Delete and the layer and all of its objects are deleted. When you delete a layer, the layer below it on the list becomes the active layer.

Moving or Copying Objects or Text from One Layer to Another
The procedures are the same for moving and copying objects and text from one layer to another. First, you must select the object you want to move or copy. You can tell which layer it is on by the displayed message on the status line. Next, from the Layers roll-up window, click on the right-pointing arrow and choose either Move To or Copy To. A "To?" arrow appears. Finally, click

6

the "To?" arrow on the new layer in the Layers roll-up window where you want the object located.

Multilayering
Generally, in order to select an object, it must be on the active layer. By choosing the MultiLayer option from the Layers roll-up flyout menu, you can select and edit any object regardless of the layer on which it resides. There are two things to note about multilayering: First, locking a layer overrides the MultiLayer option's access to objects on that layer. Second, in order to perform the moving and copying features, MultiLayer must be active.

Changing the Layer Stacking Order
The order in which the layers are listed in the Layers roll-up window is the same order in which the layers are stacked in your drawing; the top being first and the bottom last. To change the existing order, drag the layer name you want to move from its present location in the scroll box, and place it on top of the name of the layer you want it to overlay in your drawing. When you release the mouse button, the list will be rearranged—as will the order of the layers in your drawing.

Welding
The Welding feature joins two or more objects as if they were one. They cannot be separated or broken apart after they are welded. The fill features of the original object created will be in effect for the new object.

Follow these steps to experiment with this feature:

1. If the wireframe mode is selected, turn it off.
2. Using the Ellipse tool, draw a circle in the left half of the page. Fill it with any pattern by clicking on the Fill tool and then clicking on the pattern you want. (Chapter 12 describes the Fill feature in depth.)
3. Using the Rectangle tool, draw a square that overlaps the circle. Fill it with a different pattern.

An example can be seen in Figure 6-24. The objects at this point are separate and can be individually selected.

4. With the Pick tool draw a marquee around both objects, taking care to include all of both objects.
5. From the Arrange menu select Weld.

As Figure 6-25 shows, both objects are combined into a single curved object and filled with the originally created object's fill pattern.

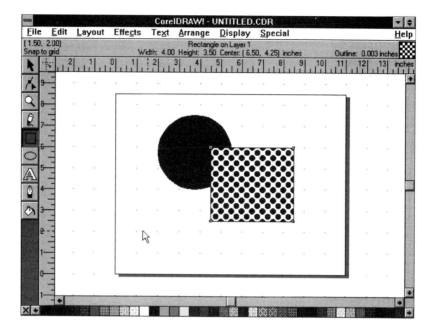

Separate
objects ready
to be welded
Figure 6-24.

By now, you have had an opportunity to practice all of the functions of the Pick tool that do not require you to change the size or structure of selected objects. In Chapter 7 you will explore the transformation mode of the Pick tool and learn to stretch, scale, rotate, skew, and mirror a selected object or group of objects.

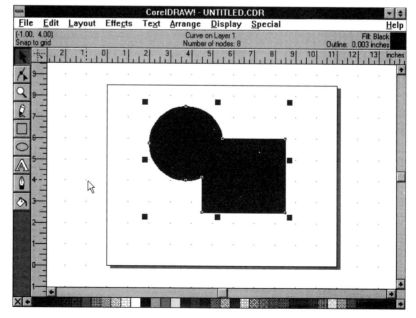

Welded
objects
combined into
one curved
object
Figure 6-25.

6

CHAPTER

COREL DRAW! 4

7

TRANSFORMING OBJECTS

In Chapter 6, you learned how to use the Pick tool to select, move, and arrange objects. In this chapter, you will use the Pick tool to transform the size or shape of selected objects.

When you transform an object with the Pick tool, you do not alter its fundamental shape; a rectangle continues to have four corners, and an ellipse remains an oval. (This is not the case when you reshape an object using the Shaping tool, which you will learn about in Chapters 8 and 9.) The five basic transformation techniques you will learn in this chapter enable you to stretch, scale, mirror, rotate, and skew an object in any direction. You will also learn how to retain a copy of the original object, repeat transformations automatically, and return an object to its original format, even if you have transformed it several times.

The exercises in this chapter introduce not only the basic skills that make up the art of transformation, but also the alternative ways you can practice them. CorelDRAW! lets you customize the way you work when transforming objects. If you like to work interactively, you can carry out these functions using the mouse and keyboard alone. For a little extra guidance, you can look to the status line and rulers. And, if you have to render a technical illustration that requires absolute precision, you can specify transformations using the commands and dialog boxes in the Effects menu.

Throughout most of this chapter, you will practice each skill using a simple text string that you create in the following section. However, the stretch, scale, rotate, and skew functions of CorelDRAW! work exactly the same way with multiple selected objects as with single ones. In later exercises, you can practice combining transformation operations with other skills you have learned in previous chapters.

Stretching and Mirroring an Object

As you discovered in Chapter 6, a rectangular highlighting box, made up of eight black boundary markers, surrounds an object when you select it. These boundary markers, shown in Figure 7–1, have special functions in

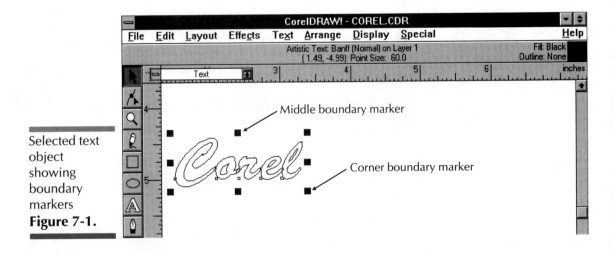

Selected text object showing boundary markers
Figure 7-1.

CorelDRAW!; you use them to stretch and scale objects. When you *stretch* an object, you change its *aspect ratio* (the proportion of its width to its height), because you lengthen or shorten it in one direction only. When you *scale* an object, you change the object's length and width at the same time, so the aspect ratio remains the same. To stretch an object, you must drag one of the four middle boundary markers, as shown in Figure 7-1. To scale an object, you drag one of the four boundary markers in the corners of the highlighting box.

This section covers all of the available techniques for stretching objects. You have the additional option of creating a mirror image or making a copy of the original object as you stretch it. The exercises in this section introduce you to both the interactive and menu-assisted methods for stretching, mirroring, and copying objects.

If you prefer to work interactively, bypassing menu commands and dialog boxes, you can stretch a selected object using the mouse and keyboard alone. You do not sacrifice precision when you work this way, for the status line assists you in setting precise values as you stretch an object. Practice stretching a text string interactively in the following sections.

Stretching Horizontally

You can stretch an object in either a horizontal or vertical direction. In the following exercise, you will create a text string and stretch it toward the right.

1. Make sure your page is in portrait format before you begin. If it is not, choose the Page Setup command from the Layout menu and select the Portrait option button. Then choose Letter from the Paper Size drop-down list box. Also, from the Layout menu, select Grid Setup. In the Grid Setup dialog box, turn off the Show Grid and Snap To Grid options, set the vertical grid origin to 11 inches, and click OK.

2. Make certain the Edit Wireframe command in the Display menu is still selected with a check mark and turn on Show Rulers.

3. Select Text Roll-Up from the Text menu or press Ctrl-F2. Set the font to Banff, 60 points, click on the Left justify button, and then click on Apply. When the Text Attributes dialog box appears with Artistic Text and Paragraph Text selected, click on OK. You can close the roll-up, or click the roll-up button and leave only the title bar on the screen.

4. Select the Text tool, then select an insertion point at the 1 1/2-inch mark on the horizontal ruler and the 5-inch mark on the vertical ruler. When the insertion point appears, type the text string, **Corel**.

5. Select the Zoom tool and choose 1:1 from the flyout menu.

6. Select the Save As command from the File menu, make sure you are in the directory where you save your drawings, and type **corel.cdr**.

7. Press the Spacebar to activate the Pick tool. A highlighting box surrounds the text string immediately, since it was the last object you drew. Your screen should resemble Figure 7-1.

8. Position the pointer directly over the center right boundary marker of the highlighting box. The mouse pointer changes to a crosshair like the one in Figure 7-2.

9. Depress and hold the mouse and drag the boundary marker to the right. The original object seems to stay in the same place, but a dotted rectangular box follows the pointer, which changes to a two-way horizontal arrow, as shown in Figure 7-3. As you drag, the status line displays the message: "x scale:" followed by a numeric value and a percent sign. This value is the amount you are stretching the selected object, shown in increments of 1/10 of a percentage point.

10. After you have stretched the object to the desired size, release the mouse button. CorelDRAW! redraws a horizontally stretched version of the original object, like the one in Figure 7-4.

11. Select the Undo Stretch command from the Edit menu to return the text string to its original size. The original text string remains selected for the next exercise.

To stretch a selected object to the left instead of to the right, drag the middle boundary marker at the *left* side of the highlighting box. Practice stretching the text string from the left side if you wish, but select Undo Stretch after you are finished so that the original text string remains on the screen.

Preparing to stretch a selected object horizontally
Figure 7-2.

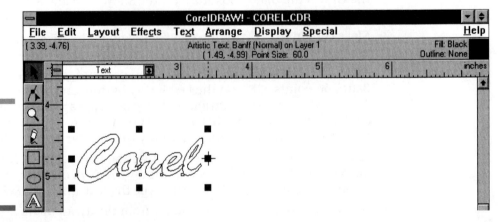

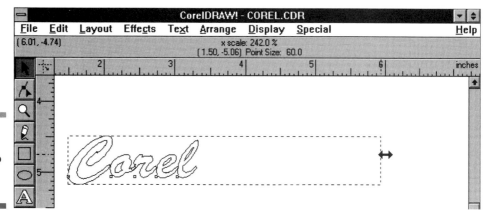

Stretching an
object
horizontally to
the right
Figure 7-3.

NOTE: When the mouse pointer is allowed to cross a window border, the object will continue to transform until the pointer is moved back inside the window. This is called Auto-Panning. If you don't like Auto-Panning, you can turn it off in the Preferences dialog box reached through the Special menu.

7

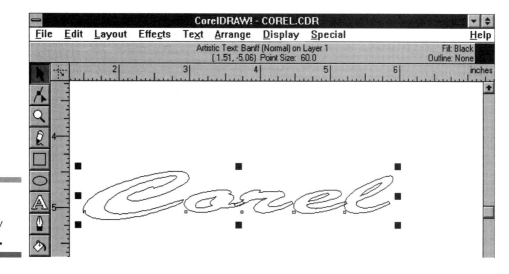

Text object
stretched
horizontally
Figure 7-4.

Stretching Vertically

You can also stretch an object in a vertical direction. The mouse pointer and status line information change to reflect the direction of your stretch.

1. Select the "Corel" text string if it is not selected already.

2. Position the mouse pointer directly over the top middle boundary marker of the highlighting box. The mouse pointer changes to a crosshair.

3. Depress and hold the mouse and drag the boundary marker upward. The original object seems to stay in the same place, but a dotted rectangular box follows the pointer, which changes to a two-way vertical arrow, as shown in Figure 7-5. As you drag, the status line displays the message: "y scale:" followed by a numeric value and a percent sign. This value shows precisely how much you are stretching the selected object in increments of 1/10 of a percent.

4. After you have stretched the object to the desired size, release the mouse button. CorelDRAW! redraws a vertically stretched version of the original object.

5. Select the Undo Stretch command from the Edit menu to return the text string to its original size.

If you wish, practice stretching the text string downward in a vertical direction. When you are finished, undo your changes to the original object and then proceed with the next exercise.

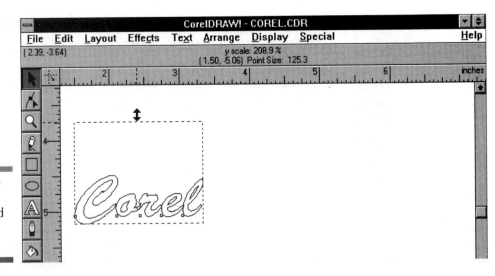

Stretching an object vertically and upward
Figure 7-5.

Stretching in Increments of 100 Percent

In previous chapters, you saw how to use Ctrl to constrain your drawing or moving operations to fixed increments or angles. The same holds true when you are stretching a selected object. To stretch an object in fixed increments of 100 percent, press and hold Ctrl as you drag the boundary marker in the desired direction. The status line keeps track of the increments in which you are stretching the object. As always, remember to release the mouse button *before* you release Ctrl, or the object may not stretch in exact increments. In the following exercise, you will triple the width of the original object using Ctrl.

1. Select the text string if it is not selected already.

2. Press and hold Ctrl and then drag the right middle boundary marker to the right. Notice that the dotted rectangular outline does not follow the two-way arrow pointer continuously; instead, it "snaps" outward only when you have doubled the width of the object.

3. When the status line displays the message, "x scale: 300.0%," as shown in Figure 7-6, release the mouse button first and then Ctrl. The text string redisplays at triple its original width.

4. Select the Undo command from the Edit menu to revert to the original unstretched object.

7

Retaining a Copy of the Original Object

A useful design technique is to make a copy of the original object as you stretch it, so that both the original and the stretched objects appear on the screen. To retain a copy of the original object, just press the + key on the numeric keypad or click the right mouse button once as soon as you begin the stretching, and the outline box appears.

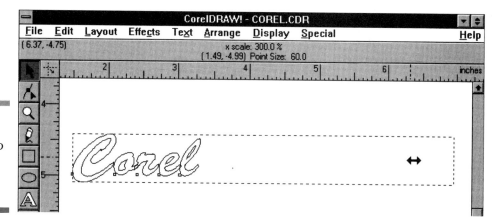

Horizontal stretch constrained to 300% of original size
Figure 7-6.

NOTE: Pressing the right mouse button while dragging to leave the original does not conflict with the function you assign to the right mouse button in the Preferences dialog box.

You can also retain a copy of the original object when using Ctrl. Try this technique now:

1. Select the text string "Corel" if it is not already selected. Position the mouse pointer over the bottom middle boundary marker and begin to drag this marker downward.

2. As soon as the dotted outline box appears, press the ⊞ key or press the right mouse button once. The message "Leave Original" appears at the left side of the status line.

3. Press and hold Ctrl and continue to drag the bottom middle boundary marker downward until the status line reads "y scale: 200.0%."

4. Release the mouse button and then Ctrl. The screen displays both the original and stretched object, as in Figure 7-7.

5. Undo your changes to the original text string before continuing.

If the stretched object does not appear in the correct proportions, you either failed to press and hold Ctrl, or you released Ctrl before releasing the mouse

Retaining a copy of the original object while stretching it
Figure 7-7.

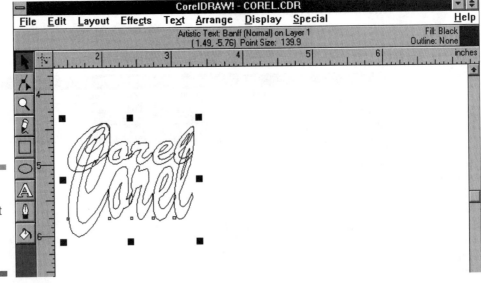

button. Keep practicing until you feel comfortable with the technique, but remember to undo your changes to be ready for the next exercise.

Creating a Mirror Image

Using the middle boundary markers on the highlighting box, you can create a horizontal or vertical mirror image of an object. You have several choices of technique, depending on your needs. If, for example, you choose to retain a copy of the original object, you need to use the ⊕ key or click the right mouse button. If you choose to make the size of the mirror image an exact multiple of the original, you need to use [Ctrl]. You can just as easily decide not to copy the original object, or make the mirrored object a custom size. In every case, however, you will drag the *opposite* center boundary marker until it "flips" in the direction in which you want the mirror image to appear.

In Figure 7-8, the original object is retained, but neither the original nor the mirrored object is stretched.

The following exercise assumes that you want to create a perfect horizontal mirror image of an object, like the one in Figure 7-8. At the end of the exercise are suggestions for obtaining other results.

1. Select the text string "Corel" if it isn't selected already.

2. Position the mouse pointer over the left middle boundary marker and begin to drag this marker to the right.

3. As soon as the dotted outline box appears, press the ⊕ key or click the right mouse button once. The message "Leave Original" appears at the left side of the status line.

4. Press and hold [Ctrl] and continue to drag the marker to the right. The [Ctrl] key ensures that the size of the mirrored object will be an exact multiple of the original, in this case the identical size (100 percent).

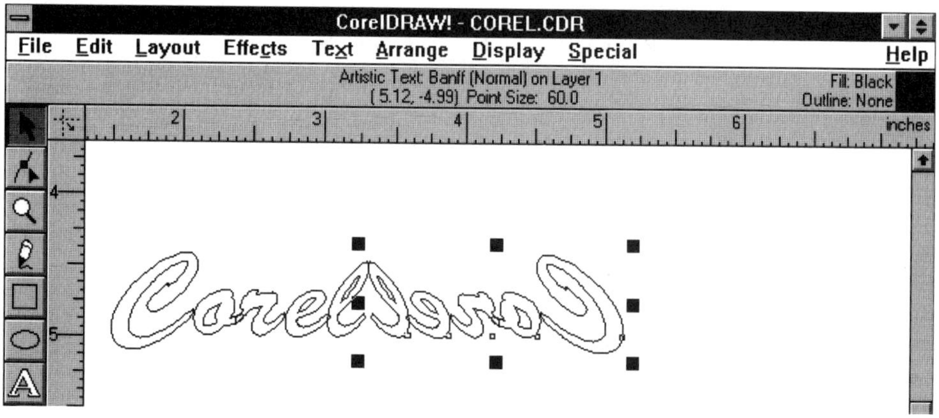

7

Retaining a copy of the original object while mirroring it
Figure 7-8.

5. When the dotted outline box "snaps" beside the original object and the status line reads "x scale: –100.0%," as in Figure 7-9, release the mouse button and then [Ctrl]. CorelDRAW! redraws the screen showing both the original and the mirrored object, as in Figure 7-8. The mirrored object is selected. If your text strings look different, select Undo and try the exercise again.

6. Press [Ctrl]-[Z] for Undo and to return the text string to its original unmirrored state.

You can vary this exercise to achieve different results. For example, to create a vertical mirror image that appears beneath the object, drag the upper middle boundary marker downward. To make the mirror image double or triple the size of the original, keep stretching the mirror object using [Ctrl]. To make the mirror image a custom size, just drag the boundary marker *without* using [Ctrl]. If you want to create a mirror image only, without retaining the original object, do not use the [+] key or the right mouse button.

If you want to create a mirror image appearing at a diagonal to the original object, you first need to be familiar with how to scale an object. See the section, "Scaling an Object" later in this chapter for instructions.

The Stretch & Mirror Command

If you find the use of the mouse and keyboard controls inconvenient, you can perform all of the possible stretch operations using the Stretch & Mirror command in the Effects menu. The dialog box that opens when you select this command allows you to choose the direction of the stretch, specify the exact amount of stretching, retain a copy of the original object, and create horizontal or vertical mirror images.

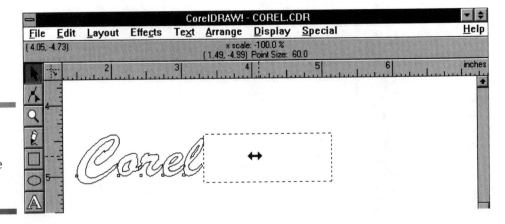

Creating a
perfect
horizontal
mirror image
of an object
Figure 7-9.

Stretching an Object

Take another look at the COREL.CDR file that you created in the first part of this chapter. Then try the following exercise to become familiar with the Stretch & Mirror command.

1. Select the "Corel" text string and then click on the Stretch & Mirror command from the Effects menu. The dialog box shown in Figure 7-10 appears. The controls in the center of the dialog box let you specify the direction and amount of stretch in increments of 1 percent. The controls at the right allow you to mirror the object horizontally or vertically. The Leave Original check box determines whether you make a copy of the original object as you stretch or mirror it.

2. Set the numeric value next to Stretch Vertically to 175 percent, using either the scroll arrow or the keyboard, and then select OK. The text string increases in height. Notice, however, that when you stretch an object using the Stretch & Mirror dialog box instead of the mouse, the stretched object is centered on the same position as the original. If you want it to appear in another location, click on the object's outline and drag it to the desired location.

3. Select the Clear Transformations command from the Effects menu to return the object to its original size. (You can also use Undo in the Edit menu or press Ctrl-Z.)

4. Select the Stretch & Mirror command again, set the Stretch Horizontally value to 175 percent, and then select OK. This time, the text string increases in width.

5. Clear the current transformation by selecting the Clear Transformations command in the Effects menu. Then select Stretch & Mirror again. This time, you will constrain the stretch of the image to an exact multiple of the original, as you did using Ctrl and the mouse button.

7

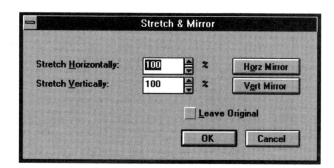

Stretch &
Mirror dialog
box
Figure 7-10.

6. Set the Stretch Vertically value to 300 and then click on the Leave Original check box to retain a copy of the original object.

7. Select OK to exit the dialog box. CorelDRAW! redisplays the original object against a vertically stretched image three times the size of the original.

Notice that when you use the Stretch & Mirror dialog box for these operations, the stretched object is superimposed on the original and both objects share a common center point, as shown in Figure 7-11. If you want the stretched object to appear above, below, or to the side of the original, you must drag its outline to the desired location.

8. To erase the transformed copy of the object so that only the unaltered original remains, select the Undo command from the Edit menu.

CAUTION: If you want to erase the copy of the original object after a transformation that leaves the original in place, use the Undo command rather than the Clear Transformations command. If you use the Clear Transformations command, the transformed object on the top layer is not erased, but instead becomes an exact copy of the original. The transformation is cleared, but not the object itself. As a result, what looks like one object on the screen is actually two superimposed objects.

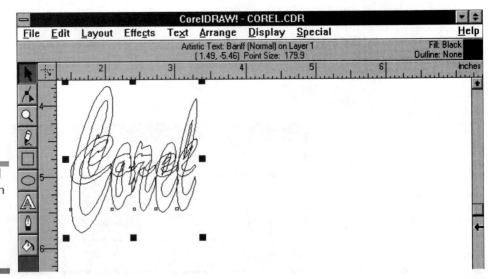

300% vertical transformation sharing same center with original
Figure 7-11.

Mirroring an Object

The following exercise shows you how to create a vertical or horizontal mirror image using the Stretch & Mirror command instead of the mouse and keyboard. When you create a mirror image, you can choose whether or not to retain a copy of the original object. You should continue working in actual size viewing magnification for this exercise.

1. With the text string in the COREL.CDR file selected, select the Stretch & Mirror command from the Effects menu.
2. Click on the Vert Mirror command button in the Stretch & Mirror dialog box. Notice that the value next to Stretch Vertically becomes a negative number automatically. Leave this value at –100 percent.
3. Select OK to exit the dialog box. A vertical mirror image of the object replaces the original, as shown in Figure 7-12.
4. Select Clear Transformations to return the object to its original state.
5. Select the Stretch & Mirror command again, but this time click on the Horz Mirror command button. Notice that the Stretch Horizontally value becomes a negative number automatically.
6. Select OK to exit the dialog box. A horizontal mirror image of the original text appears.
7. Select Clear Transformations to return the image to its original state.

You can customize the settings in the Stretch & Mirror dialog box to achieve different results.

If you want to merge a copy of the original object with the mirrored version, just click on the Leave Original check box in the Stretch & Mirror dialog box. If you want to make the mirror image larger or smaller than the original, set the Stretch Horizontally value accordingly. Remember that this value must always be a negative number if it is to result in a mirror image.

7

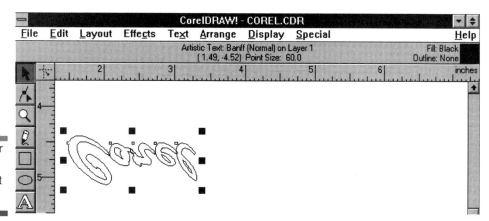

Vertical mirror image of the original object
Figure 7-12.

Keep in mind, too, that when you use the Stretch & Mirror dialog box instead of the mouse to create a mirror image, the mirror image occupies the same position as the original. If you want the mirrored object to appear above, below, or to the side of the original, you must drag its outline to the desired location.

Scaling an Object

As you have just seen, stretching an object involves changing its size in one direction (horizontal or vertical) only. When you *scale* an object, you change its size horizontally and vertically at the same time, thereby maintaining the same proportions and aspect ratio. You can scale an object interactively using the keyboard and mouse, or you can scale an object using the Stretch & Mirror dialog box. If you prefer to work more spontaneously, you will probably prefer the mouse and keyboard controls. Recall that when you stretch an object, you drag it by one of the *middle* boundary markers. Scaling an object is similar, except that you drag one of the *corner* boundary markers instead.

To practice scaling objects interactively, try this exercise:

1. Open the COREL.CDR file if it is not open already and select the "Corel" text string.

2. Position the mouse pointer directly over one of the corner boundary markers. You can scale from any corner but, for the sake of this exercise, use the lower-right corner marker. The pointer changes to a crosshair, just as when you prepared to stretch an object.

3. Drag the lower-right boundary marker diagonally downward. As you drag, the pointer changes to a four-way arrow, similar to the move arrow, except that it is rotated diagonally, as in Figure 7-13. The original object appears to stay in the same place, but a dotted outline box follows the scaling pointer. The scaling pointer increases or decreases in size, depending on the direction in which you drag the marker.

Figure 7-13 shows an object increasing in scale from the lower-right corner marker.

Note that the status line displays the message "scale:" followed by a percentage value. This value tells you precisely how much larger or smaller you are making the object.

4. When the dotted outline box is the size you want the text string to be, release the mouse button. The selected object reappears in a scaled version.

5. Select Clear Transformations in the Effects menu or Undo in the Edit menu to return the object to its original size.

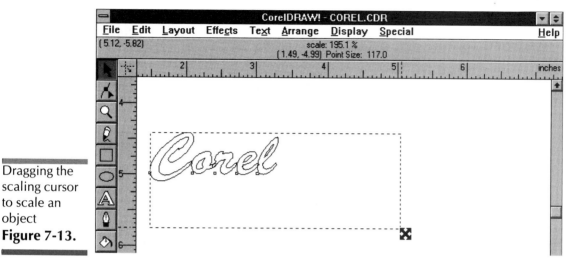

Dragging the
scaling cursor
to scale an
object
Figure 7-13.

Scaling in Increments of 100 Percent
To scale an object in increments of 100 percent of its size, all you need to do
is press and hold Ctrl while scaling the object. Just as when you stretched
objects using Ctrl, the dotted outline box does not move smoothly but
instead "snaps" at each 100 percent increment. Likewise, the message in the
status line changes only when you reach the next 100 percent increment.
Remember to release the mouse button *before* you release Ctrl, or the
increments will not be exact.

Keep in mind, too, that an object scaled to 200 percent of its original size
takes up four times the area of the original object, not twice as much,
because you are increasing both the height and width of the object by a
factor of two.

Retaining a Copy While Scaling
To retain a copy of the object in its original location as you scale it, just press
and release the ⊞ key on the numeric keypad or click the right mouse button as
soon as you begin to scale the object. The status line displays the message,
"Leave Original," just as when you leave a copy while stretching an object.

Creating a Diagonal Mirror Image
Using the corner boundary markers on the highlighting box, you can create
a mirror image that appears at a diagonal to the original object. You have
several choices of technique, depending on your needs. If you choose to
retain a copy of the original object, you need to use the right mouse button
or the ⊞ key. If you choose to make the size of the mirror image an exact

7

multiple of the original, you need to use Ctrl. You can just as easily decide not to copy the original object or to make the mirrored object a custom size. In every case, however, you drag the *opposite* corner boundary marker until it "flips" in the direction in which you want the mirror image to appear.

The following exercise assumes that you are going to create a perfect diagonal mirror image of an object like the one in Figure 7-14. In this figure, the original object remains, but neither the original nor the mirrored object is scaled beyond the original size. At the end of the exercise you will find suggestions for obtaining other results.

1. Select the text string "Corel," if it is not selected already.

2. Position the pointer over the boundary marker in the upper-left corner of the highlighting box and begin to drag the marker downward and to the right.

3. As soon as the dotted outline box appears, click the right mouse button or press the ⊕ key on your numeric keypad once to leave a copy of the original object. The message "Leave Original" appears at the left side of the status line, as shown in Figure 7-14.

The Ctrl key ensures that the size of the mirrored object will be an exact multiple of the original.

4. Press and hold Ctrl and continue dragging the boundary marker until the dotted outline box "snaps" at a diagonal to the original object and the status line reads "scale: –100.0%."

5. Release the mouse button and then Ctrl. CorelDRAW! redraws the screen showing both the original and the mirrored object. The mirrored object is selected. If your text strings do not appear in this way, try the exercise again.

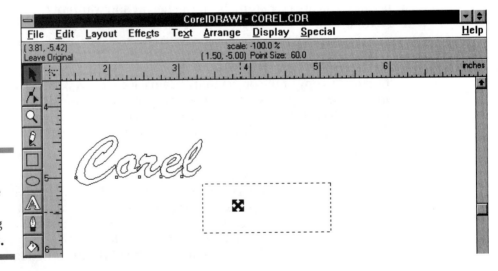

Creating a diagonal mirror image of an object while scaling
Figure 7-14.

6. Select Undo from the Edit menu or press ⌈Ctrl⌉-⌈Z⌉ to return the object to its original unmirrored state.

You can vary this exercise to achieve different results. For example, to place the mirror image at the upper-right corner of the original object, drag from the lower-left corner marker upward. To make the mirror image double or triple the size of the original, keep stretching the mirror object using ⌈Ctrl⌉. To make the mirror image a custom size, just drag the opposite boundary marker without using ⌈Ctrl⌉. If you want to create a mirror image only, without retaining the original object, do not use the right mouse button or the ⌈+⌉ key.

Scaling with the Stretch & Mirror Command

If you find the use of the mouse and keyboard controls inconvenient, you can perform all of the scaling operations precisely, using the Stretch & Mirror command in the Effects menu. You can specify the amount of scaling desired, retain a copy of the original object, and create mirror images that appear at a diagonal to the original. Work through the following exercise to become familiar with using the Stretch & Mirror command to scale an object.

7

1. With the COREL.CDR file open and in an actual size viewing magnification, select the "Corel" text string, and then select the Stretch & Mirror command from the Effects menu.

2. To scale an object, you need to set both the Stretch Horizontally and the Stretch Vertically values to the same number. Set both of these values to 150 percent, using either the scroll arrow or the keyboard.

3. Make certain that a check mark does not appear in the Leave Original check box and then select OK. The text string increases in both height and width. Notice, however, that a scaled object created with the Stretch & Mirror command appears in the same location as the original and has the same center point. If you want the scaled object to appear elsewhere, move it to the desired location.

4. Select the Clear Transformations command from the Effects menu to return the object to its original size.

Retaining a Copy While Using Stretch & Mirror

It is easy to make a copy of the original object from the Stretch & Mirror dialog box. Simply place a check mark in the Leave Original check box before you exit the dialog box.

1. Select the text string "Corel" and then select the Stretch & Mirror command. This time, you will constrain the stretch of the image to an

exact multiple of the original, as you did using [Ctrl] and the mouse. You will also leave a copy of the original object in its original location.

2. Set the Stretch Vertically and Stretch Horizontally values to 200 percent and then click on the Leave Original check box to retain a copy of the original object.

3. Select OK to exit the dialog box. CorelDRAW! redisplays the original object along with a scaled text string four times the size of the original.

4. To erase the transformed copy of the object so that only the unaltered original remains, select the Undo command from the Edit menu. If you have moved the copy of the original, select it and press [Del] to clear it.

Notice that the scaled object is superimposed on the original. If you want it elsewhere, you must drag it there.

Stretching and Scaling from the Center

In the previous stretching and scaling exercises using the mouse, the object was modified in one dimension (stretching) or two dimensions (scaling) from a fixed opposite side or sides. In other words, when you dragged the right side of the object to the right, the left side remained fixed and was in the same position as was the right side of the modified object. Similarly, when you dragged the lower-right corner down and to the right, the top and left sides remained fixed and had the same horizontal and vertical position as the modified object.

When you used the Stretch & Mirror dialog box and modified an object in one or two dimensions, the opposite sides moved proportionately. That is, with the dialog box, the object was being modified from a fixed center point instead of a fixed side or sides. When you changed the horizontal and vertical percentages, all four sides changed, leaving the same center point as the original object.

You can also stretch and scale an object from the center point by pressing [Shift] while dragging with the mouse. This is the same as drawing an ellipse or rectangle from the center by pressing [Shift] while dragging with the Ellipse or Rectangle tool.

Recall how you stretched and scaled with the mouse originally and see how this changes when you press [Shift]:

1. The COREL.CDR text object should be selected on your page in an actual size view.

2. As you did in an earlier exercise, drag the middle boundary marker on the right side to the right several inches. Notice how the left side remains fixed. Release the mouse button and press [Ctrl]-[Z] to undo the modification.

3. Press and hold (Shift) while dragging the right middle boundary marker to the right an inch or so. Notice how the left side now moves a proportionate amount—the left and right sides are moving outward in equal amounts. Release the mouse button and press (Ctrl)-(Z) to undo the modification.

The ability to stretch or scale an object from the center allows you to more easily fill a regular enclosing space.

4. Again, as you did before, drag the lower-right corner boundary marker down and to the right several inches. Notice how the left and top sides remain fixed. Release the mouse button and press (Ctrl)-(Z) to undo the modification.

5. Press and hold (Shift) while dragging the lower-right corner boundary marker down and to the right an inch or so. Notice how the top and left sides are now moving proportionately with the right and bottom sides. Release the mouse button and press (Ctrl)-(Z) to undo the modification.

Rotating an Object

When you click on an object once using the Pick tool, you can move, arrange, stretch, or scale it. In addition, the Pick tool can rotate and skew an object. *Rotating* involves turning an object in a clockwise or counterclockwise direction, at an angle that you define. When you *skew* an object, on the other hand, you slant it toward the right, left, top, or bottom in order to create distortion or three-dimensional effects.

7

As with stretching and scaling, you can rotate an object interactively, using the mouse and keyboard, or you can use the Rotate & Skew command in the Effects menu. If you feel more comfortable working with dialog boxes than with the mouse and keyboard, you can select the Rotate & Skew command after clicking on an object once. To rotate an object interactively, however, you must either click on a selected object a second time, or double-click on an object that you have not yet selected.

Practice entering the interactive rotate/skew mode now, using the text string in the COREL.CDR file.

1. With the COREL.CDR file open and displayed at the actual size viewing magnification, click once on the outline of the text string. The normal highlighting box with its eight black boundary markers appears.

2. Click on the outline of the text string a second time. CorelDRAW! replaces the eight boundary markers with eight two-way arrows, as shown in Figure 7-15. You can drag any one of the corner arrows to rotate the object but, for the sake of this exercise, you will work with the upper-right corner arrow.

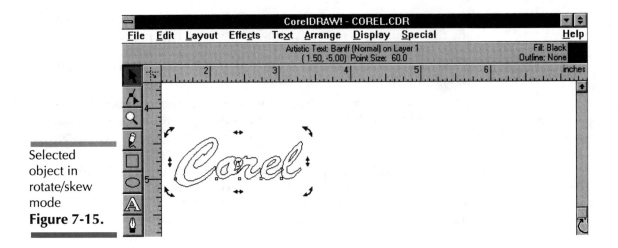

Selected
object in
rotate/skew
mode
Figure 7-15.

3. Position the mouse pointer over the two-way arrow in the upper-right corner of the rotate/skew highlighting box. When the pointer becomes a crosshair, press and hold the mouse button and drag the mouse in a counterclockwise direction. As soon as you begin to drag, the mouse pointer changes to an arc with arrows at either end. A dotted outline box representing the text string begins to rotate in a counterclockwise direction, as in Figure 7-16. Notice that the status line displays the angle of rotation as a positive number.

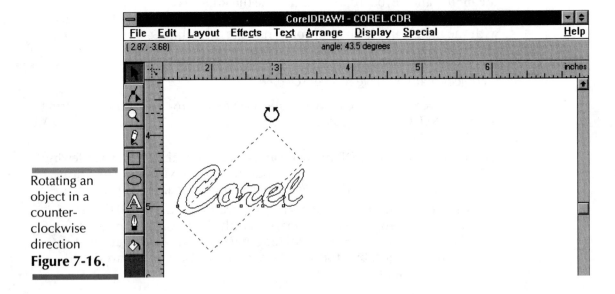

Rotating an
object in a
counter-
clockwise
direction
Figure 7-16.

4. Continue to drag the corner highlighting arrow in a counterclockwise direction until you have rotated the object more than 180 degrees. At that point, the status line begins to display a negative number for the angle of rotation, and the number begins to decrease from 180. Use the number on the status line to inform yourself how far you have rotated a selected object.

5. Continue rotating the text object until the number becomes positive again. Release the mouse button when the status line indicates an angle of about 17 degrees. CorelDRAW! redisplays the object at the selected angle of rotation.

6. Select the Clear Transformations command from the Effects menu to return the object to its original angle.

7. The text object should again appear selected, with its normal boundary markers. Click on its outline to redisplay the curved-arrow boundary markers. Drag the highlighting arrow in the upper-right corner again, but in a clockwise direction. The angle indicator on the status line displays a negative number until you rotate the text string more than 180 degrees. At that point, the number becomes positive and begins to decrease from 180 degrees downward.

8. Release the mouse button to redisplay the object at the new angle of rotation.

7

9. Select the Clear Transformations command from the Effects menu to return the object to its original angle.

NOTE: You may sometimes rotate an object several times in succession. The angle of rotation displayed in the status line, however, refers to the amount of the current rotation, not to the cumulative angle.

Rotating in Increments of 15 Degrees

As in almost every drawing or editing function of CorelDRAW!, you can use Ctrl to constrain movement in the rotation of objects. Simply press and hold Ctrl while dragging a corner arrow of the rotate/skew highlighting box, and the object rotates and "snaps" to successive 15-degree angles. The status line keeps track of the angle of rotation. As always, remember to release the mouse button before you release Ctrl, or you will not constrain the angle of rotation. You will use the constrain feature in the following exercise.

1. Double-click on the text string if it is not selected already or click once on its outline if it is selected. The two-way arrows appear to show that you are in the rotate/skew mode.

2. Position the pointer over the upper-right corner highlighting arrow until the pointer changes to a crosshair. Press and hold the Ctrl key and the mouse button and drag the highlighting arrow in the desired direction. Notice that the dotted rectangular box does not follow the rotation pointer continuously; instead, it "snaps" each time you reach an angle that is a multiple of 15 degrees.

3. When you reach the desired angle, release the mouse button first and then release Ctrl. The object redisplays at the new angle of rotation.

4. Select Clear Transformations from the Effects menu to return the object to its original angle.

Retaining a Copy While Rotating

If you like to experiment with design, you may find it useful to make a copy of the original object as you rotate it. Figure 7-17 illustrates one design effect you can achieve easily. This text pinwheel, suitable for desktop publishing applications, was created by rotating a text string in increments of 30 degrees and copying the original each time.

You can also retain a copy of the original object using Ctrl, but this operation requires a bit more coordination. Try this technique now:

1. With the COREL.CDR file open and in an actual size viewing magnification, click on the text string "Corel" if it is already selected, or double-click if it is not selected. The rotate/skew highlighting arrows

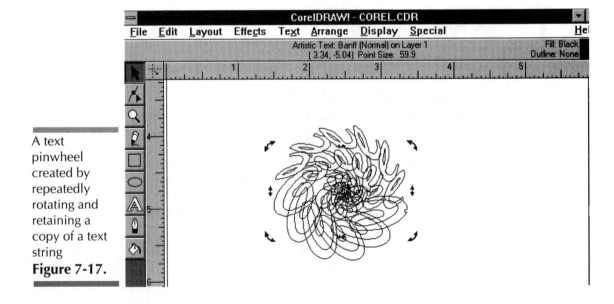

A text pinwheel created by repeatedly rotating and retaining a copy of a text string

Figure 7-17.

appear. Use the window scroll arrows to move the text object to the center of the screen. This does not change the orientation of your drawing on the page.

2. Position the mouse pointer over the upper-right highlighting arrow marker and begin to drag this marker upward. As soon as the dotted outline box appears, click the right mouse button or press the ⊞ key once to leave a copy of the original.

3. Press and hold ⌜Ctrl⌟ and continue dragging the arrow marker upward until the status line reads "angle: 30 degrees."

4. Release the mouse button and then the ⌜Ctrl⌟ key. The screen displays both the original and the rotated object, as shown in Figure 7-18.

5. Continue copying and rotating the text strings four more times at the same angle to create the design shown in Figure 7-17. Then undo your changes to the original text string before going further. Use Undo or press ⌜Del⌟ to erase the last rotation, then select the remaining objects one at a time and press ⌜Del⌟ for each object. Instead of selecting and deleting each object, it may be easier to use Open in the File menu and again open the original COREL.CDR file.

Changing an Object's Rotation

7

Look at an object on your screen when it is in rotate/skew mode. In the center of the object is a small dot surrounded by a circle. This graphic aid appears every time you activate the rotate/skew mode and represents the

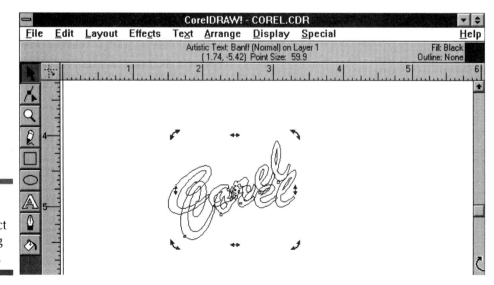

Retaining a copy of the original object while rotating
Figure 7-18.

The center of rotation does not have to be the center of the object.

center of rotation of an object. The object turns on this axis as you rotate it. If you want the object to rotate on a different axis, you can alter the center of rotation freely by dragging the center of rotation symbol to the desired location using the mouse. In the following exercise, you will create a simple text design that involves changing the center of a text string's rotation.

1. Select the text string if it is not selected already and move it to the center of the display. Click on its outlines again to access the rotate/skew mode.

2. When the rotate/skew highlighting box appears, position the mouse pointer over the center of rotation symbol until it becomes a cross. Drag the rotation symbol to the upper-right corner of the rotate/skew highlighting box, as shown in Figure 7-19. Then release the mouse button.

3. Position the mouse pointer over any one of the corner highlighting arrows and begin dragging the arrow in a clockwise direction. As soon as the dotted outline box appears, click the right mouse button or press the ⊞ key on your numeric keypad once to leave a copy of the original. Notice that because you have changed the center of rotation, the text string turns on its end rather than on its center point.

4. Press and hold Ctrl and continue dragging the marker until the status line shows that you have rotated the text string by –90 degrees.

5. Release the mouse button first, and then Ctrl. Both the original object and the rotated object display at 90-degree angles to one another.

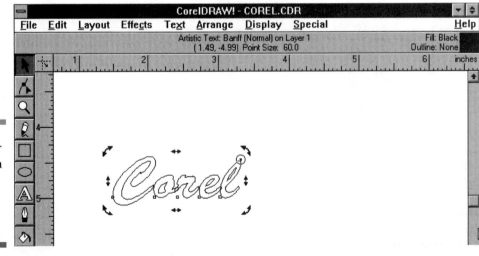

Relocating an object's center of rotation to a corner of the highlighting box

Figure 7-19.

6. Repeat this process two more times, until you have a text design similar to the one in Figure 7-20. To make all of the text strings behave as though they were one object, click on the Select All command in the Edit menu and group the text strings, using the Group command in the Arrange menu. Now reposition the group to the center of the display.

7. Save this figure as 4CORNERS.CDR.

8. Clear the screen by selecting New from the File menu.

Your new center of rotation does not have to be a highlighting arrow; you can relocate the center anywhere within the highlighting box. But a corner or boundary of the selected object often proves to be a convenient "handle" when you are performing rotations.

Rotating with the Rotate & Skew Command

If you find the use of the keyboard controls inconvenient, you can perform all of the preceding rotation operations with precision using the Rotate & Skew command in the Effects menu. You can select this command when either the normal highlighting box or the rotate/skew highlighting box is visible around a selected object. Perform the following brief exercise to familiarize yourself with the workings of the Rotate & Skew dialog box.

7

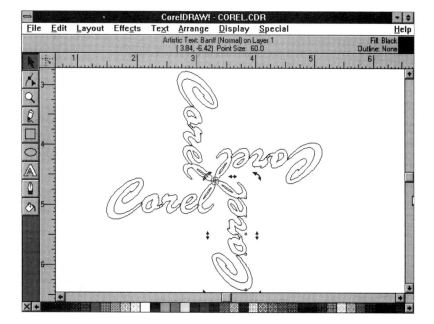

Text design created by rotating and copying an object with an altered center of rotation

Figure 7-20.

1. Open the COREL.CDR file and set the viewing magnification to 1:1. Click once on the text string to select it.

2. Select the Rotate & Skew command from the Effects menu. The Rotate & Skew dialog box appears, as in Figure 7-21.

You cannot skew and rotate an object at the same time.

3. Enter a number in the Rotation Angle numeric entry box. You can enter a number either by scrolling in increments of 5 degrees or by clicking on the numeric entry box and typing in a number in increments of 1/10 of a degree. Note that as soon as you enter a number in this box, the Skew Horizontally and Skew Vertically entry boxes become unavailable for selection.

4. If desired, click on the Leave Original check box to make a copy of the original object as you rotate it.

5. Select OK to exit the dialog box and see the results of your settings. When you are finished, select Undo to return the original object to its former angle. Leave this image on the screen for the next exercise.

That's all there is to rotating an object at the angle and axis of your choice. You can leave a copy of the original object while rotating it, just as when you copy an object that you are stretching or scaling. In the next section, you will practice skewing an object to achieve interesting distortion effects.

Skewing an Object

When you skew an object, you slant and distort it at a horizontal or vertical angle, thus warping its appearance. This technique can be useful for creating three-dimensional or surrealistic effects. As with the other techniques you have learned in this chapter, you can skew an object either interactively or by using the controls in the Rotate & Skew dialog box.

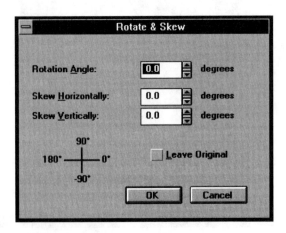

Rotate & Skew dialog box
Figure 7-21.

1. With the COREL.CDR file open and in an actual size viewing magnification, select the "Corel" text string. Then click a second time anywhere on its outline to enter rotate/skew mode.

2. To begin skewing the object horizontally, position the mouse pointer directly over the upper-middle highlighting arrow and drag it to the right. The mouse pointer changes to two half arrows pointing in opposite directions, and a dotted outline box slants to the right, the direction you are moving your mouse, as shown in Figure 7-22. The status line keeps track of the current angle of horizontal skew.

3. When you reach the desired skewing angle, release the mouse button. CorelDRAW! redisplays the object as you have skewed it, as shown in Figure 7-23.

4. Select Clear Transformations from the Effects menu to return the object to its original unskewed state.

5. Practice different angles of horizontal skewing. You can skew an object greater than 85 degrees to the right or left. If you drag one of the middle highlighting arrows along the left or right *side* of the highlighting box, you can skew the object in a vertical direction.

6. When you feel comfortable with basic skewing operations, select Clear Transformations from the Effects menu. Leave the text string on the screen for the next exercise.

7

Skewing in Increments of 15 Degrees

Once again, you can use Ctrl to introduce an extra measure of precision to the interactive transformation of objects. When skewing an object, pressing

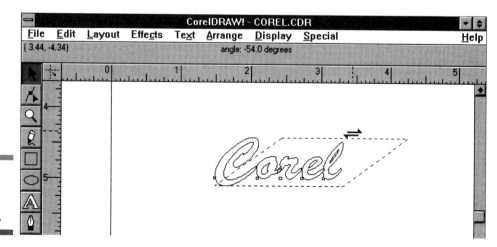

Skewing an object to the right

Figure 7-22.

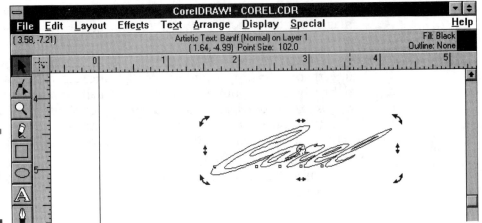

Object
skewed
horizontally to
the right
Figure 7-23.

and holding Ctrl forces the object to skew in increments of 15 degrees. Try using this constraint feature now.

1. Select the text string "Corel" and enter the rotate/skew mode.

2. Position the mouse pointer over the upper-middle highlighting arrow, press and hold Ctrl, and begin dragging the mouse to the right or left, as desired. The mouse pointer changes to the skew pointer, and the dotted outline box "snaps" in the desired direction in increments of 15 degrees.

3. When you reach the desired angle, release the mouse button first and then release Ctrl. If you release Ctrl first, you might not constrain the skewing operation to a 15-degree increment.

4. Select Clear Transformations from the Effects menu to return the skewed object to its original state. Leave the text string on the screen.

Retaining a Copy While Skewing

For an interesting design effect, you can skew an object and then make a copy of the original. As you will see in the following exercise, you can then position the skewed object behind the original to make it seem like a shadow.

1. Select the "Corel" text string and enter rotate/skew mode.

2. Position the mouse pointer over the upper-middle highlighting arrow and begin dragging the arrow to the right. As soon as the dotted outline box appears, press the ⊞ key on your numeric keypad or click the right mouse button to leave a copy of the original.

3. Press and hold Ctrl and continue dragging the marker until the status line shows a skewing angle of –60 degrees.

4. Release the mouse button first and then release Ctrl. The skewed object, which is selected automatically, appears on top of the copy of the original, as in Figure 7-24.

5. To place the skewed object behind the unskewed original, click on Order in the Arrange menu and then on To Back in the flyout menu.

6. You can manipulate the skewed object like any other object. Click once on its outline to toggle back to select mode, and then scale it to a smaller size by dragging the upper-right corner boundary marker of the highlighting box.

7. Adjust the viewing magnification to fit-in-window, and activate the preview window to obtain a WYSIWYG display of the original object and its skewed "shadow." Go to the preview window by clicking on Show Preview in the Display menu, or by pressing F9. Your preview should look roughly similar to Figure 7-25. When you learn about filling objects in Chapter 12, you can refine the appearance of skewed background images to create a clearer "shadow" than this one. To turn the preview screen off, press F9 (the toggle key that turns preview on and off).

8. To remove the transformed copy of the object so that only the unaltered original remains, click on the copy to select it and press Del.

TIP: CorelDRAW! has included the option of setting the right mouse button to toggle between the editing window and full-screen preview. If you want to do this, select the Mouse option from Preferences in the Special menu and select Full screen preview.

7

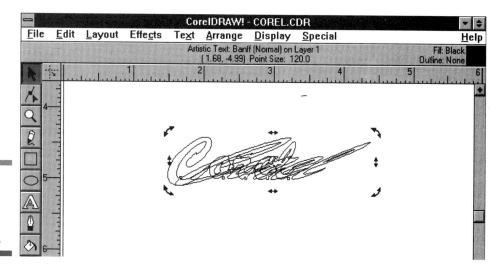

Retaining a copy of an object while skewing
Figure 7-24.

Preview of a
"shadow"
created by
skewing and
resizing an
object
Figure 7-25.

Skewing with the Rotate & Skew Command

If you find the use of keyboard and mouse controls inconvenient, you can perform all of the possible skewing operations using the Rotate & Skew command in the Effects menu. You can select this command when either the normal highlighting box or the rotate/skew highlighting box is visible around a selected object. Perform the following brief exercise to familiarize yourself with using the Rotate & Skew command to skew an object. The COREL.CDR image should still be on your screen in fit-in-window view.

A positive number results in skewing to the left; a negative number in skewing to the right.

1. Set the viewing magnification to 1:1 and click once on the text string to select it.

2. Select the Rotate & Skew command from the Effects menu. The Rotate & Skew dialog box appears.

3. First, skew the text object horizontally. Enter a number in the Skew Horizontally numeric entry box. You can enter a number either by scrolling in increments of 5 degrees or by clicking on the numeric entry box and typing in a number in increments of 1/10 of a degree. Only values between –75 and 75 degrees are valid.

4. If desired, click on the Leave Original check box to make a copy of the original object as you rotate it.

5. Select OK to exit the dialog box and see the results of your settings. When you are finished, select Undo to return the original object to its former angle (and erase the copy, if you have made one).

6. Select the Rotate & Skew command from the Effects menu once more. This time, enter a number in the Skew Vertically numeric entry box. You can adjust this value in the same way that you adjusted the Skew Horizontally value in step 3.

7. Select OK to exit the dialog box and see the results of your settings. When you are finished, select Clear Transformations from the Effects menu to return the original object to its former angle.

Repeating a Transformation

CorelDRAW! stores the most recently performed transformation in memory until you quit the current session. You can save design and drawing time by automatically repeating your most recent stretch, scale, rotate, or skew operation on a different object or set of objects. Just remember that the second object, the one on which you wish to repeat the transformation, must exist on the screen *before* you perform the transformation the first time. If you perform a transformation and then create another object and try to repeat that transformation on it, nothing happens. Perform the following brief exercise to see how this feature can work for you.

1. With the COREL.CDR file open and in actual size viewing magnification, select the Ellipse tool. Now draw a long narrow ellipse to the right of the "Corel" text string at about 5 1/2 inches on the horizontal ruler.

2. Press the [Spacebar] to activate the Pick tool. Select the "Corel" text string and then start to drag the lower-right boundary marker downward and to the right. Leave a copy of the original by using the [+] key or by clicking the right mouse button, as described earlier in this chapter. Then use the [Ctrl] key to help you scale the text string to 200 percent.

3. Select the ellipse that you drew next to the text string.

4. Select the Repeat Stretch command from the Edit menu or press the shortcut keys [Ctrl]-[R]. CorelDRAW! scales the ellipse to 200 percent, leaving a copy of the original, as shown in Figure 7-26. If the objects

7

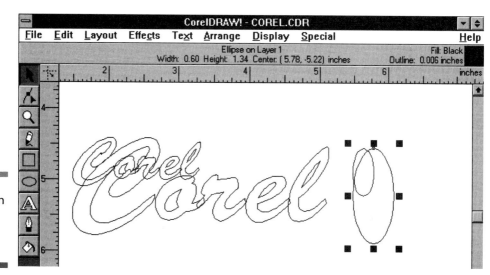

Repeating a
transformation
on a different
object
Figure 7-26.

extend beyond your viewing window, adjust viewing magnification to fit-in-window.

5. Select New from the File menu to clear the screen. Do not save any changes to your work.

You have seen how stretching, scaling, rotating, and skewing objects can lead to creative ideas for advanced designs. Continue practicing some of the techniques you have learned and see what original ideas you can come up with on your own. Chapters 16 and 17 will expand on these and other techniques and provide additional stimulation for your imagination.

CORELDRAW! 4

C H A P T E R

COREL DRAW! 4

8

SHAPING LINES, CURVES, RECTANGLES, AND ELLIPSES

The power to reshape any object to the limits of the imagination is at the very heart of CorelDRAW!. Using the Shaping tool, you can change any type of object into an image that can showcase your creativity.

The Shaping tool, the second tool in the CorelDRAW! toolbox, allows you to change the underlying shape of an object. Although the Pick tool, in transformation mode, allows you to resize, rotate, or skew an object, it leaves the fundamental shape of the object intact. When you edit an object with the Shaping tool, however, it becomes something quite different from what you originally drew.

You can apply the Shaping tool to all object types: lines and curves, rectangles and squares, ellipses and circles, text, and pixel-based (bitmap) graphics. Shaping functions for text and bitmap graphics, however, are part of a broader range of editing functions that apply specifically to those object types. You will find information specifically about shaping text in Chapter 9, and about shaping curves to fit traced bitmaps in Appendix C. This chapter covers techniques for shaping lines, curves, rectangles, and ellipses.

About the Shaping Tool

The Shaping tool performs several different functions, depending on the kind of object to which it is applied. You take advantage of the most powerful capabilities of the Shaping tool when you use it to edit curves, but it has specific effects on other object types as well.

When you are working with lines and curves, the Shaping tool is at its most versatile. You can manipulate single curve points (nodes) interactively, move single or multiple curve segments, control the angle of movement, and add or delete curve points in order to exercise greater control over the degree of curvature. You can break apart or join segments of a curve and change one type of node into another. You can even convert curves to straight lines and back again.

When you apply the Shaping tool to rectangles and squares, you can round the corners of a rectangle and turn rotated, stretched, or skewed rectangles into near-ellipses and circles. When you apply the Shaping tool to ellipses and circles, you can create pie-shaped wedges or arcs. If these shaping options for rectangles and ellipses seem limited, you will be pleased to learn that you can convert any object in CorelDRAW! to curves—and then proceed to apply the most advanced shaping techniques to it.

Selecting with the Shaping Tool

You must select an object with the Shaping tool before you can edit it. CorelDRAW! allows you to select only one object with the Shaping tool at a time. Although the Shaping tool affects each type of object in a different way, the basic steps involved in editing are similar with all object types. To select an object for editing, follow these steps:

1. Activate the Shaping tool by clicking on it or by pressing [F10]. The pointer changes to a thick arrowhead as soon as you move it away from the toolbox and toward the page area.

2. If the object you want to work with is already selected, its nodes enlarge in size automatically as soon as you select the Shaping tool, and the highlighting box around the object disappears. The number of nodes varies, depending on the object type and (in the case of curves) the way your hand moved when you drew it. If the object you want to work with is not selected, click on any part of the object's outline with the arrowhead pointer. Enlarged nodes appear on the object, while the status line shows the object type and information about the nodes on the object. If the selected object has multiple nodes, the first node appears larger than the others, as in the example in Figure 8-1. The first node is the one closest to where you started drawing the object. Often this is the farthest to the left on lines and curves, the one at the top left corner in rectangles, and at the topmost point on ellipses.

3. Refer to the chapter that covers your object type for more help on how to edit the shape of that object.

If multiple objects are selected when you activate the Shaping tool, CorelDRAW! automatically deselects all of them, and you must select a single object to edit with the Shaping tool. If you try to apply the Shaping tool to grouped objects, the outlines of the objects become dotted, and your mouse actions have no effect. The only time you can edit more than one object simultaneously is when you *combine* the objects prior to selecting the Shaping tool. You will see examples of editing combined objects in the "Shaping Lines and Curves" section of this chapter.

8

To deselect an object that you are editing with the Shaping tool, either click on the outline of a different object or select another tool from the CorelDRAW! toolbox.

Selecting an object with the Shaping tool

Figure 8-1.

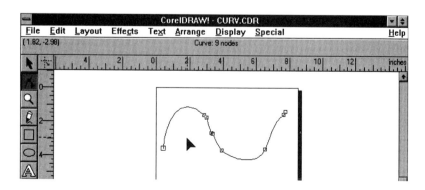

The following sections show you how to use the Shaping tool to edit specific types of objects. These sections follow the order of the drawing tools in the CorelDRAW! toolbox: lines and curves, rectangles, and ellipses.

Shaping Lines and Curves

The Shaping tool is at its most powerful when you use it to edit a curve. Ways in which you can reshape a curve include moving, adding, or deleting nodes, changing node shape, breaking nodes apart or joining them together, and manipulating the control points that define the shape of a curve segment.

You can use the Shaping tool to manipulate both nodes and curves.

You may recall that every object in CorelDRAW! has nodes, which appear when you first draw an object and become enlarged when you select it with the Shaping tool. Nodes on a curve (shown in Figure 8-1) are the points through which a curve passes, and each node is associated with the curve segment that immediately precedes it. Control points that appear when you select a single node with the Shaping tool determine the curvature of the node and of the curve segments on either side of it. (You will learn more about control points later in this chapter.)

Your options for shaping straight lines with the Shaping tool are much more limited than for curves; lines have no angles of curvature and, therefore, no control points that you can manipulate. When you edit a line segment with the Shaping tool, you can only move the nodes to stretch or diminish the length of the line segment. In the course of creating and editing a complex curve object, however, you often need to fuse curve and line segments, change curves into lines, or turn lines into curves. The Shaping tool allows you to do all of these things, and so a discussion of shaping both kinds of freehand objects belongs together.

Selecting a Line or Curve

You must select a line or a curve with the Shaping tool before you can begin to manipulate its nodes. The status line provides you with information about the number of nodes in the object.

In the following exercise, you will draw a straight line and a freehand curve and then select each object in turn. Turn off the Snap To Grid option before you begin this exercise.

1. Make certain the rulers are turned on, then activate your Zoom tool and zoom in on the upper half of the page. Now, select the Pencil tool and draw a straight horizontal line across the top half of the window, as shown in Figure 8-2.

2. Below the line, draw a freehand curve in a horizontal "S" shape. Small nodes appear on the curves.

As far as the Shaping tool is concerned, every line has the potential of becoming a curve.

3. Select the Shaping tool. The pointer changes to an arrowhead, and the S-curve is automatically selected, because it was the last object you drew. The nodes of the S-curve increase in size, and the status line displays the number of the nodes in the curve, as shown in Figure 8-2. The number of nodes in your curve may differ from the number in the figure. Notice that the node where you started drawing the curve is larger than the others.

4. To deselect the S-curve and select the line, simply click on any point of the line with the Shaping tool. Only two nodes appear on the line, one at each end. Again, the node where you started drawing is the larger. The status line displays the message, "Curve: 2 nodes," as shown in Figure 8-3.

5. Clear the screen by selecting New from the File menu. Do not save your work.

Your next step in shaping a selected line or curve is to select one or more of its nodes.

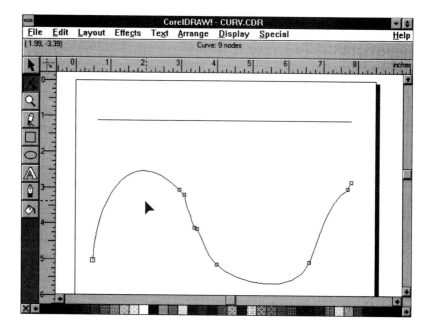

8

Displaying the number of nodes in a curve

Figure 8-2.

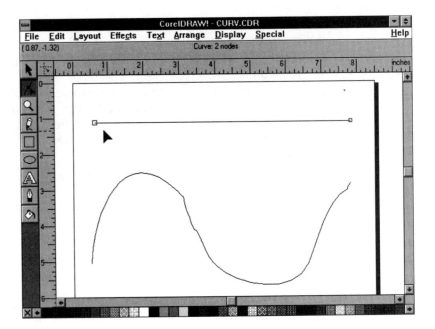

Displaying the
number of
nodes in a line
Figure 8-3.

Selecting Nodes of a Line or Curve

Although you can shape only one curve or line at a time, you can select and
shape either single or multiple nodes. The shaping options available to you
depend on whether you select one node or several. You can reshape a single
curve node interactively in one of two ways: by dragging the node itself or
by dragging the control points that appear when you select the node.
Moving a node stretches and resizes the associated curve segment(s) but does
not allow you to change the angle of curvature. Dragging the control points,
on the other hand, allows you to change both the angle of curvature at the
node and the shape of the associated curve segment(s). When you select
multiple nodes, you can move only the nodes, not their control points; as a
result, you reshape all of the selected segments in the same way.

In general, you should select single nodes when you need to fine-tune a
curve, and multiple nodes when you need to move or reshape several
segments in the same way without changing their angle of curvature.

The exercises in the following sections guide you through the available
techniques for selecting nodes in preparation for moving or editing them.
Along the way, you will become familiar with the different types of nodes
that CorelDRAW! generates and how they indicate the shape of a particular
curve.

TIP: Nodes of a straight line segment are always cusp nodes and contain no control points. They become important only when you begin adding or deleting nodes or changing a line into a curve. You will concentrate on working with curves in the next few sections.

Selecting and Deselecting Single Nodes and Identifying Node Type

When you click on a single curve node, the status line provides information about the type of node you have selected. There are three node types: cusp, smooth, and symmetrical. Their names indicate what will happen when you drag the control points to reshape a curve. In the following exercise, you will practice selecting and deselecting single nodes.

1. Using the Pencil tool, at actual size (1:1) magnification and with Edit Wireframe turned on, draw a curve object that looks roughly like Figure 8-4. The object should have sharp curves, gentle curves, and some in between. Don't worry if it doesn't look exactly like Figure 8-4.

2. Select the Shaping tool. If the curve object was selected when you clicked on the Shaping tool, it should remain selected. If your curve object is not selected, click anywhere on its outline. The status line indicates that this curve object contains 21 nodes (yours may be different).

3. Click on the node at the bottom of the half circle on the selected curve object. The node becomes a black-filled square, and two control points, tiny black rectangles connected to the node by dotted lines, pop out, as shown in Figure 8-5. (You will also see a control point extending from nodes on either side of the selected node.) The message "Selected node: Curve Cusp" appears on the status line. "Cusp" refers to the node type,

8

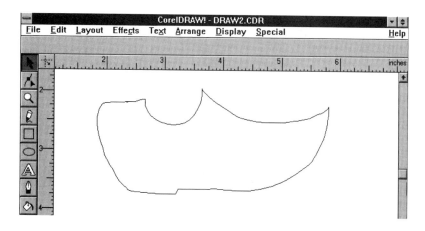

The curve object at 1:1 magnification
Figure 8-4.

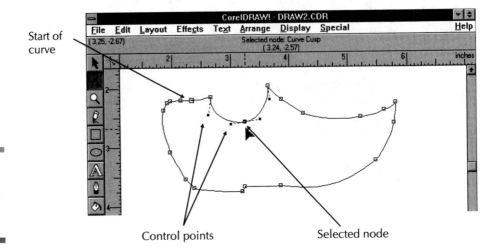

Start of curve

Control points   Selected node

**Selecting a
single node
and displaying
control points
Figure 8-5.**

which you will learn about shortly. Depending on how you drew this curve, your status line may display "Selected node: Curve Smooth." This is another type of curve and does not matter at this point.

4. Click on each node in turn to select it and deselect the previous node. Each time you select a node, control points pop out, and the status line tells you what type of node you have selected. Notice that some of the nodes are cusp nodes, while others are smooth.

5. Leave this object on the screen for the next exercise.

The names of the three different types of nodes that CorelDRAW! generates when you draw lines and curves—cusp, smooth, and symmetrical—describe both the curvature at the node and, in the case of curve objects, the way you can shape the node. Straight lines contain only cusp nodes, while curves can contain all three node types.

✦ **Cusp nodes** Cusp nodes occur at the end point of a line or curve or at a sharp change of direction in a curve. When you edit the control points of a cusp node, you can alter the curvature of the segment that precedes the node without affecting the segment that follows it.

✦ **Smooth nodes** Smooth nodes occur at smooth changes of direction in a curve. When you edit a smooth node, you alter the shape and direction of both the segment preceding and the segment following the node. The curvature of the two segments remains identical in the number of degrees, however.

✦ **Symmetrical nodes** Symmetrical nodes occur where the segments preceding and following the node curve in identical ways. (Symmetrical nodes occur less frequently than other node types in freehand drawing, but you can change any node type to symmetrical using the Node Edit roll-up, which you will learn about in a moment.) When you edit a symmetrical node, you alter the shape and direction of the curve segments before and after the node in identical ways.

You can always change the node type by using the Node Edit roll-up window, as you will see shortly. But you can also control whether the majority of nodes you generate during the freehand drawing process are smooth or cusped. To generate mostly cusped nodes (and create more jagged curves), select the Curves option from the Preferences command in the Special menu. Then set the Corner Threshold option in the Preferences-Curves dialog box to 3 pixels or lower. To generate mostly smooth nodes and create smoother curves, set the Corner Threshold option to 8 pixels or higher.

You will become familiar with techniques for moving control points in a moment. First, finish the next section to learn how to select more than one node at a time.

8

Selecting and Deselecting Multiple Nodes

You select multiple nodes with the Shaping tool in the same way that you select multiple objects with the Pick tool, using either (Shift) or the marquee technique. When multiple nodes are selected, you do not have control points to shape your object. You can only move the nodes as a group and reshape their associated curve segments by dragging the lines. Review the selection techniques in the following brief exercise.

1. Select the node that the mouse pointer is aimed at in Figure 8-5. While pressing and holding (Shift), select a node to the left and to the right of the first node. The nodes turn dark but display no control points, and the status line changes to show the total number of nodes you have selected.

2. Deselect the node farthest to the right in the selected group by holding (Shift) and clicking on the node with the Shaping tool. The other nodes remain selected.

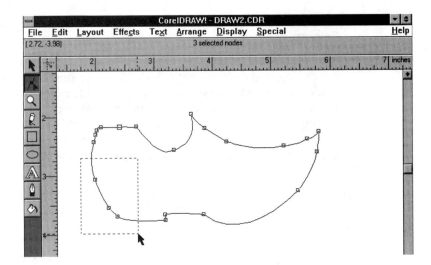

Selecting
multiple
nodes with the
marquee
Figure 8-6.

3. Deselect all of the selected nodes by releasing ⬚Shift⬚ and clicking on any
white space. The curve object itself remains selected for further work
with the Shaping tool, however.

4. Select the three nodes at the lower-left side of the object by drawing a
marquee around them, as shown in Figure 8-6. The selected nodes turn
dark after you release the mouse button, and the status line tells you
how many nodes you have selected.

5. Deselect one node at a time using ⬚Shift⬚ and the mouse button, or deselect
all of the nodes by clicking on any other node or on any white space.

6. When you are finished, clear the screen by selecting New from the File
menu. Do not save the changes.

Now that you are familiar with how to select nodes, you are ready to begin
editing a curve object. You can edit a curve by moving nodes and control
points interactively or by selecting options in the Node Edit roll-up window.

Moving Nodes and Control Points

You can reshape a curve interactively in one of two ways: by moving one or
more nodes or by manipulating the control points of a single node. You can
move any number of nodes, but in order to work with control points, you
can select only one node at a time.

You move nodes when your aim is to stretch, shrink, or move the curve
segments on either side of a node. The angle of curvature at selected nodes
doesn't change as you move them, because the control points move along

with the nodes. The end result of moving nodes is a limited reshaping of the selected area of the curve object.

The way you move control points is determined by the type of node you select.

In general, your best strategy when reshaping curves is to move the nodes first. If just repositioning the nodes does not yield satisfactory results, you can fine-tune the shape of a curve by manipulating the control points of one or more nodes. When you drag control points to reshape a curve, you affect both the angle of curvature at the node and the shape of the curve segment on one or both sides of the node. The effects of this kind of reshaping are much more dramatic.

Try the exercises in each of the following sections to practice moving single or multiple nodes, manipulating control points, and constraining node movement to 90-degree increments.

Moving a Single Node

To move a single node, you simply select the curve and then select and drag the node in the desired direction. In the following exercise, you will draw a waveform curve, select a node, and move the node to reshape the curve.

1. To prepare for the exercise, make sure that the Snap To Grid and Show Rulers options are turned off. Check to see that all the settings in the Curves option of the Preferences command are at 5 pixels. (This will result in curves with a fairly even distribution of cusp and smooth nodes.) Set viewing magnification to an actual size (1:1) ratio.

2. Select the Pencil tool and draw a waveform curve similar to the one in Figure 8-7. Don't be concerned if your curve is shaped a little differently.

3. Select the Shaping tool and then select a node near the crest of one of the curves. Elongate this curve by dragging the node (not the control

8

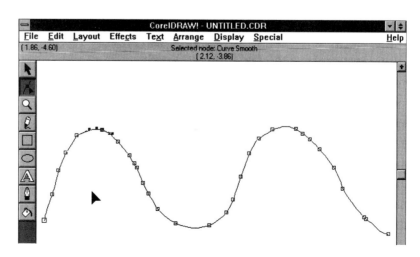

Drawing a
waveform
curve
Figure 8-7.

points) upward and to the right, as shown in Figure 8-8. As you begin to move the node, the status line provides information about *dx* and *dy* coordinates, the distance you have traveled, and the angle of movement relative to the starting point. Release the mouse button when you are satisfied with the stretch of your curve.

4. Select Undo from the Edit menu to return the curve to its original shape. Leave this curve on the screen for now. You can use it to move multiple nodes in the next exercise.

Moving Multiple Nodes

There are many cases in which you might choose to move multiple nodes instead of a single node at a time. You might move multiple adjacent nodes, for example, if you need to reposition an entire section of a curve at one time. Or you might select nonadjacent nodes and move them all in the same direction for special design effects. Whatever the case, all you need to do is select the nodes and drag them.

1. Using the mouse button and (Shift), select one node near the beginning of your waveform curve and one near the end. Again, do not be concerned if the nodes in your curve are in different positions from the nodes in the figure. The process of freehand drawing is so complex that two people rarely produce the same results.

2. Drag one of the nodes downward and to the right. Even though the two selected nodes are separated by several others, they move at the same angle and over the same distance, as shown in Figure 8-9.

3. Release the mouse button when you are finished. Select Undo from the Edit menu to return the curve object to its former shape.

Moving a
single selected
node
Figure 8-8.

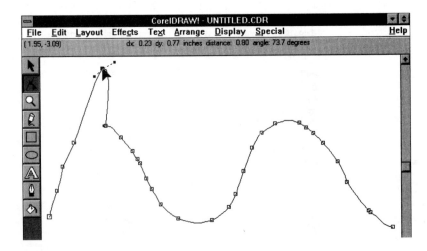

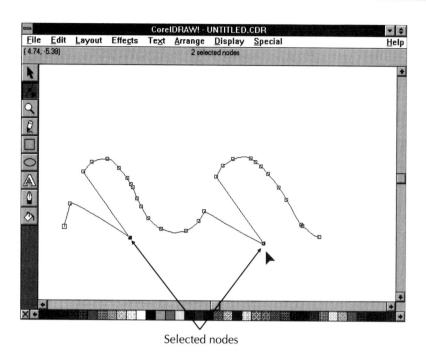

Moving
multiple
selected nodes
Figure 8-9.

Selected nodes

If you prefer to draft even the most "creative-looking" freehand curves with
precision, you may wish to exercise greater control over the angle at which
you move nodes. The next section will show you how to move nodes with
precision.

Constraining Node Movement to 90-Degree Angles

You have the option of moving nodes and their associated curve segments in
increments of 90 degrees relative to your starting point. You use the now
familiar Ctrl key to achieve this kind of precise movement.

1. Select the same two nodes you worked with in the preceding section,
   press and hold Ctrl, and drag one of the nodes to the left. At first the
   two nodes do not seem to move at all; then they "snap" at a 90-degree
   angle from their starting point. The status line in your window reflects
   this precise angle of movement, as in Figure 8-10.

2. Release the mouse button when you reach the desired angle. Select New
   from the File menu to clear the curve from the screen. Do not save your
   changes.

What if you have moved one or more nodes every which way, but you are
still not satisfied with the shape of the curve segments on either side of the

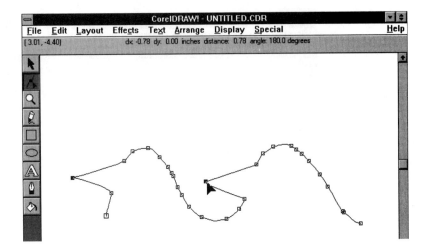

Moving
multiple
nodes by
increments of
90 degrees
Figure 8-10.

node? In the next section you will fine-tune your curves by manipulating the control points of a node.

Moving Control Points

By moving one or both control points of a node, you can control the shape of a curve segment more exactly than if you move just the node itself. The effect of moving control points varies, depending on the type of node—cusp, smooth, and symmetrical. Figure 8-11 (a through d) illustrates this difference.

The control points of cusp nodes are not in a straight-line relationship to one another. This means that you can move one control point and change the shape of one curve segment at a time, without affecting the other associated segment. The control points of smooth nodes, on the other hand, are in a straight line relative to one another. If you move one control point of a smooth node, you affect the curvature of both line segments at once, though not to the same degree. Finally, the control points of a symmetrical node are at an equal distance from the node. When you move one control point of a symmetrical node, the curvature of both associated curve segments changes in exactly the same way. Your waveform curve may not have a symmetrical node; due to the steadiness of hand required, symmetrical nodes rarely occur naturally in freehand drawing. You can practice moving the control points of smooth and cusp nodes, however, by following the steps in the next exercise.

1. Select the Pencil tool and draw a curve similar in shape to the one in Figure 8-11a. Don't be concerned if your curve has a slightly different shape. You should draw part of the curve with a steady hand and part

using more jagged movements. This will result in a more even distribution of node types.

2. Select individual nodes on your waveform curve until you find a cusp node. You will know what type of node you have selected by referring to the status line. Do not use one of the end nodes, however; end nodes have only one control point, because only one curve segment is associated with them. If you can't find a cusp node, redraw the curve to be more jagged, and then try again. For your reference, Figure 8-11a shows the waveform curve with no nodes selected and no control points moved.

3. Drag one of the cusp node's control points outward from the node as far as you can without extending it beyond the viewing window. The farther you drag the control point outward, the more angular the curvature of the associated segment becomes. Note also that the curve segment associated with the other control point does not change.

4. Drag the other control point in any direction you choose. The angle of the second curve segment associated with the node changes, independently of the first one. If you have extended both control points independently, you will see a sharp change in curve direction at the node, as in Figure 8-11b.

5. When you have practiced this technique to your satisfaction, find and select a smooth node. Notice that the two control points of this node lie along a straight line.

8

6. Drag one of the control points of the smooth node outward from the node, and notice that the other control point is not affected. Now move the control point sideways. The curvature of *both* of the segments associated with the node changes. As shown in the example in Figure 8-11c, however, the two segments do not change in exactly the same way. (The curvature of your curve segments may differ from those in the example, depending on how you drew the curve.)

7. If your waveform curve contains a symmetrical node, select it and move one of the control points outward. Notice that when you move one control point the opposite one moves the same amount. If you do not have a symmetrical node, observe the curvature changes in Figure 8-11d. The curvature of these segments changes by an identical angle.

8. When you have practiced with control points to your satisfaction, activate the Pick tool and press Del to delete the waveform curve from the screen.

Now you have a working knowledge of all the possible interactive techniques for moving and editing curves. It may sometimes happen, however, that even these techniques are not enough to shape your curve just a.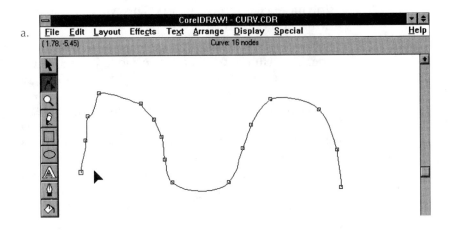

b.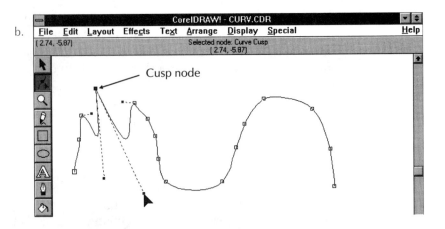

c.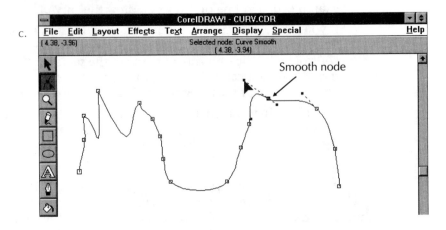

Moving
control points
of a cusp,
smooth, and
symmetrical
node
Figure 8-11.

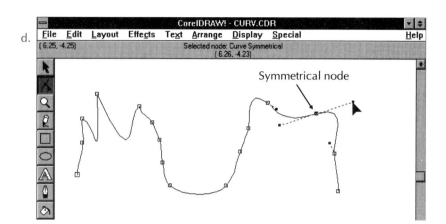

d.

Symmetrical node

Moving
control points
of a cusp,
smooth, and
symmetrical
node (*cont.*)
Figure 8-11.

as you want it. What if you are working with a cusp node and just can't
make it smooth enough? Or what if you need an additional node at a certain
point to enable you to fit a curve to an exact shape? For these and other
node-editing tasks, you can call up the Node Edit roll-up window.

Editing Nodes

Selecting a curve object and moving nodes and control points are interactive
operations that you can perform without invoking a command or menu.
There are times, however, when you need to *edit* the nodes themselves: to
change their shape or to add nodes, delete nodes, join nodes, or break them
apart. Editing nodes requires that you use the Node Edit roll-up window that
pops up when you double-click on a node or on the curve segment that
immediately precedes it.

Working with the Node Edit Roll-Up

To call up the Node Edit roll-up window, double-click on any node or on
any curve or line segment. The roll-up can be moved around the work space
to keep it away from your work by clicking and holding on the title bar and
dragging it to a clear area. It will remain in the window until you close it as
you would any window. You can also click on the roll-up arrow and keep
only the title bar visible. The Node Edit roll-up is shown in Figure 8-12.

The commands in the Node Edit roll-up allow you to add or delete selected
nodes, join two nodes or break them apart, convert lines to curves and
curves to lines, change the node type, or align sets of nodes on two separate
subpaths. Not all commands are available to you for every node, however.
Some commands appear in gray and are unavailable, depending on the

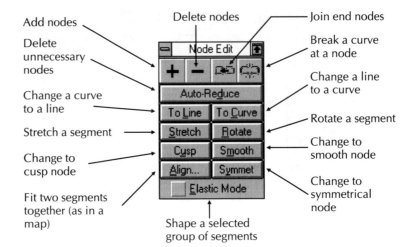

Add nodes
Delete unnecessary nodes
Change a curve to a line
Stretch a segment
Change to cusp node
Fit two segments together (as in a map)
Delete nodes
Join end nodes
Break a curve at a node
Change a line to a curve
Rotate a segment
Change to smooth node
Change to symmetrical node
Shape a selected group of segments

The Node Edit roll-up window
Figure 8-12.

number and type of node(s) you have selected. See the section pertaining to the relevant Node Edit command for more information about why particular commands are not available at certain times. To select commands that are available, click once on the command name.

TIP: When you double-click on a node or segment, you can select a command from the Node Edit roll-up by typing the underlined letter in the command name.

Except for the Align command, as soon as you select any command from the Node Edit roll-up, CorelDRAW! immediately applies the command to the selected node(s).

Try the exercises in each of the following sections to become familiar with using the commands in the Node Edit roll-up.

Adding a Single Node

In CorelDRAW!, a first node can never have a node or segment preceding it.

If you have moved nodes and manipulated control points to the best of your ability but still cannot achieve the exact shape you want, consider adding one or more nodes where the curvature seems most inadequate. You can add a single node or multiple nodes, depending on how many nodes are selected, but if the node you have selected is the first node of a line or curve, you cannot add a node to it.

The following exercise furnishes the necessary steps to add a single node between two existing nodes. Set the viewing magnification to actual size

(1:1). Make sure that the Snap To Grid is turned off for this and all of the other exercises in the "Editing Nodes" portion of this chapter.

1. Select the Pencil tool and draw a waveform curve similar to the one shown in Figure 8-13a. Activate the Shaping tool to select the curve for editing. Your curve may contain a different number of nodes than the one in Figure 8-13a.

2. Double-click with the Shaping tool on either the node or the curve segment immediately in front of the point at which you want to add a node. The Node Edit roll-up appears in your work space. Click on the title bar and drag it to a clear area, as shown in Figure 8-13b.

3. Select the Add (+) command from the Node Edit roll-up. A new node appears on the curve or line segment preceding the selected node, as shown in Figure 8-13c. If you first deselect all of the selected nodes by clicking on any white space, you can move this added node or manipulate its control points just like any other node.

4. Leave the current curve on your screen for use in the next exercise.

TIP: Independent of whether the Node Edit roll-up is open, you can add a new node by clicking where you want the node with the Shaping tool and pressing + on the numeric keyboard.

8

Adding Multiple Nodes

If you add a node to a straight line segment instead of to a curve, and then move the new node, you effectively add a new line segment.

Perform the following brief exercise to add several nodes to a curve at one time. The technique is the same as when you add a single node, except that multiple nodes must be selected.

1. You should have a waveform curve on your screen in actual size magnification along with the Node Edit roll-up and the Shaping tool, as you left them in the last exercise.

2. Select two or more nodes using either ⌗Shift⌗ or the marquee method. You will add nodes in front of each of these selected nodes. All of the squares that mark the selected nodes blacken, as in Figure 8-14a.

3. Click on the Add (+) command of the Node Edit roll-up. A new node appears in front of each of the selected nodes, as shown in Figure 8-14b. If you deselect all of the currently selected nodes and then select the added nodes individually, you can manipulate their control points to suit your drawing needs.

4. Again, leave the current curve on your screen for use in the next exercise.

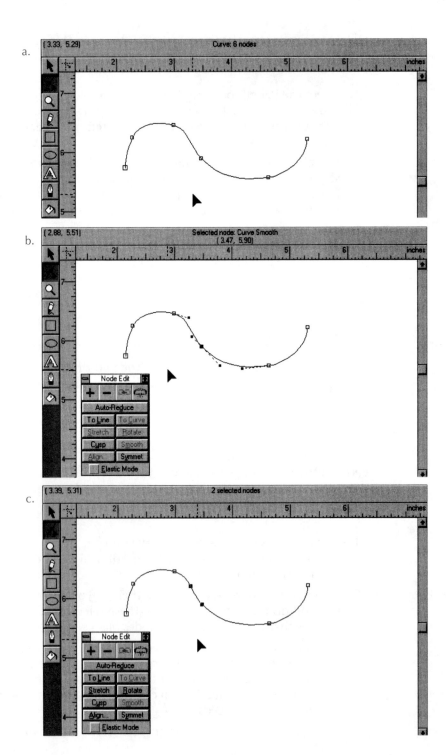

Adding a
single node
Figure 8-13.

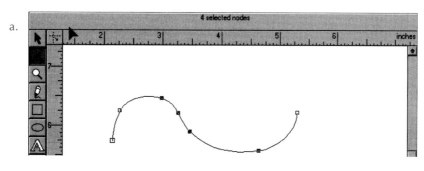

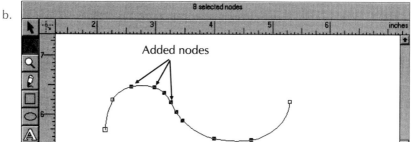

The counterpart to adding nodes is deleting them. Continue with the next
sections to practice deleting one or more nodes from a curve.

8

Deleting a Single Node

When you draw freehand curves, it is often difficult to control mouse
movement completely. Changing the Freehand Tracking, Corner Threshold,
and AutoJoin settings in the Preferences-Curves dialog box may help, but
erratic movements while you execute a curve still can produce occasional
extraneous nodes. You can smooth out an uneven curve quickly and easily
by deleting single or multiple extraneous nodes.

CAUTION: Always delete nodes with caution. Deleting a node at random,
without checking to see if other nodes are nearby, can radically alter the
shape of a curve in ways that are not always predictable.

Perform the following exercise to delete a single node from a curve.

1. You should still have a waveform curve on your screen in actual size
    magnification, and the Node Edit roll-up and Shaping tool should be
    selected as you left them in the last exercise.

2. Using the Shaping tool, click on the node that you want to delete, as in Figure 8-15.

3. Select the Delete (-) command from the Node Edit roll-up. CorelDRAW! deletes the node that you selected and redraws the curve without it. The shape of your redrawn curve could be quite different from your original one; just how different it is depends on the location of the node you selected for deletion.

4. Keep the curve on your screen for the next exercise.

Keep in mind that if you delete one of the end nodes of a curve, you delete the associated curve segment as well. If you delete either node of a straight line, you delete the entire line in the process.

TIP: As a shortcut to deleting a node, you can select a node and press ⌐Del¬ instead of invoking the Node Edit roll-up.

Deleting Multiple Nodes

You can delete multiple nodes as well as single nodes from a curve, as long as all of the nodes you want to delete are selected. To delete multiple nodes follow these steps:

1. With the previous curve still on the screen, select the nodes you want to delete, using either ⌐Shift¬ or the marquee method; Figure 8-16a shows three nodes selected. Keep in mind that if you delete an end node, you will delete the associated curve segment along with it.

2. Select the Delete (-) command in the Node Edit roll-up. CorelDRAW! immediately deletes the selected nodes from the screen and redraws the curve without them, as in Figure 8-16b. The shape of the curve can

Deleting a
single node
Figure 8-15.

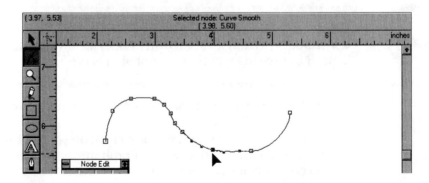

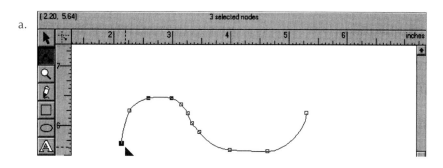

a.

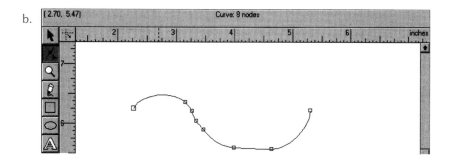

b.

Deleting
multiple nodes
Figure 8-16.

change subtly or dramatically between node positions; the extent of the
change depends on the original positions of the selected nodes.

3. Keep the curve for the next example.

You have learned to add and delete nodes when you need to reshape a curve
more than the existing nodes allow. Sometimes, though, you may want your
curve to flatten to the extent that you need to replace a curve segment with
a straight line segment. You accomplish this by converting one or more
curve segments to straight lines.

Converting a Single Curve Segment to a Straight Line Segment
CorelDRAW! allows you to convert curve segments to line segments. Before
you convert a curve to a line, you need to be able to identify whether a
selected segment is a curve or a straight line. Some important guidelines to
follow are

✦ A curve segment has two control points; a straight line segment has none.

✦ When you select the segment or its node, the status line indicates
whether the segment is a line or curve.

✦ The shape of the *selected* node identifies the type of segment that precedes it. A black fill in the selected node signifies a curve segment, while a hollow selected node signifies a straight line segment.

Perform the following exercise to gain experience in converting a single curve segment into a straight line segment.

1. Again, use the curve from the previous example. If your curve has only a couple of nodes left, add a node using the steps you recently learned, so that there is a curve segment that is a good candidate for a straight line.

2. Using the Shaping tool, click on a segment or node of a curve that you want to convert to a straight line, as in Figure 8-17a.

3. Now, select the To Line command in the Node Edit roll-up. The two control points related to the selected curve disappear, and the curve segment becomes a straight line segment, as shown in Figure 8-17b. You can reposition, stretch, or shorten this line segment by using the Shaping tool to drag the nodes at either end.

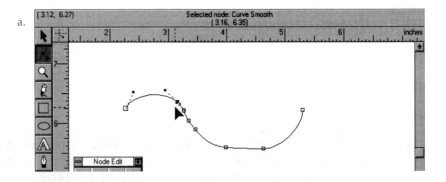

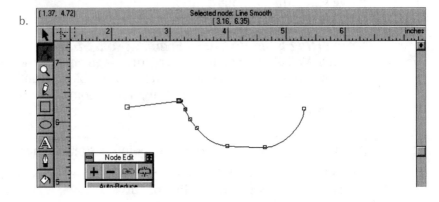

Converting a curve segment to a straight line segment

Figure 8-17.

Converting Multiple Curve Segments to Straight Line Segments

If you want a curve object in your drawing to be more angular, you can change its appearance by selecting multiple nodes or curve segments and converting them to straight lines. To convert multiple curve segments to straight line segments, follow these steps:

1. Press ⌈Alt⌉-⌈Backspace⌉ to undo making the curve segment a line and, if necessary, add a node so that there are at least two curve segments that are good candidates for straight lines.

2. Select the curve segments or nodes you want to convert to straight lines, using either ⌈Shift⌉ or the marquee technique.

3. Select the To Line command in the Node Edit roll-up. The selected curve segments convert to straight lines, and all associated control points are eliminated (straight lines do not include control points). The object becomes much more angular, as in Figure 8-18. You can now reposition, stretch, or shrink any or all of the line segments by dragging the node(s).

If your object consists of angular line segments but you want to give it much smoother contours, you can convert line segments to curves. The next section shows you how.

Converting Single and Multiple Straight Line Segments to Curve Segments

With CorelDRAW! you can convert straight line segments to curve segments through the Node Edit roll-up. Before you convert a line segment to a curve segment, you need to identify whether a selected segment is a straight line or a curve. If you are uncertain about identifying segments, review the guidelines in the previous section before you proceed. Now try the following exercise:

1. Using the Shaping tool, click on one of the straight line segments you just created, or on the *second* node of a straight line. (If you select the first node

Converting
multiple curve
segments to
line segments
Figure 8-18.

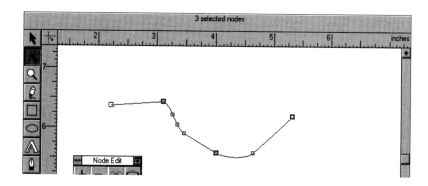

of the line segment, you will not be able to convert it to a curve.) The To Curve button is now available to you, as shown in Figure 8-19.

2. Select the To Curve command button in the Node Edit roll-up. CorelDRAW! turns the selected straight line segment into a curve, causing two control points to appear on the line segment. Drag these control points to change the segments to the shape you want.

   You can turn several straight line segments into curve segments at the same time, as long as they are part of the same object. You simply select the several segments and choose the To Curve command in the Node Edit roll-up. The selected straight line segments convert to curve lines. On the surface, the segments do not appear to have changed. However, if you deselect all nodes and then select any one of the converted nodes, two control points appear. You can reshape the peaks and valleys like any other curve.

3. Experiment with converting all the line segments to curves, and prove to yourself that now you really are working with curves.

Another group of commands in the Node Edit roll-up allows you to change the type of single or multiple nodes. These commands—Cusp, Smooth, and Symmetrical—are the subject of the next several sections.

Cusping Single or Multiple Nodes

Cusp nodes are especially useful for rendering an abrupt change in direction at a node.

When you work with a cusp node, you can move either of its control points independently of the other. This makes it possible to independently control the curvature of both of the curve segments that meet at the node, without affecting the other segment.

The following exercise shows you how to turn a single smooth or symmetrical node into a cusped node.

1. Using the Shaping tool, click on the node you want to cusp. Select any node except an end node; CorelDRAW! designates all end nodes as cusp nodes.

2. When the Cusp command button is enabled, as in Figure 8-20a, click on it. The appearance of the curve does not change. However, if you manipulate the control points of this node, as shown in Figure 8-20b, you will find that you can move one control point without affecting the curve segment on the other side of the node.

   When you want a curve object to have a relatively jagged appearance, but you do not want to turn your curves into straight lines, the next best solution is to change multiple smooth or symmetrical nodes into cusp nodes. You can then shape the cusp nodes to create a more angular appearance for the affected portions of the object.

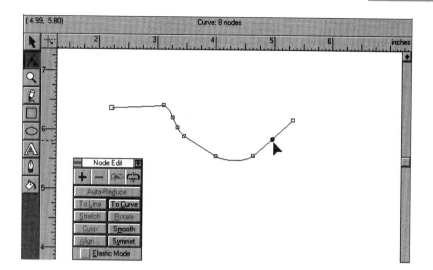

Converting a
line segment
to a curve
segment
Figure 8-19.

a.

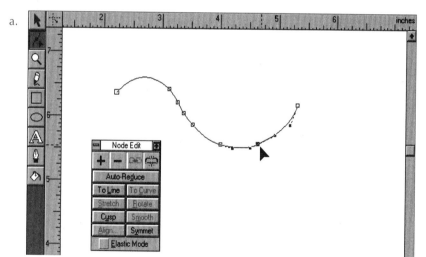

8

b.

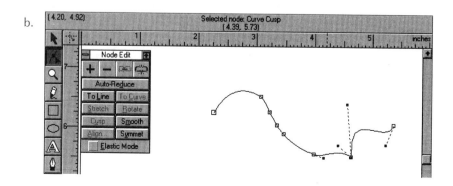

Cusping a
single node
Figure 8-20.

3. Save your drawing, using File, Save As. You can call it anything you like, for example, CH8-20. You will use it again in a later exercise.

4. Select New from the File menu to clear the screen.

In the next section, you will become familiar with changing cusped or symmetrical nodes into smooth nodes.

Smoothing Single or Multiple Nodes

In the previous section, you saw that cusp nodes are desirable when you want to create a rougher, more jagged appearance for an object. When you want to make an object's curves smoother, however, you seek out the cusped nodes and turn them into smooth ones.

A smooth node can be defined as a node whose control points always lie along a straight line. A special case exists when a smooth node is located between a straight line and a curve segment, as in Figure 8-21a. In such a case, only the side of the node toward the curve segment contains a control point, and you can only move that control point along an imaginary line that follows the extension of the straight line. This restriction maintains the smoothness at the node.

In the next exercise, you will convert a single cusp node that lies at the juncture between a straight line and curve segment into a smooth node.

1. Set viewing magnification to actual size (1:1), select the Pencil tool, and then draw a straight line connected to a curve segment, as shown in Figure 8-21a. Remember to double-click at the end of the line segment to attach it to the curve segment automatically.

2. Activate the Shaping tool. Your curve object may not include the same number of nodes as the one in this figure, but that is not important for the purpose of this exercise.

3. Using the Shaping tool, click on the cusp or symmetrical node that you want changed to a smooth node. Use the line cusp node next to the curve segment, as in Figure 8-21b. In the Node Edit roll-up, click on the Smooth command button. The curve passing through the selected node is smoothed, like the one in Figure 8-21c, and will remain smooth when you move either the node itself or its control point. The straight line segment does not change, of course.

4. Select New from the File menu to clear the screen.

To smooth multiple nodes, you simply select multiple nodes and then repeat the steps for smoothing a single node.

a.

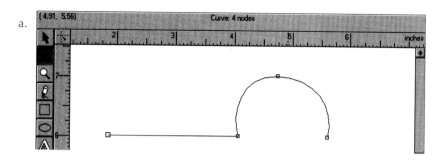

b.

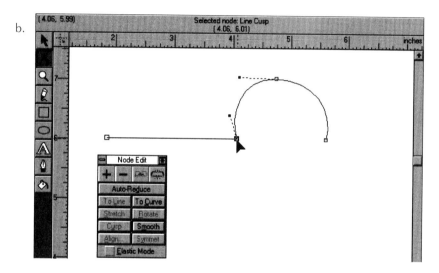

8

c.

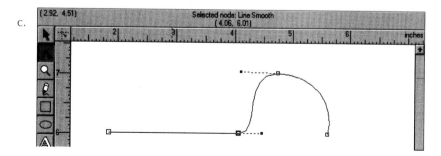

Smoothing a
single cusp
node
Figure 8-21.

Go on to the next section to learn how you can turn smooth or cusp nodes
into symmetrical nodes and how this affects the drawing process.

Making Single or Multiple Nodes Symmetrical

Symmetrical nodes share the same characteristics as smooth nodes, except that the control points on a symmetrical node are equidistant from the node. This means that the curvature is the same on both sides of the symmetrical node. As with the smooth nodes, when you move one of the control points, the other control point moves. In effect, symmetry causes the two control points to move as one.

Another important point to remember is that you cannot make a node symmetrical if it connects to a straight line segment. The node must lie between two curve segments in order to qualify for a symmetrical edit.

Perform the following brief exercise to convert a single cusp node to a symmetrical node, using the drawing with a cusp node that you saved earlier.

1. Open the cusp node drawing you saved in the earlier exercise. If its filename (possibly CH8-20.CDR) appears in the lower part of the File menu, you can open it by clicking on the name.

2. Set viewing magnification to 1:1, activate the Shaping tool, and select the curve.

3. Find a cusp node that you want to make symmetrical and then click on it, as shown in Figure 8-20b.

4. Click on the Symmet command button. The selected node is now converted to a symmetrical node and CorelDRAW! redraws the curve so that it passes through the node symmetrically, as in Figure 8-22.

5. Move the control points of this node until you have a satisfactory understanding of how symmetrical nodes work.

Making multiple nodes symmetrical is just as easy as making single nodes symmetrical. The only difference is that you select more than one node at a time, using either Shift or the marquee method.

Making a cusp
node
symmetrical
Figure 8-22.

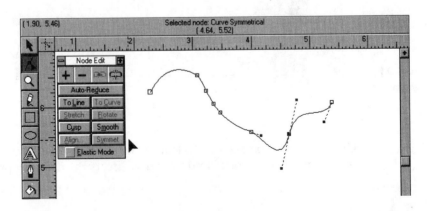

In the next sections, you will find out how to master the art of breaking nodes apart and joining them together—and why you might choose to do so.

Breaking Curves at Single or Multiple Nodes

Breaking a node involves splitting a curve at a selected node, so that two nodes appear where before there was one. Although you can move the separate sections of a broken node as though they were separate curves, CorelDRAW! does not regard them as separate. These split segments actually constitute different subpaths of the same curve. Breaking a node into separate subpaths gives the impression of spontaneous freehand drawing, yet it allows you to keep separate "drawing strokes" together as one object. Breaking curves at the nodes is also useful when you need to delete a portion of a curve and leave the rest of the curve intact.

Keep in mind that you cannot break a curve at an end node, because there is no segment on the other side of the end point with which to form a separate subpath.

When you break a node, it becomes two unconnected end nodes. You are then free to move either end node and the entire subpath to which it is connected. The two subpaths remain part of the same object, however, as you can see when you select either subpath with the Pick tool. In the following exercise, you will use the curve from the last exercise, break it at a single node, and then observe how CorelDRAW! handles the two resulting subpaths.

8

1. With the Shaping tool, select a node on the side of the curve and click on it.

2. Click on the Break command button in the Node Edit roll-up. The single node splits into two nodes. Since they are close together, however, the change is not visible until you begin to move the new end nodes.

3. Move the left end point away from the subpath to the right, as shown in Figure 8-23, and then deselect both nodes. The object itself remains selected for editing, and the status line informs you that the curve now has two subpaths.

4. Press the (Spacebar) to activate the Pick tool. Notice that the Pick tool treats these two subpaths as a single curve object, even though they look like separate curves.

   There may be times when you want to make subpaths into truly separate objects, so that you can manipulate and edit them independently. As the next step shows, CorelDRAW! provides a means for you to turn the subpaths into independent curves.

5. To separate the two subpaths into two truly distinct objects, leave the Pick tool active and then select the Break Apart command from the

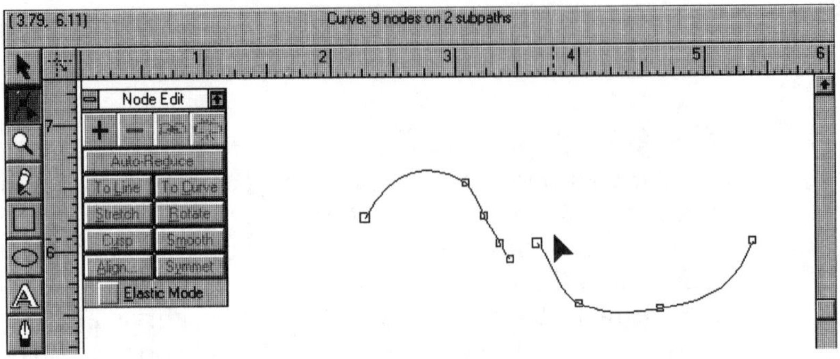

Breaking a
curve at a
single node
Figure 8-23.

Arrange menu. This command is available only when multiple subpaths
of a single curve object are selected.

6. Select New from the File menu to clear the screen. You do not need to
resave the cusp node drawing that began this last exercise.

In this brief exercise, you have seen some applications for breaking a curve at
a node. For example, you can create two separate objects from a single
object, or create separate subpaths that move together as a single object.

> **CAUTION:** If you break a closed curve object at a node, you will not be
> able to fill the object with a color or pattern.

When you break a curve at multiple nodes, the result is multiple subpaths,
which still remain part of the same object.

The reverse of breaking curves apart is joining them together. In the next
section, you will find out when you can and cannot join nodes together, as
well as some reasons why you might want to do so.

Joining Nodes

By now, you have probably noticed that the Join command is rarely
available for selection in the Node Edit roll-up. You can join nodes only
under very specific conditions.

✦ You can join only two nodes at a time, so only two nodes can be selected.

✦ The two nodes must be either end nodes of the same object or end nodes
of separate subpaths of the same object.

✦ You cannot join an end node of an open curve to a closed object, such as an ellipse or a rectangle.

When might you want to join two nodes, then? The two chief occasions are when you want to close an open path, or when you want to make a single continuous curve from the two separate paths.

Closing an Open Path   An open path, as you will recall from your previous freehand drawing experience in CorelDRAW!, is a curve object with end points that do not meet and which therefore cannot be filled with a color or pattern. To prevent open paths, you can set the AutoJoin option in the Preferences dialog box to a higher number and make it easier for end nodes to snap together as you draw. There are still times, however, when you might choose to join end points after drawing an open curve. In such cases, you use the Join command in the Node Edit roll-up. The following exercise presents a situation in which you could use the Join command to make a drawing process easier.

1. Set magnification to actual size (1:1). Select the Pencil tool and draw a more or less oval curve, but do not finish the curve—stop drawing at a point close to where you started it. See Figure 8-24 for an example.

2. Activate the Shaping tool to select this curve object and then select both of the end nodes using the marquee or Shift key technique. You can see that the Join command button in the roll-up (second from right in top row) is now available to you, as shown in Figure 8-24.

3. Click on the Join command button in the Node Edit roll-up. CorelDRAW! redraws the curve as a closed path. You can then fill this path with a color or pattern, as you will learn in Chapter 12.

4. Select New from the File menu to clear the screen.

8

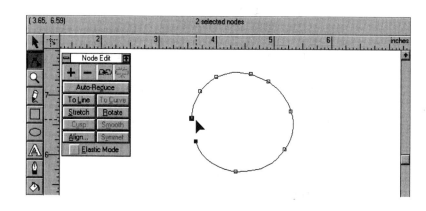

Joining nodes
to close an
open path
Figure 8-24.

It is easy to close an open path with the Shaping tool. Joining nodes from separate curves, however, is a bit trickier.

Joining Separate Subpaths (Combined Objects)   You can also join two end nodes if they are on two subpaths of the same curve. The two subpaths then become a single, continuous curve segment. A special case exists when you have two separate curve objects (not two subpaths of the same curve) and want to make them into a single curve. Knowing that you cannot join nodes from two separate objects, what do you do? Your best option is to combine the curves using the Pick tool and the Combine command in the Arrange menu. Even though the curves continue to look like separate objects, from the standpoint of CorelDRAW! they become two subpaths of a single curve. You can then join their end nodes to unite the subpaths.

1. Select actual size magnification and, with the Pencil tool, draw four separate curve segments, as shown in Figure 8-25a.

2. With the Pick tool, draw a marquee around all four curve segments to simultaneously select them. If you have a problem with this, choose Select All in the Edit menu.

3. From the Arrange menu, select Combine to make a single, broken curve out of the four segments. The result of this is shown in Figure 8-25b.

4. With the Shaping tool, select the curve. Then select one of the three pairs of end points to be joined, double-click on either of the two end points to open the Node Edit roll-up, if it is not already on the screen, and click on the Join button. Select each of the two remaining pairs and click on the Join button for each of them. The result is a single continuous curve, as shown in Figure 8-25c.

TIP: The only trick to this is to first combine the curve segments with the Pick tool and the Arrange menu before trying to join the segments with the Shaping tool.

5. Select New from the File menu; do not save the changes you have made.

Going through this process is a good way to familiarize yourself with all the steps involved in both joining nodes and breaking nodes apart. Perhaps you have some new ideas for using the Join command in some of your own drawings.

Aligning Nodes

If you want two objects to share a common edge, like two pieces in a puzzle, the Align command in the Node Edit roll-up can accomplish it for you. The

a.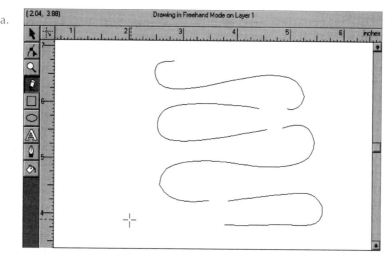

b.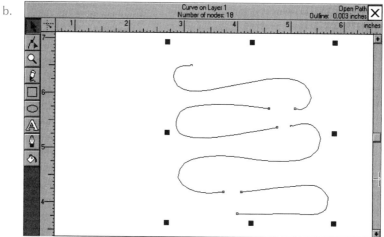

c.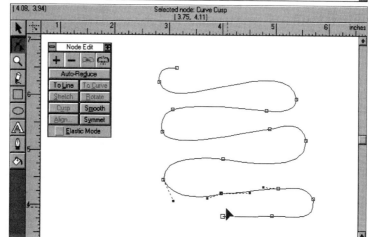

Joining nodes
to form a
continuous
curve

Figure 8-25.

two objects must first be combined with the Arrange menu, and you must add or delete nodes until there are the same number of nodes in each object in roughly the same location. Once you have completed aligning the two objects, you can break them apart.

Objects can be aligned vertically or horizontally, and they can literally share a common border through the alignment of their control points. If you want to superimpose one object on the other, you align them both horizontally and vertically *and* align their control points. The latter—aligning the objects all three ways—is the default alignment.

You can experiment with the Align command in the Node Edit roll-up in the following exercise.

1. At actual size (1:1) magnification and with the Pencil tool, draw two curve objects similar to those shown in Figure 8-26a. (Edit Wireframe should be turned on.)

TIP: Use the Spacebar to toggle between the Pick tool and any other tool you are using at the time.

2. With the Pick tool, draw a marquee around both objects to select them. Then, from the Arrange menu, select Combine.

3. With the Shaping tool, add or delete nodes until the two objects have the same number of nodes on the "mating" side, in roughly the same position as shown in Figure 8-26a.

4. For each pair of nodes you want to align, perform these steps with the Shaping tool in the order given:

   a. Select the node to be *realigned* (moved).

   b. Press Shift and select the node to *align* to (move to).

   c. Click on the roll-down arrow to open the Node Edit window.

   d. Select Align. The Node Align dialog box will open, as shown here:

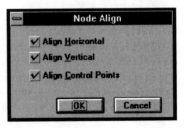

e. Click on OK to accept the default choice of all three options, which will superimpose the nodes and align the control points. You might have to tweak the control points slightly where the moved segment has reversed direction.

When you have aligned all of the node pairs you want to align, you should have a single curve segment shared by both objects, whose shape is the same as the object to which you aligned, as shown in Figure 8-26b.

5. With the Pick tool, select the combined object and choose Break Apart from the Arrange menu.

6. Click on white space to deselect the combined object and select and drag one of the original objects until you can see the two individual objects again. Now the two objects have a common, although mirror-image, shape on one side, as shown in Figure 8-26c.

7. Select New from the File menu to clear the screen; do not save the changes.

8. You are finished with the Node Edit roll-up for now. Click on its Control-menu box and click on Close.

This concludes your exploration of the techniques for shaping lines and curves. In the remaining sections of this chapter, you will try your hand at shaping rectangular and elliptical objects.

8

Shaping Rectangles and Squares

For interesting distortions, you can stretch, rotate, or skew rectangles and squares before rounding their corners.

The Shaping tool has a specific function when you apply it to rectangles and squares in CorelDRAW!. It rounds the corners of a rectangle, thus creating a whole new shape. The status line keeps track of the radius of the rounded corner as you drag. You can control the degree of rounding either interactively or by using the grid if you want to be exact.

Rounding the Corners of a Rectangle

Complete the following exercise to practice rounding rectangles and squares using the Shaping tool. You will begin by rounding corners interactively; later, you will use the grid to perform the same work.

1. For the beginning of this exercise, make sure that the Snap To Grid and Show Rulers commands are inactive, that Edit Wireframe is turned on, and that you are working in actual size viewing magnification. Then select the Rectangle tool and draw a rectangle of unequal length and width.

a.

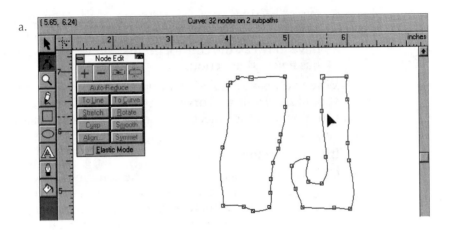

b.

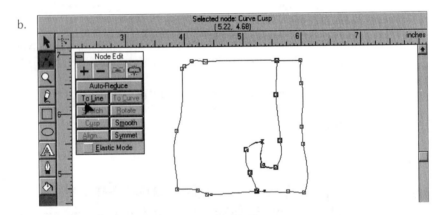

c.

Aligning the
nodes of two
curve objects
Figure 8-26.

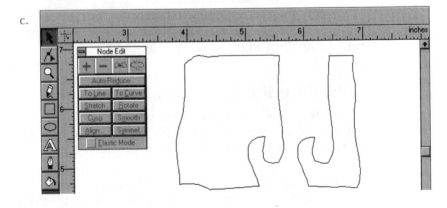

2. Activate the Shaping tool and select a node at one of the corners of the rectangle. As shown in Figure 8-27a, the status line indicates that the corner radius of this rectangle is 0.00 inches. The corner radius helps you measure the degree to which you have rounded the corners of a rectangle or square with the Shaping tool.

3. Position the Shaping pointer at this node and begin to drag the corner slowly toward the next nearest corner. As shown in Figure 8-27b, each corner node separates into two separate nodes, with each node moving farther away from the original corner as you drag. The status line also informs you just how much of a corner radius you are creating. The farther you drag the nodes from the corners, the more the corner radius increases.

4. Continue dragging the mouse until you reach the logical limit of rounding: when the nodes from adjacent corners meet at the sides of the rectangle. At this point, your rounded rectangle has become almost an ellipse, similar to the rectangle shown in Figure 8-27c.

5. Begin dragging the selected node from the middle of the line back to the former corner. As you do so, the corner radius diminishes. You can return the rectangle to its original shape by dragging the nodes all the way back to the corner.

6. Delete the rectangle from the screen, then draw a square and repeat steps 2 through 5. Notice that when you begin with a square and then round the corners to the logical limit, the square becomes a nearly perfect circle rather than an ellipse, as in Figure 8-28.

7. Press ⌈Del⌉ to clear the screen of the square-turned-circle.

8

Although the status line information helps you round corners precisely, you can gain even greater precision using the grid and rulers. The next exercise guides you through the process of rounding corners of a rectangle or square with the help of these aids.

1. Open the Grid Setup dialog box, set the Grid Frequency to 4 per inch, turn on Show Grid and Snap To Grid, and click OK. Turn on Show Rulers if they are not already on.

2. Draw a rectangle 2 inches wide by 1 1/4 inches deep. Activate the Shaping tool and select one of the corner nodes of the rectangle.

3. Drag this corner node away from the corner to round the rectangle. This time, the corner radius changes in precise increments of 1/4 inch because of the grid setting.

a.
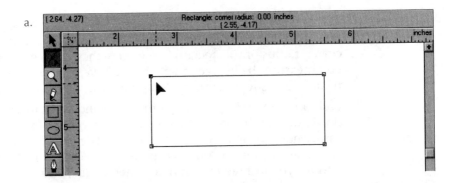

b.
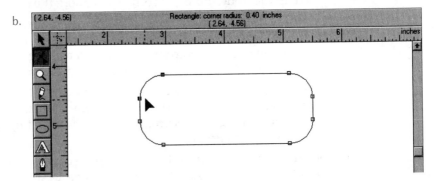

c.
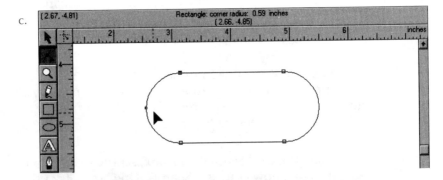

Rounding the
corners of a
rectangle
Figure 8-27.

Rounding the
corners of a
square
Figure 8-28.

4. Draw a square and round its corners. The radius of the square also changes in increments of 1/4 inch.

5. When you have finished experimenting with the rectangle and the square, select New from the File menu to clear the screen.

In the next section, you will see what can happen when you stretch, rotate, or skew a rectangle or square before attempting to round its corners.

Stretched, Rotated, or Skewed Rectangles and Squares

When you transform a rectangle or square by stretching, rotating, or skewing it with the Pick tool and then round its corners, the value of the corner radius may be distorted. The corner radius indicator on the status line is followed by the word "distorted" in parentheses. As Figure 8-29 shows, the final shape of such a rounded rectangle may also be distorted; in extreme cases it can resemble a skewed flying saucer or rotated ellipse. Figure 8-30 shows a skewed square whose corners have been rounded.

Practice this technique on your own and then go on to the next section, where you will find out how to turn a rectangle into a curve so that you can shape it in an infinite number of ways.

Converting a Rectangle to a Curve Object

8

If the shaping options for rectangles or squares seem limited to you, don't worry. You can convert any rectangle or square into a curve object and, from

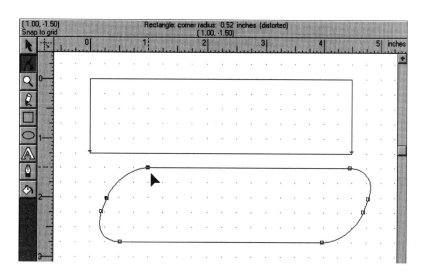

Rounding the corners of a skewed rectangle
Figure 8-29.

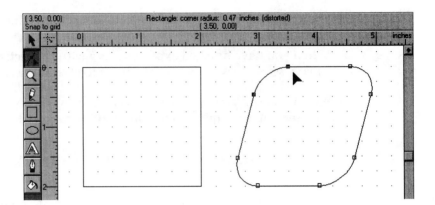

Rounding the corners of a skewed square
Figure 8-30.

that point onward, you can turn a formerly four-cornered object into anything at all. The technique is simple, as you will see in the following brief exercise.

1. Set magnification to actual size (1:1) and make sure Edit Wireframe is turned on in preparation for this exercise.

2. Select the Rectangle tool if it is not selected already and then draw a rectangle of any size or shape.

3. Activate the Pick tool by pressing the (Spacebar), and select the Convert To Curves command from the Arrange menu. The status line message changes from "Rectangle on Layer 1" to "Curve on Layer 1." Note that the new four-cornered "curve" still has the same number of nodes as when it was a rectangle.

4. Activate the Shaping tool and then select and drag one of the nodes in any direction. As the example in Figure 8-31 shows, dragging the node no longer forces the associated line/curve segment to move parallel to the other line segments.

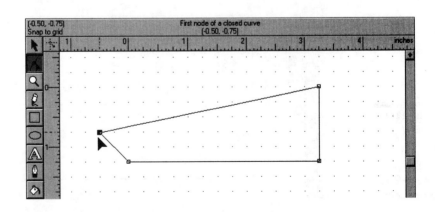

Editing a rectangle that has been converted to curves
Figure 8-31.

5. Continue warping the shape of this rectangle-turned-curve in a variety of ways. For example, you could add nodes, convert line segments to curves, create symmetrical nodes, or even turn the former rectangle into a candy cane or other hybrid object.

6. The object you have been working on should be selected. If not, select it and then press (Del) to clear the screen before going on.

Now that you have mastered the art of shaping rectangles and squares, you are ready to apply the Shaping tool to ellipses and circles for some quite different effects.

Shaping Ellipses and Circles

When you shape ellipses or circles with the Shaping tool, you can create either an open arc or a pie wedge. You can even shift back and forth between these two shapes as you draw, depending on whether the tip of the shaping pointer lies inside or outside the ellipse or circle. You also have the option of constraining the angle of an arc or pie wedge to 15-degree increments.

Creating an Open Arc

The status line provides information about the angle of the arc as you draw.

To turn an ellipse or circle into an arc, you position the tip of the shaping pointer just *outside* of the rim at the node and then drag the node in the desired direction. Make certain that the tip of the pointer remains outside the rim of the ellipse as you drag, or you will create a wedge instead of an arc. Practice creating arcs from both ellipses and circles in the following exercise.

8

1. Turn off the Snap To Grid command if it is active and set the viewing magnification to actual size.

2. Select the Ellipse tool and, by pressing (Ctrl), draw a perfect circle.

3. Activate the Shaping tool to select the circle automatically.

4. Position the tip of the Shaping tool exactly at the node, and then drag the node downward slowly, but just outside the rim of the circle, in a clockwise direction. As Figure 8-32 shows, the single node separates into two nodes, with the second node following your pointer as you drag. If the circle seems to be turning into a pie wedge instead of an arc, the tip of your mouse pointer is inside the rim of the circle. Move it outside of the rim and try again.

Note that the status line provides information about the angle position of the first and second nodes and about the total angle of the arc. This information is based on a 360-degree wheel, with 0 degrees at 12 o'clock, 90 degrees at 9 o'clock, 180 degrees at 6 o'clock, and 270 degrees at 3 o'clock.

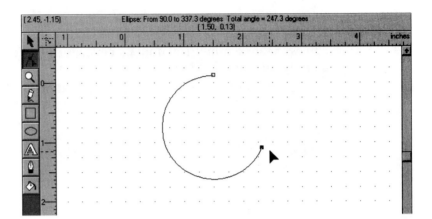

Creating an
arc from a
circle
Figure 8-32.

5. Continue to drag the shaping pointer, but now press and hold the `Ctrl` key as well. The angle of the arc snaps in increments of 15 degrees. Release the mouse button when your arc has the angle you want.

6. Select the Ellipse tool and again draw a perfect circle. Then repeat steps 4 and 5, completing this arc at an approximate 105-degree angle. If you use an ellipse instead of a circle, the "total angle" information on the status line is followed by the message "distorted" in parentheses. This message occurs because CorelDRAW! bases its calculation of an arc on a perfect circle rather than on an ellipse with different height and width. The angle assignments for arcs created from an ellipse are therefore approximate.

7. Press the `Spacebar` to activate the Pick tool and select the newly created arc. Notice that the highlighting box, like the one in Figure 8-33, is much larger than the arc itself; in fact, it seems to surround the now

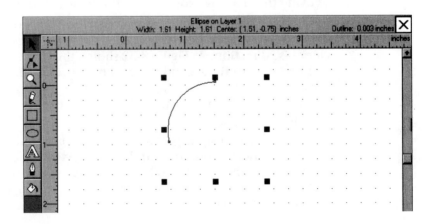

Selecting an
arc for
alignment
purposes
Figure 8-33.

invisible but complete original ellipse. The purpose of this large highlighting box is to make it easy for you to align an arc or wedge concentrically, using the Align command in the Arrange menu. The disadvantage of this large highlighting box is that when you are selecting objects with the marquee, you must make certain that your marquee surrounds the entire highlighting box.

8. Select New from the File menu to clear the screen before going on.

Creating a wedge shape from an ellipse is just as easy as creating an arc, as you will see in the next section.

Creating a Pie Wedge

The only difference between creating an arc and creating a pie wedge is that in the latter case, you position the tip of the shaping pointer *inside* the ellipse or circle as you drag. Perform the following exercise to see the difference for yourself.

1. Set magnification to actual size, select the Ellipse tool, and draw a circle. Activate the Shaping tool to select it for editing.

2. Position the tip of the shaping pointer inside the circle exactly at the node, and then begin dragging the node downward in a clockwise direction. The two nodes separate as before, but this time the circle turns into a shape like a pie missing a piece, suitable for pie charts and wedges, as shown in Figure 8-34.

3. Press and hold (Ctrl) and continue dragging the mouse. The angle of the wedge shape now moves in fixed increments of 15 degrees. Release the mouse button when you have obtained the desired angle.

4. Just as you did with the arc, press the (Spacebar) to activate the Pick tool and select the wedge. Notice the oversized highlighting box once more.

8

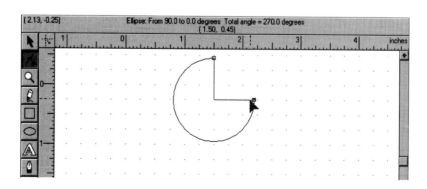

Creating a pie wedge from a circle

Figure 8-34.

Make sure to surround this highlighting box completely whenever you attempt to select a wedge with a narrow total angle.

5. Press Del to clear the screen.

That's all there is to creating arcs and wedges from ellipses and circles. If these shaping techniques are not flexible enough for you, you can always convert the arc or wedge to a curve object, as you will see in the next section.

Converting Ellipses and Circles to Curve Objects

If the shaping options for ellipses and circles seem limited to you, don't worry. You can convert any ellipse, circle, arc, or wedge into a curve object and, from that point onward, you can add and delete nodes, drag nodes and control points, or change node types. In the following exercise, you will create a wedge from a circle, convert the wedge to curves, and then reshape the new curve object into the body of a baby carriage.

1. Select the Ellipse tool and draw an ellipse that is wider than it is high, starting from the upper-left area of the rim and moving downward as you drag.

2. Activate the Shaping tool and position the arrowhead pointer over the node of the ellipse. Drag the node downward, keeping the tip of the shaping pointer inside the rim, and create a wedge with a total angle of about 240 degrees, as shown in Figure 8-35.

3. Press the Spacebar to activate the Pick tool and select the wedge, and then select the Convert To Curves command from the Arrange menu. Notice that because of the shape of the wedge, the new curve object has five nodes, whereas the ellipse had only one node.

4. Reactivate the Shaping tool and drag the node farthest to the right upward and outward, as shown in Figure 8-36. Since the segment next

A wedge created from an ellipse, with a total angle of 240 degrees
Figure 8-35.

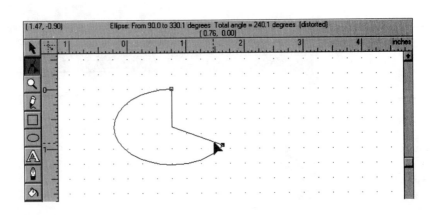

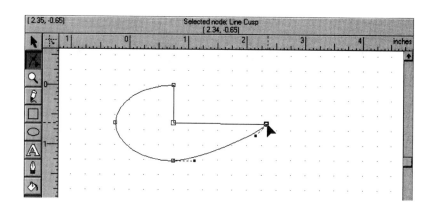

Dragging a
node to form
the top of a
carriage
Figure 8-36.

to this one is a straight line, the selected node has only one control
point. Moving this node upward and outward has the effect of
stretching the straight line.

5. The curvature of the segment associated with the node you just moved
    is not adequate to round out the bottom of the "carriage." To remedy
    this, click on the curve segment where you want the new node and
    press ⊕ on the numeric keypad. A new node appears between the
    selected node and the one below and to the left of it. It's a smooth node
    because of the existing curvature, and because the object originated as
    an ellipse.

6. Select and drag this newly added smooth node downward and to the
    right, until it forms a nicely rounded bottom to the "carriage" body, as
    shown in Figure 8-37.

Perhaps the example in the preceding exercise will stimulate your imagination
to create any number of complex objects from the basic objects available to you
through the drawing tools. The Shaping tool makes it all possible!

8

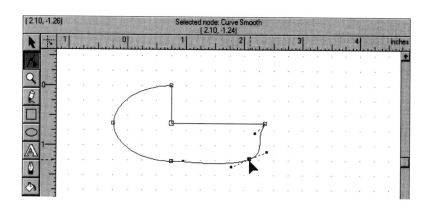

Rounding out
the bottom of
the carriage
Figure 8-37.

CHAPTER

CORELDRAW! 4

SHAPING AND EDITING TEXT

Text can be an important design element, whether you specialize in original art, graphic or industrial design, technical illustration, or desktop publishing. Every choice you make concerning font, style, spacing, alignment, type size, and placement can affect how your intended audience receives your work. You should have the option of editing text attributes at any time, not only when you first enter text on a page.

With CorelDRAW!, you do have that option. Using the

Pick tool and the Shaping tool, you can edit existing text in ways that enhance both its typographic and pictorial value. You already edited text as a graphic element in Chapters 6 and 7 by using the Pick tool to rotate, stretch, scale, skew, and reflect text strings. In this chapter, you will concentrate on editing the *typographical* text attributes (such as font and type size) of individual characters, groups of characters, and complete text strings. You will also learn to customize your text picture even further by converting a text string to a set of curves and then reshaping each curve. The Pick and Shaping tools share these editing functions between them.

Editing Attributes for a Text String

Remember the two ways you selected attributes when you first entered a text string—the Text dialog boxes and the Text roll-up window? You can also use each of these methods to change text attributes that already exist. Do this by clicking in the text string with the Pick tool and then selecting either Edit Text or Text Roll-Up from the Text menu. The changes you make will apply to every character in the text string. To change attributes for selected characters within a text string, you need to use the Shaping tool, as described in the section entitled "Selecting and Editing with the Shaping Tool."

In this first exercise, you will create a short text string that you can use in many different exercises throughout this chapter. Then, you will select the text string and change some of its attributes using the Edit Text command from the Text menu.

1. Set your viewing magnification to actual size. Turn the Show Rulers, Show Grid, and Snap To Grid commands off for this portion of the chapter. Also, ensure you are in full color mode, not wireframe.

2. Pick the Text tool and then select an insertion point midway down the left edge of your viewing window. Type the following text string on three separate lines:

   Doing
   what comes
   naturally

3. Drag across the text to select it and open the Text roll-up.

4. Change the text attributes to Cupertino italic, 65 points, and center alignment; then select Apply.

5. Because you have changed the alignment, some of the text may not appear within viewing range. If this is the case, select the Pick tool and drag the text until it fits within the viewing window, as shown in Figure 9-1.

6. Deselect the text string and save your work in a file named
   DOINWHAT.CDR. Leave the text on the screen for the next exercise.

You can change attributes for a text string as often as desired. However, as
long as you use the Pick tool to select text, any attribute changes you make
will affect the entire text string. If your work requires highly stylized text
designs, where attributes must be decided on a character-by-character basis,
you need to use the Shaping tool.

Selecting and Editing Text with the Shaping Tool

When the Shaping tool is active, you can select any number of characters
within a text string and edit their typographical attributes. Depending on
how you prefer to work, you can edit attributes either interactively, or use
the Artistic Text dialog box, the Text roll-up, or the Character command in
the Text menu. Some of these attributes, specifically, font, style, and type
size, overlap within the two dialog boxes and the roll-up. Or, you can move
letters and adjust spacing and kerning interactively, without using menu
commands, roll-ups, or dialog boxes. If all these adjustments fail to give your
text the desired look, you can gain more editing control by converting text
to curves and then manipulating the nodes and control points.

Before you can edit text attributes on a character-by-character basis, you must first use the Shaping tool to select the text string in which the characters are located. This is similar to selecting a curve object as a prerequisite to selecting one or more of its nodes. After you select a text string, you can select a specific character, multiple adjacent or nonadjacent characters, or all characters in the text string. Practice selecting different combinations of characters in the following exercise.

1. Open the DOINWHAT.CDR text file that you created in the last exercise, if it is not open already. If the Pick tool is active, make sure that the text string is not selected; it should not be surrounded by a highlighting box.

2. Activate the Shaping tool and click once on the outline of any character in the text string. A square node appears at the base of each letter in the text string, and vertical and horizontal arrow symbols appear at the lower-left and lower-right corners of the text string, respectively:

You will become acquainted with the meaning of these symbols in a moment. For now, it is enough to recognize that this change in the text string's appearance indicates that you have selected it for editing with the Shaping tool. The status line shows that you have selected all 23 characters.

3. Select a single character in the text string, the letter "n" in "naturally." Do this by clicking *once* on the node of this character. The status line now contains the message "1 character(s) selected," and the node at the bottom left of the letter turns black, like this:

4. Deselect the letter "n" by clicking anywhere outside the text string. Notice that the string itself remains selected.

5. Select the initial letter of each word. Click once on the node for the "D" in "Doing." Then press and hold the (Shift) key and click on the node for the initial letter of each of the other words. Check the status line to keep track of the number of characters you select.

6. To deselect these characters, either click on any white space, or press and hold (Shift) and click on each selected character node one by one.

7. Select the entire word "Doing" by lassoing its nodes with a marquee:

Your marquee does not have to surround the characters completely, as long as it surrounds the nodes. All the nodes of this word become highlighted after you release the mouse button.

8. Deselect these characters and then draw a marquee that surrounds all of the text string. All of the characters are now selected for editing.

9. Deselect all of the characters by clicking on any white space. Leave the text on the screen, with the text string selected for editing with the Shaping tool, but with no individual characters selected.

You may be wondering, "Why should I bother to select all the characters with the Shaping tool, when I could activate the Pick tool and change attributes for the entire text string?" You can control some attributes that way, but the Character Attributes dialog box offers you even more options for altering the appearance of text. Read on to find out how those additional attributes can enhance the design of text in CorelDRAW!.

The Character Attributes Dialog Box

9

Practically the only thing you can't do with the Character Attributes dialog box is change the characters themselves.

When you use the Character Attributes dialog box, you can control other characteristics of selected characters besides font, style, and point size. You can tilt characters at any angle, shift them up, down, or sideways, or make them into small subscripts and superscripts. In this section, you will learn how to access this dialog box and work with each of the controls in it. As you work through the exercises, you will learn about useful applications for each type of attribute. By the end of the section, you will alter the design of the DOINWHAT.CDR text string substantially.

You can access the Character Attributes dialog box either by double-clicking on a selected character node, or through the Text menu. Any attributes that you alter in this dialog box apply only to the characters you have selected. Make sure, then, that you have selected all of the characters you want to edit before accessing the Character Attributes dialog box.

1. With the Shaping tool active, select the node in front of the letter "n" in "naturally."

2. Access the Character Attributes dialog box in the way that is most convenient for your working habits. If you prefer to use menu commands, select the Character Attributes option from the Text menu. If you like using the mouse best, double-click on any of the selected nodes. The Character Attributes dialog box shown in Figure 9-2 appears.

Take a moment to become familiar with the options available to you in this dialog box and with the significance of each attribute.

Reviewing the Dialog Box

The options in the Character Attributes dialog box in Figure 9-2 allow you to control eight different types of text attributes: font, style, type size and its unit of measure, horizontal shift, vertical shift, character angle, and text placement (superscript and subscript). You are familiar with the first four attributes, but the concepts behind horizontal and vertical shifts, character angle, superscript, and subscript may be new to you. If so, browse through this section to find out more about these attributes.

Horizontal Shift   The Horizontal Shift option controls the distance, in percentage of point size, by which selected characters shift to the right or left of their original location. This unit varies, depending on the font of the selected characters.

Vertical Shift   The Vertical Shift option controls the distance by which selected characters shift above or below their starting location (baseline). CorelDRAW! expresses this distance as a percentage of the point size of the selected characters. This distance is therefore variable, too.

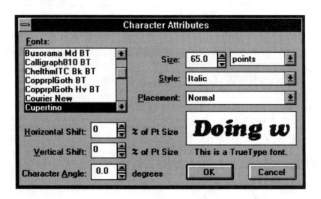

Character
Attributes
dialog box
Figure 9-2.

The baseline is
the imaginary
straight line to
which text is
normally
anchored and
with which it
aligns.

Character Angle   The Character Angle option allows you to tilt the selected characters in any direction and at any angle. You can turn characters upside down, sideways, or anywhere in between.

Superscript and Subscript   The Superscript and Subscript options, available from the Placement drop-down list box, let you place selected characters above or below the rest of the text, respectively. Superscript text bottom-aligns with the imaginary line at the top of surrounding text (for example, the "2" in $E = mc^2$). Subscript text top-aligns with the baseline of surrounding text (for example, the "2" in H_2O).

TIP: The values that display in the Character Attributes dialog box depend on how you invoke the dialog box. If you access this dialog box by double-clicking on a character, you will see the settings assigned to that character, even if you have selected other characters at the same time. If you call up the dialog box by selecting the Character command, the values displayed correspond to the first character in the selected group.

You can move between options in the Character Attributes dialog box either by using the mouse or by pressing [Tab] or [Shift]-[Tab] and the cursor keys. Of course, using the mouse is much simpler!

In the next five sections, you will have the opportunity to redesign text imaginatively, using all of the options in the Character Attributes dialog box.

9

Editing Font and Style

The fonts are
from the
CD-ROM that
comes with
CorelDRAW!. If
you have not
moved them
to your hard
disk, do so
now.

In the following exercise, you will assign a different font and/or style to each letter in the word "naturally." You selected the first letter of the word before entering the dialog box, so you will alter the letter "n" first of all.

1. Select the Aardvark font in the Font list box and then select OK. Your text string redisplays on the screen, but now the letter "n" looks quite different from the surrounding letters.

2. Double-click on the character node of the "n" once more. When the dialog box appears this time, it shows the current font of the *selected* character or characters. (See the tip in the previous section.) Select Cancel to exit the dialog box.

3. Select each of the other letters in the word "naturally" in turn. Assign fonts and styles to them in the following order: Paradise normal,

Frankfurt Gothic bold italic, Cupertino normal, Renfrew normal, Switzerland italic, Unicorn normal, USA black italic, and Banff normal. When you are finished, the word "naturally" displays an interesting patchwork of fonts:

4. Save the changes you have made by pressing Ctrl-S, and leave your work on the screen for the next exercise.

Go on to the next section to apply different point sizes to the letters whose fonts and styles you have already altered.

Editing Type Size

When you changed fonts for each letter in the word "naturally," you left the type sizes unaltered, yet the letters do not appear to be the same size. You have probably guessed by now that different fonts have different heights and widths for the same point size. The point size is only a consistent way to measure the size of characters *within* a given font.

In the following exercise, you will make the letters in "naturally" closer to one another in actual or physical size.

1. Using the Shaping tool again, double-click on the character node of the first letter "a" in "naturally." When the Character Attributes dialog box appears, change the point size for this letter to 140 and then select OK. Even though you have more than doubled its point size, this letter only now approximates the height of its neighbors. Point size is measured from the baseline of one line to the baseline above it and is not necessarily a measure of the actual type. (You may need to scroll your screen downward to see the word "naturally.")

2. In the same way, select the first letter "l" and change its type size to 75 points.

3. Finally, select the letter "y" and change its point size to 90. Now, all of the letters seem more uniform in height and size:

naturally

4. Save your work by pressing Ctrl-S, leaving the text string on screen.

To edit the word "naturally" so that it conveys a sense of a more natural state, you can shift some of the characters up or down relative to the baseline and move others sideways. In the next exercise, you will practice moving individual characters.

Horizontal and Vertical Shift

When you shift selected characters horizontally, you move them to the right or left of their starting positions, causing them to overlap with other characters on the same line. You can use this technique to convey a sense of being rushed or crowded, or simply to adjust spacing between letters precisely. When you shift characters vertically, they fall above or below the baseline, which can create a feeling of spontaneity or excitement.

In the next exercise, you will shift some of the characters in the word "naturally" to enhance the sense of spontaneity and a natural look in the text.

1. Activate the Shaping tool, if it isn't already, and then double-click on the character node for the letter "n" in the word "naturally" to enter the Character Attributes dialog box. Set Horizontal Shift to –25 percent of the point size and then select OK. Because you set the value to a negative number, the letter shifts to the left of its original position.

2. Select the character node for the next letter "a" and set Vertical Shift to 20 percent of point size. When you select OK, the position of the letter shifts above the baseline.

3. Now select the following letters in turn, changing the shift settings for each. Change the Vertical Shift of the "r" to –25 percent, the Vertical Shift of the second "l" to 10 percent, and both the Horizontal Shift and Vertical Shift of the "y" to 25 percent. Notice that a negative value for Vertical Shift causes the selected character, "r," to reposition itself below the baseline. The resulting text should now look like this:

9

4. Save your changes and leave this text on the screen.

So far, you have edited attributes for one letter at a time. In the next section, you will select a group of characters and practice positioning them as superscripts and subscripts.

Creating Superscripts and Subscripts

Perform the following exercise to simulate a superscript and subscript.

1. With the Shaping tool select the character nodes of all of the letters in the word "come" except the letter "c." Double-click on the node in front of "o" to access the Character Attributes dialog box.

2. Click on the Placement down arrow, click on Superscript, and then select OK. The selected letters have become small and appear as a superscript to the letter "c," like this:

$$c^{omes}$$

3. Select the Undo command in the Edit menu to return the selected characters to their original position.

4. Select the same characters again and return to the Character Attributes dialog box by double-clicking on the "o" node. This time, choose Subscript in the Placement drop-down list box. When you select OK, the letters display as a subscript to the letter "c."

5. Press Alt-Backspace or Ctrl-Z to return the selected characters to their original position.

In the next section, you will practice tilting the characters in the word "naturally" to different angles.

Editing Character Angle

You can tilt selected characters at any angle using the Character Angle setting in the Character Attributes dialog box. Values between 0 and 180 degrees indicate that you are tilting the characters above an imaginary horizon, in a counterclockwise direction. Values between 0 and –180 degrees indicate that you are tilting the characters below an imaginary horizon, in a clockwise direction. At a 180-degree angle, the characters are upside down. Practice adjusting character angle in the following exercise.

1. With the Shaping tool active, press and hold Shift while selecting the character nodes of the letter "n," the letter "u," and the letter "y" in the word "naturally." Double-click on one of these nodes to access the Character Attributes dialog box. Set Character Angle to –15 degrees and

then select OK. The selected characters now appear tilted toward the right.

2. Deselect these three letters and select the letter "t," the second letter "a," and the second letter "l." Double-click on one of these nodes to access the Character Attributes dialog box. Set Character Angle to 15 degrees and then select OK. These characters appear tilted toward the left. The word "naturally" now seems to fly off in all directions:

3. Save your changes and then select New from the File menu to clear the screen.

This concludes the tutorial on the use of the settings in the Character Attributes dialog box. No doubt you have come up with a few creative ideas of your own while practicing on these exercises. When you are ready to proceed, continue through the next portion of this chapter, where you will learn some convenient ways to kern text and adjust spacing interactively.

9

Kerning Text Interactively

Kerning, simply defined, is the art of adjusting the space between individual pairs of letters for greater readability. There are many possible letter pair combinations in the 26 letters of the English alphabet, but most font manufacturers provide automatic kerning for only a few hundred commonly used pairs. Occasionally you will see too much or too little space between adjacent letters. You can kern these letter pairs manually by moving one of the letters subtly to the right or left.

Using kerning as a design element can enhance the power of your message. For instance, you will draw more attention to your text when you kern letters to create special effects, such as expanded letter spacing in selected words of a magazine or newspaper headline.

The exercises in this section offer more extreme examples of kerning than you are likely to find in most text, but they will help you become familiar with the concept of kerning. Follow the steps in each exercise to learn how to kern single or multiple characters. Integrated within the exercises is information on using constraint and alignment techniques to kern more easily and precisely.

Kerning Single Characters

The following exercise lets you practice adjusting spacing between any two text characters. As you work through the steps, you will learn how to ensure that characters align properly with the surrounding text after you move them. Before starting the exercise, adjust viewing magnification to actual size. Turn on Show Grid, Show Rulers, and Show Status Line; set both the Horizontal and Vertical Grid Frequency to 8 per inch; and set the Vertical Grid Origin to 11 inches. Retain these settings for both exercises on kerning.

1. Select the Text tool and then select a text insertion point at the 1 1/2-inch mark on the horizontal ruler and the 4 1/2-inch mark on the vertical ruler.

2. Type the word **K e rning** in upper- and lowercase letters. Leave a space after the "K" and another after the "e." Press Enter to begin a new line and type the word **T e x   t** on the second line. Leave one space after the first "T," one space after the "e," and two spaces after the letter "x."

3. Select the Pick tool and open the Text roll-up if it isn't already. Set the justification to None, the type size to 72 points, and the font to Bodnoff, and click on Apply.

4. After the text string appears, as in Figure 9-3, select the Shaping tool. Since the text string was the last object you created, the Shaping tool selects it automatically. A node appears next to each character in the text string; vertical and horizontal spacing control handles appear at each end of the last line of the text string.

You need to bring the letter "e" in "Kerning" much closer to the "K" and the letters "rning" closer to the "e." You do this by dragging the "e" and the "rning" with the Shaping tool. Since you don't want to change the vertical positioning, you can prevent this by pressing Ctrl while you drag. Make sure Snap To Grid is turned off or you will not be able to get the exact positioning described in the following steps.

TIP: You can press and hold Ctrl while moving the characters, thereby constraining the text to the nearest baseline. Be sure to release the mouse button before you release Ctrl to maintain proper alignment.

Text in need
of kerning
Figure 9-3.

5. Press and hold Ctrl and then press and hold the left mouse button on
   the node in front of the letter "e." When you begin to move the mouse,
   the pointer turns into a four-headed arrow. Use the status line's *dx*
   indicator to help you drag the letter 0.69 inches to the left, as shown in
   the following illustration. A dotted outline of the letter follows the
   pointer as you drag. When you release the mouse button, the letter
   itself appears in this location.

9

6. If the "e" is not aligned as you want it, snap this letter back to its
   original position by selecting the Straighten Text command in the Text
   menu, and then repeat step 5.

The Straighten Text command erases any previous kerning information, so
use it only when you want to return text to its original location. If you forgot

to press Ctrl while dragging the "e," you can select the Align To Baseline command, also in the Text menu. When you accidentally position a character above or below the baseline, this command forces the character to align with the baseline again. Unlike the Straighten Text command, the Align To Baseline command does not erase any previous kerning information.

7. Save your kerned text as KERN1.CDR and leave it on the screen for the next exercise.

TIP: If you require a high degree of precision in the placement of kerned text, zoom in on the character(s) you want to move.

Kerning Multiple Characters

In practice, your most common use for moving and kerning multiple characters within a text string will be to move the remaining characters of a word closer to another letter that you have already kerned. However, you can select and reposition any group of characters, including nonadjacent characters, to another location in the same way.

1. With the KERN1.CDR file displayed in an actual size viewing magnification and the Shaping tool active, draw a marquee around the letters "rning."

2. Press and hold Ctrl , and then point on the node for the letter "r" and drag the mouse –1.43 inches to the left. Refer to the status line for assistance. All the letters in the selected group follow, as shown in the following illustration. If the selected characters do not line up with the adjoining text when you release the mouse button, review step 6 in the previous exercise. You may want to use both the Align To Baseline and Straighten Text commands. Deselect the letters "rning" when you have them in the desired location.

3. Use (Shift) to select the "e" and the second "t" in "Text." Click on the node in front of the letter "e" and drag .77 inches to the left, as shown here:

Both selected letters should move together across the screen without disturbing the "x." After you release the mouse button, the letters "e" and "t" will appear as shown here:

4. As you can see, the letters "x" and "t" still are not close enough to the "e." Experiment by moving these two letters on your screen until the text string appears normal.

5. Save your changes to the file by pressing (Ctrl)-(S). Then select New from the File menu to clear the screen.

Kerning is not the only text attribute that you can adjust interactively with the Shaping tool. In the next section, you will learn how to adjust spacing between characters, words, and lines for an entire selected text string.

9

Adjusting Spacing Interactively

There are two ways to edit inter-character, inter-word, and inter-line spacing of existing text in CorelDRAW!. The first way, as you will recall, is to select the text string with the Pick tool and then open the Artistic Text dialog box using either (Ctrl)-(T) or the Edit Text option in the Text menu. Using this method, you can click on the Spacing command button in the Artistic Text dialog box and set spacing in the subdialog box provided. You enjoy the advantage of precision but experience the disadvantage of going through a series of additional steps.

If you prefer to work more spontaneously, CorelDRAW! offers you an interactive method of spacing as well. This method involves selecting the text string with the Shaping tool and then dragging one of the two stylized arrows that appear at the text string's lower boundary. Keep in mind, however, that you adjust spacing for *all* of the characters in the text string when you use this technique. To adjust spacing between two individual characters, see the "Kerning Single Characters" section of this chapter.

To alter inter-character spacing interactively, you drag the horizontal arrow at the lower-right boundary of the text string. To alter inter-word spacing, you drag the same arrow while holding down Ctrl . And to alter inter-line spacing, you drag the vertical arrow at the lower-left boundary of the text string.

Adjusting Inter-Character Spacing

In the following exercise, you will create a text string and adjust the inter-character spacing, observing the changes in the CorelDRAW! window as you work.

1. Set viewing magnification to actual size, then activate the Text tool and select an insertion point near the upper-left corner of your viewing window.

2. Type **Running out of** on the first line of the text entry window and **space** on the second. Click on the Pick tool and open the Text roll-up. Set text attributes to Fujiyama normal, left alignment, and 75 points, and then select Apply. The text displays in your viewing window. If the text string is not completely visible on the display, select the text string and move it to the location shown in Figure 9-4.

3. Activate the Shaping tool. Each character node increases in size, and stylized vertical and horizontal arrows appear at the lower-left and lower-right boundaries of the text object.

4. Position the Shaping pointer directly over the horizontal arrow at the lower-right boundary of the text object, until the pointer turns into a crosshair. Then, drag this arrow to the right. Notice that, as in the example in Figure 9-5, the characters do not seem to move immediately; instead, you see a dotted outline following the two-way arrow pointer. As you drag, the status line displays the message "Inter-Character," followed by information about the horizontal distance by which you are increasing the size of the text boundary.

5. When the right boundary of the text string (represented by the dotted outline) reaches the desired point, release the mouse button. The text

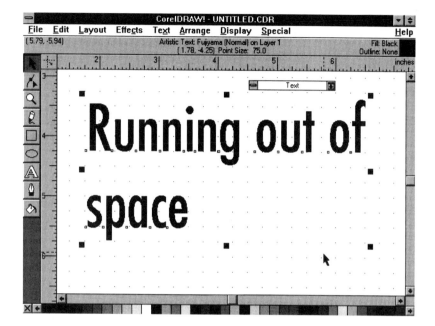

Displaying the
spacing
adjustment
arrows
Figure 9-4.

Adjusting
inter-character
spacing
Figure 9-5.

repositions itself to align with that boundary, and the space between each character increases proportionately, as shown here:

6. If you would like to know the exact inter-character spacing measurement you have obtained, select the text string with the Pick tool and access the Artistic Text and Spacing dialog boxes. This is a good way to check for precision.

7. Select the Undo command from the Edit menu to return the text to its former position. Then reselect the Shaping tool and *decrease* the space between characters by dragging the horizontal arrow to the left instead of the right. If you decrease the space drastically, letters may even overlap, like this:

8. Select Undo once more to return the characters to their original positions. Leave this text on the screen for now.

Adjusting inter-character spacing is useful when you want to fit text into a defined space in a drawing, without changing the point size or other attributes. Go on to the next section to practice changing inter-word spacing independently of the spacing between characters.

Adjusting Inter-Word Spacing

Suppose that you don't need to change the spacing between letters, but your design calls for increased or decreased spacing between words. To adjust inter-word spacing interactively, you drag the same horizontal arrow that you used for inter-character spacing. The difference is that you also hold down Ctrl at the same time. Try the following exercise, using the text string you created in the previous section.

1. With the Shaping tool active and the text string selected, position the pointer over the horizontal arrow until the pointer turns into a crosshair. Then press and hold Ctrl and drag the two-way arrow pointer to the right. The status line displays the message "Inter-Word," followed by the horizontal distance by which you are stretching the text boundary.

2. When the outline that you are dragging has the desired width, release the mouse button first and then Ctrl. (If you release Ctrl first, you will adjust the inter-character rather than the inter-word spacing.) The text redisplays with increased space between each word, as shown here:

3. Press Ctrl-Z or select the Undo command in the Edit menu to return the text to its original inter-word spacing.

4. Try decreasing the amount of inter-word spacing by dragging the horizontal arrow to the left instead of the right. When you are finished experimenting, select the Undo command once more. Leave this text on the screen for the next exercise.

You can change the spacing between lines of a text string, as well as between words or characters. The next section gives you hands-on practice in editing inter-line spacing.

9

Adjusting Inter-Line Spacing

To edit inter-line spacing with the Shaping tool, you drag the vertical arrow located at the lower left of the text boundary. Try increasing and decreasing the space between lines now, using the same text string you have been working with for the past two sections. Note that if your text string contains only one line, dragging the vertical arrow has no effect.

1. With the Shaping tool active and the text string selected, position the mouse pointer directly over the vertical arrow that appears at the lower-left text boundary and drag this arrow downward. The mouse pointer turns into a two-way vertical arrow. Simultaneously, the status line displays the message "Inter-Line," followed by the vertical distance measurement, which tells you how much you have increased the size of the text boundary.

2. When you have increased the boundary by the desired size, release the mouse button. The text repositions itself to fit the new boundary. As shown here, only the spacing between lines changes, not the length or size of the text itself:

Running out of

Space

3. To see the precise amount of inter-line spacing that you have added, press the (Spacebar) or activate the Pick tool and then select the Edit Text command in the Text menu. Then, click on the Spacing command button to see the Spacing dialog box. When you are finished, select Undo from the Edit menu to return the text string to its former inter-line spacing.

4. Reduce the inter-line spacing of the text string by dragging the vertical arrow upward instead of downward. When you are finished, select Undo to return the text to its former spacing.

5. Select New from the File menu and click on No when asked if you want to save current changes, to clear the screen before beginning the next section.

By now, you have explored all of the possible text attributes that you can change using the Pick and Shaping tools. If you need to give your text an even more customized look, however, you have the option of converting text to a curved object and then editing its nodes.

Reshaping Characters

To give messages extra flair, you might need stylized text characters that just don't exist in standard fonts. CorelDRAW! can help you create such "text pictures" easily. All you have to do is select text attributes that approximate the effect you want to achieve and then convert the text string to curves. You can then reshape the text using the Pick and Shaping tools.

The following exercise contains a simple step-by-step example of how to create stylized text pictures. Carry out the steps and give your own imagination a boost!

1. To prepare for this exercise, turn off Show Rulers, Snap To Grid, and Show Grid, and set the viewing magnification to actual size.

2. Activate the Text tool and select an insertion point about midway down the left edge of your viewing area.

3. Type **Snake** in upper- and lowercase letters and open the Artistic Text dialog box. Test each of the fonts in the Fonts list box against the sample display character. The capital "S" of the Gatineau font bears a fairly strong resemblance to a snake, so set text attributes to Gatineau bold italic, 150 points, and left alignment. Select OK to exit the Artistic Text dialog box and display your text on the page, as shown in Figure 9-6.

4. Activate the Shaping tool and double-click on the node for the letter "S" to open the Character Attributes dialog box.

"Snake" text: Gatineau bold italic, 150 points
Figure 9-6.

9

A *drop cap* is an
initial capital
letter that
stretches below
the baseline of
the remaining
text.

5. Your aim is to increase the size of the letter "S" and make it a *drop cap*. To achieve this, set the type size for the letter "S" to 250 points and set Vertical Shift to –25 percent of type size. Select OK to make these changes take effect. Your text should now look like this:

Snake

6. Activate the Pick tool (or press the [Spacebar]) to select the entire text string, and then click on the Convert To Curves option in the Arrange menu. The text redisplays with many little nodes, indicating that it has become a curve object. If you activate the Shaping tool again, the status line displays the message, "Curve: 229 nodes on 8 subpaths." This message indicates that CorelDRAW! now considers this text string to be one object with eight combined segments.

7. Activate the Pick tool again and select the Break Apart command in the Arrange menu. Each letter is now a separate object.

NOTE: The spaces inside the "a," "k," and "e," fill in because the letters are formed by two objects which you just broke apart. When the two objects are combined, their common area becomes transparent, causing the space. Remember the teacup handle example in Chapter 6. If you want the spaces to reappear, select the characters with the Pick tool and choose Combine from the Arrange menu.

8. Deselect all of the letters and then click on the letter "S" with the Pick tool. Stretch the letter vertically by dragging the middle boundary markers on the upper and lower sides of the highlighting box. Your goal is to elongate the letter, thereby enhancing the "snake-like" appearance. You may need to scroll your screen to see all of the "S."

9. Now, activate the Shaping tool and manipulate the nodes of the "S" so that you achieve the general look of the following illustration. Make

some areas of the "snake" narrower and others broader. You will want to reshape and move the snake's head, too. Make the "tail" of the snake narrower, as well.

10. You can try to match the results here exactly or develop your own creative enhancements utilizing all of the skills you have learned at this point in the book. When you are satisfied with the appearance of the snake, save the image under the filename SNAKE.CDR.

11. Select New from the File menu to clear the screen.

As you can see, the possibilities for creating custom characters for text are virtually endless. If you find yourself fired up with new ideas for your own projects, experiment until you design a word picture that best enhances your message.

9

CHAPTER

CORELDRAW! 4

10

CUTTING, COPYING, PASTING, AND OBJECT LINKING AND EMBEDDING (OLE)

So far you have learned how to select, move, rearrange, transform, and reshape objects within a single graphic. An equally important part of the editing process involves the transfer of image information within a graphic, between pictures, or between CorelDRAW! and other Windows applications. The editing functions that allow you to transfer image data include copying, cutting, and pasting objects and pictures, deleting or duplicating objects, and copying object attributes. You access these operations using the Cut, Copy, Paste, Delete, Duplicate, Clone, and Copy Attributes From options in the Edit menu.

These editing functions have many uses that will save you time and design effort. You don't have to start from scratch each time you need to duplicate an object or its style attribute. You can simply transfer image information, using the editing commands. You perform some of the transfer operations within a single picture; others allow you to transfer information between CorelDRAW! files, and even between CorelDRAW! and other Windows applications.

CorelDRAW! allows you to transfer objects to and from the Windows Clipboard. This means that you can copy or cut objects between different image files in CorelDRAW!, or from CorelDRAW! to a file in another Windows application. Conversely, you can copy or cut objects from files in other Windows applications and paste them to the page of your choice in CorelDRAW!.

This chapter covers the use of the Windows Clipboard, both within CorelDRAW! and between CorelDRAW! and other Windows applications. It introduces you to some additional object and style copying functions in CorelDRAW! that complement the use of the Windows Clipboard. You'll find out how to duplicate objects within a drawing and how to copy attributes from one object to another. You'll review the difference between cutting objects from a file and deleting them permanently. Finally you will work with Object Linking and Embedding, usually referred to by the acronym OLE (pronounced O'lay). OLE provides new ways to utilize objects from different applications.

About the Windows Clipboard

If you haven't used Windows applications before, you may be wondering how the Clipboard works. Think of the Windows Clipboard as a temporary storage place that can contain only one item at a time. When you select an object and then click on the Copy or Cut command in the Edit menu, you send a copy of the object to the Clipboard from its original place in your drawing. You can then choose Paste from the Edit menu to send a copy of the object from the Clipboard to the desired location. The copy you sent to the Clipboard remains there until you overwrite it by copying or cutting another object, or until you exit Windows and end a session.

Windows creates its own file format, called a *metafile,* out of the information that you send to the Clipboard. This standard metafile format allows you to share information between different applications that run under Windows. **A** metafile can be larger or smaller than the object you send to the Clipboard, depending on the complexity of the information you are trying to transfer. As a rule of thumb, the more complex an object is in terms of its attributes, the more memory it requires when you send it to the Clipboard.

Theoretically, all Windows applications should be able to trade information through the Clipboard. In practice, however, some types of information in objects or files transfer better than others. When you have completed the basic exercises on copying, cutting, and pasting objects within CorelDRAW!, turn to the section entitled "Working with Different Applications." There you will find tips for trouble-free transfer operations through the Clipboard.

Copy, Cut, Duplicate, Clone, or Delete

In order to duplicate or delete one or more objects, or copy or cut them to the Clipboard, you must first select the objects with the Pick tool. The Edit menu commands and their keyboard shortcuts are unavailable to you unless one or more objects are already selected.

You can select a single object, multiple objects, or all objects in a graphic for any of the Edit menu operations discussed in this chapter. To select a single object for one of the transfer operations, just click on its outline once. To select multiple objects for a transfer operation, use (Shift) or the marquee method you learned in Chapter 6. (You might also want to group the objects after you select them in order to avoid separating them from each other accidentally.) To select all of the objects in a graphic, click on the Select All command in the Edit menu.

Copying and Pasting Objects   10

The Copy and Paste commands in the Edit menu enable you to copy CorelDRAW! objects and paste them to the same file, to another file in CorelDRAW!, or to another Windows application. When you *copy* an object to the Clipboard, the original object remains in position on the page. When you *paste* the object, Windows makes another copy from the copy on the Clipboard. The copy on the Clipboard remains there until you overwrite it by copying or cutting another object or group of objects, or until you exit Windows.

To practice copying objects to the Clipboard and pasting them to the same or different pictures, you will use a file that you created in Chapter 6.

Copying and Pasting Objects Within a Picture

When you copy an object to the Clipboard and then paste it to the same picture, the copy overlays the original object exactly. The copy is selected as soon as it appears on the page, however, so you can move it safely without displacing the original object.

A more convenient way to copy an object within the same picture is to use the Duplicate command. When you invoke this command, CorelDRAW! automatically offsets the copy of the object from the original. See the "Duplicating and Cloning Objects" section of this chapter for more details.

For the exercises in this chapter, make sure that Show Rulers and Show Status Line are selected (turned on) in the Display menu and that Show Grid and Snap To Grid are selected in the Grid Setup option of the Layout menu. Then open the Chapter 6 file and practice copying a group of objects with these instructions:

1. Open the ARROW1.CDR file and group all of the text strings in the picture, using the Select All command in the Edit menu and then the Group command in the Arrange menu.

2. To copy the grouped objects to the Clipboard, either select the Copy command from the Edit menu, as shown in Figure 10-1, or press Ctrl-C. The pointer turns into an hourglass until CorelDRAW! finishes copying the selected object to the Clipboard.

3. Select Paste from the Edit menu or press Ctrl-V. The screen redraws, with the pasted object selected. You will not notice anything different because the pasted object appears exactly on top of the original.

4. To move the pasted object away from the original, press and hold the mouse button directly over any outline of the selected object and drag it

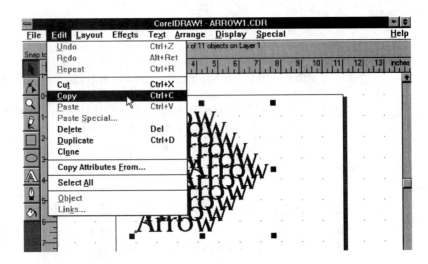

Selecting the
Copy
command
Figure 10-1.

as desired. You can now scale, rotate, stretch, skew, or otherwise edit the pasted object.

5. Select New from the File menu to clear the screen before continuing. Do not save any changes to the ARROW1.CDR document.

Next try copying an object to a different picture, and use it as a design enhancement there.

Copying and Pasting Between Pictures

In this exercise you will copy the text string from the DOINWHAT.CDR file and paste it to the KITE.CDR file.

1. Open the DOINWHAT.CDR file and select the text string.

2. Select Copy from the Edit menu or press Ctrl-C to copy the text to the Clipboard. The pointer may temporarily turn into an hourglass, or you may get a message box telling you the status, until CorelDRAW! finishes copying the text string. This lets you know it's busy.

3. Open the KITE.CDR file and drag all of the guidelines off the screen. Make sure Edit Wireframe is checked (turned on) in the Display menu.

4. From the Edit menu, choose Select All; then from the Arrange menu, select Group. The status line will tell you that there is now a group of objects.

5. Position the pointer at any of the four corner boundary markers of the group. Then drag the marker diagonally inward to scale down the kite to 50 percent of its original size.

6. Drag the kite so it is approximately centered horizontally and leaves about one-third of the vertical white space at the top. See Figure 10-2.

7. Select Paste from the Edit menu or press Ctrl-V. The text string will come into the center of the page.

8. Drag the text to the top of the page to complete this exercise, as shown in Figure 10-3.

9. Select Save As from the File menu, type **kite2**, and select OK.

10

You don't have to start from scratch to design an attractive picture.

As you can see from the preceding exercise, you can copy and paste existing objects and images to an illustration in progress, saving yourself work without sacrificing quality or originality. In the next sections, you will experiment with the Cut and Paste menu commands and see how their operation differs from that of Copy and Paste.

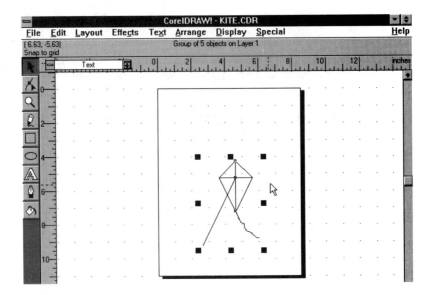

Kite
positioned to
receive pasted
text
Figure 10-2.

Cutting and Pasting Objects

When you select an object and then invoke the Cut command in the Edit
menu, the object disappears and goes to the Clipboard. When you then select
the Paste command, Windows places a copy of the cut object on the page.

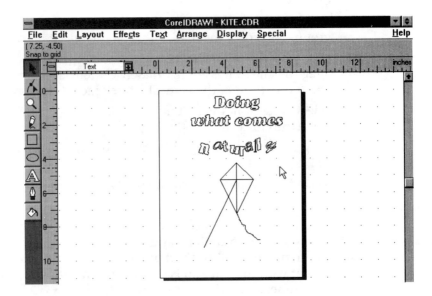

Copying and
pasting an
object to an
existing image
Figure 10-3.

The original object that you cut remains in the Clipboard until you overwrite it by cutting or copying another object, or until you end a Windows session.

To begin practicing cutting and pasting objects, you will use the LANDSCAP.CDR file you created in Chapter 3.

Cutting and Pasting Within a Picture

There are two ways to remove an unwanted object from a picture in CorelDRAW!. You can either cut it to the Clipboard using the Cut command, or delete it from the program memory entirely by using the Delete command. Use the Cut command unless you are absolutely certain that you will never need the object again. If you delete an object using the Delete command, CorelDRAW! doesn't store a copy anywhere; unless you immediately select the Undo command, you won't be able to recover the object.

CorelDRAW! always pastes a cut or copied object as the top layer of the picture. Therefore, when you cut and paste objects within an image that contains several layers of objects, remember to restore the original object arrangement using the commands in the Arrange menu.

1. Open the LANDSCAP.CDR file that you created in Chapter 3.
2. With the Pick tool, draw a marquee around the tree and its trunk to select it (make sure your marquee is large enough to completely enclose the boundary markers for the top of the tree).
3. From the Arrange menu, select Group.
4. Select Cut from the Edit menu or press Ctrl-X. The tree disappears from the drawing.
5. Select Paste from the Edit menu, and the tree comes back onto the drawing in the same place it was originally. If the tree was not on the top layer of the drawing, it will be after pasting. In that case, it is not *exactly* where it was originally.
6. Select a bird and then choose Delete from the Edit menu or press Del.

10

TIP: Once an object has been cleared or deleted from a drawing you can use Undo to restore it. If you do so, select Undo prior to doing anything else; otherwise the object is gone. Undo only remembers the last action.

7. Press Ctrl-V or select Paste again. Another tree comes onto the drawing, not the bird—the bird is not on the Clipboard; the tree still is. There will be a second tree because the second tree came in on top of the

original tree. Drag the second tree off to one side to see the other tree. Press Del to get rid of the second tree.

Go immediately on to the next section of this chapter because you will need to use the contents of the Clipboard (the tree) in the next section, where you will cut and paste objects between different pictures in CorelDRAW!.

Cutting and Pasting Between Pictures

Earlier in this chapter, you created a poster by combining the kite you drew in Chapter 2 with some text you created in Chapter 9. In the following exercise, you will add two copies of the tree you cut from the LANDSCAP.CDR drawing and the word "CorelDRAW!," which you will cut from a drawing you create.

1. From the File menu, select Open. Answer No to saving changes to the LANDSCAP.CDR file and select KITE2.CDR as the file to open.

2. Press Ctrl-V to paste the tree from the Clipboard onto the kite poster. When the tree comes onto the drawing, drag it down about a quarter of an inch.

3. Press Ctrl-V to paste a second time, drag the second tree to the right side of the poster, and then approximately align it with the first tree, as shown in Figure 10-4.

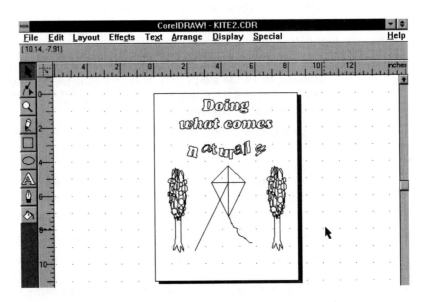

Trees pasted onto the kite poster

Figure 10-4.

4. Save the file as KITE3.CDR and then select New from the File menu. From the Display menu, click on Show Rulers to turn them off and click on Edit Wireframe to change to full color mode.

5. Select the Text tool and place the insertion point near the center of the page. Choose Text Roll-Up from the Text menu, then select the font, Times New Roman 60-point italic. Select the center-justification button and click on Apply.

6. Using all capital letters, type **CORELDRAW!**, then press F4 to go to fit-in-window magnification (the second icon from the right in the flyout menu).

7. Select the Shaping tool, then select all the characters in "DRAW!". From the Text roll-up, select the font Freeport 80 point, and then click on Apply. Close the Text roll-up. Select the Pick tool and click on any white space to deselect the text. Your screen should look similar to Figure 10-5. Select Save As from the File menu and name the drawing CDLOGO.CDR.

8. With the Pick tool, select the word "CorelDRAW!" and press Ctrl-X, or select Cut from the Edit menu.

9. From the bottom of the File menu, select KITE3.CDR, and answer No if asked whether you want to save the current file.

10. Press Ctrl-V or select Paste from the Edit menu. The word "CorelDRAW!" appears in the middle of the drawing.

11. Drag "CorelDRAW!" to the bottom of the poster. Then by dragging on one of the corner boundary markers, scale it to fit in the space available, as shown in Figure 10-6.

12. Save the completed poster as KITE4.CDR and select New to clear your work space.

10

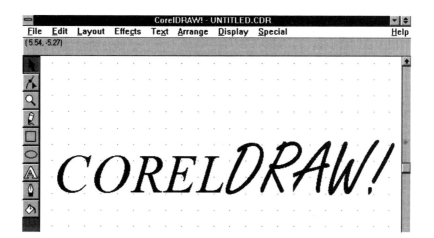

Text object,
CORELDRAW!
Figure 10-5.

Completed
poster with
four pasted
objects
Figure 10-6.

Working with Different Applications

The number of software packages running under Microsoft Windows is
increasing almost daily. These programs include such diverse applications as
word processors, desktop publishing and presentation software, database
managers and forms generators, and, of course, paint and illustration
software. If your other favorite Windows applications also support the
Windows Clipboard, you should be able to transfer data back and forth
between them and CorelDRAW!.

Features and techniques differ with every application, however; as a result,
not all visual information transfers equally well between programs. There are
too many Windows applications to catalog what happens to each file type as
it transfers to or from CorelDRAW! through the Clipboard. However, the
following sections should give you an idea of how the Clipboard handles
graphic information that you transfer between CorelDRAW! and some of the
most popular software.

Clipboard Memory Limits

There is a slight chance that at some point you may get an error message
that says "CorelDRAW! Clipboard format too large to put on Clipboard."
Should this happen, you can break the object into smaller groups of objects

and then transfer them in several passes. You can also save the object as a new drawing, then use the Import command to move it.

In most cases when you get the "CorelDRAW! Clipboard format..." message, CorelDRAW! will actually have copied the selected objects to the Clipboard in spite of the message. Check the Paste command in the Edit menu; if it is now available for selection, the objects have been successfully copied. If this command is not available, CorelDRAW! could not copy the selected object.

In general, you'll have the best chance of success when copying, cutting, and pasting CorelDRAW! objects that don't take advantage of too many advanced features at one time. An image that includes text, custom calligraphic outlines, PostScript fills, or Fountain fills, for example, will be more difficult to transfer to the Clipboard than an apparently complex geometrical image that contains none of these features.

Transferring Objects to Other Applications

When you copy or cut a CorelDRAW! object to the Clipboard, you are transferring not only the shape of an object, but also its attributes. Attributes include outline, outline fill, object fill, and text characteristics. Some attributes do not transfer well in their original form, owing in some cases to the diversity of Windows applications and in others to the complexity of CorelDRAW! features.

Most problems with transferring CorelDRAW! objects to the Clipboard have to do with objects taking too much memory. The following tips should help you avoid Clipboard memory or Windows metafile compatibility problems.

Fountain fills and PostScript fills (both discussed in Chapter 12) are extremely memory intensive from the standpoint of the Windows Clipboard, and they may go through unpredictable changes when transferred to another program. For example, when transferring an object containing PostScript fills, the object may be represented by blank or gray space when it is pasted into some applications. Even the outline disappears.

10

When an object with PostScript fill is transferred through the Clipboard, you often get the outline and then either no fill, or the little "PS"s that you see on the CorelDRAW! screen. The PostScript fill itself is not transferred in any instance.

Text sent from CorelDRAW! files to the Clipboard can be sensitive also. The greater the number of letters and/or attributes in a text string, the more likely that some information will not transfer properly. The specific program to which you want to send the text may further influence the transfer of information. As a general rule, text comes in as a graphic object rather than as editable text.

On the positive side, a number of applications such as PageMaker can import CorelDRAW!-produced lines, curves, fills, Fountain fills, and text, with all of their attributes, from the Clipboard without a problem.

Transferring Objects from Other Applications

When you transfer objects from your other favorite Windows applications to CorelDRAW!, you may not always receive exactly what you sent to the Clipboard. Sometimes this limitation depends on what the Windows Clipboard can interpret; at other times, the apparent discrepancy is specific to the interaction between the other program and CorelDRAW!.

The Clipboard, for example, has difficulty transferring special text kerning or text rotation information, pattern or flood fills, pixel-by-pixel manipulations, and combined pen colors from other Windows applications to CorelDRAW!.

Text that you import into CorelDRAW! from another Windows application comes in with the default text attributes. If you know the font, style, alignment, and other attributes you want, set these before importing the text. You can import a maximum of 4000 ASCII text characters at a time.

Some features do not transfer well into CorelDRAW!. Bitmaps, for example, often don't transfer well. Text sent from other graphics applications (as opposed to word processors) often arrives in CorelDRAW! as curves. A fill or Fountain fill from another program may transfer into CorelDRAW! as solid, or as an outline and separate fill object. Circles and ellipses may come in as connected line segments, while curves may become straight line segments. As CorelDRAW!, Microsoft Windows, and other Windows applications are constantly being upgraded, however, you can expect compatibility to improve. In the remaining sections of the chapter, you will learn about special commands in the CorelDRAW! Edit menu that make it easy for you to copy objects or their attributes within a CorelDRAW! file.

Object Linking and Embedding

Object Linking and Embedding (OLE) is similar to copying and pasting. With OLE, though, the source object is from an application other than the one you bring it into, and a connection is maintained to the source document, so that any editing in the source document will automatically appear in the destination document. Most importantly, with OLE you can double-click on an object in the destination application, and the source application will open and allow you to edit the object. With a normal copy and paste operation, you would not be able to edit the pasted object; you would have to delete the object, go to the source to change it, and then copy it back in. There are two forms of OLE: object linking and object embedding. They are the same, except that in embedding, a copy is made of the source document, and changes made to the copy do not affect the original.

Linking

When an object is linked to its source, the object is not actually copied, but rather a dynamic link is formed. When you double-click on the destination object, the link causes the source application to open with the source object, and the changes are made there. When you return to the destination application, the changes will appear. To demonstrate linking, follow these steps:

1. Switch to the Program Manager and start CorelPHOTO-PAINT!.

2. Open the file, BALLOON.PCX in the SAMPLES directory under the PHOTOPNT directory. Save this file to another name to prevent changes to the original; use the name LINKOBJ.PCX.

3. Using the Box Selection tool (the top tool in the toolbox, similar to DRAW!'s Pick tool), select some part of the picture, as shown in Figure 10-7.

4. Select Copy from the Edit menu, and switch back to the CorelDRAW! window by pressing and holding ⟨Alt⟩ while pressing ⟨Tab⟩ once or twice.

5. Select Paste Special from the Edit menu to open the Paste Special dialog

10

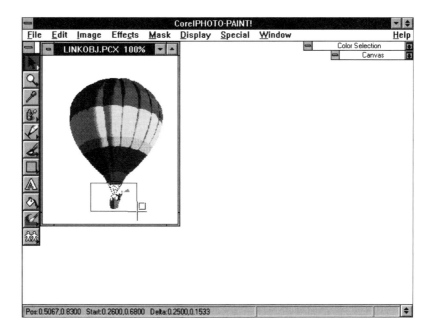

Source
application
document
Figure 10-7.

box shown here:

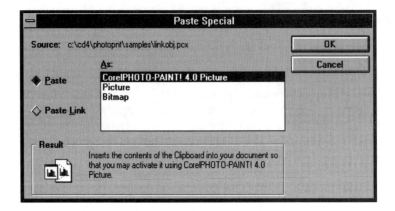

The Paste Special dialog box shows you the filename and path of the source object on the Clipboard and asks you how you want to bring it into CorelDRAW!. If you choose Paste, you will paste a *copy* of the object on the Clipboard, and you can modify it *without* affecting the original object. If you choose Paste Link, you will paste a *link* to the original object, and any modifications made will be made to the original.

6. Select Paste Link and then click on OK. The source object is now on the page. Press F4 to go to fit-in-window view. You can now size and move the object, but to change its actual contents you must use the source application.

7. Double-click anywhere on the object and CorelPHOTO-PAINT! restarts, with the object ready to be edited. When you have finished making changes, close CorelPHOTO-PAINT! by double-clicking on its Control-menu box. The changes will appear on the CorelDRAW! screen.

Embedding

Embedding is similar to linking, except that embedding makes a copy of the source object, and once the copy is pasted in the destination document, there is no connection between the copy and the source object. As in linking, you can double-click on the destination object and the source application will open. The difference is that you will be editing the destination copy and not the source object. To see object embedding in action, follow these steps:

1. Clear the screen by choosing New from the File menu and answering No to the question about saving the file. Then choose Insert Object from the File menu. The Insert Object dialog box appears, as you see here:

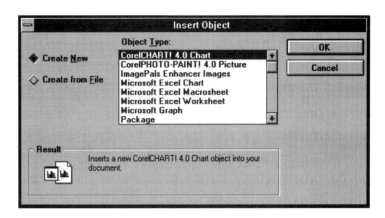

The Insert Object dialog box is very similar to the Paste Special dialog box you just used. The major difference is that Insert Object brings in objects that are not on the Clipboard. You can either go out and create a new object in some application (the Create New option) or bring in an object that is a file on your hard disk (the Create from File option). In either case you must first select the type of object you want to bring in.

2. Select CorelPHOTO-PAINT! 4.0 Picture as the type of object you want to bring in, make sure Create New is selected, and then click on OK.

   The Create a New Picture dialog box will open asking you the size and resolution of the new picture and shows you the memory required and available to hold the picture.

3. Click on OK to accept the default dimensions and CorelPHOTO-PAINT! will open with a small piece of a window title bar on the screen. Drag the piece of title bar out from under the toolbar and enlarge the window by dragging on the lower right corner. This new window is titled UNTITLED.CDR.

10

4. Once again, open the LINKOBJ.PCX. Select an object in the picture and copy it to the Clipboard. Click on UNTITLED.CDR to select it.

5. Choose Paste from the Edit menu and then click on As New Selection from the submenu that opens. The object you copied will appear in the UNTITLED.CDR window.

6. Choose Edit and Return to UNTITLED.CDR from the File menu and then click on Yes to update UNTITLED.CDR. CorelPHOTO-PAINT! will close and CorelDRAW! will open with the copied CorelPHOTO-PAINT! object in the middle of the page.

7. Double-click on this embedded object to open the source application. After making changes, go to the File menu, select Exit and Return to UNTITLED.CDR and click Yes to update it. This menu option would not

be present in the File menu if the objects had been linked instead of embedded.

If you now go back to CorelPHOTO-PAINT! and open the original object, it will not have the changes you just made. Had you linked this object rather than embedded it, the changes would have been transferred.

Duplicating and Cloning Objects

As you saw earlier in the chapter, you can use the Copy and Paste commands in the Edit menu to make a copy of an object within a picture. This process can be somewhat time-consuming if you use it frequently, because you need two separate menu commands or keyboard combinations to perform one action. A more convenient way of achieving the same end is to use the Duplicate command in the Edit menu or its keyboard shortcut, Ctrl-D.

The offset of a copy makes it easier to move the duplicate to a new location.

The Duplicate command causes a copy of the selected object or objects to appear at a specified *offset* from the original. In other words, the duplicate copy does not appear directly on top of the original, but at a horizontal and vertical distance from it, which you specify.

You can also use the Duplicate command alone or with the Combine command in the Arrange menu to achieve unusual logo or graphic designs, or special effects. In the next exercise, you will create and duplicate three different series of rectangles, each with a different specified offset. Then you will combine them to create the design shown in Figure 10-8.

1. Starting with a blank page, change the page format to landscape using the Page Setup command from the Layout menu. Also, make sure that Show Rulers and Edit Wireframe are turned on (as indicated by a check mark next to each option in the Display menu).

2. Select the Preferences command from the Special menu. Check the Place Duplicates and Clones settings at the top of the Preferences dialog

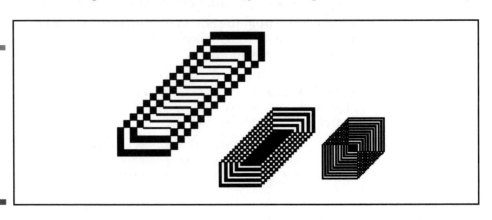

Special effects created with the Duplicate and Combine commands (with Full screen preview)
Figure 10-8.

box. The numeric entry and units boxes should each show the default value setting of 0.250 inches, as shown in Figure 10-9.

If the values are correct, select OK and exit the dialog box. If either of these settings is different, change it to 0.25 inches.

3. Select the Rectangle tool and draw a rectangle about halfway down the left edge of the page. The rectangle should be wider than it is long.

4. Press Ctrl-D or select the Duplicate command from the Edit menu. An exact copy of the rectangle appears 1/4 inch to the right and above the original. Press Ctrl-D repeatedly until you have created 14 copies of the rectangle, as in Figure 10-10.

5. Change the Place Duplicates and Clones setting in the Preferences dialog box to 0.05 inches in both the Horizontal and Vertical numeric entry boxes.

6. With the Rectangle tool still selected, draw another rectangle to the right of the first series. Then, press Ctrl-D 20 times in succession. This time, the duplicates appear at much shorter intervals, as shown in Figure 10-11, giving a smoother appearance to the transitions between the series of duplicated objects.

7. Refer to the Place Duplicates and Clones settings in the Preferences dialog box one more time, and change both values to –0.10 inches. The negative number indicates that the duplicates will appear below and to the left of the original object.

8. Draw a third rectangle between the first and second series of rectangles and then press Ctrl-D 20 times in succession. This time, the duplicates appear to the left of, and below, the original object, as shown in Figure 10-12.

10

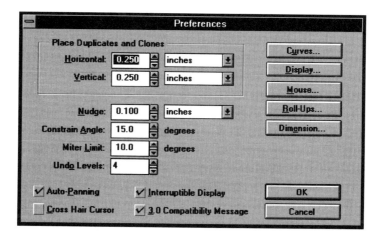

Place
Duplicates
and Clones
settings
Figure 10-9.

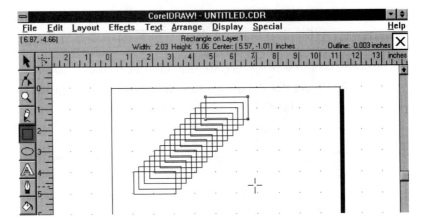

Creating and
duplicating
the first set of
rectangles
Figure 10-10.

9. Now set the right mouse button so you can toggle between the Edit
   screen and Full screen preview. Do this by selecting Mouse in the
   Preferences dialog box, then click on Full screen preview, and finally,
   click the OK buttons in both dialog boxes. With the Pick tool, select
   each of the series of objects in turn, and apply the Combine command
   from the Arrange menu to combine the series. While each object is
   selected, open the Fill tool at the bottom of the toolbox and click on the
   black solid fill in the bottom row of fills. You will recall from Chapter 6
   that using the Combine command causes alternating objects in a group
   to become transparent.

10. When you have combined all three series of objects, click the right
    mouse button to toggle to Full Screen Preview. As you can see from
    Figure 10-8, the various offsets lead to different special effects when you
    combine each group of rectangles.

11. Save this file as DUPECOMB.CDR and then select New to clear the screen.

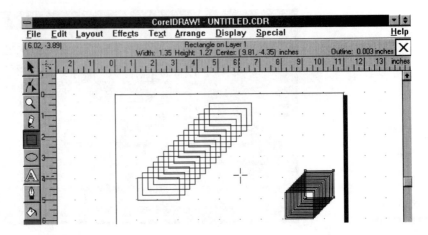

A second set
of duplicate
rectangles
with smaller
offset values
Figure 10-11.

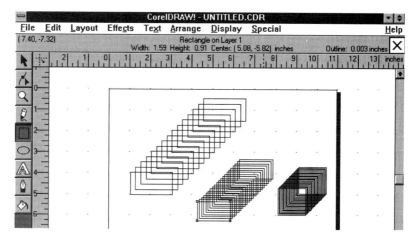

Creating and
duplicating a
third set of
rectangles
Figure 10-12.

The preceding exercise shows you only one potential use for the Duplicate
command. You can probably think of many others that will spark your
creativity and enhance your design abilities, especially since you can apply
this command to multiple or grouped objects as well as single objects.

Cloning an Object

Cloning an object is the same as duplicating; however, the resulting objects
can be used in different ways. A cloned object will still have a link to the
original object, which is called the *master*. When you make changes to the
master, those same changes will appear in the clone. The connection will
remain until some change is made to the clone itself, then the link is broken.
Try this for yourself with these steps:

1. Choose the Ellipse tool, make an ellipse near the top of the page, then
   press (Spacebar) to select it.

2. Choose Clone in the Edit menu. You see a duplicate appear on top of
   the original. Move this clone to the lower part of the page.

3. Click on the master (original) to select it, then drag one of the sizing
   handles to make the master about half the original size. The clone
   changes to match the master.

4. Now select the clone and change its size. Then go back and change the
   master. The clone will no longer follow the master.

5. Press (Ctrl)-(N) to clear the screen and open a new drawing. Answer No to
   the question of saving any changes.

10

In the next section, you will see an example of another interesting
CorelDRAW! copying technique—one that transfers attributes rather than
the objects themselves.

Copying an Object's Attributes

Suppose that you have spent a lot of time designing an object, giving it a custom calligraphic outline, special fills, or a unique combination of text attributes. You would like to give the same set of attributes to another object, but you don't want to waste time setting up all those attributes from scratch. CorelDRAW! allows you to save time and enhance the design of your image by using the Copy Attributes From command in the Edit menu. You can practice using this command in the following exercise.

1. Select the Page Setup command in the Layout menu and change the page format to portrait. Then go to the Display menu and turn off both Show Rulers and Edit Wireframe.

2. Adjust magnification to actual size (1:1), activate the Text tool, select an insertion point near the top left of the screen, and type **Corel**. Activate the Pick tool, selecting the text object, and open the Text roll-up. Set text attributes to Aardvark bold, 100 points, and alignment, None. Click on the Paragraph command button to open the Paragraph dialog box, change Character spacing to 40 percent, and click on OK. Finally, click on Apply.

3. Click on any white space to deselect the word "Corel." In the Text roll-up, set attributes to Avalon italic, 50 points, and left alignment. Click on Apply. When the Text Attributes dialog box opens, click on OK to apply this default to both Artistic and Paragraph text.

4. Select a second insertion point a little below the first one. This time type **DRAW!**. When this string appears, your screen should look similar to Figure 10-13.

5. Close the Text roll-up and activate the Pick tool. The second text string is automatically selected. Click on the Copy Attributes From command in the Edit menu. The Copy Attributes dialog box appears, as shown here:

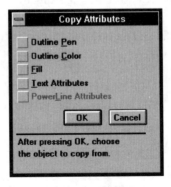

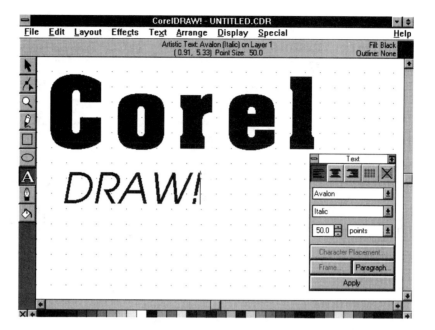

Preparing to
copy text
attributes from
one text string
to another
Figure 10-13.

The Copy Attributes dialog box contains five options: Outline Pen, Outline Color, Fill, Text Attributes, and PowerLine Attributes. You can choose to copy any or all of these attributes to the selected object. If you use the Shaping tool instead of the Pick tool to select your text, the Text Attributes option will be dimmed and unavailable.

6. Click on the Text Attributes check box to place a check mark in it. Notice that a message at the bottom of the dialog box instructs you to select the object *from* which you want to copy the attributes.

7. Click on OK to exit to the page. The pointer changes to a thick arrow containing the word "From?" This reminds you to click on the object from which you want to copy attributes.

8. Select the "Corel" text string by clicking anywhere on its outlines with the tip of the arrow. The "DRAW!" text string immediately changes to reflect the same attributes as the "Corel" text string, as shown in Figure 10-14. If you miss the outline when you click, a dialog box comes up giving you the chance to try again.

9. Select New from the File menu to clear the screen. Do not save these changes.

You will have opportunities to use the Copy Attributes dialog box again in later chapters.

10

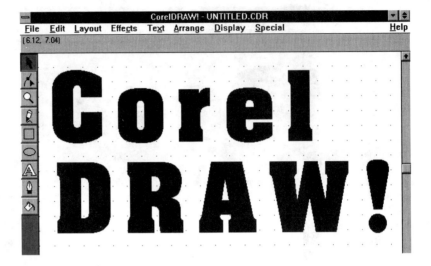

Selected
object with
attributes
copied from
adjoining
object
Figure 10-14.

You have experimented in this chapter with the available techniques for
copying, cutting, and pasting objects and attributes within or between
CorelDRAW! files, and between CorelDRAW! and other applications. In the
next two chapters, you will learn about outline width, outline fill, and object
fill—important attributes that you can assign to any new or existing object.

CHAPTER

11

DEFINING THE OUTLINE PEN

In CorelDRAW!, all objects have Outline Pen, outline color, and object fill attributes. In addition, text has its own set of attributes, as you learned in Chapter 9. All of the objects you created and edited until now had standard black fills and fixed-width black outlines. In this chapter, however, you will modify outline attributes using the CorelDRAW! Outline Pen.

The Outline Pen is actually two tools in one. In order to create an outline for any object, you need to define the

Outline Pen and the *outline color* in two separate steps. Think of the Outline Pen as a calligraphic pen having an almost infinite number of replaceable nibs. The Outline Pen, which you will explore in this chapter, represents the shape of the nib and emulates the possible ways you can slant your hand while drawing. The outline color, which you will learn about in Chapter 12, represents the ink and textures that flow from the pen.

When defining an Outline Pen for any object, you can vary the width, line style, corner shape, line ending style, and nib shape of the pen. You can also control the placement of the outline relative to the object's fill color. Only CorelDRAW! allows you so great a degree of control over the shape and appearance of your drawings. With your first try, you can create ornate calligraphic effects and simulate a hand-sketched look electronically.

Defining Outline Pen Attributes

The method you use to define Outline Pen attributes depends on whether you are creating new objects with the current default settings, editing attributes for existing objects, or altering default outline settings. The following checklist summarizes the possibilities available.

✦ To create an object with the current default Outline Pen attributes, you select the appropriate drawing tool and draw the object. You can then select the Outline Pen to view the current default outline attributes (optional).

✦ To edit Outline Pen attributes for an existing object (including grouped or combined objects), you activate the Pick tool, select the object, and then click on the Outline Pen.

✦ To begin setting new Outline Pen default attributes, you click on the Outline Pen and then on the desired icon.

Once you have selected the Outline Pen, you can choose between defining a custom Outline Pen or selecting a preset outline width. In the remaining sections of this chapter, you will practice customizing Outline Pen attributes and selecting preset Outline Pen widths for both planned and existing objects.

Using the Outline Pen

You have complete control over the attributes of the Outline Pen in CorelDRAW! thanks to a series of attributes that can be modified. There are three ways to modify these attributes:

♦ Directly from the Outline Pen flyout menu, shown in the following illustration. You use the flyout menu to make quick standard changes to an outline. All three ways of changing attributes start with this flyout menu.

♦ From a dialog box that allows the attributes to be modified with greater precision. The dialog box is displayed by clicking on the Custom Outline Pen icon, the first icon on the flyout menu, which is identical in appearance to the Outline Pen icon. By altering the settings in this dialog box, you can vary the outline's placement and width, change the shape of corners and line ending styles, design custom nibs, and create an array of calligraphic effects.

The Pen roll-up window allows you to quickly see the results of your attribute changes without opening the dialog box.

♦ From the Pen roll-up, shown in the next illustration. The Pen roll-up is displayed by clicking on the Outline Pen Roll-up icon, next to the Custom Outline Pen icon. Once the roll-up is accessed, it remains on the screen and can be rolled up or down at will.

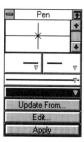

In the following exercises, you will create an object with default Outline Pen attributes and become familiar with the settings in the Outline Pen dialog box and Pen roll-up. Then you will edit Outline Pen attributes for existing objects in the sample files that came packaged with your software. Finally, you will set up new default Outline Pen attributes that will apply to objects you draw later.

If you simply want to specify outline width, without creating a custom Outline Pen, turn to the section "Selecting a Preset Outline Pen Width." There, you will find out how to alter the width of the Outline Pen quickly, without accessing a dialog box or the roll-up.

11

Creating Objects with Default Attributes

When you create a new object, CorelDRAW! applies the current default settings to it automatically. You can leave those settings as they are or edit them. When you edit Outline Pen settings for a newly created object, however, your changes apply only to that object. Other objects that you create keep the default Outline Pen attributes until you set new defaults. If you want to change the defaults themselves, refer to the section, "Customizing Outline Pen Defaults," later in this chapter.

In the exercise that follows, you will create a text string, select the Outline Pen flyout menu, access the Outline Pen dialog box, and observe the default Outline Pen attributes that are standard with CorelDRAW!.

1. Make sure that the Show Rulers, Show Grid, and Snap To Grid commands are turned off, select the Zoom tool, and set magnification to actual size (1:1).

2. Activate the Text tool and select an insertion point near the upper-left edge of the page. Type **outline pen** and then open the Edit Text dialog box from the Text menu. Set text attributes to Gatineau, normal style, 90 points, and left alignment. With the Spacing option, set character spacing to 10 percent and then select OK twice.

3. Assuming that Edit Wireframe is off (if it isn't, turn it off), the interior of the text string is black or whatever the default fill color is. For the purposes of this exercise, you want to remove the fill color to clearly view your outline. To do this, click on the X at the left end of the on-screen color palette. (If your text seems to have vanished completely, you will find a solution in the next step.)

4. Click on the Outline Pen. A flyout menu appears, as shown here:

Custom Outline Pen icon

5. Use the Pick tool to size and move the text string so that it looks similar to Figure 11-1. (The point size will be reduced.)

   The text string redisplays with just the outline. The center is hollow, as shown in Figure 11-1.

The Outline Pen flyout menu contains two rows of options. The top row consists of controls for the Outline Pen, which you will use throughout this chapter. The second row, which you will work with in Chapter 12, contains controls for the outline fill color. (If the text string has disappeared from your screen, click on the solid black icon in the second row of this flyout menu to make it reappear.)

6. Click on the Outline Pen. For the moment, ignore all but the first (leftmost) icon in the top row of the flyout menu. The seven icons after the first one allow you either to open the Pen roll-up window or to quickly specify fixed outline widths. You will practice working with outline widths later, in "Selecting a Preset Outline Pen Width." For now, click on the first icon in the top row, the Custom Outline Pen icon. It looks just like the Outline Pen icon, but it has the more specialized function of allowing you to specify all the possible attributes of the Outline Pen. The Outline Pen dialog box displays, as in Figure 11-2. Leave this dialog box on the screen for now.

The Outline Pen dialog box contains controls for nine Outline Pen attributes. The default settings on your screen should match the settings in Figure 11-2, unless you or another user has altered them since installing the software. If your dialog box shows different settings, adjust them to match the ones in the figure. Then, take a moment to become familiar with the attributes and how they function.

11

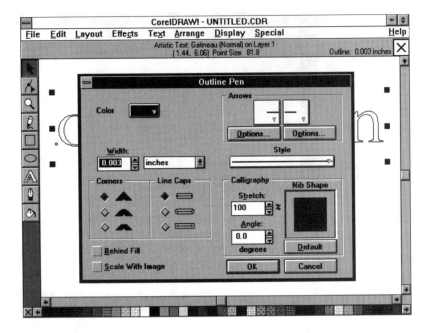

Outline Pen
dialog box
Figure 11-2.

In Chapter 12
you will learn
how the outline
coloring
features are
used.

Color   A display box at the top of the dialog box shows you the current fill color. When you click on the scroll arrow, a color palette is opened that is identical to the normal on-screen palette except for the arrangement of the color choices. At the bottom of the color display box is the More button, which opens the Outline Color dialog box, giving you access to the full range of outline coloring. In the next chapter you will learn how these features are used.

Arrows   The pair of boxes next to the color display box allow you to select or construct a line ending (such as an arrowhead) to go on either end of a line. These line endings are displayed in a flyout that you can open by clicking on either the left (line-beginning) or right (line-ending) Arrows display box. Figure 11-3 shows the left Arrows box selected. To select a line ending, scroll through the boxes of line endings until you see the one you want. Click on the line ending you want, and it will appear in its respective small Arrows display box.

Tip: To find the beginning of a line (normally the left end) or the end of a line (normally the right end) click on the line with the Shaping tool and press (Home) to highlight the beginning node. Pressing (End) will cause the ending node to be highlighted.

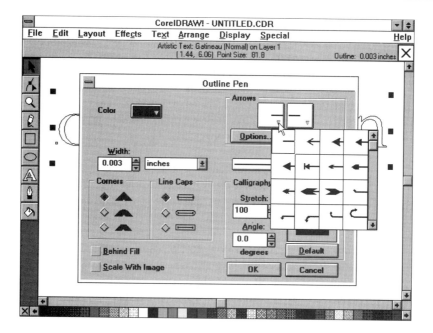

Clicking on the Options button for either the line-beginning or line-ending
arrow opens a menu that offers the same four options for each. After you
have selected a head or tail shape, the options are enabled. Choosing None
removes a line ending you previously selected. You can reverse the
beginning and ending arrows by choosing Swap. If you want to remove a
line ending from the flyout box of line endings, select it and click on Delete
From List. Clicking on the Edit option opens the Arrowhead Editor dialog
box shown here:

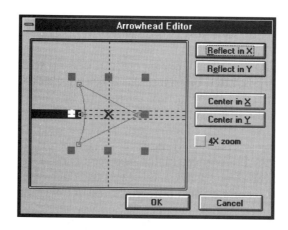

11

The Arrowhead Editor displays an enlarged arrowhead and allows you to move, scale, and stretch the arrowhead by dragging on it or one of its boundary markers. You can center the arrowhead relative to the X in the middle of the Editor, either horizontally by selecting Center in X or vertically by selecting Center in Y. Also, you can flip or *reflect* the arrowhead relative to the center, either horizontally by selecting Reflect in X or vertically by selecting Reflect in Y. Finally, you can magnify the arrowhead image by clicking on 4X zoom.

Line Width   Under the Color area of the Outline Pen dialog box are two boxes for controlling the current line width. You can change either the specific width number or the unit of measure, from inches to points, for example.

Line Style   A third box, to the right of the line width, shows the current line style. The solid line shown in the box in Figure 11-2 is the default line style. Clicking on the Style display box opens a flyout that allows you to choose from a number of dotted and dashed line styles, as you can see here:

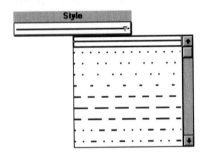

To choose a line style, use the scroll bar to display the style you want and click on that line style. You'll be returned to the Outline Pen dialog box, and the line style you choose will now be in the display box.

Corners   The Corners options pertain to objects that tend to have sharp corners: lines, open and closed curve objects, rectangles, and some angular fonts. The three option buttons in this area of the dialog box allow you to choose just how CorelDRAW! shapes those corners. The first (default) option shows a sharp or *miter* corner, where the outer edges of two joining line or curve segments extend until they meet. By altering the Miter Limit setting in the Preferences dialog box, you can control the angle below which CorelDRAW! flattens or bevels the edge of a sharp curve. When you choose the second option button, CorelDRAW! rounds the corners where two lines or curve segments meet. When you choose the third or *bevel* corner option button, corners of joining curve or line segments are flattened. The results of the Corners settings are usually subtle, unless you magnify an object or combine Corners settings with Nib Shape attributes for calligraphic effects.

Line Caps   The Line Caps options apply to lines and open curves, but not to closed path objects such as rectangles, closed curves, or ellipses. These settings determine the ending styles of lines and curves. The first or default option is a *butt line* end style, where the line ends exactly at the end point. The second option gives you *rounded line* end points. When you choose either the second or the third (*square line* end type), the line extends beyond the end point for a distance equal to half of the line thickness. When you select any of the line end caps, that style applies to both end points of the line or curve. If you have selected dashed lines as your line type for an object, each dash takes on the shape of the line end style you choose.

Calligraphy   The remaining two Outline Pen attributes—Stretch and Angle—help you define a custom pen shape, analogous to the *nib* or point of a calligraphic fountain pen. With default values of 100 percent stretch and 0-degree angle, the pen shape is square, resulting in a plain outline. On their own, these settings will not create calligraphic effects. When you alter them in combination, however, they allow you to outline objects with varying thick and thin strokes at the angle of your choice. You can set the shape of the nib by changing the values in the Stretch and Angle numeric list boxes, or interactively. Using the interactive method, you click and drag the mouse pointer inside the Nib Shape display box, where the pointer changes to a cross. The Stretch and Angle settings are automatically adjusted as you distort the nib shape. You can restore the default square nib by selecting the Default command button below the Nib Shape box. The Corners settings work with the Calligraphy settings to define the appearance of calligraphic strokes, as you will learn in "A Pen Shape for Calligraphic Effects," later in this chapter.

Behind Fill   The Behind Fill check box lets you specify whether the outline of an object should appear in front of or behind the object's fill. The default setting is in front of the fill (empty check box), but if you create objects with thick outlines, you will want to activate Behind Fill. This is especially advisable with text, where thick outlines appearing in front of the fill can obliterate empty spaces and cause text to appear smudged, like this:

11

When you place an outline behind the fill, only half of it is visible. The outline therefore appears to be only half as thick as specified.

Scale With Image   When the Scale With Image check box contains an X, the width and angle of the outline change proportionally as you resize, rotate, or skew the object. CorelDRAW! automatically updates the width and angle settings in the Outline Pen dialog box when Scale With Image is active. When the Scale With Image setting is *not* active, the width and angle of an object's outline do not change, no matter how you stretch, scale, rotate, or skew the object. This can lead to some interesting but unintended changes in appearance when you define a calligraphic pen nib for the object, as you will see in the "Scaling the Outline with the Image" section later in this chapter.

Now that you are familiar with the options in the Outline Pen dialog box, exit the dialog box by selecting Cancel. Clear the screen by selecting New from the File menu and clicking on No before going on.

Customizing Outline Pen Defaults

Different artists have different styles, and you may prefer to create most of your objects with Outline Pen styles that differ from the standard settings. If so, perform the exercise in this section to learn how to customize Outline Pen defaults. Objects that you create after changing the default attributes will then conform to the appearance that characterizes your working style.

Creating objects with new Outline Pen defaults is a three-stage process. First, you access the default Outline Pen dialog box. Then you change the Outline Pen attributes. Finally, you create new objects, which automatically adhere to the new default attributes. The dialog box that you use to edit default settings is identical to the Outline Pen dialog box, except for its title and the way you access it.

1. Start with a blank page. (If you are in an existing drawing and want to change default settings, make sure that no object is selected.) Then select the Outline Pen and click on the Custom Outline Pen icon. Since no object is selected, the dialog box in Figure 11-4 appears.

2. Click on the Artistic Text and Paragraph Text check boxes, so that all three have check marks, and then select OK to access the Outline Pen dialog box and have the defaults apply to all new objects. The contents of this dialog box are identical to the contents of the normal Outline Pen dialog box. Only the path of calling up the dialog box without a selected object is different.

3. For now don't change the defaults. As you go through this chapter you will exercise all of the options in this dialog box and become familiar

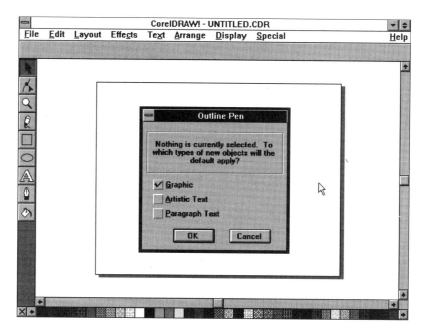

Default
Outline Pen
dialog box
Figure 11-4.

with their effects and what your likes and dislikes are. When you are finished with the chapter, you can come back here and set the defaults to what is right for you.

4. Select Cancel to close the dialog box without change and return to the work area.

CorelDRAW! encourages you to create images according to your unique working habits and style.

It's that easy to alter default settings for the Outline Pen. As with almost every other CorelDRAW! feature, customization is the key word.

On the other hand, if you are involved in technical illustration, or your normal CorelDRAW! tasks are relatively uncomplicated, you may seldom require calligraphy or other special options in the Outline Pen dialog box. The next section shows you how to change the Outline Pen width quickly and interactively, without the use of a dialog box.

11

Selecting a Preset Outline Pen Width

If width is the Outline Pen attribute you change most frequently, CorelDRAW! offers shortcuts that save you time and keep you out of the Outline Pen dialog box. The first row of the flyout menu that appears when you select the Outline Pen, as shown in Figure 11-5, contains five preset outline widths from which you can choose.

You can choose one of these options for a currently selected object, or you can set a fixed line width as a new default. When you choose a preset outline

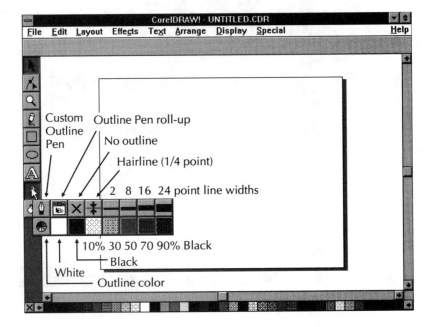

Custom Outline Pen roll-up
Outline
Pen / No outline

Hairline (1/4 point)

2 8 16 24 point line widths

10% 30 50 70 90% Black
Black
White
Outline color

Preset outline
widths
available in
Outline Pen
flyout menu
Figure 11-5.

width for a selected object, you apply that width to the selected object only. When you click on one of these options without having first selected an object, however, CorelDRAW! assumes that you want to set the option as a new default width, and the dialog box shown in Figure 11-4 pops up. Click on OK to set the selected line width as a new default for objects that you draw in the future. If you meant to select an existing object first, click on the Cancel command button instead.

The second option, next to the Custom Outline Pen icon on the left (see Figure 11-5), is the Pen roll-up, as shown here:

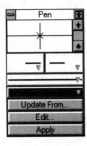

The top option in the Pen roll-up allows you to adjust the outline thickness. The default width that should appear is a hairline, shown by a thin line 1/4

point wide, met by two arrows. By clicking on the downward-pointing scroll arrow, you reduce the line thickness to zero, represented by an X through the box, signifying no outline. By clicking on the upward-pointing arrow, you can increase the line width in .01-point increments, starting with the hairline, and then a line 1 point wide. Below the outline thickness option are the familiar line ending, line style, and color options. To update the pen attributes from a given object, click on Update From and the pointer will turn into a From? arrow, which you use to click on the object. The attributes of the object then update the Outline Pen dialog box. To open the full Outline Pen dialog box, click on Edit. To apply the attributes you have set in the Pen roll-up to a selected object, click on Apply.

The next icon in the Outline Pen flyout is an X; as in the Pen roll-up window, you can click on this option when you want a selected object to have no outline at all.

The next option, similar to that in the Pen roll-up, represents a hairline or a line 1/4 point wide. The screen, however, does not display a true WYSIWYG representation of an outline this thin.

As Figure 11-5 shows, the remaining four options in the flyout menu represent fixed outline widths of 2, 8, 16, and 24 points. Think of these options as "package deals," in which each width selection includes an angle of 0 degrees and a stretch value of 100 percent in the Outline Pen dialog box.

If you have altered any of the other default Outline Pen settings using the Outline Pen dialog box, they are still effective when you select a preset Outline Pen width. For example, if you previously selected the Behind Fill or Scale With Image options as defaults, your outlines will exhibit these attributes even when you select a preset outline width. Since the Angle and Stretch settings are standardized for preset widths, however, you cannot achieve calligraphic effects.

Editing Outline Pen Attributes of Existing Objects   **11**

To define Outline Pen attributes for an existing (not newly created) object, you must select the object before you access the Outline Pen flyout menu. If you try to access the Outline Pen dialog box without having selected an object, CorelDRAW! assumes that you want to set new defaults for the Outline Pen, and any changes you make in the Outline Pen dialog box will not affect existing objects.

When you define Outline Pen attributes for an existing object that is selected, you are in effect *editing* the object's current outline style. The changes you make apply to that object only and have no effect on the default settings for objects you create later.

If you use the [Shift] method to select multiple objects in order to change their Outline Pen attributes, the Outline Pen dialog box displays the settings for the last object that you selected in the group. If you use the marquee method to select the objects, the dialog box displays the settings for the last object that you drew. Any changes you make will apply to all of the selected objects, however, so be very careful about changing Outline Pen attributes for more than one object at a time.

Each of the following sections concentrates on the effects of editing a specific attribute or related set of attributes in the Outline Pen dialog box. You will work with sample files that best demonstrate how changes to an attribute can alter the overall design and mood of a picture.

Adjusting Line Width

The line width you assign to an object's Outline Pen helps define the balance and weight of that object within a picture. In the following exercise, you will alter the line width for several elements in a text object that you create and then observe how your changes affect it.

1. Open the Outline Pen dialog box and determine whether both the Behind Fill and Scale With Image check boxes are unchecked. If either contains a check mark, click on the box to remove it.

2. Open the Text tool, click anywhere on the page, and type **Hot Tips**. Select the words "Hot Tips" using the Pick tool.

3. From the Text roll-up set the text to 60 points, BahamasHeavy. Click on Apply.

4. With the text still selected, magnify the area around the words with the Zoom tool. Your screen should now display an area similar to Figure 11-6.

5. Select the Fill tool and select the light-colored pattern, fourth from the left.

6. Select the Outline Pen and click on the line width after the hairline, a 2-point line. Now, the words "Hot Tips" should look like this:

7. Select the Outline Pen a third time and click on the third line width from the right, an 8-point line. "Hot Tips" should now look like this:

8. Select the Outline Pen again and open the Outline Pen dialog box. Notice that outline width is at 0.111 inch, which is equivalent to 8 points (a point is 1/72 of an inch or 0.014 inch), as shown in Figure 11-7. (Your screen will not have the Scale Width Image checked.) Remember that the default line width is 0.014 inch, which is 1 point.

As you can see, the variation in line width makes a big difference in how an object looks, and you can vary the line width either by selecting one of the established options on the flyout menu, or by entering an exact width in the Outline Pen dialog box.

Leave the dialog box open and the "Hot Tips" text on your screen for further use. The next section explores the design possibilities of placing outlines of objects behind or in front of their fills.

Adjusting Placement of Outline and Fill
The Behind Fill setting in the Outline Pen dialog box determines whether the outline of a selected object is placed behind or in front of the object's fill. This attribute is most important when you are working with text. Thick outlines appearing in front of the fill can clog up the open spaces in letters, making the letters appear unclear, as you saw in the 8-point example in the

11

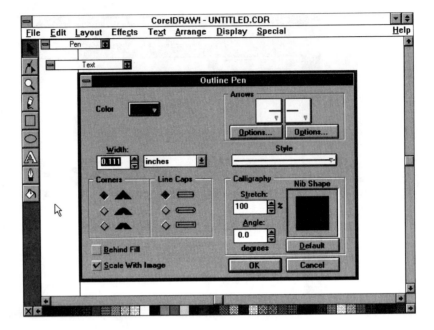

Outline Pen
dialog box
with an
8-point line
width (0.111)
Figure 11-7.

last exercise. In the following exercise, you will adjust outline placement for the letters in the "Hot Tips" text currently displayed.

1. In the Outline Pen dialog box, notice whether the Behind Fill option is selected.

2. If it is not already selected, click on the Behind Fill check box to select it and then select OK to exit the dialog box. The word reappears with a much thinner outline, as shown here:

Actually the outline is just as thick as before, but half of it is hidden behind the fill. You can see this if you watch the screen redraw (unless you have a super-fast computer).

In the next section, you will observe how the Scale With Image setting affects the appearance of resized or transformed objects.

Scaling the Outline with the Image

A wide outline, such as the 8-point width you applied in the last exercise, may be appropriate for large letters, say 75 points and above. If you scale that large type down to 24 points, however, the wide border doesn't look good at all, as you can see here:

Hot Tips

The CorelDRAW! Outline Pen dialog box has an option to scale an outline's attributes with the image. If you select Scale With Image by clicking on the check box, an outline's attributes will be appropriately scaled as you change the image. The default, though, is to not scale the attributes, and you are likely to get something that looks like the last illustration.

1. With the "Hot Tips" text still on the screen with an 8-point outline placed behind the fill, use the Text roll-up to scale the image to 24 points. You should get an image on your screen that looks like that shown in the last illustration.

2. Press <kbd>Alt</kbd>-<kbd>Backspace</kbd> to return the text to its original size.

3. Select the Outline Pen and open the Outline Pen dialog box. If it is not already selected, click on the Scale With Image check box and click on OK.

4. Again, scale the text image to 24 points. You now get a much more usable image:

Hot Tips

5. Clear the image from the screen by selecting New from the File menu; do not save the changes.

11

Setting Sharp (Miter), Rounded, or Beveled Outline Corners

The effect of changing corner attributes of the Outline Pen is so subtle that it is almost unnoticeable—unless the selected object has a thick outline as well as sharp corners. A thick outline enables you to see the shape of the object change as you cycle through the Corners options. Perform the following exercise to practice altering Corners settings for the letter "E."

1. Select the Text tool, click anywhere on the page, and type **E**.

2. Select the letter "E" with the Pick tool and select Avalon, Bold, 154 points, using the Text roll-up.

3. Move the letter "E" to the center of the printable page, magnify the character until it fills the window, select the Outline Pen, and click on the 16-point line width (the second from the right). Next click on the X to the left of the on-screen color palette, to turn off the fill.

When you have completed the preceding steps your screen should look like Figure 11-8. On the screen you see the outline of the letter "E" with 12 corners on which to test the three corner styles. The default, the sharp or miter corner, is currently displayed and is shown in Figure 11-9a.

4. Select the Outline Pen, open the Outline Pen dialog box, click on the rounded corner option button, and click on OK. You should see a distinct change in the corners, as shown in Figure 11-9b.

5. Again open the Outline Pen dialog box, select the beveled corner option, and click on OK. Once more, the corners change, as shown in Figure 11-9c.

6. Select New from the File menu to clear the screen. Do not save your changes.

In creating your own drawing, you will find the effects of the Corners options most dramatic when you assign thick outlines to objects that contain at least some cusp nodes. In the next section, you will explore when and how changes to the line end styles can alter an object's appearance.

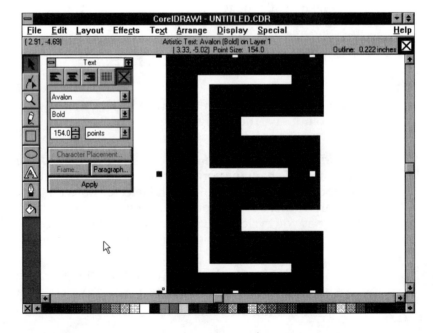

The letter "E"
set up to test
the types of
corners
Figure 11-8.

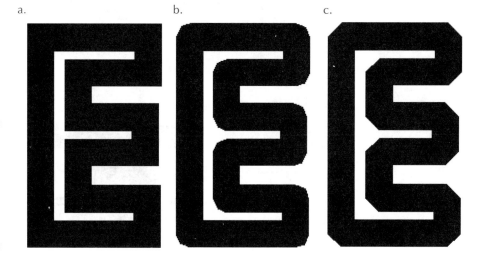

a.   b.   c.

The letter "E" with (a) sharp or miter, (b) rounded, and (c) beveled corners
Figure 11-9.

Selecting Line End Caps

Line end options (*end caps*) apply only to straight lines and open-ended curves. It is difficult to see the difference between line end types unless you create very thick lines or magnify the line a lot—you'll do both here.

1. From the Display menu select Show Rulers. From the Layout menu select Grid Setup and set the vertical grid origin to 11 inches. From the Snap To option in the Layout menu, select Guidelines.

2. Drag vertical guidelines from the ruler on the left to 2 and 4 inches.

3. Magnify the area from 1 inch on the horizontal ruler and 2 inches on the vertical ruler to 5 inches on the horizontal ruler and 4 inches on the vertical ruler.

4. With the Pencil tool, draw two straight, vertical lines down the guidelines from 2 inches to 4 inches. These should be hairline width. If they don't appear to be hairline width, select both lines and then select the hairline width icon from the Outline Pen flyout menu. Deselect these lines by clicking with the Pick tool any place in the work area except on one of the lines.

5. Select the Outline Pen and click on the far right line width, which is 24 points or .333 inch. Click on OK to apply this width to graphic objects.

6. Draw three straight, horizontal lines from 2 to 4 inches on the horizontal ruler at 2 1/2, 3, and 3 1/2 inches on the vertical ruler. Your screen should look like Figure 11-10.

11

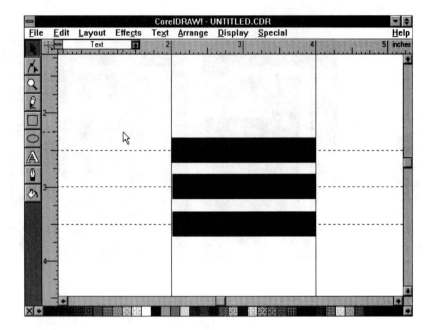

Lines prepared
for testing line
end caps
Figure 11-10.

The default line end cap, the *butt* end, is shown in Figure 11-10. The lines end exactly at the termination of the line and are squared off.

7. With the Pick tool select the middle line, open the Outline Pen dialog box, select the middle or rounded line end cap, and click on OK. The line endings on the middle line are now rounded and project beyond the termination of the line, as shown here:

8. Select the bottom horizontal line, open the Outline Pen dialog box, select the bottom or square line end cap, and click on OK. The line endings on the bottom line are now square and project beyond the termination of the line by one-half of the line width. Figure 11-11 compares the three line end caps.

9. Clear the screen by selecting New from the File menu. Don't save the contents.

If an image contains many open-ended curves, selecting rounded line end caps can soften the image, even if the lines are thin. Conversely, you can select butt or square line end styles to give an object a more rough-hewn, sharp appearance.

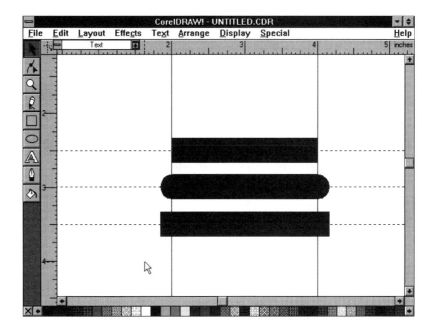

Using Different Line Styles

So far in this book, all the lines you have drawn, including the lines in the characters you have typed, have been solid lines. CorelDRAW! 4 provides a list box full of line styles and, if that is not enough, you can edit a file named CORELDRAW.DOT and add more.

In the following exercise you'll try out various line styles, look at them in various widths, and apply the different line end caps to them.

1. Select the Outline Pen, click on the Outline Pen icon, and place check marks in the Graphic and Artistic Text check boxes. Then click on OK to apply a new default line width to these two types of objects.

2. When the Outline Pen dialog box opens, change the line width to 0.014 inch (1 point) and click on OK.

   You are starting with a 1-point line because a hairline (1/4 point) is too small for demonstrating the different types of lines. The dots in a dotted line are the same height as the line is wide. Therefore, a dotted hairline has dots that are .003-inch high—three thousandths of an inch! These will print on most laser and PostScript printers, but many other printers cannot print them, and the screen does not display them correctly without magnification.

11

3. Select actual size magnification (1:1) and, with the Pencil tool, draw four straight horizontal lines, each about 3 1/2 inches long, at 4, 4 1/2, 5, and 5 1/2 inches on the vertical ruler.

4. Click on the Text tool, type **Corel** at about 6 1/2 inches on the vertical ruler, select it with the Pick tool, and use the Text roll-up to select Bodnoff normal, 60 points, and then click on Apply.

5. While the text is still selected, click on the X at the end of the on-screen palette to turn off the fill. Your screen should look like Figure 11-12.

6. With the Pick tool, click on the second horizontal line, open the Pen roll-up, and click on the third button (line style) from the top. A dashed and dotted line styles list box will open, as shown here:

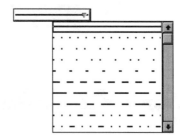

7. Select the second line type from the top. The list box closes, and a normal dotted line appears in the Pen roll-up's line styles field. Click on Apply.

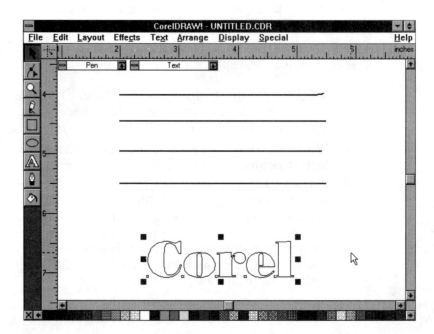

Lines and text prepared for testing line styles
Figure 11-12.

8. Select the third horizontal line and then, from the dashed and dotted line styles list box, select the second dashed line (the seventh line type). Click on Apply.

9. Select the fourth horizontal line and, from the dashed and dotted line styles list box, select the dash, double-dot line (the tenth line type). Again, click on Apply.

10. Select the text and, from the dashed and dotted line styles list box, select the first dotted line and click on Apply. Your screen should now look like Figure 11-13.

    Next, quickly look at how dotted and dashed lines look at various line widths and with various line end caps.

11. With the Pick tool, draw a marquee around the four lines (not the text).

12. From the Outline Pen flyout menu, select various line widths: first 2 points (fourth line width from the right) and then 8 points (third line width from the right). Your lines will look like this:

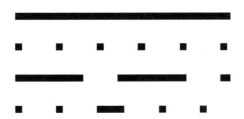

13. Select New from the File menu and No to clear the work area.

If you want to add more dotted and/or dashed lines, leave CorelDRAW!, bring up an ASCII text editor such as Windows Notepad, and edit the file CORELDRAW.DOT that is in the directory in which CorelDRAW! was installed. Instructions on adding line types are in the beginning of the file.

11

There is much variety in the styles, widths, and ends you can use with lines. In the next section you will see how you can further enhance a line with many different arrowheads and tail feathers.

Adding and Editing Arrowheads

In the earlier section, "Selecting Line End Caps," you saw one technique for ending lines. Additionally, there are a number of arrowhead and tail feather options that you can place on the end of a line. You can also customize an existing arrowhead with the Arrowhead Editor, and add new arrowheads to the arrowhead display boxes. In the next two exercises you will add some

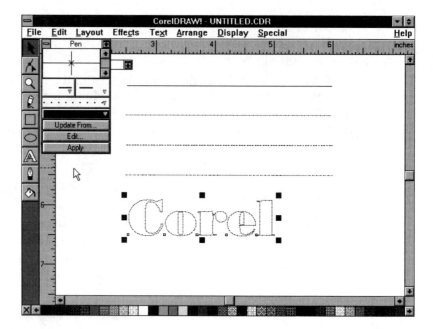

Using various
line styles
with 1-point
lines
Figure 11-13.

arrowheads and tail feathers and customize them using the Outline Pen
dialog box, Pen roll-up, and Arrowhead Editor.

1. Select the Outline Pen, click on the fourth line width from the right (2
   points), click on Artistic Text and Paragraph Text, and then OK to apply
   this to all new objects.

2. Draw three horizontal lines about 3 inches long at 2, 3, and 4 inches on
   the vertical ruler. Be sure to draw the lines from left to right so the left
   end is the beginning of the line. Set the magnification to actual size.
   Use the scroll bars to center the three lines on your screen.

3. With the Shaping tool, click on the first line and notice that the left end
   of the line has the larger node, as shown here:

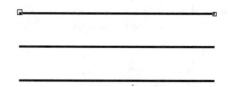

4. Change to the Pick tool. The first line should automatically be selected.

5. From the Outline Pen dialog box, click on the Arrows line-ending
   (right) display box. An arrowhead selection display box will open.

6. To put an arrowhead on the right end of this line, click on the second arrowhead from the right on the top row.

7. To add some tail feathers on the left end of the line, click on the Arrows line-beginning (left) display box, scroll the set of arrowhead display boxes by pressing the down scroll arrow three times, and then click on the last set of tail feathers on the bottom row, as shown in Figure 11-14.

8. Click on OK to return to your drawing, and click on a blank area of the screen. (Note that the last line style used in the Pen roll-up was the dash-double dot line. You might want to change this.) Your arrow should look like this:

9. Open the Pen roll-up from the Outline Pen Roll-up icon if it's not already on your screen. The second field down contains line-beginning (left) and line-ending display boxes identical to those in the Outline Pen dialog box. Click on a box and make your selection, repeat this for the other end, and then click on Apply. Use the Pen roll-up to place line endings of your choice on the second and third lines. One possible set of choices is shown in Figure 11-15.

10. With the Pick tool, draw a marquee around the three lines and set the line width, first, to 4 points. (Open the Outline Pen dialog box, change the line width to 0.056 inch, and click on OK. You can use the Pen

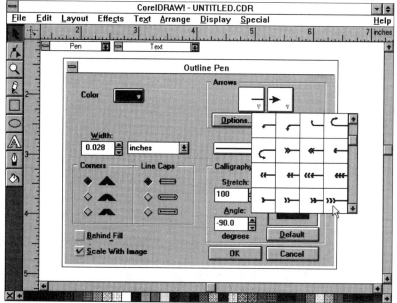

Arrowhead display box

Figure 11-14.

11

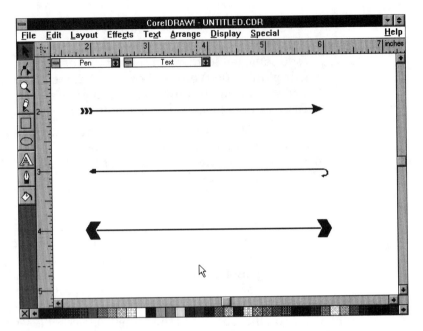

One possible
set of line
endings
Figure 11-15.

roll-up window's Edit button to open the Outline Pen dialog box, saving mouse movements and keystrokes.) Then set the line width to 8 points (you can use the third icon from the right on the Pen flyout menu). Notice how the size of the line endings changes with the size of the line.

11. Select New from the File menu (and don't save the changes) to clear the work area.

Next, use the Arrowhead Editor to modify an existing arrowhead.

CAUTION: If you close the Arrowhead Editor after modifying an arrowhead, you will have permanently modified the arrowhead you were working on. You can again modify the arrowhead to try and re-create the original, but you may not get it exactly the way it was.

TIP: To prevent permanently modifying your arrowhead file, leave CorelDRAW!, go to the CUSTOM subdirectory under the directory in which CorelDRAW! is installed, and make a copy of the file that contains the arrowheads—CORELDRW.END. Call the new file CORELDRW.EN1. Then you can modify arrowheads as you wish and when you are done, you can leave CorelDRAW! once again and copy CORELDRW.EN1 back to CORELDRW.END to restore the original arrowheads.

1. At actual size magnification, draw a horizontal line in the middle of the page.

2. Using the Pen roll-up, click on Edit to open the Outline Pen dialog box. Change to a 4-point (0.056-inch) line width.

3. Select the Arrows line-ending (right) box and click on the second arrowhead from the right on the top row. Click on the Options button and choose the Edit option.

4. By clicking and dragging on the eight boundary markers, you can modify the arrowhead, stretch out both the left and right ends, and reduce the height. In the latter operation it is likely that the arrowhead will get off center vertically. Use the Center in Y command button to correct this. Try Reflect in X to see the effect of this, and use it to return the arrowhead to its original orientation. When you are done, your dialog box should look like Figure 11-16.

CAUTION: If you click on OK and close the Arrowhead Editor, you will permanently modify this arrowhead in the Arrows display box. You can come back and move everything back to its original position (see the illustration in the "Arrows" section in the early part of this chapter to see how this should look). But unless you want to do that, choose Cancel to exit the Arrowhead Editor.

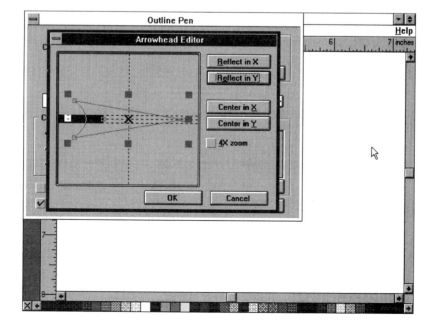

Arrowhead
Editor with
modified
arrowhead
Figure 11-16.

11

5. If you don't mind permanently modifying the second arrowhead, click on OK to close the Editor and return to the Outline Pen dialog box. Then click on the second arrowhead again to select your modifications, and click on OK to return to your drawing. Your arrow should look like this:

6. Select New from the File menu and No to clear the work area.

The Arrowhead Editor is used to stretch, scale, and position an existing arrowhead in relation to the line it will be applied to. If you want to create a new arrowhead, do so in CorelDRAW!, as you would any other object (if you build an arrowhead with multiple objects, select them all and use Combine from the Arrange menu to make one object out of them). Then use the Create Arrow command in the Special menu to save the new arrowhead at the end of the list of arrowheads. It does not matter if you have the relative size of the new arrowhead correct, because you can modify this with the Arrowhead Editor.

In the next section, you will begin working with the pen shapes—Width, Angle, and Stretch— that make calligraphic effects possible in CorelDRAW!.

A Pen Shape for Calligraphic Effects

The Stretch and Angle settings in the Outline Pen dialog box are in a separate enclosed area subtitled "Calligraphy." The Calligraphy option allows you to create variable calligraphic nibs that can be highly effective with freehand drawings and text. If you adjust both the Stretch and Angle settings in various combinations, you can approximate a freehand style of drawing.

In the following exercise, you will experiment with the Nib Shape settings, using some curves you will draw, to achieve both hand-sketched and comic-strip-style looks.

1. At actual size magnification, and with the rulers turned off, draw an approximation of the objects shown in Figure 11-17.

2. Select all the objects, group them using the Group command in the Arrange menu, set their width to 2 points (the fourth width from the right in the Pen flyout), and turn off their fill by clicking on the X at the end of the on-screen palette.

3. Save this image with the File Save As command and the name CURVES.

4. Activate the Outline Pen and open the Outline Pen dialog box. The current Calligraphy settings for this are Stretch, 100 percent and Angle, 0.0 degrees.

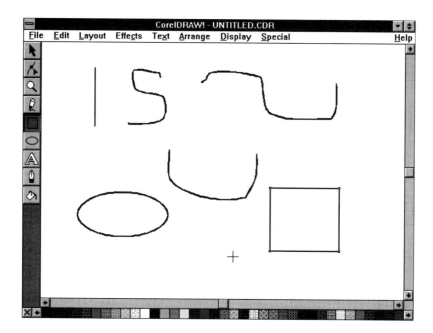

5. Leave the Width value at 0.028 inch (2 points), but change the Angle and Stretch values to 42 degrees and 14 percent, respectively. This translates into a thin outline and a relatively narrow nib with the "pen" held at a 42-degree angle. Click on OK. The effects are shown in Figure 11-18.

TIP: It is easier to use the numeric entry boxes to achieve exact Angle and Stretch settings. Interactively using the mouse pointer in the Nib Shape display box is better suited to nibs that can be approximately sized by eye.

11

6. To vary line thickness, experiment with the stretch of the nib, expressed as a percentage of the nib width. Keep decreasing the Stretch value all the way to 2 percent, and then select OK. There doesn't seem to be much change.

As the value in the Stretch numeric entry box decreases, you effectively flatten the nib in one direction; the black symbol representing a pen nib is broad in one dimension and extremely narrow in the other, which makes more extreme calligraphic effects possible. If you were to increase the Stretch value all the way to 100 percent, the curves of the image would have the same thickness everywhere, and no calligraphic effects could result.

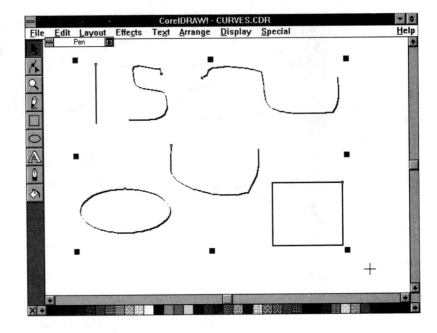

Outline Width
setting of
0.028 inch,
Angle of 42
degrees, and
Stretch of 14%
Figure 11-18.

TIP: The Stretch settings represent the relative squareness or roundness of the nib, with 100 percent representing a square nib and 1 percent representing a long and narrow nib. As the Stretch percentage value decreases, the variation in line thickness of a drawn object increases.

7. Access the Outline Pen dialog box once more. Return the Stretch to 50 percent and adjust the Angle of the nib from 42 to 0 degrees. You will recall that the Angle setting is analogous to the way you hold a calligraphic pen in your hand; at a 0-degree setting, the Nib Shape display box alters to show you a perfectly vertical nib.

8. Select OK to exit the dialog box. Now the areas that display the thickest and thinnest lines have shifted (by 42 degrees), as shown in Figure 11-19. Adjusting the Angle value is therefore a convenient way to control where thick and thin lines appear on any selected object.

9. Access the Outline Pen dialog box again and click on the Default button. This resets the Stretch and Angle settings to the default values of 100 percent and 0 degrees, respectively—a square nib with no variations in thickness. Now set Width to 0.06 inch and then select OK. The curves are redrawn with a consistently thick outline, much like a cartoon character.

10. Experiment with Stretch and Angle settings at this outline width, too. For example, to obtain greater variation in line thickness, set Stretch at a

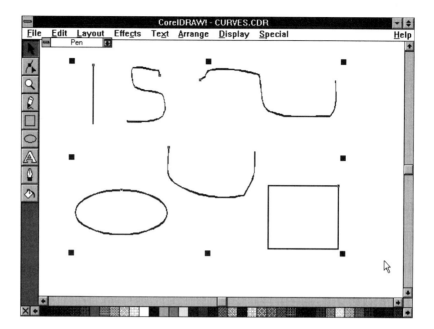

Outline Width
setting of
0.028 inch,
Angle of 0.0
degrees, and
Stretch of 50%
Figure 11-19.

reduced value, such as 4 percent, as shown in Figure 11-20. To change the placement of the thinner segments of the curve, try different Angle settings.

11. Select New from the File menu and answer No to saving the changes to clear the screen.

Appendix C
gives you more
information on
how to trace
bitmap and
scanned
images.

The possibilities for creating custom calligraphic nibs should spark your imagination. An interesting use for an image sketched faintly at 0.01-inch width might be as a background illustration in a newsletter, where the text overprints the image without obscuring it totally. You have probably seen applications like this involving outlines of scanned photographs. Appendix C will give you more information on how to outline bitmap and scanned images.

11

TIP: Avoid using 0.00-inch widths unless your draft printer is also the printer you will be using for your final output. As an outline Width setting, 0.00 inch represents the thinnest line your printer is capable of printing. For PostScript printers, this is 1 pixel or 0.03 inch, but for a Linotronic or other high-resolution imagesetter, 0.00 inch could represent something even thinner. Because of the variations among printers, this setting does not truly represent a fixed width, and the screen does not display a WYSIWYG representation of it.

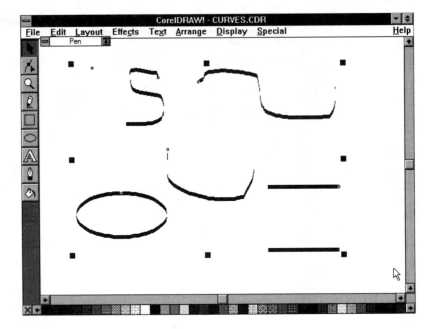

Outline Width
of 0.06, Angle
of 0.0 degrees,
and Stretch of
100%
Figure 11-20.

Angle settings are especially useful to help you fine-tune the exact location
of thick and thin lines within a drawing. With precise, degree-by-degree
control available, you can make sure that thinner areas of a selected curve
are positioned exactly where you want them.

Outline Pen Hints

The range of choices available to you makes the Outline Pen one of the
richer areas of CorelDRAW!. The following sections contain selected hints for
making the most of your choices and coordinating your settings with the
type of work you are doing.

Defining an Outline Pen for Text

Do you want text in your drawings to appear normally? Or are you aiming for
exaggerated or stylized effects? For a clean-cut look, it's best to create text
without an outline, using the X in the Outline Pen flyout menu. When text has
a visible outline, some characters appear to be drawn thicker, with the result
that spaces within letters (such as in a lowercase "a" or "e") are partially or
wholly filled in. This is especially true when you create text in small point sizes.

If your design calls for outlined text, a good way to maintain readability in
smaller point sizes is to activate the Behind Fill option in the Outline Pen

dialog box. As mentioned earlier, Behind Fill causes the outline to appear half as thick as it really is, because the other half of the outline is hidden behind the object's fill.

In some cases, you may really prefer a slightly smudgy graphic look of text with thick outlines. Let the purpose and design of your illustration be your guide in choosing how to outline text.

Varying Your Calligraphic Style

Unless you have a background in calligraphy, the wealth of Width, Angle, Stretch, and Corners settings available to you in the Outline Pen dialog box can be confusing. The following hints should help put you on the right track if you know the effect you would like to achieve.

Desktop publishers can create faint background illustrations from original artwork or scanned photos and then overprint them with text. The result is a visible but not distracting piece of artwork that enhances the mood of an article or feature. Recommended settings for this kind of graphics effect are Width, 0.03 inch or less; Stretch, 14 percent or less; and a variable Angle according to your tastes. Keep in mind that if you reduce the outline Width setting below 0.02 inch (or 1.2 fractional points), you will not be able to see an accurate representation of the calligraphy on your screen. The outline will still print according to your specifications, however.

Miter corner settings promote an angular look, while rounded corner settings create a smooth appearance.

Illustrators, cartoonists, and other artists seeking a traditional hand-sketched look should set Calligraphy options to achieve the desired variation in line thickness. For finer lines, Outline Pen width should be fairly thin, below 0.05 inch; and for blunter strokes, above 0.06 inch. Stretch should be set to 1 to 2 percent for the maximum variation in line thickness, and closer to 100 percent for minimal variation. The fine-tuning possible with Angle settings permits you to place thicker or thinner lines at exact locations.

For those who are interested in extremely broad calligraphic strokes, consider setting Stretch below 100 percent, removing the fill of an object, and then varying the Angle settings. The example text that follows has a three-dimensional look because it was created at a Width of 0.04 inch, at an Angle of 75 degrees, and with a Stretch of 10 percent:

11

TIP: When the Angle field is 0.0, the pen is vertical. When the Angle is increased, the slant of the pen increases. When the Stretch is 100 percent (the maximum value allowed), the nib shape is a square. When the Stretch is reduced, the nib becomes thinner.

Copying Outline Styles

In Chapter 10, you transferred text attributes from one text string to another using the Copy Attributes From command in the Edit menu. You can do the same with Outline Pen attributes.

You can imagine how useful the Copy Attributes From command can be if you need to copy Outline Pen styles to, or from, even larger blocks of text or groups of objects.

CORELDRAW! 4

CHAPTER

CORELDRAW! 4

12

DEFINING OUTLINE AND FILL COLOR

To define an object's outline completely in CorelDRAW!, you must define both the Outline Pen shape and the Outline Color attributes. You learned how to select attributes for the Outline Pen in Chapter 11; in this chapter, you will begin to define Outline Color. As you may recall, the Outline Pen allows you to draw with the characteristic style of a calligraphic pen, using "nibs" of various sizes. Outline Color represents the colors and textures that flow from the pen.

This chapter also introduces you to the CorelDRAW! Fill tool. The Fill tool, as its icon suggests, functions like a paint bucket with a limitless supply of paint, capable of filling the interior of any leakproof object. A leakproof object is any object that is a closed path; all CorelDRAW! objects are leakproof, except straight lines and open curves. If you draw a curve object in which the two end nodes do not join, the object remains an open path, and you cannot fill it. When you select such an object, the words "Open Path" appear at the right side of the status line. (You can close an open path by joining its end nodes, as you will recall from Chapter 8.)

Both the Outline and Fill tools offer you a choice between two different color systems—Spot color and Process color—for assigning color to an object. In the *Spot color* system, each color is assigned a unique name or number. Spot color works best for images that contain only a few colors, such as headings in newsletters or single-color objects within black-and-white graphics. The *Process color* system, on the other hand, specifies colors in terms of a mix of primary colors or color properties. Process color is more appropriate to use when you plan traditional four-color printing of images that contain a large number of colors.

You will find more information about color systems and color separation principles in Chapter 13.

Included with CorelDRAW! are three standard color-matching systems used in the printing industry: the PANTONE Spot and Process Color Matching Systems and the TRUMATCH Process Color System.

Your options for assigning outline and fill colors do not end with Spot and Process colors, however. Unlike a hand-held pen, the CorelDRAW! pen not only dispenses "ink" in all colors of the rainbow, it can lay down an assortment of halftone screens for PostScript printing. In addition, the Fill tool can dispense other types of fills that the Outline Color tool does not provide: fountain fills in any combination of colors, two-color and full-color pattern fills from the CorelDRAW! library, texture fills, and 42 different gray-scale PostScript texture fills. You will learn more about these types of fills in "Custom Fountain Fills," "Bitmap and Vector Fill Patterns," and "PostScript Texture Fills" later in this chapter.

The exercises in this chapter give you practice in specifying Spot color, Process color, gray shades, and PostScript halftone screen patterns for your object outlines and fills. The exercises also give you practice using fountain fills, bitmap fills, vector pattern fills, and PostScript texture fills for objects. The CorelDRAW! window faithfully reproduces your settings, unless you have chosen a PostScript halftone screen or texture fill. Since you cannot preview these types of outlines or fills, you must print out your work on a PostScript printer in order to view it. See Chapter 13 for assistance with printing.

Defining an Object's Outline Color Attributes

You define colors in CorelDRAW! using the Outline Color dialog box, shown in Figure 12-1, which you access from the Outline Pen flyout menu. This dialog box allows you to choose between Spot color and Process color, to select a color *model* (the method of defining color) as well as a color, and to select from among several options. The options available in the Outline Color dialog box are determined by the color model or system selected in the Show drop-down list box. You will be using the Outline Color dialog box throughout this chapter; its features will be covered in detail as they are used.

TIP: If your Outline Color dialog box does not look like Figure 12-1, it has been previously used and left in another mode. You will see how to change this in a moment.

Your first step in defining Outline Color attributes is to determine whether you want to define the attributes for existing objects or for objects not yet rendered. (An existing object can be one that you have just drawn or one that you have saved previously.) When defining Outline Color attributes for an existing object, you are in effect editing its current attributes. The changes you make apply to that object only, not to additional objects you may create later.

On the other hand, when you click on an option in the Outline Pen flyout menu without first selecting an object, CorelDRAW! assumes that you want to change the standard or default attributes for objects that you draw in the future. The object or series of objects that you draw next will automatically incorporate the newly defined Outline Color attributes.

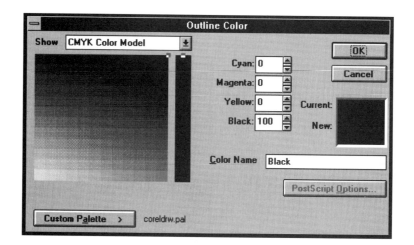

Outline Color
dialog box
with Process
color settings
Figure 12-1.

12

TIP: Always work in full color mode when you alter Outline Color attributes. Wireframe mode does not show you how the selected outline color looks. For most attributes, full color mode lets you see the result of your changes instantly.

Outlining with Spot Color

Use Spot color with a PostScript printer since it gives you access to special PostScript halftone screen patterns.

You should base your choice of a color system (Spot or Process color) in CorelDRAW! on the number of colors in your picture. If an image contains more than four colors, you would probably find Spot color too expensive and time-consuming to produce; choose Process color instead. If an image contains four or fewer colors, and you require close color matching, use the Spot color system to assign a unique PANTONE color name to each color.

Setting New Outline Color Defaults

In the following exercise, you will define the default Outline Color attributes using the Outline Color dialog box and then create objects with those defaults.

1. If necessary, clear the screen by selecting New from the File menu and then click on the Outline Pen tool. When the Outline Pen flyout menu appears, select the Outline Color icon, the first icon in the second row. It looks like a color wheel. The dialog box shown in Figure 12-2 appears, asking you which default settings you want to change.

2. Verify that Graphic is selected and click on OK. The Outline Color dialog box is displayed.

3. Select Spot color by clicking on the down arrow to the right of the Show drop-down list box and then clicking on PANTONE Spot Colors. The Outline Color dialog box should now look like Figure 12-3.

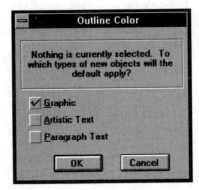

Outline Color default dialog box

Figure 12-2.

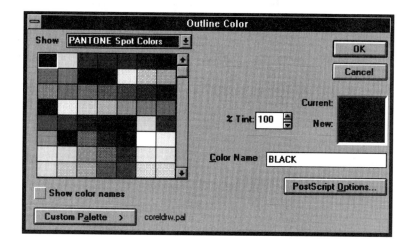

Outline Color
dialog box for
Spot color
Figure 12-3.

There are some differences between the Outline Color dialog box with the Spot color method selected (as shown in Figure 12-3) and the same dialog box with the Process color method selected (as shown in Figure 12-1). These differences are largely a function of the color model and will be covered in detail later in this chapter. Only the Spot color dialog box allows you to adjust the percentage of tint and to select a PostScript halftone and its attributes (see "Outlining with PostScript Halftone Screen Patterns" later in this chapter). All versions of the Outline Color dialog box have a Custom Palette button that opens the menu shown here:

The Palette menu allows you to add colors to or delete colors from the current palette, and to load a palette from your hard disk or save it to disk.

Once you have made changes in the Outline Color dialog box, those changes will be reflected in its settings the next time you open the dialog box. Therefore, you can make decisions on Spot versus Process color and the

12

model and palette you want to use when you begin a drawing, and those changes will keep displaying in the dialog box until you change them.

The colors you select using the Spot color system are from the PANTONE Matching System. Since the colors that appear in the color display box are only approximations, you should use the PANTONE Color Reference Manual to evaluate your choice of colors before printing. In addition, you can specify a percentage of the tint of any Spot colors you select. The effect of settings below 100 percent is to render a lighter shade of the selected color on your monitor or color printout.

Continue setting the Outline Color defaults with these steps:

4. Click on the first color from the left in the top row of the color palette. The selected color appears in a color display box on the right of the dialog box. The % Tint numeric entry box shows a value of 100 (the default value). The PANTONE identification name or number for this color, in this case "BLACK," displays in the Color Name text box.

5. Click on OK to set the default Outline Color attributes and exit the Outline Color dialog box.

    New objects that you create will now have the default outline color. Follow the next steps to create a new object:

6. From the Outline Pen flyout menu select the 2-point width (top row, fourth from the right), click on OK to have it apply to graphic objects, then, at actual size (1:1) magnification, draw several curves, as shown here:

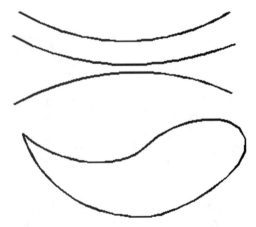

The curves are created with the default black outline color and 2-point line width. In the next section you will learn how to change the outline color for existing objects.

Assigning Spot Color Outlines

In the following exercise, you will assign Spot colors and shades of gray to the outline of your existing CorelDRAW! objects (created in the previous exercise.)

1. Drag a marquee around all of the objects you created in the previous exercise to select them, and choose Group from the Arrange menu.

2. To begin editing the existing Outline Color attributes, click on the Outline Pen and the Custom Outline Color icon, or press [Shift]-[F12]. The Outline Color dialog box appears.

TIP: If an item is selected, you can immediately open the Outline Color dialog box by pressing the shortcut keys [Shift]-[F12].

3. Click on the fourth color from the left in the top row of the color palette. The PANTONE identification name or number for this color, in this case "PANTONE Rubine Red CV," displays in the Color Name text box. If you have the PANTONE Color Reference Manual, you can compare what you see on the screen with what you see in the manual. There probably is a difference since most color monitors are not perfectly calibrated.

4. Click on OK in the dialog box. Notice that the curves have changed from black to Rubine Red.

5. Open the Outline Color dialog box again. This time, click on black (the first color in the top row) and set the tint value to 51 percent. The color preview window in the dialog box now displays a 51 percent gray shade in the lower part of the window, which you can compare with the current color in the top of the window.

6. Click on OK. If you have a VGA or Super VGA display card, you will see an actual representation of a 51 percent gray shade in the drawing, as shown in Figure 12-4.

7. Open the Outline Color dialog box once more, reselect PANTONE Rubine Red (fourth color in the top row), and then return the tint value to 51 percent. You have just selected a lighter tint of PANTONE Rubine Red.

8. Select OK to exit the dialog box with the new Outline Color setting.

9. Save this as CURVES2 and clear the screen by selecting New from the File menu.

12

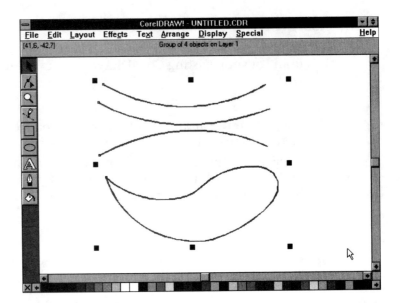

Both the Outline Pen shape and color defaults must be set before creating an object. In the next section you will set both defaults and use them with Artistic Text.

Setting New Spot Color Outline Pen Defaults

In this exercise, you will change defaults for both the Outline Pen and Spot Outline Color attributes, and then create new objects that exhibit those defaults automatically.

1. Begin with an empty page by choosing New from the File menu and not saving the curves you drew. Set the display magnification to actual size (1:1).

2. Without creating or selecting any objects, click on the Outline Pen and on the Custom Outline Pen icon in the first row of the flyout menu. A dialog box similar to the one you saw in Figure 12-2 appears, asking whether you want to change default Outline Pen values. Select Artistic Text (you can leave Graphic Text selected in addition) and click on OK to access the Outline Pen dialog box.

3. When the Outline Pen dialog box appears, set the Outline Pen attributes as follows: Width, 0.15 inch; Style, solid line; Corners, sharp (miter); Line Caps, butt; Stretch, 10 percent; Angle, –45 degrees. Do not check either Behind Fill or Scale With Image.

4. Click on the Color button at the top of the dialog box. The color drop-down palette opens, as shown here:

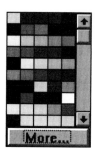

This color palette, although smaller, has the same colors to choose from as the color palette in the Outline Color dialog box.

5. Click on the More button at the bottom of the color palette. The Outline Color dialog box appears.

6. Verify that PANTONE Spot Colors is selected, then choose Blue CV Color (first box from the left in the second row), and tint value of 100 percent. Select OK twice to save these settings and exit both the Outline Color and Outline Pen dialog boxes.

7. Activate Show Rulers, make sure Edit Wireframe is off, and then click on the Text tool. Click in the lower left of your screen.

8. Open the Text roll-up window from the Text menu and select the following text attributes: no justification, Banff normal, 300 points. Click on Apply, roll up the Text window, type a capital **A**, and select the Pick tool. The letter "A" should be selected. If you followed all the steps up to this point, the text should have a default fill of black. Your screen should look like Figure 12-5, except that the color of the outline is blue. Remember that *all* of the new Outline Pen and Color attributes you have selected apply to the new object automatically.

9. Clear the screen by selecting New from the File menu. Do not save your work.

If you create the same kinds of images regularly in your work, you probably have strong personal preferences for what you would like default outlines to look like. If you wish, start a new drawing on your own, setting up the Outline Pen and Outline Color default attributes that will apply to the basic elements in your drawing. You can edit settings for objects that should have different outline fills by selecting them after you draw them and accessing the appropriate dialog boxes. If you are not satisfied with the results of your Outline Pen or Outline Color attribute settings, you can make any adjustments during the drawing process.

12

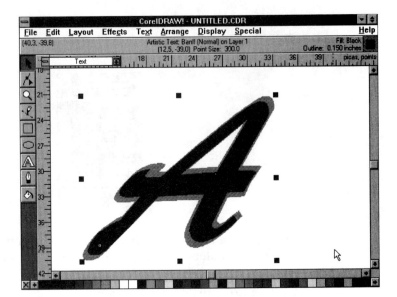

Letter created
with new
default
PANTONE
Spot color
outline
Figure 12-5.

You may find selecting a particular Spot color from the color palette difficult—it could be hard to find a particular PANTONE color from the more than 700 that are shown. If you have a PANTONE Color Reference Manual or know the PANTONE name or number of a particular color, there is another way to select a Spot color. Select Show color names in the Outline Color dialog box, and a list of PANTONE color names, as shown in Figure 12-6, is provided. When you select a color on the list, it is displayed in the color display box to the right of the list. Also, you can enter a few characters of a PANTONE name or number in the Search String box, and that name or number will be highlighted in the list while the color is shown in the display box.

If you click on OK to leave the Outline Color dialog box, you are returned to your drawing. The next time you select the Outline Color icon from the Outline Pen flyout menu, you will get the list of PANTONE colors that you just left (Figure 12-6), not the palette shown in Figure 12-3. If you want to return to the palette when you next select the Outline Color icon, deselect Show color names before leaving the Outline Color dialog box.

Using the Pen Roll-Up for Outline Color

The Pen roll-up, which you'll remember from Chapter 11, opens from the Outline Pen flyout menu (second icon from the left in the top row). It provides two ways to select or change outline color. The first is the color button (fourth bar up from the bottom), which opens the same color palette you accessed from the Outline Pen dialog box.

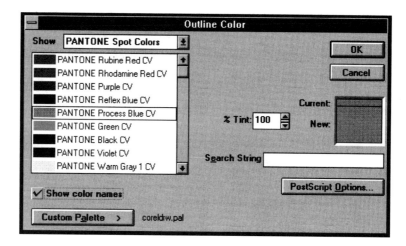

Outline Color
dialog box
listing Spot
colors
Figure 12-6.

Clicking on a color in the Pen roll-up palette, and clicking on Apply, will apply the color to the outline of the selected object. Clicking on More will access the Outline Color dialog box.

The second method of applying outline color from the Pen roll-up is to click on the Edit button (second from the bottom), which opens the full Outline Pen dialog box. Click on the Color button to open the color palette and then click on More to open the Outline Color dialog box. This is, of course, the same dialog box you get by clicking on the Outline Color icon in the Outline Pen flyout menu, or by pressing (Shift)-(F12).

If you own or use a PostScript printer, go on to the next section to learn how to assign a PostScript halftone screen as an outline color. This option is available only when you choose the Spot color method, and it takes effect only if you have a PostScript printer. You cannot see it on the screen.

Outlining with PostScript Halftone Screen Patterns

If you work with a PostScript printer, you can elect to fill an outline with a halftone screen pattern of the currently selected Spot color. This option is available only when you have selected Spot color as your Outline Color method. The CorelDRAW! window displays PostScript halftone screen patterns as solid colors only; to see the patterns, you must print the images on a PostScript printer.

The concept of a *halftone screen* is probably familiar to you already: it is a method of representing continuous tone or color by patterns of dots.

12

Black-and-white and color photographs in newspapers and magazines are examples of halftone images that you see every day.

CorelDRAW! offers ten different types of halftone screen patterns.

You define a PostScript halftone screen by clicking on the PostScript Options command button in the lower right of the Outline Color dialog box. You can vary the frequency (number of occurrences per inch) and angle of any screen to achieve dramatic differences in outline appearance, even within a single pattern.

Defining a PostScript halftone screen outline requires the following steps:

1. Select the Spot color (and tint, if desired) in which you want to print a screen pattern.
2. Click on the PostScript Options command button at the lower right of the Outline Color dialog box.
3. Specify a halftone screen pattern from among the 15 available patterns.
4. Select the frequency or number of occurrences of the pattern, per inch.
5. Determine the angle at which the pattern should print.

Since you cannot view the results of your selections on screen, this section does not feature any exercises. However, some guidelines for selecting halftone screen patterns, frequency, and angle are presented in the next section. Chapter 13 has more instructions on printing with PostScript printers.

Selecting Halftone Screen Patterns

To begin defining a halftone screen outline, make sure you have selected the Spot color and tint in which you want to print your outline. Then click on the PostScript Options command button at the lower right of the Outline Color dialog box. The PostScript Options dialog box shown in Figure 12-7 appears. This dialog box contains settings for Type, Frequency, and Angle attributes of patterns.

Selecting Halftone Screen Type

The Type option in the PostScript Options dialog box features 15 halftone patterns that are available for your Outline Color work. Your choices are Default, Dot, Line, Diamond, Diamond2, Dot2, Elliptical, Euclidian, Grid, Lines, MicroWaves, OutCircleBlk, OutCircleWhi, Rhomboid, and Star. (Default is a separate, plain or "constant" screen without a pattern in it.) To select a halftone screen type, scroll through the list until you see the name of the desired pattern and click on the name to highlight it.

PostScript
Options
dialog box
with default
settings
Figure 12-7.

Selecting Halftone Screen Frequency

The Frequency option in the PostScript Options dialog box allows you to determine how many times per inch the pattern should occur within the outline. The available range is from 0 to 1500 per inch, and the default setting is 60. The number you select depends upon the resolution of your ultimate output device; refer to Chapter 13 for more details on frequency settings for PostScript halftone screens.

Setting Halftone Screen Angle

The third option in the PostScript Options dialog box allows you to specify the angle of the screen pattern when you print it. Keep in mind that the halftone screen angle remains constant, no matter how you transform an object. If you stretch, scale, rotate, or skew an object after assigning it a halftone screen outline, you could alter its appearance significantly. If you do not want this to happen, remember to change the screen angle after performing a transform operation, to match the offset of the transformed object. You will achieve the best results by setting your screen angle at 0, 45, 90, and 180 degrees.

Outlining with Process Color

12

With the Process color system, you specify color in terms of either a set of primary colors or a set of color properties. CorelDRAW! provides three methods or models for defining Process color: CMYK (cyan, magenta, yellow, and black), RGB (red, green, and blue), and HSB (hue, saturation, and brightness). Both CMYK and RGB define a color in terms of the constituent colors in the model, while HSB defines a color in terms of color properties. For example, "brick red" is defined as 0 percent cyan, 60 percent magenta, 80 percent yellow, and 20 percent black in the CMYK model. In RGB, it is 80 percent red, 20 percent green, and 0 percent blue; and in HSB, it is 15 degrees of hue, 100 percent saturation, and 80 percent brightness. You can use any of the three models you are most comfortable with, but CorelDRAW! will convert RGB and HSB to CMYK. Therefore, CMYK will be the primary focus of this book.

CMYK is the
four-color
standard for
the printing
industry.

You can specify over 16 million colors by using various CMYK percentages. As mentioned previously, you should specify Process color instead of Spot color when your drawing includes more than four colors and you plan to reproduce it through the four-color printing process.

CorelDRAW! supports color separation for Process as well as Spot color. When you specify color in CMYK terms, your printer generates only four sheets (one each for cyan, magenta, yellow, and black) for every image page, no matter how many colors the image contains. When you specify in Spot color terms, on the other hand, the printer generates a separate page for every single color used in the drawing. You will learn more about printing Spot and Process colors and their separation in Chapter 13.

To specify Process colors for an existing object, you select or create the object, click on the Outline Pen, and click again on the Outline Color icon in the flyout menu. When the Outline Color dialog box appears, you select one of the Process models or color systems to use in defining the color you want. If you pick CMYK, RGB, or HSB, you will be able to create a color by defining a mixture of the constituent colors or color properties, using a dialog box that looks like Figure 12-1. If you pick PANTONE or TRUMATCH Process Colors for the color model, you can select a color from a palette or from a list of names similar to the palette and list you saw with Spot color.

For each color model, the Outline Color dialog box looks a little different. The Outline Color dialog boxes for HSB and RGB look, and operate, very much like the one shown in Figure 12-1 for CMYK. In the upper-left corner of the dialog box is a color selector that consists of two boxes (one circle and one box in the case of HSB) filled with varying shades of color. By dragging a marker in each box you can define a Process color. The marker in the square box or circle can be moved in two directions (left or right and up or down) while the marker in the rectangular box can be moved only up or down. In the CMYK model the square defines percentages of cyan and magenta, while the rectangle defines the percentage of yellow (black is automatically defined). In the RGB model the square defines percentages of red and green, while the rectangle defines blue. In the HSB model the circle defines the hue (it is specified in degrees from 0 to 360 around the circle) and the percentage of saturation (specified by the distance from the center), while the rectangle defines brightness.

To the right of the visual selector is a set of numeric entry boxes and scroll arrows for selecting the desired percentages of constituent colors or properties. If you are using a Process color reference chart such as the TRUMATCH Colorfinder, you can look for a color in the chart and then enter the percentages that create that color.

In the following exercise, you will specify both the Outline Pen and Process Outline Color for a text string.

1. At actual size magnification with rulers turned off, select the Text tool, click in the middle of the left side, and type **CorelDRAW!**. Activate the Pick tool to select the text string.

2. Open the Text roll-up and select Banff normal, 70-point type. Click on Apply and move or close the roll-up.

3. From the Fill tool flyout menu, click on X to turn off the fill. From the Outline Pen flyout menu, open the Outline Pen dialog box. Select rounded corners and set Width at 0.083 inch (6 points), Stretch at 14 percent, Angle at 0 degrees, and click on OK.

   When you are back in the drawing, your screen should look like this:

Your settings resulted in a moderately thick text outline, and by the calligraphic Nib Shape, an "artistic" look. The rounded corners setting adds a more polished look to the outlines of corners of angular letters. The current color does not do it justice, so you will change it now.

4. With the text string still selected, click on the Outline Pen once more. This time, select the Outline Color icon in the second row of the flyout menu to open the Outline Color dialog box.

5. If necessary, select the CMYK Color Model to switch color selection methods. The options in the dialog box change instantly. Take a moment to again familiarize yourself with the Outline Color dialog box. Move the markers in each of the visual selector boxes and notice how the color changes in the color display box, and how the percentages in the numeric entry boxes change as well. Using the scroll arrows or your mouse and keyboard, set the following color mix: Cyan 40 percent, Magenta 40 percent, Yellow 0 percent, and Black 60 percent. The color

12

display box shows a real-time approximation of changes to the color, as you scroll to or enter each specified value. When you have specified all of the values, the color display box shows a deep navy blue and the name confirms it.

6. Click on OK to exit the dialog box. The text string's outline displays as a deep navy blue, providing a contrast to the light background.

7. Press (Shift)-(F12) or click on the Outline Color icon in the Outline Pen flyout menu.

8. Select first RGB and then HSB from the Show drop-down list box and notice that Deep Navy Blue has been defined in each of these models.

Next, define your own color and add it to the custom color palette. Leave the CorelDRAW! text string on your screen and the Outline Color dialog box open. You can use the text string to test your new color.

Defining a New Color and Adding It to the Custom Palette

The custom color palette in the Outline Color dialog box displays 90 colors and 10 shades of gray. This is a far cry from the more than 16 million possible colors available with the CMYK model. The color selector in the Outline Color dialog box is Corel's answer to this discrepancy. You have seen how you can define a new color with this color selector when you want to apply it to an object. But if you want to use a color over and over, say a special corporate color you've defined, you will want to add this color to the Outline Color custom palette.

In the following exercise you will truly define a new color. In the last exercise the color you entered was already on the palette and in the name list. The new color you will define is Deep Royal Blue.

1. Select CMYK Color Model from the Show drop-down list box.

2. Type in the numeric entry boxes, or use the scroll arrows, to define a color mix of 100 percent cyan, 55 percent magenta, 0 percent yellow, and 45 percent black. The color display box will show the color, but the Color Name text entry box is empty because the color is not defined.

3. Click on the Color Name text entry box and type **Deep Royal Blue**. Your dialog box should look like that shown in Figure 12-8.

4. Click on OK to return to your drawing and see your new color. More important, clicking on OK defined your new color and added it to the color palette and the name list. See for yourself with the next step.

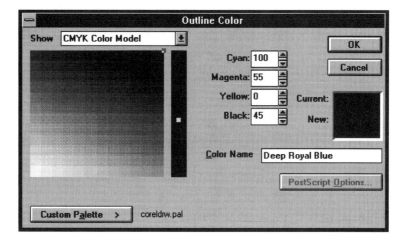

Deep Royal
Blue being
defined
Figure 12-8.

5. Press Shift-F12 to reopen the Outline Color dialog box and then select
   Custom Palette as the model. The Outline Color dialog box will open
   with a new color highlighted at the bottom of the palette and the name
   Deep Royal Blue in the Color Name text entry box.

   While it is nice to have a new color in the palette, having it at the end
   of the list is not very handy. CorelDRAW!, though, allows you to rearrange
   colors by dragging them around the palette. You can drag a color to any
   existing location and release the mouse button, and all the existing
   colors shift to the right and down to accommodate the new color.

6. Point on the new color you just defined, press and hold the mouse button
   while dragging the new color beyond the top of the palette and then
   bringing it down to the fourth row, fourth color from the left. When you
   are there, release the mouse button. Now Deep Royal Blue (your new
   color) is right next to Deep Navy Blue, as shown in Figure 12-9.

7. Assure yourself that your newly defined color is in the list of named
   colors by selecting Show color names. If necessary, click on the scroll
   bar beside the scroll box until you see Deep Royal Blue, as shown in
   Figure 12-10.

8. Click on OK to close the dialog box and return to the drawing. Leave
   the text string on your screen to use in the next exercise.

12

When specifying Process colors, you can include as many colors in the
picture as you like. When you finally print the image, the results will still be
separated into no more than four sheets.

In the next section of this chapter, you will learn a shortcut to specifying Outline
Color that will be useful if you usually print to a black-and-white printer.

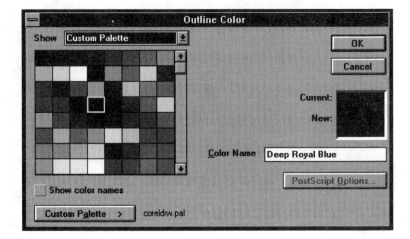

Result of
dragging Deep
Royal Blue up
next to Deep
Navy Blue
Figure 12-9.

Outlining with Black, White, or Gray

When you worked with the Outline Pen in Chapter 11, you saw how the
first row of the Outline Pen flyout menu contained five preset outline widths
that you could select simply by clicking on the desired icon. The
arrangement of the second row of the Outline Pen flyout menu is similar.
Following the Outline Color icon is a series of seven symbols that let you
select a preset Outline Color (gray shade) quickly, without having to set
attributes in a dialog box. As Figure 12-11 shows, the seven Outline Color
options are white, black, and 10, 30, 50, 70, and 90 percent gray.

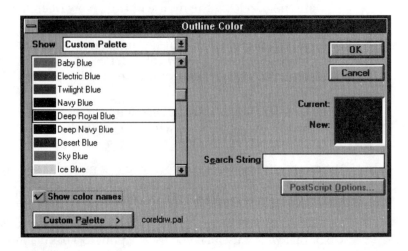

Newly defined
color in
named list of
colors
Figure 12-10.

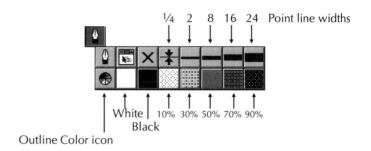

¼ 2 8 16 24 Point line widths

Preset black,
white, and
gray shades in
the Outline
Pen flyout
Figure 12-11.

White | 10% 30% 50% 70% 90%
Black

Outline Color icon

To select a preset Outline Color for an existing object, you select the object, access the Outline Pen flyout menu, and then click on the appropriate icon. To select one of these options as the default outline color, click on the desired icon in the Outline Pen flyout menu without first selecting an object.

In the following exercise, you will select several of the preset Outline Color options and apply them to the text string you created in the previous exercise.

1. Re-create the "CorelDRAW!" text string if you did not leave it on the screen after the last exercise. Magnify the area containing the text as before.

2. Select "CorelDRAW!," and then select the Outline Pen. When the flyout menu appears, click on the black square in the second row of the menu. The outline of the text string changes from dark blue to solid black.

3. Select the Outline Pen again and this time click on the 50 percent gray symbol (the third symbol from the right in the second row). Now the text outline shows a much lighter color, as in Figure 12-12.

4. Experiment with different preset Outline Color settings. Leave the text string on the screen for the next exercise.

Remember that you are not limited to these preset shades of gray if you use a black-and-white printer. You can use either the Spot color or Process color system to define other shades of gray. To define shades of gray using the Spot color method, access the Outline Color dialog box and set shades of gray by clicking on black and setting % Tint in increments of 1 percent. To define custom shades of gray using the Process color method, define a percentage for black only, leaving cyan, magenta, and yellow all at 0 percent.

12

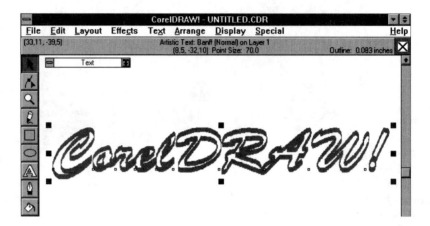

You can also use the preset shades of gray in the Outline Pen flyout menu in combination with the PostScript halftone screens.

Copying Outline Color and Pen Styles

In previous chapters, you learned how to use the Copy Attributes From command in the Edit menu to copy text or Outline Pen attributes from one object to another. You use the same command to copy Outline Color attributes between objects, as you will see in the following exercise.

1. With the "CorelDRAW!" text string still on the screen from the previous exercise, zoom out to reduce the size enough to draw a rectangle around the string.

2. With the Rectangle tool, draw a rectangle around the word "CorelDRAW!"; then turn off the fill by clicking on the X in the Fill flyout menu. The result is a rectangle around the text string. The rectangle is selected, by default.

3. Select the Copy Attributes From command in the Edit menu. When the Copy Attributes dialog box appears, click on both the Outline Pen and the Outline Color check boxes, and then click on OK. The pointer turns into an arrow containing the word "From?" to indicate that the next object you select will copy its outline attributes to the previously selected rectangle.

4. Click on the "CorelDRAW!" text string. The rectangle redisplays to show the same outline thickness and color as the text string, as shown in Figure 12-13.

Rectangle
with outline
color and pen
styles copied
from text string
Figure 12-13.

If your rectangle does not come out like Figure 12-13, it could be that the specifications on your text have been changed. They should be a 6-point line width, with a 50 percent gray outline color, and no fill.

5. Clear the screen by selecting the New command and not saving the changes.

For more practice with the Outline Color tool, you can go back to the LANDSCA4.CDR file or any other landscape drawing that you created and edited in earlier chapters. The default outlines and fills or the objects in those files are black, but you can begin to differentiate objects by varying their outlines. You can give custom outlines to interior objects or copy outline styles to multiple objects at one time.

Defining Fill Color Attributes

The Fill tool can only fill "leakproof" objects—those with a closed path.

The final step in completing an object in CorelDRAW! is to define its fill attributes. The Fill tool is similar to the Outline Color tool in that it can dispense Spot color, Process color, and PostScript halftone screen patterns. In addition, the Fill tool can apply various fountain, pattern, and texture fills.

The Fill tool flyout menu, shown in Figure 12-14, is accessed from the Fill tool icon. The first icon in the top row of the Fill tool flyout menu is the Uniform Fill icon. This icon opens the Uniform Fill dialog box that lets you define custom Spot and Process color fills and PostScript halftone screen patterns. The next icon opens the Fill roll-up window, which gives you access to the color palette and to certain other tools in the Fill flyout menu. The last five icons in the top row of the flyout menu let you access dialog boxes to apply and edit fountain, two-color pattern, full-color pattern, texture, and PostScript texture fills. The first icon of the second row (the X

12

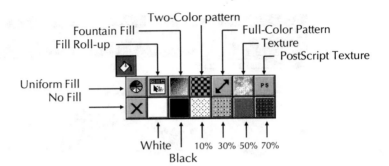

Icons in the
Fill tool flyout
Figure 12-14.

icon) causes an object to have a transparent (or no) fill. The next two icons
in the second row let you specify preset fill colors of white and black. The
remaining icons in the bottom row let you specify one of four preset shades
of gray (10, 30, 50, and 70 percent) as the fill.

Setting default fill attributes is accomplished in the same manner as outline
defaults; settings defined without any objects being selected become the new
default fill attributes. Objects you create in the future will be filled with the
default fill attributes automatically. When defining fill attributes for an
existing object, you are editing that object's current fill. The changes you
make apply to that object only, not to additional objects you may create
later.

TIP In general, it's a good idea to define fill color for one object at a
time. If you define fill colors for multiple objects that you have selected
using the ⟨Shift⟩ key technique, the fill colors of all of the objects change to
match the fill of the last object you selected. If you select multiple objects
using the marquee, the fill colors of all the objects change to match the fill
of the most recently drawn object in the group.

The remaining sections in this chapter offer you practice in working with
each dialog box and selecting fill attributes for each of the major types of
fills. Whether you are setting fill attributes for selected objects or altering
default attributes for objects you haven't drawn yet, the main steps involved
are similar.

Filling an Object with Uniform Spot Color

To fill an object with Spot color, Process color, or a PostScript halftone screen
pattern, you use the settings in the Uniform Fill dialog box. This dialog box
appears when you click on the Uniform Fill icon, the first icon in the Fill
tool flyout menu. You can also open the Uniform Fill dialog box with the

shortcut keys ⟨Shift⟩-⟨F11⟩. The name "Uniform Fill" distinguishes this type of fill conceptually from fountain, pattern, texture, and PostScript texture fills, which involve multiple hues or patterns rather than a single color. Except for the title, the Uniform Fill dialog box is identical in appearance and function to the Outline Color dialog box you worked with previously.

TIP: You will recall that Spot color is the preferred color system when an image contains fewer than five colors or if you want to use PostScript halftone screen patterns. If you do not have a PostScript printer at your disposal and your work does not require Spot color or four-color printing, you can use either the Spot or Process color system to specify fill colors.

As mentioned previously, an object must be a closed path in order for you to fill it. However, a closed path does not assure a solid object. If you combine two or more objects, as you learned to do in Chapter 6, "holes" result where the combined objects overlap. You can then create interesting design effects by surrounding the "holes" with outline and fill colors. Perform the following exercise to create a logo with transparent text, outline it, and assign a uniform fill Spot color to it. You will edit this logo throughout the rest of the chapter as you learn new ways to use the Fill tool flyout menu.

1. To prepare the screen, set magnification at actual size (1:1). Activate the Snap To Grid command and set both Horizontal and Vertical Grid Frequency to 1 per pica. If the units boxes display a unit of measurement other than picas, select picas from their drop-down list boxes. Activate both Edit Wireframe and Show Rulers from the Display menu; because of the grid settings, the rulers display in picas rather than inches.

2. Before beginning to draw, set the default Outline Pen and Outline Color attributes back to the original CorelDRAW! defaults. To do this, click on the Custom Outline Pen icon in the Outline Pen flyout menu. When the default Outline Pen dialog box appears, select Graphic and Artistic Text and click on OK. Adjust settings in the Outline Pen dialog box as follows: black color; Width, 0.003 inch; Corners, sharp; Line Caps, butt; no Arrows; Style, solid line; Angle, 0 degrees; and Stretch, 100 percent. No check boxes should be filled. Click on OK to make these settings the default Outline Pen attributes.

3. Select the Ellipse tool and position the pointer at the 24-pica mark on the horizontal ruler and the 33-pica mark on the vertical ruler. Draw a perfect circle from the center outward, starting from this point, by holding both the ⟨Shift⟩ and ⟨Ctrl⟩ keys down while dragging the mouse. Make the circle 22 picas in diameter or the largest circle you can draw, using the information on the status line to help you.

12

4. Activate the Text tool. Select an insertion point near the left edge of the circle, at the 18-pica mark on the horizontal ruler and the 32-pica mark on the vertical ruler. You do not have to position the pointer exactly, because you can align the text and circle later. Choose Edit Text from the Text menu or press Ctrl-T. When the Artistic Text dialog box appears, type **The World of Corel DRAW!** in the text entry window, one word per line. Then select the following text attributes: Aardvark bold, 40 points, center alignment. Click on the Spacing command button, set Character spacing to 20 percent and Line spacing to 80 percent, and then select OK twice. The text appears centered vertically and horizontally within the circle, as shown in Figure 12-15. If the text is not centered perfectly within the circle, then with the text still selected, activate the Pick tool and drag the text as necessary to center it.

Depending on the type of display and display adapter you have, the diameter of the circle and the point size you can fit in the circle may differ from what is described and shown here. Draw the biggest circle and use the largest type size needed to fill your screen at actual size magnification.

5. Click on both Show Rulers and Edit Wireframe in the Display menu again to deactivate them. You cannot clearly distinguish the text from the circle now, because they have the same outline and fill colors.

6. Select the Preferences command in the Special menu (or press Ctrl-J).

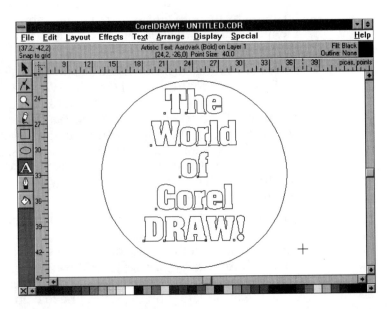

Centering a text string within a circle
Figure 12-15.

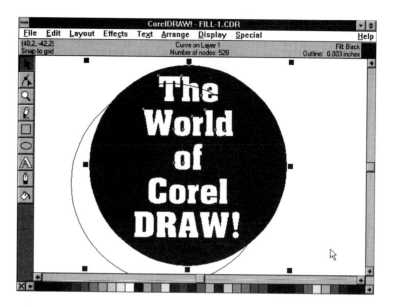

Combining
two objects to
form a curve
object with
transparent
"holes"
Figure 12-16.

When the Preferences dialog box appears, adjust both of the numeric
settings beside the Place Duplicate and Clones option to –2,0 picas and
points. Make sure that you place a comma rather than a period after the
2. Duplicate objects that you create with this setting are offset from the
original by the specified amount (in this case, 2 picas below and to the
left of the original). Click on OK to exit the dialog box.

7. Activate the Pick tool, select the circle, and then click on the Duplicate
   command in the Edit menu. A duplicate of the circle appears below and
   to the left of the original, and is selected immediately.

8. Change the fill of this duplicate circle to none by clicking on the X at
   the left of the color palette at the bottom of your screen.

9. Select both the original circle and the text string again using the Shift
   key, and click on the Combine command in the Arrange menu. The
   message in the status line changes from "2 objects selected" to "Curve on
   Layer 1." The "Fill:" message at the right side of the status line displays a
   default fill of black, but the text now appears white, as shown in Figure
   12-16. In combining the two objects, you have converted both the circle
   and the text string to curves. The area behind the text has become not
   white but transparent.

10. Select the Save command in the File menu. When the Save Drawing
    dialog box appears, type the name **FILL-1** in the File Name text box
    and then click on OK.

12

11. With the curve object still selected, click on the Fill tool and again on the Uniform Fill icon (you can also press [Shift]-[F11]). The Uniform Fill dialog box appears. Select PANTONE Spot Colors from the Show drop-down list box and deselect Show color names if it is selected. Then select the second color in the top row of the palette, PANTONE Yellow CV, and set the tint to 55 percent. Your settings should match those in Figure 12-17.

12. Click on OK to exit the dialog box. Now you can see some contrast between the black outline and the fill colors. The text has the same outline style as the circular shape because CorelDRAW! treats the text curves as "holes" or edges within the single combined object. The outline is very thin, however, so you will thicken it in the next step.

13. With the curve object still selected, click on the Outline Pen. Access the Outline Pen dialog box by clicking on the Custom Outline Pen icon (or by pressing [F12]). Change the Width setting for the Outline Pen to 5 fractional points. Select the Behind Fill option and then click on OK to apply these settings to the object. Now you see a heavier outline around both the outer rim of the circle and the text, as shown in Figure 12-18. Because you activated the Behind Fill option, the "ink" of the outline doesn't completely clog up the transparent spaces in the text.

14. You are ready to give the finishing touches to the curve object. Press [Shift]-[F12] to access the Outline Color dialog box. PANTONE Spot Colors should still be the color model. Select Show color names and type **293** in the Search String text box to select PANTONE 293 CV as the color (a medium blue). Set the tint to 52 percent and click on OK to exit the dialog box.

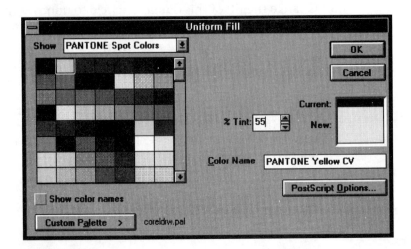

Setting for a
Spot color
uniform fill
Figure 12-17.

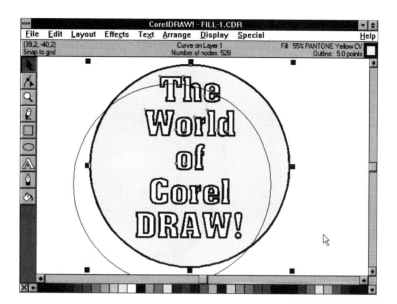

Outline
appearing
behind fill for
clearer text
appearance
Figure 12-18.

15. Select the duplicate circle. Press Shift-F11 to access the Uniform Fill dialog box. Scroll to PANTONE 281 CV (a dark purplish blue), and leave the tint at 100 percent. Click on OK to select this setting and exit the dialog box.

16. When you return to the image, you see that the circle that you thought was behind the combined text-circle curve object is really in front of it, and now covers part of the curve object. Choose To Back from the Order submenu of the Arrange menu to fix this situation.

17. The image redisplays to show the background circle creating a dramatic "shadow" effect behind the curve object. The alignment is not quite right yet, however; white space may be visible behind the upper portion of the word "The." To remedy this situation, deactivate the Snap To Grid command and adjust the position of the background circle slightly so that it fills the word "The" completely. Now all of the transparent spaces behind the letters in the curve object have fill behind them.

18. To see this apparent fill more closely, turn on full screen preview by pressing F9. Your screen should look similar to Figure 12-19.

19. Again press F9 to turn off full screen preview and then press Ctrl-S to save the changes you have made to this graphic. Leave the graphic on the screen to use in the next exercise.

The kind of object you have just created makes an excellent specimen for outline and fill experiments of all kinds. In the next section, you will add an

12

Apparent fill
of transparent
areas using a
background
object
Figure 12-19.

interesting design effect by specifying a PostScript halftone screen pattern for the background circle in FILL-1.CDR.

Filling an Object with PostScript Halftone Screen Patterns

When you choose the Spot color rather than the Process color system in the Uniform Fill dialog box, another set of fill specifications becomes available. If you work with a PostScript printer, you can fill an object with a halftone screen pattern of the currently selected Spot color. You will recall from your work with Outline Color that the CorelDRAW! preview window displays PostScript halftone screen patterns as a solid color; to see how they actually look, you have to print them on a PostScript printer.

You define a PostScript halftone screen pattern by clicking on the PostScript Options command button at the lower-right side of the Uniform Fill dialog box. You can choose from 15 different screen options, and you can vary the frequency (number of occurrences per inch) and angle of any screen pattern to achieve dramatic differences in the appearance of a Spot color fill.

In the following exercise, you will assign a PostScript halftone screen pattern of a specified angle and frequency to the foreground curve object in the FILL-1.CDR image and save the altered image under a new name. If you have a PostScript printer, you can print this image once you have mastered the printing techniques covered in Chapter 13.

1. With FILL-1.CDR still on the screen, select the foreground curve and press (Shift)-(F11).

2. When the Uniform Fill dialog box appears, click on the PostScript Options command button at the lower-right side of the dialog box. The PostScript Options dialog box appears.

3. Scroll through the Type list box until the MicroWaves halftone screen type is visible and then select it.

4. Adjust the Frequency setting to 20 per inch. This is a very low frequency (the minimum is 0, the maximum 1500) and will display a dramatic pattern on a 300 dpi PostScript printer.

5. If necessary, use the scroll arrows to adjust the number in the Angle numeric entry box to 45 degrees. This will cause the screen pattern to tilt at a 45-degree angle.

6. When your settings match the ones in Figure 12-20, click on OK to exit the PostScript Options dialog box. Click on OK again to exit the Uniform Fill dialog box and return to the screen image. You will not notice anything different, because the preview window cannot display PostScript patterns.

7. Select the Save As command in the File menu and type **FILL-2** in the File Name text box of the Save Drawing dialog box. Click on OK to save the file under this new name. After you complete Chapter 13, you can print this file to see the results of your settings if you have a PostScript printer. Your results should look like Figure 12-21.

When you assign PostScript halftone screen pattern fills to objects, base your choice of frequency on the resolution of the PostScript printer you will use. On any PostScript printer, low frequencies result in more dramatic pattern

12

Defining a custom PostScript halftone screen pattern
Figure 12-20.

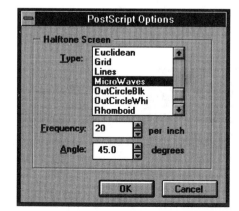

Printed image
of the
PostScript
halftone screen
Figure 12-21.

effects, while high frequencies result in the pattern being hardly visible. The
resolution of the printer, not any absolute number, determines what
constitutes a low or a high frequency. To achieve the same visual effect on
different printers, you should vary the frequency assigned to a screen. For
example, you should assign lower screen frequencies when the printer
resolution is 300 dpi, higher frequencies for the newer 600 dpi printers, and
higher still for imagesetting equipment at resolutions of 1270 dpi and above.
Table 12-1 provides information on the number of visible gray levels for
each printer resolution at a given screen frequency.

You can specify a PostScript halftone screen pattern as a default fill in the
same way that you would specify a normal Spot color. In the next section,
you will change the fill and outline colors of both of the objects in the
original FILL-1.CDR file, using the Process color system instead of Spot color.

Printer
Resolution
and Number
of Gray Levels
Visible for
PostScript
Halftone
Screen Patterns
Table 12-1.

Selected Frequency	Number of Gray Levels		
	300 dpi	600 dpi	1270 dpi
30 per inch	101	401	1600
60 per inch	26	101	401
100 per inch	10	37	145
120 per inch	7	26	101

Filling an Object with Uniform Process Color

As you will recall, Process color is the term used for expressing colors as percentages of other colors or color properties. CMYK Process color is the industry standard for four-color printing. In general, you should specify Process color instead of Spot color when your drawing includes five or more colors or when you plan to reproduce it through the four-color printing process.

CorelDRAW! supports color separation for Process as well as Spot color. When you specify color in CMYK terms, your printer generates only four sheets (one each for cyan, magenta, yellow, and black percentages) for every image page, no matter how many colors the image contains. When you specify color in Spot color terms, on the other hand, a separate page is printed for each color used in the drawing. Spot color is more exact for purposes of color matching than Process color but also more expensive to produce if more than a few spot colors are used.

Specifying Process fill colors is accomplished in the same way as setting Process outline colors, as explained previously in "Outlining with Process Color."

In the next exercise, you will specify fill and outline colors for the original FILL-1.CDR file using Process color instead of Spot color.

Assigning Process Color Uniform Fills

If you plan to generate color separations for an image in preparation for printing, remember to specify outlines and fills for all objects in terms of the same color system. In the following exercise, you will change fill color specifications for FILL-1.CDR from Spot to Process color.

1. Open the original FILL-1.CDR file that you created earlier in this chapter.

2. Magnify the image using the Fit-in-Window icon in the Zoom tool flyout menu. Deselect all objects and then select the background circle.

3. With the background circle selected, press (Shift)-(F11) or click on the Fill tool and then the Uniform Fill icon. The Uniform Fill dialog box appears, displaying the object's current Spot color fill as a named color.

4. Select CMYK Color Model in the Show drop-down list box. CorelDRAW! attempts to define the Spot color in terms of a Process color. Here you see the same color in the display box, but the Color Name text box is blank in place of the "PANTONE 281 CV." You see a color definition of 100 percent cyan, 72 percent magenta, 0 percent yellow, and 38 percent black.

5. Adjust the color values to 55 percent cyan, 55 percent magenta, and 45 percent black. Leave yellow at 0 percent. The color preview display box

12

shows a very dark blue. Select OK to redisplay the background circle with the new fill color.

6. Select the foreground circle and text and access the Uniform Fill dialog box again. Select the CMYK Color Model, set fill color values to 30 percent magenta and 10 percent yellow (leaving cyan and black at 0 percent), and then select OK.

7. Whenever you are preparing an image for four-color printing, make sure that *both* outline and fill colors are specified using the Process color system. In the present illustration, the outline color for the curve object is still specified with Spot color. To switch color systems for the circle's outline, press ⦅Shift⦆-⦅F12⦆ to access the Outline Color dialog box. Select the CMYK Color Model and set outline fill color values to 35 percent cyan, 30 percent magenta, and 10 percent black (leaving yellow at 0). Click on OK to exit the dialog box and redisplay the image. If you turn on full screen preview, the image should appear similar to Figure 12-22.

8. Select the Save As command in the File menu. When the Save As dialog box appears, type **FILL-3** in the File Name text box and then click on OK.

Specifying Process color uniform fills is easy; you will work more with color separation for Process color in Chapter 13. Many CorelDRAW! applications require only black-and-white graphics, however. In the next section, you will learn a shortcut for specifying fill color that will be useful if you usually print to a black-and-white printer.

Curve object
with Process
color outline
and fill
Figure 12-22.

Filling with Black, White, or Gray

In filling, as in outlining, you can specify preset black, white, and gray colors from the Fill tool flyout menu. The seven icons in the second row (refer to Figure 12-14) allow you to choose from no fill, white, black, and 10, 30, 50, and 70 percent gray, without having to set attributes in a dialog box.

To select one of these preset uniform fill colors for an existing object, simply select the object, access the Fill tool flyout menu, and then click on the appropriate icon. If you previously assigned a PostScript halftone screen fill to the selected object, the pattern remains the same but now has the new shade that is assigned to it.

To select one of the preset options as the default uniform fill, click on the desired icon in the Fill tool flyout menu without first selecting an object. Again, if the previous default fill involved a PostScript halftone screen pattern, that pattern remains active but in the new default gray shade.

The next section introduces you to one of the most creative types of fills in CorelDRAW!: fountain fills, which involve a smooth transition of two different colors through the interior of an object.

Custom Fountain Fills

When you specify fill colors using the Uniform Fill dialog boxes, you are limited to one color per object. When you select the Fountain Fill icon in the Fill tool flyout menu, however, you can define a fill that blends two different colors or shades of color. If you are familiar with state-of-the-art paint programs or business presentation slides, you have probably seen *fountain fills,* which are smooth transitions of two different colors or tints. CorelDRAW! makes the color drama of fountain fills available to you through the Fountain Fill dialog box.

By adjusting settings in the Fountain Fill dialog box, you can fill any object with two different colors or tints in such a way that the colors blend evenly from one extreme to the other. CorelDRAW! allows you to create three different types of fountain fills: linear, radial, and conical. In a *linear* fountain fill, the color transition occurs in one direction only, determined by the angle that you specify. In a *radial* fountain fill, the blend of start and end colors proceeds concentrically, from the center of the object outward or from the outer rim inward. In a *conical* fill, the blend of colors is made of wedge-shaped steps that radiate in clockwise and counterclockwise directions. Whichever type of fountain fill you select, you can specify colors using either the Spot color or Process color system. If you choose Spot color, you can also define PostScript halftone screen patterns to add an extra visual "punch" to your fountain fills.

12

The following exercises provide practice defining linear, radial, and conical fountain fills using Spot color, PostScript halftone screen patterns, and Process color.

Defining Linear Fountain Fills

When you specify a linear fountain fill, the start color begins at one edge of the object and the end color appears at the opposite side. In between, the colors blend smoothly along an imaginary line extending from one edge to the other. The direction of the color blend depends on the angle of the fill, over which you have complete control.

You can also control the speed and fineness of the display that defines the fountain fill in the CorelDRAW! window. You do this by choosing Preferences from the Special menu, clicking on Display, and adjusting the Preview Fountain Steps settings. A low setting (2 is the lower limit) causes the fountain fill to display rapidly with a small number of circles. A high value (256 is the upper limit) causes the filled object to redraw very slowly in the preview window, but it also results in a very finely graded transition of color. For all output devices except PostScript printers, the Fountain Steps setting also determines the resolution at which the fountain fill will print. You will have the opportunity to practice adjusting this setting and viewing the results on the screen in the "Fill Tool Hints" section of this chapter.

As with other outlines and fills, you can define a linear fountain fill for existing objects or you can set defaults for objects that you have not yet created. The exercises in the next few sections use existing objects as examples.

Spot Color Linear Fountain Fills

To open the Fountain Fill dialog box for either future or existing objects, press F11.

Theoretically, you can select any two colors as the start and end colors when you specify a linear fountain fill using the Spot color system. In practice, however, it's best to select two tints of the *same* color if you intend to send color separations of the resulting image to a commercial reproduction facility. The reason for this has to do with the way Spot color is physically reproduced, which makes it difficult to blend two discrete colors evenly.

In the following exercise, you will define a Spot color linear fountain fill for the objects in the FILL-1.CDR file, which you created earlier in the chapter.

1. Open the original FILL-1.CDR file you set up earlier in this chapter (not one of the edited versions). Your screen displays a curve object containing a PANTONE Yellow CV Spot color at 55 percent tint and a blue PANTONE 293 CV outline at a 52 percent tint. A darker blue (PANTONE 281 CV) fills a circle behind the object.

TIP: To check the current fill colors for an existing object at any time, just ungroup and select the object, click on the Fill tool, and click on the Uniform Fill icon to display the Uniform Fill dialog box.

2. Adjust the viewing area to fit-in-window magnification.

3. Deselect all objects and reselect the circle curve object alone.

4. Click on the Fill tool and then on the Fountain Fill icon in the Fill tool flyout (third from the left), or press F11 . The Fountain Fill dialog box displays, as shown in Figure 12-23.

   The Fountain Fill dialog box contains controls for selecting the From and To colors of the fill, the type of fountain fill (linear, radial, or conical), and the angle, which determines the direction of the fill. A display box shows the current fill, and other controls for several fill options are available. The default settings are Type, Linear; Angle, 90 degrees; From color, black; and To color, white. These settings would result in a fill that is white at the top, blending gradually into solid black at the bottom.

5. Leave the Type and Angle settings at the defaults. Click on the From color button and then click on More. In the Fountain Fill color dialog box, select PANTONE Spot Colors as the model and PANTONE Yellow CV (second color in the list) at 100 percent tint. Similarly, set the To color to PANTONE Yellow CV, but at 0 percent tint, which will look virtually white. Remember that when you define color using the Spot color method, both the start and end colors should be different tints of the same color.

The (default)
Fountain Fill
dialog box
Figure 12-23.

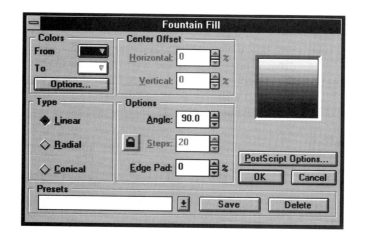

12

Spot color
linear fountain
fill at a
90-degree
angle
Figure 12-24.

6. Click on OK to exit the Fountain Fill dialog box with the new settings. The circle object now shows a darker yellow fill at the bottom, with a gradual transition to white at the top, as shown in Figure 12-24.

7. Access the Fountain Fill dialog box again (F11). This time, change the Angle setting to 45 degrees and then click on OK to exit the dialog box. Now, the curve object redisplays with a fountain fill that is lighter at the upper right and darker at the lower left.

8. For an interesting enhancement, create a fountain fill for the background circle that runs in the opposite direction from the fill for the curve object. To do this, select the background circle and press F11. When the Fountain Fill dialog box appears, set the From color to PANTONE 281 (use the scroll bars or Search String text box) at a 100 percent tint. Similarly, set the To color to PANTONE 281 at a 30 percent tint. Change the Angle setting to 135 degrees, the exact opposite of the 45-degree setting you chose for the fill of the curve object. This will result in a fill running in the exact opposite direction from the fill for the foreground object.

9. Click on OK to exit the dialog box. When the objects are redrawn, you can see that the area behind the letters is a richer color at the lower right than at the upper left. This arrangement adds some visual tension to the mock logo, as shown in Figure 12-25.

10. Select the Save As command from the File menu. When the Save Drawing dialog box appears, type the filename **FILL-4** in the File Name

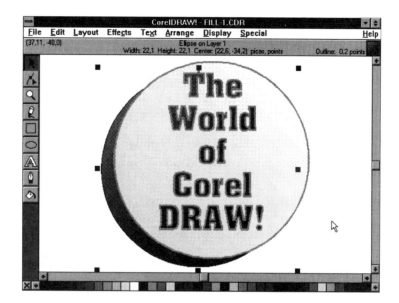

Background
linear fountain
fill at a reverse
angle from
foreground
Figure 12-25.

text box, and then click on the OK command button to save the altered
picture under this new name.

TIP: If you plan to use a commercial process to reproduce images that
contain Spot color fountain fills, make the start and end colors two tints
of the same color. If you do not plan to reproduce your images by a
commercial process, however, this restriction does not apply.

When you select the Spot color method of assigning start and end colors,
you can create a fountain fill from black to white by specifying colors as 0 or
100 percent black. Spot color is especially useful for black-and-white linear
fountain fills if you are interested in assigning a PostScript halftone screen
pattern to the object at the same time. In the next section, you will review
the process of specifying a PostScript halftone screen pattern with a linear
fountain fill.

12

Spot Color Linear Fountain Fills with PostScript Halftone Screens
You will recall from your previous work with outline fill colors that the
preview window cannot show you how a selected PostScript halftone screen
pattern will look when printed. You must actually print the object with such
a fill on a PostScript device in order to see the results. The same is true of
PostScript halftone screens when you combine them with fountain fills,
which is possible when you use the Spot color system to specify start and

end colors. Here are some tips that should help you achieve a better design on the first try:

✦ Set the angle of the PostScript halftone screen either at the same angle as the linear fountain fill or at an angle that complements it in a design sense. (You do not want the eye to travel in many directions at once.) Sometimes, you can determine the best angle only by experimentation; varying the angle of the halftone screen from the angle of the fountain fill can produce unexpected results.

✦ If you want the halftone screen to be visible when you print it, use a low frequency setting in the PostScript Options dialog box. This is most important if the Fountain Stripes setting in the Preferences dialog box, which controls the fineness of the fountain fill itself, is high.

Go on to the next set of sections to experiment with fountain fills that radiate from the center outward or from the rim inward.

Defining Radial Fountain Fills

When you specify a radial fountain fill, the start color appears all around the outer area of the object and the end color appears at its center, or vice versa. The blending of colors or tints occurs in concentric circles. Because color density in radial fountain fills changes gradually in a circular pattern, a 3-D look is easy to achieve.

You cannot specify an angle when you select a radial fountain fill, but you can control the location of the fill's apparent center. You'll see one way to change the center of a radial fountain fill in this chapter and two others in Chapters 15 and 16.

You can use either Spot color or Process color to define a radial fountain fill. When you use Spot color, you have the additional option of selecting a PostScript halftone screen pattern. The tips contained in the previous section, "Spot Color Linear Fountain Fills with PostScript Halftone Screens," apply to radial fountain fills, too.

You can control both the speed and fineness of the display that defines the fountain fill in full color mode by adjusting the Preview Fountain Steps setting in the Preferences dialog box, as discussed under "Defining Linear Fountain Fills," earlier in this chapter.

As with the linear fountain fill, you can define a radial fountain fill for existing objects or set defaults for objects that you haven't yet created. The exercises in the next few sections use existing objects as examples.

Spot Color Radial Fountain Fills

Here, you will define a black-and-white Spot color radial fountain fill for the objects in the FILL-1.CDR file that you created earlier in the chapter.

1. Open the FILL-1.CDR file.

2. Adjust viewing magnification to fit-in-window. Select the curve object and press F11.

The Angle numeric entry box dims and is not accessible when the Radial option is selected.

3. Click on the Radial option button. Click on the From color button and then click on More. Select Spot as the color model, black with 100 percent tint as the color, and then click on OK to return to the Fountain Fill dialog box. For the To color, also select Spot, 20 percent black, and OK. Then select OK again to exit the Fountain Fill dialog box. The curve object redisplays with a brighter area (the 20 percent black of the color range) in its center, as you can see in Figure 12-26. The apparent play of light you achieve with this kind of fill creates a 3-D effect, making the surface of the "globe" appear to curve outward.

4. Select the Save As command in the File menu. When the Save Drawing dialog box appears, type **FILL-5** in the File Name text box and then press Enter.

As long as you choose the Spot color method of specifying color, you can select a PostScript halftone screen pattern with a radial fountain fill. The added 3-D effect possible with radial fountain fills can lead to quite dramatic results when you add a halftone screen.

Spot color radial fountain fill with lighter shade at center
Figure 12-26.

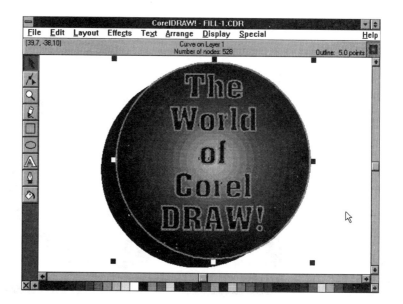

12

You can change the center of a radial fountain fill to create an off-center highlight for the object. You'll look at one method next. Two other methods for accomplishing this effect are available; both are included among the techniques discussed in Chapter 16.

Edge Padding and Radial Offset

The Fountain Fill dialog box allows you to add edge padding and to offset the center of a radial fill. You may have noticed that when CorelDRAW! creates a fountain fill, it is initially rectangular, filling an object's entire boundary box. When the creation process is complete, the excess is clipped off to fit the shape of the object, for example, the circles in this chapter. As a result, the starting and/or ending bands of the fill may be clipped off. *Edge padding* allows you to increase the percentage of an object's boundary box that is to be occupied by the starting and ending bands up to a maximum of 45 percent. Explore edge padding with the following brief exercise.

1. With FILL-5.CDR still on your screen and the curve object still selected, press [F11] to open the Fountain Fill dialog box.
2. Type **20** in the Edge Pad numeric entry box and click on OK. Your drawing should look like Figure 12-27. Compare this with Figure 12-26 and you will see the impact of adding 20 percent edge padding.

The other function of the Fountain Fill dialog box is offsetting the center of a radial fill. Look at that next.

First and last bands of fountain fill set at 20% of the object
Figure 12-27.

3. Again, press (F11) to open the Fountain Fill dialog box. (Be sure the Radial button is still selected.)

4. Type **20** in both the Horizontal and Vertical numeric entry boxes under Center Offset and click on OK.

5. You should see the center of the radial fountain fill offset to the upper-right corner, as shown in Figure 12-28.

6. Save the current image as FILL-6.

Defining Conical Fountain Fills

When you choose a conical fountain fill, the start color appears in a wedge shape from the outer edge to the center of the object. The end color is also a wedge shape from the outer edge to the center of the object on the side opposite from the start color. The blending of colors radiates in both clockwise and counterclockwise directions from the start color.

You can specify an angle and control the location of the fill's apparent center when you select a conical fountain fill. You can also use either Spot color or Process color to define a radial fountain fill and a PostScript halftone screen pattern. The tips contained in the earlier section, "Spot Color Linear Fountain Fills with PostScript Halftone Screens," apply to conical fountain fills, too.

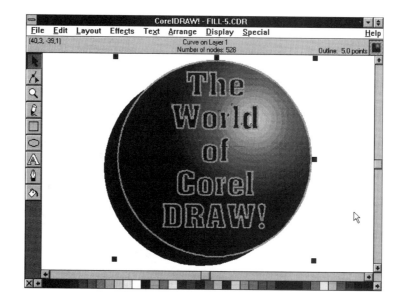

Center of a radial fountain fill offset 20 degrees to the right and 20 degrees up

Figure 12-28.

12

As with the other fountain fills, you can define a conical fountain fill for existing objects or set defaults for objects that you haven't yet created. The exercises use existing objects as examples.

Spot Color Conical Fountain Fills

In the following exercise, you will define a black-and-white Spot color radial fountain fill for the objects in the FILL-6.CDR file that you created earlier.

1. Open the FILL-6.CDR file, if it is not still on the screen.

2. Adjust viewing magnification to fit-in-window. Select the curve object and press F11.

3. Click on the Conical option button. Set the Center Offset values to 0, and click on OK to exit the dialog box. The curve object redisplays with a conical fill, as shown in Figure 12-29.

4. Select the Save As command in the File menu. When the Save Drawing dialog box appears, type the name **FILL-7** in the File Name text box and then press Enter.

As long as you choose the Spot color method of specifying color, you can select a PostScript halftone screen pattern with a conical fountain fill.

Conical
fountain fill
Figure 12-29.

Bitmap and Vector Fill Patterns

CorelDRAW! has two more ways to fill objects: bitmap fill and vector patterns and textures. Bitmap and vector refer to two methods of forming a graphic image in a computer. *Bitmap* images are formed by defining each point (or bit) in an image. *Vector* images are formed by defining the start, end, and characteristics of each line (or vector) in an image. CorelDRAW! comes with a number of bitmap and vector images that can be used to construct fill patterns. You can create your own or modify existing bitmap and vector images and then use them in fill patterns.

Bitmap and vector patterns are formed by repeating an image many times—*tiling*—so that each image is a single tile. CorelDRAW! provides the means of selecting existing bitmap and vector images, of sizing, editing, and offsetting both kinds of images, and of creating, importing, and coloring bitmap images.

Using Bitmap Fill Patterns

Bitmap images are the most numerous and the most easily manipulated, and CorelDRAW! provides the most capability to handle them. Look at bitmap fill patterns with the following exercise.

1. FILL-7.CDR should still be on your screen with the curve object selected.
2. Select the Fill tool and the Two-Color icon. The Two-Color Pattern dialog box opens.
3. Click on the display box and then on the flyout window's scroll bar to scan through the more than 48 patterns that are included with CorelDRAW!. Then select the Corel image shown here:

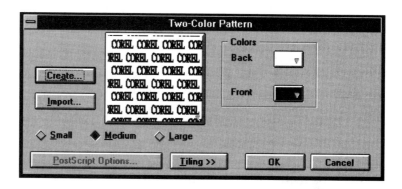

12

4. First click on Small, then Medium, and then Large to see the difference the three sizes make. Click on Tiling and type in your own sizes in the

numeric entry boxes. The height and width do not have to be the same, but for most images you probably want them to be. The maximum size is 15 inches square. (Keep the Medium size.)

Tile size is the size of each tile or image in the pattern. Different sizes work for different patterns. On some patterns, Small causes the images to looked smudged, while on others, Large causes straight lines to have jagged edges. You need to pick the size that is right for the image and for what you are trying to achieve.

Clicking on either the Front or Back buttons under Colors, or the More buttons, allows you to assign a color to either the foreground (Front)—the word "Corel" in the selected pattern—or the background (Back). The default is a black foreground and white background. The Colors buttons open the color palette, and More opens a color dialog box that is very similar to other color dialog boxes you have used in this chapter. You can choose between Spot and Process color, choose a color from a palette, specify % Tint, if you are using Spot color, and specify a custom Process or named color. Also, if you are using Spot color, you can select a PostScript halftone screen.

5. Select 50 percent black tint for Front, keep the default white for Back, and click on OK. You will return to your drawing and see the bitmap pattern provide the fill for the curve object. The text in the curve object is hard to read due to the lack of contrast among the new fill, the outline of the curve object, and the fill for the duplicate circle. Change the last two to improve the contrast.

6. Select the Outline Pen and select the white icon to change the Outline Color to white.

7. Select the duplicate circle and the Fill tool, and select the black icon to change the circle's fill to black. Your screen should look like Figure 12-30

8. Save your current drawing with the filename FILL-8.

The Import command button in the Two-Color Pattern dialog box opens a file selection dialog box. If you select a file, the image is added to the set of images that you can access in the Two-Color Pattern dialog box. You can offset (stagger) both the horizontal and vertical starting position of each image in the pattern, as well as offset neighboring rows or neighboring columns.

The Create button allows you to create a new bitmap image to use in constructing a fill pattern. When you activate the Create button, the Two-Color Pattern Editor opens, as shown in Figure 12-31. The Two-Color Pattern Editor provides for three different sizes of drawings: 16 pixels ("dots" on your screen) square, 32 pixels square, and 64 pixels square. The more diagonal or curve elements in your image, the larger the size you will need.

Medium-sized
two-color fill
pattern
Figure 12-30.

From a practical standpoint you should use the smallest size possible because
the larger sizes take longer to draw and take more room on disk. To draw,
click the left mouse button to make a pixel black and the right mouse button
to make a black pixel white again. If you want to erase an unfinished
drawing, change the size, say, from 16 by 16 to 32 by 32. You can then
change the size back, and all of the pixels will be clear. When you are done
with a drawing, click on OK, and the image will be saved as one of the

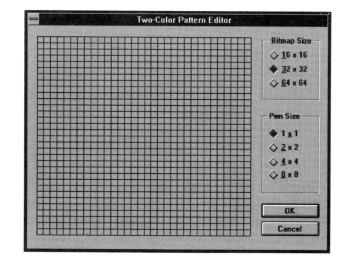

Bitmap Pattern
Editor
Figure 12-31.

12

bitmap images that are available from the Two-Color Pattern dialog box. You can then select it to create a fill pattern.

Using Full-Color Patterns

CorelDRAW! also provides full-color fill patterns. Change the fill in the curve object to a full-color pattern in the following exercise:

1. With FILL-8.CDR still on your screen and the curve object selected, open the Fill tool flyout menu and select the Full-Color Fill icon. The Full-Color Pattern dialog box will open, as shown here:

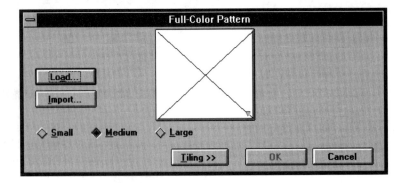

2. The Full-Color Pattern dialog box lets you open disk files with a .PAT extension. Click on the display box to look at the patterns that are available.

3. Select the Corel balloon pattern and click on OK in the display box menu. The balloon pattern will fill the display box.

4. Open the Full-Color Pattern dialog box, click on the Tiling button, select Small, then Medium, then Large. Notice that the default tile sizes in the numeric entry boxes are not square like two-color patterns are. For now, select Medium and click on OK. Your full-color filled drawing will appear, as shown in Figure 12-32.

5. Save the changed drawing with the name FILL-9.

Using Texture Fills

You can also select from over 100 bitmap texture fills with CorelDRAW!. While two- and full-color fills consist of tiled patterns, textures are created with a mathematical formula. Textures for water, clouds, minerals, and others are included. Each texture can be modified in a number of ways, including by texture number. Each texture has 32,767 texture numbers. To see their effect, change the texture number, then click on the Preview button underneath the preview box.

Full-color
pattern fill
Figure 12-32.

Other parameters, such as color, brightness, contrast, density, and softness can also be modified. The parameters that can be modified depend on the texture selected.

TIP: You can also change texture parameters randomly. Select the Lock icon next to the parameter you wish to modify to change it to the locked position, then click on the Preview button. Each time you click on the Preview button the texture will change.

To select a texture fill, follow these steps:

1. With FILL-9 still on the screen, select the curve object.
2. Open the Fill tool flyout and select the Texture Fill icon. The Texture Fill dialog box will open, as shown in Figure 12-33.
3. Using the scroll bar, select Flames in the Texture List box and click on OK. Your screen will now look like Figure 12-34.

12

NOTE: Texture fills require a large amount of memory and a longer time to print. You may need to limit the size and number of texture filled objects in your drawing because of this.

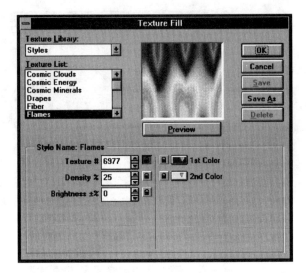

Texture Fill
dialog box
Figure 12-33.

PostScript Texture Fills

The last icon in the Fill tool flyout is the PostScript Textures icon. If you
print to a PostScript printer, you can select this icon to fill selected objects
with a choice of 42 different textures. This number is deceptive; although
only 42 basic patterns exist, you can alter the parameters for each texture to
achieve wide variations in appearance.

Texture fill
in art
Figure 12-34.

Chapter 13
contains more
information
about printing
PostScript
texture fills.

When you assign a PostScript texture fill to an object, the preview window displays the object with a small gray "PS" pattern on a white background. The Fill designation in the status line, however, indicates the name of the particular texture assigned. Unfortunately, you cannot view these textures until you print them.

Because you cannot adequately see on the screen an object filled with a PostScript texture, this section contains no practical exercise. However, it summarizes the steps involved in defining a PostScript texture fill: accessing the PostScript Texture dialog box, selecting a texture, and adjusting parameters.

1. To begin the process of defining a PostScript texture fill, select the object you'd like to fill and then click on the Fill tool and the PostScript Textures icon at the extreme right of the Fill tool flyout. The PostScript Texture dialog box shown in Figure 12-35 appears.

2. To select a texture, scroll down the list of texture names in the list box. The currently highlighted name is the selected texture.

3. Adjust each of the parameters in turn. The parameters vary, depending on the texture. You will often see references to Frequency, ForegroundGray, BackgroundGray, and LineWidth, as in Figure 12-35.

4. When you have adjusted the parameters to your satisfaction, select OK to exit the dialog box and return to your drawing.

5. Print the filled object to see whether you need to adjust parameters further. Since the mathematical algorithms used to calculate the

12

PostScript
Texture dialog
box
Figure 12-35.

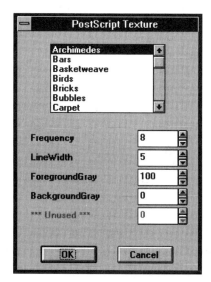

textures are very complex, some textures contain "chance" elements and may not print in a predictable way.

Working with PostScript texture fills is an adventure because of the *aleatory,* or chance, characteristics built into the mathematical formulas for the textures. Think of these textures as a way to bring more creative design elements into your drawing, even if your own drawing powers are limited.

Fill Roll-Up Window

Like many other major functions, fill color has a roll-up window. The Fill roll-up window, shown on the left, is opened by clicking on the Roll-up icon, second from the left in the top row of the Fill flyout menu.

Like other roll-up windows, the Fill roll-up window stays open on your screen until you roll it up or close it. It provides access to the Fountain Fill, Two-Color Pattern, Full-Color Pattern, and Texture Fill dialog boxes. It also allows you to edit the fill of an existing object. To use the Fill roll-up, you first click on one of the four buttons on the left side to specify the type of fill you want. Clicking the Edit button, near the bottom of the roll-up, opens the dialog box for the type of fill you have selected. Also, the display area to the right of the four fill-type buttons changes to reflect the type of fill. For uniform fill, this area is the current color palette. For the other types of fill, it provides display boxes and buttons unique to those types.

Fill Tool Hints

Finally, some hints for using the Fill tool are included in this section. These by no means exhaust the many uses to which you can put the Fill tool; rather, they are tips to help you gain speed in your work or to introduce creative effects.

Copying Fill Styles

In previous chapters, you have learned how to use the Copy Attributes From command in the Edit menu to copy text, Outline Pen, or outline fill attributes from one object to another. You can use that same command and its associated dialog box to copy fill styles between objects, too. The following summarizes how to use this feature to best advantage:

1. Select the object or group of objects *to which* you would like to copy the fill attributes of another object.

2. Select the Copy Attributes From command in the Edit menu. When the Copy Attributes dialog box appears, activate the Fill check box by

clicking on it. If you want to copy text, Outline Pen, or Outline Color attributes at the same time, activate those check boxes, too.

3. Click on OK to exit the dialog box. The pointer turns into an arrow containing the message "From?," indicating that you should select the object *from which* you want to copy the fill style.

4. Select the object whose style you want to copy to the selected object. The selected object redisplays with the new fill style.

The entire continuum of fill styles is available to you when you use this command. You can copy Spot or Process color uniform fills, PostScript halftone screens, preset shades of gray, bitmap fills, or even PostScript textures. Use this command and dialog box as a handy shortcut to defining fill attributes for one or more objects.

Using Fountain Steps to Enhance Previews and Printing

You will recall that the Preferences-Display dialog box (accessible from the Special menu) contains many useful settings to customize the way CorelDRAW! displays your work. One of these settings, Preview Fountain Steps (accessed from the Display button), applies to the use of linear, radial, and conical fountain fills.

CorelDRAW! displays a fountain fill by creating a series of concentric circles that begin at the highlighting box for the object and work their way inward. You have probably noticed this process each time the preview window redraws an object containing a fountain fill. The Preview Fountain Steps setting in the Preferences dialog box lets you determine how many circles CorelDRAW! creates to represent a fountain fill. The number ranges from 2 to 256, with 2 representing 2 circles with coarse outlines, and 256 representing a high number of finely drawn circles. As you can imagine, the window redraws more quickly when Preview Fountain Steps is set to a low number, and extremely slowly when the Preview Fountain Steps setting is high. Furthermore, if you print to a device other than a PostScript printer, the number of circles you select in the Preview Fountain Steps setting represents what will actually print. You can achieve some interesting effects by varying this setting.

12

C H A P T E R

COREL DRAW! 4

13

PRINTING AND PROCESSING YOUR IMAGES

No matter how sophisticated an image may look on your computer monitor, you can judge its true quality only after it has traveled from your hard drive to the outside world. The means by which graphics travel from your computer to your intended audience is a question of output, and until recently, output meant printer and paper. In today's world, however, paper is only one possible means by which your artwork can reach your audience. Appendix B explains how your CorelDRAW! files can be exported in various file formats that can be used in film, video tape, and 35mm slide recorders. CorelDRAW! offers you your choice of all these media and their associated output devices.

If print media remain your preferred end products, you can produce your images using the Print command in the File menu. CorelDRAW! allows you to print selected objects within an image, scale your image to any desired size, print oversize images on multiple tiled pages, print from selected layers, or print to a file that you can send to a service bureau. You can prepare color separations for Process color images, add crop marks and registration marks, print in film negative format, and add file information to your printouts. With a PostScript printing device, you can also reproduce the dotted and dashed outlines and fills, custom halftone screens, and PostScript textures you learned to use in Chapters 11 and 12.

If you want your image produced as slides or used in presentations, refer to Appendix B. You will use the Export command, not the Print command, to generate your output. CorelSHOW!, discussed in Chapter 17, allows you to assemble the slides, charts, and drawings you've created in CorelDRAW! into professional presentations.

The first part of this chapter describes the output devices and media that CorelDRAW! supports. The middle portion of the chapter guides you step-by-step through the printing process using the Print and Print Setup dialog boxes. The concluding sections of the chapter contain tips to help you achieve satisfactory printing results, based on the type of printer you use.

Output Devices

In considering how your images will travel from your computer to your audience, you are actually concerning yourself with both equipment and the product of that equipment, or with both *output device* and *output medium*. The output device you work with determines what media you can produce, or what the end product of your work will be. For example, all printers produce paper output. PostScript printers and imagesetters, however, also allow you to prepare your images as color separations or in film negative format, so that you can eliminate costly steps in the commercial printing process. CorelDRAW! supports some printing devices better than others. As you may recall from Chapter 1, Windows provides drivers for many different printers and plotters, but not all of them work equally well with CorelDRAW!. The following list shows the printing devices that CorelDRAW! supports best, in the order in which you are likely to reproduce the fullest range of CorelDRAW! features.

✦ PostScript Level 2 black-and-white printers, color printers, and imagesetters (Linotronic)

✦ HP LaserJet with Adobe-licensed PostScript Level 2 controller boards and plug-in cartridges

✦ PostScript Plus printers, such as the Apple LaserWriter II and HP LaserJet with Adobe-licensed PostScript Plus controller boards and plug-in cartridges

✦ Older PostScript printers compatible with the original Apple LaserWriter

✦ HP LaserJet printers and 100 percent compatibles

✦ HP DeskJet

✦ HP PaintJet

The PostScript printers and printers with genuine Adobe-licensed PostScript controller boards are the only ones in this list that let you generate output using PostScript printing options.

You can print your CorelDRAW! images with other printers, too, but the results may vary depending on the complexity of your images and the characteristics of a given manufacturer's device. With some of the following printers, your output may match your expectations exactly. With others, you may experience problems that are hard to predict because of the variety of standards in the industry.

✦ HP LaserJet clones that are not 100 percent compatible

✦ HP LaserJet printers, compatibles, and clones with PostScript-compatible controller boards and plug-in cartridges not licensed by Adobe

✦ Genuine HP Plotters

✦ HP Plotter clones and other plotters

✦ Dot-matrix printers

The "Hardware-Specific Tips" section of this chapter contains information about designing your images to obtain the best output results for the printer that you use. It also describes the kinds of limitations you are most likely to encounter with a specific type of printer and provides suggestions on how to solve them. The "Complex Artwork on PostScript Printers" section provides tips specific to working with PostScript printers.

13

In the next section, you will learn about general steps you can take before you print to ensure trouble-free output.

Preparing to Print

Before you select the Print command, you should make certain that your printer is correctly installed to run under Windows. You should also adjust several default settings in Windows in order to customize printing for the special needs of CorelDRAW!. Two of these other settings, called "Printer Timeouts," determine how long Windows waits before sending you messages about potential printer problems. The settings you need to review are all in the Windows Control Panel.

TIP: If you work with a PostScript printer, you should be using Windows' own printer driver or a Windows-compatible PostScript driver that came with your printer (for example, the PostScript driver for the HP4M).

Another adjustment you should make is to disable the Windows Print Manager. You do this by deselecting the Use Print Manager check box in the Printers dialog box, reached from the Control Panel. The short sections that follow will guide you through the process of reviewing and editing your printer setup.

Printer Installation and Setup

If you did not specify the correct printer and port when you installed Microsoft Windows, you will not be able to print in CorelDRAW!. To check whether your printer is correctly installed to run under Microsoft Windows, follow these steps:

1. From CorelDRAW!, press Ctrl-Esc to open the Task List and double-click on Program Manager.

2. From the Windows Main group, double-click on the Control Panel icon. The Control Panel window appears, as shown here:

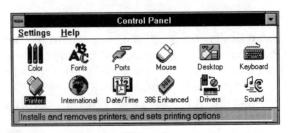

3. Double-click on the Printers icon, in the lower-left corner of the Control Panel. The Printers dialog box will open and display a list of installed printers. An example of a Printers dialog box is shown in the following illustration. The Installed Printers list box should contain the name of the printer you are going to use, and this name should be highlighted. If the name of your printer is in the list box but is not highlighted, click on it with the mouse, click on Set As Default Printer, and click on OK to return to the Control Panel. Then skip to step 5.

4. If the name of your printer is missing from the Installed Printers list box, select Add. An extensive list of printers appears. Use the scroll bar to find the printer you want (they are in alphabetical order) and then double-click on it (or highlight it and select Install). You will be asked to insert one of the original Windows Install disks so that the printer's software driver can be copied to your hard disk. When your printer appears in the Installed Printers list box, select Connect, click on the port to which the printer is attached (LPT1, COM1, and so on), and then click on OK. Repeat these steps for all the printers you will use. When you are done, click on Close to return to the Control Panel.

Refer to your printer manual for help with special settings.

5. If your printer is connected to a serial port, double-click on the Ports icon in the Control Panel. Select the port to which the printer is connected (COM1 through COM4), and click on Settings. The Settings for COM 1 (or whatever port you selected) dialog box will open, as shown next. Make sure that the Baud Rate, Data Bits, Parity, and Stop Bits are correct for your printer. More settings are available by clicking on the Advanced button, which opens an Advanced Settings dialog box. When you are finished, click on OK to return to the Control Panel.

13

If you need to alter your printer installation after performing this check, refer to your Microsoft Windows 3.1 *User's Guide* and see the chapter that discusses the Control Panel and gives the necessary instructions.

Printer Timeouts

After checking for correct printer and port assignments, you should customize the Printer Timeouts settings, found under the Printers icon in the Control Panel. These settings define how long Windows waits before sending you messages about potential printer problems. The default Printer Timeouts settings installed with Microsoft Windows may be adequate for average Windows applications, but you should customize them to improve printing performance in CorelDRAW!. To edit Printer Timeouts:

1. From the Control Panel, double-click on the Printers icon again. With your printer selected, click on Connect. The Connect dialog box will open, as shown here:

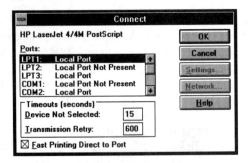

2. The Timeouts section of the dialog box shows two settings: Device Not Selected and Transmission Retry. The Device Not Selected setting determines how long Windows waits before informing you that the printer is not connected properly, not turned on, or otherwise not ready to print. Leave this setting at its default value of 15 seconds, because if the printer is not ready to perform, you want to find out as soon as possible.

3. Adjust Transmission Retry from its default value of 45 seconds to 600 seconds (equal to 10 minutes), as shown in the illustration. The Transmission Retry value determines how long the printer waits to receive additional characters before a timeout error occurs. Although 90 seconds may be long enough for most software that runs under Windows, it is not always adequate for graphics applications such as CorelDRAW!. The output file that CorelDRAW! sends to your printer can contain complex information, requiring more time to transmit.

4. The Fast Printing Direct to Port check box should be left checked—its default mode. When it is checked, Windows bypasses MS-DOS

interrupts and sends your output directly to the printer. The only time you would want to clear the check box is if you are using print spooler software that requires MS-DOS interrupts to control printing. Otherwise, clearing the check box will slow down your printing.

By verifying your printer setup and Timeouts settings each time you run CorelDRAW!, you can prevent potential printing and communications problems before you even attempt to print. You can eliminate one more potential printing pitfall by disabling the Windows Print Manager, about which you will learn in the next section.

Disabling the Print Manager

Windows is installed to print all files through the Print Manager. The Print Manager is a program that captures printing instructions and sends them to the printer. The printer then runs in the background, so that you can continue working in your application without interruption. The Print Manager doesn't always work efficiently with graphics files, however. For this reason, you can avoid printing problems if you disable the Print Manager. When the Print Manager is disabled, the printing operation runs in the foreground; you must wait until printing is complete before you can continue with your work. Printing takes place faster this way than when the Print Manager is enabled, however.

To disable the Print Manager, follow these steps:

1. If necessary reopen the Control Panel and double-click the Printers icon. The Printers dialog box will again appear.
2. Look at the check box in the lower-left corner labeled Use Print Manager. If it is checked, click on it.
3. Click on Close to return to the Control Panel and then double-click on the Control-menu box to close the Control Panel.
4. Click once on the Program Manager Control-menu box to open it, choose Switch To, then double-click on CorelDRAW!.

Now that you have customized Windows' printer settings to improve printing performance in CorelDRAW!, you are ready to set up your printer in CorelDRAW!.

13

The Print Setup Dialog Box

To prepare for printing in CorelDRAW!, you first select a printer and options to be your default CorelDRAW! printer setup. You do this by selecting the

Print Setup command from the File menu. Figure 13-1 shows the Print Setup dialog box that is displayed.

In the Print Setup dialog box you can select either the Windows default printer (selected in the Control Panel) or another printer, using the Specific Printer drop-down list box. You can also select paper size, source, and orientation. The other options will vary, depending on the printer selected.

Now you are ready to explore the options in the Print dialog box.

The Print Dialog Box

Select the Print command in the File menu to begin the process of printing in CorelDRAW!. An image must be on the screen before you can select this command. So that you can practice printing using the options in the Print dialog box, you will open a clip-art image from the CLIPART directory and then use it in the exercises that follow. Each section explores one printing option or one aspect of the printing process.

Using CorelMOSAIC!

CorelMOSAIC! is a separate program supplied with CorelDRAW! that provides visual access to CorelDRAW! files. CorelMOSAIC! can be started either from the Program Manager, by double-clicking on the CorelMOSAIC! icon in the Corel Graphics group, or from within CorelDRAW!. In this case, you'll start CorelMOSAIC! from CorelDRAW!—it is less obvious but handier for the purposes here.

The piece of clip art you will use is named CHILDREN.CDR. It is in the PEOPLE clip-art directory. With the following instructions, start CorelMOSAIC! and use it to bring this piece of clip art into CorelDRAW!.

1. Starting with a blank screen in CorelDRAW!, choose the Open command from the File menu. Click on the Options button, which allows you to access additional features.

2. Click on the Mosaic button. The program CorelMOSAIC! 4 loads and the Mosaic window opens, as shown in Figure 13-2.

3. From the File menu, click on the View Directory command. The View Directory dialog box opens, as shown in Figure 13-3. Your current directory may be different from the one shown in Figure 13-3. Use the Directory list box to locate the PEOPLE clip-art directory.

4. Highlight the PEOPLE subdirectory and click on OK. A pictorial directory will open displaying a small image for each file in the directory. Click on the arrow in the upper-right corner to enlarge the window, as shown in Figure 13-4.

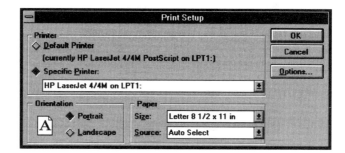

Print Setup
dialog box
Figure 13-1.

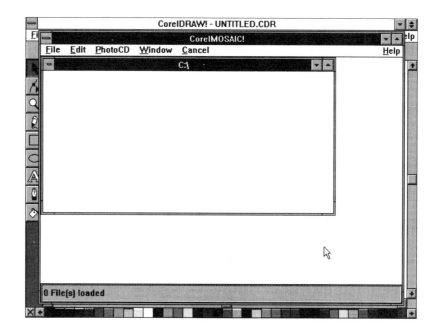

CorelMOSAIC!
window
Figure 13-2.

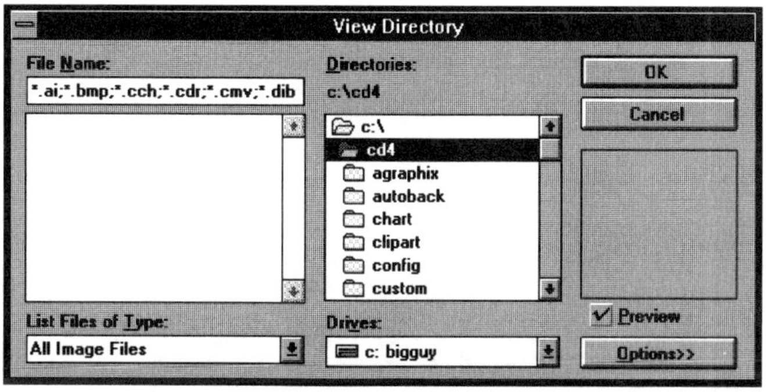

CorelMOSAIC!
View
Directory
dialog box
Figure 13-3.

13

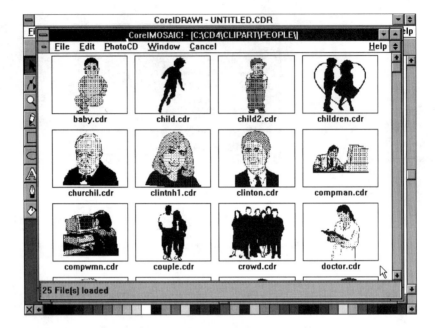

CorelMOSAIC!
pictorial
directory
Figure 13-4.

5. Double-click on the CHILDREN.CDR image. After a few moments, the
CHILDREN.CDR image will appear in your CorelDRAW! window, as in
Figure 13-5.

CHILDREN.CDR
in CorelDRAW!
Figure 13-5.

Now that you have an image ready for printing, you can select the Print command and become acquainted with the Print dialog box.

Selecting the Print Command

Select the Print command from the File menu. The Print dialog box appears, as shown in Figure 13-6.

The Print options in this dialog box are Printer (drop-down list box), Printer Information (the question mark to the right of the Printer drop-down list box), Print to File, For Mac (PostScript only), Copies, Pages, and Selected Objects Only (if you have selected an object). The Position and Size section contains settings for Preview Image, Fit to Page, Center, Tile, and Scale. Additional dialog boxes for setting color, printer, and other options are accessed using the Options, Color, and Printer command buttons. These options will be covered in detail later in this chapter.

The left side of the Print dialog box contains the Preview display box, which displays the effect of the Position and Size settings when the Preview Image option is selected. You can also change these values interactively in the Preview box by dragging any of the handles of the bounding box to the desired position. In addition, you can drag the graphic to any position on the page. These changes only affect the printed output, not the actual CorelDRAW! drawing.

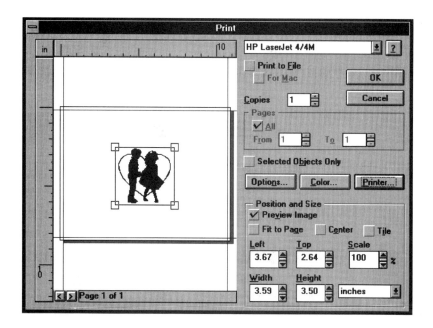

Print dialog box

Figure 13-6.

13

Before you experiment with the printing options, go on to the next section to learn how to check the printer setup.

Checking Printer Setup

Whenever you print, it is advisable to develop the habit of checking the printer setup *before* you select any print options. The Setup dialog box for your printer, which you access by clicking on the Printer command button in the Print dialog box, contains controls that allow you to define the desired number of copies, the paper size and orientation, and other settings for your printer. The other items in the Setup dialog box vary, depending on the printer you selected using the Printers icon in the Control Panel or Print Setup in the File menu. For example, the Setup dialog box shown in Figure 13-7 shows the controls available for a non-PostScript printer.

Some of the variable controls are important to know about because they help you avoid possible pitfalls when you attempt to print complex images. Later on, in the series of sections following "Hardware-Specific Tips," you will find hints on adjusting these settings to prevent or minimize printing problems. Take a moment to explore the contents of *your* printer Setup dialog box and of any nested sub-dialog boxes that are accessible by clicking on special command buttons. When you are ready, click on Cancel in the Setup dialog box.

Printer Information

More information about the selected printer is available using the Printer Information command button (the question mark to the right of the Printer drop-down list box in the Print dialog box). This opens a display box that contains detailed information about the selected printer's capabilities. This is not an interactive box; you cannot change any of the displayed settings.

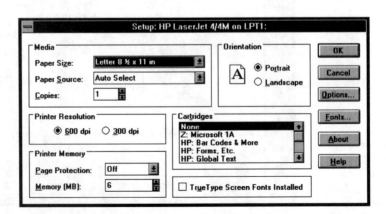

Printer Setup options for a non-PostScript printer

Figure 13-7.

Number of Copies

You can enter the number of copies you want printed at one time in the Copies numeric entry box of the Print dialog box. This can be a number from 1 through 999, and it overrides the number entered in the printer Setup dialog box.

Pages

With multiple-page documents, you can print either all the pages, a single page, or a selected range. Page ranges are entered in the From and To numeric entry boxes.

Printing Only Selected Objects

There are several reasons why you might choose to print only selected objects within a picture, rather than the entire graphic:

+ You want to save printing time and need to check only a portion of the image.

+ Your picture contains a great deal of fine detail, such as in a technical illustration, and you want to examine certain areas for accuracy.

+ Some of your picture elements contain complex or PostScript-only features.

+ You have experienced printing problems and want to locate the object or objects that are causing the trouble.

Whatever your reason, you can print just the selected objects within a picture by activating the Selected Objects Only check box in the Print dialog box. You must select the desired objects before you select the Print command, however, or you will receive an error message. Practice printing selected objects in the CHILDREN.CDR file now.

1. If the Print dialog box is still on your screen, click on Cancel to exit and return to the CHILDREN.CDR file.
2. Select any object in the image; the status line shows you that all of the objects in the picture are grouped. Choose the Ungroup command in the Arrange menu to ungroup all of the objects.
3. Using the Pick tool, deselect the object, then select just the heart by clicking on its border; it's selected if the status line changes to "Number of nodes:4".
4. Leave the heart selected and press Ctrl-P. When the Print dialog box appears, review your print setup, and then click on the Selected Objects

13

Only check box. The Preview display box shows only the selected object—the heart.

5. Select the OK command button to begin the printing process. After a short time, the image of the heart should emerge from your printer. Leave the CHILDREN.CDR image on your screen for the next exercise.

As you learn about the other options in this dialog box, you will think of effective ways to combine one or more of them with Selected Objects Only. Assume, for example, that you are working with a complex technical illustration and need to proof just a small area. If you activate both the Selected Objects Only and Fit To Page options, you can print the selected objects in magnified format in order to proof them more easily.

TIP: When you print complex, memory-intensive images, it is a good practice to use the Select All command in the Edit menu to select all objects before you click on the Print command, and then print with the Selected Objects Only option activated. Some objects in a memory-intensive image may be left out; by using the Select All command and the Selected Objects Only option, you minimize this problem.

In the next section, you will learn about a way to print proofs of a graphic that is larger than the page area.

Tiling a Graphic

You can choose from several different methods of sizing a graphic in CorelDRAW!. The most obvious method is to use rulers when creating objects. Another method involves defining a custom page size with the Page Setup command and the Page Setup dialog box. You can also use the Pick tool to scale an image to the desired size *after* you have created it.

Posters and other applications, however, require images that are larger than any paper size available for your printer. Even if you print final versions of these images on a Linotronic or other imagesetter that has fewer restrictions on paper size, how do you obtain accurate proofs? The answer is through tiling the image. Here, *tiling* refers to the process of printing an oversize image in sections that fit together precisely to form the complete picture. If, for example, you create a poster that is 11 inches wide by 17 inches high and select Tile on the Print dialog box as a printing option, the image will print on four 8 1/2-by-11-inch sheets (or on some multiple of whatever size paper you use for your printer).

In the following exercise, you will enlarge the page size for CHILDREN.CDR, scale the image to fit the page, and print the entire image with the Tile option enabled.

1. With the CHILDREN.CDR image still on your screen, click on the Select All command in the Edit menu to select all of the objects in the picture. Then select the Group command in the Arrange menu to keep all objects together.

2. Activate the Show Rulers command in the Display menu and then select the Page Setup command in the Layout menu. When the Page Setup dialog box appears, click on the Landscape option button and choose Tabloid in the Paper Size drop-down list box to activate them. Selecting Tabloid will result in a page that is 17 inches wide by 11 inches high in landscape format. Click on the OK command button to exit the dialog box. The rulers show you the change in page size, as shown in Figure 13-8.

3. With the Pick tool active, position the cursor at the upper-left corner boundary marker of the selected, grouped image. When the pointer turns to a crosshair, drag the mouse until you have scaled the image to fit the upper-left corner area of the page. Do the same for the lower-right corner boundary marker.

4. Move the scaled image so that it is centered on the enlarged page and then select the Print command from the File menu. If you get a window

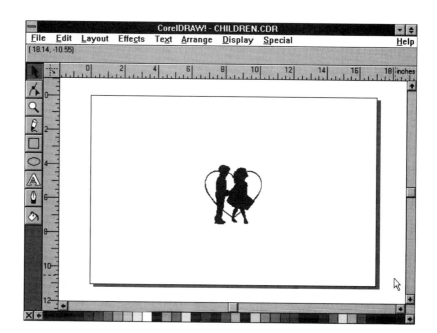

CHILDREN.CDR
on tabloid
page
Figure 13-8.

13

advising you that the printer and page orientations do not match, click on Yes to have the printer adjusted automatically.

Depending on the algorithm your printer uses, the number of sheets used for tiling may vary.

5. When the Print dialog box appears, you can see in the Preview box that the graphic is larger than the paper size. Deselect any options that are currently active, except Preview Image, and then click on the Tile option to activate it. Select OK. After a few moments, the image begins to print.

6. When the file has finished printing, deactivate the Show Rulers command, return to letter-size paper in the Page Setup dialog box, and then select Open from the File menu. Do not save the changes you have made to the picture. When the Open Drawing dialog box appears, double-click on CHILDREN.CDR to reopen this file in its original state. Leave CHILDREN.CDR on the screen for the next exercise.

Since most printers do not print to the edge of the page, you may need to use scissors or a matte knife to cut and paste the tiled pieces together exactly. Still, this method gives you a fairly exact representation of your image as it will print on the imagesetter. If your cutting and pasting skills are also exact, you may be able to use the tiled version of the image as the master copy for commercial printing.

Scaling an Image

There is a difference in CorelDRAW! between scaling an image on the screen with the Pick tool and defining a scaling value in the Print dialog box. When you scale an image visually, you are altering its actual dimensions. When you adjust values for the Scale option of the Print dialog box, however, you change only the way the file prints, not its actual size.

Perform the following exercise to print the CHILDREN.CDR file at a reduced size using the Scale option:

1. With the CHILDREN.CDR file on the screen, click on any outline within the image. As the status line informs you, the entire image is grouped.

2. Select the Print command from the File menu. When the Print dialog box appears, deselect any options, except Preview Image, that are currently active. The value in the Scale numeric entry box should be 100 percent (actual size).

3. Using the bottom scroll arrow, scroll to 10 percent, as shown here:

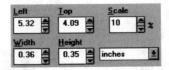

Depending on your printer, you may not be able to print as small as 10 percent. If this is the case, increase the scale until your printer accepts the image.

4. Click on OK to begin the printing process. Again, depending on your printer, the image will probably print centered on your page, but it may be slightly offset.

5. Leave the current image on the screen for further work.

You have seen how you can reduce the scale of an image to 10 percent of original size. The lower limit is 1 percent of original size. You can also increase the scale of an image to an upper limit of 999 percent of original size. If you expand the scale of an image beyond the dimensions of the page, however, remember to activate the Tile option as well.

In the next section, you will experiment with another printing option that involves image size.

Fitting an Image to the Page

Like the Scale option, the Fit to Page option in the Print dialog box does not affect the actual size of the graphic. When you select this option, CorelDRAW! automatically calculates how much it must increase the scale of the graphic or selected object(s) in order to make it fill the entire page. In the following exercise, you will combine the Fit to Page option with the Selected Objects Only option you learned about previously.

1. Select any outline within the CHILDREN.CDR image; since the entire image is grouped, you select all objects automatically.

2. Click on the Ungroup command in the Arrange menu and then click on any white space to deselect all objects. Select the three objects that make up the boy and girl by drawing a marquee around them.

3. With the boy and girl selected, choose the Print command in the File menu. When the Print dialog box appears, deselect any options, except Preview Image, that are currently active, and then activate the Selected Objects Only option.

When the Fit to Page option is selected, the centered option is also automatically enabled.

4. Click on the Fit to Page option to activate it and then click on OK to begin printing. After a few moments, the boy and girl appear on the paper, filling the entire sheet.

5. Leave the CHILDREN.CDR image on the screen for the next exercise.

13

As mentioned earlier, you can use the Fit to Page option along with Selected Objects Only when you want to blow up details within a complex graphic, such as a technical illustration.

Next you will experiment with printing an image to a file.

Printing to a File

There are two common reasons why you might choose to print an image to a file:

✦ You are creating files to send to a service bureau for output on a Linotronic or other imagesetter.

✦ Your printer is busy and you prefer to copy the print information directly to the printer at a later time.

To print to a file, you select the Print to File option in the Print dialog box and name the output file. Printer output files created in applications that run under Windows bear the extension .PRN. CorelDRAW! then displays another screen, prompting you to set printing parameters specific to the printer that will eventually print the file.

The following exercise assumes that you are going to send an output file to a service bureau for use on a PostScript imagesetter. In order to do this, you do not need to have a PostScript printer, but you must have a PostScript printer driver installed in your Windows directory. If you do not have a PostScript driver installed, use the Add command in the Printers dialog box of the Control Panel. The service bureau should be able to provide you with the correct drivers for their equipment. Refer to the discussion under "Checking Printer Setup" earlier in this chapter for assistance. Once you have the PostScript driver set up, practice printing the CHILDREN.CDR image to a file in the following exercise:

1. With the CHILDREN.CDR file on the screen, deselect all objects in the image, choose Select All from the Edit menu, then Group from the Arrange menu. Press Ctrl-P, and when the Print dialog box displays, deselect any options, except Preview Image, that are currently active. If necessary, reset Scale to 100 percent.

2. Click on the Print to File option. (Do not click on the Printers button, because any changes you make at this point will be ignored. A dialog box similar to your printer's dialog box will pop up automatically after you finish specifying an output filename.)

3. If you are going to print on a printer or imagesetter controlled by a Macintosh computer, select the For Mac option. Without this selection, the print files you produce will not work on a Macintosh.

4. Select OK; a second dialog box appears with the title "Print To File," as shown in Figure 13-9. This dialog box looks and operates similar to the Open File dialog box.

5. If the filename CHILDREN is not already in the File Name text box, type it, and then select OK. CorelDRAW! adds the file extension .PRN automatically to designate this as a printer output file.

   A third dialog box appears; the contents vary depending on the type of printer that will receive the output file. Figure 13-10 shows a dialog box set up for a PostScript imagesetter, which is the most common choice if you are sending an output file to a service bureau. If you are printing a file for use by another printer, the dialog box you see on your screen will be different.

6. Make the changes you need in the dialog box and click on OK to begin the process of printing to a file.

7. When printing is complete, select New to clear the image from the screen without saving any changes.

When printing an image to a file, you can combine several options. For example, if you are creating color separations for commercial printing, you might choose to activate the Print as Separations, All Fonts Resident, and Print to File options at the same time.

The next group of sections introduces you to advanced print options, including printing separations, which are available using the Options dialog box.

Using Print Options

The Options dialog box, accessed through the Options command button in the Print dialog box, is shown in Figure 13-11. With these options you can set the "flatness" of curves (which determines how smooth curves will appear when printed), halftone screen values, reference marks and file information

Print To File dialog box for specifying an output filename
Figure 13-9.

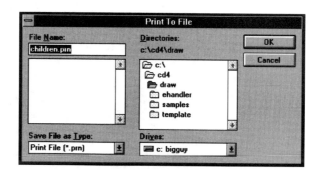

13

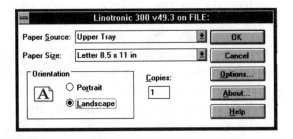

Imagesetter
setup dialog
box
Figure 13-10.

that can be printed with your drawing, and settings for printing separations
for Process color. Since you may use some of these options in combination,
the sections are ordered according to task, rather than according to their
appearance in the Options dialog box.

Printing File Information with a Graphic

If you are like most illustrators and designers, you probably revise a graphic
several times, renaming it with each revision so that you can choose the best
version later. You are therefore familiar with the bewilderment of viewing
multiple printouts of the same graphic and not knowing which sheet
represents which version.

CorelDRAW! provides a convenient solution to this common frustration. By
activating the File Information option in the Options dialog box, you can
print the filename, date, and time of printing with your image. This
information appears in 10-point Courier *outside* the top and bottom margins
of your *page,* not on your graphic (unless you select the Within page option).
If you activate the File Information option without the Within page option,
choose a page size in the Page Setup dialog box that is smaller than the
actual paper size you are printing on. This step is necessary because the file
information is visible *only* if you reduce page size below the size of the paper

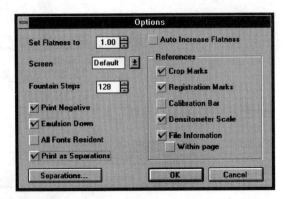

Options
dialog box
Figure 13-11.

in your printer tray. If you are using 8 1/2-by-11-inch paper, for example, you must use the Page Setup dialog box to define a custom page size of smaller dimensions, and then fit the graphic within that page. You can practice defining a custom page size and printing file information in the following exercise. You'll start by loading another CorelDRAW! clip-art file, which you will use for the rest of the chapter.

1. Open the CAR364.CDR file, which is in the TRANSPO clip-art directory. The car graphic will appear, as shown in Figure 13-12.

2. Select the Page Setup command in the Layout menu. Select Custom in the Paper Size drop-down list box, and define a page 3 inches wide (the Horizontal value) and 4 inches high (the Vertical value). Then click on OK to exit the dialog box. Reduce the size of the car so it fits on the page.

3. Press Ctrl-P, and if you get a message box advising you that the printer and page orientation do not match, click on Yes to have the printer adjusted automatically. In the Print dialog box, click on Print to File (if it is still selected), and click on the Options command button. In the Options dialog box, click on File Information and press Enter. Click on OK to begin printing. After a few moments, the image emerges from your printer. The filename, date, and time of printing appear in 10-point Courier just beyond the top and bottom boundary of the custom page, as shown in Figure 13-13.

4. Leave this image on the screen for subsequent exercises.

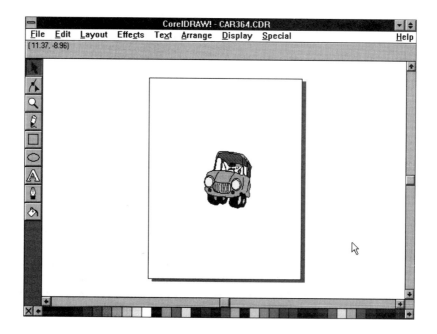

CAR364 image
Figure 13-12.

13

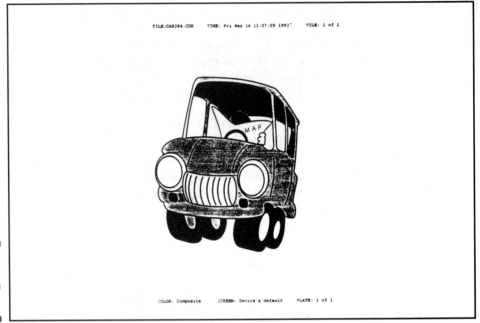

CAR364
printed with
file information
Figure 13-13.

Since CorelDRAW! generates object-oriented art, you can scale your images without distortion. It is therefore convenient to change page size so that you can print file information for your own use. Another common use for the File Information option is in conjunction with the Print as Separations, Crop Marks, and Registration Marks options.

Color Separations, Crop Marks, and Registration Marks

When you specified outline fill and object fill colors in Chapter 12, you learned about the differences between Spot color and Process color in the commercial printing process. If you plan to send output files to a PostScript imagesetter, you can reduce your commercial printing expenses by generating color separations on paper or in a file. This reduces the number of intermediary steps that commercial printers must perform to prepare your images for printing.

Put simply, *color separation* is the process of separating the colors that you specify for an entire image into the primary component colors. When you generate color separations using the Process color system (CMYK), the output is four separate sheets, one each for the cyan, magenta, yellow, and black color components of the image. The commercial printer uses the four sheets to create separate overlays for each color, in preparation for making printing plates.

When you generate color separations using the Spot color system, the output is one sheet for each color specified in the image, and the commercial printer creates overlays for each color. This process becomes very expensive as the number of Spot colors in an image increases, so it is a good idea to use the Process color system if you plan to have more than four colors in a given image.

When you generate color separations using the Print as Separations option in the Options dialog box, it is also important to include crop marks and registration marks. You can see examples of these marks in Figure 13-14. *Crop marks* are small horizontal and vertical lines printed at each corner of the image to show the exact boundaries of the image. *Registration marks,* two of which appear at each corner of an image, are crossed lines with part of a circle. Both crop marks and registration marks assist the commercial printer in aligning color separation overlays exactly; if misalignment were to occur, the final printed product would display a host of color distortions. When you activate the File Information option, CorelDRAW! prints the color for the page together with the halftone screen angle and density on the bottom and the filename, time, and date on the top.

Two other options are available in the References section of the Options dialog box—Calibration Bar and Densitometer Scale. Selecting Calibration Bar prints a bar in each color in your drawing on the page. When printed on a color printer, you can use these to adjust your monitor so that the printed colors are a close match to your monitor colors. Densitometer scales are used to check the accuracy of the printer used to print the separations. The densitometer strip on each separation page contains precise tints of the ink color for that page. These can be checked against standard reference values to determine the accuracy and consistency of the printer.

CAUTION: Just as with File Information, you can see crop marks and registration marks from your printer only if you define a custom page size that is smaller than the size of the paper you are using, unless you select the Within page option. The exception to this rule is if you are printing to Linotronic or other imagesetting equipment.

In the following exercise, you will generate color separations for the car in the CAR364.CDR file using the Print as Separations, Crop Marks, Registration Marks, Calibration Bar, Densitometer Scale, and File Information options. If you send files to a PostScript imagesetter, you may perform this exercise as well with the Print to File option activated.

13

1. With the CAR364.CDR image still on the screen, turn on Preview Selected Only in the Display menu. Select the image and, from the Arrange menu, choose Ungroup. Click in any white area to deselect the

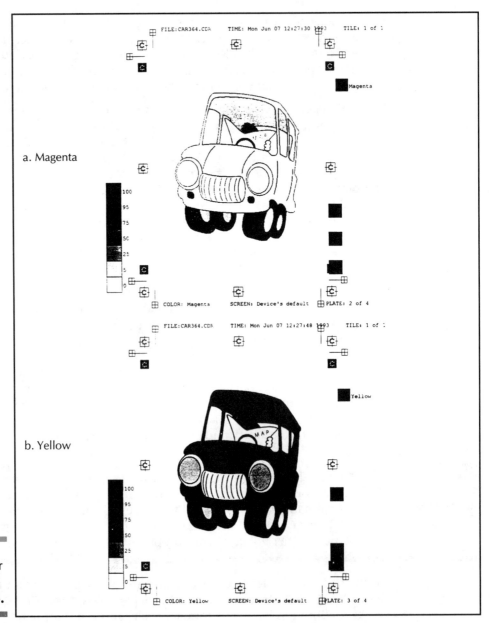

a. Magenta

b. Yellow

Process color
separations for
CAR364
Figure 13-14.

ungrouped object. Then, select various objects in turn, pressing F9 to
see just that object on the preview screen, magnifying portions of the
image if necessary for more accurate selection. When you select a color
object, open the Uniform Fill dialog box and check the Process color
values that have been specified.

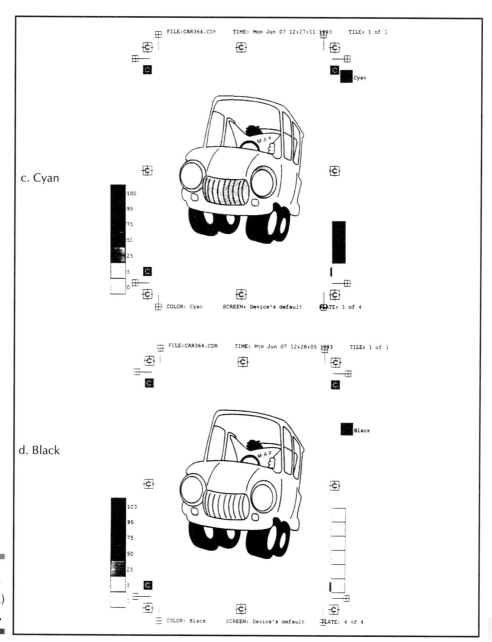

FILE:CAR364.CDR   TIME: Mon Jun 07 12:27:11 1993   TILE: 1 of 1

c. Cyan

Cyan

100
95
75
50
25
5
0

COLOR: Cyan   SCREEN: Device's default   PLATE: 1 of 4

FILE:CAR364.CDR   TIME: Mon Jun 07 12:28:05 1993   TILE: 1 of 1

d. Black

Black

100
95
75
50
25
5

COLOR: Black   SCREEN: Device's default   PLATE: 4 of 4

Process color
separations for
CAR364 (*cont.*)
Figure 13-14.

13

2. After you have observed the fill colors of various objects, choose Select All from the Edit menu and then Group from the Arrange menu to regroup the car. Then select the Print command in the File menu. When the Print dialog box appears, deselect any options, except Preview Image, that are

currently active. Open the Options dialog box, then activate the Print as Separations option. You will see that Crop Marks, Registration Marks, Densitometer Scale, Print Negative, Emulsion Down, and File Information are selected automatically when you select Print as Separations. Click on Print Negative and Emulsion Down to turn them off.

If you wish, you can select the Print to File option. (If you select Print to File, do not bother to check your printer's setup yet. Changes you make in your printer setup dialog box will not take effect until that dialog box opens automatically later in the process. You will specify your printer's setup automatically after you specify an output filename.)

3. Click on the Separations command button; the Separations dialog box is displayed, as shown in Figure 13-15.

   In the left side of the Separations dialog box is a list box containing the names of the four Process colors. (If you were preparing to print an image using the Spot color method, you would see specific color names here instead.) At the bottom of the dialog box are two command buttons: Select All and Clear All. For this exercise, leave Select All colors selected, or click on this option if all the colors are not selected already. For future reference, you can choose to print separations for either one color or a few colors at a time. To do so, just click on the Clear All command button and then on a desired color or colors in the list box. To highlight more than one color, click on the name of the first color, press and hold Shift, and click on each additional color.

   Above the Colors list box are two check boxes—Print Separations in Color and Convert Spot Colors to CMYK. If you have a color printer, you can select Print Separations in Color to print your separations in color. Convert Spot Colors to CMYK converts Spot and RGB colors in your drawing to CMYK values; the conversion isn't exact, however.

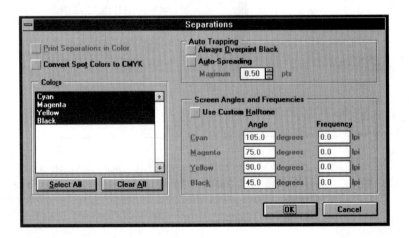

Separations
dialog box
Figure 13-15.

When the output for your drawing is to be Process color, you should use only CMYK colors.

Auto Trapping allows you to control some of CorelDRAW!'s trapping features. *Trapping* is the process of adjusting colors that print on top of each other. Normally, when objects with a uniform fill overlap, the bottom object is *knocked out*. This means that the part of the object being overlapped doesn't print, which prevents colors from interfering with each other when printed. The Always Overprint Black check box causes black to overprint; in other words, the bottom color is not knocked out. Auto-Spreading is used to minimize registration errors that can occur during printing. These show up as white spaces around colored objects. To minimize this problem, the lighter object is made larger. The overlap created makes press registration less critical. When the lighter object is on top it is made larger; this is called a *spread*. When the lighter object is on the bottom, the knockout is made smaller; this is a *choke*. Trapping can become very complicated in any but simple graphics.

Under Screen Angles and Frequencies are four screen angle and frequency values, one for each of the Process colors. Do *not* alter these values unless you are very experienced in four-color printing and know exactly what you are doing. These angles and frequencies are preset to ensure the best possible color alignment and registration.

Printing color separation sheets takes longer than simply printing the file normally.

4. Click on OK to save the Separations settings and exit the dialog box. Click on OK twice more. If you are printing directly to your own PostScript printer, CorelDRAW! now begins printing the separations. In several minutes, four sheets of paper appear. The first shows the color values for cyan, the second for magenta, the third for yellow, and the fourth for black. As shown in Figure 13-14, each sheet also contains crop marks, registration marks, filename and date information, and color and screen information.

5. If you chose to print to a file, the Print to File dialog box appears after you exit the Options dialog box and click on OK in the Print dialog box, and you are prompted to name the output file. Type **colorsep** and select OK; CorelDRAW! adds the extension .PRN automatically. The printer Setup dialog box now appears, bearing the title "PostScript Printer on FILENAME" if you are going to use a PostScript printer.

6. Adjust the file printing parameters as necessary; then click on the Options command button in the right-hand column of the PostScript Printer on the FILENAME dialog box. If you are going to use a PostScript printer, make sure that Send Header with Each Job is specified. Then, select OK twice to begin printing the file to the specified drive and directory. You can then send the file to a PostScript service bureau for output.

13

7. Leave the CAR364.CDR image on the screen for the next exercise.

CAUTION: If you fill objects with any PostScript halftone screen pattern other than the default pattern, your custom settings will have no effect when you print color separations for the objects, because CorelDRAW! uses the halftone screen function to calculate color separation angles. This limitation applies only to the objects for which you print color separations. If you require separations for only a few objects, you are free to assign PostScript halftone screen patterns to any remaining objects. If you assign non-default PostScript halftone screens to objects for which you must print color separations, your screen assignments have no effect.

Keep in mind that you can combine any number of options when you specify color separations. For example, you can tile separations for an oversize image, include file information, make selected objects fit the custom page size exactly, or scale the selected image for printing. If you are sure that the current image is in a final version, you can also print it in film negative format, as you will do in the next section.

Film Negative Format

In commercial black-and-white or color printing, the transfer of the image or of color separations to film negative is one of the last steps to occur before the printing plates are made. Think of the difference between a snapshot and the negative from which it was produced: colors in the negative appear inverted and backward. The same thing happens when you activate the Print Negative option in the Options dialog box. White image backgrounds fill with black, dark areas in the original image print as light. You can also select Emulsion Down from the Options dialog box and reverse the image horizontally, including the file Information and Registration Marks.

Use of the Print Negative option can save you money, but only if you are certain that the color separations in the image (if any) are in final form and will not need any further color correction or screen angle adjustments. If you intend to send a film negative file to a service bureau for output on a high-resolution imagesetter, ask the bureau management whether they can produce your file in film negative format automatically. Many imagesetters can print your color separation file as a film negative just by flipping a switch. This might be preferable if your aim is to achieve a higher output resolution than that provided by your own 300 or 600 dpi laser printer.

In the following exercise, you will print one color separation screen for the CAR364.CDR file in film negative format. You can print this screen directly onto paper, or create a file to send to a service bureau. Steps are provided so that you can print the film negative format to your printer and to a file.

1. With the CAR364.CDR file open, click on the Print command in the File menu. (If you printed to a file in the previous exercise and want to do that again, make sure that the Print to File option is still active.)

2. Open the Options dialog box and make sure that the print options that you used in the previous exercise—Print as Separations, File Information, Crop Marks, Registration Marks, Densitometer Scale—are still active. Then, click on the Print Negative option and click on the Separations command button.

3. You do not need to print out all four color separation sheets to see how the Print Negative option works, so click on the Clear All command button at the bottom of the dialog box. Highlight the Yellow option in the Process Colors list box and then click on OK. Click on OK to exit the Options dialog box and click on OK once more to begin printing.

   If you are printing directly to your printer, the color separation now begins to print. In a few moments, the color separation sheet for Process yellow appears in film negative format, as shown in Figure 13-16. The image in the figure shows only the graphic and its file information, but your output sheet is covered with toner all the way to the edges of the printable page area. If you elected to print to a file, the Print to File dialog box appears, prompting you to enter a filename.

4. If you are printing to a file, type **neg-yel** in the File Name text box and then click on the Print command button. The printer Setup dialog box now appears, as in the previous exercise.

5. Click on OK to generate your file. When you finish printing, leave the image on the screen, with the grouped objects selected.

You need not limit yourself to printing in film negative format when you are working with a Spot or Process color image. You can also use this printing option with black-and-white images.

Fountain Fill Steps

Try out a series of values for fountain fill steps to see which are correct for your output device.

You can use the Options dialog box to control the number of steps used to create a fountain fill on both PostScript and non-PostScript printers. The steps are numbered from 2 through 250. You may want to change the number of fountain steps for either of two reasons: to increase the smoothness of the fill and get rid of banding or to increase the speed of printing. You increase the number of steps to increase the smoothness of the fill, and you decrease the number of steps to speed up printing. The "normal" number of fountain steps depends on the resolution of your printer. For a 300 dpi laser printer, the normal value is 64, while for a 1270 dpi imagesetter it is 128. A value below 25, while fast to print, produces obvious banding. On the other end, at around 100 for a 300 dpi laser printer, you can add

13

Color
separation
sheet for
Process
yellow printed
in film
negative
format
Figure 13-16.

fountain steps without any gain in the smoothness of the image but with a
decided increase in print time.

Flatness Setting for PostScript

The Set Flatness to setting in the Options dialog box, which is only active for
PostScript printers, allows you to reduce the complexity of the curves in a
drawing and thereby improve the likelihood of being able to print the
drawing and also reduce the printing time. As you increase the Set Flatness
to setting, curves become less smooth with more straight ("flat") segments
and, therefore, less attractive in some applications.

PostScript printers have upper limits on the number of curve segments they
can handle and check for this limit. When a print image exceeds this limit,
the image won't be printed. The normal Flatness setting is 1. If you are
having problems printing a complex image, increase the Flatness setting in
increments of 3 or 4 until you can print. By about 10, the curves are
obviously less smooth. Selecting Auto Increase Flatness increases the flatness
value by 2 until the object prints or the Auto Flatness value exceeds the
Flatness value by 10. You can choose values from 0.01 to 100. Settings below
1 increase the curvature (decrease the flatness).

Screen Frequency for PostScript

The Default Screen Frequency value appears in the PostScript Halftone Screen dialog box. As you may recall from Chapter 12, you can access this dialog box whenever you assign a Spot color to an outline or object fill. The frequency of the default screen pattern determines how fine the halftone resolution will appear on the printed page. Each type of PostScript printer has a default screen frequency, with the most common being 60 lines per inch for 300 dpi printers and 90 or more for high-resolution imagesetters. The standard setting for Default Screen Frequency in the Print Options dialog box is "Device's," because in most cases it is best to let the printer you are using determine the screen frequency.

You can override this standard value, however, by clicking on the Custom option button and entering the desired value in the associated numeric entry box. Thereafter, *all* of the objects in your image will have the custom screen frequency. The most common reasons for altering this value are as follows:

✦ You want to create special effects such as the fill patterns that result from altering the halftone screen settings, as discussed in Chapter 12.

✦ You experience visible banding effects while printing objects with fountain fills and want the color transitions to occur more smoothly.

In the first case, you would increase the default screen value for the selected printer, while in the second, you would decrease it. If you have a 300 dpi PostScript printer, perform the following brief exercise to compare how reducing the default screen frequency alters the appearance of your output.

1. With the CAR364.CDR image open, click on the Print command in the File menu. The Print dialog box appears.

2. Open the Options dialog box and make sure that the Print as Separations option and its associated options are activated in the Options dialog box. Deselect any other options that show check marks in their respective check boxes and then click on the Separations command button.

3. Change the value in the Yellow Frequency numeric entry box to 45 lines per inch, click on Clear All and highlight Yellow, as you did in the previous exercise. These settings will cause only the color separation for the color yellow to print.

4. Click on OK to exit the Separations dialog box and click on OK again to exit the Options dialog box. Click on OK one more time to begin printing. After a few moments, the color separation sheet appears. If you compare this output sheet with the one produced in the "Color

13

Separations, Crop Marks, and Registration Marks with PostScript"
section, you will not notice a big difference, but if you look closely you
will see that the dot pattern of the 45-lines-per-inch screen printout
appears coarser.

5. Select New from the File menu to clear the screen of the CAR364.CDR
file. Do not save any changes to the image.

If you alter the default screen frequency in order to proof an image, be sure
to change the frequency back to Device's before sending the final output file
to a service bureau. Otherwise, your image will not appear to have a much
higher resolution than what your printer could offer.

Note, however, that if you assign *custom* PostScript halftone screen patterns
to an object while drawing, any changes you make to the *default* screen
frequency at printing time will have no effect on the screen frequency of
that object.

In the next section, you will become familiar with the uses of the All Fonts
Resident printing option. Since the example image does not contain any
text, you will not have an exercise, but the principle of the option is quite
straightforward.

All Fonts Resident for PostScript

The All Fonts Resident option in the Options dialog box is designed with the
occasional user of Adobe PostScript fonts and laser service bureaus in mind.
As you are aware, CorelDRAW! comes supplied with 750 different TrueType
and Adobe Type 1 fonts. Although the TrueType fonts are of very high
quality, they do not contain the "hints" (program instructions) that allow
genuine Adobe PostScript fonts to print at extremely small sizes with very little
degradation. Therefore, if you use text with a small type size in a drawing, you
might choose to substitute equivalent Adobe PostScript fonts for the
CorelDRAW! fonts at printing time. You activate the All Fonts Resident option
to instruct the PostScript printer to substitute the correct fonts.

The All Fonts Resident option is intended for temporary use. If you have
purchased downloadable fonts from Adobe and *always* want your printer to
automatically substitute Adobe fonts for CorelDRAW! fonts, you should alter
the [PSResidentFonts] section of your CORELDRW.INI file according to the
instructions in the section, "PostScript Printers and Controllers," later in the
chapter. If you use the All Fonts Resident option when you send output files
to a laser service bureau, make sure that the service bureau has all of the
necessary PostScript fonts downloaded. If you specify a PostScript font that is
not in the host printer's memory, the font will print as Courier instead.

CorelDRAW! also provides advanced tools for creating color separations. You will look at these tools in the next section.

Using the Color Separator

CorelDRAW!'s Color Separator, shown in Figure 13-17, is accessed with the Color command button in the Print dialog box. The Color dialog box offers advanced prepress tools for preparing graphics for printing. *Prepress* describes the process of modifying a graphic file to improve its quality when printed. With CorelDRAW! you can use virtually any combination of colors in a drawing, limited only by your imagination. When your graphic has to be printed, however, the printing process has limitations that can prevent your graphic from printing as you intended. Prepress tools prepare your graphic to minimize the problems that can arise during the printing process.

The prepress tools included with CorelDRAW! are intended for users who are familiar with the Process color printing process. If you are not an experienced user, using the prepress tools can cause more problems than they solve. In this section the different tools will be briefly explained.

At the top of the Color dialog box are two display boxes separated by color bars. The display box on the left displays your original drawing; the box on the right displays the color corrected graphic. Clicking on the color bars between the display boxes enables or disables that color. At the top of each display box is a zoom button that allows you to magnify the image in the

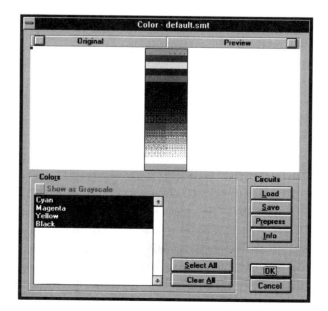

Color dialog box

Figure 13-17.

13

display box. The Colors list box below the Original display box is similar to the Colors list box in the Options dialog box. It is used to select the colors that will be modified.

Below the Preview display box is the Circuits section. Circuits are templates that contain color separation settings for modifying an image. The parameters that can be modified are Output Device Calibration, UnderColor Removal (UCR), Black Point Generation, Gray Component Replacement (GCR), Press and Paper Dot Gain, and Color Separation Quality. Circuit templates can be saved and loaded using the Load and Save command buttons. The Info command button lists detailed information about the current Circuit template.

Graphics and templates can be modified using the Prepress Tools dialog box, shown in Figure 13-18, accessed with the Prepress command button. On the left side of the Prepress Tools dialog box are controls for Gray Component Replacement (GCR) and UnderColor Removal (UCR). Both of these tools replace a portion of the cyan, magenta, and yellow inks with black ink. This is done to reduce the amount of ink used in printing and improve the quality of the finished product.

If a graphic was to be printed with 100 percent of cyan, magenta, yellow, and black inks, the ink coverage would be 400 percent. This is easy to create on the computer screen, but impossible to produce on a printing press. It is best to keep the ink coverage to under 300 percent. Equal amounts of the cyan, magenta, and yellow inks (which create black when combined) can be replaced by an equal amount of black ink to reduce the total amount of ink used. For example, if a color is made of 50 percent cyan, 70 percent magenta,

Prepress Tools dialog box
Figure 13-18.

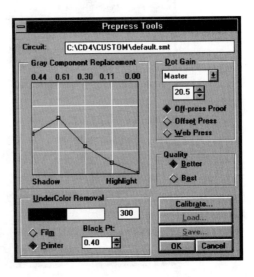

30 percent yellow, and 0 percent black, the total ink coverage for that color would be 150 percent. The same color could be made by replacing 30 percent of the cyan, magenta, and yellow with black. The new percentages would be 20 percent cyan, 50 percent magenta, 0 percent yellow, and 30 percent black, and the ink coverage would be reduced to 100 percent.

The Dot Gain section compensates for another printing problem: the fact that halftone dots "grow" in size as they move from the computer to the printing press. This is a function of the materials used in the printing process. This is compensated for by making the original halftone dots smaller than the final desired size. Different printing equipment and processes affect dot gain differently; the Dot Gain controls allow you to adjust for the particular type of equipment your graphic will be printed on.

The Calibrate command button opens a display box containing preset color patches used to adjust your monitor to match the colors produced by a color printer. This helps reduce the problems of selecting colors based on their screen representations.

In the final sections of this chapter, you will find tips for smooth printing based on the type of printer you are using and the features of your artwork.

Hardware-Specific Tips

Even if you closely follow all recommended printing procedures, such as checking the printer Setup options or setting Transmission Retry at 600 seconds, you may encounter printing difficulties on occasion. Some difficulties involve settings for your specific printer type, while others may involve features of the artwork you are trying to print. This section deals with printing problems that could be dependent on hardware and makes suggestions for solving them. The final section, "Complex Artwork on PostScript Printers," deals with printing problems that might be related to features of the artwork itself.

TIP: Regardless of the type of printer you use, you may sometimes encounter one of several error messages indicating that you should cancel the printing process. In most cases, click on the Retry command button. Repeated attempts to print often force the data through your printer.

PostScript Printers and Controllers

CorelDRAW! is designed for the PostScript Level 2 type of printer, with its 11 resident font families and at least 3MB of RAM. CorelDRAW! also runs on older versions of PostScript printers that contain only four font families, but you may experience slower performance or other limitations if the memory in your printer is not sufficient. If this happens, check with your printer dealer to see whether a memory upgrade is possible. If you run CorelDRAW! with an older model of PostScript printer, you should edit your CorelDRAW! CORELDRW.INI file to notify the program that certain PostScript fonts are not available. To do this, proceed with the following steps.

1. From the Program Manager, open the Notepad application and double-click on the CORELDRW.INI filename in the CONFIG directory where you installed CorelDRAW! to begin editing this file.

2. Go to the [PSResidentFonts] section of the CORELDRW.INI file and look at the listings of fonts that are followed by the number 3 at the end of the line. These are PostScript Plus fonts, not available for the older models of PostScript printers.

3. Change each 3 to a 0. This tells CorelDRAW! to always substitute CorelDRAW! fonts for the PostScript fonts when you print the file to a PostScript printer.

4. Save these changes to the CORELDRW.INI file and exit Notepad.

5. Exit and then restart CorelDRAW! to cause your changes to take effect.

In today's market, a number of so-called PostScript-compatible controllers and plug-in cartridges are available for the HP LaserJet and compatible printers. You should be aware that there is a distinction between genuine PostScript controller boards and cartridges (licensed by Adobe) and PostScript-*compatible* controller boards and cartridges, which are only as compatible as their interpreters. If your LaserJet printer is equipped with a genuine Adobe PostScript controller board or cartridge, you should be able to print everything that would be possible on a genuine Adobe PostScript printer. This is not necessarily true for a printer equipped with a PostScript-compatible controller board or cartridge, although some of these components work extremely well.

If you have a genuine PostScript printer, or if your printer has a genuine PostScript controller board or cartridge, the following tips should help you prevent printing problems when running CorelDRAW!. Potential problems are organized according to whether your printer is connected to a parallel or a serial port.

Parallel Printers
Printer or job timeout problems are common with PostScript printers that are parallel-connected. To avoid such problems, check for the following:

Additional tips for printing complex artwork with PostScript printers are in the "Complex Artwork on PostScript Printers" section.

✦ The Print Manager should be turned off (see "Preparing to Print," earlier in this chapter).

✦ Make sure that your printer is set up for batch processing mode, not interactive mode. Interactive mode does not permit the printing of imported bitmaps.

✦ See whether you can change Wait timeout directly from the printer as well as from the Windows Control Panel. Many PostScript printers provide utilities that let you specify these times independent of any software application.

✦ Set the Job timeout, Device Not Selected, and Transmission Retry settings as recommended in the "Preparing to Print" section of this chapter.

Serial Printers

Although most PostScript printers attach to IBM-compatible computers with a parallel cable (the faster and preferred printing method), some printers require the use of a serial cable. To ensure trouble-free printing with a serial-connected printer, compare your printer setup with the following checklist:

✦ Use the Ports icon in the Control Panel and make certain that the settings are correct. (Refer to your printer manual.) Make sure that hardware handshaking ("Flow Control") is active.

✦ Check your printer cable. Some long or unshielded serial cables do not always transmit all available data with graphics applications.

HP LaserJet Printers and Compatibles

Since the HP LaserJet and compatible printers connect to your computer by means of a parallel rather than a serial cable, you should refer to the "Parallel Printers" section under "PostScript Printers and Controllers." Printers that are guaranteed to be 100 percent LaserJet compatible perform equally well with the genuine HP LaserJet. Printers that are HP LaserJet clones and that do not guarantee 100 percent compatibility may present erratic problems, which vary with the printer driver and manufacturer.

If your LaserJet or compatible is an older model and you have only 512K of memory, you may find that you are unable to print full-page graphics with complex features such as outlines and fountain fills. Many LaserJet-type printers split a graphic that is too large for memory and tile it over several sheets. If you plan to print large graphics regularly, see whether you can

13

expand your printer's memory. If this is not possible, try reducing the size of the graphic on the page. Since object-oriented graphics can be scaled up or down without distortion, this should be a satisfactory solution. As a last resort, reduce the printing resolution of the graphic to 150 dpi, or even 75 dpi, in the printer Setup dialog box.

HP DeskJet and PaintJet

The HP DeskJet is a black-and-white inkjet printer that is almost completely compatible with the HP LaserJet. There are different versions of the software driver for this printer, however. Check to make sure that you have the latest model driver when printing graphics from CorelDRAW!. In addition, avoid designing large filled objects or layered objects; the ink for the DeskJet is water-based and could run or smear if you layer it too thickly.

Genuine HP and Other Plotters

The Windows driver for plotters seems to be written specifically for the HP Plotter line. The HP Plotter supports only hairline outlines and no fills for objects that you create in CorelDRAW!. If you have a clone from another manufacturer, the Windows driver may not work well for you when you print images from CorelDRAW!. Contact your plotter manufacturer to see if a driver for CorelDRAW! is available.

Dot-Matrix Printers

The results of printing CorelDRAW! graphics on dot-matrix printers are very erratic, owing to the large number of printer types available and the many different drivers written for them. Some dot-matrix printers cannot print complex files at all, while others print part of a page and stop. Dot-matrix printers that have multicolored ribbons do not lay all colors down on the page in the same order. This can result in muddy colors that do not match what you see on your screen. Depending on the problem, you may wish to contact your printer manufacturer to see if a driver for Windows is available.

Complex Artwork on PostScript Printers

The term "complex" artwork, when applied to CorelDRAW!, can include a variety of features. Among them are curves with many nodes, multiple fountain fills in an image, PostScript halftone screens and textures, and text converted to curves. Many printing problems that are traceable to the complexity of features are encountered chiefly with PostScript printers. This happens because the PostScript language has certain internal limits. When these are exceeded, the affected object may not print at all or may print incorrectly. For example, objects that contain more than 200 to 400 nodes may cause your PostScript print job to crash. If you are having this problem, try increasing the Flatness setting in the Print Options dialog box by increments of 3. As discussed earlier, this reduces the number of nodes in curves, and after only a couple of increments, there is a noticeable improvement.

You might not experience a problem with the same object if you are printing to an HP LaserJet printer, because the HP LaserJet does not recognize nodes; it interprets all graphic images simply as collections of pixels. Some PostScript printer manufacturers, such as QMS, allow you to run PostScript printers in LaserJet mode. If you have such a printer, try switching to LaserJet mode and printing your "problem" image again. If the file prints correctly, it is safe to guess that an internal PostScript limitation is causing printing problems in PostScript mode.

Downloadable PostScript Error Handler

You may not be aware (since it is undocumented) that both CorelDRAW! 4 and Windows 3.1 include error handlers that help you diagnose PostScript printing problems. As of this writing, CorelDRAW!'s is better. To understand how an error handler works, you need to know that PostScript prints the "bottom" or first-drawn object in the image first, followed by each succeeding layer. When you download the error handler and try to print a problem file, the printer begins with the first object and prints as far as it can. When the printer encounters an object that is problematic, it stops and prints out the objects completed so far, together with an error message. Although the messages are in PostScript code language, they are, in many cases, intelligible enough for you to decipher what the basic problem might be. The purchase of a relatively inexpensive PostScript manual, of which several are available, can help you even further.

To download the PostScript error handler to your printer and keep it resident there until you turn the printer off, follow these steps:

1. From the Print dialog box, click on the Printer command button.
2. From the Setup dialog box, click on the Options command button to access the Options dialog box.
3. From the Options dialog box, click on Advanced. From the Advanced Options dialog box, make sure the box beside Print PostScript Error Information is checked. This setting has no effect if you send a file to a service bureau, since most service bureaus use their own error handlers.

13

The PostScript error handler should be helpful in fixing problems that already exist within a graphic. However, there are other measures you can take to design a graphic that will cause no printing problems. The following sections explain a few of these measures briefly.

Printing PostScript Textures

The 42 PostScript textures described in Chapter 12 were created with highly complex mathematical algorithms. Sometimes, you may not be able to make an object with a PostScript texture print correctly. If this happens, try adjusting the parameters to avoid extremely dense patterns. If the image does not print at all, try removing excess objects. PostScript textures can be so memory-intensive that they do not tolerate many other objects within the same graphic. In general, you should use these textures as fills in a limited number of objects within a given graphic. Short text strings used as headlines (but not converted to curves) are among the best applications for PostScript texture fills.

If you are a desktop publisher, you may sometimes find that a page containing a CorelDRAW! graphic with PostScript textures does not print. Try removing everything from the page except the PostScript texture graphic, and then attempt to print the page again. Sometimes a page becomes too complex for PostScript if it contains both PostScript textures and other elements.

Printing Complex Curve Objects

As previously mentioned, the current version of PostScript may give you difficulty when you try to print images that contain objects with a large number of nodes. The exact number of nodes that will create a problem depends on the type of fill the object has. If you suspect that an object has too many nodes and could be causing problems, click on it with the Shaping tool. The number of nodes contained in the object appears on the status line. If the number of nodes seems too high or approaches the danger zone, reshape the object and eliminate any unnecessary nodes.

When you drag one or more control points of a curve object outward by a great distance, the boundary markers of the object may extend much farther outward than you can see. If you print a file containing many curve objects and some objects just do not print, it may be that you have not selected them. One remedy is to click on the Select All command in the Edit menu before you begin to print, and then activate Selected Objects Only in the Print dialog box. This procedure ensures that all objects in the graphic are selected, no matter how extensively you may have reshaped them.

Printing Fountain Fills

A common complaint when printing fountain-filled objects on PostScript printers is that *banding* can occur. In other words, the edges of each fountain stripe are clearly visible and do not blend into the next stripe smoothly. This occurs more often with 300 dpi printers than with Linotronic or other imagesetters that have a higher resolution. With LaserJet and compatible printers, solving this problem is easy: you simply increase the Preview Fountain Steps value in the Preferences dialog box to create a smoother blend. When you alter this value with a PostScript printer, however, it affects your preview window only, not the way the image prints.

To reduce banding on Fountain Fills when you print to a 300 dpi PostScript printer, increase the value for Fountain Steps in the Print Options dialog box by 10 or 20.

TIP: If you alter the default screen frequency for a draft printout on a 300 dpi printer, remember to change the Default Screen Frequency setting back to Device's before you create an output file to be sent to a high-resolution imagesetter. Also keep in mind that when you alter the default screen frequency, your image should contain no objects that have a nonstandard halftone screen pattern.

300 DPI Printers Versus High-Resolution Imagesetters

It may sometimes happen that your graphic prints on your own 300 dpi PostScript printer, but causes a high-resolution imagesetter to crash. This occurs because at higher resolutions, the amount of information in a file multiplies. It is possible that your graphic exceeds certain internal PostScript limits at these higher resolutions, but doesn't at the lower resolution. To avoid such problems, try reducing the resolution at which the imagesetter prints, by resetting the Default Screen Frequency in the printer Setup dialog box. Alternatively, you can define a custom default screen frequency for the imagesetter before you create the output file. If you do so, make certain that your custom frequency is lower than that of the imagesetter. These measures help reduce the amount of data in fills and outlines.

13

CHAPTER

COREL DRAW! 4

14

CREATING SPECIAL EFFECTS

The Effects menu, shown in Figure 14-1, is used to produce dramatic effects in your work. For example, with the Rotate & Skew feature, you can specify an angle that the selected text is to be rotated, or specify that the angle is to be skewed horizontally or vertically, as shown in Figure 14-2. The Stretch & Mirror feature allows you to elongate a text image, or cause it to mirror either horizontally or vertically, as shown here:

ABC CORPORATION

ABC CORPORATION

ABC CORPORATION

Another special effect is the Add Perspective feature. It allows you to create depth in text or graphics by stretching the borders of the object. The object seems to fade away into the distance. You can create a simple 3-D effect or a more complex version, such as that seen in Figure 14-3.

With the Envelope feature, you can cause text within the envelope to conform to any shape you make the envelope. In CorelDRAW! an *envelope* is a box that surrounds text or graphics. You can pull the envelope in different directions, distorting the shape as you might with putty. Any object within the envelope will follow the shape of the envelope. Figure 14-4 shows an example.

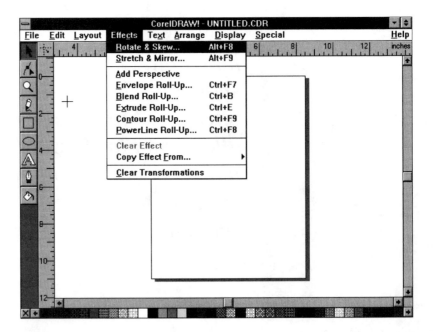

Effects menu
Figure 14-1.

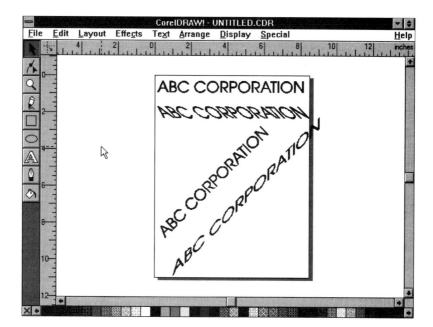

Rotated and
skewed text
Figure 14-2.

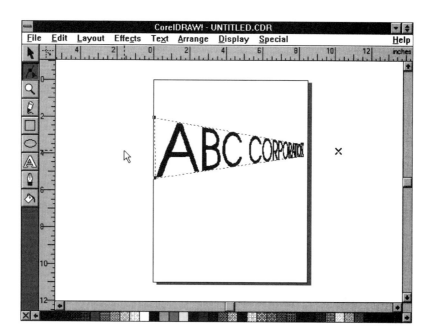

Example of
perspective
effect
Figure 14-3.

14

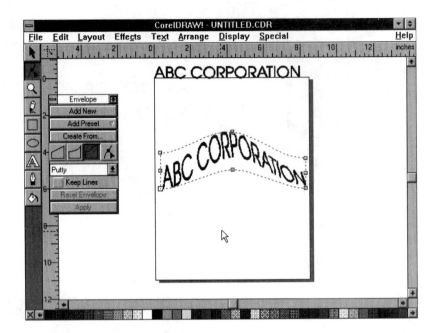

Example of
envelope effect
Figure 14-4.

Another special effect is the Blend feature, which allows you to blend one object into another, as shown here:

You define the beginning and ending points, and CorelDRAW! fills in the blend steps.

The Extrude feature gives depth to objects. An example of an open path extruded surface is shown here:

Contour, a new feature in CorelDRAW! 4, allows you to create a blended type of effect with a single graphic or text object. You can display this effect within or outside an object, or centered, as shown here:

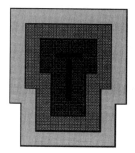

Another new feature in the Effects menu is PowerLine. This feature allows you to draw a line of varying width and darkness. It differs from the Pencil tool in that the object is a graphic having its own fill, outline, and nib attributes. An example is shown here:

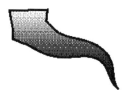

As you can see, the Effects menu contains many powerful and dramatic drawing effects. You will explore these special effects beginning with the Envelope feature. If your computer is not turned on, turn it on now and bring up CorelDRAW!.

Using an Envelope

An envelope is a bounding box with eight handles on it that surrounds the text or graphic. You pull the handles to reshape the object within the envelope.

The Envelope roll-up window contains the options for applying and editing envelopes. It contains eight basic operations, as shown in Figure 14-5.

You can add a new envelope to a selected object. You may either apply the first envelope to an object or apply an envelope over another object.

14

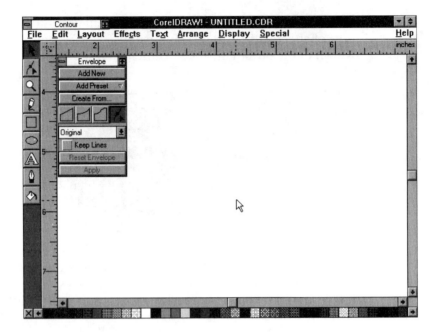

Envelope
roll-up menu
Figure 14-5.

You can select from a predefined group of envelope shapes, as shown here:

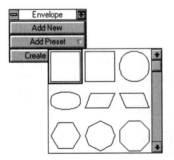

An envelope shape can be created from an existing image. In this case, you select the destination object that will conform to the new envelope before selecting the Create From option. Your pointer turns into a From? arrow, which you use to click on the source object. You can then click on Apply to copy the envelope shape from the source to the destination object.

You may select one of four editing modes that determine how the envelope can be reshaped, as shown here:

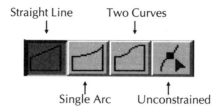

Straight Line   Two Curves

Single Arc   Unconstrained

The first three modes allow you to change the shape of a side of the envelope in a specific way. The first one allows you to pull the side in a straight line, the second in a curved line, the third in a line with two curves. The fourth envelope editing mode is unconstrained. It allows you to pull in any direction, and to change a line to a curve.

As you move the handles, the envelope changes shape. When you tell CorelDRAW! to apply the editing changes, the contents of the envelope are reshaped to conform to the new shape, as you will see shortly.

By clicking on the list box beneath the editing modes, you can see a list of mapping options, shown here:

These options control how an object will be fitted to the envelope. There are five possibilities:

✦ *Original* Maps the object's boundary box (selected handles) to the envelope's shape. It produces an exaggerated effect.

✦ *Putty* Maps only the corners of the boundary box to the envelope's corners.

✦ *Vertical* Maps the object to fit the vertical dimensions on the envelope.

✦ *Horizontal* Maps the object to fit the horizontal dimensions of the envelope.

✦ *Text* Automatically applies when working with paragraph text. The other options are unavailable. The Text option can be used to flow text around graphics.

14

You will now create and duplicate some text to use for the first three editing modes.

Creating and Duplicating Text

To prepare for the first exercise, you need to create a piece of text and then duplicate it twice.

1. Click on the Text tool and then click on the page, at about the middle left.

2. Type **Happy Birthday** and select the text by dragging on it. Open the Text roll-up and change the type size to 60 points and the font to Cupertino. Click on Apply to change the text. Now you will copy the text twice so that there are three copies, one for each of the first three editing modes.

3. From the Edit menu, select Duplicate for the first copy.

4. Press Ctrl-D to duplicate another copy. The three copies will be stacked on top of each other with the edges of the bottom copies peeking out, as shown here:

    Now you will move them apart.

5. Click on the Pick tool. Place the mouse pointer on an edge of the selected text. Press and hold the mouse button while moving the box outline to the bottom of the page. Center the outline horizontally on the page. When you release the mouse button, the selected copy of the text will be moved from the stack onto the page.

6. Click on the top of the stack to select the next text object. Repeat step 5, but move the second copy from the stack to the top of the page. The last copy will remain at the center of the page.

7. Space the three text units so that you can easily work with each one. Figure 14-6 shows an example of the screen with the three copies rearranged on the page.

Now you are ready to work with the first envelope editing mode.

Straight Line Envelope

The Straight Line editing mode allows you to pull envelope handles in a straight line. You can move one handle at a time.

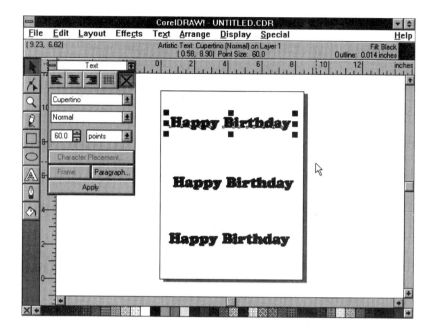

Text to be
used for
illustrating
envelopes
Figure 14-6.

*In the
Unconstrained
mode, all
handles move
in any
direction.*

As in all of the first three editing modes, the handles can be moved only in a restricted way: handles located in the center of the sides move left or right; handles located in the top and bottom center move up or down; corner handles move up or down or left or right.

The easiest way to understand the feature is to try it out. Follow these steps:

1. If the top text object is not selected, select it by clicking on it so that the selection box surrounds it.

2. Display the Envelope roll-up from the Effects menu.

3. Choose the first editing mode, Straight Line.

4. Click on Add New.

   The envelope will appear on the screen surrounding the selected text. You can see the eight handles. Also, the Shaping tool is selected, and the pointer turns into a shaping arrow.

5. Pull the top middle handle up, as shown here:

6. Pull the bottom center handle up as well.

7. Click on Apply to have the text conform to the envelope, as shown here:

You can see how the text conforms to the new straight line. Next you will see how the Single Arc editing mode differs.

Single Arc Envelope

The Single Arc editing mode allows you to create an arc by pulling the handles up, down, right, or left. You can only pull one handle at a time, and, as with the Straight Line mode, they can be moved only in a restricted way: handles located in the center of the sides move left or right; handles located in the top and bottom center move up and down; corner handles move up or down or left and right.

Follow these steps to try it out:

1. Click on the Pick tool, then select the second text copy by clicking on it so a selection box surrounds it.

2. From the Envelope roll-up, choose the second option, the Single Arc.

3. Click on Add New.

4. Pull the top middle handle up.

5. Pull the bottom middle handle up.

6. Click on Apply.

The text will conform to the Single Arc envelope, as shown here:

You can see how the Straight Line and Single Arc editing modes differ. Now try out the third editing mode.

Two Curves Envelope

The third choice allows you to create two curves by pulling one of the eight handles. You can only move one handle at a time, and the same restrictions apply as in the Straight Line and Single Arc modes.

Follow these steps to try the Two Curves editing mode:

1. Click on the Pick tool and click on the third text object so it is selected.
2. From the Envelope roll-up, choose the third item, Two Curves.
3. Click on Add New. The envelope will surround the third text object.
4. Pull the top middle handle up. Then pull the bottom middle handle up.
5. Click on Apply. The text will conform to the Two Curve envelope, as shown here:

You can see how two curves are created out of the line, shaping the text in an entirely different way. These three envelope editing modes have an additional feature that can be used to constrain the shapes.

Using Ctrl and Shift with Envelopes

You can use Ctrl or Shift with the three editing modes to produce surprising results. Three effects can take place:

✦ If you hold down Ctrl while you drag on a handle, the opposite handle will move in the same direction.

✦ If you hold down Shift while you drag on a handle, the opposite handle will move in the opposite direction.

✦ Finally, if you hold both Shift and Ctrl while dragging a handle, all four corners or sides will move in opposite directions.

You can use these keys with any of the first three Envelope options. Try the Ctrl method now with the first text object on your screen.

14

1. Click on the top text image so that the envelope and handles appear on the screen. Now experiment for a moment.

2. From the Envelope roll-up, click on Add New to get an envelope around the text. Note that it is not the right one. The previous envelope was correct.

3. Click on Reset Envelope to restore the previous envelope.

4. Press Ctrl while dragging the top middle handle down.

5. Click on Apply. The text should be changed, as shown here:

Happy Birthday

You can see two immediate effects: First, the top and bottom sides move in the same direction. You expected that. Second, and unexpectedly, the lines are *not* being shaped according to the Straight Line edit mode that was earlier applied to this particular text object. Instead, the lines are being shaped according to the Two Curves edit mode, the last mode applied to another text object. Whenever you apply a new editing mode to any envelope on the page, all new edits will be assigned the new mode as well. If you need to change the shape of an object while retaining the original edit mode, simply reselect that mode before making your changes.

Now you will try the Shift method with the second text object.

1. Click on the middle text object so that the envelope and handles appear on the screen.

2. From the Envelope roll-up, select the Single Arc option.

3. Press Shift while dragging the top right handle out to the right. The left and right sides will move in opposite directions, as shown here:

4. Click on Apply; you'll see an interesting effect.

The Shift-Ctrl method is just as easy.

1. Click on the bottom text object to select it.

2. From the Envelope roll-up, select the Two Curves option.

3. Press ⟨Shift⟩-⟨Ctrl⟩ while dragging the top right handle to the right. The top and bottom and both sides all move in opposite directions, as shown here:

4. Click on Apply.

These techniques are particularly useful when you are changing the shape of drawings, as in circles or rectangles, and you want one or all of the dimensions to be altered to the same degree.

Now you will explore the fourth envelope editing mode.

Unconstrained Envelope

The Unconstrained editing mode is the most dynamic of the four modes. The handles can be moved in any direction, and they contain control points that can be used to fine-tune and bend the objects even more dynamically. Unlike the first three Envelope options, the Unconstrained mode lets you select several handles and move them as a unit. To experiment with this, first clear the page of its contents, then follow these steps:

1. Select New from the File menu. Click on No when asked about saving the current screen contents.

2. Select the Text tool and click on the middle left of the page.

3. Type **Not Constrained**. Select the text, and from the Text roll-up, change the type size to 70 points and the font to Bangkok. Click on Apply.

4. From the Envelope roll-up window, choose the fourth submenu option, Unconstrained.

5. Click on Add New.

You will see the text object surrounded by the envelope and its handles. Also, the pointer turns into a Shaping tool, and the handles of the bounding box become nodes.

6. Pull the top middle handle or node up and then the bottom middle node down, as shown here:

You can see that a pair of control points appeared first on the top middle, and then on the bottom middle, nodes. These control points, like Shaping tool control points, allow you to alter the shape by exaggerating and bending the curve.

7. Place the pointer on the left control point of the bottom middle node and pull it down. (To experiment with it, move it down and then back up so that you will see what happens with the handle.)

8. Click on the top middle node to select it. Place the pointer on the right control point of the top middle node and pull it up, as shown here:

Now, suppose you want the last letters to curve up at the end.

9. While holding (Shift), click first on the bottom middle node and then on the bottom right node. Release (Shift). Now you can treat all three selected nodes.

10. Hold down the mouse button and pull the bottom middle node down, as shown here:

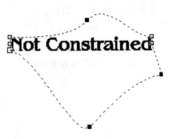

11. Click on Apply for another interesting effect.

One way that you can use the Unconstrained edit mode is to modify text to conform to a shape, for example, text within a circle or oval. First you create the circle, oval, or whatever shape you want as a border and move the text with its envelope within the border. You then manually move the control points of the text so that they correspond with the border shape. Then if you don't want the border to appear, you can delete it.

Continue to experiment until you are comfortable with the Unconstrained edit mode. Then you can move on to more Envelope features.

Adding a New Envelope

Sometimes you may want to use more than one of the editing modes on an object. Adding a new envelope allows you to do this. You apply an envelope and shape the object with it. Then you add a new envelope, which replaces the first envelope while retaining its shape. With the new envelope, you select a new editing mode and change the shape again. To try this out, follow these steps:

1. Clear the screen by selecting New from the File menu. Click on No when asked if you want to save the screen contents.
2. Select the Text tool and click on the middle left of the page.
3. Type **New Envelope**, select the text, and from the Text roll-up, set the type size to 80 points and select the Penguin font. Click on Apply.
4. From the Envelope roll-up window, attach an envelope by selecting the Straight Line editing mode and then Add New.
5. Click on the top left handle and drag it up.
6. Click on the bottom right handle and drag it down, as shown here:

7. Click on Apply.

Now you will apply a new envelope and change the shape using another editing mode on top of the Straight Line editing mode.

1. From the Envelope roll-up, select the Single Arc editing mode. Click on Add New.

   You will use Shift to move the opposite handles in opposite directions.

2. While pressing Shift, drag the upper-left handle up.

3. While pressing Shift, drag the bottom-right handle to the right, as shown in Figure 14-7.

4. Click on Apply.

One way that a new envelope can be used is with certain fonts that do not bend or reshape themselves exactly as you want. You can form the basic shape with one of the first three edit modes and then apply the Unconstrained edit mode to fine-tune the text. In this way you can manually form the letters with more precision than you might get with the font alone.

5. Remove the previous envelopes by clicking on Clear Transformations from the Effects menu.

Now you can copy an envelope to a new object.

Copy Envelope From

The Copy Envelope From command allows you to copy the envelope and its current shape to a new object. The new object does not need its own envelope. To try out this feature, you will first create a new object.

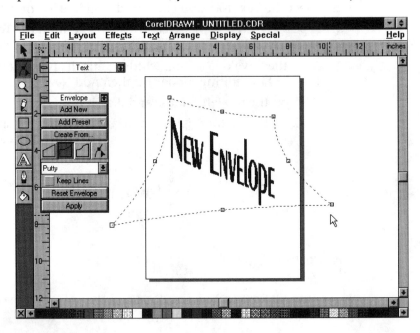

Using Add New Envelope to reshape a text object within the borders of a previous envelope
Figure 14-7.

1. Add a new envelope to the text. Specify the Two Curves editing mode, Add New, and click on Apply. Using the Shape tool pull the top middle node up and the bottom middle node down. Click on Apply.

2. Click on the Ellipse tool. Draw a circle below the text, using the Ctrl key.

3. Select Copy Effect From in the Effects menu. Select Copy Envelope From in the submenu.

   The pointer will turn into a From? arrow. You will move the arrow to the source of the envelope, which is the text.

4. Move the arrow to the text "New Envelope," and click on it.

The destination object, that is, the ellipse, will be reshaped with the new tool to match the text, as shown in Figure 14-8.

Sometimes you might want to start over again. Clearing an envelope allows you to do that.

Clearing an Envelope

The Clear Envelope command on the Effects menu (not on the roll-up) removes the current envelope and all shape changes that occurred with it. The Clear Envelope appears on the Effects menu when you have chosen the Envelope roll-up. If you have applied more than one envelope, only the most recent one will be removed.

Using Copy Envelope From to reshape a second object, in this case, a circle
Figure 14-8.

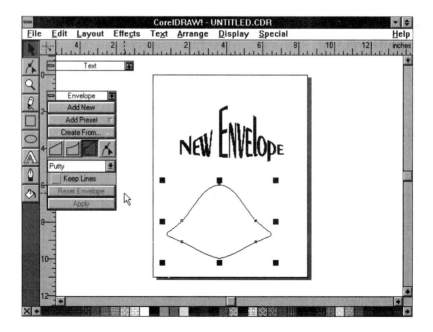

14

To clear the last envelope from the current text object, first select the "New Envelope" text with the Pick tool. Then select Clear Envelope from the Effects menu. The drawing will be returned to the previous Straight Line edit mode. However, if you have applied a perspective (perspectives are discussed shortly) to the object after applying the most recent envelope, the perspective must be removed before you can clear the envelope.

NOTE: The Clear Transformations command, found on the Effects menu, removes all envelopes, restoring the drawing to its original shape. If you have applied perspectives, they will also be removed and the original shape restored.

Creating Perspective Effects

Perspective gives an object a sense of depth, as if the object were moving away from you. This effect can be applied from one- or two-point perspective views. Figure 14-9 shows the two kinds of perspective.

The one-point perspective, on the top, gives the effect of moving away from you in a straight line. The two-point perspective, on the bottom, distorts the view so that the object is moving away and being twisted in the process.

Examples of one-point and two-point perspectives
Figure 14-9.

Using One- or Two-Point Perspective

You apply perspective in much the same way that you change the shape of an envelope. A perspective bounding box with handles surrounds the object. You can drag the handles to shorten or lengthen the object, giving the perspective you want. Follow these steps to try it out:

1. Clear the screen by selecting New from the File menu. Click on No when asked if you want to save the screen contents.

2. If the rulers are not showing, click on Show Rulers in the Display menu to display them. Pull the Zero Guides to the lower-left corner of the page. Place a horizontal guideline at 9 inches and a vertical guideline at 1 inch.

3. Select the Text tool and click at the intersection of the guidelines.

4. Type **Moving Away**, select the text, and with the Text roll-up, set the type size to 60 points and the font to Toronto. Ensure that Normal is the selected style. Click Apply when you are done.

5. Select Add Perspective from the Effects menu.

   An envelope will surround the text, and the pointer will change to the Shaping tool. When you place it on the handles, it will change to a crosshair. You move the handles according to the coordinates, which tell the location of the pointer. The coordinates are shown in the upper-left corner of the status line.

   You will now change the shape of the text object. To change to one-point perspective, drag the handle either up, down, right, or left; that is, vertically or horizontally. In the following instructions and in the next several exercises, you will see sets of coordinates. These are meant as guidelines and are approximate. The coordinates are in inches and always have the horizontal displacement before the vertical.

6. Click on the bottom right handle and drag it vertically, straight down, until the coordinates are approximately 5.7 and 8.0.

7. Drag the bottom left handle vertically, straight down, until the coordinates are approximately 1.0 and 6.0, as in Figure 14-10.

   Now you will alter the shape to add the two-point perspective. You do this by dragging the handles either toward or away from the center of the object. If you drag toward the object, the shape is pushed under; if you drag away from the object, the shape is pulled out toward you.

8. Drag the handles as close as possible to the following coordinates, as shown in Figure 14-11.

14

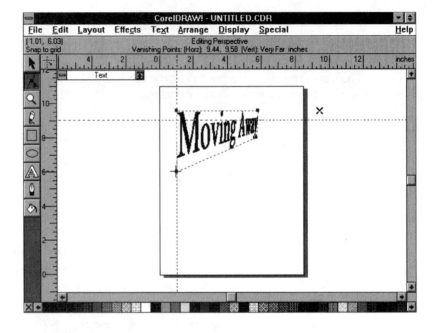

Example of
one-point
perspective
created by
dragging the
handles
straight down
Figure 14-10.

Upper-right corner: 6.9, 9.0
Lower-right corner: 6.6, 8.0
Lower-left corner: 2.0, 6.5

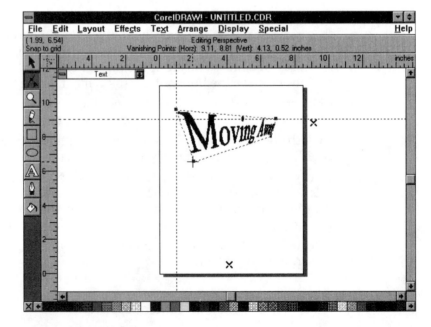

Example of
two-point
perspective
created by
dragging the
handles
diagonally
toward or
away from the
center of the
object
Figure 14-11.

You should see two X symbols, known as *vanishing points,* which you will learn about next.

Using the Vanishing Point

In Figure 14-11, just off the page on the right, is the horizontal vanishing point. On the bottom of the page is the vertical vanishing point. Each of these points is marked with an X.

You can change the perspective by moving the vanishing point itself. By moving the vanishing point toward the object, the edge closest to the point becomes vertically shorter; the edge becomes vertically longer when the point is moved away from the edge.

When you move the vanishing point parallel to the object, the far side will remain stationary, while the side nearest the point moves in the direction you drag the vanishing point.

Take a moment now to play with the vanishing point. When you are satisfied, you can explore some of the other perspective features.

Adding a New Perspective

You can add a new perspective to an object on top of one that already exists. This allows you to change the perspective, within the limits of the perspective already applied. To see how this is done, follow these steps:

1. Select Add Perspective from the Effects menu. A new, second bounding box will be applied to the object. Now you will change the perspective again.

2. Drag the handles to the following coordinates, or close to them, as shown in Figure 14-12.

   Upper-right handle: 5.6, 8.0
   Lower-left handle: 2.0, 6.3
   Lower-right handle: 8.2, 2.5

Now you will apply this perspective to a new object.

Copy Perspective From

When you select the Copy Perspective From option, you use the shape of one object to change the perspective of another one. First, you will create a form to which the perspective will be applied.

14

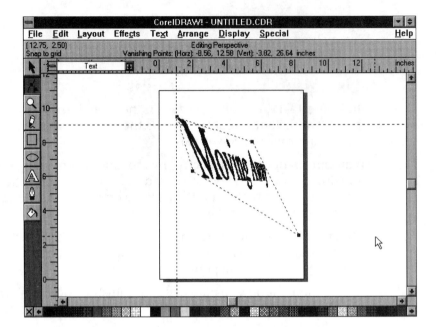

Changing
shape with
Add New
perspective
Figure 14-12.

1. Select the Ellipse tool and draw a perfect circle under the text object.

2. Select the Copy Effect From command from the Effects Menu and then select Copy Perspective From in the submenu. The From? arrow will appear.

3. Move the tip of the From? arrow to the outline of the text object and click on it. The circle will be redrawn with the new perspective.

4. Use the Pick tool to drag the circle over the text object. (It doesn't matter if the reshaped circle isn't the same size as the text.)

5. Click on no fill (the X) in the lower-left corner of your screen.

6. The results should look like Figure 14-13. (It may differ because of the work you did with the vanishing point.)

Clearing a Perspective

Clear Perspective, similar to Clear Envelope, removes the most recent perspective applied to an object. The Clear Perspecitve option appears when you have chosen Add Perspective. If you've applied more than one perspective, only the last one is removed.

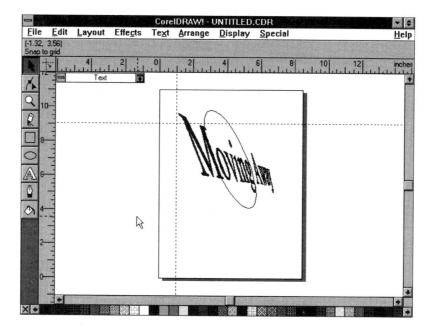

The circle
reshaped with
a copied
perspective
Figure 14-13.

If you've applied an envelope over a perspective, you must first remove the
envelope before the perspective can be removed. Before you remove the
envelope, be sure to duplicate the object in order to retain the shape you
have created with the envelope. Then you can restore the shape by using the
Copy Envelope From command after the perspective is removed.

Notice that Clear Transformations in the Effects menu will clear all
perspectives and envelopes from an object at once. This is used when you
want to restore an object to its original shape.

Now remove the perspective from the current object by following these steps:

1. Select the text and ellipse with the Pick tool.
2. Select Clear Perspective from the Effects menu. The shape will be
   changed.
3. Select Clear Transformations. See the change again.
4. Select New from the File menu. Do not save the changes.

14

Blending Objects

The Blend command causes one object to be blended into another by a number of connecting images. For example, you can turn a square into a circle with 20 intermediate images. You can also use this feature to create highlights and airbrush effects. The images can be of different colors, line weights, fills, and so on.

Before the objects are blended, you must fill them and place them where you want them on the screen. And, of course, first you must create the objects to be blended.

1. Select the Text tool and click on the upper-left area of the page.
2. Type **Happy**, select the text by dragging on it, and from the Text roll-up, set the type size to 60 points and the font to USA-Black, Normal. Click on Apply.
3. While the text object is still selected, click on the yellow in the palette at the bottom of your screen as the fill for the word "Happy."
4. With the text still selected, click on the lower center area of the page.
5. Type **Birthday**, select the text by dragging on it, and with the Text roll-up, set the type size to 60 points and the font to USA-Black. Click on Apply.
6. Click on a bright blue in the palette at the bottom of your screen for the word "Birthday."

Now you are ready to blend the two objects.

Blending Two Objects

Blending is done with the Blend roll-up window. To blend the objects, you must first select the two objects. Then you simply open the Blend roll-up window, tell CorelDRAW! how many steps are needed between the two objects, and click on Apply.

1. Select the Pick tool and then marquee-select the two objects by dragging a dotted rectangle around both objects. You must be careful that both objects are selected. If not, you will not be able to use the Blend command.
2. When both objects are selected, select Blend Roll-Up from the Effects menu. The Blend roll-up window will appear:

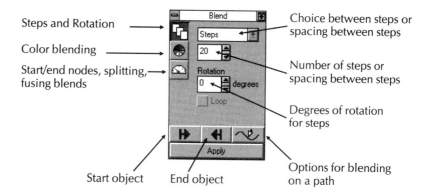

The menu contains three main modes, represented by the icons on the left of the roll-up. The first, which is displayed, displays the Steps and Rotation controls. The second displays color blending attributes, and the third provides controls for choosing start and end nodes, and splitting and fusing blends.

The Steps and Rotation controls, on your screen now, are used to control how many steps you want in the blend and what degree of rotation will occur between the two objects. The Loop check box controls where the center of rotation is to be. You'll see its effects shortly. At the bottom of the menu are three controls. The two arrows allow you to select the start (the right-pointing arrow) and end (the left-pointing arrow) objects. The rightmost icon is used to manage the blend path.

You now tell CorelDRAW! the number of intervening steps between the two objects. It assumes 20 steps, which is acceptable for this example. You will indicate the degree of rotation and whether to map matching nodes in a minute.

3. Accept the 20 steps and 0 degrees of rotation by clicking on Apply. You will see the two objects blended on the screen, as in Figure 14-14.

Next you will see what the rotation can do.

Rotating the Blended Objects

You can cause the blended objects to be rotated by putting a degree of rotation in the Blend roll-up window. You cause the intervening steps to be rotated counterclockwise if a positive number is entered; clockwise, if a negative number is entered.

14

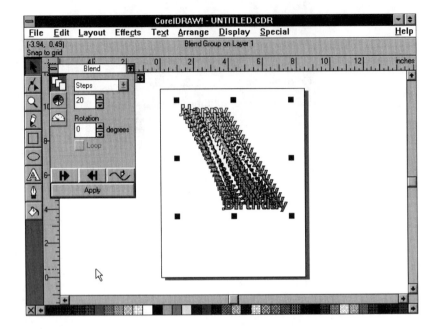

Blending of
"Happy" into
"Birthday"
with no
rotation
Figure 14-14.

The Blend roll-up window allows you to specify the degrees of rotation to be used in the intervening steps. Let's see how this is used.

1. Choose Clear Blend from the Effects menu to remove the current Blend effects. You will be left with the two unblended selected objects.

2. Change the degree of rotation to 95.0 in the Blend roll-up window. Click on Loop and click on Apply.

TIP: Clicking on the Loop option makes the blend rotate around a center point midway between the beginning and the ending object's centers of rotation. If Loop is not selected, the blend will rotate around the object's own center of rotation. Experiment to see the differences.

The effects of blending will appear on the screen, as shown in Figure 14-15.

Now try out clockwise rotation with these steps:

1. Again, choose Clear Blend to remove the current Blend effects. You will be left with the two selected objects.

2. In the Blend roll-up window, type **–90.0** for the degree of rotation and click on Loop to deselect it. Click on Apply. The results look something like Figure 14-16.

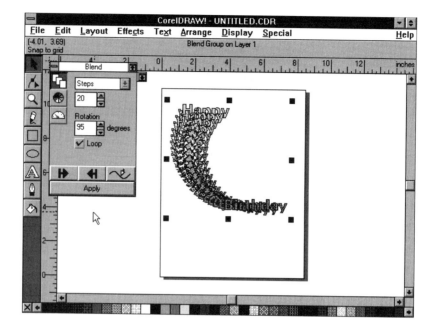

"Happy" blended into "Birthday" with 95 degrees of rotation
Figure 14-15.

3. To experiment, click on Loop and then Apply.

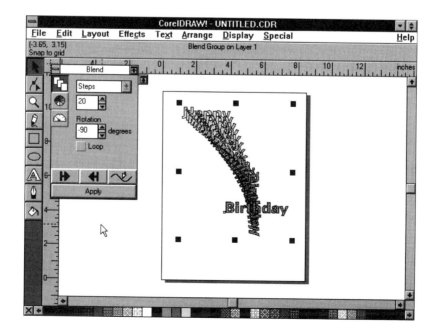

A blended arc created with −90 degrees of rotation
Figure 14-16.

14

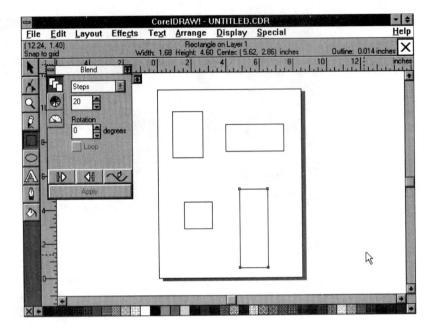

Placement of
rectangles on
the page
Figure 14-17.

One other rotation feature, discussed next, can be used to create interesting effects.

Mapping Matching Nodes

By varying the beginning nodes of both of the objects, you can create some unexpected results. The nodes identify where the blend is to begin and end. You will try two different ways of identifying the nodes.

1. Begin with a new screen by selecting New from the File menu. Click on No.

2. Select the Rectangle tool and create four different-sized rectangles on your screen, as in Figure 14-17. Make sure that all four rectangles are unfilled. Click on the X in the lower-left corner of your screen for no fill.

3. Press Spacebar for the Pick tool and marquee-select the two rectangles on the left.

4. In the Blend roll-up window, enter 20 Blend steps and 90 (positive) degrees of rotation, and click on Loop. Click on the Map Nodes option (third icon down on the left) and then on the Map Nodes button. When you move the pointer off the menu out to the page, it will become a curved arrow, and one of the selected objects will have nodes displayed on each corner, as shown here:

5. Select the upper-left corner node by moving the arrow to that node and clicking on it. The second object's nodes will be displayed.

6. Select its upper-left corner node by moving the arrow to that node and clicking on it.

7. Click on Apply in the Blend roll-up.

   You will now see one result of mapping matching nodes.

8. Marquee-select the second two objects.

9. Click on Map Nodes in the Blend roll-up.

10. With the arrow, click on the lower-right node of the first object (the one with the corner nodes selected).

11. Click on the upper-left node of the second object and click on Apply in the Blend roll-up. The blend will occur, as in Figure 14-18.

    You can continue to experiment with Map Nodes, adding a different degree of rotation if you want to see its effects. When you are finished, you can look at another major feature found on the Effects menu, the Extrude feature.

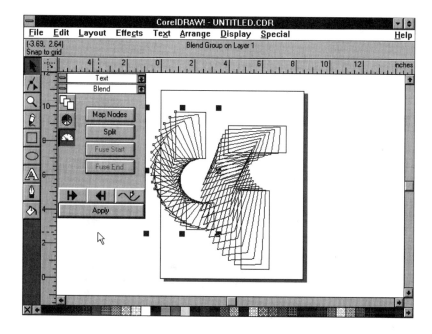

Examples of blends with two types of Map Nodes
Figure 14-18.

14

12. Renew the screen by selecting New from the File menu. Click on No. Also, close the Blend roll-up.

Extruding Objects

Extruded objects appear to have depth. You can use the Extrude feature on text, closed shapes, or open paths. The results can be very dramatic.

There are three ingredients to the Extrude feature that affect the results: the depth and direction of the extrusion, the spatial alignment of the extruded object, and the shading and coloring of the extruded object. Each of these will be investigated separately. First create the objects to be extruded with the following steps:

1. Click on the Text tool and click in the upper-left quadrant of the page.
2. Type **T**, select the letter, and from the Text roll-up, select 120 points, Nebraska font, and Normal. Click on Apply.
3. Click on Duplicate in the Edit menu to create a copy of the "T." Repeat it to make a second copy.
4. With the Pick tool, select each of the copies and drag one to the upper-right quadrant of the page; the other, to the lower-left quadrant.
5. Click on the Pencil tool and draw a wavy line in the lower part of the page. Your screen should look something like Figure 14-19.

Pressing Ctrl-D is a shortcut for the Duplicate command.

Now you are ready to experiment with extruding.

Extrude Roll-Up Window

Extruding is controlled by the Extrude roll-up window, which you open from the Effects menu. The Extrude roll-up opens in its depth and direction mode, which you can see here:

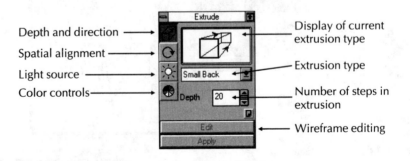

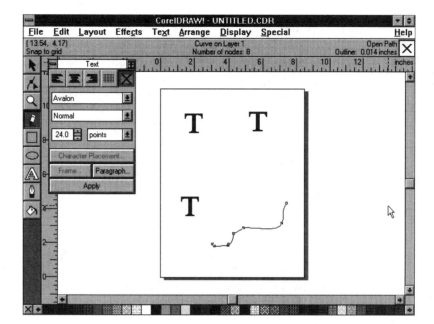

Placement of objects for experimenting with the Extrude feature
Figure 14-19.

The depth and direction mode is one of four modes that the Extrude roll-up can be in. These modes, which are activated by the four buttons on the upper-left of the roll-up, perform the following functions:

✦ Depth and direction allow you to determine the depth of the extrusion, the location of the vanishing point, whether the vanishing point is in front of or behind the object, and whether the extrusion is in a perspective or orthogonal (parallel) view.

✦ Spatial alignment allows you to rotate the extruded object in any of three dimensions.

✦ Shading allows you to determine the location of the light source and its intensity.

✦ Coloring allows you to determine if the extruded object will use the same coloring as the original object, or whether the extruded portion and its shading should be different (and what those different colors should be).

Selecting these modes significantly changes the options available in the Extrude roll-up, as you will see in the following sections.

14

Depth and Direction

Depth and direction is the default mode for the Extrude roll-up window—the window automatically opens in this mode. Should you be in another mode and want to return to this mode, you can do so by clicking on the depth icon in the upper-left of the Extrude roll-up.

Examine the Extrude roll-up window now by following these instructions:

1. With the Pick tool, click on the topmost left "T" to select it.
2. From the Effects menu, choose Extrude Roll-Up, if it is not already on your screen.

Perspective and Parallel Extrusions

You normally see an extrusion in a perspective view—it gets smaller as it extends away from you. Therefore, a perspective-type of extrusion, Small Back, is selected by default. The choices for extrusion types are shown here:

The first four extrusions are perspective types, where you are looking from front to back or back to front. If you select Back or Front Parallel type, the extrusion will be *orthogonal,* meaning that the lines forming the extrusion will be parallel to each other. See this for yourself with this exercise:

1. Click on Apply in the Extrude roll-up. The wireframe behind the "T" on the left is filled in to form a short extrusion, which narrows as it extends toward the center of the page— it is in a perspective view with a centered vanishing point, as you can see here:

2. Click on the right "T." (It takes two clicks to be selected.) From the Extrusion type drop-down list box, choose Back Parallel. Click on Apply. An extrusion is created behind the "T," extending undiminished all the way to the center of the page—it is very obviously not in perspective, as shown here:

Changing the Depth

The Depth counter is available only if you are working with an extrusion in perspective, and it determines how far toward the vanishing point the extrusion extends. You can think of this counter number as the percentage of the distance between the object and the vanishing point that is occupied by the extrusion. The Depth counter can go from 1 to 99. A value of 99 makes the extrusion extend all the way to the vanishing point, and a value of 1 creates no extrusion. A value of 0 or a negative number is not a valid entry.

Now you will reselect the "T" on the left, keeping the Small Back type.

1. With the Pick tool, click on the left-hand "T" to select it. (Again, it will take two clicks.)
2. Click on the up arrow of the Depth counter to increase the depth to 70. (If 70 is not available, drag the counter and type in 70.)
3. When the depth is at 70, click on Apply. A new, more elongated extrusion will appear, as shown in Figure 14-20.

You can also affect the depth and direction of the extrusion by working directly with the vanishing point, as you'll see next.

Moving the Vanishing Point

You can move the vanishing point on the page in two ways: by adjusting the horizontal and vertical counters in the Extrude roll-up, or by clicking on Edit and dragging the X that indicates the vanishing point. Try both techniques:

1. Select the "T" on the left, set the depth to 40, and the extrusion type to Small Back.
2. Click on the Page icon beneath the Depth numeric entry box. The following menu will appear:

14

You can set the horizontal and vertical locations by typing an absolute number into the counters. You select how these numbers are to be measured by clicking either the Page Origin or Object Center option.

3. Change the horizontal and vertical counters for the vanishing point so they both have a value of 6.5. You can do this either by clicking on the up arrows, or by dragging across the numbers and typing the new value. Keep the Page Origin default and click on Apply.

By moving the vanishing point, you've made the extrusion shift to follow it, as you can see in Figure 14-21. If you rotate the vanishing point around the object, the extrusion will also rotate. If you move the vanishing point away from the object, the extrusion will extend out following the vanishing point (although the depth value doesn't change—it is a percentage, so it merely re-scales the extrusion).

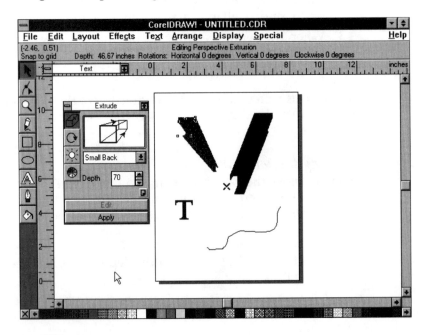

Original extrusion with Depth changed to 70
Figure 14-20.

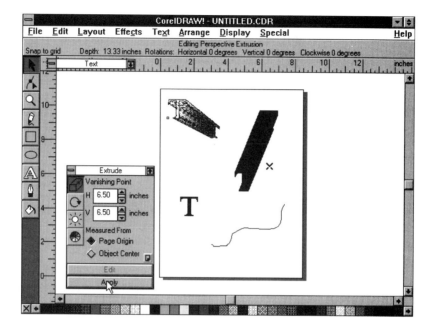

Moving the
vanishing
point with the
counters
Figure 14-21.

4. Drag the vanishing point to the upper-right corner of the page. Again, the extrusion will follow, as shown here:

5. Click on Apply to complete the extrusion.

TIP: You can also move the vanishing point by clicking on Edit and dragging the X representing the vanishing point wherever you want it. The extrusion will follow the X.

Clearing an Extrusion

If you have an extrusion that you want to remove without getting rid of the original object, you cannot just press Del, which would get rid of everything, including the object. You must use the Clear Extrude option in the Effects menu.

14

1. With the extruded "T" on the left, select Clear Extrude from the Effects menu. The extrusion is removed, leaving the original selected object.

2. Press ⏎Del to remove that letter, and to get ready for the next exercise.

3. Click on the extruded "T" on the right. Press ⏎Del, and the entire object and extrusion are removed from the page.

To prepare for the next exercise on spatial alignment, follow these steps:

4. Click on the remaining "T" to select it.

5. Click on the Page icon to return to the Depth and Dimension roll-up.

6. Select Small Back extrusion type and set the depth to 70. Click on Apply.

Now you are ready to proceed with the next mode.

Spatial Alignment

The second mode in which you can place the Extrude roll-up is spatial alignment. You change to spatial alignment mode by clicking on the second button in the left column of the Extrude roll-up. Try that now, and the Extrude roll-up will change to include the 3-D rotator that you see here:

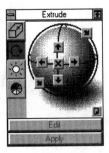

The 3-D rotator has six arrows that allow you to move the currently selected object in any of six directions—two in each of three planes. When you click on an arrow, the object is rotated five degrees in the direction of the arrow. In the center of the sphere is an X button that allows you to clear the current rotation. The 3-D rotator does not change the vanishing point, only the object and its extrusion. Try the 3-D rotator now with this exercise:

1. Click several times on the upward-pointing arrow above the X on the sphere. The wireframe representing the extrusion will rotate upward—the face of the extrusion, the original letter, moves up, while the other end of the extrusion moves down, as you can see here:

2. Click on Apply to fill in the wireframe and complete the rotation.

3. Click on the X in the center of the sphere, and then click on Apply to remove the rotation and return the extrusion to its original position.

4. Click several times on each of the arrows on the rotator to observe their behavior. Click on the center X after each, to return the extrusion to its original position.

5. When you are through, click on X and then Apply.

With the 3-D rotator, you can look at the extruded object from literally any angle.

Shading and Coloring

You may have noticed both on your screen and in the figures and illustrations in this part of the chapter, that the extruded surfaces were hard to see, and the extruded effect therefore was not very clear. The reason for this is that both the original letter and the extrusion are black, so there is no differentiation between them. You can change this by altering the shading and coloring of the extrusion. The last two modes on the left of the roll-up window provide this capability. Try them now, starting with the remaining "T" selected:

1. Click on the color wheel icon to place the Extrude roll-up window in coloring mode. The roll-up's appearance will change, as you can see here:

14

The default coloring scheme is Use Object Fill. In other words, the object's fill color is used as the color for the extrusion. This is why both are presently black.

2. Click on Solid Fill to make the extrusion a solid (not shaded) color that is independent from the original object.

3. Click on the color button just under and to the right of Solid Fill. The current color palette will open. Click on the second gray from the right in the second row, then click on Apply.

The extruded object now has clear differentiation, as shown in the following illustration. (Deselect the "T" to see it more clearly by clicking anywhere else on the screen, then select it again for the next step.)

This two-color scheme is nice, but you can improve on it with shading. When you select the Shade option, you can specify a range between two colors or shades for the extrusion. You will get a linear fountain fill along the extrusion, with the From color nearest to the original object, and the To color at the vanishing point.

4. Click on Shade to give the extrusion a shaded fill.

5. Click on the From color button and select the same gray you chose above. Then click on the To color button and choose the second from the right in the top row of the palette. Click on Apply. The extrusion changes to this:

To give your extrusion even more life, you can put a spotlight on it and change the location of that light.

6. Click on the third button in the left column of the Extrude roll-up window. The Extrude roll-up changes once more, this time to include a device for setting the light source, a slider to control intensity, and an On/Off switch:

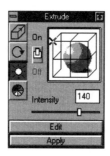

7. Click the On/Off switch to turn the light source on. Then click on the upper-left corner of the wireframe around the sphere to place the light source (represented by the X) there. Next, drag the Intensity control to 140.

8. Click on Apply. The extrusion will be redrawn like this:

Now you will experiment briefly with how an open path can be used in a creative way with extrusions.

Applying Extrusions to Open Paths

Open paths can be used to create some dramatic effects with extrusions. In this case, you will create a ribbon from your wavy line.

1. Click on the wavy line to select it.

2. Click on the color wheel in the Extrude roll-up. Then click on Shade, if it isn't selected. Make the From color a black, and the To color a gray. Click on Apply. Your wavy line will change to a shaded ribbon, like this:

14

3. To clear the screen, select New from the File menu. Do not save the drawing.

Now you will work with contours, a new feature in version 4.

Using Contours

Contours add concentric outlines either inward toward the center of an object, or outward away from the edge of it. Contours can be made to look like blending, but for a single object. They cannot be applied to groups of objects, bitmap objects, or OLE objects.

Follow these steps to get an understanding of what contours can do for you:

Fill must be on for contours to be seen.

1. Using the Ellipse tool, create three circles, each filled with black, by selecting the Fill tool and clicking on black. With the Text tool, type **L**. Select the "L" by dragging on it. From the Text roll-up, set the "L" to 120 points and ErieBlack. Click on Apply. Select the Fill tool and click on black. Your screen will look like Figure 14-22.

2. With the Pick tool, select the first circle on the upper left.

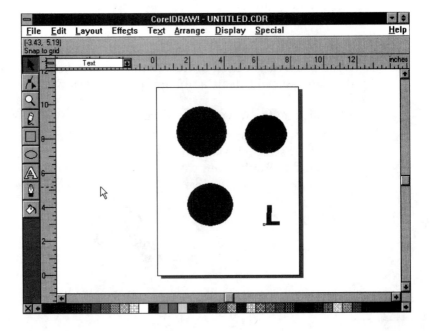

Screen set up to experiment with the Contour feature

Figure 14-22.

3. From the Effects menu select Contour Roll-Up. The roll-up looks like this:

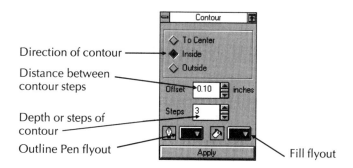

Direction of contour

Distance between
contour steps

Depth or steps of
contour

Outline Pen flyout

Fill flyout

You have a choice of where the contour is to be applied: toward the center of the object, from the edges inward (not necessarily to the center, depending on the number of steps and the Offset), and from the edge of the object outward. Offset is used to define the thickness of each layer of the contour, and Step defines the number of layers you want in the contour. You can define the outline and fill colors or patterns from the menu as well.

In some of the following illustrations, the object being displayed is not selected (it does not have a bounding box around it), in order to show it more clearly. Your screen will have the objected selected.

4. Click on To Center and set Offset to .2 inches. From the roll-up's Outline Pen flyout, select black. From the Fill flyout, select a light blue. Click on Apply. Your screen will look like this:

NOTE: Although the steps will not be used in the To Center option, you may have to have a value other than 0. If you get an error message warning you that the number of steps is between 1 and 99, set the Contour mode to Inside, type in 1 step, and click on To Center again. Then click on Apply.

14

5. Select the next circle to the right and click on Inside. Set Offset to .2 inches, set Step to 3, and click on Apply. Your circle looks like this:

6. Select the third circle, click on Outside, keep Offset at .2 inches, keep Step at 3, and click on Apply. The results can be seen in Figure 14-23.

7. Click on the "L" to select it. Click on Apply to see how the contour setting affects text. Figure 14-23 shows the results.

   The Blend effect is achieved by turning off the Outline Pen. The concentric outlines then blend into each other.

8. On the Outline Pen flyout, click on the X to turn off the outline. The black outlines are removed and the colors blend more readily.

TIP: To edit an individual contour, first select the contoured object and then select Separate from the Arrange menu. Hold down [Ctrl] and click on a contour node. A bounding box surrounds a single contour, and the status line refers to it as "Child Curve." You can then edit the contour by resizing, rotating, or changing the fill or outline.

9. To prepare for the next section, select New from the File menu. Click on No to abandon the changes. Clear the Contour roll-up from the screen.

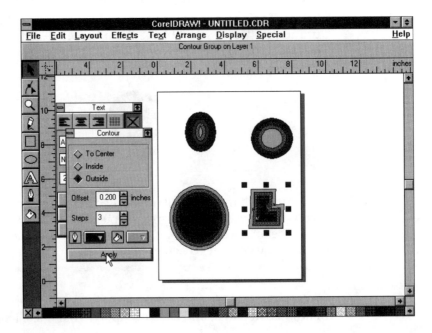

Results of contouring with and without outlines
Figure 14-23.

Another new feature in CorelDRAW! 4, PowerLine, is discussed next.

Using Powerlines

The PowerLine feature, new with version 4, gives you a tool to create graphic lines. The lines resemble those drawn by hand, varying width and darkness, such as you get with calligraphic pens or paintbrushes. Since the line contains both outline and fill, it can be treated as a graphic. CorelDRAW! comes with 23 preset powerlines, and you can create your own and then save them.

To get the powerlines, you click on PowerLine Roll-Up on the Effects menu. It looks like this:

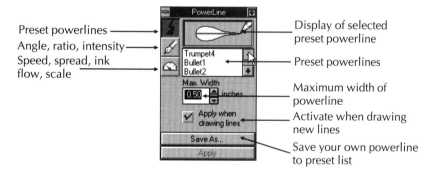

Preset powerlines
Angle, ratio, intensity
Speed, spread, ink flow, scale

Display of selected preset powerline
Preset powerlines
Maximum width of powerline
Activate when drawing new lines
Save your own powerline to preset list

The PowerLine feature has three modes or controls: The first, seen in the illustration, allows you to select preset powerlines for your own use. The second, represented by the second icon on the left, allows you to set the angle, ratio, and intensity controls for the powerline in use. The third, represented by the third icon on the left, allows you to control the speed, spread, ink flow, and scale of the powerline.

The first mode displays the powerlines available for your use. To see the whole list of powerlines, you would click on the list box down arrow. Beneath the list box is a setting for maximum width, which defines the thickness the powerlines may be. Clicking on the "Apply when drawing lines" check box allows you to apply the powerline settings to new lines you expect to create. You can save your own unique powerlines to the preset list by clicking on the Save As command button.

To begin with, you will use a circle to experiment with the effects available with this new feature.

14

Applying Powerlines to an Object

You can apply powerlines to existing objects. Follow these steps to see how you can create intriguing effects with an ordinary circle:

1. With the Ellipse tool, draw a circle. Fill it with the second-from-the-right gray, in the second row on the Fill flyout. From the Outline Pen flyout, set the width to 2 points by clicking on the icon next to the hairline icon.

2. Click on PowerLine Roll-Up in the Effects menu, if it is not already on your screen.

3. Choose Wedge 1 as the type of powerline and set the maximum width to 1 inch. Click on Apply. Your screen looks like this:

4. Click on the third icon on the left for applying speed, spread, and ink flow. The roll-up looks like this:

   You use the Speed setting to control the line sharpness on curves. The higher the number, the greater the "skid" around the curves. Use Spread to control smoothness. The higher the number, the smoother the line. A high number would be more like a paintbrush while a lower number would be more like an ink pen. Use Ink Flow to control the darkness of the line and how much ink flows as you draw the line. A high number lets more ink flow, while a lower number restricts the ink flow. Finally, use Scale with Image to resize the powerline as the values change.

5. Set Speed to 20, Spread to 50, and Ink Flow to 50. Click on Apply. The circle looks like this:

Varying the Nib

You can also vary the nib shape of the line by selecting the second icon on the left. The resulting roll-up looks like this:

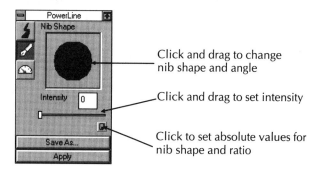

With this menu you can vary the nib shape, angle, and intensity. The display box contains a circle representing the nib shape. You can change it by placing the pointer on the display. As you drag the pointer, the nib shape and angle change. Beneath the display box is the slide control or numeric entry box for Intensity. This determines how strongly the nib is being pressed. Beneath the Intensity control is a Page icon, which displays controls for entering absolute values for the nib shape angle, ratio, and intensity.

Follow these steps to experiment with the nib shapes:

1. Click on the second icon on the left.
2. Set Intensity to 75.
3. Click on the Page icon beneath Intensity. Set the angle to 14 degrees and the nib ratio to 50. Click on Apply. The circle now looks like this:

14

4. Select the circle and press (Del) to clear the screen.

Once you have a shape, you can pull it in different directions using pressure lines.

Using Pressure Lines

For more interesting effects, you can create your own pressure lines, and you can use the Shaping tool to edit a pressure line.

1. Click on the first icon on the left in the Nib Shape roll-up to return to the first powerline mode. From the list box, select Pressure. Your pointer will turn into a hairline. Draw a squiggly line, as shown here:

2. Select the Shaping tool. Double-click on the pressure line. A Node Edit roll-up will appear, as shown here:

3. Click on Pressure Edit.

Two nodes on a straight line appear on each end of the line. You pull them along the line to broaden the line or make it more narrow.

4. With the Shaping tool move the upper-right node to the right; move the lower-left node to the left, as shown here:

5. Select black fill from the Fill tool; the line will be filled in.
6. Turn off Pressure Edit in the Node Edit roll-up.
7. Using the Shaping tool, shape the line however you wish by dragging the nodes.

An example is shown in Figure 14-24.

When you are finished, leave CorelDRAW without saving your test files.

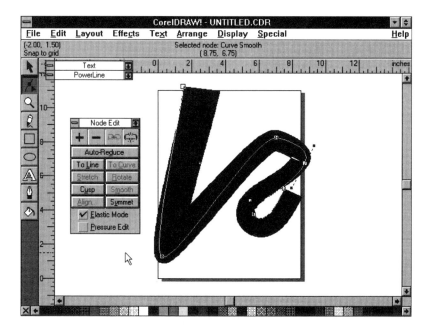

Results of shaping pressure powerlines
Figure 14-24.

14

They can easily be created again.

You can see that the Effects menu offers many dramatic ways to enhance your text and drawings. Chapter 18 introduces more special effects that you can use with CorelDRAW!, and combines many of the other features you've learned about so far.

CHAPTER

COREL DRAW! 4

15

COMBINING CORELDRAW! FEATURES

The previous chapters in this book concentrated on teaching you a specific set of skills. The key word is concentrated, for the exercises throughout the book built on skills you had already learned, even as you mastered new ones.

This chapter, however, takes a different approach. It assumes that you have mastered all of the basic skills in CorelDRAW! and are ready to explore applications that combine many different techniques. In this chapter you will find ideas, and perhaps some of these ideas may inspire you in your own work. However, you will not find a comprehensive catalog of every possible technique or special effect of which CorelDRAW! is capable. The three major exercises that make up this chapter feature text in the sample illustrations, because no other software for the PC allows you to turn text into word pictures as magnificently as CorelDRAW!.

Each of the three main sections in this chapter contains one exercise in designing a graphic. The title of the section describes the type of graphic; the introduction to each exercise briefly describes the main CorelDRAW! techniques that help you create the graphic. If you need to review certain techniques, you can refer back to the chapter or chapters that first introduced these skills. Bon voyage!

Integrating Clip Art and Line Art

In the following exercise, you will design a poster that integrates a clip-art image with line art—in this case, text. You can use this exercise to review text editing, stretch and scale, and outline and fill techniques (Chapters 4, 7, 9, 11, 12, and 14). Since the poster format is 11 inches by 15 inches, you also can brush up on the page setup, printing, and tiling skills you learned in Chapter 13. The end result of your exercise should look similar to Figure 15-1.

Completed
poster
Figure 15-1.

NOTE: The instructions that follow assume that you are using CorelDRAW! version 4. If you have an earlier version of CorelDRAW!, you cannot perform this exercise exactly as written. However, you can import another image and try your hand at merging it with the text described here.

To create the poster, follow these steps:

1. Starting with a blank screen, turn on the Show Rulers and turn off the Edit Wireframe commands in the Display menu. Also make sure the Snap To options (Grid, Guidelines, and Objects) on the Layout menu are turned off for this exercise.

2. From your CELEBRAT clip-art directory, double-click on the ANGEL2.CDR or the HAT066.CDR file to open it. (Either one will work; ANGEL2.CDR is used in this chapter.)

3. Select Page Setup from the Layout menu, select Tabloid (11x17), assure that Portrait is selected, and click on OK. In the Grid Setup dialog box reached from the Layout menu, type **17** in the Vertical Grid Origin numeric entry box to move the vertical zero point to the top of the page, and click on OK to return to the drawing.

4. Drag two horizontal guidelines down to 4 inches and 11 inches on the vertical ruler, and drag a vertical guideline to 4 1/2 inches on the horizontal ruler.

5. Drag the angel image up and to the right until the upper-right corner of the dotted frame that forms when you drag the object is in the upper-right corner formed by the guidelines and the page edge. Drag the lower-left boundary marker until the bottom edge of the boundary marker is at 11 inches vertical. Your screen at this point should look like Figure 15-2.

6. Save and name the image. Select Save As from the File menu and type **dance** in the File Name text box. Then press [Enter] or click on the OK command button to save the file and return to the CorelDRAW! screen.

7. Select the Zoom-In icon from the Zoom tool flyout menu and magnify just the part of the page to the left of the angel.

8. Activate the Text tool and select an insertion point at 6 inches vertically and 2.25 inches horizontally. Type **8th** and then activate the Pick tool. Open the Text roll-up and set text attributes to center alignment, Paragon, normal style, 250.0 points. Click on Apply. The text reappears at the insertion point.

9. Move the text to the position shown in Figure 15-3. Press [Ctrl]-[S] to save the changes you have made to the file.

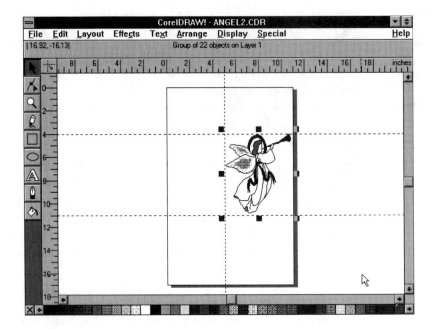

Incorporating
a piece of clip
art into a
poster
Figure 15-2.

10. With the text string still selected, click on the Outline Pen tool and then on the Custom Outline Pen icon in the flyout menu. The settings for this text string should be Color, black; Width, 0.01 inches; Line Style, solid; Corners, mitered; Line Caps, butt; Stretch, 100 percent; and Angle, 0 degrees. Both the Behind Fill and Scale With Image options should be inactive. Click on the OK command button to save these settings for the text.

11. Click on the Fill tool and then on the 50 percent gray icon in the flyout menu. (This is the third icon from the right in the second row.) The screen shows the change in the fill color of the text. Since the outline of the text is black, however, the word stands out. Save your changes by pressing Ctrl-S.

12. Activate the Text tool again and select another insertion point at 9.5 inches vertically and 2.25 inches horizontally. Type **Annual** and activate the Pick tool. In the Text roll-up, set text attributes to center alignment, Paragon, normal style, 125.0 points, and click on Apply.

13. Move "Annual" to the location shown in Figure 15-4.

14. With the "Annual" text string still selected, choose Copy Attributes From in the Edit menu. In the Copy Attributes dialog box, check the boxes for Outline Pen, Outline Color, and Fill, but not Text Attributes. Click on OK. The From? arrow will appear. Click it on the "8th" text string you entered earlier.

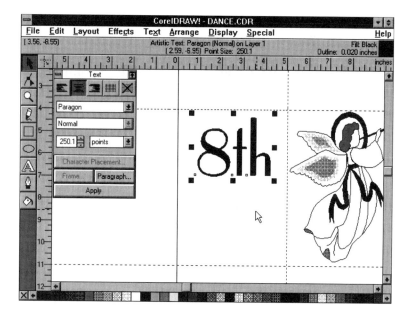

Moving "8th"
into position
Figure 15-3.

15. Scroll your screen so you can see the bottom third of the poster. Also, roll up the Text roll-up window.

16. Activate the Text tool once more and select a third insertion point at 12.5 inches vertically and 5.5 inches horizontally. Type **DINNER DANCE** and press Ctrl-T to open the Artistic Text dialog box. Set text

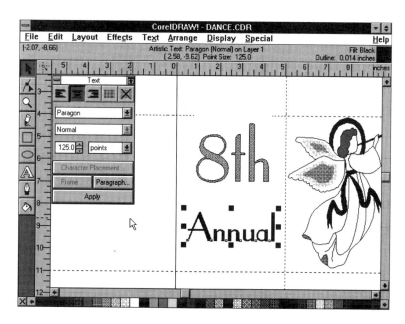

Moving
"Annual" into
position
beneath "8th"
Figure 15-4.

attributes to center alignment, Paragon, normal style, 100.0 points. Click on the Spacing command button and set Character spacing to 10 percent and Word spacing to 120 percent. Then select OK twice. The text string reappears at the insertion point.

17. Activate the Pick tool to select the text automatically. Move this text string to the position shown in Figure 15-5.

18. With the "DINNER DANCE" text string still selected, click on the Copy Attributes From command in the Edit menu. Activate only the Outline Pen, Outline Color, and Fill check boxes and then select OK. When the From? arrow appears, click on the "Annual" text string to copy its outline and fill attributes to the currently selected text string. Make certain to click on the *outline* of the object from which you want to copy the style, or you will see an error message.

19. Activate the Text tool once more and select another insertion point at 14 inches vertically and 2 inches horizontally. Type **Olympic Hotel 7pm**, press (Enter), and then type **Saturday, Dec. 23rd**. Press (Ctrl)-(T) to open the Artistic Text dialog box. Set text attributes to center alignment, Paragon, normal, 100.0 points. Click on the Spacing command button and set Character spacing to 10 percent, Word spacing to 110 percent, Line spacing to 110 percent. Then select OK twice to display the text.

20. Activate the Pick tool to select the new text string automatically. Move this text string to the position shown in Figure 15-6.

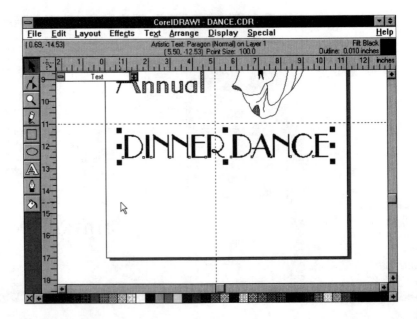

Moving
"DINNER
DANCE" into
position on
the poster
Figure 15-5.

Placing the
place and date
text string in
position
Figure 15-6.

21. With "Olympic Hotel..." still selected, choose Copy Attributes From in
    the Edit menu. Make sure Outline Pen, Outline Color, and Fill are
    turned on and Text Attributes is turned off, and then click on OK. The
    From? arrow will appear. Click it on "DINNER DANCE," which you
    entered earlier.

22. Scroll your screen so you can see the top third of the poster.

23. Activate the Text tool once more and select an insertion point at 1 inch
    vertically and 5.5 inches horizontally. Type **SEATTLE** on the first line,
    then press ⌷Enter⌷ and type **SYMPHONY** on the second line. Press ⌷Ctrl⌷-⌷T⌷
    to open the Artistic Text dialog box. Set text attributes to center
    alignment, Paragon, normal, 130.0 points. Click on the Spacing
    command button. Set Character spacing to 10 percent and Line spacing
    to 110 percent of point size and then select OK twice.

The shortcut
for Show
Preview is ⌷F9⌷.

24. Activate the Pick tool to select the new text string automatically. Drag
    the text string to the position shown in Figure 15-7.

25. Click on the Fill tool and then on the 90 percent black icon, on the far
    right, to fill the selected text with 90 percent black.

26. Click on the Zoom tool and again on the Show Page icon, and then
    press ⌷Ctrl⌷-⌷S⌷ to save your changes. Select Show Preview from the Display
    menu. Your final poster should look like Figure 15-1.

27. Press F9 and select New from the File menu to clear the screen.

You may choose to print this oversize poster on your own printer. If you do, be sure to activate the Tile option in the Print dialog box. Your poster will print on four separate sheets, each containing one quarter of the graphic. If your printer does not have enough memory to print this graphic at 11 by 17 inches, try scaling the image down. Then, change the page size to 8 1/2 by 11 inches using the Page Setup command in the Layout menu.

To add to your CorelDRAW! applications gallery, continue with the next exercise. There, you will create a color design that takes advantage of CorelDRAW! features that fit text to a path and mirror images.

Fitting Text to a Path

If you have followed this book from the first chapter onward, you have learned nearly every available CorelDRAW! drawing technique. One important (and very creative) technique remains: fitting text to a path using the Fit Text To Path command in the Text menu. You can cause a text string to follow the outline of *any* object, be it a circle or ellipse, a rectangle or square, a line, a curve, a complex curved object, or even another letter that has been converted to curves.

15

Once you have fitted text to an object, you can delete that object without causing the text to lose its newly acquired shape. If you edit text attributes later, however, the text may change its alignment. You can remedy this simply by fitting text to the same path again. You can also make the curve object transparent by selecting the X (none) icon for both the object's outline and its fill.

Fit Text To Path Roll-Up

The shortcut for Fit Text To Path is Ctrl-F.

You open the Fit Text To Path roll-up by selecting Fit Text To Path from the Text menu. There are actually two Fit Text To Path roll-up windows, depending on whether you are fitting text to an open line or open curve, or to a closed rectangle or ellipse. The roll-up for fitting text to an open line or curve is shown on the left in the following illustration; the roll-up for fitting text to a closed rectangle or ellipse is shown on the right.

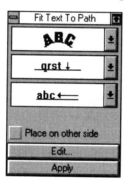 

The two roll-up windows share two drop-down list boxes: the list box at the top of the roll-up lets you determine the orientation of the text, while the second list box lets you select the distance that the text will sit above or below the path of the object. Also, both roll-ups have a check box for moving the text to the opposite side of the path. The difference in the two roll-ups is in how to align the text on the object. For an open object, you have a drop-down list of alignment possibilities, whereas closed objects have a four-sided button to set their alignment. Each of these elements will be discussed in the next several sections. Figure 15-8 shows several examples of fitting text to a path that will be referred to in these sections.

Orientation of the Text

The orientation of the text is its degree of rotation, or skew, as it follows the path it is fitted to. There are four options for orientation in the drop-down list. Most of the examples in Figure 15-8 show the first (default) orientation; in this orientation, the letters rotate to follow the path. Figure 15-8*f* shows

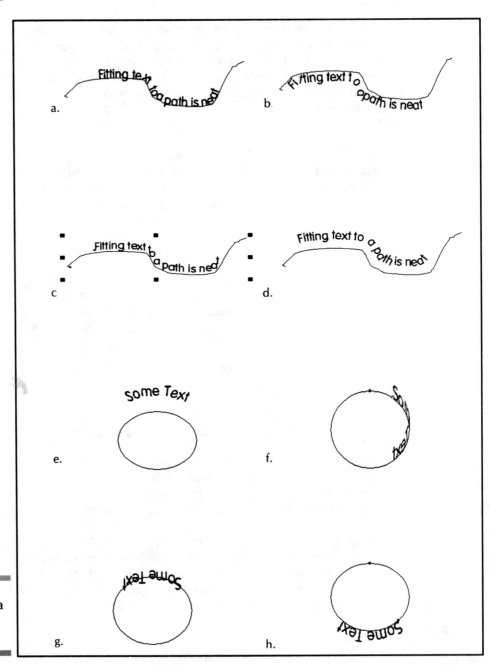

Examples of
fitting text to a
path
Figure 15-8.

the second orientation, Figure 15-8*e* shows the third, and Figure 15-8*c* and *g* shows the fourth orientation.

15

Distance of the Text from the Path

The second drop-down list box offers five alternative settings for the distance of the text from its path. (Not all five choices are always available.) Figure 15-8*a* and *f* show the first alternative, in which the text sits right on the path (the baseline of the text is on the path, and the descenders are beneath it). Figure 15-8*b* shows the second alternative: the text sits underneath the path. Figure 15-8*c* shows the third alternative, in which the text sits slightly above the path (only the descenders are on the path). Figure 15-8*g* shows the fourth alternative: the path goes through the text. Figure 15-8*d* and *e* show the fifth alternative, in which the text can be pulled away from the path either with the mouse or with the Fit Text To Path Offsets dialog box shown here:

Fit Text To Path Offsets		
Horizontal Offset:	0.00	inches
Distance From Path:	0.00	inches
OK	Cancel	

Aligning the Text on the Path

For open paths, the third drop-down list box on the roll-up provides three alternatives for aligning text on a path. Figure 15-8*b* shows the first alternative, in which the text is aligned with the left end of the path. Figure 15-8*a*, *c*, and *d* show the second alternative, in which the text is centered on the path.

For closed-path rectangles and ellipses, the text is aligned to the middle of one of four sides by clicking on the corresponding side of the four-sided button that is displayed. The text is rotated as it is moved to the right (shown in Figure 15-8f), the bottom (it is, therefore, upside down on the bottom), or the left side. If you want to flip the text to the other side of the path, click on the Place on other side check box in the Fit Text To Path roll-up. Figure 15-8*g* has this box checked and Figure 15-8h has the bottom side checked but not the Place on other side.

Using Fit Text To Path

In the following exercise, you will design a stylized "rainbow" image that consists of a series of scaled and aligned wedges. You will then fit the word "Rainbow" to a curve, combine the text string with a background object to create a mask, and overlay the transparent letters on the rainbow colors. The result after stretching and mirroring the mask and rainbow is shown later in Figure 15-18. If you have a color monitor, your results will appear more vivid than the one shown in the figures. If you have a black-and-white display adapter and monitor, you can achieve a similar "rainbow" effect by filling the wedges with the gray shades indicated in parentheses in the following steps.

1. Starting with a blank screen, select Page Setup from the Layout menu. When the Page Setup dialog box appears, click on the Landscape and Letter option buttons and then select OK. This results in a page that is 11 inches wide and 8 1/2 inches high.

2. To prepare the CorelDRAW! screen for the exercise, activate the Show Rulers and Edit Wireframe commands. Make sure that Snap To Grid from the Grid Setup on the Layout menu is activated, that the Vertical Grid Origin is set to 8.5 inches, and both Horizontal and Vertical Grid Frequency are set to 8 per inch.

3. Set new outline and fill defaults so that all of the objects you draw will be standardized. First, click on the Outline Pen tool and again on the X (for none) icon in the first row of the flyout menu. The Outline Pen dialog box appears, asking whether you want to define Outline Pen settings for objects you haven't drawn yet. Click on Artistic Text and accept the checked Graphic, so that both are selected. Select OK to set no outline as the new default for Graphic and Artistic Text objects.

4. Click on the Fill tool and then on the black icon. The Uniform Fill dialog box appears, asking whether you want to define fill colors for objects you haven't drawn yet. Click on Artistic Text and accept the checked Graphic, so that both are selected. Select OK to define a default fill color of black for all new Graphic and Artistic Text.

5. Activate the Ellipse tool, then position the pointer at the 6 1/2-inch mark on the vertical ruler and the 3/4-inch mark on the horizontal ruler. Press and hold Ctrl-Shift and drag the mouse downward and to the right until the status line shows a width and height of 3 inches. As you may recall from Chapter 3, the use of Ctrl and Shift together results in a circle drawn from the center outward. When you release the mouse button, the circle appears with the node at the top, as shown in Figure 15-9a.

6. Create a 90-degree wedge from this circle, as you learned to do in Chapter 8. Activate the Shaping tool and position the Shaping pointer

at the node of the circle. To turn the circle into a pie wedge, press and hold Ctrl and drag the node in a clockwise direction until you reach the 9 o'clock position (90 degrees on the status line). (Hold the tip of the Shaping pointer *inside* the rim of the circle as you drag, or you will see an open arc instead of a wedge.) Release the mouse button when you reach the 9 o'clock position. The wedge appears, as in Figure 15-9b.

15

7. Activate the Pick tool to select the wedge automatically. Notice that the highlighting box is much larger than the wedge, just as in Figure 15-9c. CorelDRAW! continues to treat the wedge as though it were a full circle.

8. Click again on the outline of the wedge to enter rotate/skew mode. Position the pointer at the arrow markers in the upper-right corner, press and hold Ctrl, and rotate the box frame of the wedge in a clockwise direction until the status line indicates an angle of –90 degrees. Remember to release the mouse button before you release Ctrl; otherwise, the wedge may not snap to the exact –90-degree angle. The curve of the wedge now faces upward and to the right, as shown in Figure 15-9d.

9. Click again on the wedge outline to return to stretch/scale mode. You are ready to increase the scale of the wedge and leave a copy of the original. Position the pointer at the boundary marker in the upper-right corner and scale the wedge upward and to the right, until the status line value reaches approximately 116.7 percent. When you reach the desired point, continue to hold the mouse button, but press the + key on the numeric keypad to leave a copy of the original. Then release the mouse button. The original wedge remains in position, and a scaled version overlays it, as in Figure 15-10.

10. Press Ctrl-R (the Repeat key combination) five times to create five additional wedges, each larger than the previous one. Your screen should show a total of seven wedges, resembling Figure 15-11.

11. Your next step is to align the wedges so that they form one-half of a rainbow. Click on the Select All command in the Edit menu to select all seven wedges, and then select the Align command in the Arrange menu. When the Align dialog box appears, click on both the Horizontally Center and Vertically Center option buttons, click on the Align to Center of Page check box, and then select OK. The wedges realign with a common corner point in the center of the page, as shown in Figure 15-12.

12. With the seven wedges still selected, click on the Order option in the Arrange menu and then on the Reverse Order command on the flyout. You will not see a visible change at this point, but you have positioned the larger wedges in the back and the smaller wedges in the front. When you turn on the preview window later in the exercise and begin

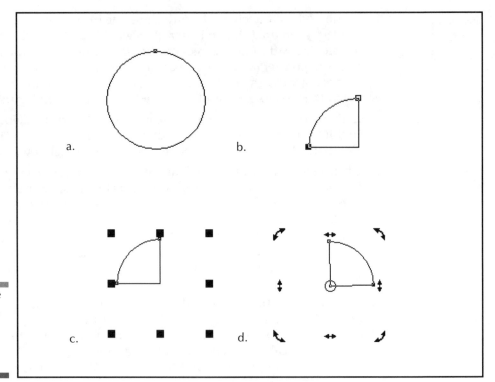

Creating a pie
wedge from a
circle and
rotating it
Figure 15-9.

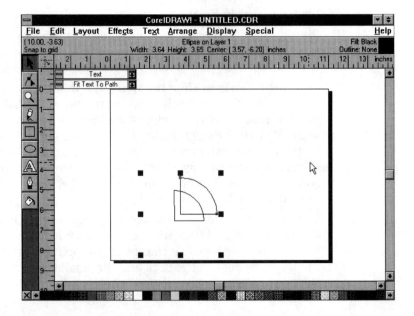

Scaling a
wedge and
leaving a copy
of the original
Figure 15-10.

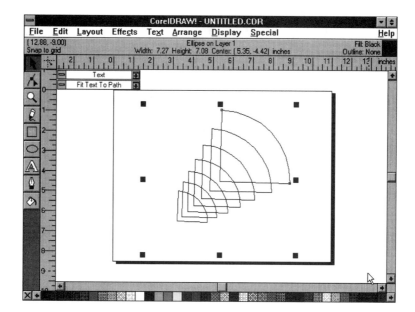

Series of
scaled wedges
created using
the Repeat key
combination
Figure 15-11.

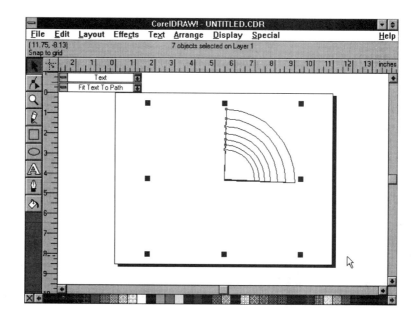

Wedges
aligned using
Horizontally
and Vertically
Center options
Figure 15-12.

to assign fill colors to the wedges, you will see each wedge as a ribbon-like band.

13. Select the Save As command from the File menu. When the Save Drawing dialog box appears, type **rainbow1** and then press Enter or click on OK.

14. To design the other half of the rainbow, you simply create a horizontal mirror image of the currently selected image. Click on the Stretch & Mirror command in the Effects menu to access the Stretch & Mirror dialog box. Then activate both the Horz Mirror command button and the Leave Original check box and select OK. The mirror image of the seven wedges appears and fits tightly against the original group of wedges, as shown in Figure 15-13.

15. You can now begin to assign fill colors to the wedges of the "rainbow." Activate the Preview Selected Only command in the Display menu. Adjust magnification to fit-in-window by clicking on the Fit-In-Window icon in the Zoom tool flyout menu.

16. Deselect all of the wedges by clicking on any white space. Then select both the largest wedge on the left half of the "rainbow" and the smallest wedge on the right half. To select both of them, click on each of their curve outlines while holding down Shift. The editing window, shown in Figure 15-14a, looks as though all of the wedges were selected, because the highlighting box of the largest wedge surrounds all of the objects. However, the preview window, reached by pressing F9, and shown in Figure 15-14b, shows you that only two wedges are selected.

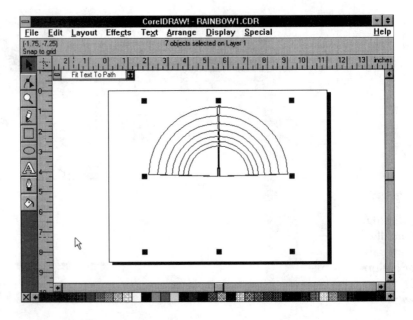

Original seven wedges with a horizontal mirror image

Figure 15-13.

17. With the two wedges selected, click on the Fill tool and again on the Uniform Fill icon. When the Uniform Fill dialog box displays, select the CMYK Color Model and set color values to 0 percent cyan, 100 percent magenta, 75 percent yellow, and 10 percent black. Select OK; the two opposite wedges now redisplay with a red fill, the hue of which varies depending on whether you have an EGA or VGA display adapter. (If you have a black-and-white monitor, set black to 80 percent and leave all other colors at 0 percent.) Press F9 again.

15

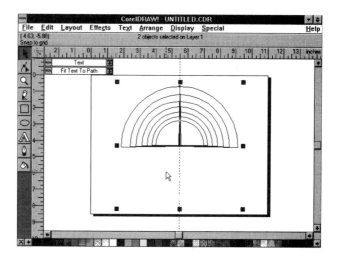

a.

Selecting pairs of wedges in wireframe mode (a.) and in full screen preview (b.)
Figure 15-14.

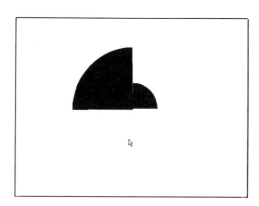

b.

You can also
see the color
by turning
Edit
Wireframe off
from the
Display menu;
then you do
not have to
use F9.

18. Deselect the previous wedges. Then select the second-largest wedge on the left half of the "rainbow" and the second-smallest wedge on the right half, and press Shift-F11 to access the Uniform Fill dialog box once more. If you have a color monitor, set Process color values to 0 percent cyan, 60 percent magenta, 100 percent yellow, and 0 percent black, and then select OK. The two wedges now show a bright orange fill. (If you have a black-and-white monitor, set black to 40 percent and leave all other colors at 0 percent.)

19. Continue in the same way with the next five pairs of wedges. If you have a color monitor, assign colors as follows: third pair, 100 percent yellow; fourth pair, 40 percent cyan and 60 percent yellow; fifth pair, 100 percent cyan, 40 percent yellow, and 20 percent black; sixth pair, 100 percent cyan, 100 percent magenta, and 10 percent black; seventh pair, 100 percent magenta and 50 percent black. Leave the colors not mentioned at 0 percent. Check your colors by pressing F9. (If you have a black-and-white monitor, assign 15 percent black to the third pair, 40 percent black to the fourth, 30 percent black to the fifth, 75 percent black to the sixth, and 100 percent black to the seventh.) When you are finished, turn off the Preview Selected Only feature and press F9. The two halves of the rainbow show an opposite sequence of colors, as you can see by the black-and-white representation in Figure 15-15.

20. Press F9, click on the Select All command in the Edit menu to select all 14 wedges, and then apply the Group command from the Arrange

Opposite
color
sequences in
each half of
the rainbow
Figure 15-15.

menu. This prevents you from accidentally moving or editing an individual wedge apart from the group.

21. Click on the Show Page icon in the Zoom tool flyout menu to display the full page.

22. Now you are ready to prepare the text that will eventually overlay the rainbow as a transparent mask. First, activate the Ellipse tool and position the drawing pointer at the 1-inch mark on the vertical ruler and the 2 1/2-inch mark on the horizontal ruler. Drag the mouse downward and to the right and draw a circle 6 inches in diameter. Remember to use Ctrl (but *not* Shift) to obtain a circle rather than an ellipse. The circle overlays most of the "rainbow" for now, but you will delete it when it has served its purpose.

23. Activate the Text tool and select an insertion point in any white space on the page. Type **Rainbow** and press Ctrl-T to open the Artistic Text dialog box. Set text attributes to Aardvark bold, 105.0 points, alignment, None. Click on the Spacing command button, set Character spacing to 10 percent, and then select OK twice to redisplay the text on the page.

24. Activate the Pick tool to select the text string automatically. Use Shift to also select the circle you have just drawn. Then press Ctrl-F or click on the Fit Text To Path command in the Text menu.

25. When the Fit Text To Path roll-up opens, make sure that all of the defaults in the roll-up are set: rotated text orientation (the first alternative in the first drop-down list); text sitting on the path (the first alternative in the second drop-down list); the top quadrant in the four-sided button; and Place on other side not checked. After verifying these settings, click on Apply. In a few seconds, the text appears right side up, but on the circle, as shown in Figure 15-16.

26. Deselect the text to leave only the circle selected and then press Del to delete the circle. The text retains its new shape.

27. Click again on the outline of the text string to select it, and then fill the text with white by clicking on the Fill tool and again on the white icon in the second row of the flyout menu.

28. Create the rectangle that will become the background of the mask. Activate the Rectangle tool and position the drawing pointer at the zero point on both the horizontal and vertical rulers. From this point, draw a rectangle 7 3/4 inches wide and 3 3/4 inches high, dragging downward and to the right.

29. Press the Spacebar to select the rectangle automatically. Give the rectangle a white fill by clicking on the Fill tool and then on the white icon in the flyout menu. Make the edge of the rectangle transparent

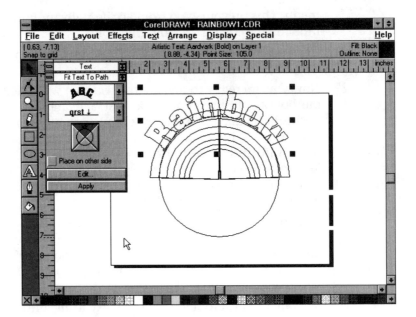

Fitting text to
a circle
Figure 15-16.

also by clicking on the Outline Pen tool and again on the No Fill icon in the first row of the flyout menu.

30. Select the text string and move it on top of the rectangle. Position it so that the bottom of the text string is 1/4 inch above the lower edge of the rectangle.

31. To center the text horizontally on the rectangle, select both objects, click on the Align command in the Arrange menu, and choose the Horizontally Center option button. Select OK to leave the Align dialog box and redisplay the newly aligned objects.

32. With both the text and rectangle still selected, move both objects into the empty space at the bottom of the page, out of the way of the rainbow wedges. Then select the Order command from the Arrange menu and choose Reverse Order to place the text behind the rectangle.

33. Press F9 to turn on full screen preview. You cannot see the rectangle because it is white, and you cannot see the text because it has a white fill and is behind the rectangle. Press F9 again to return to the editing window and, with the text and rectangle both selected, click on the Combine command in the Arrange menu. When the two objects combine, their common area, the text, becomes transparent "holes" in the white rectangle.

15

34. Move the newly combined object back over the grouped rainbow wedges and align the bottom edge of the curve object with the bottom edge of the wedges.

35. Press F9 for full screen preview. With the white rectangle invisible against the page, all you can see are the rainbow colors behind the transparent text string, as shown in Figure 15-17.

TIP: The object that is in the background when you combine two objects determines the fill color of the combined object. If you see white letters over a transparent rectangle, you forgot to place the text behind the rectangle. Select Undo from the Edit menu, use the Reverse Order command in the Arrange menu to bring the rectangle to the foreground, and then combine the two objects again.

36. Return to the editing window and then adjust viewing magnification to fit-in-window. Select both the combined object and the wedges and apply the Group command from the Arrange menu.

37. Create a mirror image of the grouped object. With the group still selected, click on the Stretch & Mirror command from the Effects menu. When the Stretch & Mirror dialog box appears, click on both the Horz Mirror and Vert Mirror command buttons, and place a check mark in

Rainbow colors appearing as fill through the mask object
Figure 15-17.

the Leave Original check box. Select OK; an upside-down and backwards version of the "Rainbow" text displays beneath the original, as shown in the full screen preview in Figure 15-18. This object is selected automatically in the editing window.

38. Press Ctrl-S to save the changes to your work, then select New from the File menu to clear your screen.

The main emphases in this last exercise have been on fitting text to a path, working with color effects, creating a mask, aligning objects, repeating operations, and creating mirror images. In the next and final sample application, you can achieve 3-D effects using fountain and contrasting fills, outlines, and repeated scalings.

Achieving Special Effects with Text and Graphics

The "FAX" image in Figure 15-19 has a vibrant, 3-D look; the graphic represents the power of facsimile to quite literally "broadcast" to the

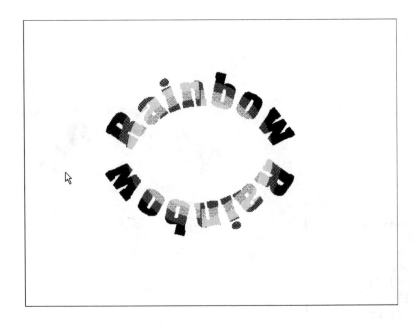

Rainbow with vertically flipped mirror image
Figure 15-18.

15

world. Several special effects techniques contribute to the dynamic quality of the image:

+ Text fitted to a curve

+ Text objects with drop shadows (shadows placed behind and offset from the original)

+ A "globe" with an off-center radial fountain fill

+ Repeated duplication and expansion of a text string

+ Judicious use of contrasting fills

+ Inclusion of a backdrop that makes the image seem to burst beyond its boundaries

You already have practiced the basic skills that make all of these special effects possible. In the exercise that follows, you will recreate this image, using the Leave Original and Repeat keys, fountain fill and node editing techniques, and the Duplicate, Fit Text To Path, Group, and Page Setup commands. For a review of shadow and fountain fill techniques, see Chapter 12.

"FAX" illustration using fountain fill, drop shadows, and a background frame to enhance 3-D effects
Figure 15-19.

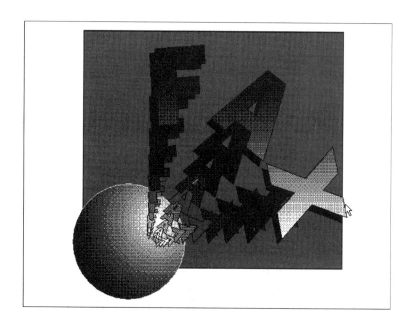

1. Starting with a blank screen, select Page Setup from the Layout menu. When the Page Setup dialog box appears, make sure that Landscape and Letter are still selected and then select OK.

2. To prepare the CorelDRAW! screen for the exercise, activate the Snap To Grid command in the Layout menu, select the Grid Setup command, set both Horizontal and Vertical Grid Frequency to 8 per inch, and set the Vertical grid origin to 8.5 inches. From the Display menu, activate the Show Rulers and Edit Wireframe options as well.

3. Change the default outline type to a hairline by clicking on the Outline Pen tool and then on the hairline icon in the first row of the flyout menu. When the dialog box appears, click on Artistic Text, accept the checked Graphic, and then click on OK.

4. Change the default outline color to black by clicking on the Outline Pen tool and then on the black icon in the second row of the flyout menu. The Outline Pen dialog box appears; select Artistic Text, accept the checked Graphic, and click on OK, as you did in step 3.

5. Create a small circle to which you will fit text. To do this, activate the Ellipse tool and position the crosshair pointer in the center of the page at 4.25 inches vertically and 5.5 inches horizontally. Press and hold Shift and Ctrl and draw a perfect circle 0.75 inches in diameter. When you complete the circle, remember to release the mouse button before you release Shift and Ctrl to ensure that you create a circle rather than an ellipse.

6. Now enter the text that you will fit to this circle. Activate the Text tool and select an insertion point about an inch above the circle. The exact location does not matter, because when you invoke the Fit Text To Path command later, the text will snap to the circle no matter where it is. Type **FAX** in all capital letters. Open the Artistic Text dialog box. Set text attributes to an alignment of None, FrankfurtGothicHeavy, Normal, 30.0 points. Click on OK to redisplay the text on the page.

7. Press the Spacebar to activate the Pick tool; the text string is selected automatically, since it was the last object you drew. While holding down Shift, select the circle as well.

8. With both objects selected, press Ctrl-F or click on the Fit Text To Path command in the Arrange menu. The Fit Text To Path roll-up will open, if it hasn't already. Accept the defaults and click on Apply. The text wraps around the outside of the circle, centering itself at the top. The result is shown in Figure 15-20.

9. Deselect the text string using Shift and then press Del to delete the circle. The text remains curved, even though the circle is no longer there.

10. Double-click on the text string to enter rotate/skew mode, and rotate the text by 45 degrees in a clockwise direction.

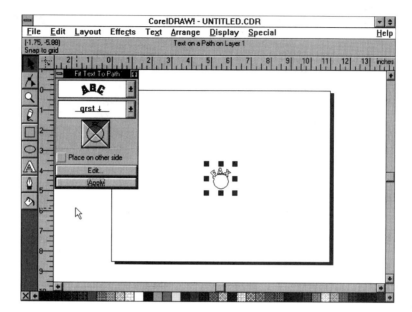

Magnified
view of text
fitted to a
small circle
Figure 15-20.

11. Move the text to the lower-left corner of the page, approximately 1/2 inch from the bottom left page edge.

12. Now you are ready to begin creating a text pattern. Turn off Snap To Grid and, with the Pick tool still active, position the pointer at the upper-right corner boundary marker of the text object and begin to scale the object from this point. As soon as the dotted outline box appears, click the right mouse button or press and release ⊞ on the numeric keypad (to leave a copy of the original). Continue scaling the text until the status line indicates a value of approximately 129 percent. Then release the left mouse button. A larger-scaled version of the text string appears on top of, and offset from, the original. You can see the proportions more clearly if you temporarily change magnification to fit-in-window.

13. Select the Show Page icon from the Zoom tool flyout menu to return to full-page view. Then press Ctrl-R, the Repeat key, ten times, to repeat the scaling and duplication of the text. Ten scaled replicas of the text string overlay one another, each one larger than the previous one. The last text string exceeds the boundaries of the page, as shown in Figure 15-21.

14. Leaving the most recently created text string selected, click on the Preferences command in the Special menu. Make certain that the Place Duplicates and Clones values are both at 0.25 inches and then select

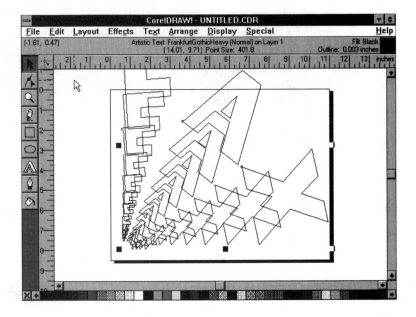

Scaled and
repeated text
strings
exceeding the
page
boundaries
Figure 15-21.

OK. These values determine the placement of a duplicate object relative to the original.

15. Press Ctrl-D to create an exact duplicate of the top text string, offset 1/4 inch above and to the right of the original. The duplicate is selected as soon as it appears.

16. Press F9 for the preview window. All of the text strings appear with black fills. Press F9 again to return to the editing window, click on the Select All command in the Edit menu and then on the Group command in the Arrange menu to group all of the text strings. Then select the white icon in the Fill tool flyout menu and turn off Edit Wireframe. The text strings redisplay with a fill of white, making it easier to distinguish them from one another.

17. With all text strings still selected, click on the Outline Pen tool and then on the Custom Outline Pen icon to access the Outline Pen dialog box. Change the Width setting to 0.01 inch, turn on Scale With Image, and select OK. The text strings redisplay with a medium outline of uniform width.

18. Ungroup and deselect all text strings and then select only the last text string you created (the top). Click on the Fill tool and again on the Fountain Fill icon to access the Fountain Fill dialog box. Choose a linear fountain fill and an angle of 45 degrees. For the From color, click on More, select PANTONE Spot Colors, then black at 0 percent Tint, and

15

click on OK. Similarly, for the To color, click on More, select Spot color, black at 100 percent Tint, and click on OK. Click on OK again to make this fill pattern take effect.

19. Now create a drop-shadow effect. Press Tab to select the text string in the layer just below the text string with the fountain fill. Assign a fill of black to this object by clicking on the black icon on the far left of the palette at the bottom of your screen. Select the Zoom-Out icon from the Zoom flyout menu to see your whole work. Figure 15-22 shows the result of your selection.

20. Continue pressing Tab to select each text string in the reverse order from which it was created. Fill the text strings in the following sequence, starting with the largest text string after the drop shadow: 90 percent black, 80 percent black, 70 percent black, 60 percent black, 50 percent black, 40 percent black, 30 percent black, 20 percent black, and 10 percent black. Fill one more text string with 10 percent black and the remaining (smallest) text strings with white. You can quickly apply these shades by using the color palette at the bottom of the screen, beginning with the second black from the left. The resulting gradation of fills and the drop shadow make the repeated text strings seem to leap out of the screen, as shown in Figure 15-23.

21. To group all text strings so that you cannot separate them accidentally, click on Select All in the Edit menu and then on the Group command in the Arrange menu. Then move the group upward and away from the

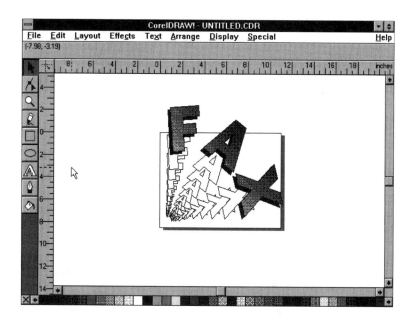

Drop-shadow effect using duplicated text and black fill
Figure 15-22.

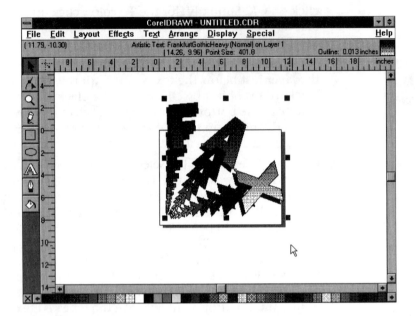

Gradation of
fills, leading to
a 3-D effect
Figure 15-23.

left side of the page. You will bring the group back later, but for now
you need room to create more objects.

22. Activate the Ellipse tool and position the pointer 4 1/2 inches from the
    top of the page and 3/4 of an inch from the left margin. Press and hold
    Ctrl and draw a circle 3 inches in diameter, starting from the upper-left
    area of the rim. Use the status line as a guide.

23. Turn the circle into a 3-D globe by giving it a radial fountain fill. To do
    this, activate the Pick tool to select the circle automatically, and then
    click on the Fill tool and again on the Fountain Fill icon. When the
    Fountain Fill dialog box appears, use the More buttons to select the Spot
    method, change the From color to black Tint 100 percent and the To
    color to white Tint 0 percent. Select a radial fountain fill, but leave the
    other settings unaltered. Select OK to make the fountain fill take effect.
    The globe reappears with a white highlight in the center and the fill
    gradually darkening toward the rim.

24. Prepare to create an off-center highlight so that the light source seems
    to be coming from above and to the right of the globe. Activate the
    Pencil tool and draw a short line segment above and to the right of the
    globe. Select both the line segment and the globe, and click on the
    Combine command in the Arrange menu to combine these into one
    object. Redo the fountain fill by repeating step 23. Whenever the
    window redraws from now on, CorelDRAW! extends the first stage of

the fountain fill as far as the line segment, as shown in Figure 15-24. This means that you can control the placement of the highlight on the globe by moving the nodes of the line segment with the Shaping tool.

15

25. If you wish to change the placement of the highlight on the globe, activate the Shaping tool and move the uppermost node of the line segment in a clockwise or counterclockwise direction. You can move either or both nodes; experiment until you find the placement you want.

26. Now make the line segment invisible. Activate the Pick tool to select the combined object automatically, and then click on the Outline Pen tool and again on the white icon in the second row of the flyout menu. The line segment seems to disappear from the screen, but you can still use it to manipulate the highlight on the globe.

27. Create a rectangle that will form a backdrop for the rest of the image. Activate the Rectangle tool and begin a rectangle at the 1-inch mark on the horizontal ruler and the 1 1/2-inch mark on the vertical ruler. Extend the rectangle downward and to the right until you reach the 7 1/2-inch mark on the horizontal ruler and the 7 1/4-inch mark on the vertical ruler, then release the mouse button. The window shows that this object lies on top of all the other objects, obscuring them from your view.

28. Activate the Pick tool to select the rectangle automatically, click on the Order option in the Arrange menu and then on the To Back command. Now, the globe appears as the top layer.

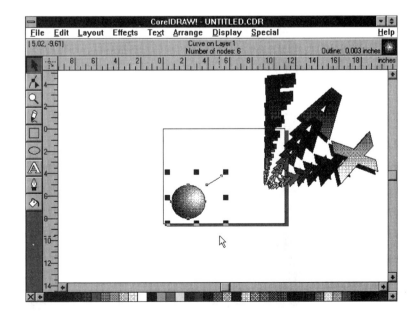

Changing the center of a radial fountain fill by combining a line segment with globe

Figure 15-24.

29. With the Outline Pen and Fill tools, assign a black outline of 2.0 fractional points and a fill of 20 percent gray to the rectangle.

30. To make the globe stand out in 3-D from the background, select it and assign an outline 0.01 inch wide, using the Outline Pen dialog box.

31. Select the "FAX" grouped text strings and move them on top of the globe, so that they seem to be emerging directly from the highlight. To make certain that the text strings are the top-layer object, click on the To Front command from the Order option on the Arrange menu. This also hides the line segment that you used as a "handle" to change the center of the globe's fountain fill, as shown in Figure 15-25.

32. Adjust viewing magnification to fit-in-window by clicking on the Fit-In-Window icon in the Zoom tool flyout menu. With the grouped object still selected, scale the text strings down until the status line displays a value of approximately 47 percent. Return to fit-in-window magnification and select Show Preview. Thanks to the insertion of the background rectangle, the text strings still seem to thrust outward in 3-D, as shown earlier in Figure 15-19.

33. Press F9 and click on the Select All command in the Edit menu and then on the Group command in the Arrange menu to group all of the objects in the image.

34. Select Save As from the File menu. When the Save Drawing dialog box appears, type **faxtrans**, and then press Enter or click on OK.

35. Select New from the File menu to clear the screen.

Grouped text strings overlaid on the globe highlight for 3-D effect

Figure 15-25.

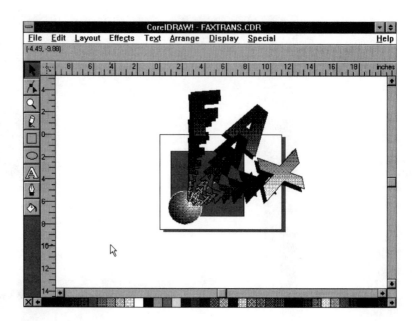

15

If you have performed all three of the exercises in this chapter, you are well on the way to understanding how to combine many different CorelDRAW! features, tricks, and techniques. Perhaps these exercises have stimulated you to create your own original designs, or given you new ideas for embellishing existing ones. Whatever your field, your work in this tutorial has given you the tools to create more effective illustrations, documents, presentations, and designs. CorelDRAW! makes it all possible!

C H A P T E R

CORELDRAW! 4

16

USING CORELCHART!

CorelCHART! is a stand-alone program for creating several different kinds of charts. Charts let you view information in pictorial form and are commonly used in publications and presentations. Many people find information presented visually, rather than numerically, easier to understand.

CorelCHART! can create 12 basic chart types using data imported from spreadsheet and database programs or entered directly into CorelCHART!. Each basic chart type is available in up to 8 formats.

Charts can be customized with titles and other text labels. Graphics can be imported, or created with CorelDRAW! or CorelCHART!, and added to the charts. Customized charts can be saved and repeatedly used as *chart templates*—that is, preformatted starting points for new charts. The chart templates for each basic chart type include the chart format, the color palette, and graphics. CorelCHART! comes with an assortment of templates for each basic chart type. You can also create and save your own templates.

The exercises in this chapter will demonstrate how to create a new chart; how to import data for the chart; how to add titles, labels, and graphics to charts; how to modify chart objects; and how to use chart templates. The different types and formats of charts will also be covered.

Charting Basics

The objective of using a chart is to present information in a graphic form that makes it easier to understand and highlights the message the information is carrying. Not all charts accomplish this objective. It is important to learn not just how to create charts, but how to create effective charts.

Each value that is plotted on the chart is called a *data point*. Data points are grouped in data series and data categories. *Data series* are groups of related data points. In a chart of sales figures from several sales offices, for example, the data points (sales figures) for one office are one data series. *Data categories* are groups containing one data point from each data series, taken at one interval. If the chart of sales figures reflects monthly sales, then one data category could be the sales from all the offices for one month.

Figure 16-1 shows a Vertical Bar chart, which displays the attendance at a series of conferences in four cities over a period of four years. The four years of attendance for each city constitute one data series. Each year constitutes one data category. This chart makes it easy to see the differences among the cities (the data series) in any year (the data category).

Figure 16-2 shows the same data as Figure 16-1, except that the data series and data categories have been reversed. Each year is now a data series and each city, a data category. This chart highlights the differences among the years (the data series) in any one city (the data category). When creating your charts, the relationship you want to emphasize will determine how you define your data series and data categories.

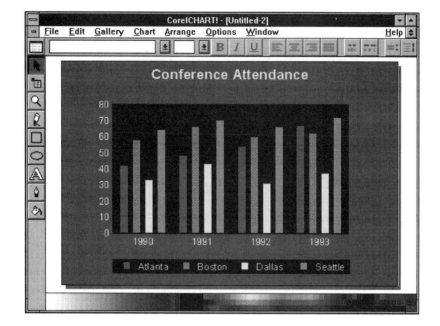

Conference
attendance
with each city
as a data series
Figure 16-1.

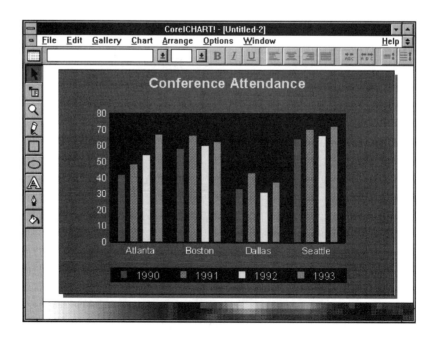

Conference
attendance
with each year
as a data series
Figure 16-2.

CorelCHART! can create both two- and three-dimensional charts. Two-dimensional (2-D) charts have two axes. The horizontal or X axis is usually the category axis. Each data category is plotted along the category axis. The vertical or Y axis is the data axis. Each data point is plotted against the data axis. The data axis usually has a scale indicating the range of values for the data points. Three-dimensional (3-D) charts have an additional axis, the Z axis, which is at a right angle to the X and Y axes, and adds depth to the chart.

Starting CorelCHART!

CorelCHART! is a separate program included with CorelDRAW!. It is installed in the Windows Program Manager's Corel 4 group along with CorelDRAW!. To start CorelCHART!, open the Corel 4 group window and double-click on the CorelCHART! icon. The initial CorelCHART! screen appears after the title screen and looks like Figure 16-1 or 16-2 without a chart. As you can see, it is similar in appearance to the CorelDRAW! window.

Across the top of the screen, below the menu bar, you see the *text ribbon,* a set of drop-down list boxes and command buttons that you use to select the text attributes—the font, size, and other characteristics—for the text used in your charts. The text ribbon is similar to CorelDRAW!'s Text roll-up and is used in the same way.

On the left side of the screen is the CorelCHART! toolbox. Many of the tools operate much like their CorelDRAW! counterparts. The first tool, which is actually in the text ribbon, is used to switch between the chart window and the data window, both of which you will learn about in a moment. The tool changes appearance based on which window is currently active. This and the other tools are explained in the following table.

Tool	Description	Function
	Chart View	Makes the chart window the active window when in the Data Manager
	Data Manager	Makes the Data Manager the active window when in chart view

Tool	Description	Function
	Pick	Selects elements in a chart
	Pop-up Menu	Accesses the chart menus related to a particular object by clicking on that object
	Zoom	Presents a flyout menu to change the magnification of the chart
	Pencil	Presents a flyout menu with four drawing modes: straight lines, polygons, freehand lines, and arrows
	Rectangle	Draws rectangles in the same manner as its CorelDRAW! counterpart
	Ellipse	Draws ellipses and circles in the same manner as its CorelDRAW! counterpart
	Text	Adds text to a chart
	Outline	Sets the line characteristics used to outline objects
	Fill	Fills the selected object with the selected color and pattern

Undo only reverses the last action taken, so use it before you continue working with the chart.

On the bottom of the screen is the color palette. To use the palette, simply select the chart element you want to change and then click on the desired color in the palette. The color of the selected element will change to the chosen color. To undo any color change, choose Undo in the Edit menu.

Creating a New Chart

When CorelCHART! is started, only the File and Help menus are available. The File menu is used to either load an existing chart or to create a new chart. This exercise will create a new blank chart. In the next exercise, data will be added to the chart with the Data Manager.

1. From the File menu, choose New. The New dialog box, shown in Figure 16-3, is presented.

On the left in the New dialog box is the Gallery list box, which is a listing of the basic chart types. To the right of the Gallery list box is the Chart Types list box. This is a pictorial display box containing specific templates for the basic chart type chosen in the Gallery list box. Both a basic chart type and a template must be chosen for a new chart. The various chart types will be covered in detail later in this chapter.

2. For this exercise, click on Bar in the Gallery list box, then click on the chart template for a Side-by-Side Bar chart in the lower-left corner of the Chart Types pictorial display box. Make certain the Use Sample Data box is *not* checked and click on OK.

This chart template will create a Vertical Bar chart. A window for the chart and a window for the Data Manager are opened, as shown in Figure 16-4.

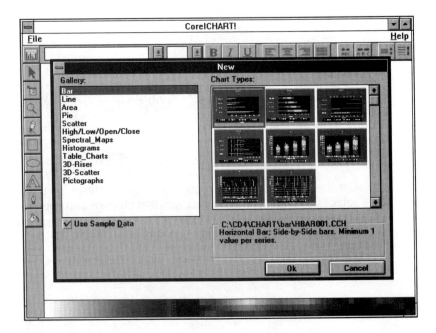

New dialog box
Figure 16-3.

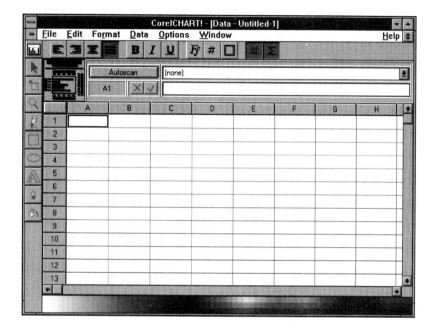

The Data
Manager
Figure 16-4.

The Data Manager is the element of CorelCHART! that is used to enter or import data for the chart. It also is used to format and prepare data for charting.

Using the Data Manager

The Data Manager presents a grid of rows and columns that hold the data for the chart. The Data Manager is arranged like a spreadsheet—data is stored on it in rows and columns, and it provides the numbers and text that will be used to create a chart.

The box where a row intersects a column is called a *cell*. Cells are usually referenced by the cell address, which is the column letter and row number, in that order. The first cell in the upper-left corner of the Data Manager is A1, meaning column A, row 1. Each cell can contain one value. The *value* may be a numeric data point to be charted in the form of a number, a formula, or text for a label.

Cells are selected by clicking on the cell—the selected cell then becomes the *active cell*. The active cell has a heavier line surrounding it. A rectangular group of contiguous cells is called a *range*. Ranges of cells are selected by clicking on the cell that is one of the corners of the range and dragging the mouse until the desired range is highlighted. Ranges are referenced by the addresses of the cells in the upper-left corner and the lower-right corner, separated by a colon. A range of cells from A1 (in the upper-left corner) to B2 (in the lower-right corner) would be referred to as A1:B2.

Use the scroll
bar to see all
the tags in the
drop-down list
box.

In the upper-left corner of the Data Manager window is an icon showing the type of chart the Data Manager will create. At the upper-right of the Data Manager window is a drop-down list box, the Chart Elements box, which is used to tag the contents of each cell. The information in each cell is *tagged* to tell CorelCHART! which values are to be plotted and which values are to be used as labels for row and column headers, titles, and other chart elements. The drop-down list box, shown in the following illustration, presents a list of the available tags.

Most of the tags are self-explanatory. The Data Range tag is used to define the range of cells containing the data points to be plotted on the chart. The other tags define cells containing text for the chart's titles.

To the left of the Chart Elements box is the Autoscan command button. When Autoscan is selected, the Data Manager is scanned for a range of cells containing data. If a range of cells containing data is found, the first row and column are tagged as the row and column headers. The rest of the range is tagged as the data range. Any text below the data range is tagged as subtitles and footnotes.

Below the Chart Elements box is the Contents box. The Contents box is used to enter and edit the contents of cells. When you select a cell and start to type information into it, the information will be entered in the Contents box. When Enter, Tab, or one of the arrow keys is pressed, the information is entered in the selected cell. When you select a cell, the contents of that cell will be placed in the Contents box, where it can be edited.

To the left of the Contents box (below the Chart Elements box) are two command buttons, one with an X, which is used to cancel the contents of the box, and one with a check mark, which enters the contents. These two buttons, "Cancel" and "Enter," are available when the Contents box is active, which occurs by clicking in the Contents box or by pressing F2.

Entering Data with the Data Manager

Data for charting can be entered directly into the Data Manager, as the next exercise shows. The data will represent attendance at a series of conferences.

1. Click on the maximize button in the data window if it is not already maximized, then select cell A1 and type **Conference Attendance** in the Contents box. Press Enter.

2. Use the arrow keys or mouse to move to cell B2.

3. In cell B2 type **1990**. Press Tab to move to the next cell in the row, C2. In cell C2 type **1991**. Repeat this step until cells B2:E2 contain the dates 1990 to 1993.

4. Use the arrow keys or mouse to move to cell A3.

5. In cell A3 type **Atlanta**. Press Tab to move to cell B3.

6. In cell B3 type **42**. Press Tab to move to the next cell in the row, C3. In cell C3 type **48**. Repeat this step until cells B3:E3 contain the numbers 42, 48, 54, and 67.

7. Select cell A1. In the Chart Elements drop-down list box, select Title to tag the selected cell as the title for the chart.

8. Select the range of cells B2:E2 by dragging the mouse across them. In the Chart Elements drop-down list box, select Column Headers to tag the selected range as the column headers for the chart.

9. Select cell A3. In the Chart Elements drop-down list box, select Row Headers to tag the selected cell as the row header for the chart.

10. Select the range of cells B3:E3. Again in the Chart Elements drop-down list box, select Data Range to tag the selected range as the data to be charted.

11. Click on the Chart View tool at the top of the toolbox to view the chart. Figure 16-5 shows the chart created from the information in the Data Manager.

12. Use the File menu to save the chart and your data.

In this chart there is one data series, the attendance in Atlanta. Each year is one data category.

Importing Data with the Data Manager

The Data Manager also allows you to import information from spreadsheets and databases to use in charts. CorelCHART! can import data in the file formats shown in the following table.

16

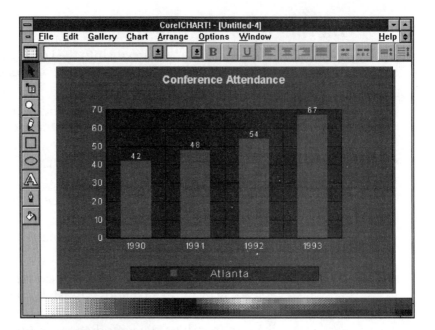

Conference
attendance in
Atlanta
Figure 16-5.

File Format	Extension
ASCII (Comma-Separated Value)	.CSV
ASCII (Space-Separated Value)	.TXT
ASCII (Tab-Separated Value)	.TXT
dBASE	.DBF
Excel	.XLS
Harvard	.CHT
Lotus	.WK1, .WK3
MSWorks	.WKS
Table	.TBL

The steps to import an Excel worksheet are as follows:

1. To import data, select File New, choose the chart type and format you want to create, and then click on the Data Manager tool to make it the active window.

2. From the File menu, choose Import. The Import Data dialog box, shown in the following illustration, will be presented. In the lower-left corner is the List Files of Type drop-down list box for selecting the file type to

import. For example, if you wanted to import an Excel worksheet, you would select "Excel (*.xls)" in this drop-down list box.

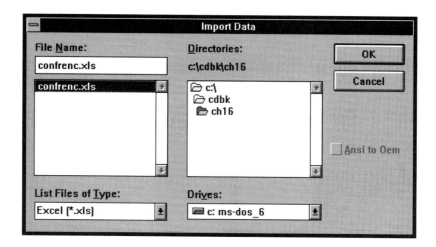

3. Select a file to import and click on OK. The imported data will replace any data already in the Data Manager.

4. The imported data needs to be tagged before it will be charted properly. This is done in the same manner as in the previous exercise: select the cell with the title and tag it as the Title. Select the range containing the row headings and tag it as the Row Headings. Select the column headings range and tag it as the Column Headings. Select the range with the data and tag it as the Data Range.

5. To see the new chart, switch to chart view by clicking the Chart View tool. The example data used here is shown in Figure 16-6.

Customizing Charts

CorelCHART! provides a number of ways to customize your charts. Text can be formatted by selecting a different font, color, size, placement, and style. Labels can be added to emphasize elements of your chart. Graphics, including arrows, can also be placed on the chart.

Formatting Text

Text is formatted with the text ribbon at the top of the CorelCHART! screen, below the menu bar. This exercise will use the text ribbon to format the chart title.

1. To format text, the chart window is the best choice. Click on the Chart View tool in the toolbox, if necessary.

2. Select the chart title, "Conference Attendance," by clicking on it.

3. Select a new font for the title with the font drop-down list box shown here:

4. Select a font by clicking on it.

5. The size of the text is set with the size drop-down list box, which is to the right of the font drop-down list box. Select 24 in the size list box by clicking on it.

6. The text is already formatted as bold. Add an underline by clicking on the underline button (U), farther to the right along the text ribbon.

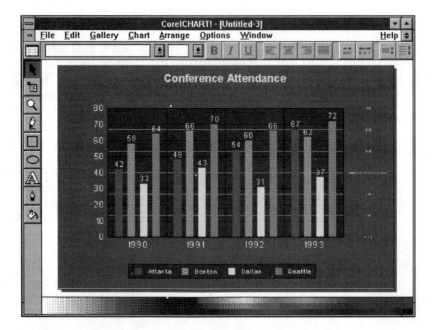

Conference attendance chart with new data
Figure 16-6.

Adding Labels

You have already seen how to define text for chart titles and headings using the Data Manager. Other text, such as labels to draw attention to a specific element of the chart, can be added using the Chart toolbox. This exercise will add a label and an arrow to identify the largest attendance on the chart.

1. To add labels to the chart, the chart window must be the active window. Once again, click on the Chart View tool in the toolbox, if necessary.

2. Select the Text tool in the Chart toolbox by clicking on it. The mouse pointer will turn into a crosshair.

3. Click on the chart in the approximate location where you want the text to be placed. (The text can be moved after it has been added to the chart.)

   This label will identify the largest attendance on the chart—which is 72, the attendance in Seattle in 1993—so click on the area above the chart on the right side. The I-beam insertion point will appear where you clicked. Type **Best Attendance** and then click on the Pick tool. The text you just typed will reflect the current text attributes (font, size, and so forth) that you selected in the text ribbon for the title. The attributes can be changed with the text ribbon while the new text is selected.

4. If the text needs to be larger or smaller, it can be adjusted in two ways. The first way is to select the text and then use the type size drop-down list box to change the size of the text. The other method is to select the text and use the edit handles to increase or decrease the size of the text box.

5. When you are satisfied with the appearance of the text, drag it into its final location with the mouse.

6. Next, add an arrow to the chart to point out the bar representing the best attendance. Click on the Pencil tool in the toolbox. The Pencil tool has a flyout menu for selecting the type of line to draw. Click on the Arrow tool on the right of the flyout menu.

7. Click on the point where you want the arrow to start (this will be the end without the arrowhead). Drag the mouse to set the length and direction of the arrow. When the line is where you want it, release the mouse button. An arrow will appear with the arrowhead where you ended the line. The arrow can be moved by choosing the Pick tool in the Chart toolbox, selecting the arrow, and dragging it with the mouse.

Figure 16-7 shows the conference chart with the label and arrow described in this exercise.

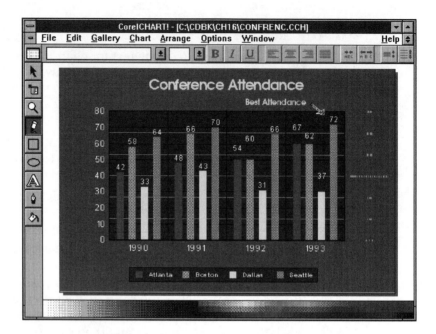

Chart with
annotation
Figure 16-7.

Adding Graphics

You can add graphics to your charts by creating them with CorelCHART!'s drawing tools or by importing them from other programs. Graphics created with CorelDRAW! can be placed directly onto a CorelCHART! chart.

Graphics and text are placed on the chart in layers, in a manner similar to CorelDRAW! drawings. The chart layer, which contains all the information on the Data Manager, is the bottom layer. All other layers are placed above the chart layer. The label "Best Attendance" and the arrow you added in the previous exercise are both above the chart layer. The next exercise will add a simple graphic to the chart, using CorelCHART!'s drawing tools. The graphic will appear behind the chart title. To do this, you will first create the background graphic and then create a new chart title to be placed above it.

1. To modify the chart, the chart window must be the active window. Click on the Chart View tool in the toolbox, if necessary.

2. Since the existing chart title will be covered by the graphic, you can turn the title off. In the Chart menu, choose Display Status. The Display Status dialog box shown here will open:

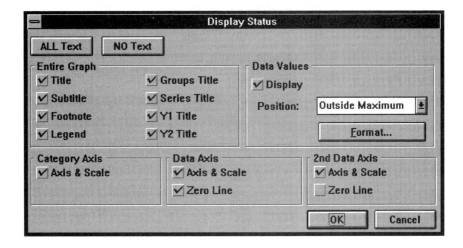

3. To turn off the chart title, click on the Title option button, so there is no longer a check mark in the box, and then click on OK.

4. Now you will create an ellipse, using the Ellipse tool. Select the Ellipse tool from the toolbox. The mouse pointer will turn into a crosshair.

5. Place the mouse pointer in the area that will be the left side of the ellipse (see Figure 16-8). The ellipse can be moved with the Pick tool after it is created, so the exact placement isn't critical.

6. Drag the mouse to the right and down. When you like the shape and size of the ellipse, release the mouse button.

7. Select the Pick tool in the Chart toolbox and drag the ellipse into position above the chart.

8. Since the ellipse was created after the text and arrow that you added earlier, it is on top of the text. To move the ellipse behind the text, leave the ellipse selected, pull down the Arrange menu, and choose To Back.

9. Now you need to add a new chart title. Select the Text tool in the toolbox and recreate the chart title, using the same steps covered previously.

Figure 16-8 shows one way the chart could appear. You should experiment with the Fill tool and the color palette to see the effects they can create.

Graphics can also be imported into CorelCHART!. Imported graphics can be in a number of different formats, as shown in the following table.

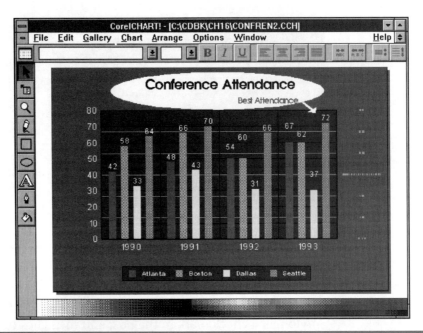

Ellipse added
to chart
Figure 16-8.

File Format	Extension
Adobe Illustrator 88, 3.0	.AI, .EPS
AutoCAD	.DXF
CompuServe GIF	.GIF
Computer Graphics Metafile	.CGM
CorelPHOTO-PAINT!	.PCX, .PCC
CorelDRAW!	.CDR
CorelTRACE!	.EPS
GEM	.GEM
HP Plotter HPGL	.PLT
IBM PIF	.PIF
Lotus PIC	.PIC
Macintosh PICT	.PCT
Targa Bitmap	.TGA
TIFF 5.0 Bitmap	.TIF
Windows Bitmap	.BMP
Windows Paintbrush	.PCX, .PCC
Windows Metafile	.WMF

Modifying Chart Elements

In the previous exercises you modified charts by adding text and graphics to them. Charts can also be modified by changing the objects on the charts. In a Bar chart, the width of the bars, the distance between bars, and the shape of the bars can all be modified. The options for modifying chart elements are in the Chart menu; the exact options displayed vary, depending on the type of chart being modified. For example, when a Bar chart is the selected chart, the Chart menu contains options that modify the bars on the chart. When a Pie chart is selected, the Chart menu contains options for modifying segments of the pie.

The commands in the Chart menu can be accessed in three different ways. For each method, you first select the chart object to be modified. You can then choose the desired option from the Chart menu, using the mouse or keyboard; or you can also select the Pop-up Menu tool in the toolbox. When the Pop-up Menu tool is selected, a pop-up menu containing the same options as the Chart menu is presented next to the selected object. The pop-up menu will contain only the options that can be used with the selected object. Figure 16-9 shows the pop-up menu presented when a bar is selected. From the submenu you can select the amount of space between each bar.

Pop-up menus can also be used *without* selecting the Pop-up Menu tool. Pressing the right mouse button while a chart object is selected will bring up the same menu.

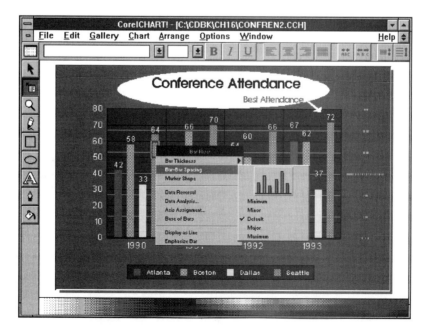

Pop-up menu
and submenu
Figure 16-9.

16

Figure 16-10 shows the example chart with the bar thickness set to Default and the marker Shapes set to several of the available shapes. Experiment with the different combinations CorelCHART! provides to discover what effects you prefer for your own charts.

Creating Chart Templates

Any chart you design can be used as a chart template. You can insert your template in the Chart Types pictorial display box in the New dialog box, so it will be available when you are creating a new chart. You can also use a chart as a template after you have created it as a regular chart.

To include your chart template in the New dialog box, you must save it to the directory where CorelCHART! stores the other chart templates. In the directory containing your Corel applications, there will be a subdirectory named CHART. The CHART subdirectory will itself contain a series of subdirectories, one for each type of chart. The chart templates are stored in these directories. If you installed CorelDRAW! using the default parameters, the path is C:\COREL40\CHART\BAR (or other chart type) *.CCH. Any chart saved to these directories will be available in the Chart Types pictorial display box.

A chart template is simply a regular CorelCHART! chart. When it is loaded as a template, if the Use Sample Data is not checked, the existing data (including text) is ignored. Only the chart type, graphics, color palette, and other modifications are presented.

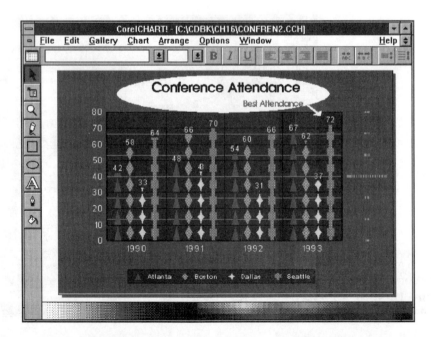

Various
shaped
markers
Figure 16-10.

Placing a template chart in the CorelCHART! directories makes it readily available when you are creating a new chart. However, any chart can be used as a chart template, no matter where it is located. If you want to use a chart as a template after you have saved it as a regular chart, follow these steps:

1. Open the chart you wish to start with, then, in the File menu, select Apply Template. The Open Chart dialog box, shown here, will be presented:

16

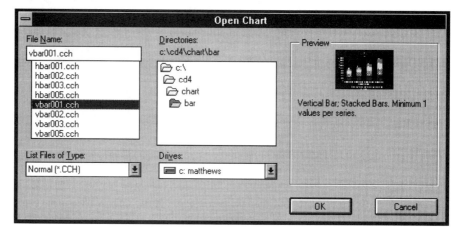

2. Select the drive and directory containing the chart file you want to use and then select the file in the File Name list box.
3. Click on the filename and then click on OK, or just double-click on the filename.

The selected chart file will apply its format characteristics to the current chart.

Chart Types

CorelCHART! can create 12 basic chart types, with most of these chart types available in several formats. Each chart type and format presents your data in a different pictorial form. The chart type that best presents your data will depend upon the kinds of relationships you are illustrating.

Bar Charts

Bar charts are used to show how values compare with one another and how they change over time. Each bar represents one data point—the value in one cell of the Data Manager. Bar charts can be configured as Vertical Bar charts, as shown in Figure 16-11, or as Horizontal Bar charts, as shown in Figure 16-12.

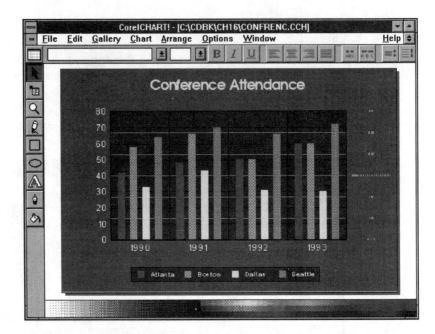

Vertical Bar
chart
Figure 16-11.

Vertical and Horizontal Bar charts have seven formats. The Bar, Line, and
Area charts have the same set of formats. These formats will be covered in
detail in this section and mentioned only briefly in the sections on Line and
Area charts.

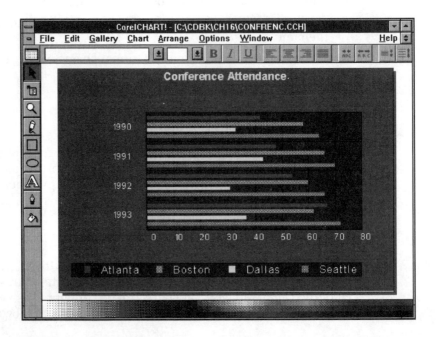

Horizontal Bar
chart
Figure 16-12.

The available formats are as follows:

✦ *Side-by-Side Bar*   The bars representing each data point are placed next to each other. Figure 16-11 is a Side-by-Side Bar chart.

✦ *Stacked Bar*   Each bar in the data category is placed on top of the previous bar, rather than next to it. Each overall bar represents the sum of values for one data category. The Stacked Bar chart is used to compare sums of data points between categories and to see the relative contribution of each data point. Figure 16-13 shows the conference data as a Stacked Bar chart.

✦ *Dual-Axis Side-by-Side*   The charts shown so far have had one category axis (the X axis) and one data axis (the Y axis). The Dual-Axis Side-by-Side format has two data axes. In a Horizontal Bar chart, one data axis is at the bottom of the chart and the other data axis is at the top of the chart. Some of the data series are plotted against the bottom data axis, and the other series are plotted against the top data axis. In a Vertical Bar chart, one data axis is on the left side and the other data axis is on the right side. Figure 16-14 shows the conference attendance as a Vertical Dual-Axis Side-by-Side chart.

✦ *Dual-Axis Stacked*   This is identical to the Dual-Axis Side-by-Side chart, except that each bar in the data category is placed on top of the previous bar, rather than next to it. Each bar represents a sum of data points.

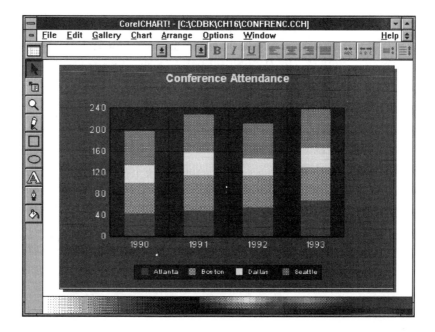

Stacked Bar chart
Figure 16-13.

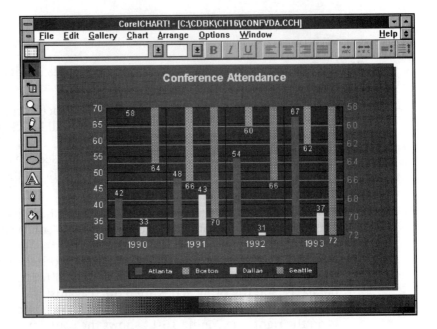

Vertical
Dual-Axis
chart
Figure 16-14.

+ *Bipolar Side-by-Side* The Bipolar Side-by-Side chart divides the chart into halves, horizontally for a Vertical Bar chart and vertically for a Horizontal Bar chart. There are two data axes; each starts at the center of the chart and increases in value toward the edge of the chart. Figure 16-15 shows a Vertical Bar Bipolar Side-by-Side chart of the conference data. As you can see, the baseline for the data axes is the center of the chart, and values increase as they approach the top and bottom of the chart. The Horizontal Bar Bipolar Side-by-Side chart is similar, except that the data values increase as they get closer to the left and right sides of the chart.

+ *Bipolar Stacked* This is identical to the Bipolar Side-by-Side chart, except that each bar in the data category is placed on top of the previous bar, rather than next to it.

+ *Percent* A Percent chart is a type of Stacked Bar chart. In the Percent chart, the sum of all the numbers in each data category is represented as 100 percent. Each number in the data category is shown as a percentage of the total, rather than its actual value. Figure 16-16 shows the conference data as a Vertical Bar Percent chart. (Note that this chart's Y-axis scale runs from 0 to 1, rather than 0 to 100.)

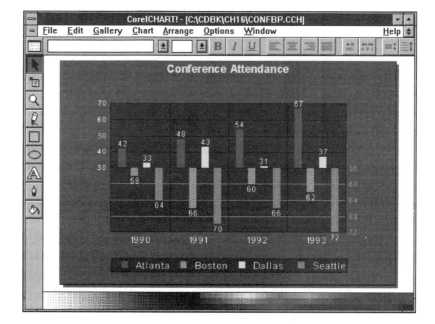

Vertical
Bipolar
Side-by-Side
chart
Figure 16-15.

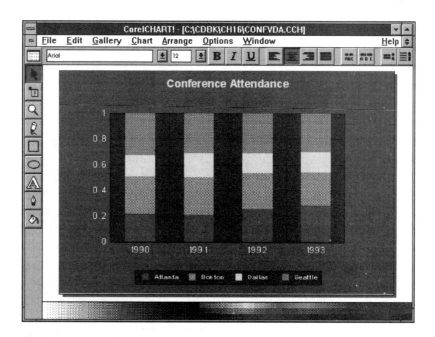

Vertical Bar
Percent chart
Figure 16-16.

Line Charts

Line charts are primarily used to show the change over time in a series of values. Each data series is plotted side by side, allowing you to readily observe trends between the data series. A marker is placed at each data point, and the markers in each data series are connected. Line charts can be either vertical or horizontal. Figure 16-17 shows the conference data plotted as a Vertical Line chart.

Vertical and Horizontal Line charts offer seven formats that are similar to the ones available for Bar charts. The Line chart formats are as follows:

✦ *Absolute* Each data value is plotted at its actual value on the data axis. The values in each category are plotted in line with each other on the category axis. Figure 16-17 is an Absolute Line chart.

✦ *Stacked* The Stacked Line chart is similar to the Stacked Bar chart—each value is plotted above the previous value in the data category, and the largest marker represents the sum of the values.

✦ *Bipolar Absolute* This is an Absolute Line chart in a Bipolar format, similar to the Bipolar Bar chart described in the previous section. The data is presented in the same manner as the Bipolar Side-by-Side Bar chart.

✦ *Bipolar Stacked* This is a Stacked Line chart in the Bipolar format. Data is presented in the same manner as the Bipolar Stacked Bar chart.

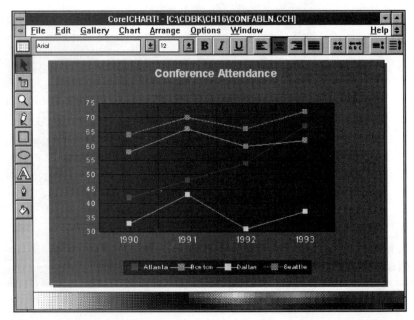

Vertical Line
chart
Figure 16-17.

◆ *Dual-Axis Absolute* This is an Absolute Line chart in the Dual-Axis format. Data is presented in the same manner as the Dual-Axis Side-by-Side Bar chart.

◆ *Dual-Axis Stacked* This is a Stacked Line chart in the Dual-Axis format. Data is presented in the same manner as the Dual-Axis Stacked Bar chart.

◆ *Percent* The Percent format shows each value as a percentage of the total, in the same manner as the Bar Percent chart.

Area Charts

Area charts are similar to Line charts. The difference is that Area charts fill the areas between the lines with a color or pattern. Area charts can also be vertical or horizontal and offer formats similar to Bar and Line charts. Figure 16-18 shows the conference data as a Stacked Area chart.

The Area chart formats are as follows:

◆ *Absolute* Each data value is plotted at its actual value on the data axis. The values in each category are plotted in line with each other on the category axis.

◆ *Stacked* The Stacked Area chart is similar to the Stacked Bar or Line chart—each value is plotted above the previous value, and the largest value marker represents the total of all the values in the data category.

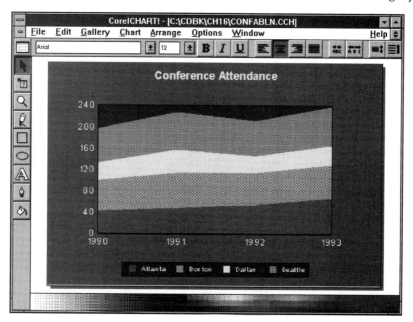

Stacked Area chart
Figure 16-18.

♦ *Bipolar Absolute* This is an Absolute Area chart in a Bipolar format, similar to the Bipolar Bar charts described previously. The data is presented in the same manner as the Bipolar Side-by-Side Bar chart.

♦ *Bipolar Stacked* This is a Stacked Area Chart in the Bipolar format. Data is presented in the same manner as the Bipolar Stacked Bar chart.

♦ *Dual-Axis Absolute* This is an Absolute Area chart in the Dual-Axis Format. Data is presented in the same manner as the Dual-Axis Side-by-Side Bar chart.

♦ *Dual-Axis Stacked* This is a Stacked Area chart in the Dual-Axis format. Data is presented in the same manner as the Dual-Axis Stacked Bar chart.

♦ *Percent* The Percent format shows each value as a percentage of the total, in the same manner as the Bar Percent chart.

Pie Charts

Pie charts show the percentage distribution of your data. The entire pie represents 100 percent of one data series. Each data point is plotted as a wedge, representing a percentage of the total. Figure 16-19 shows the conference data as Multiple Pie charts. Each Pie chart represents the data from one year.

Pie charts have six formats as follows:

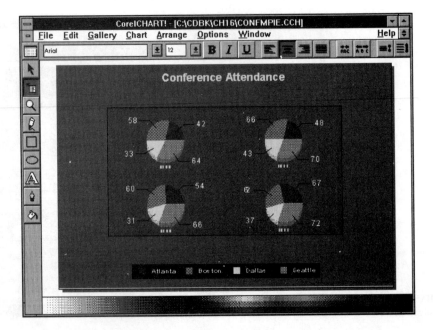

Multiple Pie charts
Figure 16-19.

16

♦ *Pie*   This is the single Pie chart.

♦ *Ring Pie*   This is identical to the single Pie chart, except that the pie is shaped like a ring with a hole in the center.

♦ *Multiple Pie*   This format uses several Pie charts together, to represent several data series.

♦ *Multiple Ring Pie*   This is like the Multiple Pie chart, but with ring-shaped pies.

♦ *Multiple Proportional Pie*   Each pie is sized in relation to the other pies. The pie that represents the largest total value will be the largest pie. The pie that represents the smallest total value will be the smallest pie.

♦ *Multiple Proportional Ring Pie*   This is like the Multiple Proportional Pie format, but uses ring-shaped pies.

Scatter Charts

Scatter, or X-Y charts, show the relationship between pairs of numbers and the trends they represent. In each pair of numbers, one is plotted on the category axis, the other on the data axis. A marker is placed on the chart at the point where the value on the category axis intersects the value on the data axis. Figure 16-20 is a Scatter chart, showing the hypothetical relationship between hours of sleep and units of production.

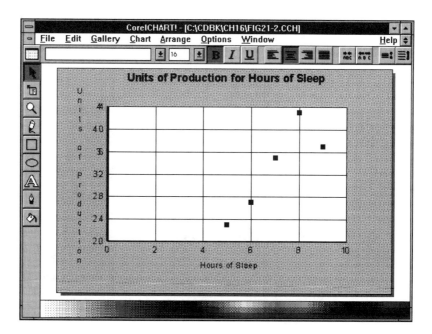

Scatter chart
Figure 16-20.

Scatter charts have four formats:

✦ *Scatter* This is the basic Scatter chart.

✦ *X-Y Dual-Axis* This is a basic Scatter chart with two data axes.

✦ *X-Y with Labels* This is a basic Scatter chart with the data points labeled.

✦ *X-Y Dual-Axis with Labels* This is a Dual-Axis Scatter chart with the data points labeled.

High/Low/Open/Close Charts

The High/Low/Open/Close chart is a type of Line chart. It is also known as a Stock Market chart because a common use for High/Low/Open/Close charts is to show opening, low, high, and closing prices for shares of stock. Figure 16-21 shows the high and low prices for two different stocks over a period of four quarters.

High/Low/Open/Close charts have six formats:

✦ *High/Low* This format plots just the highest and lowest values.

✦ *High/Low Dual-Axis* This format plots the highest and lowest values with dual axes.

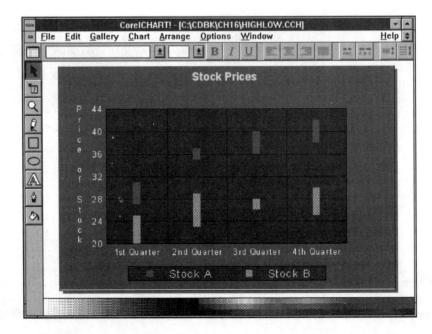

High/Low
chart
Figure 16-21.

16

♦ *High/Low/Open*   This format plots the highest, lowest, and starting values.

♦ *High/Low/Open Dual-Axis*   This format plots the highest, lowest, and starting values with dual axes.

♦ *High/Low/Open/Close*   This format plots the highest, lowest, starting, and ending values.

♦ *High/Low/Open/Close Dual-Axis*   This format plots the highest, lowest, starting, and ending values with dual axes.

Spectral Maps

Spectral Map charts are used to show relationships between sets of data. In Spectral Maps a range of values, not a data series, is marked with colors or patterns. Spectral Map charts are like topographical maps, where elevation ranges are marked with different colors. Spectral Maps have only one format. Figure 16-22 shows the conference data as a Spectral Map.

Histograms

Histograms are use to show how often values occur in a set of data. For example, if a temperature was recorded over a period of time, a Histogram could be used to show how often each temperature was recorded. Figure 16-23 shows a Vertical Histogram of the daily temperatures in the month of May. Histograms have two formats as follows:

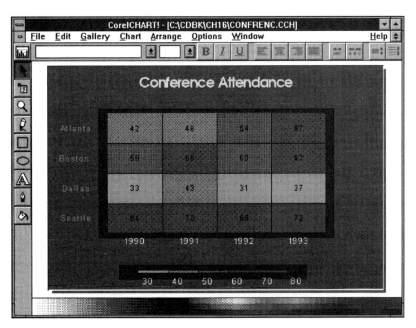

Spectral map
Figure 16-22.

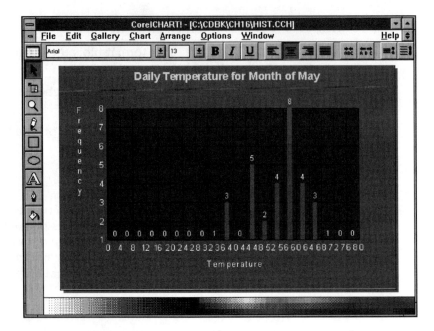

Histogram
Figure 16-23.

✦ *Vertical Histogram*   As in a Vertical Bar chart, the bars are oriented vertically.

✦ *Horizontal Histogram*   As in a Horizontal Bar chart, the bars are oriented horizontally.

Table Charts

Table charts present the data in a row and column format, similar to the way the data is contained on the Data Manager. Table charts have three formats:

✦ *Rows*   Rows are separately colored, as shown in Figure 16-24.

✦ *Columns*   Columns are separately colored.

✦ *None*   The table has no color division.

3-D Riser Charts

The 3-D Riser chart is the general name for a 3-D Bar chart. Each bar represents one data point. Figure 16-25 shows a 3-D Riser chart with octagon bars. The 3-D Riser has four formats:

✦ *3-D Bars*   Each bar is rectangular.

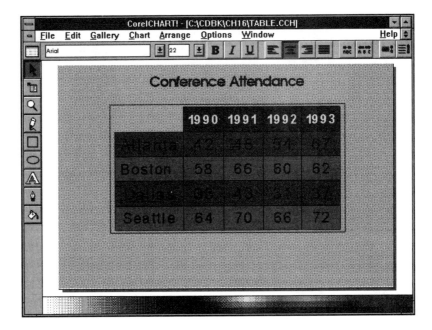

Table chart
Figure 16-24.

♦ *Pyramids* Each bar is a pyramid.

♦ *Octagons* Each bar is an octagon.

♦ *Cut-Corner Bars* Each bar is rectangular with a cut corner.

3-D Scatter Charts

The 3-D Scatter chart is similar to the normal Scatter or X-Y chart with the addition of a third axis. Figure 16-26 shows a 3-D Scatter chart. The 3-D Scatter chart has two formats:

♦ *XYZ Scatter* This is like a normal Scatter chart, but with a third data series.

♦ *XYZ Scatter with Labels* This is an XYZ Scatter chart with data labels.

Pictographs

A Pictograph uses a graphic element to replace the plain bars in Bar charts and Histograms. For example, you could display the conference data from Atlanta, using the image of stacks of computers in place of a solid bar.

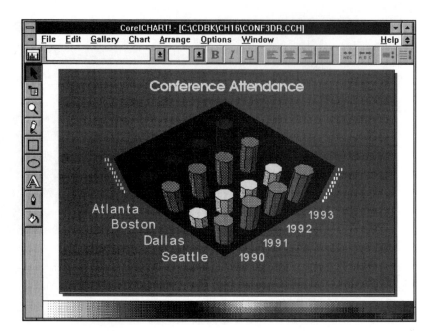

3-D Riser chart
Figure 16-25.

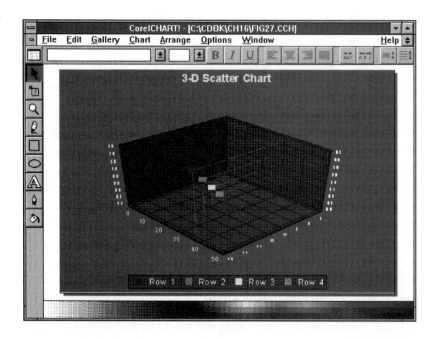

3-D Scatter
chart
Figure 16-26.

CHAPTER

17

INTRODUCING CORELSHOW!

With CorelSHOW! you can assemble drawings and graphics from other products to produce slide presentations, computer screen shows, documents (such as brochures), or overhead transparency presentations.

This chapter introduces CorelSHOW! by briefly discussing the features it offers, how you get started using it, and how to use the principal tools.

559

CorelSHOW! Overview

CorelSHOW! lets you integrate drawings, charts, and other art for the purpose of creating a presentation. CorelSHOW! has no editing or artistic tools of its own. Rather, it lets you gather art from other OLE (Object Linking and Embedding) applications, such as CorelDRAW! and CorelCHART!, and then move it around or resize it until the art is arranged for the presentation.

A presentation can be a computer screen show, where the slides are displayed on the computer screen one at a time, in a timed display. You can set the time that each screen will be displayed. If you want the presentation to ultimately be recorded on slides, overhead transparencies, or paper, you can first preview the show on your computer screen.

The OLE connection is a basic component of CorelSHOW!. (Chapter 10 explains this feature in more detail.) If you want to import a chart created with CorelCHART!, for example, you have two options for bringing it into CorelSHOW!. You can paste a *linked* copy into CorelSHOW!, which causes the contents of the original chart to be mirrored in CorelSHOW!. To make changes to the linked copy, you open CorelCHART! either directly, from within CorelSHOW!, or from Windows, and then modify the original chart. Any changes are reflected in the linked copy. Alternatively, you can *embed* a copy of the chart in CorelSHOW!. In this case, if changes are made to the embedded copy, the changes are again made with CorelCHART!, but they are not reflected on the original chart.

CorelSHOW! has some limitations: it cannot import *files* from applications that are not OLE applications. As described in the preceding paragraph, if a linked or embedded copy must be modified, this must be done in the OLE application from which it came. CorelSHOW! has no tools to modify its art. Further, if you want to assemble a document, such as a brochure, CorelSHOW! has no word processing capabilities for flowing text around graphics or changing fonts. You must do this in other OLE applications and link or embed the results into CorelSHOW!. If you must bring in something from a non-OLE application, cut or copy it to the Windows Clipboard from the originating application, then load or switch to CorelSHOW!, and paste the item. If you need to edit this item, you must leave CorelSHOW!, open the originating application, and, after editing, repeat the copy and paste procedure.

Getting Started with CorelSHOW!

CorelSHOW!

You load CorelSHOW! from the Corel 4 group in the Windows Program Manager. Once CorelSHOW! is loaded, you have the choice of opening an existing presentation or creating a new one.

Follow these steps to get started:

1. Start Windows, open the Corel 4 group if necessary, and then load
   CorelSHOW! by double-clicking on the CorelSHOW! icon.

   When CorelSHOW! has been loaded, after the initial title screen, you'll
   see the screen displayed in Figure 17-1. The dialog box allows you to
   determine whether to open an existing presentation or to start a new
   one. If you choose to open an existing file, there is one on the second
   CD-ROM:QTOUR\SAMPLES\MULTI.SHW. in the CorelSHOW! FLICS
   subdirectory.

2. Either start a new presentation or open an existing presentation by
   clicking the corresponding option button and clicking OK.

If you open a sample file, the screen shown in Figure 17-2 will be displayed.

CorelSHOW! Screen Elements

At the top of the screen, beneath the title bar, is the menu bar. It contains
seven menus: File offers various options to manage your files, presentations,
and printing; Edit provides limited editing options, such as Cut, Copy, and
Paste, plus Edit Cue, which sets the conditions for pausing and restarting a
presentation; Insert allows you to insert new pages, objects, animation, and
sound files; Arrange offers several options for rearranging objects on different

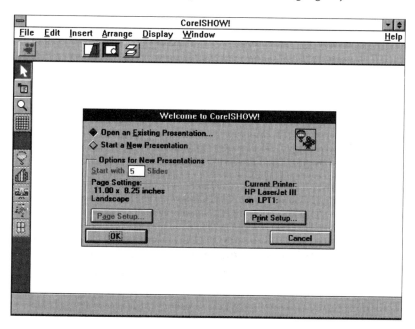

Initial
CorelSHOW!
screen
Figure 17-1.

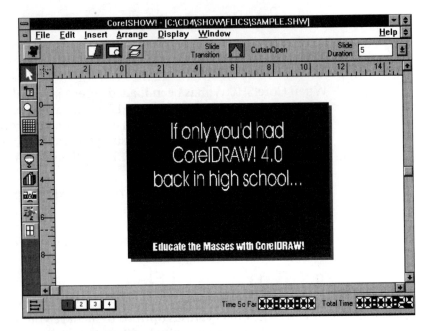

Slide view, for working on an individual slide
Figure 17-2.

levels; Display provides rulers, guidelines, and other display aids; Window offers a variety of ways to view the presentations on the screen; and Help has the standard help options.

The toolbox, discussed shortly, is displayed beneath the menu bar and along the left side of the screen. The presentation window is below and to the right of the toolbox. It contains the name of the presentation, ruler guides (if specified with the Display menu), and the contents of the current slide.

The bottom of the screen contains the Timelines icon on the far left, which displays the Timelines window. Next on the bottom are the slide number icons, which allow you to switch from one slide to another by simply clicking on the slide number you want. Also at the bottom of the screen, on the right, are the time icons, which assist you in timing your presentation by displaying the Time So Far and the Total Time for previewing the presentation.

CorelSHOW! Tools and Modes

You can view a presentation in three modes: background view, which displays art elements common to all slides; slide view, to view an individual slide (this view is shown in Figure 17-2); and slide sorter view, to display all slides. Background view is illustrated in Figure 17-3.

The toolbox controls which of the three modes you are in at any time.

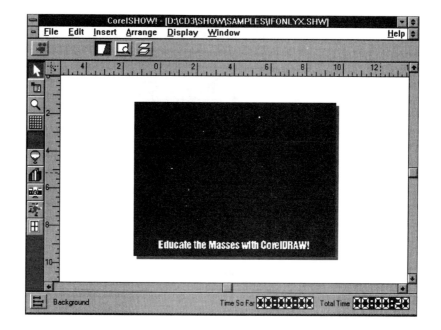

Background
view, for
working
on the
background of
a set of slides
Figure 17-3.

Background View

You can select background view by clicking on the Background View icon, the second one from the left in the top horizontal toolbox. In Figure 17-3, the text on the individual slide has been omitted, and you see only the background common to all slides.

Background view is used to create or modify the background of the slides. CorelSHOW! has a series of backgrounds from which you can select, or you can create your own in another application and then assemble it in CorelSHOW!. Once you identify and insert a background, it will appear in all slides (unless the contents of a slide cover it up).

To insert a background from the CorelSHOW! library of backgrounds, click on the Background Library icon. A dialog box displays the backgrounds that are available, as shown in Figure 17-4. You then click on the background you want, and it will be inserted for all slides.

Slide View

Slide view is selected by clicking on the Slide View icon, beside the Background View icon in the top toolbox. Use slide view to create or modify an individual slide. Figure 17-2 shows this view.

From this view, you can easily integrate a drawing, chart, or other object
from another application. This can be done either by clicking on the
appropriate icon, as shown in the following table, or by pulling down the
Insert menu, selecting Object, and choosing the file to be inserted. Click on:

	For CorelDRAW!
	For CorelCHART!
	For CorelPHOTO-PAINT!
	For CorelMOVE!
	For other OLE applications

If you click on the icon for CorelDRAW! or one of the other applications,
you will be placed within the selected application, but with a link that allows
you to easily return to CorelSHOW!. For example, clicking on the
CorelDRAW! icon and then drawing a rectangle in the slide (to identify the
area the drawing will occupy) takes you to CorelDRAW!. There, you can

create a new drawing or open an existing one and then copy it to the Clipboard. When you return to CorelSHOW! (by choosing Exit and Return from the File menu), you can then paste the drawing onto the slide. The appropriate links with CorelDRAW! are automatically established to ensure that changes to the original will be reflected in the copy. Refer to Chapter 10 for more information about how to move from one OLE application to another, and back.

If you insert a file with the Object, Animation, or Sound commands from the Insert menu, you can select the file to be linked or embedded into CorelSHOW! *without* switching to another application.

17

Slide Sorter View

Slide sorter view, shown with the sample application in Figure 17-5, displays the slides in a reduced size. (You can revert quickly to slide view by double-clicking on any slide that you want to examine in detail.) With this screen, you can manipulate the collection of slides. You can drag the slides from one position to another, thereby reordering the slides within the presentation.

An alternative way to reorder the slides is to use the Numbering icon. In this case, you click on the Numbering icon and then click on the slides in the sequence that you want them to appear.

Slide sorter
view, for
working on
slides as a
group
Figure 17-5.

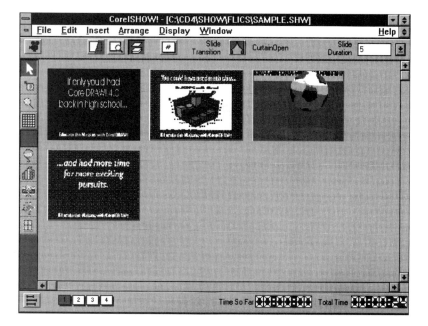

If you have more than one presentation open at one time, you can copy, cut, and paste slides from one presentation to another using the slide sorter view. The Tile command in the Window menu displays two windows side by side so that you can use the Copy, Cut, and Paste commands on the Edit menu to move slides between the two presentations.

Slide Transition

Slide transition determines how you go from one slide to another. This is accomplished with the Transition Effects dialog box shown in Figure 17-6. You open the dialog box by clicking on the Slide Transition icon in the horizontal toolbox. The dialog box allows you to apply special effects to the opening and closing of any slides. To assign a transition effect to a slide, first click on the slide to select it, then click on the Slide Transition icon.

With these options, you can create effects such as a curtain opening to reveal a slide, or closing to mask a slide. You can zoom in to a slide, or out from a slide, quickly or slowly. Or, you can open a slide with a shutter effect, in which the shutters of a blind gradually open to reveal the slide. These are just a few tricks to make a slide presentation more interesting and animated, without having actual movement in the slides.

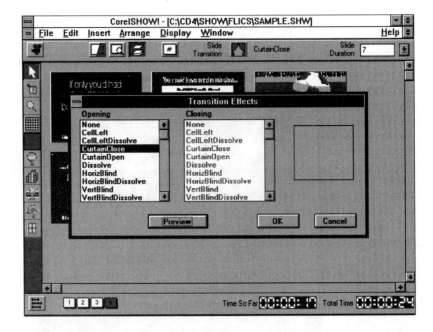

Transition Effects dialog box, for determining how to go from one slide to another
Figure 17-6.

Slide Duration

The Slide Duration list box, on the right side of the toolbox, allows you to assign the length of time each slide should be displayed. You click on the down arrow to display a drop-down list of various standard times from 1 to 60 seconds. Click on each slide, then either select a time value from the drop-down list, or enter a specific time in the entry box.

Previewing a Presentation

To preview a presentation, you can click on the Screen Show icon, at the left side of the horizontal toolbox. If you want to change defaults affecting how the presentation will run, first choose Presentation Options from the Display menu and make any desired changes in the Presentation Options dialog box. You have the options of advancing to the next slide either automatically or manually, of repeatedly running the presentation until [Esc] is pressed, of displaying a mouse pointer on the screen, and of generating the slide show in advance, so that the presentation moves from slide to slide more smoothly.

After completing the dialog box, you can click on the Screen Show icon or select Run Screen Show from the File menu.

Other Tools

There are two other tools in the vertical toolbox that have not been discussed: the Pop-up Menu tool and the Zoom tool. The Zoom tool is exactly like the Zoom tool in CorelDRAW! and has the same subsidiary tools. You can use the Zoom tool to magnify a part of a slide to better align objects you are placing on it.

The Pop-up Menu tool (under the Pick tool) allows you to click on an object and get a set of menus that relate to that object. For example, selecting the Pop-up Menu tool and clicking on the border of a slide produces this set of menus:

With these menus, you can edit or change a characteristic of the selected object. For example, click on BackGround to change the background of the current slide.

17

CHAPTER

CORELDRAW! 4

18

INTRODUCING CORELPHOTO-PAINT!

CorelPHOTO-PAINT! is another exciting product first made available with CorelDRAW! 3. It combines traditional paint capabilities with photograph enhancement features.

This chapter introduces CorelPHOTO-PAINT! by briefly discussing the features and tools, and how to get started using it.

CorelPHOTO-PAINT! Overview

CorelPHOTO-PAINT! is a multifaceted paint program. It allows you to create bitmap images with an extensive drawing-tool kit, and also enables you to enhance and retouch scanned photos. You can include the resulting images in CorelSHOW! presentations, in CorelDRAW! graphics in word processing or desktop publishing documents, or in other applications.

Getting Started with CorelPHOTO-PAINT!

To start CorelPHOTO-PAINT!, first bring up Windows, open the Corel 4 Group, and then double-click on the CorelPHOTO-PAINT! icon.

After a short time, you will see the screen displayed in Figure 18-1.

At this point you can either open an existing picture on disk or create a new one. If you want to create a new image, select the File menu and choose New; confirm or change the defaults in the Create a New Picture dialog box,

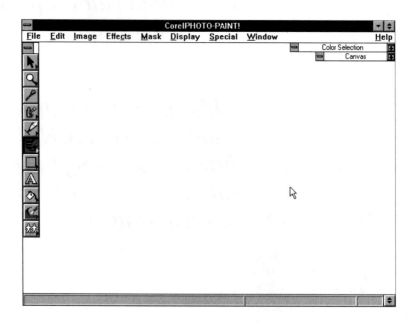

Initial
CorelPHOTO-
PAINT! screen
Figure 18-1.

shown in the following illustration. A blank window will open, where you can create the picture.

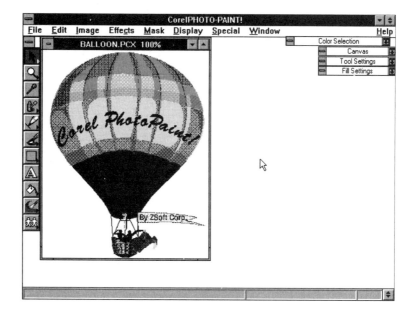

If you want to open an existing picture, select File Open and identify the file you want. Once you've loaded a picture into CorelPHOTO-PAINT!, your screen will look something like Figure 18-2. In this case, a sample file called BALLOON.PCX, from the Photo-Paint! SAMPLES directory, has been opened.

18

Opening an existing picture
Figure 18-2.

572

CorelDRAW! 4 Made Easy

CorelPHOTO-PAINT! Screen Elements

The CorelPHOTO-PAINT! window contains many features to help you create pictures or retouch photos.

At the top of the screen is the title bar. On the right are the maximize and minimize buttons, which allow you to resize or restore the screen on the Photo-Paint! window.

The menu bar, which is discussed shortly, is beneath the title bar. Beneath the menu bar is the Photo-Paint! picture window, where you can create or open a picture. The status bar, beneath the picture area, displays messages, pointer coordinates, and other useful information as you work with a picture. It is blank until a picture is being used in the window.

The menu bar contains nine menus.

The File menu, shown in Figure 18-3a, contains the file-handling and printing features. You can create a new file; open or close an existing one; save a file onto disk; and acquire images by selecting a source device, such as a scanner, and then calibrating the device or acquiring the image. With this menu you can also set up or calibrate a printer and print your CorelPHOTO-PAINT! pictures. The Prepress command allows you to work with color separations. The Edit Tone Map command displays a Tone Map dialog box for editing and creating curves and then adding them to images. These can affect such factors as the tone range, contrast, brightness, and balance of an image. Finally, from the File menu, you exit CorelPHOTO-PAINT!.

The Edit menu, shown in Figure 18-3b, offers basic editing features like Undo, Cut, Copy, and Paste. The Clear command clears the window to the background color. Using the Paste flyout, you can copy as an image or as a new selection. You can copy to and from external files with this menu.

The Image menu, shown in Figure 18-3c, allows you to retouch or add special effects to a picture or scanned photo. The Color command offers a set of suboptions for controlling filters for Brightness and Contrast; Threshold color, which changes coloring in an image to solid colors with no shading; Gamma, which adjusts middle gray-scale values; Hues, which sets a precise color; and Saturation, which sets a measured amount of a color. Sharpen filters allow you to sharpen and enhance details, and Unsharpen Mask filters work to emphasize edge details. Smooth filters are provided to smooth, soften, diffuse, or blend images. Tone filters adjust color balances of colors/grays, or equalize tones in images.

The Image menu also contains options to flip, rotate, or distort a picture. The Resample command allows you to create new images of different sizes or resolutions; the Resolution command alters the vertical or horizontal resolution of an image. The Convert To command converts to another color. You can use the Split Channels To command to separate an image into channels that you can edit; then recombine the image with the Combine Channels command. Finally, the Info option displays measurements and technical details about an image.

The Effects menu, shown in Figure 18-3d, allows you to select and apply special effects filters to pictures or cutouts. The filters include Artistic, Edge, Emboss, Invert, and Jaggy Despeckle (which scatters colors). Motion Blur filters make an image look as if there were motion in the picture; Noise filters add or remove or change the intensity of noise; Pixelate filters create block-like effects in a picture; Posterize filters remove graduations that create solid shades or colors; Psychedelic filters display color in a random order; and Solarize filters create negative images (reversals) in selected areas.

The Mask menu, shown in Figure 18-3e, applies a protective shield against filters or enhancements. These can be applied to selected areas or to the whole picture.

The Display menu, shown in Figure 18-3f, controls images on the screen. You can zoom in and out of pictures; selectively hide or show the four roll-up menus or the toolbox; and maximize the screen, thereby clearing the screen of all but pictures (the title and menu bars are hidden). Full Screen Preview shows only the active picture. Optimized Dithering fine-tunes the image on the screen when it has too many colors, thus sharpening the image. Calibrate adjusts the brightness of the monitor.

The Special menu, shown in Figure 18-3g, allows you to adjust color tolerances, select some preferences (such as units of measurement), and display system information.

The Window menu, shown in Figure 18-3h, arranges the windows and icons. You can change the active window from here. It also duplicates pictures so you can see them at different magnifications.

Finally, there is a Help menu, shown in Figure 18-3i, which has the standard help options.

The PHOTO-PAINT! window as shown in Figure 18-2 can contain four floating roll-up menus: at the top right is the Color Selection roll-up, then the Canvas roll-up, the Tool Settings roll-up, and finally the Fill Settings roll-up.

The Roll-Up Menus

The four roll-up menus, shown in Figure 18-4, can be hidden or displayed by selecting the Display menu and clicking on the appropriate roll-up menu name. If a check mark appears next to the name, the roll-up is displayed on the screen.

File menu

a)
File	
New...	Ctrl+N
Open...	Ctrl+O
Close	
Save	Ctrl+S
Save As...	
Acquire Image	▸
Print	▸
Prepress...	
Edit Tone Map...	
Exit	Alt+F4
1 c:\cd4\programs\undisp.bmp	

Edit menu

b)
Edit	
Undo	Ctrl+Z
Cut	Ctrl+X
Copy	Ctrl+C
Paste	▸
Clear	Del
Copy To File...	
Paste From File...	

Image menu

c)
Image	
Color	▸
Sharpen	▸
Smooth	▸
Tone	▸
Flip	▸
Rotate	▸
Distort	
Resample...	
Resolution	
Convert To	▸
Split Channels To	▸
Combine Channels...	
Info...	

Effects menu

d)
Effects	
Artistic	▸
Edge	▸
Emboss...	
Invert	
Jaggy Despeckle...	
Motion Blur...	
Noise	▸
Pixelate...	
Posterize...	
Psychedelic...	
Solarize...	

Mask menu

e)
Mask	
Select All	
Clear Mask	
Crop to Mask	

Display menu

f)
Display	Special	Window
Zoom		▸
100% (No Zoom)		Ctrl+1
Zoom To Fit		
Hide All		Ctrl+A
✓ Toolbox		Ctrl+T
✓ Canvas Roll-Up		F5
✓ Color Selection Roll-Up		F6
✓ Fill Settings Roll-Up		F7
✓ Tool Settings Roll-Up		F8
Maximize Work Area		
Full Screen Preview		F9
Optimized Dithering		
Calibrate...		

The menus for
CorelPHOTO-
PAINT!
Figure 18-3.

Special menu

g)

Special	
Color Tolerance...	
Preferences...	Ctrl+J
System Info...	

Window menu

h)
Window	
Cascade	Shift+F5
Tile	Shift+F4
Arrange Icons	
Duplicate	Ctrl+D
✓ 1 UNDISP.BMP 100%	

Help menu

i)

	Help
Contents	
About PHOTO-PAINT!...	

On the right of each roll-up is an arrow. If you click on it, the roll-up will be rolled down. If you click on it again, the menu will be rolled up.

The shortcut for displaying or hiding the Color Selection roll-up is F6.

The Color Selection roll-up, shown in Figure 18-4a, allows you to select outline, fill, and background colors for an image. It can be used to adjust or select a color palette. You can create a graduated effect in the colors by controlling the To/From values which are displayed when the Gradient Fill tool is selected.

The shortcut for displaying or hiding the Canvas roll-up is F5.

The Canvas roll-up, shown in Figure 18-4b, allows you to load a canvas pattern from disk or the Clipboard. When the pattern is loaded, it is displayed in the display box of the roll-up. This can be applied as a background to a painting, or it can overlay a picture for a transparency effect.

18

The shortcut for displaying or hiding the Tool Settings roll-up is F8.

The Tool Settings roll-up is used to control the width, shape, or thickness of a brush tool, depending on the tool selected. The option boxes below the width (Edge, Density, Variances, etc.) are used with the Impressionist, Impressionist Clone, Pointillist, and Pointillist Clone tools, which you will learn about later in the chapter. It is shown in Figure 18-4c.

The shortcut for displaying or hiding the Fill Settings roll-up is F7.

The Fill Settings roll-up, shown in Figure 18-4d, is used to load a picture saved to a disk or the Clipboard for use with the Tile Fill tool, which fills an enclosed area with a repeating pattern. By clicking on the Create Texture command button on the roll-up, the Texture Fill dialog box shown in Figure 18-5 is displayed. This allows you to load a specific picture or pattern.

This brief tour of the screen gives you an introduction to the software, but experimenting with the CorelPHOTO-PAINT! tools is where you will really begin to appreciate the power of the package.

CorelPHOTO-PAINT! Tools

Pressing Ctrl-T is a shortcut toggle that hides or displays the toolbox.

The CorelPHOTO-PAINT! toolbox is a floating window that you can move around on the screen. Although the toolbox is displayed by default, you can hide it by clicking on the Control-menu box in its title bar. The Control menu on the toolbox offers you an option for hiding the toolbox. Once the toolbox is hidden, you can later display it when you need it by selecting the Display menu and choosing Toolbox.

Color Selection roll-up

a)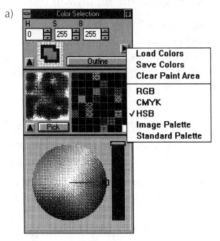

Canvas roll-up

b)

Tool Settings roll-up

c)

Fill Settings roll-up

d)

Roll-up menus
available
when loading
CorelPHOTO-
PAINT or from
the Display
menu.
Figure 18-4.

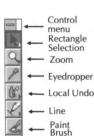

Control menu ←
Rectangle Selection ←
Zoom ←
Eyedropper ←
Local Undo ←
Line ←
Paint Brush ←
Hollow Box ←
Text ←
Flood ←
Smear ←
Clone ←

Tools within the toolbox are arranged according to function. There are 11 tools shown on the toolbox, as you can see here. Most buttons represent "groups" of tools; these can be identified by a small white or black (depending on whether the tool is selected) triangle in the lower-right corner of the tool button. When you click on a button with a triangle, a flyout menu displays the tools in the group.

The tools within the toolbox can be selected by clicking on a tool button, or in the case of group tools, by dragging the cursor on a flyout menu until the tool you want is highlighted.

The toolbox contains five types of tools: selection and display, retouching, painting, drawing, and text. A brief summary of each of the tools is provided in the following sections.

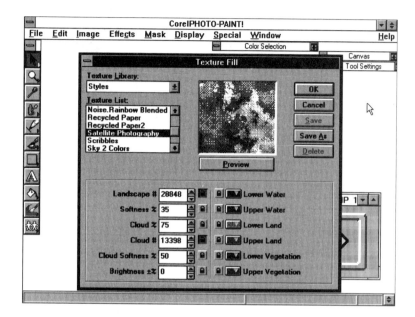

Texture Fill
dialog box
Figure 18-5.

Selection and Display Tools

Selection tools are used to select, or cut out, an area of a picture. Once
selected, an area can be cut, copied, pasted, stretched, rotated, or otherwise
manipulated. Display tools are used to manipulate the display of the picture
in some way.

There are seven selection and display tools located in the first two tool icons.
There are four selection tools:

Rectangle Selection defines a rectangular area within an image by dragging the
pointer over the area to be selected, thus placing a rectangle around it.

Magic Wand lets you duplicate a set of colors from one area or object
to another.

Lasso lets you select an irregular area by drawing a line around it in
freehand mode.

Polygon Selection lets you define an area to be selected by clicking on a spot on the picture, moving the pointer, clicking on another spot, and so on, creating a polygon around the area. The polygon may have up to 200 points.

There are three display tools:

 Zoom enlarges or reduces the size of the image.

 Locator displays the same area in any copies of a picture on the desktop.

 Hand moves a picture in any direction: up, down, to the side, or diagonally.

Retouching Tools

Retouching tools are used to refine or retouch parts of a picture (filters are generally used to retouch whole pictures). There are 11 retouching tools. The first retouching tool, found by itself, is the Eyedropper. The second group of retouching tools is found immediately below it, in the flyout of the Local Undo icon. The last group of retouching tools is found in the flyout of the Smear Paintbrush icon.

 Eyedropper picks up a color from a picture so the same shade can be applied elsewhere.

Three retouching tools are found in the flyout of the Local Undo icon:

 Local Undo cancels the last change made since a tool was selected or a command was used.

 Eraser erases or clears an area of the picture.

 Color Replacer changes the outline color to the fill color.

Finally, there are seven retouching tools found in the flyout of the Smearing icon:

Freehand Smear spreads and smears colors in an area.

 Freehand Smudge adds texture to a picture by randomly mixing colors and spraying a picture with the result.

 Freehand Sharpen sharpens or adds crispness to colors of an area.

 Freehand Contrast intensifies the brightness or darkness of an area. **18**

 Freehand Brighten adds highlights, or darkens an area.

 Freehand Tint adds an overall cast or tint of color to an area.

 Freehand Blend Paintbrush softens the contours of an area.

Painting Tools

Painting tools are the bread and butter of the Photo-Paint! program. They allow you to create and delete shapes and add color, texture, or text to a picture. There are 13 painting tools in three groups.

The first group is found in the flyout of the Paint Brush icon:

 Paint Brush, using a primary color, lets you draw outline colors in freehand. The effect is coarser than with the Outline Pen.

 Impressionist Brush paints with multicolored brush strokes, similar to those used by Vincent Van Gogh.

 Pointillism Brush creates clusters of dots for a pointillistic effect.

Artist Brush gives the appearance of an oil painting.

 Airbrush sprays color into an area, adding shading and depth.

 Spraycan adds a rough pattern to a picture by randomly splattering a color.

The second group of painting tools is found in the Flood Fill icon:

 Flood Fill fills an enclosed area with color.

 Tile Fill fills an enclosed area with a repetitive tile pattern.

 Gradient Fill fills an enclosed area with a gradient ranging from the secondary to the background color.

 Texture Fill fills an enclosed area with a bitmap text.

The last group of painting tools is found in the flyout of the Clone icon, the last icon on the toolbox:

 Clone duplicates painting or drawing strokes elsewhere within a picture, or applies them to a duplicate of a picture. As you draw, a clone is produced.

 Impressionist Clone clones colors of an area in a Van Gogh style.

 Pointillist Clone clones colors of an area of many dots.

Drawing Tools

The drawing tools create lines, curves, ellipses, rectangles, or squares, which may be filled or hollow. These 12 tools are found in two groups.

The first group is in the flyout of the Line tool icon:

Line lets you draw straight lines by establishing start and end points.

 Curve lets you create a curve by setting two points and then dragging the line between them to form the curve.

 Pen lets you draw smoothly and evenly in freehand mode.

The second group of drawing tools is found in the flyout of the Rectangle tool icon:

18

 Hollow Box creates hollow, unfilled rectangles or squares.

 Hollow Rounded Box creates hollow, unfilled squares and rectangles with rounded corners.

 Hollow Ellipse creates hollow, unfilled circles and ellipses.

 Hollow Polygon creates hollow, unfilled shapes having up to 200 rounded corners.

 Filled Box creates a square or rectangle with a border of the current primary color and filled with the current secondary color.

 Filled Rounded Box creates a square or rectangle with rounded corners, having a border of the primary color and filled with the secondary color.

 Filled Ellipse creates a circle or ellipse with a border of the primary color and filled with the secondary color.

 Filled Polygon creates a shape with up to 200 sides, having a border of the primary color and filled with the secondary color.

Text Tool
There is one text tool:

 Text allows you to type text onto the picture.

Experiment with CorelPHOTO-PAINT!

This introduction only touches on the numerous capabilities found in CorelPHOTO-PAINT!. The program contains many more surprises. Continue to experiment with it, and you will be impressed with its capabilities.

Using the ensemble of Corel products, you can DRAW, TRACE, CHART, PAINT, and finally, SHOW presentations in a professional and stunning manner.

COREL DRAW! 4

CHAPTER

COREL DRAW! 4

19

INTRODUCING CORELMOVE!

CorelMOVE!, which is new with CorelDRAW! 4, is a complete multimedia, animation program. With CorelMOVE! you can create simple or complex animations using graphics created in CorelDRAW!, you can record and edit sounds, and you can import graphics and sounds from other programs to use in your animations.

This chapter introduces CorelMOVE! by briefly discussing the basics of animation, how to get started using CorelMOVE!, and how to use its principal tools.

Animation Basics

Traditionally, animations are created by drawing a series of individual images, called *frames,* that are viewed in sequence. Each frame contains a number of cels of different objects. *Cels* are the individual images that make up an animated object. For example, to animate a walking figure, each frame would contain a cel of the figure with its legs and body in a slightly different position. First one leg would move to the front, then the other. The arms would be drawn in a similar manner. A series of ten cels might be needed to show a complete cycle of movement. To create a longer animated sequence, these same ten cels would be shown over and over again. For example, an animation 100 frames long would have the same ten cels of the figure repeated ten times. Each object in the animation has its own set of cels.

Objects in an animation are either *actors* or *props.* The difference between actors and props is that props are single objects, with only one cel, not a series of cels. This means that props cannot be animated. A chair and a tree could be examples of props. If you wanted to have a tree moving in the wind, however, the tree would have to be an actor, because it would be animated. Props can be moved around in an animation, but in each frame the prop will be identical in appearance. In other words, it would not be animated.

Actors can be either *single-cel* or *multiple-cel.* The walking figure mentioned previously is an example of a multiple-cel actor. Multiple-cel actors are used when an object changes its shape or appearance in an animation. A single-cel actor is similar to a prop; both have only one cel. Single-cel actors can be combined with multiple-cel actors to conserve resources in an animation. For example, to show a ball bouncing, a single-cel actor could be used to show the ball while it's in the air. When the ball strikes the ground, a multiple-cel actor is used to show the ball compressing and then expanding as it bounces.

Both actors and props can change position in an animation. This movement is independent of the animation of the object. If the walking figure actor is placed in the same place in each successive frame of an animation, for example, the figure will appear to be walking without moving. The feeling of movement is created either by having the actor move across the screen, or by having other objects (actors or props) move in relation to the walking figure.

You control how actors and props move in an animation by defining *paths* for the objects to follow. A path has one point in each frame of the animation, and each actor or prop has its own path. When the points of a path are close together, movement is relatively slow; when the points are farther apart, movement becomes more rapid. For example, the path for the bouncing ball would have the points of its path close together at the top and bottom of its bouncing motion, where the ball would naturally be traveling slower. In the middle of its path, where the ball is either rising or falling, the points would be farther apart, because the ball would be traveling faster.

With CorelMOVE! you can control all of these animation attributes. In the following sections you will learn more about CorelMOVE!'s animation tools.

Getting Started with CorelMOVE!

To start CorelMOVE! from Windows, double-click on the CorelMOVE! icon. After a few moments, the initial CorelMOVE! screen will be displayed.

Only the File menu is available when CorelMOVE! is started. In the File menu you can either open an existing animation file or create a new file. To become familiar with the CorelMOVE! menus and screen elements, you must first open a new file.

19

1. Select the File menu and choose New. The Select Name For New File dialog box will be displayed.

2. Click on OK to accept the default filename, UNTITLED.CMV. The main CorelMOVE! screen, shown in Figure 19-1, is displayed.

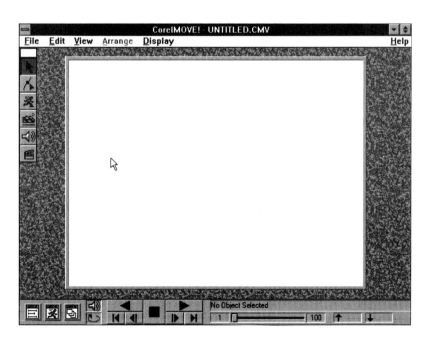

CorelMOVE!
main screen
Figure 19-1.

CorelMOVE! Screen

In the center of the CorelMOVE! screen is the Animation window. This is the work area for building and displaying your animations. Both the height and width of the window can be adjusted. The Animation window displays one frame of your animation while you are working on it. It is also where your animation is displayed when it is played. At the top of the screen is the title bar, and below that, the menu bar. To the left is the toolbox. At the bottom of the screen is the Control Panel. Each of these elements is described in the following sections.

CorelMOVE! Menus

At the top of the screen, below the title bar, is the menu bar, which contains six menus. The File menu contains the options for creating, opening, and saving files, and importing and exporting files to use in your animations. Edit offers basic editing features, such as Copy and Paste, along with options for editing CorelMOVE! objects. The View menu allows you to play animations and also view them in single-frame mode. Like CorelDRAW! drawings, CorelMOVE! animations consist of layers; the Arrange menu is used to control the layers in an animation. The Display menu opens the CorelMOVE! roll-up menus and playback options. The Help menu contains standard help options.

Many of the menu options are also available using the toolbox and Control Panel. From CorelMOVE!'s Display menu, you can open two unique and important dialog boxes: Animation Information and Playback Options.

Animation Information Dialog Box

Selecting Animation Info in the Display menu opens the Animation Information dialog box, shown in Figure 19-2. This dialog box presents information about your animation, such as the number of actors, props, sounds, and cues used, and allows you to adjust certain attributes of your animation. The width and height of the animation window can be adjusted using the Width and Height numeric entry boxes. This allows you to adjust the size of the animation to the intended output device, such as video tape or computer monitor. The number of frames in an animation can be set from a range of 1 to 5000 frames. The speed of the animation can be set from a range of .25 to 60 frames per second (fps). Grid Spacing functions much like grid spacing and Snap To Grid in CorelDRAW!, except that a list of preset values from 5 to 200 pixels is presented in a drop-down list box.

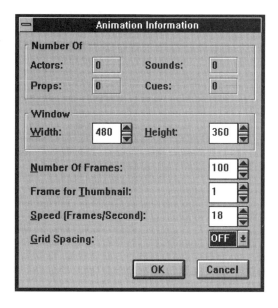

Animation
Information
dialog box
Figure 19-2.

19

Playback Options Dialog Box

Also in the Display menu is the Playback Options command. Selecting
Playback Options displays the Playback Options dialog box, which is shown
in Figure 19-3. This dialog box allows you to control how to stop the
animation, either by a mouse click or by pressing Ctrl-Break. It also allows
you to display or hide the toolbox, menu bar, and cursor, and to enable the
playing of sounds included with the animation. If the Auto Replay check
box is not checked, the animation runs through once and then stops; if it is
checked, the animation runs continuously.

CorelMOVE! Toolbox

The CorelMOVE! toolbox has some similarities to the CorelDRAW! toolbox.
The first tool in the toolbox, the Pick tool, is used for selecting objects, like
the Pick tool in CorelDRAW!. The remaining five tools are for working with
specific parts of your animation.

Path Tool

The second tool in the toolbox, the Path tool, is used to create and modify
the paths that actors and props follow. This tool is similar to the Shaping
tool in CorelDRAW!, but here it controls the movement of objects in your

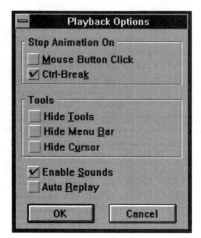

Playback
Options
dialog box
Figure 19-3.

animation. When the Path tool is selected, the Path Edit roll-up is displayed, as shown here:

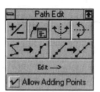

The Allow Adding Points check box is selected when you want to add points to a path using the mouse. To add a point, make sure this check box is selected, then click on the location in the path for the new point.

The Scale Path button (+/−), in the upper-left corner of the Path Edit roll-up, is also used to change the number of points in a path. The path will have the same starting and ending points, but the object's movement will be distributed over the new number of points. Selecting the Scale Path button opens the Scale Path dialog box, as shown here:

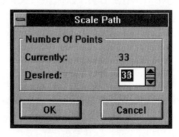

Selecting the Path Point Information button, located next to the Scale Path
button, opens the Point Information dialog box shown here:

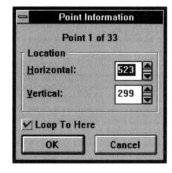

19

The location of a point on a path can be set by using the Horizontal and
Vertical numeric entry boxes in this dialog box, or it can be set directly,
using the mouse to drag the point to the desired location. When the Loop
To Here check box is selected, the selected point becomes the *loop point,* and
the object will move from the end point of the path to the loop point. The
loop point does not have to be the start point of the path. If a point in the
middle of the path is set as the loop point, the object will follow the path
from the start point to the end point. It will then jump to the loop point
and continue to the end point, where it will jump to the loop point again.
When there is no loop point in a path, the object will move along the path
once and then disappear from the animation.

The next two buttons on the Path Edit roll-up are used to mirror the selected
path vertically and horizontally.

The Smoothing button, the left button in the second row, is used to make an
angular path smoother. Repeated application to a path will make the path
flatter. Next to the Smoothing button is the Distribution button, which is
used to distribute the points in a path more evenly. This has the effect of
making the speed of an object's movement along the path more consistent.

The Edit command button opens the Edit Path menu shown here:

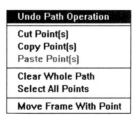

This menu contains the familiar editing commands of Undo, Cut, Copy, and Paste, which can be applied to individual points, a selected group of points, or the entire path. Copy and Paste can be used to duplicate a range of points. For example, to have a ball bounce across the screen, the path for one complete bounce would be created, then copied and pasted so that the start point of the second bounce was also the end point of the first bounce.

The Move Frame With Point command attaches the path's object to the current point. As you move the point, the object moves with it. This allows you to position your object along its path more precisely.

Actor Tool

Selecting the Actor tool, located below the Path tool, opens the New Actor dialog box, shown in Figure 19-4. When the Create New option button is selected, the Object Type list box displays the available programs you can use to create a new actor. If you select an application other than CorelMOVE!, that application is opened. The object that you create in the application will then be embedded in the CorelMOVE! animation file.

An existing object can be placed in your animation file by clicking on the Create from File option button in the New Actor dialog box, as shown in Figure 19-5. In this case, you would enter the path and filename in the File text box, or use the Browse command button to locate the appropriate file.

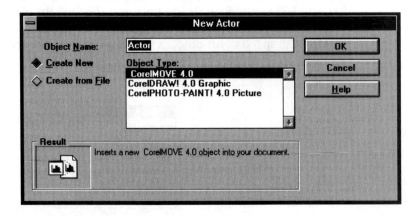

New Actor
dialog box
Figure 19-4.

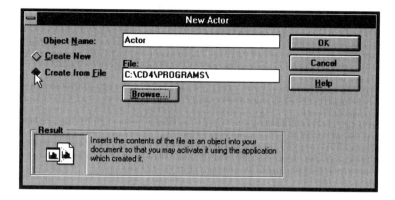

New Actor
dialog box
with Create
from File
selected
Figure 19-5.

When Create New is selected and CorelMOVE! is the selected application,
clicking on OK opens the Paint toolbox and Paint Document window
shown here:

19

The tools in the Paint palette are similar to the tools available in
CorelPHOTO-PAINT!. A brief summary of each tool follows.

 Marquee selects a rectangular section of the image.

 Lasso selects an irregular section of the image.

 Pencil draws freehand lines.

Brush draws with the current pattern and brush shape.

 Paint Bucket fills the selected object with the current color and pattern.

 Spray Can sprays the current color and pattern into an area, similar to an airbrush.

 Text adds text to an object. All the fonts available with CorelDRAW! can be used with CorelMOVE!.

 Eraser removes the parts of images it is dragged over.

 Color Pick-up changes an existing color in an image to the current color.

 Line draws straight lines.

 Rectangle draws rectangles with square corners.

 Rounded Rectangle draws rectangles with rounded corners.

 Oval draws circles and ovals.

 Curve draws free-form shapes.

 Polygon draws polygons with irregular sides.

Foreground Color Selector opens a pop-up palette for selecting the foreground color.

Background Color Selector opens a pop-up palette for selecting the background color.

 Pattern Selector opens a pop-up palette with the available patterns.

Line Width Selector selects the current line width.

Recent Color Pick-up displays the 12 most recently selected colors.

19

 Cel Cycle Arrows cycle through the cels of a multiple-cel actor. The box above the Cel Cycle Arrows displays the number of the current cel and the total number of cels.

Three menus are available for working with your animations in the Paint Document window: File, Edit, and Options. The File and Edit menus contain the familiar commands for file handling and image editing. The Edit menu also contains the Registration command, which is used to define a *registration point* for each actor. The actor will always be the set distance and direction from its registration point. It is the registration point that moves along a path. For example, if you want your animation to have two figures walking side by side, you could either create a separate path for each actor, or you could use one path and offset the registration points for each actor.

The Options menu, shown in the following illustration, offers special effects that can be applied to the actor being created or edited. Zoom allows you to zoom in for detail work. Font opens a dialog box to access all the fonts available with CorelDRAW!.

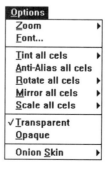

The next group of Options commands apply special effects to all of the object's cels, or to a selected area of one cel. Tint blends the selected color with either the current foreground or background color. Anti-Alias is used to smooth the edges of objects by blending the colors along the edge of an object. Rotate rotates the object either clockwise or counterclockwise in one-degree steps. Mirror flips an object either horizontally or vertically. Scale is used to change the size of an object.

Ink effects are adjusted with the Transparent and Opaque commands. When an object is *opaque,* any object underneath it is invisible; when it is *transparent,* any object underneath it is visible.

The Onion Skin command duplicates the traditional method of creating cels for animated objects. *Onion skin* refers to a type of translucent paper animators use to draw on. Each successive cel would be placed on top of the previous cel. The animator could then make sure each cel was properly aligned with the preceding cel. Selecting the Onion Skin command shows the preceding or following cel of the actor behind the current cel. The onion skin cel will be lighter than the current cel.

Prop Tool

Selecting the Prop tool opens a dialog box identical to the New Actor dialog box, with the same options for creating objects. The title bar will contain "New Prop," however. When Create New and CorelMOVE! are selected, a Paint toolbox and display window identical to the New Actor Paint toolbox and display window are displayed. The only difference between the Actor and Prop Paint toolbox is that the Prop Paint tools do not include the Cel Cycle Arrows and display, since a prop cannot have multiple cels.

Sound Tool

If you have a sound board, such as a Creative Labs Sound Blaster card or Microsoft Windows Sound System, you can record, edit, and play sounds with your animations. Selecting the Sound tool opens the New Wave dialog box. You can either select an existing sound or record a new one. Sounds can be edited using the Wave Editor, accessed from the Timelines roll-up.

Cue Tool

The Cue tool, located at the bottom of the toolbox, controls one of CorelMOVE!'s more advanced features—the ability to control the playback of an animation with external events (such as a mouse click). You could use this in a situation where the presenter wants to stop the show to make comments. The Cue Information dialog box, shown in Figure 19-6, is displayed when the Cue tool is selected. At the top of the Cue Information

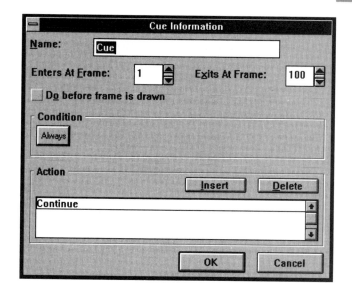

Cue
Information
dialog box
Figure 19-6.

dialog box is the Name text box. This allows you to name a cue and then reference the cue by that name. Below the Name text box are two numeric entry boxes: Enters At Frame and Exits At Frame. The values in these boxes determine the portion of the animation for which the cue will be in effect. This may be the entire animation, or just a portion of it. The "Do before frame is drawn" check box is selected if you want the action defined by the cue activated before the frame is displayed on the screen.

The section labeled "Condition" is used to define the event or events that trigger the action defined by the cue. The appearance of the Condition section will vary depending on the conditions selected. When you press the Condition button (now "Always"), you'll see this submenu:

Depending on whether you choose Wait for or If then else conditions, a different set of buttons will be displayed. The three conditions, shown in Figure 19-6, are as follows:

✦ *Always* The action is always executed without any other condition being met.

✦ *Wait for* The animation stops and waits for a condition to occur.

✦ *If then else* When the If condition is met, the then action will occur. When the If condition is not met, the else action occurs.

A second list box is displayed if you select the Wait for and If then else conditions. It shows three additional options: Time Delay, Mouse Click on, and Key Down.

✦ *Time Delay* The animation continues after a preset delay. A third list box allows you to enter a time value.

✦ *Mouse Click on*   The animation waits for a mouse click. A third drop-down list box displays the options for Mouse Click:

Anything Any mouse click will meet the condition.

Actor Named The mouse pointer must be on the named actor when clicked.

Prop Named The mouse pointer must be on the named prop when clicked.

If Actor Named or Prop Named is selected, a fourth list box is displayed which allows you to select an actor or prop from a list.

✦ *Key Down* The animation waits for a specific key to be pressed. The key is selected in the Choose A Key dialog box which is displayed when Key Down is chosen.

The Action section at the bottom of the Cue Information dialog box is used to establish the action that will occur when the defined condition is met. The options displayed vary depending on the conditions selected. When If then else is selected, actions can be set independently for each condition. The Action list box displays the selected action. Choices are made by pointing on an action in the Action list box and pressing the mouse button, as shown here:

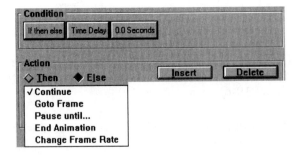

A drop-down menu is displayed, with the following choices:

✦ *Continue* The animation continues.

✦ *Goto Frame* The animation continues from the selected frame.

✦ *Pause until* The animation stops until a condition is met.

✦ *End Animation* The animation ends.

✦ *Change Frame Rate* The playback rate of the animation is changed.

You highlight the option you want and click on Insert or Delete to select or remove an action.

CorelMOVE! Control Panel

Located at the bottom of the CorelMOVE! screen is the Control Panel, shown in the following illustration. It provides controls for the playback of your animations and displays information about them.

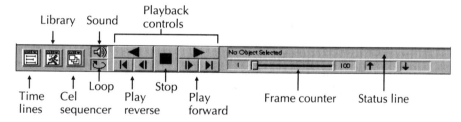

Playback Controls

The playback controls are the group of command buttons that look like the playback controls on a VCR, and they are used in the same manner as VCR controls. In the center (the black square) is the Stop button, on the right side is the Play Forward button, and on the left is the Play Reverse button. Below the Play buttons are two additional control buttons. Under the Play Forward button are the Step Forward button, which advances the animation in single-frame increments, and the Last Frame button, which advances the animation to the last frame. Similar buttons on the left side step through the animation one frame at a time in reverse and jump to the first frame.

To the left of the playback controls are the Sound and Loop icons. The Sound icon (on top) turns the sound on or off, and the Loop icon, when selected, plays your animation continuously.

To the right of the playback controls is the status line, which displays information about the animation or selected objects. Below the status line is the frame counter. A slider is used to move through the animation. The left side of the slider displays the current frame number; the right side displays the total number of frames. Two additional display boxes are visible to the right of the frame counter. When an object is selected, the left box (with the upward-pointing arrow) displays the number of the frame in which the selected object first appears in the animation; the other box displays the number of the last frame in which the object appears.

Icons for the Timelines, Library, and Cel Sequencer roll-ups are located on the left side of the Control Panel. You will learn about their functions after you open a sample CorelMOVE! animation.

Opening a CorelMOVE! Animation

If you have installed your CorelMOVE! sample files, you will find a file called SAMPLE.CMV in your MOVE\SAMPLES directory. Open the SAMPLE.CMV file now with these instructions:

1. Select the File menu and choose Open. The Open dialog box will be displayed. Display the MOVE\SAMPLES directory.

2. Double-click on SAMPLE.CMV to open the sample animation file. In a few moments your screen should look like Figure 19-7.

Before continuing, play the animation by clicking once on the Play button (to the right of Stop). Remember, if the Loop button is selected, the animation will play continuously. Either deselect the Loop button to stop the animation, or click on the Stop button, and then click on the First Frame button to jump to the first frame of the animation. In the next section you will learn more about how the different elements of an animation are combined to create a finished movie.

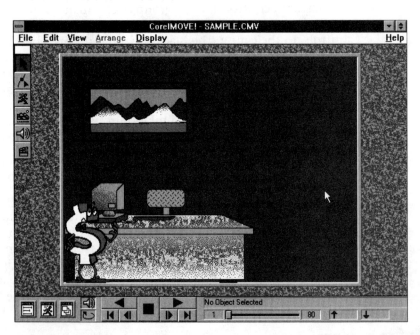

First frame of
SAMPLE.CMV
animation
Figure 19-7.

Timelines Roll-Up

The Timelines roll-up, shown in the following illustration, is used to edit
actors and props and their actions or placement at specific times in your
animations. The features of the Timelines roll-up should look familiar to
you. At the top of the roll-up are the Actor, Prop, Sound, and Cue icons.
These control which elements will be displayed in the list box below them.
Objects with a check mark are displayed in the animation window; if you
deselect an object by clicking on its check mark, it will be removed from the
animation window.

19

When you double-click on an actor, the Actor Information dialog box,
shown in Figure 19-8, is displayed. The dialog box allows you to edit when
the actor enters and exits the animation, its starting position, and path
starting point. Clicking on the Edit Actor command button opens the Actor
Paint toolbox and display window (which you saw in the "Actor Tool"
section), with the selected actor displayed.

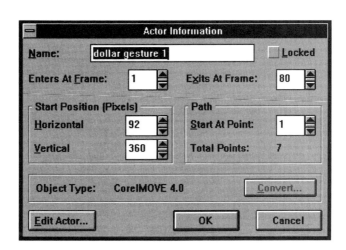

Actor
Information
dialog box
Figure 19-8.

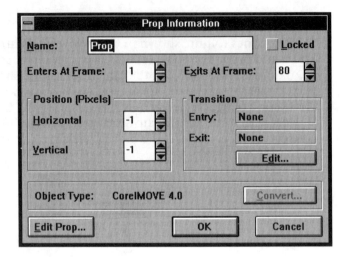

Prop
Information
dialog box
Figure 19-9.

When you double-click on a prop, the Prop Information dialog box, shown
in Figure 19-9, is displayed. This dialog box is similar to the Actor
Information dialog box. Clicking on the Edit command button in the
Transition section of the dialog box opens the Transitions for Prop dialog
box, shown in Figure 19-10.

The Transitions for Prop dialog box controls how props enter and exit an
animation. Separate transitions are established for the prop's entry and exit.
Experiment by selecting transitions from the Entry and Exit list boxes, and
clicking on Preview.

Library Roll-Up

You can create libraries (or files) of actors, props, and sounds to use in your
animations through the Library roll-up, shown here:

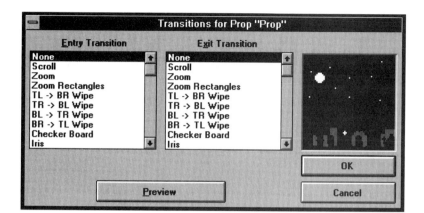

Transitions for
Prop dialog
box
Figure 19-10.

The Library flyout menu is opened by clicking on the right-pointing arrow underneath the roll-up arrow. The menu commands allow you to open a library, create a new library, or modify an existing one. Objects can be added, deleted, or renamed. The display box will display either a list of objects in the library or an image of the selected object.

Cel Sequencer Roll-Up

You use the Cel Sequencer, shown in the following illustration, to control how the cels of an actor are used in your animation. You can control the order in which cels are shown, and apply effects to individual cels or groups of cels.

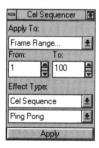

In the Apply To drop-down list box at the top of the Cel Sequencer roll-up, you select the frames the effect will apply to. This can be all the frames, an individual frame, or a group of frames. The Effect Type drop-down list box is used to select the type of effect to apply to the selected frames. Effects include scaling the size of the cel (useful for creating the impression of an actor coming toward or moving away from the viewer) and setting the cel display sequence.

APPENDIX

CORELDRAW! 4

A

INSTALLING CORELDRAW! 4

This appendix guides you through the process of installing CorelDRAW! 4. If you or someone else has installed your software already, you do not need to use this appendix. If you have an earlier version of CorelDRAW!, many of the steps are the same, but you should be aware that this discussion describes CorelDRAW! 4.

You must install Windows 3.1 or later and ensure that it is working properly before you install CorelDRAW! 4. Refer to the documentation that came with your Windows software for full instructions on installing Windows correctly.

System Requirements

Before you begin the installation procedure, review the hardware and software requirements explained in this section. You can help ensure trouble-free operation of CorelDRAW! 4 by checking to see that your system meets all of the requirements.

Computer

Your computer must be based on an 80386, 80486, or compatible microprocessor with a hard disk drive and at least one floppy disk drive (an 80286-based computer will not work).

Memory

You must have a minimum of 4MB (megabytes) of memory, and 8MB is strongly recommended. All memory above 1MB should be configured as *extended* memory. You should be running HIMEM.SYS, which comes with Windows 3.1 or DOS 5 or DOS 6. You can find out how much memory you have by exiting Windows, changing to your Windows directory, and typing **msd**. By clicking on Memory, you can see your memory usage and availability. Your Windows and DOS manuals, as well as your dealer or internal company support people, can help you change or add to your memory. Increasing the memory size beyond 4MB will speed the running of both Windows and CorelDRAW! and give you more flexibility in what you can do.

Hard Disk Space

Your hard disk must have approximately 37MB of space available for a full installation of CorelDRAW!, plus an additional 10MB for the Windows swap file, and another 10MB for the storage of temporary files. The amount of disk space for the Windows swap file may be permanently assigned and not showing as available space. You can determine this from within Windows by opening the Control Panel from the Program Manager, clicking on the 386 Enhanced icon, and then on the Virtual Memory button.

If you do not have this much space available on your hard drive, you can perform a Custom installation and selectively install the programs, features, and graphic sample files you think you will use. The amount of disk space that you will use for storage of CorelDRAW! files will be displayed.

Monitor and Display Adapter

You should have a color or paper-white VGA graphics monitor and VGA adapter that is supported by Windows 3.1, with at least a 640 by 480 resolution. A color monitor and higher-resolution video display adapter are highly recommended to take full advantage of CorelDRAW!'s full-color mode.

Drawing Device

You must have a mouse or another drawing device, such as a graphics tablet, in order to run CorelDRAW!. If you use a graphics tablet instead of a mouse, choose one that has the activation button on the side rather than on the top. This type of design gives you the best results because it minimizes unwanted movement on the screen.

This book assumes that most users work with a mouse instead of some other type of drawing device. References to a mouse therefore apply to any drawing device.

Output Device

A

Using the Print and Export commands in the File menu, you can produce your CorelDRAW! images on paper (standard printers) or in formats used by film recorders and slide generation equipment. Appendix B discusses the file formats needed to output to 35mm slide generation or presentation equipment in greater detail. If you normally print your images to paper, however, you will achieve the best results with the following types of printers:

✦ PostScript printers, imagesetters, PostScript controller boards, and PostScript plug-in cartridges licensed by Adobe Systems

✦ HP LaserJet series or 100 percent compatible printers

✦ HP PaintJet and DeskJet printers

For more information on printers, see Chapter 13.

Although Windows supports other printers as well, many of these cannot reproduce complex CorelDRAW! images exactly as expected. In addition, a few of the most complex CorelDRAW! features can only be produced on PostScript printers.

Operating System and Windows Requirements

CorelDRAW! 4 requires Windows 3.1, and the combination of DOS 6 and Windows 3.1 is recommended to make full use of CorelDRAW!'s extended memory and OLE capabilities. CorelDRAW! 4 will work with earlier releases of DOS (3.3 and above), but you won't have the high memory optimization and other features of DOS 5 or 6.

Installing the Software

The SETUP program for CorelDRAW! 4 installs CorelDRAW! program files, fonts, sample files, and clip art onto your hard disk. Depending on your choice of installation method (Full or Custom), you can install some or all of the other eight programs that make up the total CorelDRAW! 4 ensemble: CorelDRAW!, CorelCHART!, CorelSHOW!, CorelPHOTO-PAINT!, CorelTRACE!, CorelMOVE!, CorelMOSAIC!, and CCAPTURE.

The directions that the SETUP program gives you vary according to which installation method you choose. The Full installation method requires the least interaction on your part and is recommended for new users of CorelDRAW!. If disk space is a concern, you might do a minimum Custom installation and then later selectively add other CorelDRAW! programs, again using the Custom installation method, as your needs and disk space allow.

Before you begin, decide on the name of the hard disk directory in which you want to install CorelDRAW! 4, and have the Windows Program Manager on your screen. The following example assumes you will perform a Full installation.

1. Insert CorelDRAW! Disk 1 into the floppy drive from which you want to install CorelDRAW!. This book assumes that you are installing the software from drive A, but you can use any drive.

2. Click on the Program Manager's File menu, choose Run, and type **a: setup** in the Command Line text entry box. (If you are installing CorelDRAW! from a different floppy drive, type that drive name instead of **a:**.) If you are installing from a CD-ROM, type **e:\setup2**, where **e:** is replaced with your CD-ROM drive letter. Press Enter or click on OK.

3. After a short period, the initial installation window appears on your screen. Press Enter or click on Continue to proceed with the installation.

4. Type your name, press Tab, enter your serial number which appears on a pair of self-adhesive labels in the envelope with the disks, and press Enter or click on Continue.

5. The next window provides buttons for the two installation methods, Full Install (the default) and Custom Install. If you are unsure of your installation method, you can choose either button and explore some of its features before committing to the corresponding method. For example, choosing the Custom installation method accesses its menu of choices. If you decide not to continue with the Custom installation, click on the Back button to return to the window with the two installation buttons.

6. To continue with the Full installation method, press Enter or click on the Full button. You are now given the choice of installing CorelDRAW!

to the C:\COREL40 directory on your hard drive. If this is satisfactory, press [Enter] or click on Continue. If you want the CorelDRAW! files copied to another destination, backspace over this default path and type your path name in the text entry box. Press [Enter] or click on Continue to continue with the installation.

7. Choose which files you want to install from the options that are presented. When you are done press [Enter] or click Continue.

   You are next told that CorelDRAW! is ready to be installed. If you wish to precede, click on Install or press [Enter].

8. CorelDRAW! now begins copying files to the destination you established in step 6. When prompted, insert CorelDRAW! Disk 2 in drive A. Press [Enter] or click on OK. Continue to insert the remainder of the installation disks when prompted. Depending on the speed of your computer, the installation process will take approximately 30 minutes.

9. SETUP finishes by creating a Program Manager application group called Corel 4.

A

This completes the automatic installation procedure.

You should decide whether you want to make automatic backup copies of your drawings when you run CorelDRAW!. If you do not, use Windows Notepad to edit the [Config] section of your CORELDRW.INI file, which is located in the CONFIG subdirectory under the directory where you installed CorelDRAW!. Change a line in the section that reads "MakeBackupWhenSave=1." If you do not want CorelDRAW! to make backup copies of your illustrations, edit this line so that it reads "MakeBackupWhenSave=0." Look at other items in this file to see if you want to make any other changes. When you are done with your changes, select the File menu, choose Save, and then select File and Exit to close Notepad.

Creating a Directory

You need a directory in which to store the drawings created with CorelDRAW!. When you installed Windows and CorelDRAW!, directories were automatically created in which the program, font, and other files that came with Windows and CorelDRAW! are stored. While you could use these directories to store your CorelDRAW! drawings, it is unwise to do so for two reasons. First, when you get an update to Windows or CorelDRAW! you will want to remove the old program files and replace them with the new ones. The easiest way to do that is to erase the entire directory with a single command. If your drawing files were in the directory at the time, you would lose them. Second, if you want to do some file maintenance with either DOS or the Windows File Manager, the large number of product-related files will make looking for drawing files difficult.

Therefore, create a new directory now to hold your drawing files. You can name your directory anything you want as long as the name is from one to eight characters long and does not include the following characters:

+ ; , * ?

This book will use DRAWINGS as the example directory in which drawings will be stored. Your directory can be a full directory branching off the root directory, or a subdirectory under either the Windows or the CorelDRAW! directory. For simplicity, this book will assume that the DRAWINGS directory is a full directory off the root directory. Its path then is \DRAWINGS. Use these instructions to create this directory either from the DOS prompt or from the Windows File Manager.

At the DOS prompt:

1. Type **cd** and press [Enter] to make sure you are in the root directory.
2. Type **md\ drawings** and press [Enter] to create the new DRAWINGS directory.

From Windows:

1. Double-click on the File Manager icon located in the Program Manager's Main application group.
2. Select the File menu and choose the Create Directory option.
3. Type **c:\drawings** in the Name text entry box. Press [Enter] or click on OK to create the new DRAWINGS directory.

The only remaining step is to start CorelDRAW! and begin using it. Do that now by following the directions in Chapter 1.

COREL DRAW! 4

APPENDIX

B
IMPORTING AND EXPORTING FILES

As more graphics applications for IBM-compatible computers become available, the need to transfer files among different applications becomes more acute. Connectivity, or the ability of a software program to import and export data in various file formats, is rapidly becoming a requirement for graphics applications. Whether your work involves desktop publishing, technical illustration, original art, or graphic design, it is essential to be able to export your CorelDRAW! graphics to other programs, to import clip art, and to polish your work from other programs.

CorelDRAW! offers you two different methods of connectivity. In Chapter 10, you learned how to use the Windows Clipboard to transfer files between CorelDRAW! and other applications that run under Microsoft Windows. The Windows Clipboard is not your only option for transferring files, however. CorelDRAW! has its own independent import and export utilities specifically for transferring data between different graphics formats. These utilities allow you to import graphics from and export them to a variety of drawing, painting, desktop publishing, and word processing applications, even though some of these programs may not run under Windows. The use of the Import and Export commands in CorelDRAW! is the subject of this chapter.

Bitmap Versus Object-Oriented Graphics

CorelDRAW! imports from and exports to both bitmap and object-oriented applications, as well as text files. It is important to have a clear understanding of the differences between bitmap and object-oriented graphics. You then have a firm basis for choosing how and when to import and export graphics files.

There are many different graphics file formats, but only two kinds of graphics: bitmap, also known as *pixel-based,* and vector, also known as *object-oriented.* The differences between these two kinds of graphics involve the kinds of software applications that produce them, the way the computer stores them in memory, and the ease with which you can edit them.

Paint programs and scanners produce bitmap images by establishing a grid of pixels, the smallest visual unit that the computer can address, on the screen. These applications create images by altering the colors or attributes of each individual pixel. This way of storing images makes inefficient use of memory, however. The size of an image (the number of pixels it occupies) is fixed once it is created, and is dependent on the resolution of the display adapter on the computer where the image first took shape. As a result, finished bitmap images are difficult to edit when you transfer them from one application to another. If you increase the size of a finished bitmap image, you can see unsightly white spaces and jagged edges. If you greatly decrease the size of a finished bitmap image, parts of the image may smudge because of the compression involved. Distortion can also occur if you transfer bitmap graphics to another computer that has a different display resolution.

Object-oriented graphics, on the other hand, have none of these limitations. They are produced by drawing applications such as CorelDRAW! and are stored in the computer's memory as a series of numbers (not pixels) that describe how to redraw the image on the screen. Since this method of storing information has nothing to do with the resolution of a given display adapter, line art is considered to be *device-independent*; no matter what computer you use to create an object-oriented graphic, you can stretch, scale, and resize it flexibly without distortion. Object-oriented graphics also tend to create smaller files than bitmap graphics because the computer does not have to "memorize" the attributes of individual pixels.

How can you use each type of graphic in CorelDRAW!? As demonstrated in Appendix C, you can import bitmap images in order to trace them and turn them into object-oriented graphics. Alternatively, you can simply import them and incorporate them into an existing drawing. Your options for editing an imported bitmap image do not end with the editing capabilities available in CorelDRAW!, however. When you need your finished work to issue from a paint application, or if you prefer to polish your artwork in pixel format, you can export CorelDRAW! graphics back to a paint program, such as CorelPHOTO-PAINT!.

If you work with other object-oriented drawing and design programs, you can import line art in order to enhance it with advanced features that only CorelDRAW! offers. You can introduce clip art and edit it flexibly. When you are finished editing, you can export CorelDRAW! artwork back to your favorite object-oriented application or to the desktop publishing application of your choice. You can even export your CorelDRAW! graphics to a format that film recorders and imagesetters will be able to use to create professional-looking presentation materials.

B

CorelDRAW! supports an ever-growing number of file formats that include both pixel-based and object-oriented graphics. Table B–1 lists all of the file formats you can import into CorelDRAW! 4, while Table B–2 lists the file format to which you can export CorelDRAW! 4 graphics. Both tables list for each file format, the file type (bitmap or "Pixel," object-oriented or "Line," or "Text") and the file extension.

File Format	File Type	Extension
Adobe Illustrator 1.1, 88, 3.0	Line	.AI, .EPS
Ami Pro 2.0, 3.0	Text	.SAM
ASCII Text	Text	.TXT
AutoCAD	Line	.DXF
Autodesk FLIC Thumbnail	Line	.FLI
CompuServe Bitmap	Pixel	.GIF
Computer Graphics Metafile	Line	.CGM

CorelDRAW!4
Import File
Formats
Table B-1.

File Format	File Type	Extension
CorelDRAW!	Line	.CDR
CorelPHOTO-PAINT!	Pixel	.PCX
CorelDRAW!/CHART!/SHOW! Thumbnail	Line	.CDR, .PAT, .CCH, .SHW
CorelTRACE!	Line	.EPS
EPS Thumbnail	Line	.AI, .EPS, .PS
Excel For Windows 3.0, 4.0	Text	.XLS
GEM Artline	Line	.GEM
HP Plotter	Line	.PLT
IBM PIF	Line	.PIF
Joint Photographers Experts Group(JPEG)	Pixel	.JPG,.JFF, .JTF, .CMP
Kodak Photo-CD	Pixel	.PCD
Lotus Pic	Line	.PIC
Lotus 1-2-3 1A, 2.0	Text	.WKS, .WK2
Lotus 1-2-3 3.0 and for Windows	Text	.WK3
Macintosh PICT	Line	.PCT
Mac Write II 1.0, 1.1	Text	Any
Micrografx Designer 2.x, 3.x	Line	.DRW
Microsoft Rich Text	Text	.RFT
Microsoft Word 5.0, 5.5	Text	.DOC
Microsoft Word for Mac 4.0, 5.0	Text	Any
Word for Windows 1.x, 2.x	Text	.DOC
Targa Bitmap	Pixel	.TGA,.VDA, .ICB, .VST
TIFF 5.0 Bitmap	Pixel	.TIF
Windows Bitmap	Pixel	.BMP
Windows Metafile	Line	.WMF
WordPerfect Graphics	Line	.WPG
WordPerfect 5.0, 5.1, and for Windows	Text	Any

CorelDRAW!4 Import File Formats (cont.)
Table B-1.

File Format	File Type	Extension
Adobe Illustrator 88, 3.0	Line	.AI, .EPS
Adobe Type 1 Font	Line	.PFB
AutoCAD	Line	.DXF
CompuServe Bitmap	Pixel	.GIF
Computer Graphics Metafile	Line	.CGM
CorelPHOTO-PAINT!	Pixel	.PCX
Encapsulated PostScript	Line	.EPS
GEM Artline	Line	.GEM
HP Plotter HPGL	Line	.PLT
IBM	Line	.PIF
JPEG Bitmap	Pixel	.JPG, .JFF, .JTF, .CMP
Macintosh PICT	Line	.PCT
Matrix/Imapro SCODL	Line	.SCD
Microsoft Rich Text	Text	.RTF
OS/2 Bitmap	Pixel	.BMP
PostScript	Line	.EPS
Targa Bitmap	Pixel	.TGA, .VDA, .ICB, .VST
TIFF 5.0 Bitmap	Pixel	.TIF
TIFF 6.0 Four Color	Pixel	.SEP
TrueType Font	Line	.TTF
Windows Bitmap	Pixel	.BMP
Windows Metafile	Line	.WMF
WordPerfect Graphics	Line	.WPG

CorelDRAW!4
Export File
Formats
Table B-2.

B

Using Help for Importing and Exporting

You can use CorelDRAW! Help to get detailed technical information on the different formats available for importing and exporting. To get help, press Ctrl-F1 or click on the Help menu and then on Search For Help On. The Search dialog box appears. In the Search dialog box, type a search argument, such as **bmp**, and the requested subject appears in the window, as shown if Figure B-1.

You can then choose either the import or export notes and click on Show Topic to put them into the lower window. Click on OK and the help subject

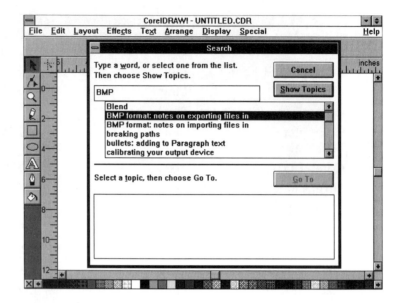

Searching for
help on
exporting to a
.BMP format
Figure B-1.

is displayed. If you need hard copy of the subject, click on Print in the
File menu.

Importing: An Overview

The process of importing into CorelDRAW! from other file formats always
involves these three steps:

1. Select the Import command from the File menu.
2. Select one of the file types listed in the Import dialog box's List Files of
   Type drop-down list box.
3. Specify the directory and filename of the file you want to import and
   click on OK.

You will
find more
information
on the
CorelDRAW!
bitmap tracing
features in
Appendix C.

Once you import the file, you have several editing options, depending on
the kind of application it comes from. If the imported object originated in a
paint program, you can trace it automatically or manually and turn it into a
distortion-free, object-oriented image.

When you select the Import command from the File menu, the Import
dialog box appears, as shown in Figure B–2. The drop-down list box in the

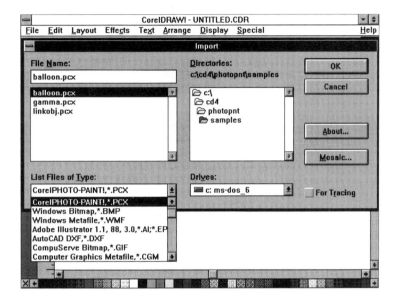

Import dialog box
Figure B-2.

B

bottom left of the dialog box contains the list of file formats available for import.

Bringing in a File

To select the format for the file you wish to import, and actually bring the file into CorelDRAW!, follow these steps.

1. Select the Import command from the File menu. The Import dialog box appears.

2. In the Directories list box, select the path to the directory that contains the file you want to import.

3. Click on the down arrow in the List Files of Type drop-down list box. If the file type you want does not immediately appear in the window, use the scroll arrows to move through the list.

4. Select the filename you want and click on OK, or double-click on the filename. The image will begin importing to the CorelDRAW! page, as you see here:

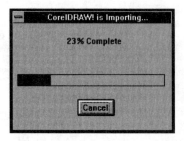

What happens to the image during the import process depends on the specific file format you have chosen.

Importing Bitmap Graphics

CorelDRAW! can import bitmap graphics in many different formats, as you saw in Table B-1. Once imported, you cannot break bitmap images down into their component parts, because CorelDRAW! treats the entire bitmap image as a single object. You can crop a bitmap after importing it, however, so that only a specified section is visible. You can also select, move, rearrange, stretch, scale, outline, and fill a bitmap as though it were any other type of object.

A rotated or skewed bitmap will only print on a PostScript printer.

In some respects, imported bitmaps behave differently from other objects when you edit them. If you rotate or skew a bitmap, the original image in the preview window changes to a series of bars, unless you are in Edit Wireframe, in which case it will appear as a gray box.

Importing Object-Oriented Graphics

The original release of CorelDRAW! allowed you to import three object-oriented graphics file formats: .CDR (the native CorelDRAW! format), Lotus .PIC graphs, and .AI and .EPS files created by Adobe Illustrator or clip-art manufacturers. Since then, the ranks of supported object-oriented file formats have swelled to include many more file formats. Table B–1 lists each supported object-oriented file format.

Specific notes on importing and working with each file format are provided in CorelDRAW! Help. Keep in mind that software applications are being upgraded continually, and that process may alter the way certain file formats interact with CorelDRAW!.

The CorelDRAW! import filters offer you a rich world of possibilities. But the uses to which you can put CorelDRAW!'s advanced graphics features are even richer when you consider the software applications to which you can export your images.

Exporting: An Overview

Connectivity is a two-way street. The ability to import any number of different file formats would be of limited use if you could not export your work to other applications as well. CorelDRAW! also has a large number of export filters. After perfecting a masterpiece in CorelDRAW!, you can send it to your favorite paint program, object-oriented drawing software, desktop publishing application, or film-recording device.

The process of exporting a CorelDRAW! file to another application always involves these five steps:

1. Open the CorelDRAW! image file you want to transfer and save it before beginning the export procedure. If you want to export only certain objects rather than the entire file, select those objects.
2. Select the Export command from the File menu.
3. Select a file type from the choices in the Export dialog box's List Files of Type drop-down list box.
4. Choose whether to export the entire file or selected objects only.
5. Specify the directory and filename for the object you want to export.

Depending on the export file format you choose, other choices in various secondary Export dialog boxes may also become available to you.

B

Preparing for Exporting

If you are planning to export an existing file, open it before you select the Export command. If the page is empty when you attempt the export procedure, you'll find you can't select the Export command.

If you are preparing to export a new file or one you have imported and edited, always save the file as a .CDR image before exporting it. This is extremely important if there is any chance that you might need to edit the image again later. In some cases you will not be able to import a file that was exported earlier from CorelDRAW!.

If you want to export only a part of the CorelDRAW! file rather than the entire image, select the desired objects before beginning the export procedure. An option in the Export dialog box will allow you to specify the export of selected objects only.

The Export Dialog Box

When you select the Export command from the File menu, the Export dialog box appears, as shown in Figure B–3.

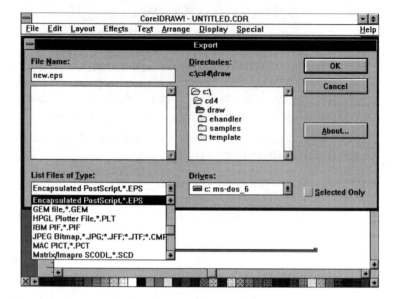

Export dialog
box
Figure B-3.

At the lower-left corner of the dialog box, the List Files of Type drop-down list box contains the names and extensions of the file formats to which you can export the current file. Depending on the format selected, there are several secondary Export dialog boxes for entering further options; these include Bitmap Export, Export EPS, HPGL Options, and Export AI, to name a few. One of these boxes will appear if you select the corresponding file type in the drop-down list and click OK.

To select and highlight the file format to which you will export the CorelDRAW! image, scroll through the list box until it appears and then click on it.

"Selected Only" Option
The Selected Only option is available for any export file format that you choose. It lets you choose to export only certain objects from your on-screen graphic. However, you must have one or more objects selected before the Selected Only option is available.

The Export dialog box in Figure B–3 indicates that an object has been selected, since the Selected Only option is available.

Specifying the Filename and Destination Directory
To specify the destination drive and directory for the exported image, click on the appropriate drive in the Drives drop-down list box and double-click on the appropriate directory in the Directories list box. Use the scroll bars if

the desired directory is not visible. The path of the highlighted drive and directory appear above the box.

To name the export image file, double-click in the File Name box to select the default extension. Then type the desired filename; CorelDRAW! will restore the correct extension. Click on OK. Select the needed options in the secondary Export dialog box, and click OK to begin transfer of the image.

Exporting to Bitmap Graphics Formats

When you have a choice of several different export file formats, your primary concern should be the end use to which you will put the exported graphic. Add to that, the CorelDRAW! features that can or cannot be retained, and the convenience of working with the image in the export file format.

The bitmap file formats are good choices for export to paint programs and can also be used with desktop publishing programs if you do not use a PostScript printer and cannot take advantage of the .EPS file format. However, one of the object-oriented formats such as .WMF is a better choice for desktop publishing applications. Unlike the bitmap formats, the object-oriented formats are easy to resize without distortion, and they preserve more attribute information. You should select a bitmap file format only when one of the following conditions applies:

B

✦ The application to which you are exporting accepts only bitmap graphics.

✦ You plan to alter the CorelDRAW! graphic using techniques available only in the pixel-by-pixel editing environment of a paint program.

As shown in Table B–2, CorelDRAW! can export drawings in many bitmap formats. When you choose a bitmap format from the File Export dialog box, the secondary Bitmap Export dialog box opens, as shown in Figure B–4.

You can export full-color and gray-scale images with these bitmap formats. The files they create, if uncompressed, would be quite large—up to several megabytes—as shown in the bottom of the dialog box. When you have the option of compressing a file, the Compressed check box will be available for selection.

Specifying a Bitmap Graphics Resolution

Assuming you have chosen a pixel-based export file format and then selected OK, you can choose the bitmap resolution from the Bitmap Export secondary dialog box. The available resolution is from 75 dpi (dots per inch), up to 300 dpi. A higher resolution is the option to choose if you want to give

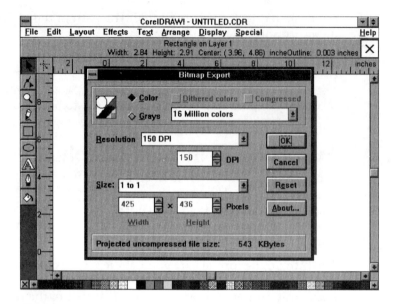

the exported image the best possible appearance—but it will also take up
more disk space.

Because of the way a computer stores pixel-based graphics, an image that is
large in CorelDRAW! can occupy an enormous amount of memory (for
example, 5MB for a medium-sized image) when you export it at a high
resolution. Rather than export the graphic at a lower resolution, consider
using the Pick tool to scale the CorelDRAW! image down to the size it should
be in the final application. For example, if you plan to export the graphic to
a desktop publishing program and know the desired image size on the page,
scale it down to that size before exporting it from CorelDRAW!. This
precautionary action will also prevent you from having to resize the bitmap
later, thereby causing its appearance to deteriorate.

Exporting to Object-Oriented Graphics Formats

As mentioned earlier, object-oriented formats transfer color, outline, fill, and
attribute information more accurately than is the case with bitmap formats.
In addition, object-oriented formats are device-independent, which means
that their images look the same despite resizing or changes in the display
resolution.

Use
CorelDRAW!
Help any time
there is doubt
about the way
the import or
export filters
handle a
particular
format.

Your main concerns when choosing an object-oriented export format are the final use to which you plan to put the image and the kinds of information you cannot afford to lose during the export process.

Exporting to an EPS Format

EPS is a good example of an object-oriented format that is widely used. As with most of the objected-oriented formats, a secondary dialog box will appear when OK is selected in the Export dialog box. The EPS Export dialog box is shown in Figure B-5.

Including an .EPS Image Header

An image header is a visual representation of a PostScript graphic for display on your screen. The Header Resolution option is available only when you select the .EPS export file format for PostScript images and the Export EPS secondary dialog box appears. While not truly WYSIWYG, the image header helps you position or crop the .EPS image in desktop publishing applications such as Aldus PageMaker and Ventura Publisher. If you choose not to include an image header, select the 0 dpi option in the Header Resolution drop-down box. In this case, you will not have a visual representation of an .EPS image in your desktop publishing application.

Choose the 0 dpi option only if you plan to use the exported .EPS image in an application that cannot display an .EPS image header.

B

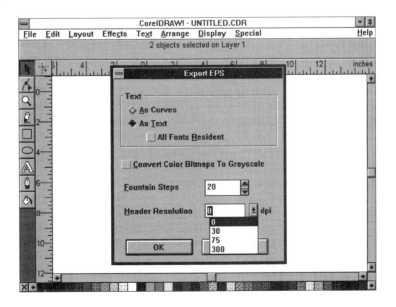

Export EPS
dialog box
Figure B-5.

The image header resolution you select does *not* affect the actual PostScript graphic. If conserving memory and disk space is a concern, you should select the Low Resolution option for the smallest image header. If accurate representation is more important to you than memory conservation, select the 300 dpi option to obtain an image header that is true to the proportions of the actual graphic. The 300 dpi Header Resolution option can result in an image header that adds more than 64K to the .EPS file.

All Fonts Resident .EPS Option

The All Fonts Resident option in the Export EPS dialog box becomes available if you choose to export text "As Text." When you activate the All Fonts Resident option, you tell CorelDRAW! to assume that all fonts used in your graphic are resident in the output device. Text strings in the exported graphic will be printed using the printer-resident fonts rather than the original CorelDRAW! fonts.

You should use the All Fonts Resident option if you have downloadable PostScript fonts and want to use them instead of CorelDRAW! fonts. You might also use this option when producing material that will be printed by a service bureau. Most laser service bureaus have access to all of the Adobe PostScript fonts and can substitute them for the CorelDRAW! fonts automatically.

CORELDRAW! 4

A P P E N D I X

TRACING BITMAP IMAGES

Appendix B described two types of graphics that can be imported into CorelDRAW!: bitmap images and object-oriented images. When you import an object-oriented image, you can edit it just as you would any picture created in CorelDRAW!. Bitmap images, however, contain no objects for you to select; they consist entirely of a fixed number of tiny dots or pixels. If you enlarge or reduce the size of the bitmap without converting it to a CorelDRAW! object, distortion or unsightly compression of the pixels results. The solution is to trace the bitmap in CorelDRAW! or CorelTRACE! and turn it into an object-oriented image. You can then change the shape of the object's outline and the color of its fill, edit it normally, and print it, all without distortion. The CorelDRAW! package offers you three different methods for tracing an imported bitmap. The newest and most sophisticated of these is CorelTRACE!, a separate program included with CorelDRAW!. You will be amazed at the speed and accuracy with which this product can turn even the most complex bitmap into a finished curve object ready for editing. CorelTRACE! will be discussed later in this chapter in the section, "Tracing with CorelTRACE!."

In CorelDRAW! itself you can choose between manual tracing and the semiautomatic Autotrace feature. These methods are slower than CorelTRACE! and require more work on the part of the user, but they offer you a high degree of control over the curves that result from your tracing. They are discussed in the earlier sections of this chapter.

Creating a Bitmap Image

CorelDRAW! treats a bitmap image as a unique object type, separate from other object types such as rectangles, ellipses, curves, and text. Unlike all of the other object types, bitmaps must be created outside of CorelDRAW!.

There are several ways to secure a bitmap image for importing into CorelDRAW!. The easiest method is to import a finished clip-art image or a sample file having one of the many extensions related to bitmap files (see Appendix B). The next easiest method is to scan an existing image from a print source, such as a newspaper or magazine. Alternatively, you can sketch a drawing by hand and then scan the image in .PCX or .TIF format. Finally, you can create your own original pixel-based images with CorelPHOTO-PAINT!.

Once the bitmap image is available, you are ready to import it into CorelDRAW!.

Importing a Bitmap Image

As you saw in Appendix B, CorelDRAW! accepts many bitmap file formats for import: .PCX, .TIF, and .BMP, to name a few. The .PCX format is native to the ZSoft PC Paintbrush and Publisher's Paintbrush family of paint software and is also used in CorelPHOTO-PAINT!. The .TIF format is the one that most scanners support, and .BMP is the Windows Paint file format. If the bitmap you want to import is in another format, you can convert it to .PCX or .TIF using an image conversion program such as Inset Graphics' Hijaak or U-Lead Systems' ImagePals.

To import a bitmap, you use the Import command in the File menu and select the appropriate bitmap file format in the Import dialog box.

The standard CorelDRAW! package includes several .TIF sample files in the C:\COREL40\CLIPART\TIFS directory. In the following exercise, you will see how to import one of the sample .TIF files.

1. Starting with a blank CorelDRAW! screen, open the Display menu and make sure that Show Rulers and Edit Wireframe are turned off (not checked). With Edit Wireframe off, the Show Bitmaps option is automatically dimmed.

2. Select the Page Setup command from the Layout menu and make certain that the page is set for Portrait and that the page size is Letter. Click on the OK command button to save these settings.

3. Select the Import command from the File menu. The Import dialog box appears.

4. Open the List Files of Type drop-down list box and select TIFF Bitmap.

5. In the Drives and Directories boxes, specify the drive and directory that contains the CorelDRAW! sample TIFF files. If you installed CorelDRAW! using the standard directory scheme, this is the C:\COREL40\CLIPART\TIFS path. Make certain that the For Tracing box is checked.

6. To open a .TIF file, double-click on the filename in the File Name list box, or highlight the filename and click on OK. After a few seconds, the image appears, centered on the page and surrounded by a selection box, as shown in Figure C-1. The status line displays the message "Monochrome Bitmap on Layer 1" (or "Color Bitmap on Layer 1" for a color TIFF file) in the center and "For Tracing" on the right.

NOTE: The file used here is named OUT_PLAY.TIF. If it is not available in your version of CorelDRAW!, select another .TIF file so that you can follow these steps.

7. Select the Save As command from the File menu. When the Save Drawing dialog box appears, change the directory to the one in which you save your CorelDRAW! drawings. Type a name, for example, **auttrace**, in the File Name text box, and then choose OK. You do this to prevent overwriting the original file.

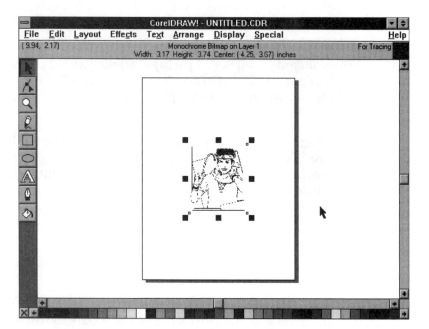

CorelDRAW! - UNTITLED.CDR

File   Edit   Layout   Effects   Text   Arrange   Display   Special   Help
[9.94, 2.17]   Monochrome Bitmap on Layer 1   For Tracing
                          Width: 3.17 Height: 3.74 Center: (4.25, 3.67) inches

Bitmap image,
imported for
tracing
Figure C-1.

Autotracing an Imported Bitmap

As mentioned earlier, CorelDRAW! lets you turn an imported bitmap image
into a resolution-independent curve object by tracing the image. You can
trace a single bitmap image either semiautomatically, using the Autotrace
feature, or manually. You can also use the fully automatic CorelTRACE!
program described later in this chapter. Manual tracing is a good choice if
you desire total control over the appearance and placement of the outline
curves. If you find it cumbersome to use the mouse for tracing long paths
manually, however, use the Autotrace feature instead. You have less control
over the results, but you will spend less time manipulating the mouse.

The Autotrace feature becomes available to you when the bitmap object is
selected. Autotrace is semiautomatic in the sense that the software draws the
actual curves for you, but you must define a number of parameters before
tracing begins. You control the shape of the Outline Pen, the color of the
outline fill, the interior fill of the object, and the smoothness of the curves.

In the following exercise, you will use Autotrace to trace portions of the
AUTTRACE.CDR image that you imported earlier from your .TIF file.

1. With the image you will use still on the screen and selected, adjust
   magnification to fit-in-window view.

2. All black-and-white bitmap objects are imported with a preset outline
   color of black and a preset fill of None. You can adjust the Outline Pen

settings as desired, but to have those settings apply to your traced objects, you must first deselect the bitmap. For the bitmap itself, the fill color applies to the background, the outline color applies to the bitmap pixels that are turned on, and outline width has no meaning. Deselect the object, click on the Outline Pen tool and then on the hairline icon in the first row of the flyout menu. This will result in hairline curves of a very fine width. Click on OK in the Outline Pen dialog box to apply this default to all graphic objects. With the object still deselected, click on the Fill tool and on the X (the no fill icon). Again, accept this as the default for all graphic objects. Now reselect the bitmap.

3. Now you can crop the bitmap so that no white space extends beyond the portion you are tracing. With the bitmap again selected, activate the Shaping tool and position it over the middle boundary marker of each edge in turn. When the pointer changes to a crosshair, drag the edges inward until the object is the size you want. The status line shows the percentage that has been cropped from each side, as shown in Figure C-2.

4. Choose the Preferences command from the Special menu and then click on Curves. In the Preferences-Curves dialog box, adjust the settings as follows: Autotrace Tracking, 5 pixels; Corner Threshold, 8 pixels; Straight Line Threshold, 3 pixels; AutoJoin, 10 pixels; and leave Freehand Tracking and Auto-Reduce at their current settings. These settings will result in smoother curves, smooth (rather than cusp) nodes, curves rather than straight line segments, and curve segments that snap together when they are as far as 10 pixels apart, as shown in Table C-1. Click on OK twice to make these settings take effect.

5. Turn on Preview Selected Only in the Display menu. Select the Zoom-In tool and magnify only the portion of your bitmap object that you want to start tracing. The editing window should show your figure, similar to Figure C-3.

6. Now you are ready to begin Autotracing. Make sure that the bitmap is still selected and then select the Pencil tool. Notice that the pointer looks different; instead of being a perfectly symmetrical crosshair, it has a wand-like extension on the right. This is the Autotrace pointer. It appears only when you activate the Pencil tool with a bitmap object selected. The phrase "AutoTrace on Layer 1" appears on the status line, indicating that you are now in Autotrace mode.

7. Position the wand of the Autotrace pointer to the left of an area that you want to trace and then click once. After a moment, a closed curve object appears, completely enclosing the contours of the area that you clicked on, as shown in Figure C-4. Press F9 while the curve is still selected, and you see the traced line similar to Figure C-5.

Cropped
bitmap
Figure C-2.

Option	Determines	Settings	
		Low no. (1-3)	High no. (7-10)
Freehand Tracking	How closely Corel follows your freehand drawing	Many nodes	Few nodes
Autotrace Tracking	How closely the Autotrace pointer follows bitmap edges	Rough curve	Smooth curve
Corner Threshold	Whether a node is cusped or smooth	Cusp nodes	Smooth nodes
Straight Line Threshold	Whether a segment should be a curve or a straight line	More curves	More lines
AutoJoin	How close together two line or curve segments must be in order to join	Less joining	More joining
Auto-Reduce	How many nodes are removed by Auto-Reduce in the Node Edit roll-up	Less nodes	More nodes

Guidelines for
Setting
Options in the
Preferences-
Curves Dialog
Box
Table C-1.

Tracing Bitmap Images

Magnified
view of a
bitmap
Figure C-3.

Autotracing a
closed
curve—editing
screen
Figure C-4.

Autotraced
closed
curve—preview
screen
Figure C-5.

Autotrace does not give you the same high degree of control available with manual tracing.

8. Position the Autotrace pointer along the remaining closed portions of your bitmap object and click on each of them. Another closed curve appears each time you click.

9. Select the Zoom-In tool and zoom in on a part of your bitmap that has many small details. Position the intersection point of the Autotrace pointer inside one of the closed regions and click. A closed curve object quickly appears.

10. Create more detailing curves in the same way and then move around the bitmap, tracing the objects you see.

11. Press Shift-F4 to show the full page. Select the Pick tool and click on the bitmap somewhere other than where you were tracing. Press Del to remove the bitmap and see your handiwork. Autotrace produces a rough approximation of your bitmap object, as you can see in Figure C-6.

12. Save your changes to the image by pressing Ctrl-S.

13. Select New from the File menu to clear the screen.

TIP: If you have trouble selecting a region that results in the curve you need, try pointing at the desired region using the tip of the wand on the Autotrace pointer instead of its center point. You will find that you can aim the wand more accurately when you are working in a magnified view.

Result of
Autotracing
part of a bitmap
Figure C-6.

As you saw in the previous exercise, the results of the Autotrace feature depend on your choice of the area to outline and on exactly how you position the Autotrace pointer. Even if you use Autotrace to trace the same area twice, CorelDRAW! may change the number and positions of the nodes each time. The path that an Autotrace curve takes can sometimes seem to be quite unpredictable, especially if the subjects within the bitmap have overlapping or connected pixels. With practice, you will gain skill in positioning the Autotrace pointer for the best possible results.

Tracing Manually

You don't have to be a superb drafter to trace a bitmap with precision in CorelDRAW!. By magnifying the areas you trace and adjusting the Lines and Curves settings in the Preferences dialog box, you can trace swiftly and still achieve accurate results. To trace a bitmap manually, you deselect the bitmap just before you activate the Pencil tool. This action prevents the Pencil tool from becoming the Autotrace pointer.

Manual tracing is faster and easier than Autotracing if the imported bitmap contains multiple subjects with no clear separations between the pixels that compose these subjects. Most commercial clip art fits this description. Using the manual method avoids the problem of Autotrace curves that extend beyond the subject with which you are working. As a result, you usually need to do less editing after your initial manual tracing than after using Autotrace.

Just as when you use the Autotrace feature, you can define the default shape of the Outline Pen, Outline Color, the interior fill of the object, and the smoothness of the curves before you begin tracing. In the following exercise, you can manually trace portions of your .TIF file.

1. Once again, import your .TIF file as you did earlier.

2. When the bitmap object appears, adjust magnification to fit-in-window. Also, make sure Snap To Grid, Show Rulers, and Edit Wireframe are turned off, and Preview Selected Only is turned on.

3. Deselect the object, click on the Outline Pen tool and then on the hairline icon in the first row of the flyout menu. This will produce hairline curves of a very fine width. Accept this setting as the default for all graphic objects.

4. Click on the Fill tool and again on the X icon to change the object fill color to none. This prevents any closed paths that you trace from filling with an opaque color and obscuring other traced areas that lie beneath. (You can edit the fill colors of individual objects later.) Again, accept this as the default and then reselect the object.

5. With the bitmap still selected, select the Shaping tool and crop the bitmap, so that only the part of the picture you want to trace is visible, by positioning the pointer directly over a corner boundary marker of a corner you want to reduce. When the pointer changes to a crosshair, depress and hold the mouse button and drag this corner diagonally. Release the mouse button when the area you want is in the box, as in Figure C-7. You might also want to drag the center boundary markers inward to get the final shape that you need.

6. Select the Preferences command from the Special menu and click on Curves. Adjust the settings as follows: Freehand Tracking, 1 pixel; Corner Threshold, 10 pixels; Straight Line Threshold, 1 pixel; AutoJoin, 10 pixels; and leave Autotrace and Auto-Reduce as they are. These settings will result in curves that closely follow the movements of your mouse. You will generate smooth (rather than cusp) nodes, curves rather than straight line segments, and curve segments that snap together when they are as far as 10 pixels apart. These settings promote ease of editing should you need to smooth out the traced curves later. Click on OK twice to save these settings.

7. Deselect the bitmap object and activate the Pencil tool. (If you see the Autotrace pointer instead of the regular Pencil pointer, you haven't deselected the bitmap.) Position the Pencil tool anywhere along the outline of a closed area, then depress and hold the mouse button, trace

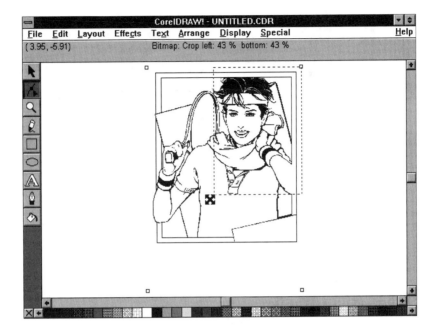

Cropping a
bitmap in
preparation for
manual tracing
Figure C-7.

all the way around, and end the curve at the starting point. Should you
make any errors, you can erase portions of the curve by pressing the
(Shift) key as you drag the mouse backward. If you end the curve within
10 pixels of the starting point, the two end nodes snap together and
form a closed path. If the end nodes are farther apart than 10 pixels, the
curve remains an open path. To close the path, activate the Shaping
tool and draw a marquee around the two end nodes, double-click on
one of them to invoke the Node Edit roll-up, and select Join, as you see
in Figure C-8.

8. Zoom in and trace more of the picture with the Pencil tool. You can
    trace the outline of small details in the bitmap as open curves and use
    Autotrace as well as manual, all in the same picture.

9. In order to do some Autotracing in your bitmap, activate the Pick tool
    and select the entire bitmap object. Remember that unless the bitmap is
    selected, you cannot enter Autotrace mode.

10. Activate the Pencil tool again with the bitmap selected. Position the
    Autotrace pointer inside one of the small detail areas of your bitmap
    and click to trace a curve around this tiny area automatically.

11. Using Autotrace, trace a few more small details of your picture. When
    you have finished, your screen should look roughly similar to the way it
    looked in the previous section, "Autotracing an Imported Bitmap." Save
    the image at this point under the filename, MANTRACE.

Joining the
ends of a curve
object
Figure C-8.

12. Select the Pick tool and click on the bitmap somewhere other than
where you were tracing. Press [Del] to remove the bitmap and see your
handiwork. Your screen should show the curve objects, as you see in
Figure C-9.

13. Save your changes by pressing [Ctrl]-[S], and then select New from the File
menu to clear the screen.

As you have just seen, it is possible and sometimes even preferable to
combine both the manual and Autotrace methods when tracing complex
bitmap images. Manual tracing is best for obtaining exact control over the
placement of curves in bitmaps that contain several subjects close together,
as is the case with most clip art. The Autotrace method is useful for tracing
small closed regions, like the details of the bitmap in the previous exercises.
The Autotrace method is also more convenient to use when the bitmap
image has a single, clearly defined subject with sharp contours.

Whether you use the Autotrace feature, manual tracing, or a combination of
both methods, you can always edit the curve objects you create.

Tracing with CorelTRACE!

A third method of tracing bitmap images is available to you—one that is
more rapid, sophisticated, and efficient than either the manual or Autotrace

Combining
Autotracing
with manual
tracing
Figure C-9.

*CorelDRAW!
comes with
sample files
with which you
can practice
changing the
tracing
parameters.*

method. The CorelTRACE! batch tracing utility allows you to trace one or more bitmaps automatically at high speeds and save them in the Adobe .EPS format. You can choose from two default methods of tracing, or you can customize tracing parameters to suit your needs. When you are finished tracing files, you can edit the resulting object-oriented images in any drawing program that can read the Adobe .EPS file format, including CorelDRAW!.

The following sections provide instructions for preparing to use CorelTRACE!, for selecting and tracing bitmaps, and for customizing and editing tracing parameters.

Preparing to Use CorelTRACE!

CorelTRACE! is installed in the same directory and Windows group where you installed CorelDRAW!. Before you begin using CorelTRACE! for the first time, check the amount of free space available on your hard drive. When you trace bitmaps using CorelTRACE!, temporary files are generated on your hard drive. If you trace large bitmaps, or more than one bitmap during a session, you are almost certain to require several megabytes of hard drive space for these temporary files. You should have at least 5MB of space free, and 10MB is recommended.

If your selected hard drive does not have enough space available, you can either remove unnecessary files or, if you have one, specify a different hard drive where CorelTRACE! can place the large temporary files it generates. For example, if CorelDRAW! and CorelTRACE! are installed in drive C and you wish to locate temporary files in the TRASH directory of drive D, you would first open your AUTOEXEC.BAT file in a text editor. Then either add the following line, or edit any existing "set temp=" line to match the following:

```
set temp=d:\trash
```

This statement tells Windows always to place temporary files in the specified drive and directory. Be sure to reboot after you edit the AUTOEXEC.BAT file in order to make your changes take effect. Also be sure that the directory you named exists on the specified hard drive.

CAUTION: Never select the Windows directory as the directory in which to store the temporary files that Windows applications generate. Errors could result that might cause your system to crash unexpectedly.

Loading CorelTRACE!

Unless you have over 2MB of memory, do not run any other Windows applications in the background while you are running CorelTRACE!. This means that you should leave CorelDRAW! while running CorelTRACE!; not just switch out of it. CorelTRACE! requires a large amount of memory to work efficiently. If you run other applications concurrently, CorelTRACE! may not run or may function very slowly.

To load CorelTRACE!, double-click on the CorelTRACE! icon in the Corel 4 group window. The opening screen appears and is then replaced by the main window, shown in Figure C-10.

The main window of CorelTRACE! contains six menus: File, Edit, Settings, Trace, Display, and Help. To obtain information on running CorelTRACE!, click on the Help menu or press F1 at any time.

Opening Files to Trace

In order to trace one or more bitmaps, you must open the files in CorelTRACE! by clicking on Open in the File menu. Alternatively, you can click on the Batch Files roll-up button (the first button in the row of buttons under the menu bar) and then on the Add button in the Batch Files roll-up. In either case, the Open Files dialog box appears, as shown in Figure C-11. There are two unique options available in this dialog box: first, the Preview

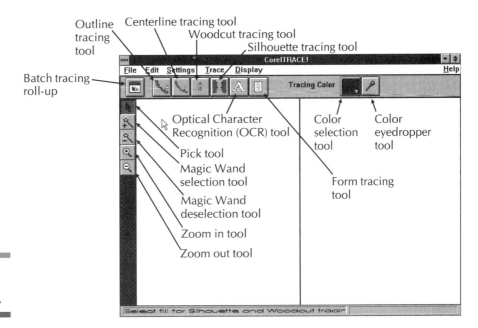

C

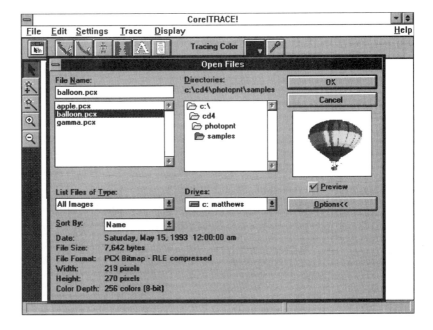

check box allows you to see the image before it is opened, and second, the Options command button displays all the properties of the selected file.

Tracing a Bitmap with CorelTRACE!

Tracing one or more bitmaps involves several steps:

1. Click on Open and specify the source directory of the file(s) you want to trace, using the Directories list box if necessary.

2. Select one or more files to trace by clicking on their names in the File Name list box while holding down Ctrl. Then click OK. If you selected more than one file, the Batch Files roll-up appears.

3. Edit the tracing options, if desired, by selecting an option from Modify in the Settings menu.

4. Click on one of the trace buttons (second and third buttons in the top row) to begin tracing the selected file(s). If there is more than one file to trace, use the Trace All button in the Batch Files roll-up.

In the following exercise, you will tell CorelTRACE! to *batch trace* (trace one after the other) two bitmap files. You can use any two bitmap graphics files that are available to you.

1. Click on Open and change to the drive and directory where your bitmap files are located.

2. While holding Ctrl, click on two filenames in the File Name list box at the left side of the dialog box. Click on OK, and the Batch Files roll-up will appear with the selected filenames listed and the first of the two images in the roll-up, as shown in Figure C-12.

3. Choose Modify in the Settings menu and then click on Batch Output. The Batch Output dialog box appears, as you see in Figure C-13. Here you tell CorelTRACE! where to send the traced files and whether to replace an older version of the same filename. You are also given the opportunity to make the files "Read Only" and to decide how text is to be handled.

4. Click on OK to close the Batch Output options.

5. Other settings can be changed with the Modify option, but for now click on Default Settings in the Settings menu.

The Default Settings option tells CorelTRACE! to trace a line around each of the black or white regions of the bitmap image, and then fill each area with black or white to match the original bitmap. The Outline method is best for tracing bitmaps with thick lines, many fills, and a hand-sketched look. The

Tracing Bitmap Images

Batch Files
roll-up
Figure C-12.

C

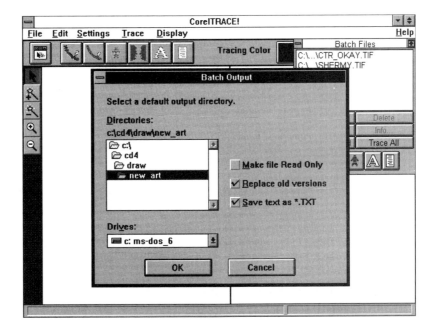

Batch Output
dialog box
Figure C-13.

Centerline method, on the other hand, is best for architectural or technical illustrations that have thin lines of fairly uniform thickness and no fill colors. See the next section of this chapter for more details on the differences between the Outline and Centerline methods of tracing.

6. Click on the Trace All command button in the Batch Files roll-up to begin tracing the two sample files. After a few seconds, the window on the left side of the screen contains the first of the two bitmaps. When the tracing is complete, the first bitmap disappears automatically and is replaced by the second bitmap. When both tracings are done, both images will disappear—they will be saved as .EPS files, which you can edit from another program such as CorelDRAW!.

The preceding exercise gave you a glimpse of what CorelTRACE! can do. In the next section, you will learn more about how you can customize the options that determine the smoothness, fineness, and clarity of the curves during the tracing process.

Customizing Your Tracing Options

The buttons at the top of the CorelTRACE! window contain two default tracing options, Outline and Centerline. If you wish, you can modify the parameters associated with these two options to define your own custom tracing methods. When you modify a tracing option, you can save your result as a new option in the Settings menu, using the Save As option.

Outline Tracing

When you select the Outline button (second from the left in the top row) as the tracing method, CorelTRACE! seeks out the *outlines* of areas and traces around them. Every curve becomes a closed object that is then filled with black or white, a color, or a gray shade to match the original bitmap as closely as possible. This method is most appropriate when the images that you trace contain many filled objects or have lines of variable thicknesses.

Centerline Tracing

When you select the Centerline button (third from the left) as the tracing method, CorelTRACE! seeks out the *center* point of lines in a bitmap and traces down the middle of those lines. No attempt is made to close paths or fill them. The resulting accuracy and attention to fine detail makes this tracing method the best choice for scanned images of technical or architectural drawings. Centerline is also appropriate for tracing drawings in which line thicknesses are fairly uniform.

Other Types of Tracing and Tools

Besides Outline and Centerline tracing, there are four other types of tracing you can perform with CorelTRACE!: Woodcut, OCR, Silhouette, and Form. These tools are selected with the fourth through the seventh buttons in the horizontal toolbox at the top of the screen and are described as follows:

Button	Description
	Woodcut tracing produces a special effect similar to old-fashioned hand woodcuts.
	Silhouette tracing produces an outline of the traced area filled with a single color that can be selected with either the color selector or the eyedropper (described a little later)
	Optical character recognition (OCR) converts text brought in as graphics to text that CorelDRAW! can edit as text.
	Form tracing allows you to trace the lines and text of a form and then edit them with CorelDRAW!.

When you use Woodcut or Silhouette tracing, you can choose a color for the area you are tracing (*before you do the tracing*) by either selecting it from the Color selection tool or by using the Eyedropper tool to pick it up from the original image (just click on the color with the eyedropper). This works well with the Magic wands which select (the wand with a plus sign) and deselect (the wand with a minus sign) areas of the object to be traced that are a constant color. Therefore, to do custom tracing, you select the area to be traced with the Magic wand selector, pick the color, either by choosing it from the palette that appears when you click on the Color selection tool or by using the Eyedropper tool to pick up the original color, and then click on the Silhouette tool to do the tracing.

Defining a Custom Tracing Method

What if the image you want to trace contains both filled areas and line art? In CorelTRACE!, you can adjust a variety of tracing options by selecting the Modify option in the Settings menu. Follow these steps to access this command and define a custom tracing option:

1. Load CorelTRACE! from the Program Manager.

2. You can modify the tracing settings at any time by clicking on Modify in the Settings menu and then choosing the menu item you want to change, as you see in Figure C-14. Each of these items has a dialog box associated with it in which you can make the appropriate changes.

3. When you are finished editing, select the Save As option in the Settings menu to save the new tracing options under a new name. This will now appear in the Load Settings dialog box, as shown in Figure C-15.

As you use your custom tracing settings, the Settings menu maintains a list of the last three that were used. These three are listed directly under Default Settings and can be selected at any time without going through the Load Settings dialog box.

Editing parameters for tracing options saves time when you import traced graphics into CorelDRAW! and edit them. For example, if you know in advance that you need to invert colors of a particular bitmap or that you require a larger or smaller number of nodes in the traced graphic, you can change tracing parameters to give you the desired results automatically.

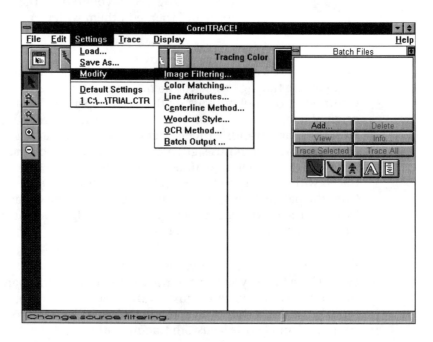

Modify options
in the Settings
menu
Figure C-14.

Tracing Bitmap Images

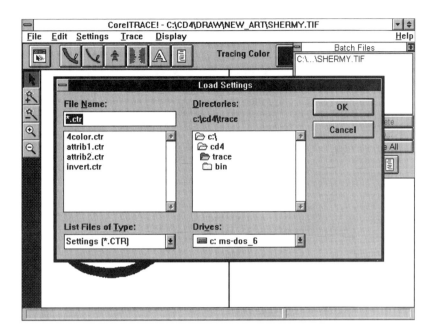

Load Settings
dialog box
Figure C-15.

INDEX

A

Aardvark font, 99
Active cell, 531
Actor Information dialog box (CorelMOVE!), 601
Actor tool (CorelMOVE!), 592-596
Actors (animation), 586
Actual Size tool, 126, 136-137
Add Color menu, 353
Add Perspective feature, 444-445
Align dialog box, 174-177
Aligning to a node, 252
Aligning nodes, 250, 252-254
Aligning objects, 64-66, 173-177
Aligning text, 90-93
All Fonts Resident for PostScript, 432
Animation basics, 586-587. *See also* CorelMOVE!
Animation Information dialog box, 588-589
Application icons, CorelDRAW! OLE, 564
Area charts, 549-550
Arrange menu, 8
Arrow mouse pointer, 10
Arrowhead Editor, 319-320, 335-340
Arrowhead Editor dialog box, 319
Arrowheads
    adding and editing, 335-340
    display box of, 319, 337
    examples of, 338
Arrows option (Outline Pen), 318-319
Artistic Text dialog box, 84-85, 133
    moving around in, 86-87
    review, 103-104
Aspect ratio, 185
Attributes
    copying, 308-309
    creating objects with default, 316-322
    defining for Outline Pen, 314
    editing, 266-269
    editing Outline Pen, 325-344
    paragraph, 115-116
AutoJoin feature, 45-48
    adjusting the threshold, 46-48
    setting, 74
Auto-Panning feature, 187
Autotrace feature, 632-637
Autotracing a closed curve, 635-636
Avalon font, 98-99

B

Background Library (CorelSHOW!), 564
Background view (CorelSHOW!), 563
Banding, 441
Bar charts, 543-547
Batch Files roll-up (CorelTRACE!), 645
Batch Output dialog box (CorelTRACE!), 645
Beginning of a line, finding, 318
Behind Fill option (Outline Pen), 321-322
Bevel, 320
Beveled corners, 331
Bézier mode
    drawing curves in, 37-40
    drawing a polygon in, 31-32
    vs. Freehand mode, 22
    straight lines in, 30-31
Billiard table drawing, 173-177
Bipolar side-by-side bar chart, 546-547

Bipolar stacked bar chart, 546
Bitmap, 391
Bitmap Export dialog box, 624
Bitmap graphics
     creating, 630-631
     exporting, 623-624
     fill patterns, 391-396
     importing, 620, 630-632
     vs. object-oriented graphics, 614-615
     tracing, 629-649
Bitmap Pattern Editor, 393
Blend feature, 446, 466-472
     mapping matching nodes, 470-472
     rotating blended objects, 467-472
Bold type, selecting, 101
Boundary markers, 184-185, 196
Bounding box, 108
Breaking apart objects, 170-172
Breaking curves at nodes, 247-248
Butt line, 321

C

Calligraphic pen, 340-344
Calligraphy option (Outline Pen), 321
Cancel button (Artistic Text), 86
CAR364 image, 424
     changing the screen frequency, 431-432
     color separations for, 423-425
     with file information, 421-422
     film negative color separation, 428-430
Cel sequencer roll-up (CorelMOVE!), 603
Cell, 531
Cels (animation), 586
Centering text, 91-92, 372
Center-justified text, 91-92
Centerline tracing, 646
Character Attributes dialog box, 269-275
Character option (Spacing dialog box), 104-105
Character Reference Chart, 121-122
Characters (text)
     angle editing, 271, 274-275
     editing fonts and style, 271-272
     editing type size, 272-273
     entering special, 121-122
     horizontal and vertical shift, 273
     kerning, 275-279
     reshaping, 284-287
     shaping and editing, 265-287
     superscripts and subscripts, 274
Chart menu, 541
Chart templates, 526, 542-543
Charting basics, 526-528. *See also* Charts;
     CorelCHART!
Charts. *See also* CorelCHART!

adding graphics, 538-540
adding labels, 537
with annotation, 538
area, 549-550
bar, 543-547
data series for, 526-527
ellipse added to, 540
high/low/open/close, 552-553
line, 548-549
modifying chart elements, 541-542
pie, 550-551
scatter, 551-552
table, 554-555
3-D Riser, 554-556
3-D Scatter, 555-556
types of CorelCHART!, 543-556
various shaped markers for, 542
Check boxes in dialog boxes, 11-12
Choke, 427
Circles
     centering text in, 372
     converting to curve objects, 262-263
     creating an arc from, 260
     creating a pie wedge from, 261
     drawing, 72-74
     drawing from the center, 73-74
     drawing from the rim, 73
     fitting text to, 512
     practice using, 74-78
     shaping, 259-263
Classes of objects, 15
Clear Transformations command, 194
Clearing the screen, 27
Click, 3, 22
Clicking the mouse, 3, 22
Clip art, integrating, 494-500
Clipboard (Windows), 290-291
     memory limits of, 298-299
     for transferring CorelDRAW! objects, 299-300
Clone, 7
Cloning objects, 307
Closed curve objects
     autotracing, 635-636
     drawing, 35-36
Closing an open path, 35-36, 249
CMYK process color system, 362, 422
Color dialog box, 433
Color model, 351
Color option (Outline Pen), 318
Color palettes, 6, 357, 364-366
Color separations, 422-428
     in film negative format, 428-430
     printing, 427
Color Separator, 433-435
Color sequences for a rainbow, 510
Coloring extruding objects, 479-481
Color-matching systems, 350

Colors. *See* Outline Color; Rainbow example; Spot colors
Column text, creating, 114-115
Combine command, special effects using, 304
Combining CorelDRAW! features, 493-523
Combining objects, 148, 170-172, 373
Command buttons (dialog box), 11-12
Complex curve objects, printing, 440
Conical fountain fills, 381
    defining, 389-390
    Spot color, 390
Connect dialog box (Windows), 406
Connectivity, 613-614
Constrain, 26
Constraining a line to an angle, 26-27
Context-sensitive help, 10
Contour feature, 447, 482-484
Contour roll-up, 483
Control Panel (CorelMOVE!), 599-603
Control Panel window (Windows), 404
Control points (on curves), 37
    displaying, 224
    moving, 226-233
    and node types, 227
Control-menu box (CorelDRAW!), 5
Copies to print, selecting, 413
Copy Attributes dialog box, 308
Copy command, 291-294
Copying an object, 189-190
    and moving it, 163-166
    and pasting it, 291-294
    and pasting it between pictures, 293-294
    and pasting it within a picture, 291-293
Copying an object's attributes, 308-310
Copying fill styles, 398-399
Copying Outline Color and Pen styles, 368-369
Copying outline styles, 346
Corel 4 icon, 2-4
Corel Graphics group window, 3
CorelCHART!, 525-556. *See also* Charts
    creating a new chart, 530-531
    customizing a chart, 535-540
    Data Manager, 531-535
    formatting text, 535-536
    New dialog box, 530
    starting, 528-529
    toolbox, 528-529
CorelDRAW! menus, 7-10
CorelDRAW! screen, 4-7
CorelMOSAIC!, 408-410
CorelMOVE!, 585-603
    Actor tool, 592-596
    Control Panel, 599-603
    Cue tool, 596-599
    getting started, 587
    main screen, 587-588
    menus, 588-589

opening an animation, 600
Path tool, 589-592
playback controls, 599-600
Prop tool, 596
Sound tool, 596
toolbox, 589-599
CorelPHOTO-PAINT!, 569-582
    drawing tools, 580-581
    getting started, 570-571
    initial screen, 570
    opening a picture, 571
    painting tools, 579-580
    retouching tools, 578-579
    roll-up menus, 573-576
    screen elements, 572-573
    selection and display tools, 577-578
    text tool, 581
    tools, 575-581
CorelSHOW!, 559-567
    getting started, 560-561
    and OLE, 560
    previewing a presentation, 567
    screen elements, 561-562
    Slide view, 562
    tools and modes, 562-567
CorelTRACE!, 630. *See also* Tracing bitmap images
    customizing tracing options, 646-648
    loading, 642
    opening files to trace, 642, 644
    preparing to use, 641-642
CorelTRACE! window, 643
Corner attributes (Outline Pen), 329-331
Corner boundary marker, 184, 196
Corner radius indicator, 257
Corner settings (Outline Pen), 345
Corners
    examples of, 331
    rounding rectangle, 253, 255-257
    rounding square, 256
Corners option (Outline Pen), 320-321
Create a New Picture (CorelPHOTO-PAINT!), 571
Crop marks, 423
Cropped bitmap, 634
Ctrl
    constraining lines with, 26-27
    use of, 26
    using with envelopes, 453-455
Cue Information dialog box (CorelMOVE!), 597
Cue tool (CorelMOVE!), 596-599
Curve objects. *See also* Curves
    aligning the nodes of, 254
    converting ellipses to, 262-263
    converting rectangles to, 257-259
    joining, 250, 640
    at 1:1 magnification, 223
    printing complex, 440
Curve segments

converting straight line segments to, 241-243
converting to straight line segments, 239-241
Curves, 22. *See also* Curve objects
    breaking at nodes, 247-248
    displaying control points, 224
    displaying the nodes in, 221
    drawing, 32-40
    drawing in Bézier mode, 37-40
    drawing closed, 35-36
    drawing multisegment, 35
    drawing practice with, 48-54
    drawing a waveform curve, 227
    erasing portions of, 34
    flatness of, 419
    joining automatically, 45-48
    moving nodes and control points, 226-233
    selecting, 220-221
    selecting nodes of, 222-226
    shaping, 220-253
Cusp nodes, 224, 232, 242-244
    making symmetrical, 246
    smoothing, 245
Custom color palette, 364-366
Custom fountain fills, 381
Custom Outline Pen icon, 316
Custom text characters. *See* Text characters
Customizing charts with CorelCHART!, 535-540
Customizing Outline Pen defaults, 322-323
Customizing tools, 18
Cut command, 294-298
Cutting and pasting objects, 294-298
    between pictures, 296-297
    within a picture, 295-296
Cycling through objects, 153-156

D

Data categories (charting), 526
Data Manager (CorelCHART!), 531-535
    entering data with, 533
    importing data with, 533-535
Data point (charting), 526
Data series (charting), 526-527
Default Outline Pen dialog box, 323
Defaults, custom Outline Pen, 322-323
Defining the Outline Pen, 313-346
Deleting a layer, 179
Deleting multiple nodes, 238-239
Deleting a single node, 237-238
Deselect, 145
DeskJet printers, 438
Device-independent graphics, 615
Dialog boxes, 11-14
Dimension Lines features, 40-42
Directory, creating, 609-610

Display boxes in dialog boxes, 12-13
Display menu, 8
Display Status dialog box (CorelCHART!), 539
"Distorted" corner radius indicator, 257
Dot-matrix printers, 438
Double click, 4, 28
Double clicking the mouse, 4, 28
Drag, 33
Dragging the mouse, 33
Dragging the scaling cursor, 197
Drawing device requirements, 607
Drawing tools, 14-17
Drop cap, 286
Drop-down list boxes in dialog boxes, 11-12
Drop-shadow effect, 519
Dual-axis side-by-side bar chart, 545
Dual-axis stacked bar chart, 545-546
Duplicate command, special effects using, 304
Duplicating and cloning objects, 304-307
Duplicating text, 450

E

Edge padding (radial fountain fills), 388-389
Edit menu, 7
Edit Path menu (CorelMOVE!), 591
Editing tools, 17-18
Effects menu, 8, 443-444
Ellipses
    added to a chart, 540
    converting to curve objects, 262-263
    creating a wedge from, 262
    drawing, 70-72
    drawing from the center, 71-72
    drawing from the rim, 70-71
    practice using, 74-78
    shaping, 259-263
Ellipse tool, 16
Embedding with CorelSHOW!, 560
Embedding an object, 302-304
End caps, 331
End of a line, finding, 318
Envelope, 444
Envelope feature, 444, 446-460
    adding a new envelope, 457-458
    clearing an envelope, 459-460
    Copy Envelope From, 458-459
    creating and duplicating text, 450
    editing modes for, 449
    mapping options, 449
    single arc envelope, 452
    straight line envelope, 450-452
    two curves envelope, 453
    unconstrained envelope, 455-457
    using   and Shift 453-455

Envelope roll-up menu, 448
EPS format, exporting to, 625-626
Erasing portions of a curve, 34
Erasing portions of a line, 25
Error handler, downloadable, 439-440
Exiting CorelDRAW!, 18-19
Export dialog box, 621-622
Export EPS dialog box, 625
Export file formats, 617
Exporting files, 613-626
    to bitmap graphics formats, 623-624
    to EPS format, 625-626
    help with, 617-618
    to object-oriented graphics formats, 624-626
    overview of, 621-623
Exporting text to a word processor, 110-113
Extended memory, 606
Extending a line using status line indicator, 26
Extracting text to a word processor, 110-113
Extrude feature, 446
Extrude roll-up window, 472-473, 479
Extruding objects, 472-482
    clearing an extrusion, 477-478
    depth and direction, 474-477
    shading and coloring, 479-481
    spatial alignment, 478-479
    using open paths, 481-482

F

FAX image, 514-515
File formats
    export, 617
    import, 534, 615-616
File information, printing, 420-422
File menu, 7, 18
Files
    importing and exporting, 613-626
    printing to, 418-419
    retrieving, 55-56
    saving, 54-55
Fill colors
    checking, 383
    defining, 369-370
Fill patterns
    full-color, 394-395
    texture, 394-398
Fill roll-up window, 398
Fill styles, copying, 398-399
Fill tool, 18, 350, 398-399
Fill tool flyout icons, 370
Filling with uniform Process color, 379-380
Filling with uniform Spot color, 370-376
Fills
    black/white/gray, 381

custom fountain, 381-390
    gradation giving 3-D effect, 520
    outline appearing behind, 375
    placement of, 327-328
    PostScript halftone screen patterns, 376-378
    rainbow colors through a mask, 513
    for Spot color uniform fill, 374
Film negative format, 428-430
Find dialog box, 119
Find feature, 118-119
Finding the beginning or end of a line, 318
Fit Text To Path Offsets dialog box, 503
Fit Text To Path roll-up, 501, 503
Fitting an image to the page, 417
Fitting text to a circle, 512
Fitting text to a path, 500-514
    aligning the text, 503
    distance of text from path, 503
    examples of, 502
    rainbow example, 504-514
    text orientation, 501, 503
    using a small circle, 517
Fit-in-Window tool, 127, 138-139
Flatness of curves, 419
Flatness setting for PostScript, 430
Flyout, 14
Font dialog box (CorelMOVE!), 595
Font drop-down list box (CorelCHART!), 536
Fonts, 85
    Aardvark, 99
    Avalon, 98-99
    comparing the tone of, 96
    editing, 271-272
    Frankfurt Gothic, 96, 100
    Frankfurt Gothic italic and bold, 101
    Gatineau, 104
    Paradise, 96, 98-99
    selecting, 95-99
    symbol, 99
Fonts list box (Artistic Text), 85
Fountain Fill dialog box, 382-383
Fountain fill steps, 399, 429-430
Fountain fills, 381-390
    conical, 389-390
    custom, 381-390
    linear, 382-386
    printing, 441
    radial, 386-389, 521
Four-color standard (CMYK), 362, 422
Frame Attributes dialog box, 115
Frames (animation), 83, 108, 586
Frankfurt Gothic bold-italic, 103
Frankfurt Gothic font, 96, 100
Frankfurt Gothic italic and bold, 101, 103
Freehand mode, 22
Freehand Tracking
    adjusting, 69

setting, 74
Full color mode, 36-37
Full screen view, 509
Full-color fill patterns, 394-395
Full-Color Pattern dialog box, 394
Full-page view, 125, 139-140

G

Gatineau font, 104
Gradation of fills giving 3-D effect, 520
Gray shade outline, 356
Grids
    adjusting frequency, 64-65
    changing settings, 43-44
    displaying, 43-44
    practicing with, 64-66
Grouping objects, 148, 168-170
Guidelines, 51
Gutter, 84

H

Halftone screen patterns
    filling with, 376-378
    outlining with, 359-361
    selecting, 360-361
Halftone screens, 359
    and color separations, 428
    defining, 377
    printed image of, 378
Handles, 144
Hard disk space required to run CorelDRAW!, 606
Hardware requirements to run CorelDRAW!, 606-607
Hardware-specific printing tips, 435-438
Help Contents, 10
Help with importing and exporting, 617-618
Help menu, 9-10
Highlighting box, 144
High/low/open/close charts, 552-553
Histograms, 553-554
Horizontal bar chart, 544
Horizontal Grid Frequency, 42
Horizontal Shift (Character Attributes), 270
Hot zone, 116
HP DeskJet and PaintJet printers, 438
HP LaserJet printers, 437-438
Hyphenation, 116

I

Imagesetter setup dialog box, 420
Import button (Artistic Text), 86

Import Data dialog box (CorelCHART!), 535
Import dialog box, 619
Import file formats, 615-616
Imported graphics formats, 540
Importing bitmap graphics, 620, 630-632
Importing data with Data Manager, 533-535
Importing and exporting files, 613-626
Importing files
    help with, 617-618
    overview of, 618-620
Importing object-oriented graphics, 620
Importing text into CorelDRAW!, 113-114
Insert Object dialog box, 303
Insertion point, 84
Installing CorelDRAW!, 605-610
Installing and setting up printers, 404-406
Inter-character spacing, adjusting, 280-282
Inter-line spacing, adjusting, 283-284
Inter-word spacing, adjusting, 282-283
Italic type, selecting, 101

J

Joining combined objects, 250
Joining curve objects, 45-48, 250, 640
Joining lines
    automatically, 45-48
    and preventing accidental joins, 46-48
Joining nodes, 248-251

K

Keeping drawing strokes together as one object, 247
Kerning, 275
    multiple characters, 278-279
    single characters, 276-278
    text characters, 275-279
Kite drawing, 48-54
Knocked out (object bottom), 427

L

Labels, adding in CorelCHART!, 537
Landscape page format, 74, 76
LaserJet printers and compatibles, 437-438
Layer Options dialog box, 179
Layer stacking order, changing, 180
Layers
    creating or editing, 178-179
    deleting, 179
    moving objects between, 179-180
    using, 177-180
Layers roll-up, 178

Layout menu, 7-8, 74-75
Leading, 105
Leakproof object, 350
Leaving CorelDRAW!, 18-19
Left alignment of text, 90-91
Left-justified text, 90-91
Library roll-up (CorelMOVE!), 602-603
Line art, integrating clip art with, 494-500
Line caps option (Outline Pen), 321
Line charts, 548-549
Line end caps
    examples of, 333
    selecting, 331-332
Line option (Spacing dialog box), 105
Line segments. *See* Straight line segments
Line spacing, adjusting, 283-284
Line Style option (Outline Pen), 320
Line styles, selecting, 333-335
Line types, Outline Pen, 321
Line Width option (Outline Pen), 320, 326-328
Linear fountain fills, 381-386
Lines (straight), 22. *See also* Outline Pen; Outlining
        objects
    constraining with   , 26-27
    displaying the nodes in, 222
    drawing, 22-32
    drawing multisegment, 27-28
    drawing practice, 48-54
    drawing using Dimension Lines, 40-42
    erasing portions of, 25
    extending, 23
    extending using the status line indicator, 26
    joining automatically, 45-48
    nodes on, 23
    preventing from joining accidentally, 46-48
    selecting, 220-221
    selecting nodes of, 222-226
    shaping, 220-253
Linking, with CorelSHOW!, 560
Linking an object, 301-302
List boxes in dialog boxes, 12
Load Settings dialog box (CorelTRACE!), 649
Logo example, 371-399
Loop point, 591

M

Markers, chart, 542
Marquee, 128
    selecting an area with, 129
    selecting multiple nodes with, 226
    selecting objects with, 151-153
Master object, 307
Maximize button (CorelDRAW! screen), 5

Memory requirements to run CorelDRAW!, 606
Menu bar (CorelDRAW! screen), 5
Menus, CorelDRAW!, 7-10
Merging text into CorelDRAW!, 113-114
Metafile, 290
Middle boundary marker, 184, 196
Minimize button (CorelDRAW! screen), 4-5
Mirror image
    creating, 191-196
    diagonal, 197-199
    of a pie wedge, 508
    of rainbow-colored text, 514
Miter, 320
Mitered corners, 331
Monitor, to run CorelDRAW!, 607
Mouse
    clicking, 3, 22
    double clicking, 4, 28
    dragging, 33
    entering text with, 88-89
Mouse button, setting to zoom in, 130
Mouse pointer, 10
Move box, dragging, 157
Moving control points, 230-233
Moving nodes
    on curves, 226-233
    multiple nodes, 228-229
    in 90-degree angles, 229-230
    a single node, 227-228
Moving objects, 156-166
    between layers, 179-180
    and copying while moving, 163-166
    multiple objects at once, 157-161
    90 degrees, 159-161
    a single object, 156-157
    using the keyboard, 162
    using precise measurements, 162-163
Multilayering, 180
Multiple curve segments, converting, 241
Multiple nodes
    adding, 235, 237
    cusping, 242-244
    deleting, 238-239
    making symmetrical, 246-247
    moving, 228-229
    selecting, 225-226
    smoothing, 244-245
Multiple objects
    grouping, 169
    moving, 157-159
    selecting, 148-153
Multiple pie charts, 550
Multiple straight line segments, converting, 241-243
Multiple-cel actors (animation), 586
Multisegment curves, drawing, 35
Multisegment lines, drawing, 27-28

N

Negative film format, 428-430
Nested submenus, flyout of, 14
New actor dialog box (CorelMOVE!), 592-593
New dialog box (CorelCHART!), 530
Nib, 321
Nib shapes
    calligraphic pen, 340-344
    varying with PowerLine, 487-488
Node Align dialog box, 252
Node Edit roll-up window, 233-253, 488
Node types
    and control points, 227
    identifying, 223-225
    moving control points of, 232-233
Nodes, 22-23
    adding multiple nodes, 235, 237
    adding a single node, 234-236
    aligning, 250, 252-254
    breaking curves at, 247-248
    cusping, 242-244
    deleting multiple, 238-239
    deleting single, 237-238
    displaying, 221-222
    editing, 233
    ellipse, 70-71
    joining, 248-251
    making symmetrical, 246-247
    moving, 226-233
    moving multiple, 228-229
    moving in 90-degree angles, 229-230
    moving single, 227-228
    selected, 229
    selecting, 222-225
    selecting multiple, 225-226
    smoothing, 244-245
Nudge feature, 162
Numeric entry boxes in dialog boxes, 11-12

O

Object linking and embedding (OLE), 300-304
Object-oriented graphics, 614
    vs. bitmap graphics, 614-615
    exporting, 624-626
    importing, 620
OLE
    application icons, 564
    and CorelSHOW!, 560
One-point perspectives, 460-462
Onion skin, 596
Opaque object, 596

Open arc, creating, 259-261
Open Chart dialog box, 543
Open Drawing dialog box, 56
Open Files dialog box (CorelTRACE!), 643
Open paths
    applying extrusions to, 481
    closing, 35-36, 249
    message, 35
Opening a saved drawing, 55-56
Operating system requirements, 607
Option buttons in dialog boxes, 11-12
Outline Color, 314
    copying, 368-369
    defining, 349-399, 351-352
    resetting defaults, 352-354
    using the Pen roll-up for, 358-359
Outline Color dialog box, 351-352
    custom color palette, 364-366
    listing Spot colors, 359
    shortcut access, 355
    for Spot color, 353
Outline Color icon, 367
Outline corners, setting, 329-331
Outline Pen, 314
    adding and editing arrowheads, 335-340
    adjusting line width, 326-328
    calligraphic pen, 340-344
    customizing, 322-323
    defining, 313-346
    defining attributes, 314
    defining for text, 344
    editing attributes of, 325-344
    hints for defining, 344
    hints for using, 344-346
    line types, 321
    outline and fill placement, 327-328
    resetting for Spot color, 356-358
    scaling outline with image, 329
    selecting line end caps, 331-333
    selecting line styles, 333-335
    selecting a preset width, 323-325
    setting outline corners, 329-331
    varying calligraphic style, 345
Outline Pen dialog box, 317-322, 328
Outline Pen flyout, 315, 324, 367
Outline styles, copying, 346
Outline tool, 18
Outline tracing, 646
Outlining objects, 145
    with black/white/gray, 366-368
    with PostScript halftones, 359-361
    with Process color, 361-366
    with spot color, 352-359
Output devices, 402-404, 607
Output medium, 402

P

Page boundaries, exceeding, 518
Page formats, changing, 74, 76
Page Setup dialog box, 75
Pages
    fitting images to, 417
    selecting to print, 413
PaintJet printers, 438
Panning, 139-140
PANTONE Spot and Process Color Matching
    Systems, 350, 358
Paradise font, 96, 98-99
Paragraph attributes, 115-116
Paragraph dialog box, 116
Paragraph mode
    bounding box, 108
    features of, 107-108
Paragraph text, 83-84
Paragraph Text dialog box, 109-110, 114
Paragraph Text tool, 108
Paragraphs, working with, 107-119
Parallel extrusions, and perspective, 474
Parallel PostScript printers, tips for, 436-437
Paste, 291
Paste button (Artistic Text), 86
Paste Special dialog box, 302
Pasting objects, 291-298
Pasting text into CorelDRAW!, 113-114
Path Edit roll-up (CorelMOVE!), 590
Path tool (CorelMOVE!), 589-592
Paths (animation), 586
Pen. *See* Outline Pen
Pen roll-up window, 315, 324, 358-359
Pencil tool, 16, 21-56
Percent bar chart, 546-547
Perspective effects
    adding a new perspective, 463-464
    clearing a perspective, 464-465
    Copy Perspective From, 463-465
    creating, 460-465
    one- and two-point perspective, 460-462
    and parallel extrusions, 474
    using the vanishing point, 463
Photograph enhancement. *See* CorelPHOTO-PAINT!
Pick tool, 17
    editing text attributes with, 266-267
    modes, 144
    selecting objects with, 144-156
    to size and shape objects, 183-214
    transformation mode, 147
    using, 100, 102
Pictographs, 555
Pie charts, 550-551
Pie wedges
    aligning, 507
    creating, 261-262

    creating and rotating, 506
    with a mirror image, 508
    repeating, 507
    scaling and copying, 506
Pixels, 45
Pixel-based graphics, 614
Place Duplicates and Clones settings, 305
Playback Options dialog box (CorelMOVE!), 589-590
Plotters, tips for using, 438
Point Information dialog box (CorelMOVE!), 591
Point line widths (Outline Pen flyout), 367
Pointer, mouse, 10
Polygons, drawing, 29, 31-32, 48-54
Portions of a line, erasing, 25
Portrait page format, 74, 76
PostScript
    All Fonts Resident setting, 432
    complex artwork with, 438-441
    defining a halftone screen, 377
    downloadable error handler for, 439-440
    flatness setting for, 430
    printers and controllers, 435-437
    screen frequency for, 431-432
    using Spot color with, 352
PostScript halftone screen patterns
    and color separations, 428
    filling with, 376-378
    with fountain fills, 385-386
    outlining with, 359-361
    printed image, 378
    table of, 378
    texture fills, 396-398, 400
PostScript Options dialog box, 361, 377
PostScript Texture dialog box, 397
PowerLine feature, 447, 485-489
    applying powerlines to an object, 486
    using pressure lines, 488-489
    varying the nib, 487-488
PowerLine roll-up, 485-486
Precision
    increasing, 43
    using the status line for, 24-25
Preferences-Curves dialog box, 47, 634
Prepress, 433
Prepress Tools dialog box, 434
Pressure lines, using, 488-489
Preventing lines from joining, 46-48
Preview Fountain Steps, 399
Preview mode, 36
Preview Selected Only, 150
Previewing a slide presentation, 567
Print dialog box, 408-419. *See also* Print Options
    dialog box
    checking printer setup, 412
    fitting an image to the page, 417
    options, 411
    printing to a file, 418-419

printing selected objects, 413-414
scaling an image, 416-417
selecting number of copies, 413
selecting pages to print, 413
tiling a graphic, 414-416
using CorelMOSAIC!, 408-410
Print Manager (Windows), disabling, 407
Print Options dialog box, 419-435. *See also* Print
    dialog box
    changing the screen frequency, 431-432
    color separations, 422-430
    Color Separator, 433-435
    printing file information, 420-422
    using film negative format, 428-430
Print Setup dialog box, 407-409
Print To File dialog box, 419
Printers. *See also* PostScript; Printing
    installation and setup, 404-406, 412
    300 dpi vs. high-resolution, 441
    timeouts, 406-407
Printers dialog box (Windows), 405
Printing, 401-441. *See also* PostScript; Print dialog
    box; Print Options dialog box; Printers
    color separation sheets, 427
    complex curve objects, 440
    to a file, 418-419
    fountain fills, 441
    hardware-specific tips, 435-438
    output devices, 402-404
    preparing for, 404-407
    selected objects, 413-414
Printing devices supported, 403
Process color
    filling an object with uniform, 379-380
    outline and fill example, 380
    outlining with, 361-366
Process color separations. *See* Color separations
Process color system, 350, 362, 422
Program Manager window (Windows), 3
Prop Information dialog box (CorelMOVE!), 602
Prop tool (CorelMOVE!), 596
Props (animation), 586

Q

Question mark mouse pointer, 10
Quitting CorelDRAW!, 18-19

R

Radial fountain fills, 381, 521
    defining, 386-389
    Radial offset, 388-389
    Spot color, 387-388

Rainbow example, 504-514
    aligning the pie wedge, 507
    color sequences for, 510
    colors as fill through a mask, 513
    creating and rotating a pie wedge, 506
    fitting text to a circle, 512
    full screen view, 509
    mirror image of a pie wedge, 508
    scaling and copying a pie wedge, 506
    using mirror image, 514
    using the Repeat key, 507
    using wireframe mode, 509
Range (Data Manager), 531
Realigning a node, 252
Rectangle tool, 16
Rectangles
    converting to curve objects, 257-259
    creating and duplicating, 306-307
    drawing, 60-62
    drawing from any corner, 60-62
    drawing from the center outward, 62
    practice using, 66-69
    rounding the corners of, 253, 255-257
    shaping, 253-259
Reflect, 320
Registration marks, 423
Registration point (animation), 595
Reordering superimposed objects, 166-168
Repeat key, using, 507
Repeated text exceeding page boundaries, 518
Repeating a transformation, 213-214
Replace dialog box, 119
Replace feature, 118-119
Reshaping text characters, 284-287
Retrieving a file, 55-56
Right mouse button, setting to zoom in, 130
Right-aligned text, 92-93
Right-justified text, 92-93
Roll-up windows, 13-14
Rotate & Skew command, 207-208, 212
Rotate & Skew dialog box, 208
Rotate & Skew feature, 443, 445
Rotating blended objects, 467-472
Rotating an object, 201-208
    and changing the axis, 205-207
    in increments, 203-204
    and retaining a copy, 204-205
    in rotate/skew mode, 201-207
    with Rotate & Skew, 207-208
Rotating a pie wedge, 506
Rounded line, 321
Rounding corners, 331
    of a rectangle, 253, 255-257
    of a skewed rectangle, 257
    of a skewed square, 258
    of a square, 256
Rulers (CorelDRAW! screen), 6, 43-45, 65

S

Sample characters display box, 85
Save Drawing dialog box, 55
Saving a drawing, 54-55, 69
Saving a file, 54-55
Scale Path dialog box (CorelMOVE!), 590
Scale With Image option (Outline Pen), 322
Scaling, 185, 196-201, 416-417
    from the center, 200-201
    in increments, 197
    a pie wedge, 506
    and retaining an original, 197
    with Stretch & Mirror, 199-200
    with text exceeding page boundaries, 518
Scaling cursor, dragging, 197
Scatter charts, 551-552, 555-556
Screen, clearing, 27
Screen frequency for PostScript, changing, 431-432
Scroll bars (CorelDRAW! screen), 6
Scroll bars (dialog boxes), 13
Select mode, 17, 144
Selecting
    all objects in a graphic, 153
    an arc for alignment, 260
    a line or curve, 220-221
    multiple nodes, 225-226
    multiple objects, 148-153
    nodes of a line or curve, 222-226
    objects, 291
    objects with the marquee, 151-153
    objects with the Pick tool, 144-156
    with the Shaping tool, 218-220
    single objects, 145-148
Separations dialog box, 426
Serial PostScript printers, tips for, 437
Settings for COM1: dialog box (Windows), 405
Settings menu (CorelTRACE!), 648
SETUP, 608-610
Shading extruding objects, 479-481
Shaping
    characters, 284-287
    ellipses and circles, 259-263
    lines and curves, 220-253
    rectangles and squares, 253-259
Shaping tool, 17
    editing text attributes with, 267-269
    selecting with, 218-220
    using, 217-263
    using to adjust spacing, 280-284
Shift key
    selecting objects with, 148-151
    using with envelopes, 453-455
Show Page tool, 127, 139
Show Preview shortcut, 499
Side-by-side bar chart, 545-546
Single arc envelope, 452

Single-cel actors (animation), 586
Size of type
    editing, 272-273
    selecting, 94-95
Skew, 201
Skewed rectangle, rounding the corners of, 257
Skewed square, rounding the corners of, 258
Skewing an object, 208-211
    in increments, 209-210
    and retaining a copy, 210-211
    with Rotate & Skew, 212
Slide presentation (CorelSHOW!)
    duration, 567
    preview, 567
    slide sorter view, 565-566
    slide transition, 566
    slide view, 562-565
Smoothing nodes, 224-225, 232, 244-245
Snap To property, turning on, 43-44
Snapping away, 72
Sound tool (CorelMOVE!), 596
Spacing, adjusting, 279-284
Spacing adjustment arrows, 281
Spacing button (Artistic Text dialog box), 86
Spacing dialog box, 102-107, 133
Special characters, entering, 121-122
Special effects, creating, 304, 443-490, 514-523
Special menu, 8, 74
Spectral maps, 553
Spelling Checker, 116-118
Spelling Checker dialog box, 117
Spot colors
    assigning outlines, 355-356
    conical fountain fills, 390
    filling an object with uniform, 370-376
    linear fountain fills, 382-386
    listed in Outline Color dialog box, 359
    Outline Color dialog box, 353
    Outline Pen defaults, 356-358
    outlining with, 352-359
    radial fountain fills, 387-388
    uniform fill setting, 374
    using with a PostScript printer, 352
Spot color system, 350
Spread, 427
Square line, 321
Squares
    drawing, 62-64
    drawing from the center outward, 63-64
    drawing from any corner, 62-63
    practice using, 66-69
    shaping, 253-259
Stacked area chart, 549
Stacked bar chart, 545-546
Starting CorelCHART!, 528-529
Starting CorelDRAW!, 2-4
Starting CorelMOVE!, 587

Starting CorelPHOTO-PAINT!, 570-571
Starting CorelSHOW!, 560-561
Status line codes, 24-25
Status line indicators (CorelDRAW! screen), 5-6
    when drawing a line, 26, 62
    when drawing a rectangle, 62-63
    when drawing a square, 62-63
    using for precision, 24-25
Straight line envelope, 450-452
Straight line segments
    converting curve segments to, 239-241
    converting to curve segments, 241-243
Straight lines. *See* Lines (straight)
Stretch, 185
Stretch & Mirror dialog box, 193
Stretch & Mirror feature, 192-196, 443-444
    and retaining an original, 199-200
    scaling with, 199-200
Stretching an object, 184-194
    from the center, 200-201
    horizontally, 185-187, 189
    incrementally, 189
    and mirroring, 192-196
    and retaining an original, 189-190
    vertically, 188-191
Style drop-down list box, 85
Styles (type), 86
    editing, 271-272
    selecting, 100-102
Submenus (nested), flyout of, 14
Subscripts, 271, 274
Superimposed objects
    cycling through, 153-154
    reordering, 166-168
Superscripts, 271, 274
Symbol font, example of, 99
Symbol library, using, 119-121
Symbols roll-up, 120
Symmetrical nodes, 225, 233, 246-247
System requirements to run CorelDRAW!, 606-607

T

Table charts, 554-555
Tagged cell (Data Manager), 532
Teacup drawing, 67
    drawing, 67-69
    editing, 130-134
    selecting objects in, 149-151
    using the Combine command, 171-172
Templates, chart, 526, 542-543
Text attributes, editing, 266-269
Text Attributes dialog box, 95
Text characters
    angle editing, 274-275

editing fonts and style, 271-272
editing type size, 272-273
entering special, 121-122
horizontal and vertical shift, 273
kerning, 275-279
reshaping, 284-287
shaping and editing, 265-287
superscripts and subscripts, 274
Text cursor, 85
Text dialog box
    entering text in, 87
    in Paragraph mode, 109-110, 114
Text entry area, moving around in, 87-89
Text entry boxes in dialog boxes, 11-12
Text menu, 8
Text outline. *See* Outline Pen; Outlines
Text ribbon, 528
Text roll-up window, 89-90
Text tool, 17, 82-83
Text window, 110
Texture Fill dialog box, 396, 577
Texture fills, 394-398
Thesaurus, using, 118
Thesaurus dialog box, 118
3-D effects, 520, 522
3-D Riser charts, 554-556
3-D Scatter charts, 555-556
300 dpi printers, 441
Tiling, 391, 414
Tiling a graphic, 414-416
Timelines roll-up (CorelMOVE!), 601-603
Title bar (CorelDRAW! screen), 4-5
Toolbox icons, 14
Toolboxes, 6, 14-18, 528-529
Tools
    for customizing, 18
    drawing, 14-17
    editing, 17-18
    ellipse, 16
    fill, 18
    outline, 18
    pencil, 16
    pick, 17
    rectangle, 16
    shaping, 17
    text, 17
Tracing bitmap images, 629-649. *See also*
    CorelTRACE!
    with Autotrace, 632-637
    combining Autotracing with manual, 641
    with CorelTRACE!, 640-649
    manually, 637-640
Transferring objects
    from other Windows applications, 300
    to other Windows applications, 299-300
Transformation mode, 17, 144, 147
Transformations, repeating, 213-214

Transforming objects, 183-214
    by mirroring, 194-196
    by rotating, 201-208
    by scaling, 197-201
    by skewing, 208-212
    by stretching, 184-194
Transition Effects dialog box (CorelSHOW!), 566
Transitions for Prop dialog box, 603
Transparent object, 596
Trapping, 427
TRUMATCH Process Color System, 350
Two curves envelope, 453
Two-Color Pattern dialog box, 391
Two-column text, creating, 114-115
Two-point perspectives, 460-462
Type design, selecting, 95-107
Type size
    editing, 272-273
    selecting, 94-95
Type size selection box (Artistic Text), 85-86
Type styles, 86
    editing, 271-272
    selecting, 100-102

U

Unconstrained envelope, 455-457
Undo command, 189, 194
Units of measurement, changing, 42
Unjustified text, 93-94
UNTITLED.CDR, 4

V

Value (Data Manager), 531
Vanishing points, 463
    moving, 475-477
    using, 463
Vector, 391
Vector fill patterns, 391-396
Vertical bar chart, 544
Vertical bar percent chart, 547
Vertical bipolar side-by-side bar chart, 547
Vertical dual-axis bar chart, 546
Vertical line chart, 548
Vertical Shift (Character Attributes), 270
Vertical transformation, 194
Views

actual size, 136-137
full-page view, 125, 139-140
options for viewing, 125
panning, 139-140
using the Zoom tool, 125-128
using the Zoom-In tool, 128-134
using the Zoom-Out tool, 134-136

W

Waveform curve, drawing, 227
Wedge (pie). *See* Pie wedge
Welding feature, 180-181
Window border (CorelDRAW! screen), 4-5
Windows
    fitting graphics in, 138-139
    roll-up, 13-14
Windows applications
    transferring objects from, 300
    transferring objects to, 299-300
    using with CorelDRAW!, 298-304
Windows Clipboard, 290-291
    memory limits of, 298-299
    for transferring CorelDRAW! objects, 299-300
Windows (Microsoft)
    Connect dialog box, 406
    Control Panel window, 404
    disabling Print Manager, 407
    Printers dialog box, 405
    Program Manager window, 3
    requirements to run CorelDRAW!, 607
    Settings for COM1: dialog box, 405
    Window menu, 3
Windows Write, CorelDRAW! text in, 112
Wireframe mode, 36
    vs. full color mode, 36-37
    pairs of pie wedges in, 509
Word option (Spacing dialog box), 105
Word processor, extracting text to, 110-113
Word spacing, adjusting, 282-283

Z

Zero points, 45
Zoom tool, 125-128
Zoom-In tool, 126, 128-134
Zoom-Out tool, 126, 134-136